# THE BRITISH ECONOMY
## SINCE 1945

# THE
# BRITISH ECONOMY
# SINCE 1945

Edited by
N. F. R. CRAFTS and N. W. C. WOODWARD

*with the assistance of B. F. Duckham*

CLARENDON PRESS · OXFORD
1991

Oxford University Press, Walton Street, Oxford OX2 6DP
Oxford New York Toronto
Delhi Bombay Calcutta Madras Karachi
Petaling Jaya Singapore Hong Kong Tokyo
Nairobi Dar es Salaam Cape Town
Melbourne Auckland
and associated companies in
Berlin Ibadan

Oxford is a trade mark of Oxford University Press

Published in the United States
by Oxford University Press, New York

British Library Cataloguing in Publication Data
The British economy since 1945.
1. Great Britain. Economic conditions, history
I. Crafts, N. F. R.   II. Woodward, N. W. C.   III. Duckham, B. F.
330. 941
ISBN 0–19–877274–2
ISBN 0–19–877273–4 (Pbk.)

Library of Congress Cataloging in Publication Data
The British economy since 1945 / edited by N. F. R. Crafts and
N. W. C. Woodward with the assistance of B. F. Duckham.
p. cm.
Includes bibliographical references and index.
1. Great Britain—Economic conditions—1945-   2. Great Britain—
Economic policy—1945-
I. Crafts, N. F. R.
II. Woodward, N. W. C.   III. Duckham, Baron Frederick.
HC256.5.B725 1991     330.941'085—dc20      90–48643
ISBN 0–19–877274–2
ISBN 0–19–877273–4 (Pbk.)

Typeset by Aurelec Data Processing Systems, Pondicherry, India
Printed in Great Britain by Bookcraft (Bath) Ltd.,
Midsomer Norton, Avon

# Contents

# 1

# The British Economy since 1945: Introduction and Overview

N. F. R. CRAFTS AND N. W. C. WOODWARD

## 1. Introduction

The central aim of this chapter is to provide a context in which the more detailed studies that follow can be placed. Our approach is necessarily one which sketches some of the main outlines of recent economic history rather than one which seeks to offer an exhaustive treatment. In reviewing post-war British economic development our emphasis will be on changes in three areas: the structure and institutions of the economy, economic policy, and economic performance. In order to develop greater perspective on British experience we also introduce some international comparative material.

It is clear that since 1979 there have been considerable changes in the direction of policy, and moreover in economists' thinking, such that earlier post-war conventional wisdoms no longer command respect. Accordingly the late 1980s provide a particularly interesting vantage point from which now to look back on the post-war period and in that light to reflect on recent developments. On many of the key issues relating to the success or otherwise of the Thatcher governments the jury is still out, of course, but economic history is a vital ingredient in forming an assessment and we hope that this chapter, and indeed the book as a whole, can contribute to this as well as introduce a fascinating period for historians to study.

## 2. Economic Policy Then and Now

It is probably very difficult for students whose formative years have been entirely in the Thatcher era to empathize with the basic preconceptions and prejudices of the 'post-war economic settlement' and the policy-making of governments of both parties from the 1940s through the 1960s. Major developments in economic analysis and the sadness and wisdom of experience to a significant extent place professional economists in a similar position.

At the risk of excessive simplification, it is useful to highlight three major shifts in policy stance since the 1950s of which there were stirrings in the 1970s but which have only been fully consummated in the 1980s. These are:

(1) the downgrading of the role of demand management in economic policy and a switch in the role of fiscal policy from a demand to a supply-side instrument.

(2) the move to a greater emphasis on supply-side policy with less weight

placed on correcting market failures but more attention given to cost reduction with an awareness that regulation itself might sustain inefficiency.

(3)  the much-reduced weight placed on distributional considerations in equity/efficiency trade-offs.

Each of these requires some exposition and explanation.

After the ending of the most severe wartime controls, beginning in the early 1950s, there was a lengthy period of demand management based on discretionary fiscal policy, aimed at fine tuning the economy and seeking to respond to changing economic conditions to ensure both that demand was high enough to avoid a return to the high unemployment of the 1930s and also to smooth out business-cycle fluctuations. It was generally accepted that the government had the ability to lower unemployment by expanding the level of demand in the economy. Mainstream British academic thinking at this time was firmly set in what would now seem to have been an 'unreconstructed Keynesian' mode, although this by no means prevented authors in this tradition from arguing that fiscal policy had contributed little or nothing to the achievement of either objective (Dow, 1964; Matthews, 1968). Moreover, the performance of the economy in terms of unemployment and inflation worsened somewhat as the 1960s wore on.

Something of a reaction against this Keynesianism started to emerge in the 1960s when first the Macmillan and then the Wilson Governments sought to supplement demand management with policies to promote faster growth. It was, however, the events of the 1970s which truly undermined the erstwhile 'Keynesian Consensus' with a drastic deterioration in economic performance heralded by the unsustainable boom created by Conservative fiscal and monetary policy in the early 1970s and exacerbated by the oil-price shock of 1973/4. Keynesian policies appeared not to offer an adequate response to the stagflationary situation.

Also during the 1970s developments in economic analysis were demonstrating the inadequacy of post-war Keynesian macroeconomics. First a range of economic theories were put forward which purported to explain certain political developments but which also implied weak productivity performance within Keynesian social democratic regimes. Second, increasing theoretical attention was given to the role of aggregate supply in the analysis of inflation and unemployment. This work increasingly led economists to question whether there was a significant role for demand management. The idea of the natural rate of unemployment suggested that appropriate microeconomic policies might be the best way to sustain low levels of unemployment; work on the credibility of policy stance pointed to the danger that employment targets would undermine counter-inflationary strategies; while, finally, work on expectations formation argued that anticipated policy changes would be ineffective as a means of influencing employment and real GDP.

The implications of the new analysis were taken seriously by the Treasury under Chancellors Howe and Lawson (Begg, 1987) and were clearly set out in the latter's Mais Lecture (Lawson, 1984). The Conservatives of the 1980s would abandon discretionary fiscal and monetary policy for pre-announced rules (the Medium Term Financial Strategy), which would focus on achieving low inflation while accepting that anticipated demand management policy was ineffective in increasing employment. Meanwhile microeconomic policies (including taxation and trade union reform) would be assigned to increasing sustainable levels of employment and growth through raising incentives and improving the supply side of the economy. By the mid-1980s, then, macroeconomic thinking, in government circles at least, seemed to have much more in common with that of the pre-Keynesian 1930s than of the 1950s and 1960s.

By contrast, with regard to the working of markets and the efficient use of resources the direction of policy in the 1980s has moved distinctly away from the tendencies of both the 1930s and the early post-war period. The interwar years saw governments increasingly seeking to insulate the economy from the pressures of competition, through imposing tariffs, encouraging cartels, and regulation of industries like coal and cotton. The 1945–51 Labour Governments sought further escape from market failure through nationalization of major industries such as coal, gas, and the railways.

There was, of course, an early revival of competition policy with the Restrictive Practices Act, the establishment of the Monopolies Commission, and Britain's participation in international tariff-cutting agreements. Nevertheless the main thrust of policy should still be seen to have been geared towards correcting market failures in the efficient allocation of resources and this was reflected in the growth through the 1960s of interventions in the form, for example, of regional and industrial policies such as subsidized investment in selected areas and inducements to mergers to achieve economies of scale, or in the 1967 rules based on marginal cost pricing for the operation of nationalized industries.

The outcome of these policies came during the 1970s to be widely regarded as most unfortunate. In particular it was argued that the rapidly growing subsidies had been captured by producer groups to prop up inefficient and declining activities (Morris, 1983) and that the nationalized industries' costs were much too high, while political pressures made controls upon them ineffective (NEDO, 1976). Economic theorists began to stress the existence of conflicts between the efficient allocation of resources and improvements in productivity given that Whitehall had imperfect information on what could be achieved (Vickers and Yarrow, 1988). Thus, while pricing at marginal cost would prevent exploitation of monopoly power, it would offer no inducement to management to pursue cost reductions through higher productivity; by contrast, profit incentives would encourage management to discover that costs could be lowered but at the expense of departures from marginal cost pricing. In sum, regulation, ostensibly in the interests of allocative efficiency, brought with it the prospect of underperformance and excessive costs.

Since the late 1970s but obviously particularly under the Thatcher Governments there has been a considerable effort to make underperformance less attractive in both public and private sectors (in marked contrast to British policy in the 1930s in the aftermath of an equally severe recession). Both tight financial targets for nationalized industries and privatization with RPI–X-type regulation can be seen in this vein, as can the ending of foreign exchange restrictions in 1979 (with its attendant requirement to make returns attractive by world standards) together with the large reduction in regional and investment subsidies. The new climate was clearly signalled by the government's conduct of the 1980 steel strike and is underlined by privatizations of natural monopolies like water.

A central concern of economic policy in the 1940s was the attempt to achieve a 'fairer' society characterized by the abolition of poverty and a substantially more equal distribution of after-tax incomes than had obtained between the wars. The Beveridge Report of 1942 led to major increases of transfer payments and of entitlements to non-means-tested benefits while high taxation during wartime paved the way for a relatively large government budget thereafter, even under Conservative administrations (Peacock and Wiseman, 1961). In the 1950s there was a widely shared sense of satisfaction at the apparent achievement of these redistributive aims (Crosland, 1956).

Up to the end of the 1970s, although there was a retreat from the Beveridge system towards greater reliance on means-tested benefits like Supplementary Benefit, these post-war arrangements remained relatively unchallenged and most benefits grew *pari-passu* with earnings, leading to significantly higher spending than Beveridge had originally proposed (Dilnot *et al.*, 1984). The British tax system was characterized throughout by exceptionally high marginal tax rates for top earners together with tax reliefs for approved uses of savings which were not conducive to the efficient allocation of resources (Kay and King, 1986).

Against this background the changes to tax and benefit policies in the 1980s seem quite radical, even if in some ways diluted by comparison with some rightwing proposals. Until very recently a top marginal income tax rate of 40 per cent, a poll tax, the indexation of benefits to prices rather than wages, and the widespread sell-off of council houses would have been generally regarded as politically inconceivable as well as distributionally unacceptable.

In sum, the policy stance of the Conservatives under Mrs Thatcher is markedly different from that of the Conservatives under Churchill, Eden, and Macmillan. The disappointing performance of the economy in the 1970s has promoted major experiments in the 1980s as the government has distanced itself from the beliefs of the Butskellite era and from the corporatist tendencies of the 1960s and 1970s.

## 3. Macroeconomic Performance

In this section we examine the performance of the economy as a whole in the context both of earlier periods and of other countries. In doing so we concentrate on five indicators—unemployment, inflation, short-run output fluctuations, long-run growth, and the balance of payments—all of which were important concerns of policymakers, albeit with varying degrees of priority, for at least part of the post-war period.

Fig. 1.1 displays in detail the behaviour of unemployment rates and inflation over time. Measures of unemployment are heavily dependent on the way in which the count is taken and this has changed radically over time. An official series on today's basis is only available back to 1971 and we have made adjustments to the earlier data to render them broadly comparable. The 1946–70 figures were adjusted on the basis of comparisons of the current and previous definition series for the 1970s and a further correction was made to allow for the restricted scope of the interwar national insurance scheme, as proposed by Metcalf *et al.* (1982). The corrections are large and this emphasizes how misleading it would be simply to report the raw data collected at the time, as is so often done.

Fig. 1.1 shows that until the 1980s unemployment was lower than in the inter-war years but equally clearly by the 1970s the economy no longer achieved the exceptionally low unemployment of the early post-war period. This relatively favourable experience was succeeded in the 1980s, however, by an episode of unemployment

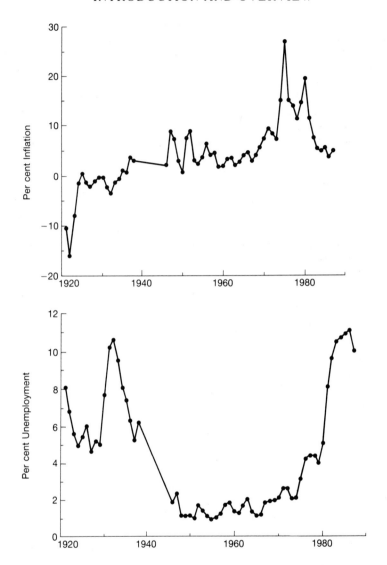

FIG. 1.1.    *Inflation and unemployment 1921–1987*

*Notes*:    Unemployment figures as estimated in 1988; pre-1971 adjusted from the original insurance data:
1921–38 × 0.478; 1946–70 × 0.765.

*Source*:    Feinstein (1972, *Economic Trends* 1989).

roughly on a par with the worst years of the 1930s but lasting twice as long until the
sharp falls of 1987–9. It seems that both supply and demand conditions in the
labour market have varied markedly over time, a topic which is explored in depth
in chapter 7.

   Turning to inflation, it is apparent from Fig. 1.1 that the post-war years have
been very different from the era of falling prices which prevailed from the early

1920s through the Depression of the early 1930s. Nevertheless despite the existence of very low levels of unemployment the 1950s and 1960s were years of relatively modest inflation to which the economy has recently returned following the severe deflation of the early 1980s. The intervening years represent Britain's worst peacetime inflationary experience, the shock of which has profoundly influenced economists and politicians alike. Varying inflationary outcomes reflected changes in the labour market and in world commodity prices, and trends in monetary policy, and these factors are explored in detail in Chapters 3 and 8.

Taking unemployment and inflation together it is apparent that ever since the early 1970s the 'misery' of the two combined has been far in excess of the earlier years and that while inflation in the 1980s has returned to 1960s levels unemployment very definitely has not.

Table 1.1 allows us to develop an international perspective on British unemployment and inflation. British unemployment is seen to have been below the average of the other four countries only in the first period and distinctly the highest by the 1980s. It is also clear that there has generally been higher unemployment since the end of the post-war boom in 1973 with the European countries suffering decidedly more than Japan or the United States.

TABLE 1.1. *International comparisons of inflation and unemployment rates*

| International comparisons of inflation (%) | | | | | | | |
|---|---|---|---|---|---|---|---|
| 1950–64 | | 1965–73 | | 1974–81 | | 1982–7 | |
| USA | 2.2 | USA | 4.3 | Germany | 4.7 | Japan | 1.1 |
| Germany | 3.2 | Germany | 4.5 | Japan | 7.0 | Germany | 2.8 |
| UK | 4.0 | France | 5.0 | USA | 8.4 | USA | 3.6 |
| Japan | 4.2 | UK | 5.9 | France | 11.0 | UK | 5.3 |
| France | 6.0 | Japan | 6.2 | UK | 16.0 | France | 7.1 |
| Standardized unemployment rates (%) | | | | | | | |
| 1950–64 | | 1965–73 | | 1974–81 | | 1982–7 | |
| Japan | 1.8 | Germany | 0.9 | Japan | 2.0 | Japan | 2.6 |
| France | 1.9 | Japan | 1.2 | Germany | 3.3 | Germany | 6.8 |
| UK | 2.5 | France | 2.1 | France | 5.1 | USA | 6.8 |
| Germany | 3.6 | UK | 3.1 | UK | 5.7 | France | 9.5 |
| USA | 4.8 | USA | 4.4 | USA | 6.8 | UK | 11.3 |

*Sources:* 'Standardized unemployment' attempts to correct for different national conventions in counting unemployment and is based on Maddison (1982) and OECD (1989b); inflation is measured by the rate of change of the GDP deflator and comes from OECD (1989a) and OECD (1970).

Similarly, to an extent there is a common pattern in inflationary trends with a general tendency to some increase in the Vietnam War period, a further rise, marked in some cases, during the years beginning and ending with the two OPEC oil shocks, followed by a substantial decrease in inflation in the 1980s. The UK has had higher than average inflation throughout and coped least well with the difficult 1970s period, but has achieved a creditable reduction in inflation in the 1980s.

As noted in section 2, in the period of demand management governments sought to smooth out short-term fluctuations in economic activity, in particular wishing to ameliorate recessions, which had been severe between the wars. Whether or not they were successful, Table 1.2 shows that the years up to 1973 were remarkable in that the disturbances were 'growth recessions' which involved a slowdown in the rate of growth rather than absolute reduction in the level of production. This was in marked contrast to the inter-war years and also to the post-1973 period, when there was a significant decline in output in both 1973–5 and 1979–81. In the latter case the recession was of a similar magnitude to the notorious years of 1929–31 during the World Depression.

TABLE 1.2. *Average growth rates in downswings*
(%/yr)

|  | GDP | Industrial production |
|---|---|---|
| 1920–38 | −1.2 | −8.3 |
| 1951–64 | 0.6 | −0.9 |
| 1964–73 | 1.9 | 1.4 |
| 1973–87 | −2.0 | −4.4 |

*Sources*: *Economic Trends* (1989); Mitchell (1975).

Increases in living standards depend upon long-run growth in real GDP per person and in turn this is based on productivity growth. Table 1.3 gives a long view of British economic growth and highlights the relatively strong performance in the years of the post-war boom, 1951–73, when productivity growth was at an alltime high. Growth slowed markedly in the 1970s but in the 1980s recovery has seen a very respectable, although not spectacular, rise in living standards and a return towards 1960s labour productivity growth.

TABLE 1.3. *Average annual growth rates*
(%/yr)

|  | GDP | GDP per person | GDP per employee | Total factor productivity |
|---|---|---|---|---|
| 1856–73 | 2.2 | 1.4 | 1.3 | 1.5 |
| 1873–1913 | 1.8 | 0.9 | 0.9 | 0.6 |
| 1924–37 | 2.2 | 1.8 | 1.0 | 0.6 |
| 1951–73 | 2.8 | 2.3 | 2.4 | 2.2 |
| 1973–9 | 1.3 | 1.3 | 1.1 | 0.5 |
| 1979–87 | 1.8 | 1.7 | 2.1 | 1.1[a] |

[a] Business sector only, 1979–86.

*Sources*: Economic Trends Annual Supplement (1989); Matthews *et al.* (1982); Englander and Mittelstadt (1988).

Exceptionally fast growth in the 1950s and 1960s followed by a marked slowdown was, of course, a universal experience among OECD countries, as Table 1.4 shows. Conditions for growth after the war were particularly favourable with widespread

opportunities to imitate American technology, to contract low productivity agriculture, and to exploit cheap energy in a rather stable macroeconomic environment of
freer and rapidly growing world trade—circumstances which have not prevailed
since the early 1970s and which on the whole did not obtain between the wars.

One of the most disappointing aspects of British economic performance over the
post-war period is that the rate of economic growth has been slower than that of
other countries. Table 1.4 provides an invaluable perspective on British performance
and reflects a long period of relative British economic decline through to the end of
the 1970s. Thus, although British growth in the 1950s and 1960s was impressive by
our own historical standards it was depressingly poor relative to that of other
countries, GDP growth being the lowest of the sixteen countries and GDP/person–
hour growth thirteenth of the sixteen. It should be noted, however, that the
slowdown since 1973 has affected some countries rather more than the UK so that
our productivity growth has risen to sixth best.

TABLE 1.4. *Annual average growth rates*
(%/yr)

|  | 1913–50 | | 1950–73 | | 1973–86 | |
|---|---|---|---|---|---|---|
|  | GDP | GDP/ person hr | GDP | GDP/ person hr | GDP | GDP/ person hr |
| Australia | 2.1 | 1.6 | 4.7 | 2.7 | 2.8 | 1.8 |
| Austria | 0.2 | 0.9 | 5.4 | 5.9 | 2.3 | 2.8 |
| Belgium | 1.0 | 1.4 | 4.1 | 4.4 | 1.8 | 1.7 |
| Canada | 2.9 | 2.4 | 5.2 | 2.9 | 3.4 | 1.5 |
| Denmark | 2.5 | 1.6 | 4.0 | 4.1 | 2.0 | 1.5 |
| Finland | 2.4 | 2.3 | 4.9 | 5.2 | 2.8 | 2.5 |
| France | 1.0 | 2.2 | 5.1 | 5.0 | 2.3 | 3.4 |
| Germany | 1.3 | 1.0 | 6.0 | 6.0 | 1.9 | 3.0 |
| Italy | 1.4 | 1.7 | 5.5 | 5.5 | 2.3 | 2.1 |
| Japan | 1.8 | 1.7 | 9.7 | 7.6 | 3.6 | 3.1 |
| Netherlands | 2.4 | 1.7 | 4.8 | 4.3 | 1.9 | 1.8 |
| Norway | 2.9 | 2.5 | 4.0 | 4.3 | 4.2 | 3.3 |
| Sweden | 2.8 | 2.8 | 3.8 | 4.4 | 1.7 | 1.6 |
| Switzerland | 2.0 | 2.7 | 4.5 | 3.3 | 0.9 | 1.6 |
| UK | 1.3 | 1.6 | 3.0 | 3.2 | 1.4 | 2.5 |
| USA | 2.8 | 2.4 | 3.7 | 2.4 | 2.5 | 1.2 |

*Source*: Maddison (1982, 1989).

Table 1.5 highlights this comparatively poor performance in a rather different way
by looking at income levels adjusted for differences in the cost of living. Whereas in
1950 the UK ranked fifth, by 1973 we had fallen to tenth, and by 1987 to thirteenth.

Finally in Table 1.6 we briefly report on the balance of payments. For much of the
post-war period one of the most closely watched economic statistics was the current
account of the balance of external payments which, although not an objective in
itself, was taken to be a major constraint on economic policy and frequently dominated policy debate in the context of economic crises. With that in mind the striking
feature from the perspective of the late 1980s is that the deficits seen in Table 1.6

TABLE 1.5. *GDP per capita in international dollars*
(UK = 100)

|  | 1950 | 1973 | 1987 |
|---|---|---|---|
| Australia | 105.2 | 103.8 | 103.9 |
| Austria | 50.9 | 86.8 | 95.8 |
| Belgium | 74.7 | 93.6 | 95.5 |
| Canada | 115.6 | 126.1 | 138.4 |
| Denmark | 93.3 | 105.8 | 108.4 |
| Finland | 62.6 | 91.8 | 103.5 |
| France | 70.5 | 100.7 | 103.2 |
| Germany | 60.1 | 102.5 | 108.6 |
| Italy | 55.7 | 92.1 | 98.3 |
| Japan | 26.8 | 89.3 | 106.3 |
| Netherlands | 85.2 | 104.6 | 100.2 |
| Norway | 82.4 | 95.4 | 127.0 |
| Sweden | 93.5 | 111.8 | 112.5 |
| Switzerland | 126.0 | 142.4 | 129.7 |
| USA | 160.6 | 148.1 | 147.6 |

*Source*: Maddison (1989).

generally appear relatively modest with the exception of the immediate post-war crisis years, the Korean War period, and the aftermath of the first oil price shock in the mid-1970s.

TABLE 1.6. *UK balance of payments current account/GDP*
(%)

| 1946 | −2.3 | 1957 | 1.1 | 1968 | −0.6 | 1979 | −0.3 |
|---|---|---|---|---|---|---|---|
| 1947 | −3.6 | 1958 | 1.5 | 1969 | 1.0 | 1980 | 1.4 |
| 1948 | 2.2 | 1959 | 0.7 | 1970 | 1.6 | 1981 | 2.7 |
| 1949 | 0.0 | 1960 | −0.9 | 1971 | 1.9 | 1982 | 1.7 |
| 1950 | 2.4 | 1961 | 0.1 | 1972 | 0.3 | 1983 | 1.3 |
| 1951 | −2.5 | 1962 | 0.5 | 1973 | −1.4 | 1984 | 0.6 |
| 1952 | 1.0 | 1963 | 0.4 | 1974 | −3.8 | 1985 | 0.9 |
| 1953 | 0.9 | 1964 | −1.1 | 1975 | −1.4 | 1986 | 0.0 |
| 1954 | 0.7 | 1965 | −0.2 | 1976 | −0.7 | 1987 | −0.7 |
| 1955 | −0.8 | 1966 | 0.3 | 1977 | −0.1 | 1988 | −3.3 |
| 1956 | 1.0 | 1967 | −0.7 | 1978 | 0.6 |  |  |

*Source*: *Economic Trends* (1989).

## 4. The Evolving Structure of the Economy

In this section we examine some key structural characteristics of the economy, namely the composition of aggregate expenditure, the deindustrialization of employment, and the distribution of income. We select these both because they have attracted substantial attention from economists writing in the past fifteen years or so and because they are particularly interesting in the context of the discussion of the previous two sections.

Tables 1.7 and 1.8 give details of shares of investment and total government outlays (including both expenditure on goods and on transfer payments) in GDP in a comparative international framework. Relatively low investment coupled with or even caused by a large public sector has frequently been claimed to be a major factor underlying relative economic decline in Britain, for example by Bacon and Eltis (1978).

TABLE 1.7. *Shares of investment in GDP*
(%)

|         | 1950–9 | 1960–7 | 1968–73 | 1974–9 | 1980–7 |
|---------|--------|--------|---------|--------|--------|
| UK      | 14.6   | 17.7   | 19.1    | 19.3   | 16.9   |
| USA     | 17.4   | 18.0   | 18.4    | 18.7   | 17.9   |
| France  | 17.5   | 23.2   | 24.6    | 23.6   | 20.5   |
| Germany | 20.7   | 25.2   | 24.4    | 20.8   | 20.5   |
| Japan   | 23.3   | 31.0   | 34.6    | 31.8   | 29.0   |

*Sources:*  OECD (1970, 1989a); *Economic Trends* (1989).

TABLE 1.8. *Government outlays as a share of GDP*
(%)

|         | 1950–9 | 1960–7 | 1968–73 | 1974–9 | 1980–7 |
|---------|--------|--------|---------|--------|--------|
| UK      | 35.1   | 34.7   | 39.6    | 44.3   | 46.7   |
| USA     | 26.4   | 28.3   | 31.0    | 32.6   | 35.9   |
| France  | 32.1   | 37.4   | 38.9    | 43.3   | 50.6   |
| Germany | 30.9   | 35.7   | 39.8    | 47.5   | 48.0   |
| Japan   | 14.9   | 18.7   | 20.5    | 28.4   | 33.3   |

*Source:*  as Table 1.7.

Table 1.7 confirms that post-war Britain has tended to invest a somewhat lower share of GDP than other countries. At the same time, it should be noted that this was by no means a new feature of the British economy but rather was a long-established characteristic dating from at least the mid-nineteenth century (Crafts, 1985). Again there is a common international pattern of rising investment shares through the 1970s and a fall in recent times.

Table 1.8 demonstrates that there has indeed been a large rise in the British government budget relative to GDP since the early 1960s. In turn early post-war government spending levels showed a substantial jump from those of the 1930s (Peacock and Wiseman, 1961). More significantly, perhaps, Table 1.8 reveals that a rising share of government in GDP since 1950 is universal and that both the levels and rates of increase in this ratio are higher in France and Germany than in Britain. It is fair to say therefore that government spending has not been exceptionally high and that Britain has invested relatively little. Although this appears to support a widely held belief that Britain needed to invest more, it should be noted that rates of return were also disappointing. Finally, in both investment and government spending the unusual experience has been that of Japan.

The recession of the early 1980s saw a large fall in employment in British manufacturing and heightened awareness of the de-industrialization of the British economy in terms of falling absolute and proportional employment in industry. Changes in the structure of employment linked in part to international trade have been an important aspect of development throughout the century and in the long run have had a profound effect on both the British economy and society. Table 1.9 gives a longer term view of these changes.

TABLE 1.9. *Shares of employment in selected sectors* (%)

|  | 1911 | 1931 | 1951 | 1971 | 1988 |
|---|---|---|---|---|---|
| Agriculture | 8.1 | 6.3 | 5.1 | 2.7 | 1.3 |
| Mining | 6.2 | 5.7 | 3.8 | 1.6 | 0.8 |
| Food/Drink/Tobacco | 1.8 | 3.4 | 3.4 | 3.1 | 2.5 |
| Metals/Engineering/Vehicles | 10.1 | 11.0 | 16.7 | 17.8 | 12.1 |
| Textiles/Clothing/Footwear | 13.8 | 10.7 | 7.9 | 4.7 | 2.4 |
| Construction | 6.2 | 5.0 | 6.3 | 7.0 | 4.6 |
| Distributive trades | 9.1 | 14.5 | 12.1 | 12.7 | 15.3 |
| Financial services | 1.3 | 2.1 | 2.0 | 4.0 | 11.3 |

*Sources*: Lee (1979); Department of Employment *Gazette* (1989).

From Table 1.9 it is possible to get a sense of both what are long-standing tendencies and what are relatively recent developments. Sectors in a long-term relative decline, which has continued throughout the post-war period, include agriculture, mining, textiles, and, to a lesser extent, transport. Long-term relative growth belongs to the service sector in the form of distributive trades and financial services. Since 1971 the distinctly new features are the very rapid advance in financial services and the sharp decline—reversing earlier trends—in the metals, engineering, and vehicles sector. Whereas in 1951 financial services accounted for only 2.0 per cent of employment while metals etc., mining, and textiles amounted to 28.4 per cent, by 1988 their shares were 11.3 per cent and 15.3 per cent respectively with a likelihood of parity in shares in the early 1990s.

Table 1.10 deals with a higher level of aggregation and introduces international comparisons. De-industrialization in the UK is seen to have been much more rapid since 1970 but was already taking place prior to that date and starts from an unusually high proportion of the labour force in industry, as was typical of Britain in the nineteenth century (Crafts, 1985, pp. 62–3). The tendency to a marked decline in the industrial share of the labour force since 1970 is shown to be a quite general experience, although the British change is certainly more pronounced. It is clear that rich countries in the 1980s all have far more workers in services than Britain did in 1950 and that a substantial part of the shifting structure in employment in Britain can be seen as a 'normal' part of economic development.

Nevertheless contrasting fortunes in international trade undoubtedly explain some of the differences between the UK and Germany evident in Table 1.10.

TABLE 1.10. *Deployment of the labour force*
(%)

|  | UK | USA | France | Germany | Japan |
|---|---|---|---|---|---|
| *1950* |  |  |  |  |  |
| Agriculture | 4.9 | 11.9 | 27.4 | 23.2 | 41.0 |
| Industry | 49.4 | 35.9 | 37.0 | 44.4 | 24.2 |
| Services | 45.7 | 52.2 | 35.6 | 32.4 | 34.8 |
| *1970* |  |  |  |  |  |
| Agriculture | 3.2 | 4.5 | 13.9 | 8.6 | 17.4 |
| Industry | 44.8 | 34.4 | 39.7 | 48.5 | 35.7 |
| Services | 52.0 | 61.1 | 46.4 | 42.9 | 46.9 |
| *1987* |  |  |  |  |  |
| Agriculture | 2.4 | 3.0 | 7.1 | 5.2 | 8.3 |
| Industry | 29.8 | 27.1 | 30.8 | 40.5 | 33.8 |
| Services | 67.8 | 69.9 | 62.1 | 54.3 | 57.9 |

*Sources*: Bairoch (1968); OECD (1989b); figures for France and Japan are for 1954 and 1955 respectively not 1950.

Table 1.11 shows that between 1950 and 1970 the UK experienced a major decline in her share of world manufactured trade especially in the face of German and Japanese expansion. The situation has stabilized in recent years but with the UK at a much lower market share than Germany.

TABLE 1.11. *Share of world manufactured exports*
(%)

|  | 1950 | 1960 | 1970 | 1979 | 1988 |
|---|---|---|---|---|---|
| UK | 25.5 | 16.5 | 10.8 | 9.1 | 8.3 |
| USA | 27.3 | 21.6 | 18.5 | 16.0 | 14.9 |
| France | 9.9 | 9.6 | 8.7 | 10.5 | 9.1 |
| Germany | 7.3 | 19.3 | 19.8 | 20.9 | 20.6 |
| Japan | 3.4 | 6.9 | 11.7 | 13.7 | 18.1 |

*Sources*: Brown and Sheriff (1979) and DTI (1989).

In section 2 it was noted that the early post-war years were characterized by much public and political sympathy for the notion of a relatively egalitarian society whereas in the 1980s the pendulum has swung back again. In this context it is interesting to consider trends in the distribution of income over the last fifty years, as reported in Table 1.12.

The picture that emerges is a striking one. The available data suggest a distinct reduction in inequality in the late 1940s compared with the late 1930s and on these measures this seems to have been accentuated somewhat through to the 1970s. The 1980s has seen a sharp reversal of this trend, notably in original income where the share of the top 20 per cent now appears to be slightly higher than in 1938. Both the revival of profits as a share of national income and the rise of unemployment can

Table 1.12. *Distribution of income*
(%)

|  | Original Income | | | Gross Income | | |
|---|---|---|---|---|---|---|
|  | Top 20% | Bottom 20% | Gini | Top 20% | Bottom 20% | Gini |
| 1938 | 50 | | | 50 | | 46 |
| 1949 | | | | 47 | | 41 |
| 1961 | | | 40 | 45 | 5.3 | 40 |
| 1973 | 44 | | 42 | 42 | 6.2 | 37 |
| 1979 | 45 | 0.5 | 45 | 42 | 6.3 | 35 |
| 1986 | 51 | 0.3 | 52 | 44 | 6.1 | 40 |

|  | Disposable Income | | | Final Income | | |
|---|---|---|---|---|---|---|
|  | Top 20% | Bottom 20% | Gini | Top 20% | Bottom 20% | Gini |
| 1938 | 46 | | 43 | 41–3 | | |
| 1949 | 42 | | 36 | | | |
| 1961 | 42 | 6.5 | 33 | 42 | | 33 |
| 1973 | 39 | 6.8 | 33 | 39 | | 32 |
| 1979 | 39 | 6.5 | 33 | 38 | 7.1 | 32 |
| 1986 | 42 | 6.2 | 36 | 42 | 6.3 | 36 |

*Notes*:   'Original income' is income from value added; 'gross income' also includes transfer payments
in cash; 'disposable income' is gross income less income tax and national insurance
contributions; 'final income' is income after allowing for all taxes and transfers.

*Sources*:   Barna (1945); Lydall (1959); *Economic Trends* (various issues); Royal Commission (1979).

be presumed to have played a part in this turn around. Nevertheless it is also worth noting that, in response to these pressures, the social security safety net seems to have achieved a greater redistribution in the 1980s than in the 1960s as measured by the difference between the Gini coefficients for Original and Final Income.

A fuller discussion of inequality must also take into account the distribution of wealth, although it should be remembered that in this context measurement problems are formidable. The most reliable long-run estimates are those of Atkinson *et al.* (1989) reported in Table 1.13 which show a very high concentration of wealth between the wars, which has subsequently declined considerably but is still much greater than that of income. Analysis suggests that the major reason for declining inequality over time is the spread of 'popular wealth' in the form especially of home ownership. This leads Atkinson *et al.* (1989, p. 331) to argue that when data for the 1980s become available there will have been a further appreciable erosion in the share of the top 1 per cent and that, in contrast to the trends in income distribution, the reduction in wealth inequality is still continuing.

## 5. Institutional Changes in the Post-War Economy

An important lesson of economic history is that institutional arrangements matter both of themselves and in the constraints they place on governments' policy choices. There have been a number of highly significant changes over time in this context which form an important part of the background to the chapters that follow.

TABLE 1.13. *Distribution of wealth in*
*Great Britain*
(%)

|        | Top 1% | Top 5% | Top 10% |
|--------|--------|--------|---------|
| 1923[a] | 60.9   | 82.0   | 89.1    |
| 1938   | 55.0   | 77.2   | 85.4    |
| 1950   | 47.2   | 74.4   | na      |
| 1960   | 34.4   | 60.0   | 72.1    |
| 1970   | 30.1   | 54.3   | 69.4    |
| 1980   | 19.6   | 42.8   | 59.8    |

[a] England and Wales.

*Source*:   Atkinson *et al.* (1989, p. 318).

From a macroeconomic perspective we wish to draw attention to developments in four areas in particular. First, and most obvious, is the exchange-rate regime, which is dealt with more fully in Chapter 5. Under the Bretton Woods agreement there was a fixed exchange rate of $2.80 to the pound from September 1949 to November 1967, of $2.40 to December 1971 and of $2.60 until the currency switched to the present floating rate in June 1972; although the fixed exchange rate mechanism of the European Monetary System was established in 1979, the pound has not participated in this arrangement so far.

Operating under a fixed exchange rate has important consequences for the conduct of economic policy. In the long run if the exchange rate is to be maintained, there is not much scope for the inflation rate to diverge from that of competitor countries and thus relatively little freedom for monetary policy. The fixed exchange rate can be thought of as a discipline on the government and on wage bargaining. It is also true that in the short run fiscal policy tends to be more powerful than monetary policy as an instrument for altering the level of demand in the economy because of the impact on international capital flows. Operating with a floating rate may be similar if in practice the government has an exchange-rate target to which it subordinates other policy instruments, or at the other extreme with a free float there is complete discretion over monetary policy and indeed monetary policy tends to become the more powerful instrument for demand management. Thus the monetary targets used by policymakers in the 1980s were essentially predicated on flexible exchange rates whilst after 1972 the discipline of the fixed exchange rate system was lost.

Second, and closely related to the preceding discussion, the degree of capital mobility between countries has a significant impact on the conduct of fiscal and monetary policy. In the limit with perfect capital mobility there can be no differences in real interest rates; under fixed exchange rates monetary policy becomes completely ineffective as a means of demand management; and under flexible rates fiscal policy becomes impotent (Dornbusch and Fischer, 1988, ch. 6).

There have clearly been major increases in the degree of capital mobility in the post-war period with the pound a non-convertible currency until 1958 but, from 1979 and the abolition of foreign exchange restrictions, there has been unrestricted movement of funds into and out of the UK. Since the mid-1960s there has also been a dramatic increase in the volume of international capital movements reflected, for example, in the rise of foreign assets of deposit banks in the OECD from 1.5 per cent of GDP in 1964 to 17 per cent of GDP by 1984. The result has been a substantial reduction in real interest-rate differentials between Britain and elsewhere since the 1970s (Fukao and Hanazaki, 1986, pp. 8, 16).

A third key area of change, particularly over the past 20 years, concerns financial institutions and is discussed fully in Chapter 4. The period up to the early 1970s can be broadly characterized as one of heavy regulation and of attempts to control monetary growth through quantitative restraints on banks that operated in a non-competitive mode. The era ushered in by Competition and Credit Control in 1971 saw a retreat from this stance but a reluctance to accept the monetary consequences of loosening the authorities' grip. By contrast in the 1980s the emphasis has been on deregulation and instilling more competition in financial markets in the interests of the efficient allocation of resources resulting in a much more rapid rate of financial innovation. Paradoxically then in the early post-war period when monetary policy was 'out of fashion' it was relatively easy to predict both the supply of and demand for money while in the days of monetary targets in the 1980s it became extremely difficult either to interpret monetary statistics or to achieve the desired rate of monetary growth.

The fourth notable area of institutional development relating to macroeconomic performance is industrial relations. The early post-war years were a time of relatively strong central control in trade unions with the TUC much more willing than it was later on to pursue policies of wage restraint. From the mid-1950s onward bargaining became much more decentralized and power gravitated away from central leaderships towards shop stewards while from the late 1960s to the late 1970s union membership and militancy are generally perceived to have increased. Subsequently the Conservatives have stressed union legislation as a key institutional reform and, in an era of much higher unemployment, union membership, strike frequency, and, in the early 1980s, bargaining power have all fallen steeply.

There are strong reasons to believe that these developments have had important consequences for employment and productivity. (Chapters 7 and 9 respectively explore these claims in more detail.) From the mid-1950s to at least the early 1980s the industrial relations situation is widely argued to have steadily raised the level of unemployment consistent with stable inflation (Layard and Nickell, 1985; Minford, 1983). The 'cold climate' for trade unions in the 1980s seems to be associated with a surge in productivity previously unachievable through restrictive practices (Wadhwani, 1989) and, perhaps, a permanent increase in the sustainable growth rate of productive potential.

From a microeconomic perspective we group institutional changes in terms of two areas of interest, namely trends in competition and in the market for corporate control. These aspects of the organization of production are both of major significance not only for the efficiency of the economy at any point in time but also for the ability of the economy to eliminate inferior performance over time through the entry into an industry of new firms or new management teams. The person in the street aware of the existence in the 1980s of giant modern corporations and the post-war growth in scale of many industrial activities tends to believe that there has been an inexorable decline in competition ever since Victorian times. In fact, there have been countervailing forces in the post-war world. In the United States, for instance, Shepherd concluded that despite a substantial rise in aggregate and market industrial concentration up to 1970 the scope of competition rose notably as a result of anti-trust policy, import competition, and deregulation so that by 1980 77 per cent of national income was produced under conditions of effective competition whereas in 1939 and 1958 the fractions were only 52 per cent and 56 per cent respectively (1982, p. 619).

Comparable calculations do not exist for the UK but it is possible to review evidence on the factors identified by Shepherd. (Our brief discussion here is amplified substantially in Chapter 10.) As in the United States concentration increased markedly after the war until about 1970. The share of the top 100 firms in manufacturing rose from 22 per cent of output in 1949 to 41 per cent by the late 1960s since when it has remained constant (Prais, 1976; Mann and Scholefield, 1986). Similarly the average domestic 5-firm concentration ratio had reached 49 per cent by 1970 but was only 50 per cent in 1983 (Ferguson, 1988, p. 38).

The increases in concentration up to 1970 tended to reduce competition and were associated with rising market power (Cowling and Waterson, 1976). Nevertheless the opportunity to exploit market power has surely been checked by the growth of import penetration, particularly since 1970. The share of imports in home demand for manufactures was only 4.7 per cent in 1955, had risen to 16.6 per cent by 1970 and 35.2 per cent by 1987 (Scott, 1963, p. 41; Hewer, 1980, p. 108; *Annual Abstract of Statistics*, 1989, p. 219). Allowing for imports the average CR5 was 41.3 per cent in 1970 but only 35.9 per cent in 1983 (Ferguson, 1988, p. 38).

Indeed tariff barriers to the entry of imports which dated from the inter-war period were significantly reduced after Britain joined the European Free Trade Association in 1960 and then the European Economic Community in 1973. Average tariffs on dutiable goods were about 20 per cent in the 1950s and only 40 per cent of imports were duty free, whereas by 1966 tariffs were 14.9 per cent and 61 per cent of goods were duty free and by 1985 the figures were 8.3 per cent and 77 per cent respectively. Subsidies which were 2.7 per cent of GDP in 1952, fell to 1.9 per cent in 1960, 1.8 per cent in 1972, and 1.2 per cent in 1988 (Hufbauer, 1983; *Economic Trends*, 1989). These trends were, however, offset somewhat by the development of non-tariff barriers to trade which were negligible before 1970 but affected 5 per cent of manufactured imports by 1986 (Jones, 1987).

Anti-trust institutions have been strengthened over time, particularly between 1956 and 1973 with legislation to combat Restrictive Practices, including the cartel arrangements which proliferated in Britain in the 1930s and 1940s, successive strengthening of the Monopolies and Mergers Commission, and the establishment of the Office of Fair Trading. Deregulation has been an increasingly prominent feature of the 1980s especially in the formerly nationalized sectors and in financial services where competitive pressures have been introduced or increased.

Overall there is some uncertainty as to the net effect of these developments. It certainly seems highly likely that competition and trade policy has had favourable effects since the mid-1950s and that the worst results of rising concentration were probably felt in the 1960s. Since 1970 stable domestic concentration, rising imports, and deregulation have perhaps been a pro-competitive combination. One index of market power is the price-cost margin which Cowling estimates to have risen by about a third from 1948 to 1973 but to have stabilized thereafter (Cowling, 1982, 1983).

The threat of takeover is potentially a vital means of eliminating inadequate managerial performance, especially if new entry through the product market is difficult. The potency of takeover as a disciplinary device depends, however, on institutional arrangements both in terms of legal considerations and also on the efficiency of shareholders in monitoring and evaluating management. Indeed before the war takeover was virtually unknown and incumbent management was not well monitored by shareholders (Hannah, 1974).

The 1948 Companies Act paved the way for the development of the hostile takeover by requiring much fuller disclosure of information. The 1960s, early 1970s, and the mid-1980s saw episodes of spectacular expenditure on company acquisitions rising to 1.2bn. in 1968 and 1972 and to 1.75bn. in 1988 all at 1962 prices. Throughout the post-war period the proportion of shares held by institutional investors has risen from a trivial level before the war to 17 per cent in the late 1950s, 34 per cent in 1969 and 59 per cent in 1985 (Cosh et al., 1989, pp. 76–7). In the 1980s innovations in methods of financing have seen a major increase in the size of companies vulnerable to hostile bids culminating by 1989 with the 13bn. bid for British American Tobacco, a company which would have been regarded as impregnable by virtue of its size until very recently.

There are, however, reasons to doubt the efficiency of this market for corporate control, especially during the first merger boom from the mid-1950s through to the early 1970s. Two points in particular stand out. First, in this period size rather than profitability-performance appears to have been the best protection against takeover (Singh, 1975). Second, studies of post-merger performance are generally rather pessimistic and fail to find evidence that on average efficiency was improved (Cowling et al., 1980; Meeks, 1977) despite the stockmarket's ex-ante optimism that profits would be enhanced by mergers (Franks and Harris, 1986). Together these points suggest that the picture was one more of empire-building by ambitious managers than of effective disciplining of inferior performance.

Through the 1970s then it is arguable that the advent of the hostile takeover had not really fulfilled the role envisaged for it in obviating persistent management failure and relative economic decline. Recent developments suggest a more mature capital market in which this may be changing, although the evidence is at the moment only suggestive. In particular, the rise of institutional shareholdings seems to be associated with some increase in the role of profitability as a determinant of takeover and also with better post-merger results (Cosh et al. 1989).

## 6. Key Issues

In this chapter we have highlighted some of the most important changes which have taken place over the post-war period. First there were important structural changes. For example, we have drawn attention to post-war de-industrialization; to higher levels of public expenditure and investment as compared with the inter-war years; to the increased levels of industrial concentration, although this did not inevitably imply a diminuition in competitive pressures; and finally to a more active market for corporate control although it remained doubtful whether this activity had done much to enhance economic performance.

Second, there have been significant changes in the direction of economic policy.

For example the early post-war period saw the birth of the Beveridge welfare state and for most of the period there had been an explicit goal to reduce inequality, which seems to have met with some modest success. Similarly, there was a much greater emphasis upon economic management, although there has been a significant change in direction. At the beginning of the period demand management and market supporting supply-side policies held the centre of the stage. However, by the mid-1980s most of these had been downgraded in favour of a strategy in which market-enhancing supply-side policies and financial restraint were central. This change in the direction of economic policy, moreover, coincided with a change in the policy environment: the switch from fixed to floating exchange rates in the early 1970s, greater international capital mobility, a more liberal trade regime, and the emergence of decentralized wage bargaining.

Finally, the period has been one of contrasting macroeconomic performance. The 1950s and 1960s, for example, have occasionally been labelled 'The Golden Age' in view of the low misery (discomfort) index and the low degree of cyclical amplitude. The rate of economic growth was also high when judged against earlier periods, although Britain continued to decline relative to other countries. During the 1970s and 1980s, however, there was a deterioration in economic performance; the misery index rose while the rate of growth declined. The main source of optimism at this time was an improvement in Britain's relative growth performance.

It is these performance patterns that pose the most interesting challenges for the economic historian. And in the remainder of this chapter we shall be concerned with raising two important sets of questions:

(1)  Why has Britain undergone a further period of relative decline over the post-war period?
(2)  Why was the misery index low during the Golden Age? Why did the position deteriorate subsequently?

These issues are both complex and controversial, and inevitably the answers are likely to be coloured by political prejudices. Nevertheless it might help the student to make up his or her mind if we present two fairly simple—somewhat crude—sets of answers. The first are those of the 'Thatcherites'. The term is not used to describe the views of an individual but rather to describe the position of those who broadly accept the Conservative government's policy prescriptions and analysis of the post-war period. The second set of answers are those of the 'centrists'—those towards the centre-left of the political spectrum. This group has been less critical about the fundamental direction of post-war policy, although not necessarily about its details, and more inclined to draw attention to the importance of market failures and historical developments. These schools obviously do not lie at extreme points along a continuum so that it is possible to entertain other viewpoints, including numerous eclectic ones.

On the issue of relative decline, we have already drawn attention (in section 2) to the contrasting nature of the economic policies introduced by the Conservatives; the emphasis upon market-enhancing policies; and the rejection of the earlier 'policy consensus' with its emphasis upon distributional justice, and the welfare state, its enthusiasm for the mixed economy with a large state sector and interventionist industrial policies, its commitments to voluntarism in industrial relations, and, especially, to full employment.

In support of this position Thatcherites believe that the single most important cause of Britain's post-war decline was the nature and extent of economic policy. They do not deny that Britain may have entered the post-war period with an unfavourable historical legacy. But they do believe that the subsequent failure to effect a rapid adjustment and modernization was principally due to subsequent policy. This was misdirected in two fundamental ways.

First, there was little or no recognition of the possibility that the most effective way to correct market failures is often to use a market solution. That is, open up the economy to competitive pressures, so that backward firms are penalized at the expense of those who are more efficient and which have had more foresight.

Second, post-war policy was misguided because it was a growth-reducing strategy. For example, the commitment to economic management encouraged governments to enter the vote market with the result that Britain became overgoverned with the associated problems of high interest rates, penal tax rates, and excessive bureaucratic control (D. Marquand, 1988). Similarly, it was rarely recognized that attempts to correct market failure invariably resulted in regulatory failure which created inefficiencies more serious than those it was aimed to correct. Finally, Thatcherites point to the political payoffs implicit in the post-war consensus and would stress the strategic interactions between interest groups and governments. This would highlight the point that regulatory failure is always a serious problem in a mixed economy. Crucially concerns to avoid rising unemployment frequently put government in a weak bargaining position when confronted by vested interests, as indeed was also been true in the 1930s (Tolliday, 1987), besides undermining management incentives and abilities to remove inefficient working practices.

Few centrists, of course, would reject out of hand this line of argument. They would probably concede that there was too much reliance upon co-operative solutions in policy formation. Neither would they deny that the post-war settlement carried some costs in terms of efficiency losses and foregone growth. Nevertheless on a number of issues they would take a different line. In the first place they would tend to place much less faith in market solutions, arguing that Britain's decline has been due to supply-side weaknesses—poor industrial relations, inadequate training and education, low levels of non-military research and development, for example—which by their nature need to be corrected by government intervention. In any case they would deny that history implies that market solutions are inevitably effective in reversing economic decline.

Second, they argue that it is not clear to what extent policy failures were the result of unfortunate policy errors and how far they came from fundamental attributes of the political economy of the post-war settlement. For example, it could be argued that poor performance in the nationalized industry sector stemmed from inexperience in Whitehall in setting up sensible policy rules for operation and for coping with a world of incomplete information and X-inefficiency. Similarly it might be claimed that the design of industrial policy did improve over time but its effects failed to show through because of the macroeconomic shocks coupled with the support of lame duck firms. Again it might be suggested that policymakers' enthusiasm for mergers in the 1960s and 1970s was basically sound but was undermined by as yet unrecognized weaknesses in the capital market. Capital and product market failures did need to be rectified.

Nevertheless there are aspects of policy of which they are critical. They would, for example, question the assumption, which was implicit in much post-war policy-making, that it was necessary to maintain a high pressure of demand in order to reverse relative decline. Similarly, they would be critical of the preoccupation of post-war governments with investment, not recognizing that high growth tends to generate its own investment. The most serious criticism, however, is that much post-war policy simply was not directed at the underlying supply-side failures that were responsible for relative decline, and, when it was, it tended to be half-hearted and misdirected. The result, for example, was that Britain's management and labour force remained relatively undereducated; there was an underinvestment in research and development; and industrial relations remained adversarial.

When we turn to the question of the changing level of 'misery', the issues become both more interesting and more complex. For the Thatcherite the key to the Golden Age again is policy—including financial policy, both at home and overseas. Important here was the fact that for most of the period up to the mid-1960s financial policy in the United States was both restrained and exhibited a high degree of stability. This ensured that the world rate of inflation was low while at the same time, with the exception of the Korean boom, the world economy was not exposed to any sudden shocks or major disturbances on either the demand or supply sides.

At the same time British governments were committed to maintaining a fixed exchange rate under Bretton Woods and this ensured that the British inflation rate was kept close to that of the other Western countries. This financial discipline, moreover, had some beneficial side-effects. First, it gave credibility to counter-inflationary policies, so that on the few occasions when inflation rose to unacceptable levels it proved possible to reduce it again with only relatively modest transition costs in terms of foregone output and unemployment. Second, the low rates of inflation helped to maintain a stable business environment while sustaining relatively high levels of profitability, both of which helped to support relatively rapid employment growth.

Another possible reason for the low rate of wage inflation is that labour, conditioned by the deflation and relatively low productivity growth of the inter-war years, was subject to money illusion while real wages rose faster than anticipated. This helped to satisfy wage aspirations while making inflation easier to accept. It is also likely that at this time the natural rate of unemployment was fairly low. However, as time passed it was inevitable, given the contradictions within Keynesian Social Democracy, that government policy would increasingly distort the workings of the labour market. Thus from the late 1960s there was a conspicuous rise in the natural rate of unemployment as governments introduced distorting incomes policies, raised the replacement ratio, priced workers out of employment via the tax wedge, and failed to check the growing power of the trade unions.

The Thatcherites, therefore, believe *some* deterioration in the index was inevitable during the 1970s, as money illusion disappeared and the distorting effects of consensus policies became more pronounced. Nevertheless the major cause of the increased misery was financial policy that became increasingly expansionary as governments, both at home and abroad, increasingly tried to exercise discretion. At home this had started in the mid-1960s and resulted in the devaluation of 1967, the monetary explosion of the early 1970s, and the Heath–Barber boom of 1971–3. Abroad the most important developments were the ambitious social programmes of the Kennedy–Johnson administrations together with the inflationary financing of the Vietnam war. The inevitable consequence was a rise in the world inflation rate as well as a breakdown in the Bretton Woods system.

The other obviously inflationary factor in the 1970s was, of course, the supply-side shocks. Thatcherites, however, tend to discount these, arguing that these disturbances created inflationary problems only because of the underlying financial policies. Furthermore by the time the shocks appeared British governments had undermined the counter-inflationary credibility of their economic policies, by adopting stop–go financial policies and by trying to short-cut financial discipline by their continual adherence to incomes policies. The result was that by the mid-1970s wage inflation had become less sensitive to deflationary policies than it had during the 1950s and 1960s. The rise in inflation also takes the Thatcherite part of the way in explaining why unemployment rose from the late 1960s onwards. These inflationary disturbances not only reduced company profitability but created business uncertainty and impaired the workings of the market economy, further raising the natural rate of unemployment.

Nevertheless most Thatcherites would probably argue that for much of the 1970s and 1980s the level of unemployment was above the natural rate as a result of the major downturns of 1973–5 and 1979–81. These brought about reduced employment in the downturns with 'jobless growth' in the upturns. This was in contrast with the experience in a number of other Western countries, which over the same period experienced quite rapid employment growth. Thus what was significant about the two downturns was not that they took place or that they were severe by post-war standards, but that they demonstrated the inflexibility of the British labour market. But this again was a direct consequence of consensus labour-market policies which had not only raised the natural rate but had also impeded adjustment capabilities of the economy in the face of sudden disturbances.

As the economy enters the 1990s, however, the Thatcherite would argue that there are grounds for optimism. As a result of the 'monetarist' policies adopted in the 1980s financial discipline was restored, bringing down inflation while restoring counter-inflation credibility. At the same time the supply-side strategy was applied enthusiastically to the labour market, improving its flexibility while tending to reduce the natural rate of unemployment.

How then do centrists react to this story? Again there are areas of agreement. Few would deny that the low misery index of the Golden Age was partly due to the absence of external economic shocks or to the importance of a restrained financial policy in the United States. Neither would they deny the importance of the Bretton Woods system in maintaining financial discipline. Indeed we suspect that the typical centrist would have a stronger preference for a fixed exchange rate regime.

However, he is likely to take a slightly different position on the impact of economic policy. He would probably concede that Demand Management may not have been wholly successful. But this was in large part due to policy errors and to learning problems—associated with failings of data, quantification of policy effects and of forecasting difficulties associated with the primitive state of macroeconomic modelling—rather than the use of discretionary demand management per se. Furthermore much has been learned from this and later experience to suggest that Keynesian techniques still have a role to play under the appropriate circumstances.

The centrist would also probably argue that the adoption of Keynesian type policies, by raising business confidence, helped to sustain the long post-war boom upon which low unemployment partly rested. He might also point to other policy successes of the period: to the managed decline of the nationalized industries during the 1960s in contrast to the chaos during the 1980s, for example, and to the success of regional policy in reducing unemployment differences.

Perhaps the biggest difference between the two groups, however, concerns wage bargaining. For Thatcherites wage bargaining is of peripheral interest; what really matters is the maintenance of financial discipline and policies to maintain the flexibility of the labour market. Centrists, however, while not denying the importance of these factors, go further by arguing that wage determination cannot be treated like any other area of price formation, being influenced not only by the shape of policy but also by traditions and values and being strongly conditioned by historical developments.

Furthermore it is central to their position that wage determination is the key to any explanation of the success of the Golden Age. Specifically, it is argued that over this period, trade unions exercised wage restraint. The result was that not only was wage inflation contained but that, as a result, business profitability remained relatively high. This not only acted as an incentive for employers to expand employment, but also helped to maintain high levels of investment upon which the post-war boom was based.

Why the trade unions were prepared to exercise wage restraint at this time remains a somewhat open question. One obvious explanation is that labour was conditioned by the unemployment experience of the inter-war years (Newell and Symmons, 1989). Another related explanation is that as a result of wartime experience an 'implicit contract' was made, in which the trade unions agreed to exercise wage restraint in return for which the government would pursue full-employment policies and respect the voluntarist tradition. The unions at this time were able to uphold their part of the bargain in that the contract enjoyed the support of the membership while the prevalence of industry-wide bargaining enabled them to exert some control over the direction of wage bargaining (Flanagan et al., 1983).

Nevertheless the economic success of the Golden Age rested upon very uncertain foundations because even as Britain entered the post-war period it was clear that wage bargaining left much to be desired. On the one hand Britain was faced with a fairly low degree of 'social cohesion'. At the same time the bargaining structure—the multi-unionism, strong workplace organization, and yet weak national unions—gave the economy an inflationary bias. The only reason that neither inflation nor unemployment emerged as problems is that the implicit contract was effectively in operation. But as the period progressed the position gradually deteriorated. Underlying support for the implicit contract declined, while at the same time private-sector wage bargaining became increasingly concentrated at the place of work, out of the direct control of the formal trade unions. Thus by the late 1960s the implicit contract had effectively broken down.

Even in the early post-war period it was recognized that there was a need to reform industrial relations. In principle such reform might have moved in one of two directions. The first was to adopt centralized bargaining of the Austrian or Swedish variety by deliberately attempting to strengthen and rationalize the trade-union movement in the hope that trade unionism would become all-embracing, thus allowing wage problems to be contained through corporatist solutions. The other alternative was to move towards a Japanese-type system of decentralized company bargaining (and co-operative industrial relations), in the hope that local unions would become more responsive to market conditions.

Yet until the late 1960s there were no attempts to improve industrial relations or to reform wage bargaining, apart from the introduction of a number of norm-with-exception type incomes policies. These, however, did little to change the underlying system of wage bargaining; if anything they supported the status quo. No doubt part of the reason for the lack of progress was a genuine respect for the voluntarist tradition. It is also likely that there was very little consensus about the direction in which reform should move. Yet the most obvious reason for the lack of progress is that reform might very well have threatened the very existence of the implicit contract, which had been one of the principal reasons for the economic success. Thus, with the benefit of hindsight, the governments of the 1950s and 1960s cannot be blamed for not having reformed wage bargaining.

So going into the 1970s, Britain was ill-equipped to deal with the problems which were about to arise. Like the Thatcherites the centrists tend to be critical of some aspects of domestic financial policy: the inflationary monetary policy and the Heath 'dash for growth' in 1971–3 (with the adoption of floating). They also tend to be critical of the Monetarist experiment as an example of 'overkill'. Yet they would also probably concede that the supply-side policies of the 1950s and 1960s left the economy unprepared for the disturbances which were about to occur, in as much as these had been implicitly based upon the assumption that the long boom would continue. As a result they were not designed to promote flexible responses in the face of shocks.

Centrists also tend to place a good deal of emphasis upon changes in the international environment: the inflationary financing of the Vietnam War, the breakdown of Bretton Woods in 1973, and the subsequent US policy of benign neglect. They would also give much greater weight to the severity of the stagflationary shocks (common throughout the OECD) coming from wages in the 1960s, and oil prices in the early 1970s.

Nevertheless the crucial development had come earlier with the breakdown of the implicit contract. This was important because, first, it led to increased wage pressures and thus raised the natural rate of unemployment. Equally, if not more serious it left the government without an adequate strategy with which to counter the inflationary shocks of the 1970s. Britain now paid for not having reformed her wage bargaining earlier.

In effect there were two possible options open to deal with the inflationary problem, neither of which was very attractive. The first was a Corporatist incomes policy. This was tried in the mid-1970s. However, it had only a limited chance of success because the emergence of decentralized bargaining had effectively taken wage bargaining out of the hands of the official trade unions; while the failure to find a solution to the problems of public-sector pay in periods of wage restraint proved to be destabilizing. At best therefore this option offered a temporary breathing space. It is surprising that it had as much success as it did.

The second option was the 'market solution' of a short (if not too sharp) deflation, which was tried by the Thatcher Government in the late 1970s. This, however, also came up against the problems of the wage-bargaining system. In the initial stages of the policy nominal wages proved to be sticky, thus bringing about a massive shake-out of labour and the emergence of a structural unemployment problem. Subsequently, real wages proved to be insufficiently flexible, leading to an insider-outsider problem and a period of 'jobless growth'.

Nevertheless centrists do not condemn out of hand the changed policy stance of the 1980s, welcoming the return to better financial policies and giving guarded support to some of the supply-side policies. Overall, however, they remain sceptical whether the reforms have been wholly successful, arguing that recent experience does not suggest that the underlying weaknesses of the wage bargaining system have been corrected. Consequently they have serious doubts, as we enter the 1990s, whether there are very strong grounds for optimism.

Obviously the issues raised in this section are very large ones which go right to the heart of many political debates. Readers of this book will not, of course, find any ready-made answers—the evidence is at once too complex and inadequate. Nevertheless we hope that what is presented in the following chapters will serve to inform better judgements both on these topics and on British post-war economic history generally.

# 2

# Reconversion, 1945–51

## SIR A. CAIRNCROSS

When the war with Germany ended in May 1945 the full seriousness of the economic situation facing the United Kingdom was not widely appreciated. The strain of six years of war created expectations of better things when peace returned that it was not possible to fulfil.

The first and most compelling problem was how to pay for the imports indispensable to recovery. As Keynes put it, Britain was in danger of 'a financial Dunkirk', with total earnings of foreign exchange in the autumn of 1945 paying for only 40 per cent of expenditure abroad. This problem was aggravated by the disturbed state of the world, the need to maintain British troops in many different countries from Germany to Indonesia, and the growing distrust of Russian intentions both in Europe and in Asia. There was also in 1945–7 a world-wide shortage of food to add to procurement difficulties.

The domestic front also posed many awkward problems. The labour tied up in the armed forces and supply services, totalling nearly 9 million in June 1945, would have to be run down to a peace-time level so as to allow workers to be absorbed into civil employment without more than a brief transitional spell of unemployment. It was to be hoped also that the jobs they would find would be in the industries it was most important to man up. In parallel with this, industry had to be converted from making munitions and army supplies to meeting civilian market requirements at home and abroad, and reconstructed with an eye to future international competition. Industries such as coal-mining, textiles, and building which had been contracted in wartime had now to be rapidly expanded while others, which had expanded in wartime, especially the metal and engineering industries, were badly in need of an extensive overhaul. A third domestic problem was the heavy arrears of maintenance and renewal throughout the economy, the extensive bomb damage to housing, and the further investment that would be required if there was to be enough capacity to allow the level of employment to be raised and the surplus manpower of pre-war days to be offered full employment. This would make it necessary to achieve a high rate of industrial investment and, still more, of capital formation of all kinds. How, fourthly, was this to be financed when consumers would be in no mood to save and had accumulated unspent funds in wartime which they would wish to bring into use as soon as the goods they wanted were on sale? Was there not a danger that the pressure of demand would become excessive and find vent in inflation? Would full employment not add to this danger by opening the door to wage inflation? In war-time various controls had helped to limit the rise in prices but no one contemplated their indefinite retention. There was thus yet another problem of dispensing with the controls without letting loose uncontrollable inflation.

These were all problems arising out of the war. But the world had changed and new aspirations had been born. These included not just full employment but social security on a comprehensive scale. The public looked to the government to implement the Beveridge Plan and usher in what is now referred to as 'The Welfare State'. On the international plane also, change was in the air and relations with the United States, the Commonwealth, and Europe all needed reconsideration.

It fell to a new government elected in July 1945 shortly after the end of war with Germany and shortly before the end of war with Japan, to confront these problems and give expression to popular aspirations. It was the first Labour Government to enjoy a clear majority and it intended to use that majority to carry through a full programme of legislation. Not much of its programme bore on the acute economic problems listed above. It was a social, not an economic revolution, at which it aimed. Nationalization and full employment were its first concerns; but what was to be done with the industries nationalized, and how full employment was to be secured, had been given little consideration. Similarly, although there was much talk of planning, hardly any member of the government was sure what it meant except perhaps the continuation of physical controls. What dominated thinking as the government took office was the expectation of an early slump in the United States such as had occurred after the First World War. The danger of inflation was correspondingly discounted. Even the external situation, to which we now turn, appeared more manageable than it proved to be: there was little expectation of a world-wide shortage of dollars.

I

**The External Situation**

Large changes had taken place in Britain's command over imports from abroad. Not only had the war wrought havoc in many parts of the world from which she drew her imports, so that supplies were much reduced, but other countries could now be expected to re-enter world markets and bid for the reduced supplies. More troubling still was Britain's impoverishment, indeed her near-bankruptcy, in the form of inability to settle accounts with her suppliers.

First and foremost, there was a huge external debt such as no other belligerent had incurred: it was the largest external debt in history. The cumulative deficit in the balance of payments on current account from the outbreak of war to the end of 1945 amounted to £10,000m.; and although more than half of this had been met by the United States under Lend-Lease arrangements, not far short of £5,000m. had had to be found by borrowing in sterling or in dollars or by selling foreign investments. Most of the borrowing was in sterling from poor countries like India and Egypt and reflected large military expenditures in those countries. It was this borrowing that gave rise to the chronic post-war problems of the sterling balances— funds held in London on short-term by foreign banks and official holders. At the outbreak of war these liabilities had been roughly equal to the gold and dollar reserves at about £500m. At the end of the war they were over five times as great: not far short of £3,500m. while the gold and dollar reserves were just over £600m.

Second, the debt was still mounting. As Attlee told the House of Commons shortly after the Japanese surrender, British earnings from exports were currently no more than £350m. a year to which other receipts of foreign exchange might add a further £450m. in 1945. Total outgoings, on the other hand, including military expenditure abroad and the food and other supplies previously paid for by the United States, were running at the rate of £2,000m. a year. This left a gap of £1,200m. a year to be met by fresh borrowing abroad.

The external deficit reflected the intensity with which resources had been mobilized for the prosecution of the war. Manpower had continued to be withdrawn from the export industries until, by 1944, the volume of exports had fallen to 30 per cent of its pre-war level. This was made possible by the provision of Lend-Lease aid by the United States and by extensive borrowing abroad. The resulting division of labour between the allies, while it was no doubt to the mutual advantage of Britain and America, left the British economy in a very exposed position when the war ended and Lend-Lease was suddenly withdrawn. Britain had counted on continued American financial support in virtue both of the heavy dependence on foreign aid that her role in allied strategy implied and of undertakings by Roosevelt to Churchill at the Quebec Conference in 1944. No such support was offered when Lend-Lease came to an abrupt end in August 1945.

Official forecasts suggested that the deficit in the balance of payments would continue for at least three years. Over those years a cumulative deficit of perhaps £1,250m. was likely to be incurred before balance was restored. Even so, it would be necessary to keep the volume of imports below pre-war levels throughout and to regain the pre-war level of exports by the end of 1946. On a long-term view nothing less than a 50 per cent increase in exports—and more probably a 75 per cent increase—would do, and this would require a fivefold increase or more in volume in comparison with 1944.

A disproportionate rise in exports was required because of a third change in Britain's international accounts. In pre-war years exports had covered only 55 per cent of the cost of imports, the balance being largely met from a surplus on invisibles, mainly net shipping earnings and income from foreign investments (see Table 2.1). These two items alone had paid for 35 per cent of the value of pre-war imports. In the war, however, half Britain's merchant marine had been sunk, sales of investments abroad had exceeded £1,000m., and interest had to be paid on the large debts to other countries that had been run up. A large drop in invisible income was inevitable and, given the purchasing power of what was left over, imports had been halved. It was to make up for this loss on invisibles that Britain would have to push up her exports. To do so would mean fighting for a higher share of world trade and remaining competitive once Germany and Japan recovered.

A further reason for seeking a big increase in exports was the need to cater for a larger working population and one that it was hoped would be more fully employed and more productive than in pre-war years. With a higher GNP there was likely to be a higher demand for imports, and to pay for additional imports still more exports would be required.

The restoration of external balance faced yet another problem. The wars had dislocated the economies of many other countries and left nearly all of them, like Britain, in deficit. Only the United States and Canada were in surplus. Other countries had to draw on their reserves or borrow abroad in order to sustain their imports; and the source to which one and all turned for additional supplies was

TABLE 2.1. *UK balance of payments 1936–1938 and 1946*
(£ million)

| | 1936–8 (average) | 1946 (forecast) | 1946 (actual) |
|---|---|---|---|
| Imports[a] | −866 | −1300 | −1063 |
| Exports[a] | +477 | +650 | +960 |
| Trade deficit | −389 | −650 | −103 |
| Government expenditure overseas (net)[b] | −7 | −300 | −223 |
| Net income from overseas investments | +203 | | +85 |
| Net income from shipping | +105 | +200 | +9 |
| Other invisibles | +44 | | +2 |
| | −44 | −750 | −230 |

[a] Import and export prices were assumed to be about double pre-war prices in the forecast in col. 2 and turned out to be slightly higher than this. Re-exports and imports for re-export are excluded from the figures in cols. 1, 2, and probably 3. Imports and exports of silver bullion and specie are excluded from col. 1.

[b] In col. 2 the figure relates only to war expenditure. In the *Annual Abstract of Statistics 1953* military expenditure overseas in 1946 is given as £374 million but if war disposals, etc. are deducted, the net figure works out at £210 million. The figure in col. 3 excludes interest paid or received by government.

*Sources*: Col. 1　HM Treasury, 1945.
　　　　　Col. 2　Keynes, 1979, p. 555.
　　　　　Col. 2　*Economic Trends Annual Supplement* (1981).

North America. Such supplies, however, were obtainable only for dollars and a shortage of dollars grew out of the shortage of supplies.

### The Dollar Shortage

In those circumstances what came to dominate Britain's international accounts was not the balance of payments deficit but the drain of gold and dollars from the reserves. There was ample sterling around the world to pay for exports from Britain; but if payment was made in sterling, Britain was no further on in finding the means to settle accounts with the United States, her principal supplier. Payment in other currencies that were equally inconvertible into dollars was also of limited value unless supplies were offered in return that limited the need to buy from America. In a world of inconvertible currencies it was only too easy to end up with a large export surplus to countries making payment in 'soft' currencies and a deficit in 'hard' currencies that could be met only by drawing on reserves. Exports in total might then exceed imports in total without disposing of the balance of payments problem because the reserves continued to drain away in settlement of the deficits with hard-currency countries like the United States.

　　The dollar shortage did not come to the forefront immediately after the war, partly because most countries had substantial reserves and partly because the

United States was pouring out dollars through the United Nations Relief and Rehabilitation Administration, foreign loans, and in other ways throughout 1946. It was only gradually that the imbalance in British trade was seen to be part of a wider international imbalance that was reflected in an excess of American exports over imports and created the strains in settling accounts with other countries that were christened 'the dollar shortage'.

From the British point of view the dollar shortage had a double significance. On the one hand, it meant that sterling was less acceptable than dollars in international dealings and restricted Britain's freedom of manoeuvre in financing transactions with other countries. On the other hand, it meant that it was no longer possible to rely on a triangular or multilateral settlement of accounts such as had enabled Britain before the war to apply surpluses in trade with other continents to meeting a deficit with North America, or indeed with the whole of the Western Hemisphere. It was necessary to take direct measures to reduce that deficit, by reducing imports or expanding exports, within the limits of what could be furnished in settlement. This was not easy when so much of what Britain imported came from North America and so little was exported to North America in return. In 1938 imports from the United States and Canada had been more than four times as large as exports to those two countries; in 1945 they were not far short of ten times as big and even in 1946 nearly six times. Indeed, exports to the United States in the early post-war years did not even cover the bill for imports of American tobacco. Yet since the markets of North America were highly competitive—far more competitive in those years than the markets elsewhere in the world—it was peculiarly difficult to effect a large increase in exports to them except in traditional lines such as Scotch whisky, of which there was only a limited supply.

On the import side, the difficulties were just as great. North America had been before the war and remained after the war a major source of raw materials and foodstuffs, supplying a little over one-fifth of British imports in 1938 and nearly one-third in 1946. The rise in the proportion was an indication of the difficulty of procuring supplies elsewhere. Buying as much as possible in non-dollar markets, the government could procure in 1946 only two-thirds of the pre-war volume of imports and any further compression of dollar purchases meant a corresponding reduction in rations or a more acute shortage of raw materials.

## Negotiations for an American Loan

Given the international situation as seen at the end of the war, with the prospect of a large and obstinate deficit stretching out over several years, the need for a substantial loan (or grant) seemed inescapable. Since no other country, except perhaps Canada, was in a position to lend, this meant approaching the United States for assistance.

The incoming Labour administration, which took office on 26 July 1945, hoped at first for a grant; and shortly after the cessation of Lend-Lease in August it despatched a Mission under Lord Keynes to conduct negotiations in Washington. The Mission's instructions gave it no authority to propose a loan while the Americans made it clear that they were not prepared to offer an outright grant or interest-free loan. They insisted that Congress would not entertain such a possibility and would only accept the case for further assistance to the United Kingdom if it could be persuaded that this was to the advantage of the United States. For this purpose it would be necessary for the United Kingdom to support the American vision of a multi-lateral trading system with convertible currencies and trade that was free from discriminatory trade restrictions. In concrete terms this would mean acceptance of the Bretton Woods Agreement, the introduction of sterling convertibility within one year from the ratification of a Loan Agreement, and the abandonment of dis-crimination between imports that cost dollars and those that did not.

The negotiations were long and troubled. After a brilliant initial exposition of Britain's economic situation, Keynes wore himself out in coping with the misunder-standings of American negotiators in Washington and British Ministers in London. Agreement was not reached until December 1945 and not approved by Congress until July 1946. It was not well received in the United Kingdom and had a rough passage in Parliament where the only convincing defence of it came from Keynes in the House of Lords. In the United States, approval came only after a swing in American opinion as differences with the USSR began to multiply and the threat of Soviet expansionism raised the value of a reliable European ally.

The loan was for a smaller sum than the Government's advisers had thought necessary—$3,750m. rather than the $5,000m. that had been contemplated—but it was made up to $5,000m. by the Canadian government, at considerable risk to its own balance of payments. In addition, the United Kingdom was to pay $650m. in final settlement of Lend-Lease obligations and credit for this amount would be added to the American loan. The rate of interest on the loan was nominally 2 per cent, beginning after five years, and repayment, which was also to begin after five years, was to be completed in 50 years. Annual instalments of interest and capital worked out at $140m. and were equivalent actuarially to an interest charge of 1.6 per cent over the life of the loan.

While these terms fell short of Ministerial hopes they were not only generous by commercial standards but allowed the United Kingdom to borrow on a scale that was several times larger than what might have been raised on commercial terms (e.g. from the Export–Import Bank). The additional dollar obligation, which seemed so formidable a burden in 1945–6, was subject to a complex waiver clause that suspended it when exports fell short of about 160 per cent of the pre-war volume. While it was large in relation to current dollar earnings in 1945–6, it has to be seen against a total value of British exports of nearly £1,000m. in 1946, £2,700m. in 1951 when payments began, and total foreign exchange earnings of £40,000m. in 1976, half-way through the life of the loan. The service of the loan speedily became a matter of little importance except in one or two acute balance of payments crises in the 1950s.

More important in the long run were the conditions attached to the loan. Under the Bretton Woods Agreement Britain would have been free to defer making the pound convertible until the end of a period of transition, generally expected to last five years. The Loan Agreement, however, obliged Ministers, much against their will, to shorten the period of transition and adopt convertibility by mid-1947. As we shall see, this was an undertaking that could not be fulfilled and the effort to carry it out had the effect of discrediting convertibility as an aim.

The loan provided a breathing-space but did not by itself produce any of the adjustments that were necessary in order to restore external balance. These depended on the economic recovery of Britain's trading partners, on a redeployment of domestic resources, and in the meantime on a limitation and rationing of imports to what the country could afford.

### Balance of Payments Crises

The process of readjustment of the external balance was far from smooth. It was punctuated by a succession of exchange crises in 1947, 1949, and 1951–2. Even before the first of these, the recovery of exports was interrupted by a fuel crisis in February 1947 which cut off electricity from a large section of British industry for three weeks and knocked at least £100m. off exports during the year. While industry was recovering the drain on the reserves accelerated, especially after the resumption of convertibility in mid-July. In the last full week of convertibility before its suspension on 20 August, the loss of reserves reached $230m. and by the end of the year the total had reached $4,100m.—more than the whole amount of the American loan. After an anxious winter and a long period of suspense, the drain was staunched by the first payments of Marshall Aid in 1948. The dollar deficit was cut to $1,700m. and in 1949 to $1,500m. But these were still formidable amounts, even with $1,500m. in Marshall Aid over the two years and it was necessary to draw on the limited gold and dollar reserves. The reserves, indeed, proved quite insufficient to withstand a fresh exchange crisis in the summer of 1949, brought on by a brief depression in the United States when it seemed as if the dollar and sterling worlds might be torn apart. A devaluation from $4.02 to $2.80 to the pound took place on 18 September after a long struggle. Most other countries devalued simultaneously against the dollar so that although the par value fell by 30 per cent, the trade-weighted devaluation of sterling was very much less—about 9 per cent.

The improvement in 1950 following devaluation was greatly assisted by the recovery of the American economy and its restocking with materials from the outer sterling area. For the first time there was a large-scale replenishment of reserves. At the end of 1950, this moved the United States to discontinue Marshall Aid which had brought £652m. to the support of the balance of payments over the previous three years. Six months previously, at the end of June 1950, war had broken out in Korea, an event that almost coincided with two other major developments at that time: the announcement of the Schuman Plan for a European Coal and Steel Community and the formation of the European Payments Union on 7 July. The Korean War soon overshadowed both of those events and led to a major effort of rearmament. By January 1951 the government was aiming to multiply the output of munitions by a factor of four, there were acute shortages of raw materials, primary commodities of all kinds had risen steeply in price, and the terms of trade were in course of shifting against the United Kingdom by nearly 20 per cent. This created a major sterling crisis that lasted well into 1952. It was in the middle of this crisis that the Labour government lost power in October 1951 and the Conservatives began what proved to be a 13-year tenure of office.

The deficits just quoted represent the deficit of the entire sterling area, not just of the United Kingdom. Other members of the sterling area could draw from the central pool of gold and dollars held by the Bank of England and make payment for the dollars from their sterling balances except where such drawings were subject to an agreed limit. In pre-war years the outer sterling area had paid dollars into the pool in exchange for sterling (as continued to be true after the war of the colonial territories). But in the early post-war years things worked the other way: the independent members of the sterling area drew heavily on the dollar pool, adding to the United Kingdom's difficulties. In 1947, for example, they drew $1,100m. (less gold sales by South Africa) out of a total drain of $4,100m.; and it was not until 1950, when the United Kingdom itself was in surplus, that they were able to make a net contribution to the dollar pool.

The fluctuations in the current balance of payments were much less violent than those in dollar outgoings except at the end of the period. On current account the deficit reached a peak of £380m. in 1947, virtually disappeared in 1948–9, changed to a surplus of £300m. in 1950 and plunged again in 1951 into a deficit of £370m. The dollar drain, on the other hand, rose much more alarmingly from $900m. in 1946 to $4,130m. in 1947, then fell steeply to $1,700m. in 1948. There was also a much bigger improvement in the dollar deficit in 1950 (from a drain of $1,500m. in 1949 to a gain of $800m.) and the turnaround in 1951 although nearly matched by the swing in the current account, was equally dramatic.

The frequency of exchange crises in spite of exchange control was the almost inevitable consequence of lack of reserves (which never reached $3bn. until the end of 1950), heavy short-term indebtedness in the form of sterling balances (amounting to $16bn. at the time of devaluation in 1949) and violent swings in the terms of trade. These made sterling vulnerable to balance of payments deficits, which were usually reinforced by speculative pressure in the form of 'leads and lags', and could only be countered by strong and immediate action. Usually this meant cutting the import programme and trying to limit outgoings on capital account (not, however, very effectively especially as there were no restrictions on capital flows to the rest of the sterling area).

The weakness of sterling could only be overcome in the long run by a sustained improvement in the balance of payments and it was a prime object of the government to accomplish this by administrative means. It did its best to encourage exports, first in general and later to dollar markets; and it held down imports well below the pre-war level. With an eye on the long-term difficulties of enlarging Britain's share of world trade in manufactures to the extent necessary to pay for imports on the pre-war scale, the government launched a major agricultural expansion scheme in 1948.

The priority that it attached to eliminating the external deficit is apparent from Table 2.2, which shows the changes over the six years 1946–52 in the allocation of resources between the main categories of demand. While exports increased in volume by 77 per cent over those years (they had already more than recovered to the pre-war level by the end of 1946), and imports were held down to an increase of only 14.5 per cent, the rise in consumption over those six years was no more than 6 per cent. Roughly speaking half of the increase in gross domestic product went to improving the balance of payments. For a country that had been at war for six years and emerged exhausted but victorious this was no mean achievement.

TABLE 2.2. *Change in allocation of resources, 1945–1952*
(£m. at 1948 constant market prices)

| | 1946[a] | 1947 | 1948 | 1949 | 1950 | 1951 | 1952 | 1946–52 | 1952–5 |
|---|---|---|---|---|---|---|---|---|---|
| Consumers' expenditure | (750) | 274 | −48 | 145 | 209 | −45 | −49 | 486 | 1065 |
| Public authorities' current expenditure | (−2450) | −816 | −12 | 154 | −16 | 149 | 219 | −322 | −12 |
| Gross domestic fixed capital formation | (650) | 246 | 126 | 133 | 78 | 6 | 24 | 613 | 453 |
| Value of physical increase in stocks and work in progress | (325) | 414 | −181 | −112 | −251 | 588 | −395 | 63 | 225 |
| Exports of goods and services | (650) | 93 | 416 | 238 | 324 | 129 | −55 | 1145 | 378 |
| Total final expenditure | (−75) | 211 | 301 | 558 | 344 | 827 | −256 | 1985 | 2109 |
| Imports of goods and services | — | −144 | 28 | −172 | −37 | −384 | 292 | −417 | −680 |
| Gross domestic product | (−75) | 67 | 329 | 386 | 307 | 443 | 36 | 1568 | 1429 |
| Net property income from abroad | — | 35 | 50 | −20 | 115 | −105 | −50 | 25 | 46 |
| Gross national product | (−75) | 102 | 379 | 366 | 422 | 338 | −14 | 1593 | 1475 |

[a] The figures for 1946 are based on the data in Feinstein (Table 5) and are not intended as more than a rough guide to the change in the allocation of resources in that year. The increments at 1938 prices have been recalculated at 1948 prices and adjusted to yield a fall in GDP of the same magnitude as in Feinstein.

Sources: *Years of Recovery*, based on *National Income and Expenditure 1957*, Table 12; Feinstein (1972), Table 5.

II

**The Domestic Situation**

This brings us to a consideration of the domestic situation at the end of the war. Here, too, the true situation was not widely appreciated. The experience of the 1930s was still vividly recalled as well as the short boom and deep slump that had followed the First World War. Well into the post-war period Ministers continued to express anxiety that that experience might recur and instructed their officials to bring to their attention any signs of deflation. In fact, however, there was never any serious danger of unemployment except from a shortage of fuel and power or of the materials needed to keep the factories busy. At no time did unemployment reach the 3 per cent that Beveridge had suggested to a sceptical public as a norm, apart from a week or two in the fuel crisis of February and March 1947. From the beginning it was excess demand and inflation that was the principal threat.

**Full Employment**

Employment policy, nonetheless, was what dominated the government's thinking in 1945. It had proved possible in wartime to reduce unemployment well below 100,000 and much thought had been given to maintaining full employment, although not to this degree, once peace returned. In May 1944, after prolonged debate at the official level, a White Paper on Employment Policy had been issued by the Coalition Government. This foresaw 'no problem of general unemployment immediately after the end of the war in Europe' although some increase was likely while demobilization was in progress. A greater danger was that excess demand would bring on an inflationary boom as happened after 1918 and that there would then follow the kind of slump that had raised unemployment to over 20 per cent in 1920 and proved so difficult to climb out of thereafter. The danger of inflation made it desirable to retain wartime controls over prices and consumption, to encourage a high rate of saving, and to regulate the flow and direction of investment. Since full employment would change the balance of power in the labour market in favour of organized labour, there was also a risk of inflation from the side of costs unless there was 'moderation in wage matters'.

It was not, however, the passages in the White Paper on inflation that commanded attention but the commitment of the government for the first time to 'a high and stable level of employment' as a primary aim and responsibility. It was a commitment to which the government had many reservations. It recognized that the level of demand and employment depended on conditions elsewhere in the world over which the United Kingdom had no control. If workers did not move to places and occupations where there were jobs, increased public spending might merely drive up prices; and if wages and prices could not be kept 'reasonably stable' it would be 'fruitless' to try to preserve full employment by increasing the flow of government expenditure.

What seemed at the time an even bigger reservation was the reluctance of the government to commit itself to full use of fiscal and monetary policy in the management of demand. Full employment was to be preserved by stabilizing the flow of total expenditure, or final demand, and this was to be done by operating on the main components of the total such as consumer spending and capital investment. But on the instruments to be used for this purpose the White Paper provided only a rough sketch and studiously avoided any commitment to unbalance the budget or raise interest rates. It contemplated little more than an effort to stabilize investment through a mixture of public works and jockeying larger enterprises into parallel action. Consumption was to be regulated through hire-purchase restrictions and other expedients. It took some years before the government worked out the techniques of influencing demand in what remained throughout the post-war period an overloaded economy. At no time until 1953 was it faced with the problem of *raising* the level of employment.

### Excess Demand

The pressure of demand was acute throughout the post-war period. In the early stages of reconversion demobilization was rapid but failed to remove the shortage of labour. In the eighteen months after the end of the war, over 7 million workers were released from the Armed Forces or from making supplies to meet military requirements. The numbers in other civil employment increased by 5 million, or over 40 per cent, while most of the 2 million women workers who had taken paid jobs in wartime withdrew from the labour market. During this upheaval unemployment rose to 400,000; but after the fuel crisis in February/March 1947 when the figure rose to over 2 million and another 500,000 were stood off from work but continued to receive their pay, unemployment fell to below 300,000 in the second half of the year and fluctuated over the next three years between a minimum of a little under 300,000 and a maximum of just over 400,000.

During these three years, 1948–50, there would appear to have been some slight easing of pressure. But in 1951, with the onset of rearmament after the outbreak of war in Korea in June 1950, the pressure again became intense. At the seasonal low point in July unemployment touched 210,000 before beginning a fresh climb that carried the total for the first time to over 500,000 in the spring of 1952. This turn of events was largely due to the deflationary effect of soaring import prices. Rearmament in Britain increased the pressure on domestic resources but rearmament worldwide squeezed the incomes of consumers by raising commodity prices and turning the terms of trade against importing countries like the United Kingdom.

### Inflation

The sustained pressure of demand had its inevitable impact on prices. Not that there was the violent inflationary surge of 1919–20. In 1946 consumer prices were up by only a modest 3 per cent above the 1945 level. But the rise persisted, with peaks in 1947 and 1951, when prices rose by 11.6 per cent and 12.5 per cent respectively, more gradual increases of around 3 per cent in 1949 and 1950 and intermediate rates of increase in 1948 and 1952 when inflation was subsiding from a peak in the previous year. By 1951 the cumulative increase was 35 per cent. This was a good deal less than the rise of 50 per cent in the six years of war and compared favourably with post-war experience in most other countries. It did not necessarily, however, do full justice to the inflationary pressure still remaining in the system in 1951.

## The Price Structure

The persistence of such pressure is evident from the controls by which price rises continued to be held in check. These controls are discussed below at pp. 38–44. It is also evident in the distortion of the price structure in comparison either with pre-war years or with the position in 1945. Export and import prices had roughly doubled in the course of the war and capital goods had risen in price by about 80 per cent, while other price indices—for consumer goods, the services of public authorities, final output, gross domestic product—were all up by about 50 per cent. These divergent trends continued after the war. By 1952 exports and imports had again risen most in price, exports by 85 per cent, imports by 118 per cent, while the indices for consumer prices, public authorities, final output, and GDP were grouped around a 45 per cent rise and capital goods again occupied an intermediate position with an increase of about 65 per cent.

The rapid climb in international prices put pressure on domestic costs. The biggest single influence on the inflation of those years was the rise in import prices which doubled in wartime and more than doubled again by 1952. This influence is particularly apparent in the two peak years 1947 and 1951 when import prices rose in the first by 22 per cent—three times as fast as consumer prices—and by 33 per cent in the second—a rise nearly equal to that in consumer prices over the entire post-war period to 1951.

## Wage Inflation

These increases not only raised costs and prices directly but reacted back on wages in so far as the government was obliged to acquiesce in some rise in domestic prices and could not hold down all prices by subsidy. The food subsidies introduced during the war to stabilize the cost of living had risen to about £200m. in the last year of the war and, together with the subsidies to agriculture, had reached £450m. in 1948 at which point the government called a halt. Subsidies on this scale were equivalent to one-fifth of consumers' expenditure on food, about 4½ per cent of GNP, and a heavy burden on the Exchequer. There can be no doubt that the food subsidies played an important part in keeping wage increases within modest limits and averting the danger of a wage–price spiral. But the rise in import prices was on such a scale that it was almost beyond the power of the government to offset it completely; and it already involved a damaging distortion of prices both directly and because of the high level of indirect taxation necessary in order to meet the cost. In the absence of additional subsidies, higher import prices had a large impact on the cost of living and eventually on wages.

Pressure on wages came also from two other directions. The rise in export prices, although falling short of the rise in import prices, far outran the rise in domestic costs. This left exporters with a profit that disposed them to bid for additional labour; and what the export industries paid in wages other industries had to match.

This was an illustration of a more general influence at work, namely the shortage of labour resulting from excess demand. The shortage, under conditions of full, if not over-full, employment, put organized labour in a strong bargaining position, and, as had been foreseen from the beginning, this was only too likely to start off an accelerating rise in wages.

No such rise occurred. It is true that money wage-rates rose by no less than 33 per cent in the first six post-war years. But this was rather less than the rise in consumer prices so that real wages actually fell. Moreover the response of money wages to conditions of excess demand was remarkably moderate. In 1947 when other prices were roaring up, the increase in wage-rates was no more than 3.6 per cent and over the four years 1947–50, the biggest increase in any one year was 5 per cent in 1948. The government used its influence with the trade unions, especially after the devaluation of 1949, to moderate the rise in wages; and it was only after the wage freeze of 1949–50 broke down and rearmament had begun in 1951 that the first double digit increases occurred. In the first five post-war years the rise in wage-rates averaged only double the rate in the last five pre-war years (4.4 per cent as against 2.2 per cent per annum) although unemployment had fallen from 2 million before the war to 350,000 or so after the war.

## Labour Shortages

The shortages of dollars and of manpower were accompanied by other more specific shortages. Within the manpower shortage, for example, some industries found it particularly difficult to attract sufficient manpower and were labelled 'undermanned'. These industries included agriculture, textiles, and coal-mining. Of these, agriculture had taken on more labour in wartime and employed a substantial number of prisoners of war. As these were repatriated, the shortage was intensified. It deepened still further when the government embarked in 1948 on a major expansion programme in order to relieve the balance of payments by cutting down imports of food. Curiously enough, employment in agriculture fell steadily from 1948 onwards while agricultural expansion nevertheless continued. The textile industries had lost about one-third of their labour in wartime and as major exporters were encouraged to re-expand. They did not, however, regain the pre-war level of employment before they, too, began to shed labour, beginning in 1952. Coal-mining proved to be the most difficult case of the three. It had lost about 5 per cent of its manpower during the war and unlike almost every other industry continued to lose labour when demobilization was at its height. After the fuel crisis in 1947 there was some recovery and employment was almost back to the pre-war level by the end of 1948. But from then on, as with agriculture and textiles, employment was at first more or less flat for some years and then began to fall steeply in the 1950s.

## Commodity Shortages

In the commodity markets there were similar shortages. In the case of manufactured goods they might simply be unobtainable, as with motor cars, supplies of which to the home market were severely restricted by agreement with the manufacturers, so that second-hand cars sold for twice the price of new ones. Most of the staple foodstuffs were rationed, the size of the ration varying with the supply currently available. Clothing and sweets were also rationed and some other commodities were released for sale only against a licence of some kind.

The most serious shortages from the point of view of production were of raw materials. Coal, steel, timber, and many other materials were in short supply and were allocated by official agencies. Some of these shortages resulted from a contraction in available supplies from abroad either because of war damage and dislocation or because they would have involved a higher outlay in dollars than the government could afford. Some reflected also a higher level of demand than in pre-war days, now that employment had expanded well above the pre-war level. In yet other cases the source of the shortage lay in domestic arrangements: the output of steel was limited by a shortage of fuel which in turn was aggravated by lack of labour and transport.

### The Rationale of Controls

All of these shortages, whether general or specific, could have been handled in one of two ways: either through the price mechanism or by administrative action. In wartime when the priorities that mattered were those of the government and could not find adequate expression in market dealings, it was natural to co-ordinate activity in relation to those priorities by administrative action. But when production was for the benefit of private consumers was there any reason why their preferences should not find free expression in market prices which were always capable of balancing supply and demand and eliminating shortages?

Those who thought in those terms would have dismissed the dollar shortage as a blind to conceal overvaluation of the pound sterling (and other currencies): the dearer the dollar the less the shortage. Similarly, they would have dismissed the shortage of labour as excess demand, easily cured by tight money or a budget surplus. Devaluation and a good dose of deflation would have put things straight. As for specific shortages, higher prices would soon have done the trick by confining supplies to the highest bidders and offering a stronger incentive to suppliers.

Ministers in 1945 would have had little sympathy with those views. They were not prepared to entrust the direction of the economic system to the unplanned operation of the price mechanism. They wanted a planned economy and planning was impossible without control. They did not at first visualize the possibility of control through the budget and the management of demand although by the time he left office in 1950 Cripps had come round to that approach and regarded the budget as 'the most powerful instrument for influencing economic policy which is available to the government'. Dalton, four years earlier, had taken satisfaction from the leverage over the economy afforded by the various controls inherited from the war; and most of his colleagues regarded them as natural to a planned economy. They would have objected strongly to the removal of controls if it meant a rise in prices, both from fear of open inflation and because higher prices were unfair to those who could not afford them and unfair also in the gains they yielded to sellers of scarce goods.

The Ministerial line of argument was not very convincing. They might not like open inflation but they were quite prepared to accept suppressed inflation. They saw nothing wrong with overloading the economy—nor, for that matter, did the Governor of the Bank of England or senior Treasury officials—and rather liked a little excess demand while protesting their horror of inflation. They had not suspended the price mechanism, raising the prices of controlled materials when costs increased and leaving large tracts of the economy uncontrolled. More than half of what consumers spent on food, for example, was not rationed at any time; and even at its most extensive in 1948 rationing never covered more than one-third of consumer spending.

Moreover the government provided no very coherent explanation of how the controls were intended to fit together or how long they were intended to last. There was much talk of planning but no published plan. The economy seemed to move from one economic crisis to another in a way that made nonsense of the idea that it was planned.

The various 'bonfires' of controls that began in 1948 made it clear that the continued use of controls after 1945 was essentially a *transitional* strategy. It was not intended to maintain the controls indefinitely or to perpetuate the shortages with which they dealt. On the contrary, most of the controls would disappear as supply recovered to a more normal level without any change in price. Until recovery was well under way and supply and demand were nearer to balance, there was no point in distorting the price structure in an effort to procure instant balance. Higher prices might do little to hasten an expansion in supply that was already in progress; and the substitution of rationing by price for rationing by government might provoke unrest that with patience could be avoided.

There was also a danger that once the price structure was set in motion by violent changes in particular prices, the whole system of prices might lose its normal inertia and begin to rise. A change in price that restores equilibrium in one market may create disequilibrium in other markets. In the labour market in particular a rise in wages in one industry may set off parallel claims in other industries that are difficult to resist so that the rise spreads throughout the system. In such a major upheaval as the transition from war to peace there was much to be said for holding price relationships as steady as possible even if this meant prolonging wartime controls.

We can apply the same reasoning to the dollar shortage. It might appear that such a shortage would disappear if only dollars were dear enough, that is if the pound were sufficiently devalued. But to devalue at a time when exports could not respond strongly because the necessary manpower was still locked up in the Armed Forces would have been counter-productive. It would have raised the sterling price of imports and so increased inflationary pressure, turned the terms of trade against the United Kingdom, and in all probability enlarged the deficit in the balance of payments because of the low elasticity of supply and, even more, of demand.

It might well prove, however, that an eventual devaluation against the dollar would prove necessary and helpful. Once there had been time for the full deployment of domestic resources and for the normal sources of imports to resume production, there might still be a shortage of dollars, that is, a disequilibrium in the United States' balance of payments. In such circumstances a devaluation of the pound (and other currencies) against the dollar would operate not only on the volume of exports and imports in total but more powerfully on the markets to which exports were directed and from which imports were procured. This in fact is what happened when devaluation did occur in 1949, four years after the end of the war. Most currencies moved with sterling so that what took place was as much a revaluation of the dollar as a devaluation of the pound. The dollar shortage did not disappear at once; but the new price relationships made possible a gradual transformation from shortage to surplus in the course of the next ten years.

## Controls

The controls of which the government made use in the post-war period came under five main headings.

First there was price control over all items purchased and sold by government and over about half consumer spending or, making allowance for items already under the influence of government or not susceptible to control, about 60 per cent. There was little relaxation until 1949–50 when some items such as non-rationed foodstuffs and ironmongery were removed. In July 1951 during the Korean War control was reimposed on various items and an effort was made to tighten the controls. But apart from rents, bus and railway fares, coal and a few other items, price control was effectively abandoned in 1952–3. Control was tightest over rationed goods and where, as with the utility schemes, it was possible to specify precisely the items controlled. It could not hope to contain all the pressures towards higher prices but does seem to have been successful in keeping prices more or less in line with costs.

Next there was consumer rationing: either 'single line' rationing of specific items, points rationing of canned and processed foodstuffs, clothing, and furniture, or limitations on the amount that could be spent, for example on holidays abroad or on housing repairs. The extent of consumer rationing varied. The proportion of consumer spending covered by the various schemes was never more than one-third and from 1949 never more than one-eighth. Bread and potatoes, which had not been rationed in wartime were put on ration after the war, the first for two years from July 1946, the second in the winter of 1947–8. But the main effect of this was probably to reduce the amount fed to animals. Food consumption in the aggregate had regained the pre-war level by 1947 and consumption per head was above the pre-war level by 1950, long before the end of rationing. Clothing was de-rationed in June 1948, furniture in March 1949, but fats, butter, cheese, bacon, and meat were not de-rationed until the summer of 1954.

A third form of control was over investment. In principle the government was in a position to control investment in the public sector but in practice did not find it at all easy to vary public investment over periods only a year or two ahead. Control of private-sector investment was exercised through building licensing, allocations of steel and timber, and pressure on manufacturers to give preference to exports. The first of these was rendered ineffective in the first three post-war years by an enormous over-issue of licences. The shortage of building materials, however, operated in the opposite direction. Allocation of steel and timber gave the government power to influence the scale and pattern of investment and the division of output between home and export markets. It could divert building activity in favoured directions (e.g. house-building), or to favoured areas (e.g. the development areas); limit the input of timber per house; require car manufacturers to export three-quarters of their output; and put pressure on engineering firms to meet specific requirements at home or abroad. From 1948 onwards the investment programme was the subject of careful planning even if the government was not always sure how far investment was diverging from programme.

Apart from their use in the control of investment, raw material allocations provided a fourth form of control over production. Nearly all raw materials except coal and steel were imported, either by the government itself or under licence from the government, and nearly all were at first subject to allocation. Of fifteen main raw materials 94 per cent by value were subject to allocation in 1946 and 47 per cent in 1950, but with the Korean War the proportion rose again to 64 per cent in 1952. Aluminium, wool, and rubber ceased to be allocated in 1947, tin, cotton, and most hardwoods in 1949. The process of derestriction was brought to a halt by rearmament, which made it necessary to renew some of the features of a war economy. In February 1952 the allocation of steel, which had been discontinued in May 1950 (except for sheet and tinplate), was reintroduced along with control over many other materials. The renewal of control was short-lived. The allocation of steel and some other materials ceased in 1953 and by 1954 the only allocation schemes remaining were for coal and tinplate.

Among the most important forms of control, given the central importance of the balance of payments was that over imports. This had several different aspects. Apart from the need to keep imports within the limits of what could be afforded, there was also the need to switch as far as possible to non-dollar sources of supply, often at higher cost, and to engage in bilateral deals with individual countries. The Labour government was also anxious to continue the bulk purchase of imports on long-term contracts in the expectation of driving a better bargain than private traders. All this made for the retention of a large proportion of the import trade in government hands. In 1946 four-fifths both of food and of raw-material imports were on government account. All imports of manufactures, although in private hands, required a government licence. Oil imports, which were also in private hands, were subject to quota limitations. Only some 4 per cent of imports were left uncontrolled.

Import restrictions remained largely unchanged during the first four years of peace apart from some shift back from direct government purchase to private trade under government control. In 1949, however, the members of the OEEC (the forerunner of the OECD) agreed on a programme to 'liberalize' imports from each other, that is to free imports from control. The concessions made by the United Kingdom were extended to other non-dollar countries outside the Soviet bloc while imports from dollar countries continued to be restricted. This meant undisguised discrimination against dollar countries; but since imports from sterling area countries were already admitted more freely than from other areas, it was by no means the beginning of such discrimination.

Liberalization proceeded rapidly in 1950, when half the imports made by private traders and a quarter of total imports were unrestricted. In 1951 the process was at first carried further. But in the payments crisis that accompanied rearmament in 1951–2 it was halted for a time and reversed as import cuts totalling £600m. were made in November 1951, January 1952, and again in March 1952. About a quarter of the cuts made were designed to fall on goods that had previously been liberalized. Once the crisis had passed, liberalization was resumed, the proportion of imports free from control reaching 50 per cent in 1953.

Import control varied in severity with the state of the balance of payments. Cuts were made in each successive balance of payments crisis, sometimes, as in 1949 and 1951, in association with other sterling area countries, and always with a view to reducing outgoings in dollars. At other times, when a more hopeful view could be taken, imports were increased without any change in the system of control.

Of the effectiveness of import controls there could never be any doubt. In 1947, to take one example, cuts in dollar imports produced a fall in their value of nearly 30 per cent in 1948 and reduced the proportion of imports coming from the Western Hemisphere from 43 per cent to 30 per cent. Similarly in 1951–2 it has been estimated that of the fall in imports by £400m. in 1952, £250m. can be attributed to cuts in the import programme. It is likely also that the low level of imports in post-war years owed something to import control even if most of it was the result of structural changes that reduced the importance of industries like textiles that had high import requirements or increased the output of industries like agriculture that provided substitutes for imports.

Finally there were some residual labour controls. In wartime the government had enjoyed, but rarely used, powers to direct labour. It had put a 'ring fence' round certain industries to prevent workers from leaving or being dismissed from essential work except with the consent of the Ministry of Labour and had required recruitment to certain employments to be made through the Labour Exchanges. From December 1945 these powers were largely abandoned and over the next eighteen months further relaxations were made. The powers retained by the government were by then confined to coal-mining and agriculture under Essential Work Orders and to these industries and building and civil engineering under the Control of Engagement Order. These powers were extended, but to little effect, after the convertibility crisis of 1947, but abandoned completely at the beginning of 1950.

The government found it more fruitful to rely on other means of influencing recruitment to an industry. As in wartime it was possible to persuade applicants for work at the Labour Exchanges to take jobs conforming to a list of 'first preferences'. The government could also offer training facilities, deferment of call-up, better rations, more housing in designated areas, etc., and it could promote immigration, from Eire or from the refugee camps in Europe, to specified jobs.

## Financial Controls

The history of post-war economic management is essentially the story of how physical controls were gradually replaced by financial controls. Under the Labour governments this meant primarily increased reliance on budgetary policy as physical controls were relaxed or discontinued. In particular it meant an attempt to close what was seen as 'the inflationary gap' by running a large budget surplus. Control of investment and of imports on the one hand and a growing volume of public sector savings on the other were the pivots of economic management in the late 1940s.

The budget surplus that emerged for the first time in 1947–8 was of Dalton's making. He had begun with a budget deficit of £2,200m. in 1945–6 but in his four budgets transformed this into a surplus of £636m. in 1947–8. Cripps's achievement over the next three years was to maintain a surplus of this dimension against strong criticism from his own party and Ministerial colleagues. By the time he handed over to Gaitskell in October 1950 the central importance of what came to be called 'the budget judgment' was widely recognized.

The 'budget judgment' was essentially an exercise in demand management. It rested on a forecast of the prospective change in the pressure of demand based on an assessment of the likely increment in each of the main categories of demand on resources (consumer spending, fixed investment, stockbuilding, current expenditure of public authorities on goods and services, and exports) and the simultaneous increment in the flow of supplies from current production (gross domestic product) and from imports. If the forecast pointed to excessive pressure, the increase in output leaving too narrow a margin of unused labour and capacity, the judgement would be that purchasing power should be withdrawn through the budget. Since inflationary pressure remained high throughout, the issue did not arise whether more purchasing power should be *released* even if a budget deficit resulted. The question was rather how far to go in running a budget surplus, against which Ministers were liable to rebel, especially as they felt in their bones that a deep depression was just round the corner.

In the early post-war years Ministers preferred to base economic management decisions on a manpower budget. This was possible so long as they had a buffer stock of manpower in the armed forces, but not when demobilization was complete and they had no direct control over the supply and distribution of manpower. The alternative technique of national income forecasting which had begun to take shape in the war, came gradually to the fore but remained crude and uncertain in its application, partly because of weaknesses in the statistical data, partly because the concept of excess demand was more ambiguous than it seemed. Nevertheless the management of demand had become a central preoccupation of government by 1950 and the budget was seen (by Cripps at least) as the most powerful available instrument for influencing economic policy.

Monetary policy was seen differently. Not much importance was attached to the influence of monetary conditions on investment or economic activity: the main object of the government was to reduce the burden of interest charges on the Exchequer. The government had far less need to borrow than in wartime, had the benefit of a large loan from the United States, and believed that, so far as interest rates did affect economic activity, lower rates would be appropriate after the period of transition had passed and given way to the danger of deflationary conditions.

These considerations led Dalton to embark on a campaign to lower interest rates. He cut the rate on Treasury Bills from 1 per cent to ½ per cent in November 1945, and short-term rates remained unchanged thereafter until the incoming Conservative government increased the Bank Rate to 2½ per cent in November 1951, the first increase since 1932. He then brought pressure on the market to reduce the long-term rate from the 3 per cent at which it had been held, quite deliberately, in wartime to 2½ per cent. For a brief interval in the autumn of 1946 he was successful and the price of consols reached a peak of 99 in October. But by that time the public had become net sellers of gilt-edged, the money supply, already much swollen, was increasing at a rate that alarmed the City, and a new issue of undated Treasury Stock at 2½ per cent had had a disappointing reception. The bond market began to weaken in November and weakened further in the fuel and convertibility crises of 1947. By the spring of 1948 gilt-edged were 25 per cent below the peak reached eighteen months earlier and the Dalton 'experiment' had clearly failed.

Under Cripps no fresh attempt was made to manoeuvre a fall in long-term interest rates. £300m. in long-term debt was redeemed in March 1948 and some gilt-edged was taken in by the government broker to steady the market in 1949. But in the main, the government used its stronger budgetary position to redeem short-term debt and slow down the growth of the money supply. Over the two financial years 1948–9 and 1949–50 the growth was stopped. But from then until the change of government the money supply increased slowly.

The main way in which the government sought to make use of monetary policy was through pressure on the banks to limit credit creation. This could not be done by using the pre-war system of ratio control. Nor would the Bank of England have taken to the idea of issuing a directive putting a ceiling on advances. Instead, the Chancellor wrote a number of letters to the Governor asking for his collaboration in holding inflationary policies in check by limiting advances for speculative purposes.

In general, monetary policy after Dalton was a by-product of fiscal policy and exercised little independent influence on economic activity.

## Resource Allocation

The various controls, physical and financial, were designed to promote certain adjustments in the economy: elimination of the external deficit, reduction in inflationary pressure, etc. What adjustments did take place? How fast did the economy grow and how was the growth allocated between different purposes?

Table 2.2 shows the changes from year to year in the allocation of resources between the main categories of demand.

In the first two years output, as measured by GDP, grew very little. Civil employment at first grew rather slowly as women returned to household duties, the net increase over the first year of peace and demobilization being only 1 million. But in the next six months nearly another million entered employment and after one more year, at the end of 1947 civil employment had expanded by 2½ million since June 1945. Productivity, however, suffered from the large-scale adjustments that had to be made over this period and from the shortages and bottle-necks that arose. Additionally, the severe winter of 1946–7 and the fuel crisis that arrested industrial production for weeks in many parts of the country, caused an appreciable loss of output.

It was only after some of the excess demand was chopped off in the autumn of 1947 that industry was able to advance on a more even front. The housing programme in particular had been allowed to get out of balance, with more houses started than could be finished. Drastic cuts were made in the entire investment programme with the unexpected result that investment nevertheless increased in 1948. By that time GDP was growing at a fast rate of about 3½ per cent per annum and continued to grow at or above it over the next two years, dipping slightly in 1951 and ceasing to grow at all in 1952. Over the six years 1945–51 GDP increased by 15 per cent or about 2½ per cent per annum and output per head at about 1 per cent lower, say 1½ per cent per annum.

The period started off with a big drop in government claims on resources with demobilization and a winding up of munitions production. Some of the benefit of this was conveyed to the consumer by Dalton's first two budgets in October 1945 and April 1946 which reduced taxation by about £530m. Consumers' expenditure rose by about £1,000m. (at 1948 prices) and had probably returned to the pre-war level or a little above it by 1948 in spite of the hardships of rationing, licensing, and other restrictions. Fixed capital formation rose by almost as much as consumption from a far smaller base and it, too, had regained the pre-war level by 1948. The contraction in fixed investment in wartime had been on a par with the contraction in exports and so, too, was its recovery in 1945–7. After 1947, however, fixed investment was more tightly controlled and grew more slowly. Exports, on the other hand, after an initial leap in 1946 were held back by the fuel crisis in 1947 and then made rapid progress during Cripps's three years at the Exchequer before their growth petered out in 1951. Stockbuilding, the most erratic element in demand, reached its peak in 1947, contributing to the aggravation of inflationary pressure and the big increase in the external deficit in that year. In the next three years of rising exports, stockbuilding subsided, only to explode again in 1951 and contribute once more to a balance of payments crisis. Imports increased in each of the three crisis years 1947, 1949, and 1951 but were more or less unchanged in the even years 1946, 1948, and 1950, with a sharp dip in 1952 that reflected the import cuts made in the exchange crisis during the winter of 1951–2.

The economy depicted by the table is one in which the running is made by exports and investment with the rise in consumption after the first post-war year held within narrow limits. Indeed, consumption absorbed only a quarter of the resources that were made available by 1952 for exports and fixed investment. One of the first questions that the table raises is how it was possible to keep such a tight control over consumption.

The question is the more natural in view of the changes taking place in personal incomes and in savings. At the end of the war, weekly wage earnings were roughly 80 per cent higher than in 1938 while prices were only about 50 per cent higher. In wartime much of the increase in income remained unspent and was banked in savings accounts against the day when consumer goods would again be freely available. Personal savings as a proportion of disposable income had risen from about 3.5 per cent in 1938 to over 16 per cent in 1944. But what if all this were now reversed and there was a rush to buy? If nothing were done the only check to consumption in those circumstances would be inflation. Personal savings did in fact fall steeply: at their lowest point in 1948 they were virtually zero. On the other hand, the budget had by that time moved into surplus and the surplus continued thereafter throughout the transition period. The withdrawal of purchasing power on an increasing scale from 1945 to 1950 allowed public saving to take the place of private. Consumer spending increased by only 1 per cent per annum after 1946 because real after-tax incomes rose even less. This was the result of somewhat higher taxation and a large adverse swing in the terms of trade by about 16 per cent over the six years, a steep rise in import prices eating into consumer incomes, especially in 1946–8 and again in 1949–51.

The developments we have so far discussed were not foreshadowed in the original programme on which the government was elected. That programme was more concerned with the enlargement of the public sector through nationalization and the expansion of the social services—what is now thought of as the creation of the Welfare State.

## Nationalization

Nationalization occupied much of the time of Parliament and the administration. First the Bank of England was taken into public ownership early in 1946, then the coal, gas, and electricity industries over the next three years, with rail and canal transport and long distance haulage at the beginning of 1948 and civil aviation and telecommunications a year or so previously. Thus apart from the Bank of England, which was already a semi-public body, the programme was confined to fuel and power on the one hand and transport and communications on the other: that is, to the most capital-intensive sectors of the economy. The only manufacturing industry—and the only source of really violent political controversy—was the steel industry, which did not pass into the public domain until February 1951.

The nationalization measures were very dear to the Labour Party. They persevered with them even when it meant splitting a country they were trying to unite behind their economic policy and when it endangered American goodwill. The decision to proceed with nationalization of the steel industry was taken when the convertibility crisis was at its most acute and dollars were draining away at nearly $1bn. a month. Arrangements for the nationalization of the coal industry took up scarce managerial time all through the year before the coal crisis finally broke in February 1947. What did the measures accomplish?

They added nearly 2½ million workers to the public sector and gave the government direct control over the basic industries of the country. But the government was not at all clear to what purpose such control should be put. The legislation seemed to envisage a group of public-spirited monopolies, free in most matters to run their own affairs on the model of commercial undertakings. There was no very apparent gain in efficiency, no revolution in industrial relations, no reinforcement of the government's grip on the economy.

The main immediate consequence of the measures, as might have been expected, was on investment. A far higher proportion of the total investment programme was now within the public sector—it eventually reached 50 per cent in the 1960s—and large amounts of capital from the budget surpluses were needed to recondition some of the newly nationalized industries such as coal, railway transport, and steel. The increased importance of public investment may have seemed welcome as a means of ironing out fluctuations in the total; but in practice it proved difficult to make quick changes in these mammoth projects. Whatever the merits of public ownership in the longer run, an extensive programme of nationalization did not fit very well into a policy of post-war reconstruction.

The coal industry, in this respect, may have been an exception. There was a desperate need for more coal both for domestic use and for export to European neighbours who were even more in need of fuel. Even small amounts were of the utmost value in bilateral trade agreements. But the output of deep-mined coal had fallen year by year throughout the war to a level 25 per cent below that of 1939. It was clear even in 1945 that a crisis was imminent if manpower was not increased and manpower continued to fall. Perhaps a new deal for coal, with public ownership, high investment, shorter hours, and freedom from call-up, would attract more labour and increase output.

Things did not prove quite so easy. Much of the reconstruction work itself required mining labour and the cut in hours involved some sacrifice in output. For a year or two, in 1947–8, there was a trickle of additional labour but in 1951 there were no more men in the mines than at the low point five years previously. The output of coal expanded slowly but left little for export and rationing of domestic consumers continued. Anxiety over coal supplies was never far away and in the autumn of 1950 it looked for a time as if there might be a replay of the 1947 crisis. Yet if coal in those years was the weak spot in British industry things might have been worse in the absence of nationalization and the increased investment that this brought, small though it was for so large an industry.

## The Welfare State

The other main extension of the public sector was in the provision of social services. These did not, of course, originate in the post-war years; public expenditure on health, education, pensions, etc. had grown from £35m. in 1900 (nearly all education and poor relief) to over £400m. in 1936. State contributory pension schemes went back before the First World War.

Some of the changes introduced after the war derived from the work of the wartime Coalition government. This passed the 1944 Education Act which laid the basis for modern secondary education although it was not until 1947 that the Labour government raised the school-leaving age to fifteen. The National Health Service had similarly been accepted in principle by the Coalition government but it was left to the Labour government to give substance to it. The main changes associated with the idea of the Welfare State were founded on the wartime report on *Social Insurance and Allied Services* by (as he then was) Sir William Beveridge. The central idea of his report was to unite a wide range of social services that were previously unconnected with each other into a comprehensive system of national benefits. These benefits would extend 'from the cradle to the grave' and cover maternity, sickness, unemployment, retirement, death, and other contingencies. The cost of these benefits was to be met from national insurance contributions— indeed, these contributions also met a small part of the cost of the National Health Service. The extra burden on the taxpayer came partly from the added cost of education and health services but much more, under the Labour government, from the need to cover the cost of the food and agriculture subsidies. By 1950 this exceeded total expenditure on national insurance and was also larger than expenditure on the health services.

Between 1936 and 1950 expenditure on the social services in Great Britain increased from about £400m. to £1,500m., excluding expenditure on food and housing subsidies, but since prices had doubled in the meantime the increase in real terms was much less, probably about 80–90 per cent. The main source of this large increase was the National Health Service which rapidly outstripped initial estimates and in the last three years of the Labour government was costing an average of £460m. a year. It was the weight of this burden on the Exchequer that drove successive Chancellors to propose the introduction of health charges, a proposal strongly and at first successfully resisted by Aneurin Bevan, the architect of a free National Health Service; and it was over the principle of a free Health Service (as well as the rearmament programme) that Bevan resigned in April 1951.

The food subsidies, which imposed an even larger burden, were allowed to increase under Dalton until they were well on the way to £500m. a year. In 1948 Cripps accepted the need to impose a ceiling on the total and from then onwards the subsidies were held at £465m. No reduction was made, however, until after the Conservatives took office.

These expenditures have to be seen against a total for ordinary expenditure by the central government of about £3,000m. in the late 1940s. Excluding debt charges and defence expenditure, the total for all civil purposes rose from £1,650m. in 1946–7, before the expansion in the social services had got very far, to £2,060m. in 1949–50 when most of the changes had already been made. This may give a more accurate picture of the additional financial burden on the Exchequer. But it excludes the cost of subsidies on the one hand and exaggerates the additional burden on national resources on the other.


### International Economic Relations

We turn finally to Britain's economic relations with other countries in the period of transition.

The war had cut off many traditional markets and sources of supply and it was a long time before normal conditions of trade could be re-established. Nearly all European countries had difficulty in finding the means of paying for the imports they so badly needed and turned to the American hemisphere, and particularly the United States, for indispensable imports not obtainable elsewhere. This was true not only of foodstuffs and raw materials but also of the capital equipment they badly needed in order to provide productive capacity for a more fully employed labour force.

The resulting dollar shortage and inconvertibility of currencies drove countries to make bilateral trade and payments agreements with one another. The effort to balance accounts country by country distorted the pattern of trade flows, reduced the total volume of trade, and hit with particular severity countries that had been accustomed to the blessings of multilateral trade and the settlement of deficits with one group of countries out of surpluses with others. Countries like Belgium, Sweden, and Switzerland, with their pre-war economy largely intact, were in a relatively strong position since they could supply what other countries most required and they might even, like Belgium, try to obtain settlement in gold. Other European countries ran substantial deficits against loans, credits, and what reserves of gold and dollars they could spare.

Britain's main suppliers and markets fell into three groups: North America, the sterling area, and Western Europe. Other countries, in Latin America, Eastern Europe, and elsewhere, although important for particular purposes played a subordinate role. The changes in Britain's trade with those groups between 1938 and 1946, and again between 1946 and 1950, is shown in Table 2.3.

The table tells its own story. It shows the increased reliance on imports from North America after the war and the subsequent drop as supplies from Western Europe and other parts of the world began to recover. The sterling area remained the main source throughout and was an even more important source in 1950 than in 1938. The post-war percentages, however, are of a much diminished volume of imports so that the movement of the percentages is not a good guide to changes by volume. For example, imports from North America were little if at all greater by volume in 1946 than in 1938 and supplies from the sterling area were quite appreciably lower. It is also not apparent from the percentages that the sterling area made the biggest contribution to the doubling in the value of imports between 1946

TABLE 2.3. *The pattern of British trade, 1938, 1946, and 1950*

| | Percentage of total imports by value from | | | | Percentage of total exports by value to | | | |
|------|------------------|-------------------|------------------|------------------|-------------------|-----------------|------------------|
| | North America | Western Europe | Sterling area | Rest of world | North America | Western Europe | Sterling area | Rest of world |
| 1938 | 21.7 | 24.0 | 31.2 | 23.1 | 9.3 | 23.4 | 44.9 | 22.4 |
| 1946 | 33.1 | 14.9 | 32.8 | 19.2 | 7.5 | 28.3 | 45.3 | 19.0 |
| 1950 | 15.0 | 25.1 | 38.0 | 25.9 | 11.0 | 28.3 | 47.8 | 12.9 |

*Source: Annual Abstract of Statistics* (1953), Table 211 and 212.

and 1950, accounting for 42.5 per cent of the increase while Western Europe accounted for 35.5 per cent.

The picture for exports shows the sterling area in an even more dominant position, taking a proportion of British exports higher than before the war and one approaching 50 per cent in 1950. By contrast, North America took a relatively small proportion that was raised from 7.5 to 11 per cent between 1946 and 1950 only with the greatest difficulty. Western Europe, in the absence of German competition, took a higher proportion of British exports than before the war and continued to do so in 1950 when the total volume of exports was about 75 per cent higher than in 1946. Even so, it was the sterling area that took the lion's share—roughly half—of the increase in British exports over those four years.

British recovery thus rested heavily on an expansion in trade with the sterling area, most members of which were also members of the Commonwealth, and to a lesser extent on the recovery and continued growth of trade with Western Europe. It was by such means that she hoped to put an end to her shortage of dollars. Apart from drawing in imports in substitution for imports from America there was also the possibility of earning some gold and dollars directly from South Africa, Malaya, and some of the colonial territories.

There was however a price to be paid in the need to supply, as part of the general sterling area arrangements, capital for the development of sterling area countries. That large sums flowed abroad is obvious when one compares the cumulative drain of gold and dollars over the years 1945–52 with the cumulative deficit on current account. The gap between the first, amounting to \$9.2bn. and the second, amounting to no more than £700m.—at most \$3bn.—indicates either an error in the figures or an outflow of capital equal to the difference between the two. Over the seven years the net outflow of capital was probably about £1,700m. of which £900m. went to the sterling area and most of the rest to Western Europe. More was lent or invested abroad than had been borrowed in North America. The United Kingdom had run a large current account surplus with non-dollar countries but the surplus had brought in only a limited quantity of gold and dollars; most of it had been provided in one form or another as capital.

The pattern of British trade exercised an important influence on Britain's attitude to Europe. The United States had hoped when Marshall Aid was launched that the United Kingdom would take the lead in integrating Europe. There was no sign in the middle of 1947 that France would ever think of assuming that rôle: the French were then bitterly opposed to American efforts to put Germany back on her feet. The rôle proposed was not one that the British government found attractive. It was hard enough for Britain to pay her own way; and to tack on a group of countries in much deeper trouble would be an aggravation of the difficulty. Association with North America and the Commonwealth seemed a better bet and was not easily reconciled with leadership in the economic integration of Europe. When the French, under the influence of Jean Monnet, came round to a different way of thinking about Germany and Europe they were satisfied that the United Kingdom was unlikely to be a helpful partner. The Schuman Plan was devised in the full expectation that the United Kingdom would not be a participant.

In those years the United Kingdom occupied a position in Europe very different from that of today. As late as 1951 her industrial production was still as great as that of France and Germany combined and so, too, were her exports. By comparison, in the mid 1980s France's industrial production was double that of the United Kingdom, and Germany's three times as large. Similarly, while France, Germany, Italy, and the Netherlands struggled with large and persistent deficits throughout the post-war period, the United Kingdom had balanced her current account by 1948. She saw herself, quite mistakenly, as cast in the rôle of creditor almost indefinitely in her dealings with the continent and thought it more important to mount a joint programme for freer trade in Europe combined with a joint attack on the dollar problem than to follow the path of union with Europe.

In 1949–50 under the auspices of OEEC in Paris, the British government collaborated in a programme of trade liberalization which gave a new boost to intra-European trade (although from 1949 onwards the recovery of Germany was much the most powerful factor and the largest single contribution to the elimination of the dollar shortage). The Americans brought pressure for schemes to settle intra-European payments on a multilateral rather than a bilateral basis and although the early schemes were not altogether satisfactory, a fresh initiative at the end of 1949 led to the creation in July 1950 of the European Payments Union.

The scheme was not altogether to the liking of the Bank of England and was at first opposed both by Britain and Belgium. The Belgians hankered after settlement in gold and dollars of any surpluses or deficits while the British would have liked to see a complete absence of gold and dollars from such settlements. The Bank of England also feared for the use of sterling and the future of the sterling area. It had helped to devise a system of bilateral agreements under which each side offered limited credit to the other and settlement beyond these limits was made in sterling. These arrangements would be superseded under the European Payments Union and there was a question how far other countries might use their holdings of sterling to make a settlement through the Union. In the end it was agreed to bring all payments in currently earned sterling, whether with the United Kingdom or the rest of the sterling area, within the scheme. A country in deficit (within the limits of its quota) would settle half the deficit in gold and receive credit from the EPU on the other half. On this basis, the British were satisfied and it was the Belgians whose acceptance was most difficult to obtain. In spite of many upsets the scheme was a great success until it disappeared with the introduction of convertibility at the end of 1958.

## Conclusion

The adjustments necessary at the end of the war had not been fully completed by the end of 1951. The position was obscured by the distortions introduced by an enormous rearmament programme. But in the light of after events it is clear that the dollar problem was on the way to a solution; the economy, although temporarily in heavy deficit, would swing back into balance as soon as the terms of trade returned to a more normal relationship, and the transfer of resources to sustain high levels of exports and investment had been made on an adequate scale. The consumer boom that began soon after 1951 was itself a testimony to the completion of the necessary adjustment in the use of resources.

# 3

# The Budget and Fiscal Policy*

## T. J. HATTON AND K. ALEC CHRYSTAL

In any discussion of the post-war economic history of the United Kingdom, government expenditure and taxation policy must be accorded a central place. Whether the public authorities' budget was the most important single influence on the evolution of the economy is debatable. However, there can be no doubt at all that fiscal policy received the most attention, both from policy-makers and from students of economic policy. It is the evolving role of this budgetary activity that is the subject of this chapter. We are not primarily concerned with the administrative or political process involved in the making of fiscal policy. Rather, it is the evolution of the government budget itself and the motivation behind this evolution that is our central interest.

## Introduction

There are two different aspects of government activity that we shall be examining. The first concerns the government as a producer and distributor of goods and services, and the second is concerned with the government's attempts to act as a regulator or stabilizer of the entire economy. Fiscal policy is concerned both with the financing of a desired level of public expenditure and with influencing activity outside the public sector by changes in fiscal stance (deficit or surplus in the government's accounts), though it is important to be aware that causation between the government budget and the economy runs both ways. For example as the economy expands, tax revenue rises and some expenditures (unemployment benefit, for example) fall. Even if there were no attempt by governments to influence the rest of the economy by fiscal policy, there would still remain the issue of the appropriate level of state activity and how it should be financed.

The modern debate about the appropriate role of the state in the economy goes back at least to Adam Smith. In *The Wealth of Nations* (1776) he defined three roles for the central government. First, to provide for the external defence of the country. Second, to ensure that law and order were maintained inside the country. Finally, came the '. . . duty of erecting and maintaining certain public works and certain public institutions, which it can never be for the interest of any individual, or a small number of individuals, to erect and maintain, because the profit could never repay the expense to any individual or small number of individuals, though it may frequently do much more than repay it to a great society' (bk. iv, ch. 9, p. 311).

* We are grateful to Geoffrey Wood and Andrew Gamble (as well as the editors) for comments on an earlier draft. Peter Else kindly supplied some of the data for one of the tables. We are indebted to Pam Hepworth and Wendy Rogerson for secretarial assistance.

For the rest of economic affairs Smith supported a policy of *laissez-faire*. This meant that market forces should be left unimpeded to determine the production and consumption pattern of the economy.

This tradition in economic thought was carried on in the nineteenth century by the classical economists and utilitarians such as Mill and Bentham. Though exceptions were increasingly found, *laissez-faire* remained the general rule and interventionist measures were specific departures which had to be justified individually.

In comparison with the twentieth century, the nineteenth century can be regarded as an age of *laissez-faire* though the degree to which such principles were adhered to in economic thought and policy has been debated (see Taylor, 1972). In the late nineteenth century there was a gradual erosion in the dominance of ideas based on economic individualism and a growth in socialist ideas influenced by writers such as Marx. In addition, the growing voice of the working class, reinforced by extensions to the franchise, led to a heightened awareness of issues such as public health, education, poverty, and unemployment as appropriate spheres for state intervention and provision. Until the liberal welfare reforms before the First World War, social services remained the province of local government and, apart from defence, the intervention of the national government was confined largely to providing a regulatory framework in a narrow range of industrial and commercial spheres.

During the inter-war period *laissez-faire* was seen by many observers as an inadequate response to a wide range of economic problems which went beyond those of providing for the poorer members of society. Some came to believe that the market mechanism could not efficiently allocate, or effectively reallocate, resources among alternative uses. Booms, slumps, and the protracted unemployment of the 1930s gave rise to renewed criticism of unfettered capitalism. Some observers inspired by the Russian revolution pressed for a completely centrally planned economy on the model of the Soviet Union (see for example Lange and Taylor, 1938). Others such as Hayek (1935, 1944) argued that while socialism might ameliorate cycles in activity, it would create even greater problems of rigidity and inefficiency resulting in slow growth. Between these extremes there were several strands of middle opinion which advocated limited central planning and a greater role for central government in a 'mixed' economy. Such proposals were outlined by the Liberals in their report of 1928, by moderate Labour groups and by radical Conservatives such as Harold Macmillan (Booth and Pack, 1985, chs. 2, 3, 6). Though this middle opinion is sometimes seen as a precursor of the post-war consensus on the mixed economy it was not sufficiently unified or politically focused to bring about dramatic changes before the Second World War.

Despite this the inter-war period can be seen as one of transition. The role of the state had vastly increased since the turn of the century albeit largely through the expansion of social welfare programmes. But while many of the precepts of the Victorian era were still held to, the principle of public parsimony was in retreat. The pressing claims of programmes for housing, education, health, and unemployment insurance conflicted with the desire to minimize the burden of taxation and balance the budget. Though the size of the government sector and the scope of government intervention had increased, the budget had not assumed the mantle of a tool of conomic management. The influence of the new economics of Keynes on fiscal policy was belated and incomplete. This partial retreat from *laissez-faire*, which was reached through an uneasy social and political compromise, was influenced more by reaction to economic crisis than by the application of new ideas.

These historical antecedents provide a background to the evolution of the public authorities expenditure and taxation policies in the post-war period. But the structure and scope of government activity owes much to developments which emerged from the Second World War. The provision of welfare services became universally applied rather than restricted to certain sections of the population and with this the notion of state protection against hardship and deprivation 'from the cradle to the grave' became established. The nationalization of major industries such as coal, railways, steel, and public utilities signalled a major break with the past, when, with the exception of the Post Office and some municipal public utilities, the state refrained from direct control of major industries. It should be remembered however that though this marks a significant extension of state control, because these industries sell their output on the open market, they only add to government (consumption) expenditure in so far as they make losses which have to be financed by the exchequer. With few exceptions, such as steel, which was transferred from public to private ownership and back again, and the effective purchase of ailing firms such as Rolls Royce and British Leyland in the 1970s, the scope of public ownership remained broadly unchanged until the 1980s. The Conservative government's privatization programme, which has gathered pace since 1983, represents a reversal in the trend of state control. In addition the demand for smaller government, through reducing expenditure on transfers and services and the withdrawal of state interference in other areas represents a partial return to the doctrine of *laissez-faire*.

A similar cycle can be observed in the approach to using the government's budget to control the level of economic activity through fiscal policy. Ideas stemming from Keynesian macroeconomics gained ascendancy in the early post-war period. Successive governments accepted the 1944 commitment to control fluctuations in activity and maintain high employment using fiscal policy as the principal tool of demand management. The faith in the efficiency of fiscal policy as *the* tool for achieving full employment diminished from the late 1960s as inflation gathered pace and unemployment grew despite ever larger budget deficits. Though some economists have downgraded the extent of fiscal influence on activity, government policy has remained more pragmatic. Fiscal policy is still recognized as a powerful weapon in demand management but there is a greater consciousness of adverse side-effects and of the importance of supply as well as of the demand side of the economy. Moreover much of the popular debate has failed to distinguish clearly between the effects of changes in the size of the government relative to the economy and changes in the budget deficit. Though changes in the size of the public sector will have macroeconomic effects which can be considered under the heading of fiscal policy, such policies are motivated more by long-run considerations of resource allocation and as such are conceptually separate. In what follows we briefly examine trends in the size of government before turning to fiscal policy and demand management.

THE BUDGET AND FISCAL POLICY

## Long-Term Growth of Government

The growth of government, and the consequent increasing cost of supporting government activity through taxes, has been of interest for at least the last century and probably much longer. One of the most famous early contributors to the debate about government growth was the German economist Adolf Wagner. He has the distinction of having had a 'Law of Increasing State Activity' named after him. There is some dispute about what this law actually says. It clearly involves the growth of government. Some have interpreted it to say that government will grow faster than the rest of the economy (as, perhaps, measured by GNP). However, Wagner's own words seem to support the interpretation that, once government has reached a certain size, it will tend to grow in line with national income.

There is thus a proportion between public expenditure and national income which may not be permanently overstepped. This only confirms the rule that there must be some sort of balance in the individual's outlays for the satisfaction of his various needs. For in the last resort, the state's fiscal requirements covered by taxation figure as expenditure in the household budget of the private citizen. (A. Wagner, 1883, in Musgrave and Peacock, 1962)

One might think that the relationship between the size of government and GNP should be very simple to test. Unfortunately the evidence is confused by a number of statistical issues. It is simplest to illustrate these statistical issues by reference to some data. Fig. 3.1 shows real GNP and real government expenditure on goods and services on an annual basis from 1900 to 1985. The dominant feature is the growth of spending during the two world wars. However, we want to concentrate on the long-term trend during peacetime. It may appear that GNP has grown faster than government spending, but this is deceptive. In fact, over the entire period, government spending grew 5.7-fold and GNP grew 4.1-fold in volume terms. However, since 1948 GNP has grown 2.5-fold whereas government spending has grown only 2-fold. This is particularly surprising given the widespread belief that government has grown much faster than the rest of the economy in the post-war period. Indeed, it is quite easy to find alternative statistics which can be used to paint a very different picture. If we look at the same statistics in current price, as opposed to constant price terms, a somewhat different picture emerges. From 1948 to 1985, GNP in money terms increased about 29-fold, whereas government current expenditure on goods and services increased over 40-fold.

The reason for the substantial difference between these two measures is quite straightforward. It is known as the Relative Price Effect. If we set the price deflators for GNP and government current expenditure at 100 in 1948, the value in 1985 for GNP was 1,190, but for government expenditure it was 2,030. In other words, the prices of the things bought by government spending had risen almost twice as much as the prices involved in spending as a whole. (Since the imputed output of government is about 20 per cent of GNP it is likely that government prices rose by more than double the rise in private-sector prices).

Thus we can generate a very different picture of government spending depending upon whether we use a volume measure or a value measure. Neither is uniquely the 'correct' measure to use. However, the fact that any relative growth of government consumption (at least since the Second World War) is largely due to this relative price effect is in itself very interesting. Does it imply that government has been inefficient in conceding higher price rises, or is it the inevitable result of the nature

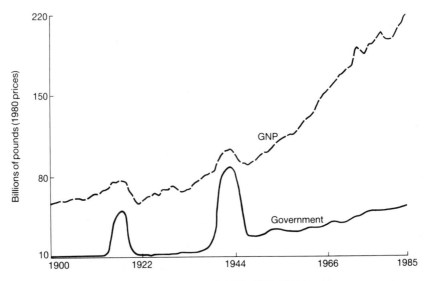

FIG. 3.1.    *Real government consumption and GNP, 1900–1985*

of the things governments do? We do not have clear answers to these questions, but it is worth pointing out that government spending is probably more labour intensive than the rest of GNP and so this effect may be explained by the rise of wages relative to goods prices. Whatever the causes of the relative price effect may be, it is clear that the volume of services provided by government has grown no faster than GNP as a whole since the war.

Current expenditure on goods and services is only part of total government expenditure, albeit the largest part. Table 3.1 shows total taxes and expenditures as a percentage of GDP at factor cost. (Note that these are ratios of current money values so the relative price effect is included). Column 1 is total tax revenue from all sources including social security contributions. Column 2 is revenue from profits of nationalized industries and other income sources such as rents. Column 3 is government current expenditure on goods and services. The 4th column shows public-sector investment in things such as house and road building. Finally column 5 shows total public expenditure. This includes debt interest and some other small items in addition to those in columns 3, 4, and 5.

TABLE 3.1. *Taxes and government spending as a percent of GDP*

|  | Revenue | | Expenditure | | | |
|  | Tax (1) | Other (2) | Consump. (3) | Inv. (4) | Transf. (5) | Total (6) |
|---|---|---|---|---|---|---|
| 1950 | 39.2 | 4.5 | 18.7 | 3.8 | 10.6 | 39.4 |
| 1960 | 31.7 | 3.7 | 18.5 | 3.7 | 9.4 | 39.1 |
| 1970 | 43.4 | 4.8 | 20.5 | 5.6 | 12.2 | 47.5 |
| 1980 | 41.3 | 5.1 | 24.5 | 2.8 | 16.5 | 52.1 |
| 1985 | 44.6 | 4.8 | 24.5 | 2.4 | 18.9 | 52.1 |

*Source*: *Economic Trends*. Annual Supplement (1987).

These data show several interesting trends. Column 3, for example, shows how government current spending on goods and services has grown in value terms relative to GDP. Six years of a Conservative Government made no impact on this ratio, since in 1985 it was the same as in 1980. Public expenditure as a whole grew sharply in the 1960s and continued to grow in the 1970s. It has levelled off in the 1980s, but has not fallen, despite some claims to the contrary. The biggest growth has been in transfer payments. The 1985 proportion was double the 1960 figure. This reflects both the rise in the numbers of old people and the increase in unemployment as well as some improvement in the quality of provision. Public investment rose in the 1960s but declined sharply in the 1970s. Most of the cuts in this area were introduced by the Labour Government of James Callaghan after 1976 under alleged pressure from the IMF. (The extent to which the cuts were IMF-imposed, rather than the Labour Government using the IMF as a scapegoat for what they had already instituted is controversial.) These cuts fell most heavily on public-sector housing. Tax revenue as a proportion of GDP fell between 1950 and 1960, but rose sharply by 1970. It dipped a little by 1980 but was as high as ever in 1985. The rise in taxes in the early 1980s was not so much a result of high tax rates but, rather, reflected the substantial boost to government revenues generated by North Sea oil.

Figures such as the last entry in column 6 have caused some people to comment that the government is spending over half of the national income, since it shows that total government spending is 52.1 per cent of GDP. However, figures like this must be interpreted with great caution. If 52.1 per cent is taken by government one might think that only 47.9 per cent is left for the private sector. Such a conclusion would be incorrect. Not all government spending consumes resources. Indeed, none of the expenditures in column 5 involves any direct consumption by the government (apart from the administrative costs which appear in column 3). Rather, it is income passed on to private citizens who then consume resources themselves. Thus column 5 reflects money redistributed within the private sector and not money taken from the private sector and consumed elsewhere.

Transfer payments even include some money which is raised in taxes and paid back to the same people who paid the tax. The clearest example of this is Child Benefit. This was intended to replace an income-tax deduction for each child with a cash payment of equal value. Such a scheme could, in principle, have raised both tax revenue and government expenditure but have left everybody with exactly the same income as they had before (except for administrative costs). This means that the figure in column 5 could exceed 100 per cent. Therefore it should not be interpreted as the government's slice of the national cake. Either column 3 or columns 3 plus 4 would be a better measure of the government's resource use. These latter figures are nothing like as large on their own and so are rarely reported by those who wish to exaggerate the size of government.

Without exaggerating it is true, nonetheless, that there has been a steady growth in the size of government, especially in value terms. The latter is at least as important as the volume measure since the higher expenditures have to be paid for. It is thus the value measure which matters for the tax implications of government spending. Indeed, taxes have to pay for transfers as well as for resource-consuming expenditures. Average tax rates may have significance for the real economy independently of the composition of government spending. (Note that while marginal tax rates are probably of most significance for incentive reasons, any one average tax rate for the economy as a whole is consistent with an infinite number of marginal tax structures.)

Even more controversial than the trends themselves are attempts to explain the trends in government growth. Most of the literature takes it as given that government has grown relative to national output and attempts to explain this growth. Theories of government growth have been developed from a number of different perspectives—ideology of elected governments, vested interests of state-employed bureaucrats, asymmetries of expansion and contraction with Keynesian fiscal policy, etc. We do not have space to discuss all of these theories. (For a comprehensive survey see Larkey, Stolp, and Winer, 1981.) Rather we shall mention three attempts to explain the growth of government which have obvious testable implications.

The most influential study in the post-war period of UK public expenditure was by Peacock and Wiseman (1961). They presented a detailed analysis of trends in public expenditure from 1890 to 1955. Their work is most remembered for the identification of a phenomenon which they referred to as the Displacement Effect. This arose because it appeared from their evidence that public spending grew roughly in line with GNP during peacetime. During wars public spending rose substantially but was never fully reversed on the cessation of hostilities. Fig. 3.2 is their figure which shows most clearly this displacement or ratchet effect.

There is no reason to doubt the existence of a displacement effect in the historical period examined. However, it is not intended as a general framework for understanding trends in government spending during long periods of peace. Indeed, since the Peacock and Wiseman data period ended, we have had over 30 years of continuous peace. One comment on the displacement effect is warranted. Notice that it relates to total expenditures and not just resource consuming or exhaustive expenditures. The ratchet effect is much less marked if government consumption alone is considered. This may reflect two phenomena. One is the changed debt position of government after wars, and the other is a greater acceptance of redistribution as a result of the common sacrifices of wartime.

In 1978 Frey and Schneider published an attempt to explain the behaviour of government in the context of what they called a Politico-Economic Model. This involved governments pursuing their ideological goals subject both to re-election constraints and to costs. Their model had two parts: first, a relationship between the state of the economy and the popularity of the government; and, second, equations which determine tax revenue and major components of government expenditure in terms of popularity as measured by opinion polls, the complexion of the party in power and various cost elements such as wage rates.

This framework has obvious appeal in that it combines both political and economic objectives of elected governments in the determination of policies. Differences between parties in spending and taxing are potentially revealed and the timing of policy changes can be influenced by election timing as well as by the needs of stabilization policy. Unfortunately their results were inconclusive in a number of respects. First, there appeared to be no well-defined differences between political parties. Second, the estimates of popularity functions and policy functions proved to be highly sensitive to the data period chosen. Finally, the behaviour of government which was central to the model was extremely implausible given the institutional constraints that operate. According to Frey and Schneider, governments are supposed to change their policies whenever they are behind the opposition party by

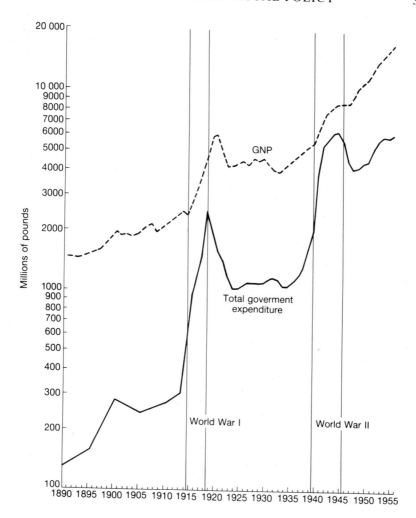

FIG. 3.2. *Total government expenditure and GNP at current prices, 1890–1955*
Source: Peacock and Wiesman (1961).

more than a critical amount in the opinion polls. This implies a flexibility of policy-making which is quite unrealistic as a description of how government works.

It was largely as a counter example to the politico-economic model that Chrystal and Alt (1979, 1983) put forward the Permanent Income Hypothesis for government spending. Fig. 3.3 shows the ratio of government consumption, government transfers, and tax revenue to GDP from 1946 to 1987. Two things stand out. First, it is clear that most of the cycle in fiscal policy is coming through tax revenue and not government expenditure. Second, with regard to expenditures, what has to be explained is not so much why government expenditure varies but, rather, why it is so stable a proportion of GDP (especially government consumption). This stability

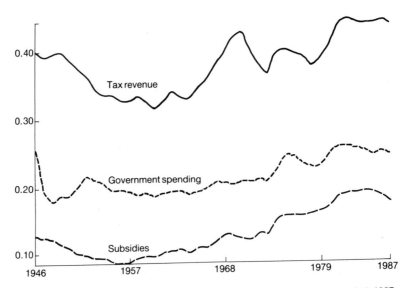

FIG. 3.3.   *Tax, government spending, and subsidies as proportion of GDP, 1946–1987*

was not accidental. The Public Expenditure Survey Committee (PESC) system, which was established following the Plowden Report of 1961, planned for public spending to rise over a five year horizon '. . . in relation to prospective resources'. Thus, as Price (1978) reports, although Keynesians talked about using government spending changes as a way of regulating economic activity, in fact government spending was planned to be neutral in fiscal policy terms. The regulatory function fell to the taxation side of the budget:

Public expenditure enjoyed an unchallenged pre-eminence in the original blueprint for postwar stabilisation policy, but in practice it surrendered this position to taxation and the manipulation of consumer demand (by measures like hire purchase restrictions) . . . By the end of the 1950s the avowed strategy had become to ensure that public spending was neutral vis-a-vis internal stability, with the public sector expanding at a rate consistent with the long-run growth of the economy, so that at least one sector would be free from cyclical disturbances. (p. 77).

These institutional realities in combination with the observed stability of public spending make it obvious that a good first approximation to an hypothesis of government spending growth would be that governments maintain a constant proportion of public spending in relation to national income. Of course, since there are time lags involved, what actually happens is that public spending plans are related to expected or forecast national income. The out-turns for either may involve unexpected or transitory components which create a need for subsequent readjustment. A similar relationship for the personal sector between planned consumption and expected income was first proposed by Milton Friedman (1957). It is from his work that the term 'Permanent Income' is derived.

The permanent income hypothesis is not without its critics. (See, for example, Burton, 1985. He argues that government spending has grown much faster than GNP, though he is concerned with total spending including transfers. As we have already seen this is factually correct. The problem remains of how to interpret these facts in the light of the relative price effect.) However, it does provide the basis for a statistical explanation of government expenditure behaviour which alternative theories must compete with or augment. It performs extremely well as an explanation for government consumption expenditure in volume terms but fails to explain the relative price effect. It is not entirely appropriate for explaining transfer payments because these are affected more severely by cyclical factors, such as the level of unemployment, and also by demographic influences, such as the number of people of pensionable age. These are determined more by the numbers of the population in need (old people and unemployed) than by plans of government resource use.

It is worth concluding this section by a comment on the apparent inability of governments to have a major impact on the trends in public spending. At the time of writing the United Kingdom has had a Conservative Government for over ten years. This Government was committed to a radical reduction in the share of resources taken by the public sector. Yet as Table 3.1 shows, by 1985 the Thatcher Government had been unable to turn the tide of public spending growth. This illustrates just how strong are the forces for the preservation of public services. It also shows that governments which have a hit list for cuts typically also have pet areas they wish to nourish.

The major changes in the composition of public spending are shown in Table 3.2. Notice that the total includes both transfers and exhaustive expenditures but excludes debt interest. There are two obvious changes between 1953 and 1983. These are the decline in the proportion of defence-related expenditures and the rise in expenditure on health and social security. The decline in defence spending actually bottomed out in the mid-1970s and subsequently recovered a little. The rise in health and social-security spending is partly due to the inclusion of transfer payments. The growing numbers of old people and the post-1980 rise in unemployment are significant influences on this growth. However, there has also been a real growth of spending on the increasingly expensive health service.

The proportions of expenditure going to industry and to education rose up to the early 1970s but then suffered a relative decline. Housing expenditure also suffered

TABLE 3.2. *Distribution of public expenditure, excluding debt interest*

|  | percentage of total expenditure less debt interest | | | | | |
|  | 1953 | 1963 | 1970 | 1975 | 1979 | 1983 |
|---|---|---|---|---|---|---|
| Defence and external relations | 31.8 | 21.5 | 15.1 | 12.3 | 14.8 | 14.8 |
| Industry, agriculture and trade | 12.8 | 15.7 | 18.4 | 18.4 | 12.1 | 10.9 |
| Housing and environmental services | 14.3 | 11.0 | 11.7 | 14.0 | 12.4 | 9.4 |
| Education and research | 9.0 | 14.5 | 16.2 | 15.6 | 14.3 | 13.9 |
| Health and social services | 26.1 | 32.2 | 33.1 | 31.9 | 38.3 | 42.6 |
| Other | 6.1 | 5.1 | 5.5 | 7.8 | 8.1 | 8.4 |
| Total | 100.0 | 100.0 | 100.0 | 100.0 | 100.0 | 100.0 |

*Note*: The figures for 1953, 1963, and 1970 are not exactly comparable with those for later years because of classification changes.

*Source*: *National Income Blue Book* (various issues).

severe cutbacks, especially after 1976 when public-sector housing took the brunt of the cuts imposed by Labour Chancellor Dennis Healey. In general, however, the pattern seems to be that from the early 1950s until the mid-1970s expansion in domestic programmes of all kinds were enabled by declines in the proportion of public spending going to defence. By the mid-1970s defence had been trimmed as much as could be considered prudent and major choices had to be made about social priorities. What emerged, deliberately or not, was a policy of protecting health and social-security expenditure at the expense of other areas.

### Government and the Private Sector: Crowding Out?

The reason why government growth is viewed with alarm in some quarters is that it may be harmful to the rest of the economy. We shall discuss the main channels through which the expansion of government is likely to affect the private sector. This is obviously an area of considerable controversy which is related to differing views about the efficiency of the market mechanism as opposed to the central direction of resources.

There is nothing novel about the suggestion that government expansion is bad for the private sector. Throughout classical economics there was a presumption that expansion of resource use in the public sector would lower the output of the private sector. Adam Smith argued that government deficit spending, financed by borrowing, led to '. . . the destruction of some capital which had before existed in the country, by the perversion of some portion of the annual produce which had before been destined for the maintenance of productive labour, towards that of unproductive labour' (Smith, 1776, p. 878).

Smith is clearly correct, even as a short-run statement, in an economy in which all markets are continuously cleared by price adjustments. If there were no excess supply of resources in the private sector, then any resources purchased by the government must be lost to the private sector. Government expansion would inevitably mean private-sector contraction. This presumption was quite prevalent in Britain up to the 1930s when it could be associated with the conventional 'Treasury view'. However, following the Keynesian revolution (see below) the objections to extra government spending were weakened by the Keynesian macroeconomic analysis which predicted a positive 'multiplier effect' of extra public spending. As a result of this effect, an increase in public spending would also increase the output of the private sector, possibly by even more than the increase in public spending.

Reactions against this Keynesian approach were associated with monetarist and new-classical schools of thought. Both of these perceived that the aggregate level of output (at least in the long run) would tend to some 'natural' or equilibrium value which was independent of aggregate demand. Hence public sector consumption would crowd out private consumption one for one. Some went even further than this and argued that an expansion of the public sector inevitably reduces total output and its rate of growth because public sector resource use is inefficient:

Reduction in the output of the private sector could, in principle, be offset by the increased output of the public sector. . . . It does not happen. Instead, there are loans or subsidies to enterprises that earn no profit or suffer large losses. . . . Absorption of labour by the government does not substitute public output for private output of equivalent value. Much public employment has the opposite effect. Complex rules and regulations absorb the time of civil servants and create the demands in the private sector for lawyers, accountants, negotiators and clerks to keep abreast of the rules, to fill out the forms and hopefully obtain more favourable interpretations than competitors have obtained. Employment is generated in the process, but much of the output produced by the employees has little value to society. More efficient output is crowded out, replaced by records, completed forms and administrative decrees that in the aggregate subtract more than they add to wealth and to welfare. (Brunner and Meltzer, 1976, p. 769)

A slightly different version of the crowding-out story was popularized in the United Kingdom by a series of articles in the *Sunday Times* in November 1975. The authors of the articles also expanded the ideas into a book (Bacon and Eltis, 1976). They divided the economy into two sectors, one of which produces 'marketed' outputs and the other which does not. 'The economy's market sector must produce all export . . . all investment and all the goods and services that workers buy. It is to be noted that the market sector will include the nationalized industries in so far as these cover their costs through sales of output, as well as the private sectors of modern economies. It will exclude the public services which are provided free of charge' (Bacon and Eltis, 1976, p. 123).

Bacon and Eltis expressed their idea in terms of the following identity:

$$i_m + b_m = e_m - c_u - i_u$$

where $e_m$ is the net output of the market sector (net of the inputs required to produce the output and of the consumption of output by those supported by employment or capital in the market sector) $i_m$ is the reinvestment into the market sector of market sector output, $b_m$ is the net exports of market sector output, $c_u$ is the consumption of market sector output by the non-market sector and $i_u$ is the investment in the non-market sector of market sector output.

The interpretation of this structure is quite straightforward. The market sector has to produce sufficient output both to satisfy its own consumption needs, provide for its own investment, and produce for export; and on top of this it has to have sufficient surplus to provide for the consumption and investment needs of the non-market sector. Bacon and Eltis used this framework to argue that the expansion of the non-market sector placed an excessive burden on the market sector and was, by implication crowding out market sector re-investment and exports. The connection between the public sector and the non-market sector is easy to make.

There may be some truth in this argument. However, one aspect of the Bacon/Eltis thesis looks a lot less plausible now than it did in 1976. This relates to the argument that private sector employment has been crowded out by the expansion of public sector employment. It was hard to sustain this argument in the mid-1970s since unemployment had drifted up from under 2 per cent in the early 1960s to about 5 per cent in the mid-1970s. However, since the end of 1979, the manufacturing sector has shed well over 1.5m. employees. At the same time the public sector has hardly expanded at all in employment terms. Nothing could be much more unlikely than that public sector employment has crowded out private sector employment, or indeed market sector employment, over this period.

The labour market is not the only channel through which crowding out can occur. There are three other mechanisms which could create at least partial crowding out of some component of private sector output or expenditure. First, high marginal tax rates are alleged to be a disincentive to income-generating effort. Some, such as Arthur Laffer, have suggested that lowering tax rates may actually increase tax revenue. The reason is that with lower tax rates people produce more and end up paying more tax in total even though it is a smaller proportion of their increased income. The possibility of this Laffer effect arising in the United Kingdom was dismissed by traditional Keynesians. However, it is the case that reductions in tax rates for the highest income earners by the 1979–83 Thatcher Government led to an increase in tax yields in these income brackets.

The second channel is through the effect on interest rates of higher government spending. An expansion of public spending funded by borrowing will put upward pressure on interest rates. This in turn will reduce private-sector investment below what it would otherwise be. If the economy is at less than full employment the result may be an increase in private incomes and private consumption, but the higher interest rates will inevitably lower investment (see Chrystal, 1979). A simultaneous expansionary monetary policy could perhaps reduce interest rates temporarily, but the ultimate effect of this would be higher inflation.

The third channel of crowding out is related to the second but will show up in different ways. It arises in an economy which has a floating exchange rate and efficient capital markets. An expansion of government demand for resources creates a current account deficit in the balance of payments. Foreign exchange market equilibrium requires a capital inflow of equal value to the current account deficit. This capital inflow will only be induced by higher domestic interest rates. At the same time the domestic exchange rate must appreciate to a point from which it is expected to depreciate. (Mundell, 1963, Branson and Buiter, 1983. This is because the expected depreciation just compensates for the fact that domestic interest rates are higher than those overseas. If it did not money would continue to flow across the foreign exchanges and exchange rates would change.) It is this appreciation which hurts the private exporting or import competing sector. It amounts to a loss of competitiveness and so also a loss of demand. Note that this loss of competitiveness resulting from a fiscal expansion depends on holding monetary policy constant. An expansionary monetary policy could reverse the effect on competitiveness, though with potentially disastrous consequences for inflation in the long run.

There may be no general mechanism for crowding out which is independent of the level of demand in the economy at the time a policy is introduced. Obviously, the less slack there is in an economy, the more likely is an expansion of government to crowd out some component of private-sector resource use. Analyses which assume that an economy will return to full market clearing automatically in the long run would inevitably predict that a larger public sector would necessitate a smaller private sector. However, economic policy analysis during the first 30 years of the post-war period was dominated by a view of the economy which had no assumption of an automatic return to full market clearing (especially in the labour market). The Keynesian Revolution was intended to solve the problem of persistent unemployment. Expansionary fiscal policy was the major tool available for the implementation of this intended solution. It is to this that we now turn.

## The Keynesian Revolution

The publication in 1936 of the *General Theory of Employment Interest and Money* by John Maynard Keynes triggered a radical change in economic thought and policy. Keynesian economics became the macroeconomic orthodoxy for at least three decades after the Second World War. The *General Theory* sought to give a new theoretical explanation for the persistence of mass unemployment, such as had existed in the depressed years before the war. A basic premiss was that in an advanced industrial economy the decisions of individual agents were not sufficiently coordinated by the price system to ensure the clearing of all markets simultaneously. By implication, Adam Smith's invisible hand of the price system needed the helping hand of government macroeconomic management. The theory devised by Keynes predicted that situations could arise in which a deficiency of aggregate demand in the economy would cause unemployment. This 'effective demand failure' could be caused by a fall in export demand coming from overseas, or it could result from a decline in domestic spending in the private sector on consumption or investment. Whatever the cause, the solution was straightforward. This was for the government to expand demand by running an expansionary fiscal policy. In practice, this meant cutting taxes or increasing public spending or both.

The principle of using the public authorities budget as a tool of economic management was not accepted without resistance. Sceptics of this new approach in the 1930s can be found among economists, politicians, and, most important, among government economic advisors. Above all, senior officials in the Treasury remained largely unconvinced of the efficacy of deficit spending as deliberate policy for economic recovery. The 'Treasury view' as for example expounded in 1929 by Churchill, the then Chancellor of the Exchequer, was 'the orthodox Treasury doctrine which has steadfastly held that, whatever the political or social advantages, very little additional employment and no permanent additional employment can in fact and as a general rule be created by State borrowing and State expenditure' (*Parliamentary Debates*, 15 April 1929). This belief was based on the idea that government borrowing to finance public works would simply deny investment funds to private industry and consequently a rise in government employment would be matched by a fall in private employment. Furthermore there were practical objections: public works would be difficult to implement and budget deficits would be positively dangerous as they would upset financial markets through a loss of confidence (see Middleton, 1985, ch. 3).

The war altered the scale of government intervention and at the same time transformed the nature and urgency of economic problems and this brought with it changes in economic decision making. The number of economic advisors increased and included many who had been influenced by Keynes (as well as Keynes himself who became a Treasury advisor). In 1940 the Economic Section and the Central Statistical Office were established as separate cabinet offices and, with the rise in power of the war ministries and the establishment of a small war cabinet (from which the Chancellor of the Exchequer was excluded), the influence of the Treasury waned. In his influential pamphlet 'How to Pay for the War', first published in 1939, Keynes pointed out that the expansion of government spending for war would soon lead to demand exceeding the economy's resources and an 'inflationary gap' would emerge. (The term 'inflationary gap' refers to a situation where aggregate demand exceeds aggregate output at existing prices.) In order to prevent procurement plans from being frustrated or leading to uncontrolled inflation, private purchasing power would have to be curtailed by taxation, by the encouragement of saving, and by allocating goods through a system of rationing.[1] This necessitated the development of a system of national accounts in order to estimate the potential

[1] Keynes emphasized the reallocation of resources which would arise from rationing and the inadequacy of voluntary savings campaigns. In addition to an increase in taxation he

inflationary gap. Work along these lines was undertaken principally by Meade and Stone in the Economic Section. The new national accounts provided the background for Sir Kingsley Wood's budget of 1941, which is often regarded as the first Keynesian budget. But it must be remembered that this was developed to meet problems which were the opposite of those prevailing in the 1930s and did not, therefore, represent a conversion to deficit financing as a cure for economic slumps. Furthermore the budget which provided for £150m. of extra tax went only part way to closing the estimated inflationary gap of £500m. and throughout the war much of the burden of matching demand to resources fell on rationing.[2]

The commitment to Keynesian budgetary policy for peacetime is often thought to have emerged in 1944 with the White Paper on *Employment Policy* (Cmd. 6527). In this the government accepted 'as one of their primary aims and responsibilities the maintenance of a high and stable level of employment after the war' (p. 3). The origins of the White Paper go back three or four years earlier. The central questions of employment policy had been the focus of discussion between the Economic Section and the Treasury for some time. The final result represented something of a compromise between the two, its publication having been brought forward to pre-empt that of Beveridge's *Full Employment in a Free Society* (1944). It has been argued that, even as late as 1944, the Treasury and its permanent secretary, Sir Richard Hopkins, held strong reservations about the peacetime application of such policies (see Booth, 1983; Peden, 1983). Nevertheless, the commitment to high employment is symbolically important (Keynes regarded it as *the* most important part of the document). Unlike Beveridge (1944), the final draft White Paper did not specify a particular level of unemployment as being the full employment level. Keynes thought that a figure as low as the 3 per cent assumed by Beveridge might not be achievable and others took the view that it was wildly optimistic and would lead to an inflationary spiral (Hutchison, 1968, pp. 26–33).

The White Paper did not lay out a plan for immediate action—intervention was not expected to be necessary until after the post-war boom—but represented a statement of general methods and principles. Considerable stress was laid on the expansion of exports and the intention of avoiding the emergence of significant balance of payments deficits. In reality balance of payments deficits were to haunt successive governments for the next three decades, but in the early post-war period, the government at least had at its disposal many of the wartime controls. As for wage and price setting, the White Paper stressed that 'the stability of these two elements is a condition vital to the success of employment policy; and that condition can be realized only by the joint efforts of the Government, employers and organized labour' (p. 19). As far as budgetary policy was concerned the major tool in stabilizing demand was to adjust the rate of investment in public works. In this respect the policy was similar to that contemplated in pre-war proposals—public

recommended a system of deferred pay which would be accredited in the form of blocked deposits in friendly societies or other approved savings accounts. These would be released when the post-war depression arrived and the budgetary impact ameliorated by a capital levy. 'Thus the system of deferment will be twice blessed; and will do almost as much good hereafter as it does now in preventing inflation and the exhaustion of scarce resources' (1940, p. 405).

[2] According to Dow 'from the economic discussions of the war years it is clear that considerable reliance was placed on direct controls to hold back demand; and that budgetary policy was devised after making allowance for this effect' (1964, p. 8).

works would be varied to compensate for variations in private investment. To provide short-run stabilization the main policy considered was an automatic mechanism linking social insurance payments (inversely) to the rate of unemployment. Other instruments considered were varying tax rates or regulating hire-purchase terms. Though these were seen initially as no more than possibilities, in reality they turned out to be the most commonly used instruments.

The coming of peace in 1945 saw the new Labour government committed to nationalization of the 'commanding heights' of the economy (coal, steel, railways, gas, and electricity) and economic planning over a wider sphere as well as the expansion of the welfare state, particularly the health and educational services. Given these priorities and the problems of rapid demobilization and an immediate balance of payments crisis, economic policy during the first two years resembled that of wartime. Budgetary policy took a minor role. By 1947, with a further balance of payments crisis looming, inflation had become more of a preoccupation. Dalton's last budget shifted the emphasis to more austere budgetary policy. In addition, 1947 saw an important shift in the focus of economic responsibility and control away from the wartime pattern. With the appointment of Sir Stafford Cripps to the new post of Minister for Economic Affairs and then (in addition) to the Chancellorship the responsibility for economic policy became more concentrated. This also marked the re-emergence of the Treasury as the key department in economic policy and the introduction of a new structure of economic planning.[3] When Gaitskell arrived as Chancellor in October 1950, new problems were appearing—the Korean War boom in commodity prices was threatening the balance of payments while at the same time rearmament was expanding the budget. The 1951 budget saw a rise in direct and indirect tax as well as cuts in public expenditure. This marked a partial return to wartime Keynesianism but, just as during the war, fiscal policy went only part way to closing the inflationary gap. Thus during the six years of the Labour government, in so far as Keynesianism existed, it was directed to deflation and not inflation. But demand management for the purpose of stabilization had not yet fully emerged and fiscal policy played only a secondary role. Over this period it was the balance of payments and the vulnerability of sterling which provided the main policy problem and this clearly foreshadowed events to come. (The Labour Government felt forced to devalue sterling in 1949. See Cairncross and Eichengreen, 1983.)

The 1951 election brought the Conservatives to power for what was to be a 13-year period of office, during which there were six different Chancellors of the Exchequer.[4] The Conservatives continued with essentially the same approach to economic management as had developed under Labour. Apart from the denationalization of steel and road transport there was a broad consensus both on the mixed economy and the

[3] Earlier in 1947 saw the publication of the Economic Survey which provided macroeconomic estimates and projections as background to the budget. In addition interdepartmental economic planning was to be strengthened with the appointment of a joint planning director Sir Edwin Plowden. With the ascendancy of Cripps to Chief Planning Officer the Economic Planning Staff and the Economic Information Unit became part of the Treasury and the Economic Section, though still a Cabinet office, became much more closely attached to it (see Chester, 1951, pp. 344–50).

[4] These were R. A. Butler (from Oct. 1951), Harold Macmillan (from Dec. 1955), Peter Thorneycroft (from Jan. 1957), D. Heathcoat Amory (from Jan. 1958), Selwyn Lloyd (from July 1960), and Reginald Maudling (from July 1962 until Oct. 1964).

use of policy tools to regulate the level of demand. These years saw the continuation of the relaxation of direct controls over raw materials, imports, and the rationing of consumer goods, as well as a gradual move towards the full convertibility of sterling at the fixed rate of $2.80 established in 1949. (Full current account convertibility was restored in 1958, though exchange controls on capital transactions remained until as recently as 1979.) Relaxation of direct controls placed more of the burden of demand management on fiscal policy, which was focused mainly on the tax side with frequent variation in both direct and indirect taxes. In addition, the variation of hire-purchase terms for durable goods, usually the percentage deposit, became a popular tool mainly because of the ease with which it could be used and its apparent effectiveness in dampening or stimulating consumer demand for durable goods. 1951 also saw the revival of monetary policy as interest rates which had remained at 2 per cent were increased in successive steps to 4 per cent. But interest rates were thought to be an uncertain tool for demand management, a view espoused in the *Radcliffe Report* of 1959. By contrast the Report paid more attention to the concept of liquidity and emphasized the effects of bank credit to consumers and businesses. With these basic tools successive administrations grappled with the major dilemma of macroeconomic management which had already been clearly foreshadowed in the recovery years. This was the problem of reconciling a high level of internal demand and resource utilization with a manageable balance of payments under fixed exchange rates.

This dilemma was reflected in the so called 'stop–go' policy cycle. The expansion of domestic demand aimed at increasing or maintaining economic activity contributed to rising incomes and prices. High domestic demand tended to lead to a deficit on the current account of the balance of payments. This is because high domestic spending leads to greater imports and may also cause supply constraints in exporting (or import-substitute production) industries. Under the fixed exchange-rate system, the Bank of England had to provide the excess spending overseas out of its foreign-exchange reserves. Whenever foreign-exchange reserves were found to be flowing out too fast a crisis was created which would typically force an immediate reversal in policy. Such crises occurred in 1952, 1955, 1957, 1961, 1966 (and to a lesser extent in other years) each differing in certain respects, but two illustrations will suffice. After the Korean war-boom inflation moderated and a recession began to develop. In his 1953 budget the Chancellor, R. A. Butler, cut the standard rate of income tax by 2½p (from 9s. 6d. to 9s. in the pound) and purchase tax by one-sixth. In addition, he restored investment allowances, which had been cut in 1952, and further relaxed direct controls. The upturn in the economy gathered pace in 1954 and further tax reductions were announced in the 1955 budget, despite the deterioration in the balance of payments. After the May election a reserve crisis developed. The immediate response was a tightening of credit and trade restrictions. An autumn budget raised purchase tax by 20 per cent. A similar cycle was repeated in 1958–60. Under Heathcoat Amory cautious reflation was undertaken to offset the recession which was developing in 1958. Hire-purchase restrictions were eased and followed in 1959 with a reduction in purchase tax, in the duty on beer and a 9d. (3.75p) cut in the standard rate of income tax. The policy reversal began in 1960 with an increase in profits tax, a rise in Bank Rate to 6 per cent and hire-purchase restrictions. In 1961 the sterling crisis became more severe and in the summer a package including a 10 per cent rise in purchase tax, a curb on government spending and a further rise in Bank Rate to 7 per cent was announced. Once more the crisis passed and boom turned to recession.

By the early 1960s this approach to demand management, lurching successively from expansion to contraction began to be regarded as inadequate if not positively damaging. However the principle of demand management was still widely accepted: what·was needed were more tools and better means of control. It was recognized that, when crises threatened, demand management required more frequent adjustment than the annual spring budget supplemented by an autumn mini-budget. An important step in this direction was the introduction in 1961 of the 'regulator' by means of which the Chancellor could vary purchase tax on consumer goods by ten per cent in either direction in between budgets. But on the expenditure side there was a growing doubt about both the practicality and desirability of using public expenditure as a counter cyclical tool. The budgetary process was such that spending departments planned their expenditure largely in isolation and not as part of an overall government spending programme. Once these annual spending plans had been set they had to be accommodated into the budget usually without major revision. Thus decisions on public expenditure lay largely outside the control of the Chancellor and the Treasury (see Pliatzky, 1982, pp. 33–9).

The 1961 Plowden Report on *The Control of Public Expenditure* (Cmd. 1432) criticized the decentralized process determining public expenditure. Instead of the annual round, plans for public expenditure as a whole should be based on surveys looking four to five years ahead and should be related to 'prospective resources' (meaning the expected growth in national income). As a result of this recommendation the Public Expenditure Survey Committee (PESC) was introduced. Total public spending was grouped into functional programmes and related to long-term objectives to form estimates for five years ahead of expenditure measured in constant prices. The Plowden Report also emphasized that, to promote economy in public expenditure and efficiency in public services, spending plans should not be subject to the vicissitudes of stop–go policy. The Report serves to emphasize the shift away from the counter-cyclical public works policy envisaged in the 1944 White Paper. In practice public expenditure plans were cut in times of major crisis but, as we have seen above, the out turn of public expenditure growth over time followed a remarkably smooth trend and was broadly in line with national income growth. (See Price, 1978, for a graphic illustration of how public expenditure plans were always based on overoptimistic assumptions about 'prospective resource' growth and were repeatedly having to be trimmed back).

The 1960s also saw the emergence of concern about Britain's growth performance relative to other countries (especially Western Europe and Japan) and with inflation. These worries led to attempts at economic planning and incomes policy. The perceived implications for macroeconomic policy are shown by two statements issued by the Labour Government on coming into office in October 1964. In the first of these the new government rejected 'any policy based on a return to stop–go economics' and in their Statement of Intent, issued jointly with the TUC and employers' associations in December, the economic objective was 'to achieve and maintain a rapid increase in real incomes combined with full employment'. These objectives differed little from the approach of the outgoing Conservatives (Brittan, 1969, pp. 187–91 *et seq.*). The desire for planning was reflected in the setting up of the National Economic Development Council. In 1963 NEDC adopted a growth target of 4 per cent per annum for 1964–6. The same 4 per cent target, this time for 1964–70, appeared in Labour's National Plan of 1965, which was produced by the new Department of Economic Affairs. Indicative planning, however, provided little in the way of policy tools for achieving growth targets and the burden fell on demand management. Incomes policies were used from time to time to help hold down domestic wage pressure, but there is no evidence that these policies had any but the most temporary effect.

The basic problem of the balance of payments had not been solved and the underlying position was deteriorating as balance of payments deficits became larger with each 'go' phase. Reginald Maudling's 'dash for growth' of 1962–4 had been intended to generate sustained growth and somehow break out of the stop–go cycle. However, the outcome was a substantial balance of payments deficit. (Recent revisions to the statistics have revealed that the deficit was nothing like as large as was reported at the time.) The incoming Labour Government chose not to devalue but resorted to a variety of measures aimed directly at the balance of payments including a 15 per cent surcharge on imports (plus a small export rebate), a rise in Bank Rate from 5 to 7 per cent as well as further restrictions on capital movements and a limit of £50 worth of foreign exchange for each tourist going abroad. Fiscal measures to deflate domestic demand began in 1965 and became more severe in the 1966 Budget, which also introduced Selective Employment Tax. (This was an employment tax levied exclusively on the non-manufacturing sectors like services and construction. It was the brain child of Nicholas Kaldor). The idea was to divert employment into the manufacturing sector. Despite the tightening of fiscal policy, July 1966 saw a major sterling crisis in the midst of a seamen's strike and an even tighter fiscal stance had to be adopted. These developments meant that as early as 1966 the National Plan had been formally abandoned.[5] However, with rapid growth in public expenditure, the limited success of incomes policy and deteriorating export performance, devaluation was forced upon the government in November 1967. Even though the balance of payments pressure was ultimately relieved there was no return to expansionary fiscal policy. The theory was that domestic 'absorption' had to be reduced in order to divert resources towards exports. By June 1970, when the Labour Government was defeated in a general election, Britain had a healthy balance of payments surplus and the government budget was also in surplus for the first time since 1950 (this feat was not repeated until 1989).

The boom–bust cycle of 1962–6 was repeated again in 1972–6, though this time it was even more pronounced. An inflationary boom was initiated by the Conservatives (the so-called Barber boom—named after Anthony Barber, now Lord Barber, who was Chancellor of the Exchequer from 1970 to 1974). The subsequent Labour Government, after attempting for a short period to maintain growth and employment, felt forced, by high inflation and a plummeting exchange rate, to turn to domestic deflation. The fiscal stimulus enacted by the March 1972 budget was a reaction to the fact that unemployment had risen above a million for the first time

---

[5] According to Brittan the National Plan was a dead letter even earlier: 'It was a result of the July 1965 package—a full year before the famous 1966 measures—that many students became finally convinced that the government had abandoned its growth and employment objectives and would be prepared to deflate to the extent necessary to maintain the exchange rate. Thus the National Plan was written off by many people two months before it was published' (1969, p. 199).

since the war. Monetary policy was also extremely inflationary following the introduction of the 'Competition and Credit Control' reforms in September 1971. Some
argued that this boom was going to be different because reserve losses would not
trigger a policy reversal. In August 1971 the dollar had been 'floated' for several
months and so floating exchange rates were now considered acceptable. A boom in
the UK economy would no longer be aborted by a reserve crisis.

There was a short sharp rise in output during 1972–3 but real investment stayed
flat and unemployment only fell modestly. However, inflation accelerated and
reached over 25 per cent by 1975. Monetary policy was reversed at the end of 1973
but the government budget deficit continued to expand—by 1975 it was in excess of
10 per cent of GDP. It was this episode above all which undermined confidence in
Keynesian style counter-cyclical demand management. Without the constraint of
the fixed exchange rate, which had incorrectly been perceived as a restraint upon
economic growth, British economic performance had been worse than at any time
in the post-war period.[6] The pound was floated in June 1972 and has been floating
ever since. Floating exchange rates had not actually eased policy choices at all.
Rather they had made the impact on prices of excess monetary demand more direct.
The cost of this economics lesson was high.


## The Counter-Revolution

The period 1974–9 marked a collapse in confidence in Keynesian demand management. This growing disillusion is epitomized by a famous statement made by Labour
Prime Minister James Callaghan in his 1976 speech to the Labour Party Conference:

We used to think that you could spend your way out of recession and increase employment by
cutting taxes and boosting government expenditure. I tell you in all candour: that option no
longer exists. And in so far as it ever did exist it worked by injecting inflation into the
economy. And each time that happened unemployment rose. . . . The cozy world which we
were told would go on for ever, where full employment would be guaranteed by the stroke of
the chancellor's pen is gone for ever.

While this statement has been seen more as an attempt to convince international
opinion (in particular the IMF) of the government's resolve to conquer inflation, it
encapsulates a wider change in attitudes among politicians, policy advisors, and
economists.

Though the soaring inflation of the mid-1970s left an indelible mark, a number of
factors contributed to the shift in economic policy. From the late 1960s the view
gained ground that the major source of instability in the economy lay not with the
private sector but with the government itself and was largely associated with swings
in budgetary policy. Such views were highlighted in evidence presented by representatives of the New Cambridge and Monetarist schools of thought to the Public
Expenditure Committee in 1974. The former consisted of a modified Keynesian

---

[6] It was widely recognized that the fiscal and monetary expansion of 1972–4 had been too
sharp and had been badly timed as it coincided with an upswing in the world economy. But
equally the subsequent crisis of stagflation was overlain by the first shock increase in oil prices
and world recession. The charge against demand management in these years is not that it was
the sole cause of stagflation but that it contributed to the build up of price expectations which
made it more difficult to cope with external shocks without excessive inflation or unemployment.

approach with the difference that private-sector savings was viewed as relatively stable: in consequence a budget deficit would be largely reflected in a balance of payments deficit.[7] The monetarist approach emphasized the link between money stock growth and inflation. In both cases the government by its attempts to stabilize employment was seen as directly contributing to deteriorating economic performance.

Monetarism turned out to be both more influential and more enduring: in so far as policy was influenced by developments in economics these were in monetary theory. This served to focus attention on the sources of monetary growth and in particular on the monetary implications of budget deficits. Depending on how they are financed deficits can lead directly or indirectly to increases in the money stock and in any event may raise interest rates as the government draws on private savings. Such arguments were not entirely new: the link between fiscal and monetary policy imposed by the 'government budget constraint' had often been stressed and had previously influenced fiscal policy though largely as a result of external pressure. At the time of the 1967 devaluation and under the influence of the IMF the concept of Domestic Credit Expansion was adopted as a target variable. Similar pressure in 1976 prompted the shift in attention to the Public Sector Borrowing Requirement which replaced the (closely related) Financial Deficit as the key budgetary concept. The government's letter of intent to the IMF gave commitments on the future growth in the money supply. What was new in 1976 was that the monetary implications of the budget gained ascendancy over the conventional Keynesian fiscal implications.

In retrospect it also appears that the change in policy approach must also be attributed partly to the severity and nature of economic fluctuations since 1970. The two major recessions of 1974–6 and 1979–81 were triggered by substantial increases in the price of oil. There is still substantial disagreement about what the appropriate macroeconomic response would have been. The problem is that supply shocks, as in the case of oil, are usually associated with *relative* price changes. Since aggregate demand policies can do little to correct sectoral imbalances it is far from clear that the traditional Keynesian policies are appropriate. Nonetheless the soaring inflation of the mid-1970s and early 1980s, if not actually caused by public policy, have been seen as exacerbated by excessively expansionary fiscal and monetary policies. Thus the eclipse of fiscal policy was hastened not so much by its ineffectiveness in influencing aggregate demand but because of its failure as a tool to counteract supply shocks.

In part the retreat from Keynesian fiscal policy was influenced by the long-run deterioration in the supply side as reflected in the trend increase in the equilibrium unemployment rate. From the 1950s onwards there was a school of thought claiming that the economy was being run at too high a pressure of demand—an issue which was at the heart of the resignation of Conservative Chancellor Peter Thorneycroft in 1958. In the 1960s a rate of unemployment of 2–2½ per cent was regarded by some economists as an appropriate target and by the mid-1970s this was being raised to 4–5 per cent.[8] Though James Callaghan's speech quoted above reflects a grudging

[7] For an explanation of the New Cambridge approach and a discussion of its shortcomings see Chrystal, 1979, ch. 6.

[8] In the earlier years the leading advocate of running the economy at a lower level of demand was F. W. Paish who argued that a target of 2–2½ per cent of unemployment would be consistent with price stability, avoid repeated balance of payments crises, and allow the economy to grow at its trend rate (see Paish, 1962, chs. 7, 17). In the 1970s similar notions gained ground under the rubric of the 'natural rate' of unemployment (see ch. 7).

acceptance of permanently higher unemployment, the Labour government remained ostensibly committed to controlling employment. The final retreat from the commitment to full employment came with the Thatcher government in 1979. This was the first administration since 1979 not to make 'full employment' (however loosely defined) one of its explicit objectives. In the White Papers on the government's Expenditure Plans issued in November 1979 (Cmd. 7746) and March 1980 (Cmd. 7841) there was no mention of maintaining (or increasing) the level of employment but instead priority was given to reducing the inflation rate by controlling government spending and the growth of the money supply.

Policy was not transformed immediately but emerged gradually with the strengthening of the monetarist camp in key cabinet positions. In 1979 the public sector pay award, recommended under the previous government by the Clegg Commission, was honoured, as well as the Conservatives own promised cut in income tax while shifting the tax burden by raising the rate of VAT from 8 to 15 per cent. These initiatives both worsened the budget deficit and immediately threw the so-called Medium Term Financial Strategy off course. It was not until 1981 when income tax was raised again and petrol duty increased that the new strategy was reflected with full force in budgetary policy. The government continued to tighten fiscal policy even though the economy was in a major recession and unemployment was rising fast. Cash limits on government expenditure had been introduced by the previous government and a target increase of 5 per cent was inherited in 1979. In 1981 these were imposed more rigorously with greater controls over local authorities' spending as well as external financial limits on public corporations and an overall cash limit of 6 per cent, even though inflation was still running at twice this figure. During the first two years, cash limits were applied only to the year ahead while the old PESC system was retained for subsequent years but from 1981 future expenditure plans were specified in cash, based on assumptions about the future rate of inflation.

By 1983 it appeared that the old 'Treasury View' of the 1930s had re-emerged as the orthodox approach to policy.[9] The Conservatives had been returned to office with a greatly increased majority despite a rise in unemployment from 1.2m. to 3m. However, as with the original Keynesian revolution, the counter-revolution occurred as a gradual process and is still not complete. Under Chancellors Howe and Lawson there has been a strong commitment to reducing gradually the PSBR (Public Sector Debt Repayment) and by 1989 a substantial surplus had emerged. While the budgetary principles of the 1950s and 1960s are no longer accepted, the short-run influence of budgetary policy is widely acknowledged. The concept of 'fine tuning' however has been deliberately eschewed in favour of a medium-term strategy. This can be seen as a shift from 'discretion' to 'rules' as the guiding principle of budgetary policy. Two interpretations can be placed on this. The first is that recognizing the powerful effects of monetary expansion on activity, particularly if unanticipated, and of the significant lags involved, stabilization requires stable growth in the

[9] There are differing views on the degree to which policy has turned full circle. It has been argued that the Keynesian Revolution failed to fully legitimate large budget deficits and that the Keynesianism of the 1950s and 1960s represents only a partial conversion to these principles (Tomlinson, 1985, pp. 98–105). On the other hand it has been argued that the late 1970s saw a major shift in approach which marked a return to the 1920s (Ham. 1981, esp. p. 1; 135). As far as balancing the budget is concerned, it has been argued that the Thatcher government can be seen as aiming to balance the inflation-adjusted budget (see p. 79 below) rather than the budget as conventionally defined (Miller, 1981).

money supply following announced targets. Though this may have been the original intention, attempts to control the nominated money supply indicator, M3, proved embarrassingly difficult to achieve, indeed, the M3 target was abandoned in 1986. The only explicit target retained was for the monetary base, M0, but even this target was exceeded in 1987–8. In addition under Chancellor Lawson an important discretionary element returned to monetary policy in an effort to manage the exchange rate—a policy reminiscent of the 1930s. Monetary aggregates ceased to be the main guideline of monetary policy. Interest rate manipulation returned to the centre of the stage.

A second interpretation arises from the notion that the private sector and particularly those involved in wage and price setting ultimately reneged on an implicit agreement whereby the government maintained employment in exchange for wage and price moderation. If the government always accommodated cost inflation with expansionary monetary and fiscal policies, the private sector as a whole would have little incentive to stick to its side of the bargain. This was reflected in the successive failure of incomes policies since the 1960s, culminating in the so called 'winter of discontent' of 1978–9 which sealed the fate of the Labour Government. With the breakdown of cooperation the government had to give a clear signal that it would no longer adjust demand to accommodate inflation. The credibility of this strategy was established by the imposition of cash limits, by the commitment to medium-term budgetary objectives, and by the refusal to reflate the economy using fiscal policy in the early 1980s.[10]

### Deficits and Public Debt in the Long Run

At this stage we turn from the official approach to fiscal policy to the measurement of fiscal stance and its effects on the economy. But first it is necessary to dispel certain myths about the long-run effects of the Keynesian revolution which have frequently entered the rhetoric of political debate. It is often alleged that during the plateau of official Keynesianism in the 1950s and 1960s full employment was sustained by levering up the level of demand through fiscal policy. It is also sometimes claimed that this engendered public profligacy in the shape of substantial budget deficits. As a result public debt was piled up at a rate which could not be sustained in the long run and which represented a severe burden on future generations. Finally, the very solvency of the state could be threatened. As we shall see there is little substance in such claims.

What is true is that the post-war years saw relatively high employment (perhaps excess demand for labour) so that from 1946 through the end of the 1960s, unemployment averaged 1.5 per cent and rarely rose above 2 per cent. At that time R. C. O. Matthews raised the question of 'whether the high level of demand that actually occurred was due to government action or whether it was due to other forces as a result of which government action was not needed' (1968, p. 556). Employing a simple version of the multiplier theory he examined various components of 'autonomous expenditure' as shares of 'full employment' national income

[10] An interpretation along these lines can be found in Begg (1987) and is consistent with Matthews and Minford (1987). For a useful survey of the progressive breakdown of incomes policies see Jones (1987).

at various dates before and after the Second World War. In so far as the rise in the employment rate (relative to the 1930s) was due to these components of demand he concluded that it was investment and, to a lesser extent, exports that were responsible. In comparison government spending played only a minor role. As is well known the unemployment rate showed an upward trend from the mid-1960s onwards. A later study along similar lines to Matthews's found that the movement away from full employment from the mid-1960s to 1975–7 could not be attributed even in part to the budget. The public sector made a positive contribution to the growth in demand partially compensating for the reduction in demand from the domestic private sector and the external sector (Taylor, 1978).

Such simple Keynesian models are far from convincing when applied to such long periods when the economy might be expected to exhibit some tendency towards equilibrium through the adjustment of wages and prices. Instead we may simply ask if the period of Keynesian policy was associated with large budget deficits. This can be done with the aid of Table 3.3 which provides various budgetary measures as shares of GDP in five-year averages. The public-sector figures in the first five columns include central government, local authorities, and public corporations. The first column shows the overall financial surplus (receipts minus payments). In the era up to 1970 deficits averaged 2 per cent of GDP compared with nearly 5 per cent in the subsequent period. This serves to emphasize that the post-war Keynesian era was not one of massive deficits though one might argue that, given the buoyancy of private-sector demand, the public accounts should have been in surplus.

TABLE 3.3. *Public sector deficit and national debt*
(% GDP)

| | Pub. sector financial surplus | Pub. sector saving | Pub. sector borrowing requirement | Pub. sector debt | National debt | General govt. debt interest |
|---|---|---|---|---|---|---|
| 1946–50 | 0.0 | 3.9 | n/a | n/a | 244.4 | 5.4 |
| 1951–5 | −3.1 | 4.5 | n/a | n/a | 177.4 | 4.5 |
| 1956–60 | −2.7 | 4.1 | n/a | n/a | 133.0 | 4.3 |
| 1961–5 | −2.7 | 4.8 | n/a | n/a | 107.4 | 4.4 |
| 1966–70 | −1.2 | 8.7 | 2.0 | 105.7 | 87.2 | 4.6 |
| 1971–5 | −4.4 | 5.0 | 6.3 | 76.4 | 57.7 | 5.1 |
| 1976–80 | −5.6 | 2.1 | 6.2 | 64.9 | 50.8 | 5.0 |
| 1981–4 | −4.0 | 1.8 | 3.8 | 62.1 | 50.9 | 5.7 |

*Sources*: *Economic Trends*, Annual supplement (1985); *Annual Abstract of Statistics* (various issues).

Two alternative measures are given in columns 2 and 3. Public sector saving nets out public investment and capital transfers and the result indicates that the public sector has consistently saved, though this saving has declined since the late 1960s. To the extent that this saving represents investments which yield a flow of future social benefits, it cannot be argued that deficits purely represent a burden on future generations—a point to which we shall return below. On the other hand, deficits however incurred must be financed and this is reflected in the public sector borrowing requirement, figures for which are available from 1977. This is of the same order of magnitude as the financial deficit for the years shown but fell dramatically relative to the latter in 1985–7 because of receipts from privatization which are not counted in the financial deficit.[11]

Concern with the extent of borrowing was reflected in renewed emphasis on the public sector debt. In the late 1960s this was a little larger than national income but had fallen to less than two thirds of GNP by the early 1980s. The national debt is a narrower concept than the public sector debt and comprises the liabilities of the central government.[12] Column 5 shows that this declined continuously relative to national income until the the late 1970s. By that time it had reached a level similar to that of the 1900s—before the debt was vastly increased to finance two World Wars. The recent trend is all the more striking since it contrasts sharply with that of most other OECD countries where, typically, the debt ratio has been rising since 1970. As a result Britain's debt/income ratio had fallen to about the average for developed countries by 1985 from four times the average in 1970. Since, at any point in time, the debt is fixed in nominal terms, the debt/income ratio can be decomposed into the rate of growth of debt (as a result of budget deficits) less the rate of real income growth and less the inflation rate.[13] Over the period 1948–84 deficits added to the debt at about the same rate as real income increased so that (in an arithmetic sense) the reduction in the debt ratio was entirely due to inflation (Buiter, 1985, p. 19).

While the ratio of debt to income declined in the post-war period the burden of servicing it did not. Column 5 shows that debt interest paid by central and local governments remained at about 5 per cent of GDP. If the real rate of interest exceeded the real growth rate of the economy then the government would need to run a surplus on the primary budget (i.e. receipts minus payments excluding debt interest) in order to prevent the debt/income ratio rising. Since the reverse has typically been the case, modest deficits are sustainable in the long run. Even if the combination of deficit, interest rate and growth rate of 1985 were sustained indefinitely, the debt would ultimately stabilize at about 100 per cent of GDP (Bispam, 1986, p. 60). The debt/income ratio alone is a poor indicator of the financial solvency of the public sector since (as reflected in the figures for public saving) it also accumulates assets which can be set against outstanding liabilities. Valuing public assets is a difficult task particularly where there is no existing market for them and the public balance sheet also needs to take into account the present value of future streams of contractual payments and receipts as liabilities and assets. One estimate taking into account items such as future oil revenues and future pension payments (under existing obligations) indicates that in 1982 prices net liabilities totalled 275bn. in 1957, 285bn. in 1966, 70bn. in 1975, and 105bn. in 1982 (maximum

[11] The financial deficit is the increase in the public sector's net financial indebtedness while the PSBR is the public sector's net borrowing from the rest of the economy. These differ because the former is assessed largely on accruals and the latter on payments and because certain kinds of capital transaction are included in the latter but not the former. For an annual comparison of these measures 1970–84 see Biswas, Johns, and Savage (1985), p. 51.

[12] The national debt represents the liabilities of the National Loans Fund (established in 1968). It includes sterling government guaranteed stocks of nationalized industries as well as official holdings (i.e. holdings of central government debt by other central government funds). The public sector debt includes the whole of public sector indebtedness to the private sector but excludes public sector holdings of debt. For the relationship between the PSBR and the public sector debt see D. J. Reid (1977).

[13] The deficit may also be financed partly by money creation but this seigniorage component has been relatively insignificant (see Buiter, 1985).

estimates, see Hills, 1984, p. 35). Thus in 1982 government liabilities exceeded assets by a sum equal to 45 per cent of GDP. However this ratio declined significantly from 1957 and, if physical and financial assets and liabilities are taken alone, the government had accumulated net assets in excess of GDP by 1982. Given that the government has it in its power to be a net saver in the future as it has in the past such statistics do not seem cause for alarm.

The balance-sheet approach to the public sector also provides a perspective on the Conservative Government's recent privatization programme. One of the reasons for privatization cited both by the Chancellor and the Treasury is to reduce the PSBR. If the government sells an asset (such as British Telecom, privatized in 1985) it receives a payment but forgoes the future net revenues which that asset would yield. If the assets sold are valued by the stream of future returns then both sides of the balance sheet would be reduced by the same amount and hence the net asset position would be unchanged. Hence the PSBR is a misleading measure of the deficit in the presence of large scale privatization. Between 1981 and 1987 assets totalling 7.2bn. in 1981 prices were sold. In financial year 1987–8 a forecast surplus of 2bn. on the PSBR was more than accounted for by some 5bn. from privatization.

## The Budget and Fiscal Stance

In any year the out-turn for the budget depends on the rates of tax and expenditure set in framing budgetary policy, but the yield of taxes and the level of some expenditures will depend on the level of economic activity. Hence the budget deficit automatically decreases as income rises (assuming the change in activity itself originated in the private sector). It has been estimated for instance that in 1964 the budget deficit would decrease by 320m. for an increase in aggregate income of 1,000m. and in 1978 the improvement from the same rise in income would have been 416m. (Similar orders of magnitude have been estimated for the 1930s.)[14] What these estimates suggest is that, given the tax and expenditure schedules of the 1960s and 1970s, rates of unemployment such as prevailed in the 1930s would have led to budget deficits which were higher by approximately 3–4 per cent of GDP than those actually observed. This approach provides estimates of what the budget would have been in each year, if activity had been such as to produce a constant rate of employment. Assuming for the sake of illustration that only taxes depend on income such that the total tax yield $T = tY$. The 'constant employment' or 'cyclically adjusted' budget deficit can be expressed proportionately as $ABD = (G - T^*)/Y^*$ where $T^* = tY^*$, $Y^*$ is constant employment income. Comparing this constant employment budget deficit with the actual budget deficit gives an indication of the likely breakdown between discretionary and induced changes in fiscal stance. However the results will depend on what is defined as a neutral or no-change policy, for example, whether elements of government expenditure are assumed to grow automatically with the growth of income over time or whether tax allowances are raised with inflation.

---

[14] For 1964 and 1978 the figures are those calculated by Ward and Nield (1978, p. 24) and are based on the change in receipts (rather than accruals) for a deviation in income from the full employment level caused by a change in exports. For the 1930s Middleton (1981, p. 276) estimated values of 0.440 for 1930/1 and 0.356 for 1938/9.

Series for the actual budget deficit and the adjusted budget deficit estimated by Ward and Nield (1978) are graphed for 1949–77 in Fig. 3.4.[15] This excludes the two severe depressions of the 1930s and 1980s and covers only the period of Keynesian fiscal policy. Two things stand out. The first is that since the standardized level of unemployment was taken as 2½ per cent, the adjusted deficit exceeds the actual until 1968, after which unemployment was consistently above this level and the reverse occurs. On this comparison, fiscal stance in the mid-1970s was similar to the mid-1950s. Second, fluctuations about the trend are similar in both series. This indicates that during the era of Keynesian demand management, fluctuations in the budget reflected for the most part changes in discretionary policy rather than the relatively mild fluctuations in economic activity. This is rather different from the pattern which emerged in the violent slumps of 1929–31 and 1979–81 when the adjusted deficit indicates a much more severe tightening of fiscal stance than the unadjusted deficit (see further below). The main features of the years covered in the graph are the expansionary shift in the adjusted deficit around the Korean war which was not reversed and the tightening of fiscal stance in 1967–70 which was reversed over the following five years.

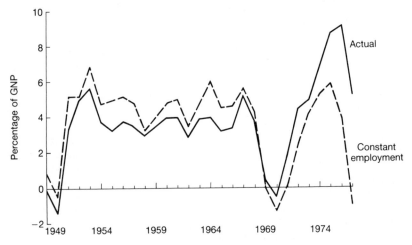

FIG: 3.4.    *Actual and constant employment budget deficits*

While the adjusted budget deficit corrects for the effect of variations in activity on the public accounts, changes in this index do not necessarily provide a good guide to the effect of the government on aggregate demand. The reason is that different taxes and expenditures have differential effects on spending. The spending impact of a set of fiscal policy changes may be estimated by weighting the various

[15] Ward and Nield used a slightly different measure of the actual deficit than the financial deficit of Table 3.2 and relate this to GNP rather than GDP. Since nominal full employment income grows over time both because of the growth of productive capacity and inflation, their definition of fiscal neutrality assumes that all tax allowances benefits and National Insurance contributions are indexed to the price level and rise in line with real income as do all fixed expenditures. For full details of these and other adjustments see Ward and Nield (1978), ch. 3.

taxes and expenditures according to their impact effect on aggregate demand. In the simplest case where government spending is only on goods and services and tax is only on income, the weighted budget deficit as a proportion of income is $WBD = (G - bT)/Y$, where b is the marginal propensity to spend out of disposable income. This may be adjusted on to a constant employment basis as before to give the adjusted weighted budget deficit as $AWBD = (G - bT^*)/Y^*$. One additional modification arises from variations in the real value of the public debt consequent on inflation. A rise in inflation will tend to be accompanied by a rise in the nominal interest rate on public debt. While the increased interest payments will be reflected as a rise in the deficit, the capital gain to the government (the inflation tax) from the declining real value of its nominal debt will not. It is extremely controversial as to whether the inflation tax should be included in estimates of fiscal stance. If any one of these indicators were to be selected as most representative of discretionary fiscal stance, we would recommend the weighted and cyclically adjusted budget deficit but excluding the inflation adjustment.

Estimates of these different budgetary measures made at the National Institute for Economic and Social Research (NIESR) for 1965–84 appear in Table 3.4. The adjusted figures are based not on a constant rate of employment but on a trend rate of growth of GDP of 2.7 per cent for 1965–73 and 2 per cent thereafter. In 1965–7 the weighted deficit appears to show fiscal policy to have been expansionary but, in contrast, the cyclically adjusted deficit suggests that it was contractionary. All four definitions show a substantial tightening in fiscal stance in the post-devaluation years 1967–70 followed by expansion to 1974 with unadjusted measures indicating continued expansion through to 1975. However, if the inflation adjustment is taken into account, by subtracting column 5 from either the unadjusted or the cyclically adjusted deficit, the picture changes sharply.[16] The post-devaluation period appears even more contractionary but, owing to the sharp rise in inflation in 1974–5, the inflation adjustment dominates. Thus, if the erosion of the real value of the debt is included in the measure of the deficit, the expansionary fiscal stance virtually disappears. If the cyclically adjusted deficit is used it appears like a substantial contractionary shift. However if we take the weighted measures then it is appropriate to weight the inflation adjustment before subtracting it. The appropriate weight is the propensity to spend out of real wealth—in this case taken as 0.2. This substantially reduces the impact of inflation such that the change in fiscal stance 1970–5 now appears only mildly contractionary.

If we concentrate on columns 3 and 4 these show a steady trend of relaxation in fiscal stance from 1970 to 1975. These also show the severe tightening of fiscal stance in 1976 and 1977 which was further tightened in 1980–2. These suggest that the fiscal squeeze during Mrs Thatcher's first Government was no more severe than that introduced after the 1976 crisis. It is also of interest to compare these recent episodes with fiscal policy during the slump of 1929–32 for which comparable measures (for central government only) are available (see Middleton, 1981; Broadberry, 1984). In 1929–32, as in the years after 1979, the government sought to counter the incipient rise in the deficit. While the actual deficit rose by 1.6 percentage points of GDP the cyclically adjusted deficit fell by 2.1 percentage

---

[16] We do not recommend taking this case too seriously since any government following a highly inflationary policy of funding a big deficit by money printing would appear to be following a deflationary course once the inflation tax was added to its revenue.

TABLE 3.4. *Adjusted financial deficits*
(% GDP)

| | Unadjusted | Weighted | Cyclically Adjusted | Weighted + Cyclically Adjusted | Inflation Adjustment | |
| | | | | | Unweighted | Weighted |
|---|---|---|---|---|---|---|
| 1965 | 2.18 | 0.48 | −1.37 | 0.44 | | |
| 1966 | 2.17 | 0.74 | −1.79 | 0.51 | | |
| 1967 | 3.54 | 2.19 | −0.68 | 1.79 | 1.98 | 0.40 |
| 1968 | 2.14 | 0.43 | −1.81 | 0.32 | 5.24 | 1.05 |
| 1969 | −1.06 | −1.99 | −5.01 | −2.24 | 1.70 | 0.82 |
| 1970 | −1.36 | −2.17 | −6.14 | −2.86 | 5.22 | 1.04 |
| 1971 | 0.49 | −1.33 | −4.91 | −2.43 | 4.61 | 1.12 |
| 1972 | 2.50 | −0.08 | −2.63 | −1.10 | 4.82 | 0.96 |
| 1973 | 3.78 | 0.19 | −0.06 | −0.02 | 5.37 | 1.07 |
| 1974 | 5.64 | 2.21 | 0.26 | 1.12 | 11.04 | 2.21 |
| 1975 | 7.24 | 3.11 | 0.03 | 0.97 | 11.30 | 2.26 |
| 1976 | 6.73 | 1.81 | −0.46 | −0.30 | 5.88 | 1.18 |
| 1977 | 4.18 | −0.44 | −2.41 | −2.22 | 6.55 | 1.31 |
| 1978 | 4.93 | −0.59 | −0.78 | −1.96 | 3.99 | 0.80 |
| 1979 | 4.40 | −0.72 | −0.73 | −1.82 | 7.55 | 1.51 |
| 1980 | 4.83 | −0.10 | −2.07 | −2.06 | 5.92 | 1.18 |
| 1981 | 3.58 | −0.47 | −4.79 | −3.50 | 4.84 | 0.97 |
| 1982 | 2.82 | −0.70 | −5.36 | −3.77 | 2.68 | 0.54 |
| 1983 | 3.60 | −0.29 | −4.34 | −3.18 | 2.23 | 0.45 |
| 1984 | 4.04 | −0.84 | −3.99 | −3.64 | 2.32 | 0.44 |

*Source*: Biswas, Johns, and Savage (1985), p. 50.

points. Thus the mid-1970s and early 1980s exhibit similar degrees of fiscal tightening in the face of a major slump as in the pre-Keynesian era.

How are changes such as these and those of earlier years to be understood? They must be examined in the light of governments' objectives and of actual or prospective developments in the economy itself. The most obvious objective from a Keynesian point of view is the stabilization of income and employment. Since fiscal policy takes time to implement and there are lags in its effects, we need to examine the government's ability to forecast future developments when evaluating policy effectiveness. In reality, however, policy objectives are more complex. Fiscal policy was often intended to serve more than one purpose and was typically used in conjunction with other policy tools to attempt to achieve several ends simultaneously. Evaluating fiscal policy in relation to economic targets becomes even more complex if these are frequently changed in reaction to perceived crises or in order to gain electoral advantage. It is to these issues that we now turn.

### Fiscal Policy and the Business Cycle

At the time of the 1944 White Paper it was expected that a short post-war boom would be followed by a protracted slump. For 30 years this failed to emerge. Though government policy may have contributed something to this experience, it was not the primary explanatory factor. Fiscal policy became focused on 'fine tuning' the economy with the objective of smoothing out economic fluctuations rather than in sustaining a higher or lower average level of demand. The pattern of business cycles which emerged was also quite different from the pre-war period. From 1870 to 1913 business cycles usually lasted for seven to ten years from peak to peak and in the intervening depressions there were typically several years of relatively high unemployment (precise comparisons with the post-World War Two situation are hampered by limitations in the statistics). The overall pattern between the two World Wars, though characterized by two severe slumps and much higher average levels of unemployment, was not dissimilar. By contrast, in the post-war era cycles were to become shorter in duration—about four years peak to peak—and involved much smaller variations in unemployment. Though fluctuations in output were somewhat greater than those in employment, up to 1975 the only year when real GNP fell was 1958 and then only by a very small margin. Only after 1970 did the severity of boom and slump resemble the pre-war experience. Prior to this (1945–70) the business cycle took the form of variations in the rate of growth of output around an upward trend. This raises the question already discussed briefly above: to what extent did fiscal policy contribute to the dampening of fluctuations and the stabilization of the economy?

In 1964 a study of the impact of demand management from 1945 to 1960 came to the conclusion that fiscal policy had, on balance, been more of a destabilizing influence than a stabilizing one.

. . . the rapid expansion of demand and output in the years 1952–55, and that in 1958–60, were both due, directly and indirectly, to the influence of policy. Though this is less certain the same may be true of the slow expansion of demand and output in years 1955–58; even if due to causes other than policy, policy was certainly not directed to counteract them. The major fluctuations in the rate of growth of demand in the years after 1952 were thus chiefly due to government policy. This was not the intended effect; in each phase, it must be supposed, policy went further than intended, as in turn did the correction of these effects. . . . As far as internal conditions are concerned then, budgetary and monetary policy failed to be stabilising and must on the contrary be regarded as destabilising. . . . Had tax changes been more gradual and credit regulations less variable, demand and output would probably have grown much more steadily. (Dow, 1964, p. 384)

In a study of the years 1959–73 Price (1978, p. 211) compared the intended change in the weighted full employment budget deficit with the change in world exports and private domestic investment. The result of regression analysis indicated a positive and significant relationship between the two. This means that typically fiscal stance was loosened when autonomous expenditures were increasing suggesting that, on average, fiscal stance moved perversely over these years.

If fiscal policy has at times moved in a destabilizing manner then it is important to ask why. A first step would be to examine taxes and public expenditures separately to see which of these accounted for the perverse movement in fiscal stance. For most of the period public expenditure appears to be the major culprit. In the period to the mid-1960s the tendency for total public expenditure on goods and services to move pro-cyclically was noticed and widely commented on (see Prest, 1968). The same holds for the period 1960–74. For these years it has also been found that public investment tended to have a destabilizing effect on total investment in the sense that total investment exhibited greater variation than private investment alone. This was largely due to the rapid growth of public investment from 1962 to

1967, which at least in its early stages coincided with an upswing in private investment. Both public and private investment declined after the devaluation crisis of 1967.

Decisions on public expenditure were designed largely to serve ends other than demand management but it is worth noting that, changes to plans for public investment and the difference between planned and realized investment made public investment less destabilizing than otherwise. Hence both discretionary revisions to public investment and shortfalls and overruns on expenditure plans tended to be stabilizing. Similarly, much of local authority expenditure is beyond the control of central government and this saw rapid increase from 1960 to 1968 (Holmans, 1970). However, dividing changes in fiscal leverage between central government and other public authorities, the Musgraves (1967, p. 42) found that most of the instability was due to the former.

We have seen that after the implementation of the Plowden Report it was intended to maintain a stable growth of public spending in line with the growth of the real economy. In this context it is natural to expect taxes to be the main counter-cyclical tool of policy. Even without deliberate changes in tax rates, the tax system itself should be stabilizing because tax revenues rise automatically with income. However, to examine tax *policy* the impact of discretionary changes in tax schedules needs to be assessed. One approach to examining the stabilization effects of policy is to estimate the impact of all the discretionary changes in taxes on demand and use these to construct counter-factual estimates of what GDP and its components would have been if no discretionary changes had been made. This counter-factual series $Y^*$ can then be compared with the actual series Y. If the regression of $Y^*$ on a trend line produces a closer fit than that of Y, then discretionary tax policy could be seen to be destabilizing and vice versa. One such test performed by Bristow (1968) for quarterly data for 1954–65 produced the result that discretionary tax changes had a mildly stabilizing effect. Another study by Artis (1972) found that for 1965–70 tax policy was marginally destabilizing. But in both cases the differences in $R^2$ between actual and counter-factual series were so small as to suggest that tax changes overall had at most minor effects on the variation in national income.[17]

Changes in economic policy have to be determined in the light of prospective developments in the economy and it is therefore necessary to construct forecasts. Such forecasts must be based on projections of the past taking into account any expected future changes as well as changes in policy itself. Unanticipated events could easily mislead policy, a concern raised by Dow (1964) and by Bristow's (1968, p. 308) finding that discretionary tax changes would have been more stabilizing if undertaken a year earlier. (Of course, the appropriate information may not have been available at the time, as statistics take time to collect. However, for whatever reason, the evidence is that governments typically acted too late to do any good and in some cases made things worse.) As we have seen, from 1947 on, forecasts were an integral part of budgetary policy and from then until 1951, the forecast for the ensuing year was published in the economic survey accompanying the budget. From that time until 1968 when the policy was re-instituted, forecasts made by the Treasury and used by the Chancellor were not published and have to be inferred. Forecasts were initially made for the following whole year. Initially these were in

[17] Bristow found that for 1954–65 $R^2$ was higher for the counter-factual series by only 1 per cent and Artis that for 1965–70 it was lower by the same amount.

nominal, but later in real, terms. In the late 1950s quarterly forecasts were released for up to a year or eighteen months ahead. Finally in 1976 the Treasury was required under the Industry Act to provide forecasts on a wider range of indicators and for longer periods. (For a detailed description of the relation between forecasting and the annual budgetary cycle see Brittan, 1969, ch. 3, esp. p. 62).

Fig. 3.5 shows the published or inferred forecast of the percentage growth in real GDP made a year earlier and the actual growth in GDP over the same period.[18] At the time the forecasts were made the effects of policy changes which were anticipated are included and they have been further adjusted for budgetary interventions made after the forecast, so that deviations from the actual are not due to policy itself. The overall impression is of a fairly close correspondence between the two, certainly as regards the direction of change, but it should be remembered that an error of as little as 1 or 2 per cent in the out-turn, which was due to unforeseen events, could seriously mislead policy. In fact the average error (regardless of sign) was 1.1 per cent—equivalent to the impact of a change in income tax of 5p in the pound (Prest and Coppock, 1984, p. 33). It might have been expected that with better and more up-to-date information, accumulated knowledge of the economy and improved fore-casting techniques, the accuracy of forecasts would have improved over time. It appears that this was not the case and no significant improvement can be found in the 1960s or 1970s over the previous decade.[19] But it can be argued that earlier in the period when actual variations in activity were smaller, changes were easier to predict than after 1970, when greater volatility emerged. It is not clear how far policy was misled by poor forecasting but it appears to have been partly responsible in 1952 when the sharp decline in stocks was not foreseen and in 1954 when rapid growth in demand was not anticipated. Perhaps the clearest example is in 1959 when the sharp recovery was underestimated despite the fact that it was largely the result of tax reductions in the budget and the earlier relaxation of credit (Dow, 1964, pp. 140–2). Less important for policy but still of significance was the under-estimation of growth in 1963 and overestimation in 1972 (Price, 1978, pp. 199, 205). The same might be said of the forecasting errors of 1974 and 1979 when oil-price shocks influenced the outcome in both cases.

Even if we were to look at the original (uncorrected) forecasts it is clear that from year to year these would follow a broadly cyclical pattern. This suggests that at least to some extent the cycle was anticipated. It may be an exaggeration to see forecasts as an indicator of the desired level of income a year ahead but it is clear that the 'target' level of activity changed from year to year. This was partly because the full adjustment was not expected to occur within the year, and partly because fiscal policy was often aimed at goals other than the stabilization of income or employ-ment. Every government held a series of macroeconomic objectives of which stabi-lization was just one. Others would be a 'satisfactory' outcome for the balance of payments, and later in the period, the avoidance of excessive inflation. Hence one could equally ask whether fiscal policy served to attenuate swings in the balance of payments or control variations in inflation. If one knew the weights attached by policy makers to these different and sometimes conflicting goals, it would be

[18] For the period when forecasts were not published by the Treasury the forecasts given are based on those of the National Institute.

[19] The average absolute percentage error calculated from the data in the table was exactly the same figure (1.1) for 1955–69 as for 1970–84.

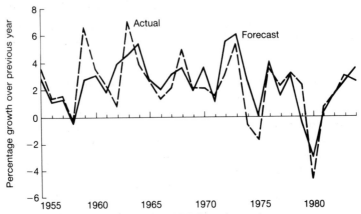

FIG. 3.5.   *Actual and forecast growth in GDP from the previous year*

possible to judge fiscal policy in relation to them all simultaneously. On the other hand it can be argued that policy tended to respond to 'crises' such as record figures for unemployment or inflation or to unsustainable balance of payments deficits and hence that the policy goals changed accordingly. Empirical evidence for 1946–73 indicates that changes in taxation were directed principally to relieving unemployment when crisis levels were reached and primarily to the balance of payments when this was the most pressing concern. Public investment also responded to the crises in balance of payments but not in the unemployment rate. (Moseley, 1984, p. 104). Not surprisingly, after 1973 when the exchange rate was floated and unemployment gave way to the priority of inflation, tax changes were directed more to controlling inflation.

It could be argued that, during the era of 'fine tuning' from 1946–73, fiscal policy ought nevertheless to be judged on the grounds of stabilization because it was principally assigned to this goal. Since there were other tools of macroeconomic management, such as the exchange rate and credit controls, these should have been aimed at and judged in relation to other goals. However, if several instruments are being used simultaneously then they should be used jointly to achieve the different policy goals. Thus, although demand management was sometimes criticized when fiscal and monetary policy were varied in opposite directions (in terms of their effects on domestic demand), such a stance might be perfectly appropriate when there is more than one macroeconomic objective (see Mundell, 1963). Hence, the achievement with regard to stabilization and other targets, such as inflation or the balance of payments, could only be assessed in relation to macroeconomic policies as a whole. Furthermore, if, as is sometimes suggested, one (or more) of the tools was not used (such as the exchange rate before 1967), was used inappropriately, or proved ineffective (such as incomes policy) then this would affect the 'ideal' setting of fiscal policy. To evaluate policy combinations one would need a full macroeconomic model in which the optimal combinations of instruments can be analysed.

An impression of the implications of different sets of policies can be gained from a symposium which took place in 1977. A number of macromodelling groups were asked to specify policies which would have been preferable to those actually followed during the two historical episodes 1964–9 and 1970–5. (In the former period they had been primarily aimed at avoiding balance of payments crisis and in the latter period there was the Barber Boom followed by the reactions to the oil crisis.) Three different views were given by the Cambridge Economic Policy Group (CEPG), the London Business School (LBS) and the National Institute of Economic and Social Research (NIESR) (Cripps, Fetherston, and Godley, 1978; Ball and Burns, 1978; Surrey and Ormerod, 1978). The choice of alternative policies differed in each case because of differences in the importance attached to different objectives, the tools used, the theoretical underpinnings and the structure of the macromodels. All three agreed that with the fixed exchange rate, the stance of fiscal policy as inherited in 1964 was too expansionary given the underlying balance of payments position. While the LBS suggested a tightening of fiscal stance the two other groups recommended devaluation at the beginning of the period rather than waiting until it was forced in 1967. In the view of the CEPG the implication for fiscal stance would have been as follows: 'If a devaluation strategy had been adopted immediately then actual fiscal stance would have been about right overall: of course with devaluation in late 1964 faster growth would have occurred during this period. In 1967, however, the actual fiscal stance was probably too lax mainly due to a sharp rise in public expenditure despite the famous cuts of 1966' (Cripps, Fetherston, and Godley, 1978, p. 11). NIESR asserted that devaluation would have needed the accompaniment of incomes policy from 1966 and in concert with these policies fiscal stance should have been tightened in 1965–6 and then relaxed until 1968. All groups took the view that in 1970 the fiscal stance inherited from the previous administration was too tight and recommended more expansionary policy in 1971–2. The actual loosening of policy in 1972–3 had been too sharp and (excepting NIESR) too large. While it was also agreed that the monetary expansion which came in the wake of Competition and Credit Control (see ch. 4) should have been avoided, different policies were recommended to cope with the oil shock of 1973–4. While CEPG recommended import controls, and NIESR incomes policy, to accompany strong counter-cyclical fiscal policy, LBS recommended a more modest fiscal expansion than actually took place.

Even greater controversy surrounds the causes of and remedies for the 1980–2 depression. The depression was more severe in Britain than in other industrial countries. What is still unclear is the extent to which this was due to tight domestic aggregate demand policies as opposed to what has come to be known as 'Dutch Disease'. One prominent pair of academic economists (Buiter and Miller, 1981b) at first put the blame on excessively tight monetary policy. However, they later changed their minds (1983) and shifted the emphasis to tight fiscal policy. The latter explanation itself is problematic as the tightening of fiscal policy did not occur until 1981–2 and yet the collapse of output was almost over by 1980 (see Chrystal, 1984). It seems likely that the effect of North Sea oil revenues on the exchange rate, the downturn in world trade and fiscal and monetary policy contributed to the contraction. One recent macromodel-based evaluation suggests that the government's tight deflation programme made only a minor contribution to the recession of 1980–1 more than half of which could be attributed to such external shocks as the fall in world trade and the rise in real interest rates abroad. It was suggested nonetheless that the tightening of 1981 was too severe despite an overall sympathetic assessment of the Thatcher Government's macroeconomic strategy (Matthews and Minford, 1987).

## The Political Business Cycle

To return to policies actually pursued rather than those which might have been chosen, the question is sometimes raised as to how these differed according to the party in power. Just as with macromodelling groups, differences between parties might depend on the implicit view of the economic system, the policy tools which were regarded as most effective and the different priorities accorded to economic objectives. Though economic policy is sometimes seen as lurching from one extreme to the other, for most of the period this was not the case. While there were differences over the use of direct controls in the 1940s and a different attitude to nationalization, the more striking feature is the parallel change in the attitudes of both parties. In the first post-war decade both sought to throw off direct controls and both embraced fiscal fine tuning, while in the 1960s, the desire for planning and experimentation with incomes policy was common ground. In the 1970s, the increasing priority given to inflation and monetary control affected each though to different degrees. Indeed, it was the Labour Chancellor Denis Healey who introduced monetary targets and he was at least as successful in sticking to them as his Conservative successors (see Gamble and Walkland, 1984, pp. 58–76). It might have been expected nonetheless that the Labour party (given its greater base of Trade Union and working-class support) would place greater emphasis on the employment target. Though one might have expected lower unemployment under Labour, particularly in the light of the dramatic rise after 1979, the difference between administrations is dominated by the long-term upward trend. It might also have been expected that Labour would have adopted a more expansionary fiscal stance. Once again the contrast between 1974–9 and 1979–84 would support this conclusion but comparisons before 1979 would not—indeed some of the most deflationary budgetary measures ever taken, such as in the late 1940s, mid-1960s, and 1975–6, were undertaken by Labour Chancellors.

A more difficult question is whether governments have used economic policy to gain temporary electoral advantage at the cost of increased instability. There is a widespread belief that pre-election budgets tend to be more expansionary than would otherwise be the case. The hypothesis of a pre-election boost is based on the notion that a temporary boom will earn electoral popularity and, therefore, that voters either do not take into account or are unaware that policy may of necessity be reversed after the election. The phenomenon of a pre-election boom followed by a post-election tightening is known as a 'political business cycle'. It is hard to identify the extent to which pre-election budgets have been more expansionary than otherwise since the economic circumstances surrounding each instance differ and no government would openly admit to such a policy. There is some evidence that the elections from 1955 to 1970 and 1979 were associated with abnormal growth in real per capita income in the preceding twelve months but this may reflect the choice of election dates at times of expansion rather than the effects of deliberate policy (Moseley, 1984, pp. 184–6). It is more difficult to identify systematic fiscal expansions as directly preceding elections although a case might be made out for 1955 and 1959 and perhaps 1964 and 1972–3. In any case the effects of such strategies are far from clear: an overtly electioneering budget could reduce the government's credibility, while more subtle changes in policy might be lost on the electorate.

The notion of the political business cycle implies two separate but related hypotheses: first that the government's popularity depends largely on cyclical variables which can be influenced by demand management policy and second that governments have reacted systematically in response to their popularity (or lack of it) when determining economic policy. These two relationships have provided the basis for a number of empirical studies. These have typically focused on the percentage lead of the government over the principal opposition party as measured by the Gallup poll. As well as economic variables, the tendency for the government to lose popularity in mid-term and then regain it as the election approaches needs to be taken into account. Using this approach a number of studies have found popularity to be inversely related to both inflation and unemployment and positively related to the growth in per capita income. In addition changes in the exchange rate and in the average tax rate have also been found to affect popularity (see for instance Frey and Schneider (1978); Pissarides (1980); Moseley (1984)).[20] The effects of popularity on policy are more controversial but it has been claimed that the various categories of government expenditure as well as total tax receipts can in part be explained by the government standing in the polls. Such findings have been heavily criticized. In particular, it has been pointed out that government expenditure can be better explained as dependency on income according to the permanent income approach discussed above (Frey and Schneider 1978, 1981; Chrystal and Alt 1981a, 1983). The fact that the trend in government spending is so smooth over time suggests that it is either too difficult to change spending at short notice (especially in the light of temporary swings in opinion polls) or governments do not even try.

As we have seen, earlier governments have frequently framed their fiscal policy according to the developing economic situation and in particular in response to crises in the balance of payments, unemployment, or inflation. The weights attached to these have clearly changed over time and priorities have shifted from one election to the next. In responding to such stimuli they have attempted to follow what would be regarded at the time as the most popular policies. But the traditional pattern of stop–go can hardly be viewed as a political business cycle. In a political business cycle the government would respond to its popularity rating only in the pre-election year by creating a boom (if necessary to win the election) and then switching to a contractionary stance thereafter. It would be rash to dismiss such effects entirely since economic decisions are taken in a political framework. However, electoral motives have not been the overriding influence on fiscal policy and have had little effect on the pattern of business cycles.

## Conclusion

In the period since 1945 the government budget has been seen as serving a range of different purposes, including the provision of social services, the redistribution of

---

[20] In his study Pissarides (1980, p. 575) found that all five variables affected the government's lead but that the traditional variables used in such studies, unemployment and the change in inflation were less important than the growth rate of consumption, changes in the exchange rate and the ratio of tax to GDP. Using the sample means of the variables (eliminating fluctuations) the model predicted a government lead of between 3.86 points and −4.3 points. This suggests that the government would need to engineer an improvement in at least some of these indicators to be sure of winning the election. Notice, however, that these numerical effects are very sensitive to the data sample chosen.

income, the control of major industries and, above all, management of the macro-economy. Yet, in relation to national income, the public sector has grown only slightly (depending on the measure used) despite frequent claims to the contrary. Ideological shifts and changes in government have had little effect on public expenditure which can be seen to have grown roughly in line with 'permanent income' (so long as transfer payments are excluded). In the long run, the growth of public employment will inevitably crowd out private employment but there is little evidence of crowding out over major cyclical phases in the post-war period. On the contrary, public expenditure has moved largely in phase with national income.

The Keynesian revolution laid emphasis on the employment-creating aspects of government spending and, in particular, on counter-cyclical budget deficits. The Keynesian demand management policies which emerged following the 1944 White Paper, and evolved through to the 1970s, were different in character from what had been anticipated. The object became to 'fine tune' variations in activity, rather than to counter major slumps. This was instituted largely through changes in taxes and other policies to control private spending, rather than through public expenditure. Thus high employment in the early post-war period was not the result of a significant fiscal stimulus in the absence of which the depression conditions of the 1930s or 1980s would have reappeared.

Disillusionment with fiscal policy as a tool of macroeconomic management arose, not because of its ineffectiveness in influencing aggregate demand, but because of the inability to reach several targets simultaneously. This, in part, may have been due to the failure to find other complementary policies, or to use them effectively. The experience of the 1970s convinced many observers that macroeconomic management was positively harmful as it appeared to have exacerbated inflation and also to have destabilized output. From a Keynesian perspective it may seem ironic that when the conditions that Keynesian demand management was originally conceived to cope with arose, the policy was given up, while in the 1950s and 1960s when it was hardly necessary it was, at least nominally, in use.[21]

Such judgments would, however, be too simplistic. The changes in economic priority away from employment towards inflation, the floating of exchange rates, and the associated rise in monetarism as the economic orthodoxy, are key elements in the changing policy stance. Concentration on the monetary implications of the budget and the recognition of the potential destabilizing influence of budgetary policy led to a policy emphasizing the application of simple rules rather than frequent discretionary adjustments. This may have been a temporary phase in the evolution of policy, as the Thatcher Government abandoned monetary targets in 1986, though it is too early to say whether they or their successors will return to more active demand management, especially using the tools of fiscal policy.

---

[21] There was little room for discretionary fiscal policy in the 1950s and 1960s owing to the binding constraint imposed by the fixed exchange rate regime. Excessive expansion of domestic demand would be rapidly reversed following losses of foreign exchange reserves. Stability and low inflation resulted from the conservative policies in the rest of the world (especially the United States) and the absence of any major supply shocks.

# 4

# British Monetary Policy since 1945*

## N. H. DIMSDALE

## 1. Introduction

During the post-war period there have been changes in the priorities placed on different macroeconomic objectives and also changes in the emphasis put on monetary policy. Together with fiscal policy, direct controls, and incomes policy, monetary policy has been a major element in demand management. In the early post-war years the main objective of macroeconomic policy was the maintenance of full employment. However, once fears of a post-war slump started to fade, increased emphasis was placed on the control of inflation and the avoidance of balance of payment difficulties. The chronic nature of the UK balance of payments problem became apparent during the 1960s combined with a rise in the underlying rate of inflation. Following the oil price shock of 1973–4 and the acceleration of inflation which followed it, governments increased the priority attached to the reduction of inflation and consciously sacrificed the objective of full employment. The downgrading of demand management policy which began under the Labour Government in 1976 was reinforced in the Conservative Government's initial Medium Term Financial Strategy (MTFS) of 1980. Control of inflation rather than attainment of full employment has been the main aim of macroeconomic policy in the 1980s, leaving employment creation to policies affecting the supply side of the economy. Macroeconomic policy became increasingly directed to medium-term objectives in contrast to the emphasis on short-term management in the 1950s and 1960s.

The role of monetary policy was initially slight, as fiscal policy and physical controls were the main instruments of policy. However, during the 1950s monetary policy in the form of credit restrictions and movements in short-term interest rates played an enhanced but still subordinate role in supporting fiscal policy, which bore the main responsibility for stabilizing the economy. The balance of payments difficulties experienced before and after the devaluation of 1967 led to increasing emphasis on monetary restriction to rectify external imbalance.

Following the upsurge of inflation in the 1970s and the collapse of the voluntary incomes policy of the Labour Government, monetary policy in the form of one-year targets for monetary aggregates became a major element of macroeconomic policy. The dominance of monetary over fiscal measures in a medium-term framework was asserted in the initial version of the MTFS, introduced in 1980. From 1982 the design of monetary policy has become more pragmatic as the MTFS became more relaxed. The single monetary aggregate £M3 adopted in 1980 was followed by the inclusion of targets for both narrower and broader definitions of the money supply.

* I am grateful to Nick Horsewood and Nicola Ralph for assistance in drawing the charts and to Nick Crafts for helpful editorial comments.

Other indicators, such as the exchange rate and the growth of nominal income were recognized as influencing policy decisions. The abandonment of monetary targets for £M3 in the mid-1980s followed from the persistent failure to achieve stated targets and the emerging conflict between the targeting of monetary aggregates and of the exchange rate.

## 2. Some Basic Theory

### (a) Keynesians and Monetarists

The evolving roles of demand management and of monetary policy have reflected an ongoing debate on monetary theory. In the *General Theory* (1936) Keynes had challenged the traditional quantity theory, which provided the monetary component of classical economic theory. Irving Fisher's famous equation of exchange stated that $MV = PQ$, where $M$ is defined as the money stock, $V$ is its velocity of circulation, $P$ is the price level and $Q$ is the volume of final output. Velocity which relates the money stock to $PQ$, the value of expenditure, was regarded as being determined by institutional factors governing the periodicity of payments, such as whether wages and salaries are paid weekly or monthly. According to classical theory, $Q$ is determined by the supply-side potential of the economy determined by technology, the size of labour force, and of capital stock. Given $V$ and $Q$, the price level $P$ varies directly with the money supply, which consists of gold coins and also bank deposits under a fractional reserve banking system. The quantity theory pointed to the dependence of the price level on the money supply. This result depended upon $V$ being fixed and the economy being approximately full employed.

Keynes questioned both assertions. He contested the classical claim that the goods and labour markets would adjust to maintain full employment. He substituted the liquidity preference theory of the demand for money for the quantity equation. Like the quantity theorists he postulated that the demand for money was related to the need to finance current payments, which he denoted as the transactions demand for money. In aggregate the transactions demand varied directly with the level of total expenditure. In addition he asserted that money will be held as an asset by investors as an alternative to holding interest-yielding bonds. The higher the rate of interest, the greater will be the demand for bonds and the lower the demand for money. Keynes also argued that investors would hold money rather than bonds when they expected interest rates to rise, which would cause capital losses to bond holders. Such speculative factors could lead to difficulty in bringing about rapid changes in long-term interest rates, which would be necessary to offset fluctuations in the confidence of those responsible for investment decisions. Sticky long-term interest rates could not match the varying 'animal spirits' of entrepreneurs, so limiting the ability of monetary policy to maintain full employment. Keynes, therefore, recommended the use of fiscal measures to stimulate a depressed economy, on account of the slow adjustment of long-term interest rates. His followers also argued that investment decisions were likely to be unresponsive to changes in interest rates, although Keynes himself believed that investment was strongly influenced by the rate of interest.

Keynesian economists refined the arguments of the *General Theory*. Changes in the money supply are envisaged as having a ripple effect on the yields of other assets which will in due course influence the price of equities and so create incentives for adding to the stock of capital goods. Despite these modifications Keynesians have continued to favour fiscal policy rather than monetary measures as the main way to achieve full employment through demand management. Changes in the money supply were regarded as being only weakly related to changes in national income as argued in the Radcliffe Report (1959), which sought to discredit the notion of the velocity of circulation and to downgrade the importance of the money supply.

The Keynesian orthodoxy has been challenged by Monetarists led by Milton Friedman of the University of Chicago. Friedman (1956) restated the quantity theory of money which had been dismissed by Keynesians, most notably in the Report of the Radcliffe Committee. Friedman claimed that the demand for money was a stable function of a small number of variables, which implied that the velocity of circulation was not fixed as in the earlier version of the quantity theory, nor purely passive as claimed by the Radcliffe Committee, but rather a stable predictable relationship.

Friedman (1969) claimed that there was a well-established statistical correlation between changes in the money supply and changes in nominal income, and argued that causation ran from money to income and not vice versa. He restated the classical position that variables, such as output and employment, depended upon real factors such as productivity, and individuals' decisions about saving and the labour supply, while nominal variables, such as the price level, depended upon the money supply. Monetary changes could have powerful short-run effects on output but in the longer term their impact would be on prices rather than output. In place of the Keynesian emphasis on nominal interest rates Friedman urged that policy makers should pay more attention to monetary aggregates. Control over the money supply was, he argued, a precondition for the control of inflation.

Monetarists have generally challenged the effectiveness of fiscal policy, arguing that a rise in public expenditure financed by bonds would raise interest rates, so displacing or crowding out private spending (Carlson and Spencer, 1975). Friedman (1959) argued that rules were to be preferred to discretion in policy-making, and the rule he favoured was a steady growth in the money stock at a low predetermined rate. His policy prescriptions therefore differed sharply from the post-war Keynesian orthodoxy which emphasized demand management. Monetarist views gained increasing influence as inflation accelerated during the late 1960s and the early 1970s. Friedman (1968) also questioned the existence of a stable trade-off between inflation and unemployment as postulated in the Phillips curve.

These views were reinforced by the arguments of the New Classical school of macroeconomists during the 1970s. Economists, such as Lucas (1973) and Sargent and Wallace (1976) advanced the new doctrine of Rational Expectations in contrast to the adaptive expectations, which underlay the gradualist prescriptions of the previous generation of monetarists. In a world of Rational Expectations economic agents formed expectations on the basis of the best available economic models and data and did not make systematic errors. The presence of systematic errors would lead immediately to re-examination and correction of the underlying model.

Rational Expectations combined with perfectly flexible wages and prices yielded striking theoretical results. They implied no trade-off between inflation and unemployment even in the short run. Expectations would rapidly adjust to a faster growth of aggregate demand, which would be reflected in a higher rate of inflation, with only a temporary positive shock to output. Also systematic monetary policy was shown under these assumptions to be ineffective in influencing output and employment. Monetary policy should therefore be conducted in accordance with Friedman's constant-growth rule to minimize disturbances to the real economy.

Monetarist doctrines were a major influence on monetary policy in the 1970s and 1980s, while the influence of New Classical theories can be seen in the early versions of the Conservative Government's Medium Term Financial Strategy.

## (b) *Monetary Policy in an Open Economy*

During the 1950s and the 1960s Britain was on fixed exchange rate. The pound was maintained within a narrow band as agreed under the Bretton Woods system. Under this system of fixed exchange rates monitored by the IMF, devaluation was only permitted when a country's balance of payments was in 'fundamental disequilibrium'. The pound was devalued on these grounds in both 1949 and 1967. Apart from these episodes a fixed exchange rate was maintained. As the dollar shortage of the early post-war years grew less acute, countries removed restrictions on trade and payments culminating in a general move towards convertibility in 1958. The relaxation of restrictions in short-term capital movements allowed short-term funds to move more readily between financial centres in response to interest differentials. Fears of exchange-rate changes meant that funds might not move until interest differentials were wide enough to cover the cost of obtaining forward cover against the risk of devaluation.

Economists began to explore the consequences of international capital mobility for the operation of monetary policy under both fixed and flexible exchange rates. J. M. Fleming (1962) and Mundell (1963) independently developed a Keynesian model which showed that monetary policy would be largely ineffective in an economy with a fixed exchange rate under conditions of international capital mobility. Expansion of the money supply through open market operations by the central bank would tend to reduce domestic interest rates relative to those in the rest of the world leading to a capital outflow. The central bank would have to maintain the exchange rate by purchasing domestic currency from investors seeking higher returns abroad, leading to a reduction in its foreign exchange reserves. A rise in interest rates would be needed sooner or later to check the fall in the reserves. Thus monetary policy would be ineffective as purchases of domestic bonds by the central bank would be offset by loss of reserves, leaving the money supply and the interest rate unchanged.

The situation was quite different under a floating exchange rate, in that monetary expansion through open market operations would not be offset by central bank intervention in the foreign exchange market. When interest rates fell below the international level, there would be an outflow of capital depreciating the exchange rate. Exports would become more competitive leading to a rise in income and employment. Income would rise until the transactions demand for money had expanded to push up the demand for money to restore the rate of interest to its initial level. Thus in a Keynesian model assuming fixed prices, monetary policy would be powerful under a floating exchange rate, but largely ineffective under a fixed exchange rate in the presence of freedom of capital movements.

The corresponding Monetarist analysis, known as the Monetary Approach to the

The corresponding Monetarist analysis, known as the Monetary Approach to the Balance of Payments, was developed principally by H. G. Johnson (1976) and led to broadly similar conclusions about the effectiveness of monetary policy in an open economy. Under a fixed exchange rate, domestic prices were held in line with those in the rest of the world by the need to maintain uniform prices for competing goods. Domestic monetary expansion must lead to an offsetting capital outflow to maintain the purchasing power parity of the currency and so leave the money supply unchanged. Under a floating exchange rate a larger money supply was reflected in a lower exchange rate and a higher price level so leaving competitiveness or the real exchange rate unchanged. In contrast to the Mundell model monetary policy affected prices rather than output.

In the 1970s and 1980s monetary policy was more powerful than in the 1950s and 1960s largely on account of the introduction of flexible exchange rates following the breakdown of the Bretton Woods system in the early 1970s. Rapid monetary expansion following the decision to float sterling in 1972 was associated with a depreciation of the exchange rate. This pointed to the need for monetary restriction and implied a greater role for monetary policy than under the previous regime of fixed exchange rates.

### (c) *The Money Supply*

[This section is more technical than the rest of the chapter and can be used as a reference.]

The money supply in a modern industrial economy is determined by a complex process of interaction between the banking system, the central bank, the government, and the non-bank private sector. There are several approaches to the analysis of this process. A brief account will be given here of two of the most frequently used approaches, the money multiplier and the flow-of-funds system of identities.

A convenient starting point for the discussion is the simplified balance sheet of the commercial banks and the central bank, which are shown below. The commercial banks have liabilities consisting of current accounts, deposit accounts, and non-deposit liabilities, such as capital reserves and other internal funds. They hold assets consisting of reserves, which are a liability of the central bank, government securities, and loans to the private sector. The central bank has liabilities in the form of currency and bank reserves. These liabilities are readily convertible and for simplicity all currency is assumed to be held by the non-bank private sector. The central bank has assets consisting of foreign exchange reserves and government securities. The liabilities of the central bank are known as the wide monetary base and can be changed by purchases or sales of either government securities (open-market operations) or of foreign exchange (intervention in the foreign exchange market).

*Commercial Banks*

| *Liabilities* | *Assets* |
| --- | --- |
| Current Accounts | Reserves |
| Deposit Accounts | Government Securities |
| Non Deposit Liabilities | Loans to the private sector |

*Central Bank*

| *Liabilities* | *Assets* |
| --- | --- |
| Currency | Foreign Exchange Reserves |
| Bank Reserves | Government Securities |

From the balance sheets we obtain directly three definitions of the money supply, M0, the monetary base, M1, narrow money, and £M3, broad money.

(1)   M0 = Currency + Bank reserves
(2)   M1 = Currency + Current accounts
(3)   £M3 = M1 + Deposit accounts = Currency + Bank deposits

The Bank of England's definition of £M3 excludes foreign currency deposits and overseas sterling deposits, which are excluded from our simplified balance sheet, but which are included in M3. £M3 can also be looked at from the asset side of the balance sheet of the commercial banks.

(4)   £M3 = Currency + Reserves + Government securities + Loans to the private sector − Non-deposit liabilities

According to the money-multiplier approach the banks hold a uniform ratio $\beta$ of reserves to deposits, for either mandatory or prudential reasons. It is assumed that, following British practice, the reserve ratio does not differ between current and deposit accounts. The non-bank public hold currency in a fixed proportion to deposits $\alpha$. The monetary base M0 is controlled by the central bank. We have therefore:

(5)   $\alpha = \dfrac{C}{D}$ and $\beta = \dfrac{R}{D}$ where $C$, $R$ and $D$ are currency, bank reserves, and deposits respectively

(6)   M0 = Currency + Reserves = $\alpha D + \beta D = (\alpha + \beta)D$

(7)   £M3 = Currency + Deposits = $(\alpha + 1)D$

From (6) $D = \dfrac{M0}{\alpha + \beta}$ , which when substituted into (7) gives:

(8)   £M3 = $\dfrac{(1 + \alpha)\, M0}{\alpha + \beta}$

The money multiplier is given by the response of £M3 to the change in M0

(9)   £M3 = $m \triangle M0$ where $m = \dfrac{(1 + \alpha)}{(\alpha + \beta)}$

For example, if $\alpha = 0.20$ and $\beta = 0.10$, m = 4. and a rise in M0 of £1bn. generates a rise in £M3 of £4bn. According to this approach, a rise in the monetary base initiated by the purchase of government securities by the central bank from either the banks or the non-bank public will raise bank reserves. This increase in the monetary base will generate an expansion of the money supply as banks respond to larger holdings of reserves by expanding their earning assets, government securities, and loans to the private sector. The expansion of bank assets and liabilities is restricted by the size of the banks' reserve ratio $\beta$ and the drain of reserves into currency. The non-bank public will raise its holdings of currency as the volume of bank deposits increases as determined by the size of $\alpha$, so checking the rise in bank deposits.

This view of the money supply process has been criticized as being too mechanical (Tobin, 1963). The non-bank public may not be willing to increase their borrowing from the banking system nor to increase their holdings of bank deposits. $\alpha$ and $\beta$ are not constant as the simple version of the theory supposes and M0 is not determined exogenously by the central bank. It will be affected by changes in foreign exchange reserves under a system of fixed exchange rates or when there is any intervention in the foreign exchange market by the central bank, which is not neutralized by equal and opposite purchases or sales of government securities. The PSBR (Public Sector

Borrowing Requirement) will also affect the monetary base unless fully offset by sales of gilts to the non-bank public or the banking system. Nevertheless, the money-multiplier approach forms the basis of the analysis of the money supply of those economists who advocate monetary base control (MBC).

The theory also features in elementary accounts of the British banking system, where it is emphasized that a decline in bank reserves due to open-market sales of securities by the central bank will prompt the banks to withdraw money at call from the discount market (Crouch, 1963). The discount houses will seek to make good the loss of call money by borrowing from the Bank of England. The Bank will be able to choose between relieving the cash shortage at the penal Bank Rate or at the current interest rate ruling in the market. Should relief from the Bank not be available, contractionary open-market operations could, it is argued, lead to unacceptably wide fluctuations in interest rates, which could disturb the working of the financial system (Bank of England, 1979).

The Bank of England has developed the supply side or counterpart approach to the determination of £M3. It concentrates upon the flow of funds between sectors and is framed in differences. The change in £M3 is given from (4) by:

(10)  $\triangle$£M3 = $\triangle$Currency + $\triangle$Bank deposits
         = $\triangle$Currency + $\triangle$Reserves + $\triangle$Bank holdings of government securities
      + $\triangle$Bank lending to the private sector − $\triangle$non-deposit liabilities

The change in bank reserves is a form of lending to the government and can be combined with the change in bank holdings of government securities to give the change in bank lending to the government. This represents the contribution of the banks to the finance of the PSBR, which is the budget deficit, including also some capital transactions. The PSBR is financed by increases in currency, sales of securities to the non-bank public, increased borrowing from the banks, and the sterling proceeds of a reduction in foreign exchange reserves.

(11)  PSBR = $\triangle$Currency + $\triangle$Borrowing from non-bank public + $\triangle$Borrowing from the banks − $\triangle$Foreign exchange reserves

This relationship can be solved for $\triangle$Borrowing from the banks which is then substituted in (10) to obtain the fundamental identity for £M3.*

(12)  $\triangle$£M3 = PSBR − $\triangle$Borrowing from non-bank public + $\triangle$Bank lending to the private sector + $\triangle$Foreign exchange reserves − $\triangle$Non-deposit liabilities

This may be summarized as:

(13)  $\triangle$£M3 = PSBR − Sales of gilts + Increase in bank lending − External finance − Change in non-deposit liabilities

The flow-of-funds approach to the money supply relates monetary and fiscal policy, showing how the PSBR and sales of gilts to non-banks affect £M3 and also the impact of a rise in bank credit. In the analysis presented here changes in foreign exchange reserves are the only external flow, which is a considerable oversimplification. A more complete analysis would include additional items such as government borrowing overseas and foreign-owned sterling deposits. The important conclusion

*(11a)  $\triangle$Reserves + $\triangle$Bank holdings of government securities = $\triangle$Borrowing from the banks = PSBR − $\triangle$Currency − $\triangle$Borrowing from the non-bank public + $\triangle$Foreign exchange reserves

Note that when this is substituted in (10), $\triangle$Currency drops out.

which may be drawn from this wider analysis is that, even when there is a floating exchange rate, £M3 will not be isolated from external flows. For further discussion, see Artis and Lewis (1981) and Goodhart (1978).

The IMF has favoured an alternative measure of broad money known as DCE (Domestic Credit Expansion). Like £M3 it can be looked upon as a measure of the change in bank liabilities or alternatively as a measure of credit extended on the asset side of the balance sheet of the banking system. From the first viewpoint, DCE is the change in the money stock adjusted for external flows. External finance, which is excluded from $\triangle$£M3, is included in DCE:

(12)   DCE = $\triangle$£M3 + External finance + $\triangle$Non-deposit liabilities

On the credit side DCE is given by:

(13)   DCE = PSBR − $\triangle$Borrowing from non-bank public + $\triangle$Bank lending to the private sector

DCE is useful in drawing attention to the expansionary impact of monetary policy under fixed exchange rates, which is reflected in a decline in foreign exchange reserves rather than an expansion of bank liabilities. This raises DCE but not $\triangle$£M3. A curb on DCE will be particularly effective in strengthening the balance of payments which is the main concern of the IMF. Like $\triangle$£M3 it relates changes in credit extended by the banking system to the PSBR and the purchase of gilts by the non-bank public. From an historical point of view DCE was the precursor of the targeting of £M3, being introduced by the IMF in 1967, well before the coming of monetary targets in 1976.

(d) *Alternative Targets for Monetary Policy*

In the Keynesian approach to economic policy followed during the 1960s policy makers set policy instruments in order to achieve the desired level of goal variables. Instruments included those of monetary policy, such as the discount rate and open-market operations, and those of fiscal policy, such as the level of government spending and tax rates. The goal variables included the level of employment and output and the price level. It was not sufficient to have enough instruments to match the number of goal variations, it was also necessary to assign the instruments appropriately to policy objectives, as shown by Mundell (1962). With a fixed exchange rate, fiscal policy should be assigned the task of determining domestic balance, while monetary policy, which had a major impact on capital flows, should bear responsibility for external balance. This was the solution which policy-makers had reached before the formal solution was developed by Mundell, as shown for example in the recommendations of the Radcliffe Committee (1959).

Two major lines of criticism operated to undermine this approach to economic policy. Friedman (1953) argued that discretionary policy was unlikely to be effective on account of lack of knowledge of the structure of the economy. As previously discussed, he argued for a monetary growth rule in place of setting instrument levels to achieve desired goals. He also challenged the notion that monetary policy could affect the level of real variables, such as output and employment, emphasizing the impact of monetary growth on inflation.

New Classical economists have strengthened the case for targeting monetary aggregates. By modifying the expectations of both employers and wage earners, it was argued that the rate of inflation could be reduced with minimal impact on output and employment. The attainment of this outcome depended upon the credibility of policy, which was dependent upon the resolution of the government in not reneging upon previously announced targets. Although the authorities might gain temporarily from cheating, in the long term they would benefit from adhering to their declared strategy (Minford, 1980).

The second line of criticism arose from practical experience with stabilization policy. The implementation of such policy was restricted by lags in the availability of information about the goal variables in a world where the economy was subject to unforeseen disturbances. Further difficulties arose from the structure of the economy not being fully understood by policy-makers and being subject to change over time. It was suggested that the authorities should adopt a two-stage approach to economic policy by choosing an intermediate variable which was closely related to the goal variables and also readily observable. The chosen intermediate variable or target should be controllable by the authorities. For policy makers with monetarist leanings, who gave priority to the control of inflation over the attainment of real goals, such as output and employment, the obvious candidate for selection as a target was a monetary aggregate, such as broad money. A target for the nominal interest rate might be taken as a Keynesian alternative to targeting the money stock (Bryant, 1980; Courakis, 1981).

During the 1980s the heroic or dogmatic phase of monetarism gave way to a more pragmatic approach to economic policy as the rate of inflation subsided. Alternative intermediate variables were suggested. First the Medium Term Financial Strategy was associated with an over-appreciation of the exchange rate which led to the suggestion that the exchange rate should be targeted rather than the money supply. Any attempt to combine exchange rate and monetary targets could, however, lead to inconsistency. For example, an attempt to keep sterling in line with the Deutschmark would require monetary contraction if sterling–DM exchange rate was weakening, but this might not accord with the announced monetary target.

Second, a persistent problem with relying upon a monetary target is that the relationship between money and nominal income is variable and difficult to predict. This has led to the suggestion that nominal income or $MV$ should be targeted rather than $M$. Nominal income has the advantage of being more closely related to the goal variables of output and prices than the money supply on account of the variability of velocity.

In the event the evolution of policy in the 1980s has led to attention being paid to a number of economic indicators, such as broad money, the exchange rate, and the course of nominal income. While this is not a return to the discretionary policy of the 1960s, it is far removed from the setting of a single monetary target, which is intended to act as an anchor for inflationary expectations.

## 3. Monetary Policy 1945–60

(a) *The Development of Monetary Policy under
the Labour Government: 1945–51*

The guidelines for monetary policy in the post-war period were discussed by the National Debt Enquiry Committee in 1945 which was greatly influenced by Keynes's evidence (Howson, 1987). The Committee favoured the maintenance of low interest rates on both long-dated and short-dated securities. Low interest rates were needed on account of the heavy burden of debt which had been accumulated during wartime. In addition, there were fears of a post-war world slump starting initially with a setback in the United States and later spreading throughout the world economy. Since there were problems, as Keynes had emphasized, in reducing long-term rates rapidly, the best course of action seemed to be to keep down interest rates in anticipation of a decline in world economy activity. Low short-term rates might create difficulties in the event of a rise in interest rates in the rest of the world but movements of short-term capital could be restricted by appropriate exchange control regulations. The implication of maintaining low long-term interest rates of about 3 per cent per annum and pegging Bank Rate at 2 per cent was that inflationary forces within the economy would have to be controlled by a combination of physical restrictions and budgetary policy.

Dalton's attempt to reduce the long-term rate of interest to 2½ per cent went beyond the recommendations of the National Debt Enquiry Committee. Following the failure of the cheap money drive gilt-edged prices drifted downwards.[1] The authorities did not need to be concerned about the weakness of the bond market because they did not need to issue new debt. This was a major change from the wartime and immediate post-war situation in which the government was a heavy borrower in order to finance a massive budget deficit. From 1948–50 the government, as a result of tightening fiscal policy, ran a budget surplus which enabled it to repay debt. In addition the proceeds of the post-war American loan and Marshall aid reduced the need to borrow internally. The surplus was used to limit the growth of the money supply, as measured by the deposits of the London clearing banks, but no attempt was made to reduce the liquidity of the banking system (Cairncross, 1985).

Monetary control was in theory exercised through the cash ratio which the clearing banks were required to hold at the Bank of England.[2] The cash ratio had traditionally been set at 10 per cent but was reduced to 8 per cent in 1946 and made mandatory. In wartime the Bank of England had undermined the cash ratio as a control device through its willingness to lend to the discount houses at ½ per cent on the market's initiative, known as the 'open back door policy' (Sayers, 1958). The banks paid more attention to their liquidity ratio, conventionally 30 per cent, which included cash, money at call with the discount market, and holdings of Treasury and commercial bills. At the end of the war the liquid assets ratio was only 25 per cent, which reflected the Bank of England's concern about the excessive liquidity of the banking system. It had, therefore, introduced Treasury Deposit Receipts which did not count as liquid assets but earned only ½ per cent and represented 29 per cent of deposits in 1946. The banks wished to reduce their holdings of TDRs and to increase their advances which stood at only 17.4 per cent of deposit in 1946 as compared with 42.9 per cent in 1938. In the early post-war years the financial system was under growing pressure as the banks sought to raise their advances relative to deposits. The Bank of England had some sympathy for the desire of

[1] The cheap money policy is discussed in Cairncross (1985), C. M. Kennedy (1952), Paish (1950), and Sayers (1957).
[2] The money supply process envisaged was the simple money multiplier explained in section (c) of the Introduction.

bankers to increase their lending to the private sector and therefore opposed suggestions from the Treasury for ceilings on bank advances (Cairncross, 1987).

As the 1940s drew to a close the rigid interest rate policy followed by the authorities looked increasingly inappropriate. No attempt was made to counter the severe convertibility crisis of 1947 by raising short-term rates, even though outward capital movements which were an important factor in the crisis might have been discouraged by a higher Bank Rate.[3] Similarly, monetary measures were not enforced in 1949 to make the devaluation of sterling effective. The Bank of England favoured a tighter fiscal policy, and the Treasury favoured restrictions on bank lending, but no attempt was made to push up sharply the yield on gilt-edged securities (Cairncross, 1987). It was, however, increasingly recognized that inflation rather than a post-war slump was the major threat to the economy and that a higher short-term rate could make some contribution to buttressing sterling when the balance of payments was weak. The abandonment of low pegged interest rates in the United States in the face of inflationary pressures meant that the British authorities would encounter more difficulty in holding down short-term interest rates (see Table 4.1).

### (b) The New Monetary Policy under the Conservatives during the 1950s

The Conservative Government elected in 1951 resolved to rely to a greater degree on monetary policy. Bank Rate was raised from 2 per cent to 2½ per cent in November and it was announced that the 'open back door' policy would be discontinued. The Bank of England would intervene in the money market at market rates at its own discretion, but it reserved the right to force the money market to borrow at the penal Bank Rate, if it wished to do so (Sayers, 1957). The reduction in the clearing banks' holdings of TDRs had led to a rise in the liquid assets ratio to 37.5 per cent in 1951 as Treasury bill holdings had risen. The Bank of England issued £1,000m. of Funding stock to curb the excessive liquidity which could result in an upsurge of bank lending. Bank advances rose by 105 per cent between 1946 and 1951, which underlined the need for improved control.[4]

In March 1952 there was a further rise in Bank Rate to 4 per cent which was intended both to curb inflationary pressures and to strengthen sterling. The movement of the economy into recession in 1952, the improvement in the balance of payments and the reduction in the rate of inflation was attributed by some observers to the tightening of monetary policy in November and March. As demand pressures eased so market rates of interest declined and Bank Rate was reduced to 3½ per cent in September 1953 and 3 per cent in May 1954 to keep it in line with market trends.

Monetary policy became more expansionary when controls on hire purchase, introduced in March 1952, were withdrawn in July 1954 at the request of the Board of Trade. The result was an upsurge in spending on consumer durables which necessitated the reintroduction of controls within a year. The economy recovered vigorously from the recession of 1952 as the revival of consumer durable spending was

---

[3] Cairncross (1985) does not regard this passive policy as surprising.

[4] Monetary policy in the 1950s is well described in the Radcliffe Report, paras. 399–435 and in C. M. Kennedy (1962), and Dow (1964).

TABLE 4.1. *Additional indicators 1946–1960*

| | Percentage of nominal GDP | | Unemployment % | Sterling–Dollar exchange rate ($) | Treasury bill rate | Discount rate Fed. Res. Bank NY |
|---|---|---|---|---|---|---|
| | PSBR | Current balance | | | | |
| 1946 | | -2.29 | 2.5 | 4.03 | 0.50 | 0.75 |
| 1947 | | -3.54 | 3.1 | 4.03 | 0.51 | 1.00 |
| 1948 | | 0.22 | 1.8 | 4.03 | 0.51 | 1.25 |
| 1949 | | -0.01 | 1.6 | 3.68 | 0.52 | 1.50 |
| 1950 | | 2.35 | 1.5 | 2.80 | 0.52 | 1.63 |
| 1951 | | -2.53 | 1.2 | 2.80 | 0.56 | 1.75 |
| 1952 | 5.02 | 1.03 | 2.1 | 2.79 | 2.20 | 1.75 |
| 1953 | 3.48 | 0.85 | 1.8 | 2.81 | 2.30 | 1.88 |
| 1954 | 2.06 | 0.65 | 1.5 | 2.81 | 1.79 | 1.75 |
| 1955 | 2.43 | -0.80 | 1.2 | 2.79 | 3.75 | 2.00 |
| 1956 | 2.74 | 0.99 | 1.3 | 2.80 | 4.95 | 2.75 |
| 1957 | 2.20 | 1.05 | 1.6 | 2.79 | 4.81 | 3.25 |
| 1958 | 2.13 | 1.56 | 2.2 | 2.81 | 4.56 | 2.37 |
| 1959 | 2.35 | 0.71 | 2.3 | 2.81 | 3.37 | 3.25 |
| 1960 | 2.76 | -0.89 | 1.7 | 2.81 | 4.88 | 3.50 |

*Sources:* PSBR, 1952–60: Bank of England (1970).
Current balance, Money GDP: *Economic Trends*, annual supplement (1988).
Unemployment: LCES (1971).
Sterling–Dollar exchange rate: *Economic Trends*, annual supplement (1988).
Average Treasury bill rate 1946–59: LCES (1971), 1960–70 *International Financial Statistics Yearbook* (1976).
US Discount Rate (FRBNY): LCES (1971).

followed by a boom in fixed investment. Bank advances rose steeply to both the personal and company sectors and the Bank of England responded by raising Bank Rate in two stages to 4½ per cent in February 1955 and hire purchase controls were also reintroduced. Although the volume of bank deposits did not rise rapidly the clearing banks increased their loans by reducing their holdings of gilt-edged, which offered a lower return than advances to the private sector. The two rises in Bank Rate in early 1955 did not prevent further sales of investments by the clearing banks to expand advances.

Demand continued to rise leading to a balance of payments crisis in the autumn as the current account slipped into deficit. Pressures on sterling were increased by the decision taken in February to support the exchange rate for transferable sterling as a move towards sterling convertibility. Support for the transferable rate established *de facto* convertibility for non-residents making sterling more vulnerable to short-term capital movements.

In the general election held in May 1955 the Conservatives were re-elected but the tax cuts introduced in March were substantially reversed in the autumn budget. In raising taxes the Chancellor recognized that his expectations of the impact of monetary policy at the time of the Budget had been excessive. As bank advances continued to rise in the summer, there was a sharp difference of opinion between the Bank and the Treasury over the need for quantitative restriction of credit (Cairncross, 1987). The Treasury did not feel that the Bank of England was making a sufficiently strong case to the clearing banks on the need to restrict credit to the point where both bankruptcies and unemployment would rise. The Chancellor pressed for a decline in bank advances of 10 per cent and a reduction by this percentage was agreed by the end of the year. The delay in securing agreement on credit restriction aggravated the exchange rate crisis in the autumn. It also underlined the differences between the Bank of England and the Treasury. The former emphasized the need for a counter inflationary fiscal policy largely in the form of cuts in government expenditure, while the latter emphasized the need for restricting bank lending to the private sector. The over-optimism of Butler's policies which resulted in the sterling crisis of the end of 1955 led to his replacement as Chancellor by Macmillan.

In 1956 the Governor of the Bank called for curbs on public spending rather than a higher Bank Rate to reduce the level of demand and raise foreign confidence in sterling. Lower government expenditure would reduce the need for borrowing and hence the dependence of the Bank of England upon the sentiment of the gilt-edged market. Failure to sell gilt-edged securities forced the Bank to borrow by the issue of Treasury bills which were chiefly held within the banking system, so expanding liquid assets, which made bank lending difficult to control. While the Treasury pressed for such measures as a variable liquidity ratio and quantitative restrictions on bank lending, the Bank emphasized the need for a tight fiscal policy.

The outcome of these discussions was an introduction of a package of restrictive measures in February 1956 when the new Chancellor, Macmillan, announced a rise in Bank Rate by 1 per cent point to 5½ per cent, combined with the tightening of hire-purchase restrictions. Fiscal policy was also tightened by the withdrawal of initial allowances on investment and by cuts in public investment. In July the Chancellor took the unprecedented step of bypassing the Bank of England and of summoning representatives of the banks to a meeting to obtain their assurance that credit restriction would be vigorously enforced (Dow, 1964). The result was a temporary reduction in bank advances in the second half of 1956, while the easing of external pressures allowed Bank Rate to be reduced to 5 per cent in February 1957. Such a relaxation proved to be premature in the face of the major crisis of confidence in sterling which developed in the autumn of 1957.

Pressure on sterling built up following a devaluation of the French franc in August and widespread expectations of an appreciation of the Deutschmark and a possible fall in the pound. The response of the authorities to the decline in the reserves, which reflected adverse short-term capital movements, since the current account was in surplus, was an upward jerk of Bank Rate by a full 2 percentage points to 7 per cent. Although the origins of the crisis were external, the cause of the diminished confidence in sterling arose from concern about the lack of resolution of the government in the face of powerful wage demands. The rate of inflation was below 4 per cent, but there were fears that the rate would rise with wage concessions to organized labour. Thorneycroft, who had succeeded Macmillan as Chancellor, argued that inflation should be checked by tight control over the money supply (Cairncross, 1987).

The rise in Bank Rate was accompanied by a requirement that banks should hold their advances at the average level of the preceeding 12 months and hire-purchase regulations were tightened. The economy moved into recession in 1958, while a world-wide decline in commodity prices moderated the rate of inflation. Thus the fears of inflation and overheating which had dominated the discussion of monetary and fiscal policy in the second half of 1957 appeared largely misconceived in retrospect. Under the new Chancellor, Heathcoat-Amory, Bank Rate was reduced from 7 per cent to 6 per cent in March, followed by a series of four reductions by ½ per-cent point to 4 per cent in November. In July restraint on bank advances was relaxed, following a two-year period of stagnation since 1956.

A new measure of monetary control was introduced in 1958 in the form of Special Deposits, the result of extensive discussion of the need for a variable liquidity ratio. The Bank of England could call on the banks to make Special Deposits which would earn interest at the Treasury bill rate but would not count towards the liquid assets ratio. In return, the banks undertook to maintain the conventional liquid asset ratio. (It was understood that the Bank of England would purchase Treasury bills from the banks to ensure that Special Deposits operated to restrict liquid assets rather than cash.) It was intended that calls for Special Deposits would provide a way of discouraging banks from engaging in excessive expansion of advances and would obviate the need for official ceilings on lending. Banks were now free to increase loans for the first time since the Second World War. There was a similar relaxation of hire-purchase controls when all restrictions were suspended in October 1958. They had been in force continuously, but with varying terms from February 1952, apart from a seven-month period of suspension from July 1954 to February 1955.

Relaxation of monetary controls was accompanied by an expansionary Budget in April 1959 which included tax concessions to stimulate both consumers' expenditure and investment. The result of these stimulating measures was a rapid recovery in economic activity and fall in unemployment.

In the first half of 1960 it was becoming increasingly apparent that restrictive measures were called for. Bank Rate was raised by 1 percentage point to 5 per cent in January, followed by the reintroduction of hire-purchase restrictions and the first call for Special Deposits in April. A second call for Special Deposits was made in June, when Bank Rate was raised by a further point to 6 per cent. Fiscal policy had not been tightened in the 1960 Budget, and so the main burden of restraining the boom fell on monetary measures. The use of Special Deposits to check the rise in advances was only moderately successful. Advances grew less vigorously in 1961 than in the two previous years, but there was a tendency for the banks to react to a call for Special Deposits by selling investments rather than reducing advances.[5] Although the authorities had not expected this reaction by the banks, they were willing to see a fall in the price of gilt-edged, since a rise in long term interest rates would exert some downward pressure on demand.

### (c) *Debt Management and the Money Supply in the 1950s*

During the mid-1950s the authorities began to take a more positive approach to the yield on government securities. This contrasted with their policy in the late 1940s, following the failure of the Dalton experiment, which was one of largely ignoring the behaviour of long-term interest rates (Dow, 1964). The yield on consols rose from an average of 2.60 per cent in 1946 to 3.78 per cent in 1951. The rise in nominal interest rates reflected the slower growth in the money supply than in nominal income, which resulted in a rise in income velocity from 1.26 in 1946 to 1.69 in 1951. During the 1950s the authorities became used to the need to borrow regularly from the gilt-edged market, as the ratio of the PSBR to nominal GDP settled down to about 2½ per cent. Monetary growth continued to lag behind the rise in nominal income, so that velocity rose steadily from 1.69 in 1951 to 2.44 by 1960, while the yield on consols followed a rising trend going up from 3.78 per cent to 5.42 per cent between 1951 and 1960 (see Table 4.2 and Figs. 4.1 and 4.3). The ratio of debt to GDP declined throughout the period from 178 per cent in 1951 to 99.5 in 1961. The Bank of England did not attempt to force up interest rates to check inflation, which proceeded at a moderate pace during the 1950s with the exception of the Korean war boom of 1951 and the sharp boom of 1954–5 (see Table 4.2 and Fig. 4.2.)

Faced with the need to finance the PSBR, the Bank of England was resolved to keep down the growth of Treasury bills which would increase the liquidity of the banking system. It therefore sought to encourage the gilt-edged market to take up stock when conditions were favourable, that is when bond prices were rising. The Bank did not accept that the demand for gilts would be stimulated by a lower price but argued rather that a decline in price would generate expectations of a further decline and so discourage purchasers (*Radcliffe Report*, 1959, para. 553; Dow, 1964, pp. 234–5). It emphasized the problem of selling gilts when the rates of interest were following a rising trend and therefore sought to take advantage of any strength in the market to sell government stock to the non-bank public. During 1957–9 when interest rates were tending to fall, the Bank of England sold stock to prevent the bond market from rising and in 1960–1, when its call for Special Deposits led to sales of bonds by the banks, it welcomed the resulting rise in interest rates.

---

[5] Gibson (1964) discusses the working of Special Deposits.

TABLE 4.2. *Monetary indicators 1946–1960*

| | MO | \| Nominal GDP | Real GDP | GDP deflator | Velocity M3 | Treasury bill rate | Yield on consols |
|---|---|---|---|---|---|---|---|---|
| | | M3 | Nominal GDP | Real GDP | GDP deflator | Velocity M3 | Treasury bill rate | Yield on consols |

Annual percentage rate of change

| | MO | M3 | Nominal GDP | Real GDP | GDP deflator | Velocity M3 | Treasury bill rate | Yield on consols |
|---|---|---|---|---|---|---|---|---|
| 1946 | 6.0 | 14.3 | 1.5 | −4.4 | 2.3 | 1.26 | 0.50 | 2.60 |
| 1947 | −0.7 | 3.5 | 7.0 | −1.5 | 9.9 | 1.31 | 0.51 | 2.76 |
| 1948 | −7.0 | 2.2 | 9.8 | 3.2 | 6.7 | 1.40 | 0.51 | 3.21 |
| 1949 | 2.7 | 0.3 | 5.7 | 3.7 | 2.6 | 1.48 | 0.52 | 3.30 |
| 1950 | 5.9 | 3.1 | 4.5 | 3.6 | 0.8 | 1.50 | 0.52 | 3.54 |
| 1951 | −1.1 | −1.0 | 11.6 | 1.8 | 9.2 | 1.69 | 0.56 | 3.78 |
| 1952 | 4.7 | 1.8 | 8.5 | 0.6 | 7.7 | 1.80 | 2.20 | 4.23 |
| 1953 | 6.3 | 4.2 | 7.8 | 3.8 | 2.9 | 1.86 | 2.30 | 4.08 |
| 1954 | 5.5 | 3.9 | 5.5 | 4.2 | 1.4 | 1.89 | 1.79 | 3.75 |
| 1955 | 2.7 | −2.9 | 7.6 | 3.7 | 4.1 | 2.10 | 3.75 | 4.17 |
| 1956 | 4.9 | 1.4 | 8.0 | 1.2 | 6.6 | 2.23 | 4.95 | 4.73 |
| 1957 | 5.5 | 3.5 | 5.7 | 1.6 | 3.7 | 2.28 | 4.81 | 4.98 |
| 1958 | 2.4 | 3.5 | 4.3 | −0.2 | 4.2 | 2.30 | 4.56 | 4.98 |
| 1959 | 3.3 | 4.4 | 5.4 | 4.0 | 1.1 | 2.32 | 3.37 | 4.82 |
| 1960 | 5.0 | 0.6 | 6.0 | 5.5 | 1.1 | 2.44 | 4.88 | 5.42 |

*Sources:* MO, M3, Year End: Capie and Collins (1985).
Nominal GDP, Real GDP, GDP deflator: *Economic Trends*, annual supplement (1988); extended to 1946 using Feinstein (1972).

M3 Velocity = Nominal GDP
⎯⎯⎯⎯⎯⎯⎯⎯
M3

Average Treasury bill rate: LCES (1971), 1946–59 *International Financial Statistics Yearbook* (1960).
Yield on consols: *Annual Abstract of Statistics* (various issues).

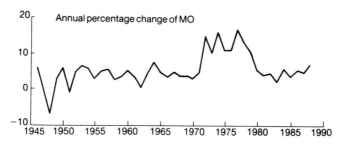

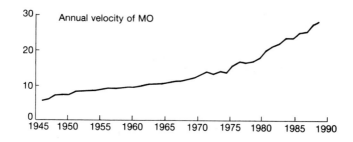

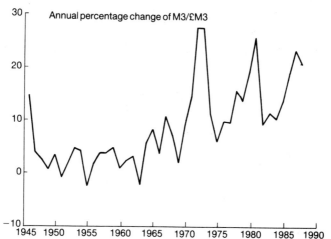

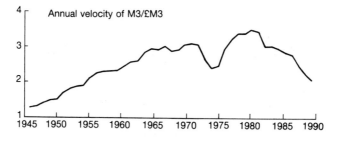

FIG. 4.1.

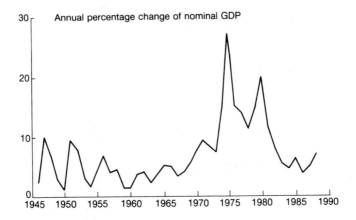

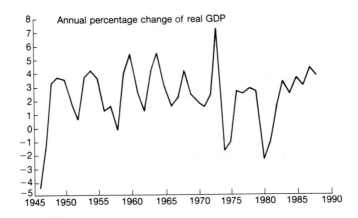

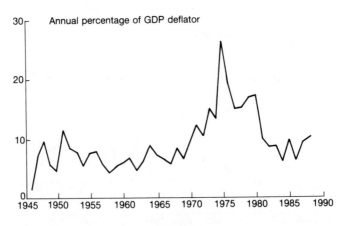

FIG. 4.2.

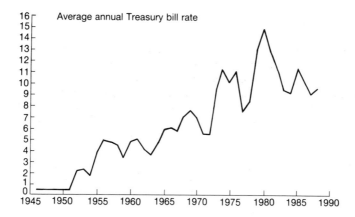

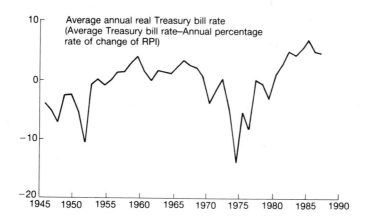

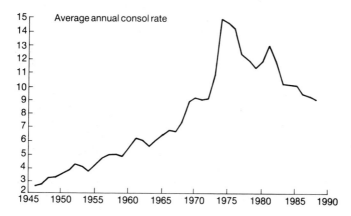

FIG. 4.3.

(d) *The Radcliffe Committee and the Operation of Monetary Policy*

When monetary measures were used to curb the boom and inflation of 1951–2, the authorities were over-impressed by what was achieved. This was made clear in Butler's ill-fated attempt to use Bank Rate and credit controls to curb the boom of 1954–5, following the expansionary Budget in the spring of 1955. There was growing recognition that the mechanism of monetary policy was not well understood. The role of monetary policy was extensively examined by the Radcliffe Committee, which was appointed in April 1957 following the difficulties with monetary control in 1955–6.

The Committee, which reported in 1959, concluded that monetary policy should play a subordinate role to fiscal measures in the context of demand management policy, aiming to achieve full employment with reasonable price stability (*Radcliffe Report*, 1959, paras. 511, 516). Monetary measures were seen as acting on the level of demand through altering the liquidity position of the public and hence their expenditure decisions. The Committee explicitly downgraded the role of the quantity of money and argued that the velocity of circulation could vary without limit. They emphasized the significance of liquidity, without clearly defining the meaning of the concept. Liquidity was influenced by movements in the structure of interest rates which affected the willingness of lenders to lend (paras. 387–91). They were therefore unimpressed by the Bank of England's tactics of smoothing movements in gilt-edged prices. While accepting the need for a package deal of monetary and fiscal measures to deal with a financial emergency, they were concerned about the distorting effects of quantitative controls. They therefore recommended that the authorities should not rely for long periods on restrictions on bank lending or on hire-purchase regulations. They recognized that such physical controls could, in the course of time, lead to major distortions in the financial system (paras. 436–41, 513, 527–8.). They also allowed that fluctuations in Bank Rate might have an impact on short-term capital flows and hence on the strength of sterling but did not consider that business investment was sensitive to interest rates.

The Radcliffe Committee undertook a comprehensive review of British financial institutions and the techniques of monetary control and provided an excellent picture of the banking system at the end of the 1950s.

Because of the priority attached by the Bank of England to the control of short-term interest rates and in particular the Treasury bill rate, the conventional 8 per-cent cash ratio had lost much of its significance. Loss of reserves by the clearing banks as a result of an open-market sale of securities by the Bank of England did not generally operate to reduce the volume of bank deposits. The banks responded to a shortage of cash by calling in money at call from the discount houses. The latter had the privilege of being able to borrow from or discount bills at the Bank of England, but the Bank determined the terms under which the assistance was offered. The Bank could lend to the discount houses either at market rates or enforce the penal Bank Rate. Since it attached great importance to the discount market covering the total issue of Treasury bills, the Bank of England generally dealt freely between cash and Treasury bills in the bill market. It did not therefore deny the money market the cash which it needed to make good the loss of money at call to the banks. In return, by covering the tender through a single syndicated bid, the discount houses assured the Bank that the residual financial needs of the public sector would be met. This would avoid the need to resort to 'Ways and Means' advances by the central bank to the government which would expand the monetary base (paras. 374–80, 583–5).

When the Bank wished to tighten credit, it over-issued Treasury bills, so putting pressure on the discount houses and forcing them to borrow at an increased penal Bank Rate. Treasury bill rates rose in sympathy and so also did other short-term interest rates which were related to Bank Rate by administrative convention. The rate of interest paid on deposit accounts at the clearing banks was determined by a cartel among the banks and related directly to Bank Rate as also were the rates charged on bank advances.

Loss of reserves by the clearing banks resulting from open-market sales of securities by the Bank of England did not necessarily lead to a decline in advances, since a shortage of cash could be made good by calling in money at call from the discount market. Whether loans or investments were reduced depended upon whether the banks held more liquid assets than the conventional 30 per-cent ratio. A contraction of deposits or advances could only be forced by the central bank, if liquidity were reduced below the conventional minimum (paras. 376, 143–6).

## 4. Monetary Policy during the 1960s

### (a) *The Main Episodes*

During the 1960s monetary policy continued to be used as a tool of demand management in a subordinate role to fiscal policy as recommended by the Radcliffe Committee (Goodhart, 1973; Kareken, in Caves, 1968; Tew 1978*a*). The problems of managing the economy in the early 1960s appeared much the same as during the late 1950s. Monetary measures were used to protect the balance of payments at the peak of each cycle and policy became more relaxed when the authorities wished to promote recovery during the subsequent recession which was associated with an improvement in the balance of payments. There were, however, differences between the problems of the 1960s and those of the previous decade. Managing the economy with an overvalued exchange rate led to increasing reliance upon monetary restraint in the mid-1960s. Following the devaluation of sterling in November 1967, monetary policy in combination with restrictive fiscal measures was used to bring about a fundamental improvement in the balance of payments. Increasing reliance was placed upon monetary policy because of the need to contain the rising trend in inflation in the later 1960s. Thus the economy was subjected to deflationary policies for much of the second half of the decade (Bank of England, 1969).

There were major changes in the working of financial markets, which arose from the greater mobility of international capital following the announcement of the formal convertibility of sterling and of other European currencies in the late 1950s. The dollar shortage which had dominated the international monetary scene since the Second World War gave way to a massive outflow of dollars. The rapid growth of the market in Euro-dollars, followed by markets in Euro-currencies, contributed to the creation of an international market in short-term capital.[6] Short-term rates of

[6] For an excellent analysis of the Euro-dollar market, see Johnston (1983).

interest came to be increasingly influenced by international factors reducing the
scope for national divergencies under the Bretton Woods system of fixed exchange
rates.

The development of new financial markets for local authority deposits, sterling
inter-bank funds, and negotiable certificates of deposit was associated with changes
in financial institutions. Between 1959 and 1968 the share of the deposit banks in
the total sterling deposits of the UK banking system declined steeply from 85 per
cent to 50 per cent, while there was a sharp rise in the share of sterling deposits of
accepting houses, overseas banks, and other banks. The growth of these institutions
had policy implications, since lending ceilings imposed on the clearing banks
became increasingly inequitable and ineffective as other banks, which were not
subject to controls, expanded their lending. There were also problems in applying
conventional balance-sheet reserve rates to banks which were not engaging in retail
banking and achieved liquidity through matching the term structure of assets and
liabilities rather than by holding reserves. The introduction of sterling certificates
of deposit by these banks in the late 1960s was to have important implications for
both the behaviour of banks and the operation of monetary policy (Bank of
England, 1969).

During the 1960s the Bank of England used the same monetary techniques as in
the late 1950s, namely variations in Bank Rate, calls for Special Deposits, ceilings
on bank lending, and hire-purchase restrictions (Kareken, in Caves, 1968). Lending
ceilings and hire-purchase restrictions were imposed when Bank Rate was increased
but the relaxation of policy tended to be more gradual and piecemeal. The general
course of monetary policy can be assessed by examining the movements in Bank
Rate which were largely in response to pressures on the reserves which in turn were
associated with the current balance and the pressure of domestic demand (see
Tables 4.3 and 4.4).

During the vigorous recovery from the recession of 1958 Bank Rate was raised to
6 per cent in June 1960, which was followed by two reductions of ½ percentage
point to 5 per cent in December. Pressures on sterling forced the Bank to raise
Bank Rate to 7 per cent in July, which was accompanied by renewed restrictions on
bank lending and a call for Special Deposits. The lending request was stated in
general terms and was addressed to the non-clearing banks as well as to the London
clearing banks and the Scottish banks. Following the restoration of confidence
in sterling, there was a gradual reduction in Bank Rate by five steps of ½ percentage point to 4 per cent in January 1963. Lending restrictions were lifted in
October 1962 when it was clear that the economy was moving into recession, and
lending was encouraged by a reduction in the liquidity ratio from 30 to 28 per cent
in May 1963.

The economy revived strongly in 1963 and 1964 when there was a rapid expansion
in bank lending (see Tables 4.3 and 4.4). Fiscal policy was relaxed both before and
in the 1964 Budget. The recovery of the economy led to growing fears about the
state of the balance of payments which was reflected in a rise in Bank Rate to 5 per
cent in February. However, despite growing evidence of overheating, no further
action was taken in the run up to the October election in which the Conservative
Government was defeated. The incoming Labour administration faced a severe balance of payments deficit and high level of domestic demand (see Table 4.4 and Fig.
4.4). Bank Rate was raised by 2 percentage points to 7 per cent in November,

TABLE 4.3. *Monetary indicators 1960–1970*

| | Annual percentage rate of change | | | | | | | |
|------|------|--------|----------------|-------------|----------------|-------------------|----------------------|---------------------|
| | MO | M3/£M3 | Nominal GDP | Real GDP | GDP deflator | Velocity M3/£M3 | Treasury bill rate | Yield on consols |
| 1960 | 5.0 | 0.6 | 6.0 | 5.5 | 1.1 | 2.44 | 4.88 | 5.42 |
| 1961 | 3.2 | 2.1 | 6.7 | 2.7 | 3.4 | 2.56 | 5.13 | 6.20 |
| 1962 | 0.3 | 2.8 | 4.8 | 1.2 | 3.8 | 2.61 | 4.18 | 5.98 |
| 1963 | 4.3 | -2.4 | 6.3 | 4.1 | 2.1 | 2.84 | 3.66 | 5.58 |
| 1964 | 7.5 | 5.3 | 9.0 | 5.5 | 3.6 | 2.94 | 4.61 | 6.03 |
| 1965 | 4.5 | 8.1 | 7.4 | 3.0 | 4.9 | 2.92 | 5.91 | 6.42 |
| 1966 | 3.2 | 3.4 | 6.7 | 1.6 | 4.7 | 3.01 | 6.10 | 6.80 |
| 1967 | 4.7 | 10.5 | 5.8 | 2.2 | 3.1 | 2.88 | 5.82 | 6.69 |
| 1968 | 3.6 | 7.1 | 8.6 | 4.2 | 3.9 | 2.92 | 7.09 | 7.39 |
| 1969 | 3.7 | 1.8 | 6.8 | 2.5 | 5.4 | 3.07 | 7.64 | 8.88 |
| 1970 | 2.8 | 8.6 | 9.7 | 1.9 | 7.5 | 3.10 | 7.01 | 9.16 |

*Sources:* MO: Capie and Collins (1983).

M3 1960–2: Capie and Collins.

£M3 1963–70: *Economic Trends*, annual supplement (1988).

Nominal GDP, Real GDP, GDP deflator: ETAS (1988).

M3 Velocity = Nominal GDP

$$\frac{M3}{}$$

Average Treasury bill rate: *International Financial Statistics Yearbook.*

Yield on consols: *Annual Abstract of Statistics* (various issues).

TABLE 4.4. *Additional indicators 1960–1970*

| | Percentage of nominal GDP | | Unemployment % | Sterling–Dollar exchange rate ($) | Treasury bill rate | Euro-dollar rate |
|---|---|---|---|---|---|---|
| | PSBR | Current balance | | | | |
| 1960 | 2.76 | −0.89 | 1.7 | 2.81 | 4.88 | 4.18 |
| 1961 | 2.56 | 0.17 | 1.6 | 2.80 | 5.13 | 3.58 |
| 1962 | 1.90 | 0.54 | 2.1 | 2.81 | 4.18 | 3.77 |
| 1963 | 2.72 | 0.41 | 2.6 | 2.80 | 3.66 | 3.95 |
| 1964 | 2.94 | −1.12 | 1.7 | 2.79 | 4.61 | 4.32 |
| 1965 | 3.26 | −0.21 | 1.4 | 2.80 | 5.91 | 4.81 |
| 1966 | 2.48 | 0.33 | 1.5 | 2.79 | 6.10 | 6.12 |
| 1967 | 4.55 | −0.70 | 2.3 | 2.79 | 5.82 | 5.46 |
| 1968 | 2.85 | −0.60 | 2.4 | 2.39 | 7.09 | 6.36 |
| 1969 | −1.14 | 1.03 | 2.4 | 2.39 | 7.64 | 9.76 |
| 1970 | −0.10 | 1.54 | 2.6 | 2.40 | 7.01 | 8.52 |

*Sources:*  PSBR, 1952–62: Bank of England (1970); 1963–70 *Economic Trends*, annual supplement (1988).
Current Balance, Money GDP: ETAS (1988).
Unemployment: LCES (1971).
Sterling–Dollar Exchange Rate: ETAS (1988).
Average Treasury bill rate: *International Financial Statistics Yearbook*.
Euro-dollar Rate, 3 months: IFS.

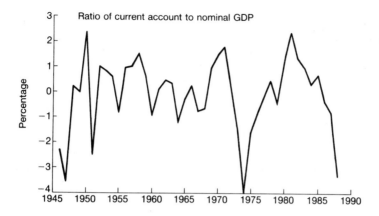

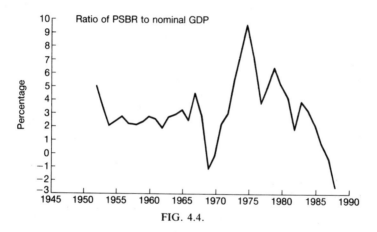

FIG. 4.4.

followed by the re-introduction of restrictions on lending in May 1965. The regulations were stated in quantitative form and froze lending at 105 per cent of the current level for the next 12 months and were to apply to all banks and to the larger finance houses. The ceilings applied to holdings of commercial bills as well as to bank lending (Tew, 1978*a*, Artis, 1978). Bank Rate was temporarily reduced to 6 per cent in June but the continuing weakness of sterling forced a rise to 7 per cent in July 1966 which was accompanied by a tightening of lending ceilings and of hire-purchase restrictions, combined with reductions in public spending. Some relaxation occurred in the first part of 1967, Bank Rate came down to 5½ per cent in May after three reductions of ½ percentage point. There was also some relaxation of lending restrictions on the clearing banks.

Renewed pressure on sterling, culminating in the devaluation crisis of November 1967, forced a rise in Bank Rate to 8 per cent and the reimposition of lending ceilings.[7] Bank Rate was maintained within a narrow range of 7–8 per cent from November 1967 to April 1970 and lending ceilings were in continuous operation

[7] The devaluation of 1967 is discussed in Cairncross and Eichengreen (1983) and Tew (1978*b*).

throughout this period, although redefined from time to time. The correction of the balance of payments deficit, following the devaluation of sterling by 14.3 per cent from $2.80 to $2.40 in November 1967, gave little scope for relaxing either short-term interest rates or credit controls. It was only after the turn-round in the current account in 1970 that interest rates could be brought down and credit ceilings be relaxed (see Tables 4.3 and 4.4 and Fig. 4.4). Bank Rate was reduced from 8 per cent to 7½ per cent in March 1970 with a further three reductions to 5 per cent in September 1971. Credit restrictions were relaxed in April 1971 having been in continuous operation since May 1965.

The recounting of the variation of monetary instruments in the 1960s serves to emphasize the changing nature of the problems facing the authorities. During the years up to 1965 monetary measures were being applied in a similar fashion as in the 1950s to deal with periodic crises in the balance of payments which coincided with a high level of domestic demand. During the subsequent recession interest rates were reduced and credit controls relaxed, as the balance of payments improved and the authorities became increasingly concerned about the level of unemployment. However from 1965 until the end of the decade the British economy suffered from chronic balance of payments difficulties. The Wilson Government attempted to head off pressures on sterling by imposing a deflationary package in 1966. When speculative pressures against sterling forced devaluation upon the authorities in November 1967, the process of correcting the balance of payments proved long and painful, requiring a sustained application of restrictive monetary and fiscal measures.

During the 1960s the Bank of England made greater use of credit restrictions than recommended by the Radcliffe Committee (*Report*, paras. 511–13, 524) which had argued that lending ceilings should be imposed only temporarily in times of emergency (Tew, 1978a). The Radcliffe Committee were arguing on the basis of the experience with stop–go cycles in the 1950s and not the persistent balance of payments problems encountered in the later 1960s. Credit ceilings were applied to a wider range of financial institutions than the London clearing banks and the Scottish banks. Other banks and major finance houses became subject to credit controls. The Bank also prepared a Cash Deposit Scheme which would have enabled it to call for Special Deposits from a wider range of financial institutions. However, the scheme was never put into effect.

Hire-purchase restrictions continued to be heavily relied upon to contain credit-financed consumer spending. Restrictions were tightened as part of a package deal to check home demand and to improve the balance of payments in July 1965 and 1966 and in November 1967 and 1968. Restrictions were relaxed in June and August 1967 and were discontinued in July 1971. Econometric evidence suggests that consumers' expenditure may have been temporarily reduced by up to 2½ per cent as a result of the imposition of hire-purchase restrictions. Restrictions on advances have also been shown to have had impact on fixed investment, but it is less easy to find a major effect on investment of changes in interest rates. Thus credit restrictions appear to have been more effective on regulating home investment than variations in the cost of borrowing. One area where short-term interest rates did have a significant impact was on the flow of funds into building societies. Flexible short-term rates fluctuating with market conditions showed greater variability than the deposit and loan rates of building societies. A rise in market rates acted to reduce the inflow of funds into the societies and led to rationing of credit to house buyers.

The availability of mortgage finance was an important factor affecting the demand for private residential constructions which was a major component of private-sector capital formation (Artis, 1978).

The chief impact of variations in Bank Rate was on international movements of short-term capital. The relationship between the Euro-dollar rate and the yield on 3-month local authority deposits, which was related to Bank Rate, became increasingly relevant for capital flows. Such flows were also influenced by the confidence effects of a rise in Bank Rate which showed that the authorities intended to defend the sterling exchange rate. This factor was at least as important as interest differentials in influencing short-term capital movements. As fears of devaluation mounted in the mid-1960s, the Bank of England intervened extensively in the forward market for sterling in order to induce inward movements of short-term funds to bolster sterling (Tew, 1978b).

During the 1960s the main impact of monetary measures was on external flows as short-term interest rates were regulated in order to maintain the fixed exchange rate. On the domestic side, monetary policy acted as a support for fiscal policy in demand management, chiefly through restricting credit to borrowers. The main channels through which the process operated were financial constraints on borrowing by the personal sector through hire-purchase controls and credit rationing by building societies, in addition to the impact on companies of ceilings on bank lending (Artis, 1978).

## (b) Bank Liquidity and Debt Management Policy

The Radcliffe Committee had been concerned about the problem of excess liquidity within the banking system, which resulted in the liquidity ratio of the clearing banks being comfortably in excess of the conventional minimum of 30 per cent. This meant that the banks were in a position to increase advances by reducing their holdings of liquid assets. During the 1960s progress was made in reducing the liquid assets ratio of the banking by funding the short-term debt, as market Treasury bills holdings were reduced and the stock of long-term debt was increased. Thus between December 1959 and 1969 the Treasury bill holdings of the London clearing banks declined from £1,157m. to £394m. However, the liquid assets ratio declined only from 33.2 per cent to 32.1 per cent, on account of the expansion of holdings of commercial and other bills and of money at call with the discount market. The discount market also increased the size of its commercial bill portfolio, so that within the banking sector as a whole liquid assets became increasingly composed of private rather than public debt (Tew, 1978a). One consequence of restricting bank lending was to encourage bill finance by companies which provided the banks with additional liquid assets. The response of the Bank of England was to include restrictions on commercial bills holdings in its directives on bank lending in 1965. This multiplication of restrictions on the banking system and weakening of control through the liquid assets ratio pointed to the need to redefine reserve ratios and to review techniques of control, a need which was recognized in the discussions which preceded the introduction of Competition and Credit Control in 1971.

During the 1960s the Bank of England paid considerable attention to the problems arising from the management of the long-term debt. In retrospect it would appear that debt management reasserted its dominance over monetary policy to almost the same extent as in the years 1945–51. During the 1950s the Bank had developed a policy of selling gilt-edged securities upon a rising market in order to finance the capital needs of the public sector. It had been criticized by the Radcliffe Committee for not attempting to sell gilts by adjusting prices downwards (*Report*, paras. 557–67). In response the Bank had argued that it was inadvisable to press stock on a falling market, because of the extrapolative expectations of the gilt market. These views were reasserted in the 1960s when the Bank adopted a policy of 'leaning into the wind', whereby it only sold gilt-edged on a rising market and intervened to support a declining bond market (Bank of England, 1966). It argued that the long-term demand for gilts was maximized if holders of gilts were cushioned against volatility in interest rates. Intervention was directed towards smoothing the course of gilt-edged prices, but the Bank did not attempt to resist a trend in the market (Goodhart, 1973). During the 1960s long-term interest rates continued to rise. The yield on consols rose from 5.42 per cent in 1960 to 6.69 per cent in 1967. There was a similar upward trend in average Treasury bill rates during this period from 4.88 per cent to 5.82 per cent (see Table 4.3 and Fig. 4.3). Since there was no comparable rise in the rate of inflation, there was a gradual upward movement in real interest rates which had been negative during the 1950s.

Since the authorities were primarily concerned about problems of debt management, they did not exercise control over the money supply. When sterling was weak and this weakness was communicated to the gilt-edged market, the Bank intervened in the bond market to cushion security prices, so expanding the liquidity of the banking system. The official policy of supporting bond prices encouraged banks to sell gilt-edged securities when they wanted to increase their advances and also to respond to calls for Special Deposits by reducing holdings of gilts rather than loans to the private sector. The authorities did not fully recognize the connection between financial markets. Thus when Bank Rate was raised during a time of emergency, to strengthen the reserves, there was a tendency for gilt-edged prices to fall. By intervening in the gilt market the Bank raised bond prices and encouraged sales of gilts and the outward movement of funds, so depleting the reserves. It has been shown that any benefit to the reserves by raising short-term rates could largely have been reversed through the Bank's intervention in the bond market (Nobay, 1987).

The policy of smoothing movements in long-term interest rates had implications for the relationship between the PSBR and the money supply. The PSBR averaged about 2–3 per cent of GDP from 1960–9 which was not very different from the percentage in the 1950s. Since it was the policy of the authorities to stabilize the gilt market, the money supply had to grow broadly in line with the rise in debt holdings of the public. There was nothing inevitable about this process which merely reflected the priority given by the authorities to debt management. However, despite the general lack of concern about monetary aggregates in the 1960s, velocity continued on its upward trend from 2.44 in 1960 to 3.10 in 1970 (see Table 4.3 and Fig. 4.1).

### (c) *The IMF and DCE*

The Bank's attitude towards debt management and monetary aggregates was subject to increasing pressure following the devaluation of 1967. A Letter of Intent was sent to the IMF by Chancellor Jenkins in connection with the negotiation of drawing rights to support sterling. The Letter stated that the growth of the money supply in 1968 would be limited to its estimated rate of growth in 1967. During 1968 there were discussions with the IMF about Domestic Credit Expansion (DCE) and in his second Letter of Intent of May 1969 the Chancellor set a target for the growth of DCE of £400m. for 1969–70 (Tew, 1978a).

DCE can be regarded as a measure of the money supply adjusted for the balance of payments and is a useful measure of the stance of monetary policy in an open economy with a fixed exchange rate.[8] (Artis and Nobay, 1969). When monetary policy is expansionary, it will generate a capital outflow, so that the measured growth in the domestic money stock understates the scale of the expansion. By including the change in the external element, DCE gives an improved measure of policy stance and by emphasizing the relationship between public-sector borrowing and the change in a monetary aggregate, it provided a basis for the co-ordination of monetary and fiscal policy which had hitherto been lacking.

The implementation of the targets agreed with the IMF led to a sharp fiscal contraction which turned the PSBR of 4.55 per cent of GDP in 1967 into a surplus of 1.14 per cent in 1969. Fiscal contraction was associated with a decline in the rate of growth of £M3 from 10.5 per cent in 1967 to 1.8 per cent in 1969, while the current account swung from a deficit of £183m to a surplus of £484m. (see Tables 4.3 and 4.4, and Figs. 4.1 and 4.4). In his Budget statement in April 1970 Chancellor Jenkins reported that DCE had turned out to be negative in 1969/70 due to the movement of the current account into surplus. He predicted DCE of less than £900m. for 1970/1 and a reduced rate of growth for the money supply, measured by M3. In April 1971, when the external position of sterling had been greatly strengthened, the Chancellor did not feel it necessary to set a target for DCE and the concept was not revived until November 1976 when there was a renewed application for assistance to the IMF.

The DCE targets introduced in 1969–70 and 1970–1 were the first examples of the use of monetary aggregates as intermediate variables. The achievement of the intermediate target was seen as an essential element in the attainment of the goal of equilibrium in the balance of payments. This episode was short-lived on account of its success in correcting external imbalance, but it persuaded the Bank of England of the need to take account of the behaviour of monetary aggregates and of the need to revise its tactics in the gilt-edged market. 'Leaning into the wind' or intervention to support a sagging bond market was understood to be in conflict with the control of either DCE or the money supply, since purchases of gilts by the Bank would raise the volume of bank deposits (Bank of England, 1969).

## 5. The New Approach of Competition and Credit Control

During the 1960s a variety of problems had arisen in the operation of monetary policy. The Bank of England became increasingly aware of the difficulties occurring under the existing arrangements and it therefore introduced a widespread reform of the monetary system in 1971 known as Competition and Credit Control (CCC).

[8] For a more formal statement of DCE, see the section on the Money Supply in the Introduction.

The Bank was aware that it had relied too heavily upon restriction of bank lending and that regulations had fallen unduly heavily upon the London clearing banks and the Scottish banks. The result had been a distortion of the financial system, favouring the development of secondary or fringe banks which were less subject to control. Further distortions arose in the field of finance of consumer durables, which were subject to credit restrictions of varying severity during the 1960s. The Crowther Committee (1971) strongly criticized reliance upon such restrictions, repeating the arguments which had impressed the Radcliffe Committee on the basis of experience in the 1950s. The fixing of deposits and loan rates by a cartel of the London clearing banks was criticized by National Board for Prices and Incomes in its report on bank charges (1967). The cartel which dated back to the First World War was also criticized by the Monopolies Commission in its report on the proposed merger between Barclays, Lloyds, and Martins (1968). The authorities were reluctant to accept these criticisms because of the convenience of tying the deposit and lending rates to the Bank Rate which gave them a tight control over short-term interest rates. However tight the control may have been in the 1950s, it had become eroded during the course of the 1960s with the development of the new markets for money, such as for local authority temporary money, inter-bank deposits, and certificates of deposit. The rates of interest on these funds were determined by competitive forces and were not related in any direct way to Bank Rate. Thus the administratively set deposit and loan rates threatened to be out of touch with rates determined in more competitive financial markets.

The Bank of England had encountered problems with the liquidity ratio, on account of the growth of commercial bill finance during the 1960s (Tew, 1978a). It had sought to restrict the growth of commercial bill holdings by the banks from 1965, but there was a need to redefine the ratio and to extend its application to a wider range of banks. The Bank had also been forced to recognize the problems inherent in its policy of supporting the gilt-edged market.

The new approach to monetary policy was set out in the Bank's consultative document published in June 1971 and the scheme was introduced in September (Bank of England, 1971c). Lending ceilings on banks and finance houses, which had been in operation almost continuously from the mid-1960s, were removed, although the Bank retained the right to give qualitative guidance on lending. Hire-purchase regulations were discontinued in July as recommended by the Crowther Committee. The cartel among the London clearing banks was abolished and their deposit and lending rates were no longer to be directly related to Bank Rate.

The reserve ratios of the banking system were redefined. The liquid assets ratio observed by the clearing banks and reduced from 30 per cent to 28 per cent in 1963, was replaced by the Reserve Asset Ratio (RAR) under which all banks held 12½ per cent of their eligible liabilities in reserve assets. Reserve assets included balances at the Bank of England (excluding Special Deposits), money at call with the discount market, Treasury bills and commercial bills (up to a maximum of 2 per cent of eligible liabilities), local authority bills, and British government securities with less than one year to maturity. Eligible liabilities were defined as the sterling liabilities of the banking system excluding deposits with a maturity of more than two years. The London clearing banks, unlike other banks, were to hold 1½ per cent of their eligible liabilities in the form of non-interest bearing deposits at the Bank of England. This ratio replaced the former 8 per cent cash ratio and was suitably reduced to take account of the exclusion of notes and coins held by the banks. All banks were to be subject to calls for Special Deposits, and the larger finance houses were required to maintain a reserve ratio of 10 per cent (Bank of England, 1971c).

There were changes in the markets for Treasury bills and gilt-edged securities. The discount houses were to continue to cover the tender issue of Treasury bills but they would no longer submit a single agreed bid. The retention of the cash ratio meant that the authorities would continue to exercise their control over Treasury bill rates by regulating the terms under which a cash shortage was relieved. The discount houses were to be required to hold 40 per cent of their assets in public-sector debt. A further change which was not introduced until 1972 was the replacement of Bank Rate by Minimum Lending Rate (MLR). MLR was directly related to the Treasury bill rate and would vary automatically with market interest rates and, therefore, be more responsive to changing conditions than the administered Bank Rate.

Turning to the gilt market, the Bank announced in May that it no longer felt any obligation to provide support for gilt-edged stocks which had more than a year before maturity. It stated that it would no longer facilitate movements out of gilt-edged by the banks, even if sales of government debt were to depress bond prices. The Bank, therefore, indicated that it would not normally step in to support a weak bond market, although it might intervene at its own discretion. The new policy went beyond a return to the tactics used before the introduction of 'leaning with the wind' in the 1960s. The redefined reserve ratio was not intended to bring about a multiple contraction of deposits but rather to provide a means of putting pressure on bank liquidity. Banks were expected to respond to such pressure by reducing loans and/or selling securities. In the past monetary policy had been chiefly concerned with bank lending and the gilt-edged market was of secondary importance. However, the increased emphasis on monetary aggregates created the need for more flexible interest rates, and reduced the scope for smoothing gilt-edged prices. The aim of the new policy was to exert a generalized influence on credit through variations in interest rates.[9]

The Bank of England undertook a thorough investigation of the Keynesian and Monetarist theories. It adopted a compromise position, concluding that money had an important influence on the economy but without accepting the main precepts of Monetarism. At the same time the Bank estimated econometrically money demand equations for both M1 (narrow money) and M3 (broad money). Bank economists appeared to have estimated money demand equations, which were sufficiently reliable for policy purposes. This implied that by varying interest rates the authorities could control the money supply, without needing to rely upon quantitative restrictions on credit. It appeared that sufficient variation in interest rates would enable the central bank to control the money supply. In accepting the stability of the demand for money function, the Bank had implicitly rejected the views of the Radcliffe Committee on the instability of the velocity of circulation (Bank of England, 1970, 1972).

The new monetary arrangements were introduced at a time when economic policy

---

[9] The aims of the reforms are discussed in Bank of England (1971a, 1971b), and market operations in Bank of England (1971c, 1971d).

was becoming more expansionary, following the stagnation of output in 1969–70, when the current balance moved strongly into surplus. Chancellor Jenkins achieved a negative PSBR during these years as fiscal policy was tightened. Such financial orthodoxy did not impress the electorate, which voted for a Conservative Government in the 1970 election. The new administration embarked on a cautiously expansionary policy. Bank Rate which stood at 7 per cent in April 1970, was reduced to 6 per cent a year later, followed by a further reduction to 5 per cent in September. The rate of growth of £M3 rose to 8.6 per cent in 1970, compared with only 1.8 per cent in 1969, and there was a similar acceleration in the rate of growth of M1. Fiscal policy was relaxed as the ratio of PSBR to GDP rose to 2.3 per cent. However, the pace of recovery was not sufficient to prevent unemployment from rising from 617,000 at the end of 1970 to 799,000 a year later. The new Chancellor, Barber, aimed in his March 1972 Budget to raise the growth of output to 5 per cent per annum, compared with the sluggish rise in GDP of 1.5 per cent in 1971. The aim of lower unemployment was not to be frustrated by a deterioration of the balance of payments, since sterling was floated in June and was allowed to depreciate as domestic recovery gathered pace (see Tables 4.5 and 4.6 and Fig. 4.5).

The new arrangements therefore began against a background of economic revival after a period of stagnation. Banks liberated from the lending ceilings which had been in effect continuously since the mid-1960s expanded their advances rapidly under a regime which encouraged competition in the financial sector. Initially the authorities were not concerned about the expansion of bank lending. The previous removal of restrictions in 1958 had led to a surge in lending and something similar was only to be expected in the 1970s. Moreover, the clearing banks, freed from discriminatory regulations, might well have been expected to seek to win back both deposits and loans which had been diverted into other financial institutions. In both 1972 and 1973 there was a strong tendency for banks to seek to channel funds to themselves and away, for example, from inter-company loans and building societies; such activity was known as reintermediation. The rapid expansions of bank lending, which rose by 33 per cent in 1973, led to a massive increase in £M3 which surged by 27 per cent in both 1972 and 1973, the growth of M1 was slower at 14.2 per cent in 1972 and still more so at 5.1 per cent in 1973 (see Table 4.5 and Fig. 4.1) The unprecedented behaviour of broad money in the first phase of CCC caused the authorities growing concern. Their attempts to restrain monetary growth were to reveal major defects in the new approach. In achieving their objective of encouraging greater competition in the banking system, they appeared to have surrendered monetary control.[10]

The first signs of tightness in the money market occurred in mid-1972, when the three-month inter-bank rate rose by 3½ per cent between May and July. Minimum Lending Rate, which replaced Bank Rate, rose from 7¼ per cent to 9 per cent in December, before easing back to 7½ per cent by May 1973. There were also calls for Special Deposits in November and December. In the second half of 1973 money-market conditions became more restrictive as MLR moved up to 9 per cent and then 11½ per cent in July. Finally, in November the Bank of England overrode the formula and raised MLR to a record 13 per cent by administrative action. In addition there were renewed calls for Special Deposits in July and November. The rapid

---

[10] The operation of the banking system under Competition and Credit Control is discussed in Spencer (1986).

TABLE 4.5. *Monetary indicators 1970–1988*

| | Average percentage rate of change | | | | | Velocity | | Treasury bill rate | Yield on consols |
|---|---|---|---|---|---|---|---|---|---|
| | MO | £M3 | Nominal GDP | Real GDP | GDP deflator | MO | £M3 | | |
| 1970 | 2.8 | 8.6 | 9.7 | 1.9 | 7.5 | 12.7 | 3.10 | 7.01 | 9.16 |
| 1971 | 4.6 | 14.0 | 12.3 | 1.5 | 9.2 | 13.6 | 3.05 | 5.57 | 9.05 |
| 1972 | 14.8 | 27.2 | 10.7 | 2.4 | 8.1 | 13.1 | 2.66 | 5.54 | 9.11 |
| 1973 | 10.1 | 27.1 | 15.2 | 7.3 | 7.2 | 13.7 | 2.41 | 9.34 | 10.85 |
| 1974 | 16.0 | 11.0 | 13.7 | −1.7 | 14.6 | 13.4 | 2.47 | 11.37 | 14.95 |
| 1975 | 10.9 | 5.7 | 26.4 | −1.0 | 27.2 | 15.3 | 2.95 | 10.18 | 14.66 |
| 1976 | 11.0 | 9.5 | 19.3 | 2.7 | 15.0 | 16.5 | 3.22 | 11.12 | 14.25 |
| 1977 | 16.7 | 9.4 | 15.2 | 2.5 | 13.9 | 16.3 | 3.39 | 7.68 | 12.31 |
| 1978 | 13.1 | 15.4 | 15.3 | 2.9 | 11.3 | 16.6 | 3.39 | 8.51 | 11.93 |
| 1979 | 10.4 | 13.4 | 16.9 | 2.7 | 14.5 | 17.6 | 3.49 | 12.98 | 11.39 |
| 1980 | 5.3 | 18.9 | 17.2 | −2.3 | 19.8 | 19.5 | 3.44 | 15.11 | 11.88 |
| 1981 | 3.8 | 25.3 | 10.2 | −1.0 | 11.5 | 20.7 | 3.03 | 13.03 | 13.01 |
| 1982 | 4.3 | 9.0 | 8.8 | 1.5 | 7.5 | 21.6 | 3.02 | 11.47 | 11.90 |
| 1983 | 2.0 | 11.1 | 8.9 | 3.4 | 5.2 | 23.1 | 2.96 | 9.59 | 10.24 |
| 1984 | 5.7 | 10.1 | 6.4 | 2.5 | 4.3 | 23.2 | 2.86 | 9.30 | 10.16 |
| 1985 | 3.4 | 13.2 | 9.9 | 3.7 | 5.9 | 24.7 | 2.78 | 11.56 | 10.11 |
| 1986 | 5.2 | 18.7 | 6.5 | 3.1 | 3.6 | 25.0 | 2.49 | 10.37 | 9.47 |
| 1987 | 4.8 | 22.8 | 9.6 | 4.4 | 4.7 | 26.1 | 2.24 | 9.25 | 9.31 |
| 1988 | 8.0 | 20.5 | 10.5 | 3.8 | 6.6 | 26.7 | 2.05 | 9.78 | 9.12 |

*Sources:* MO: 1970–82 Capie and Collins (1983); 1983–6 *Economic Trends*, annual supplement (1988), *Economic Trends* (1989).
£M3: ETAS (1988), ET (1989).
Nominal GDP, Real GDP, GDP deflator: ETAS (1988), ET (1989).
Average Treasury bill rate: *International Financial Statistics Yearbook.*
Yield on consols: *Annual Abstract of Statistics.*

TABLE 4.6. *Additional indicators 1970–1988*

| | Percentage of nominal GDP | | | | Sterling | | |
|---|---|---|---|---|---|---|---|
| | PSBR | Current balance | Unemployment % | Sterling–Dollar exchange rate ($) | effective exchange rate (1975 = 100) | Treasury bill rate | Euro-dollar rate |
| 1970 | −0.10 | 1.54 | 2.55 | 2.40 | 128.1 | 7.01 | 8.52 |
| 1971 | 2.28 | 1.89 | 2.78 | 2.44 | 127.9 | 5.57 | 6.58 |
| 1972 | 3.04 | 0.30 | 3.08 | 2.50 | 123.3 | 5.54 | 5.46 |
| 1973 | 5.54 | −1.38 | 2.10 | 2.45 | 111.8 | 9.34 | 9.24 |
| 1974 | 7.68 | −3.95 | 2.15 | 2.34 | 108.3 | 11.37 | 11.01 |
| 1975 | 9.57 | −1.49 | 3.35 | 2.22 | 99.9 | 10.18 | 6.99 |
| 1976 | 7.06 | −0.73 | 4.48 | 1.80 | 85.6 | 11.12 | 5.58 |
| 1977 | 3.75 | −0.09 | 4.48 | 1.75 | 81.2 | 7.68 | 6.00 |
| 1978 | 5.01 | 0.57 | 4.68 | 1.92 | 81.5 | 8.51 | 8.73 |
| 1979 | 6.45 | 0.34 | 4.28 | 2.12 | 87.3 | 12.98 | 11.96 |
| 1980 | 5.13 | 1.26 | 5.43 | 2.33 | 96.1 | 15.11 | 14.36 |
| 1981 | 4.17 | 2.48 | 8.48 | 2.03 | 94.9 | 13.03 | 16.51 |
| 1982 | 1.78 | 1.46 | 9.85 | 1.75 | 90.5 | 11.47 | 13.11 |
| 1983 | 3.87 | 1.11 | 10.78 | 1.52 | 83.2 | 9.59 | 9.60 |
| 1984 | 3.20 | 0.46 | 11.08 | 1.34 | 78.6 | 9.30 | 10.78 |
| 1985 | 2.14 | 0.83 | 11.28 | 1.30 | 78.3 | 11.56 | 8.34 |
| 1986 | 0.61 | −0.26 | 11.13 | 1.47 | 71.6 | 10.37 | 6.77 |
| 1987 | −0.35 | −0.70 | 9.98 | 1.64 | 70.5 | 9.25 | 7.11 |
| 1988 | −2.54 | −3.20 | 8.05 | 1.78 | 74.8 | 9.78 | 7.91 |

*Sources:* PSBR, Current Balance, Nominal GDP, Unemployment, Sterling/Dollar Sterling Effective Exchange Rates: *Economic Trends*, annual supplement (1988), *Economic Trends* (1989).
Average Treasury bill rate, Euro–dollar Rate: *International Financial Statistics Yearbook*.

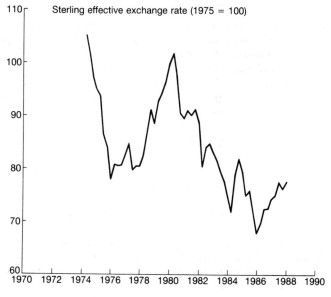

FIG. 4.5.

growth of bank lending was finally checked by resorting to quantitative restrictions, which were not in the spirit of CCC (Tew, 1978a).

As banks experienced pressure on their reserves from mid-1972, they responded by bidding vigorously for wholesale deposits and certificates of deposit. They and the discount market also bid for reserve assets, such as Treasury bills, which would enable them to support a larger volume of lending. The result was that yields on certificates of deposits and wholesale deposits rose relative to the yield on short-term public debt. The attempt by the banks to attract deposits when subjected to pressure on their reserves (so called liability management) had not been envisaged by the architects of Competition and Credit Control. It had been supposed that banks would respond to reserve pressures better by raising lending rates, leading to a decline in advances, or by selling public sector debt, so raising the yield on such securities relative to the return on holding bank deposits. The non-bank public would then have an incentive to hold more public debt and lower bank deposits. These portfolio changes did not occur in practice (Bank of England, 1982a). Although yields on Treasury bills and gilts rose, the relative rate of return did not rise on account of the upward pressure on competitively determined deposit rates. The interest bearing component of the money stock could increase rather than decline as interest rates rose, on account of the movement in interest differentials in favour of bank deposits. This explains the contrasting growth in £M3 and M1 in 1973. The former increased under the impetus of rising interest rates and the latter slowed down, as the non-bank public moved away from non-interest bearing current accounts of which M1 largely consisted.

The Bank of England attempted to narrow the excess of the certificate deposit rate over the Treasury bill rate, which opened up in mid-1972 as a result of the banks and the discount houses bidding for reserve assets. The reserve ratio of the discount houses was redefined in July 1973. They were no longer required to observe a public-sector lending ratio but their holdings of non-public sector assets were limited to twenty times their reserves plus capital. This change was intended to discourage the discount market from bidding down the yield on Treasury bills and hence the MLR, in order to increase their assets and hence the capacity to provide money at call for the banks. The new reserve requirements did not prevent the persistence of a substantial differential in favour of CDs in 1973 and 1974, which was aggravated by calls for Special Deposits.

A second and more important distortion arose as a result of the relative inflexibility of bank lending rates compared to deposit rates. During 1973 renewed upward pressure on money-market rates due to liability management by the banks led to a situation in which first-class borrowers were in a position to arbitrage between bank loans and sterling certificates of deposit, since the cost of borrowing at base rate plus 1 per cent was less than the yield available on CDs. This distortion, known as 'round tripping' inflated the growth of M3 (Bank of England, 1982a; Goodhart, 1981).

The Bank of England recognized that it was necessary to restrict the upward pressure on deposit and CD rates and that further calls for Special Deposits would merely aggravate the situation. They therefore introduced Supplementary Special Deposits (SSD) in December 1973. The scheme, known as the Corset, imposed penalties in banks and finance houses whose interest bearing eligible liabilities (IBELS), that is approximately interest-bearing sterling deposits, grew faster than a prescribed rate. The penalties in the form of compulsory non-interest bearing deposits at the Bank of England became increasingly severe the greater the excess of growth in IBELS over the prescribed rate. Initially, the allowable growth rate was 8 per cent over the first six months of the scheme, then rising at 1½ per cent per month. The Corset was a form of quantitative restriction designed to check the rapid growth of broad money which resulted from the vigorous competition among the banks for interest-bearing deposits. Such a measure combined with the raising of MLR to 13 per cent in November was felt to be necessary on account of the growing evidence of overheating in the economy in addition to the explosive growth of M3.

Fiscal policy continued to be expansionary in 1973, when the PSBR rose to 3 per cent of GDP. The growth of output surged to 7.3 per cent and unemployment had fallen by the end of the year to below 500,000. The current account moved into a heavy deficit of £1,000m., which was aggravated by the rise in world commodity prices, as well as the strength of domestic demand. Consequently sterling, which had been floated in June 1972, weakened against the US dollar. In the face of fears of higher inflation and excessive economic activity, fiscal policy was tightened at the end of the year and hire-purchase controls also were introduced to check the boom in consumer spending (see Tables 4.5 and 4.6 and Fig. 4.4).

So ended the first period of Competition and Credit Control. In retrospect and in the light of subsequent experience with financial deregulation, it is clear that the Bank of England seriously underestimated the credit expansion which was likely to follow from a removal of long-established lending ceilings. What made the situation particularly acute was that the deregulation was partial, in that lending rates were less flexible than deposit rates so aggravating credit expansion through opening up opportunities for arbitrage by first class borrowers.[11]

## 6. Monetary Policy in the 1970s

### (a) *Towards Monetary Targets*

During the early 1970s there was an upward trend in the rate of inflation, which was accentuated by both the rise in world commodity prices of 50 per cent in 1973 and the quadrupling of oil prices in 1973–4. These shocks to the supply side of the economy followed the massive rise in broad money which had resulted from the deregulation introduced under Competition and Credit Control.

The response of the Labour government, elected in 1974, to rising inflation and declining output was to maintain a relatively relaxed fiscal stance, allowing the ratio of the PSBR to GDP to rise from 5.5 per cent in 1973 to 9.6 per cent in 1975. Following the breakdown of the initial voluntary policy, an incomes policy was introduced in 1975 combined with a tightening of fiscal policy. Inflation as measured by the GDP deflator fell from a peak of 27 per cent in 1975 to 15 per cent in 1976 (see Tables 4.5 and 4.6).

The role of monetary policy during this period of crisis was secondary. Following its rapid expansion in 1973, the rate of growth of £M3 fell to 11.0 per cent in 1974 and to 5.7 per cent in 1975. The slowdown was due largely to the reduced demand for bank advances as the economy moved into recession in 1974–5. In addition the Corset discouraged banks from bidding for deposits and so checked monetary growth. As the demand for credit was further reduced by the recession, the competitive pressure among banks continued to decline, allowing the Corset to be

[11] The crisis in the secondary banking system which followed the rapid growth of bank credit is described in M. Reid (1982).

suspended in February 1975. MLR which had been raised to 13 per cent in December 1973 remained in the range 10–11 per cent in 1974 and 1975, while the Treasury bill rate averaged 10–11 per cent. This relative stability of short-term interest rates at a time of rising inflation led to real interest rates becoming negative. Thus in 1975 the real return on Treasury bills fell to −14 per cent (see Table 4.5 and Fig. 4.3).

During 1976 there was growing concern at home and abroad about the continuation of a high rate of inflation combined with a massive PSBR, which approached 10 per cent of money GDP (see Fig. 4.4). Whereas in 1974/5 the PSBR had been largely financed by sales of debt to the non-bank public and by borrowing from overseas, in 1975/6 borrowing from the banking system became more important, at a time when the growth of £M3 was increasing from a moderate 5.7 per cent in 1975 to 9.5 per cent in 1976. Against a background of weakening financial confidence, the sterling effective exchange rate declined from 105.2 in the first quarter of 1975 to 78.1 in final quarter of 1976, a fall of 25.8 per cent (see Fig. 4.5).

In response to the deteriorating financial conditions, Chancellor Healey wrote a Letter of Intent to the IMF in December 1976 introducing formal financial targets as a precondition of obtaining a loan of $3.9bn. from the Fund. According to the Chancellor's letter the PSBR was to be reduced to £8.5bn. compared with £10.6bn. in 1975/6, followed by further reductions in the next two financial years. As in 1969 Domestic Credit Expansion (DCE) was to be brought under tighter control. It was to be reduced from £9bn. in 1976/7 to £7.7bn. in 1977/8 and £6bn. in 1978/9. The Letter of Intent stated that the rate of increase of £M3 was expected to be within the range of 9–13 per cent in 1976/7. The expected growth rate was rapidly elevated to the status of a monetary target (D. Savage, 1979).

The growth of the money supply was to be restrained by a reduction in the PSBR combined with other restrictive measures. In November the Corset had been reintroduced, setting the maximum permitted rate of growth of IBELS (or interest bearing deposits) which would not incur penalties at 3 per cent over a period of six months. During the period of prolonged pressure on sterling, MLR had been pushed upward by stages from 9 per cent in March 1976, culminating in a rise of 2 percentage points from 13 per cent to 15 per cent in October. The high level of short-term interest rates assisted the finance of the PSBR, through encouraging sales of gilt-edged to the non-bank public in 1977. MLR was progressively reduced from 14 per cent in January 1977 to 7 per cent in August through a large number of small reductions. In the gilt market investors bought bonds in anticipation of further reductions in interest rates which would generate capital gains for bond holders (Savage, 1979; Dennis, 1980). The resulting strong demand for gilts enabled the authorities to achieve bond sales to the non-bank public in excess of the PSBR, known as Overfunding, which reduced the growth of the money supply. As a result the rate of growth of £M3 was only 7 per cent in 1976/7, below the lower end of the target range of 9–13 per cent. The reduction in short-term interest rates increased the demand for non-interest-bearing deposits, leading to an acceleration of the rate of growth of M1 (narrow money), but the demand for bank credit remained moderate, enabling the Corset to be suspended in August.

The out-turn for DCE in 1976–7 was £4.3m., compared with the target of £9.0bn. in the Letter of Intent to the IMF. The reason for the undershooting was the strong turn-round in the balance of payments as the current account improved sharply.

This led to a renewal of confidence in sterling, as the decline in the effective exchange rate was halted in 1977 and the exchange rate started to appreciate. Thus the impact of the measures introduced at the end of 1976 led to a rapid improvement in financial confidence, which was reflected in the sentiment of both the foreign exchange market and the bond market.

## (b) *The Rationale for Monetary Targets*

The introduction of monetary targets as the result of negotiations with the IMF accorded with the views of the Bank of England and the Treasury. The Bank, following the explosive growth of £M3, which was associated with CCC, monitored monetary aggregates closely. It was, as Fforde (Bank of England, 1983) has noted, a small but significant step in moving from an unpublished target for M3 to a published target which would act as an overriding constraint on economic policy.

The Governor examined the rationale for monetary targeting in the Mais Lecture (Bank of England, 1978). Control of monetary aggregates was seen as contributing to the achievement of goal variables. The goals of economic policy were defined differently from those recommended by the Radcliffe Committee. Greater emphasis was put on the control of inflation in the medium term through monetary measures rather than the maintenance of full employment through an active policy of demand management, as proposed in the *Radcliffe Report*. The objectives of monetary policy were not to be achieved by quick-acting measures but rather by the coordination of monetary, fiscal, and incomes policy over the medium term. The chief function of monetary targets was to provide a framework for economic stability. They would indicate that excessive wage claims would not be accommodated by faster monetary expansion and would merely result in higher unemployment. In this way monetary targets were seen as reinforcing incomes policy. The Governor emphasized the broad relationship between monetary growth and inflation without accepting a specifically Monetarist standpoint. He referred to the need to provide an anchor for policy which was required once the discipline of a fixed exchange had been removed.

In considering the implementation of policy the Governor recognized the difficulties of estimating a reliable money-demand function and emphasized the counterpart approach to the money supply. In the flow-of-funds scheme used by the Bank the change in £M3 is defined as:[12]

| $\triangle$ £M3 = PSBR | − Sales of gilts to non-bank private sector | + Increase in bank lending in sterling to the private sector | + Net external finance | − Increase in banks' non-deposit liabilities |
|---|---|---|---|---|

The Bank envisaged using short-term interest rates to influence the non-bank public's demand for gilt-edged and also the demand for bank loans. In addition fiscal policy affected the size of the PSBR and exchange-rate policy influenced net external flows. The counterpart approach therefore provided the authorities with a

---

[12] For the derivation of this identity which explains the connection between the balance sheet of the banks and the PSBR, see the section (c) in the Introduction.

co-ordinated framework for monetary control which related monetary and fiscal policy. Such a framework could only be constructed for broad money (£M3) and this was the major reason for choosing it rather than narrow money (M1) as the targeted monetary aggregate. This choice was made despite the breakdown of estimated money-demand functions for broad money and the sensitivity of £M3 to relative interest rates, which the authorities found difficulty in controlling[13] (Artis and Lewis, 1981).

### (d) *Monetary Targets under the Labour Government*[14]

The revival of financial confidence in 1977 led to the first real test of the Labour Government's commitment to monetary targets. As the exchange rate showed signs of strengthening during the first half of the year there was a conflict between the desire of the government to hold sterling at a competitive level and the requirements of monetary targeting. This is an example of a conflict between targeting the money supply and the exchange rate which is discussed in section (d) of the Introduction. The Bank of England intervened in the foreign exchange market to check the appreciation of sterling as shown by the sharp rise in its reserves. Unless fully neutralized by domestic sales of securities, such intervention would raise the money supply. The restoration of external confidence in sterling occurred when the British interest rates were high relative to those in the rest of the world, encouraging a massive capital inflow. The government announced that domestic monetary targets could be endangered by large-scale inflows of funds and discontinued the policy of holding sterling at a competitive level. Although the money supply was no longer subject to pressures from capital inflows, there was an overshoot of public borrowing towards the end of the financial year, which resulted in growth of £M3 of 16 per cent in 1977/8 in excess of the target range of 9–13 per cent.

It was announced in the April 1978 Budget that monetary targets which had been fixed annually since December 1976 would be subject to review every six months. Chancellor Healey announced that the rate of growth of £M3 in 1978/9 would be narrowed slightly to 8–12 per cent, while the PSBR would be raised from £5.5bn. in 1977/8 to an estimated £8.2bn. in 1978/9.

The combination of relaxing the PSBR, while tightening the target range for monetary growth was ill-considered, particularly since MLR stood at the historically low level of 7½ per cent. The weakening of sterling combined with rising interest rates in the United States led to the expectation that interest rates would rise and encouraged the bond market to postpone purchases of gilts until the increase had taken place. The authorities were obliged to introduce restrictive fiscal measures in June.[15] In addition MLR was raised by 1 percentage point to 10 per cent, following two increases to 9 per cent in May, and the Corset was reactivated. This tightening of policy enabled the sales of gilts to be resumed. £M3 which had initially been growing faster than its target range of 8–12 per cent ended up rising in 1978/9 at 11 per cent just within its upper limit.

---

[13] Institutional developments are not discussed here, reference should be made to the *Report* of the Wilson Committee (1980).
[14] Monetary targeting under the Labour Government is discussed in Spencer (1986).
[15] For an account of the gilt-edged strike, see Browning (1986), pp. 114–15.

While the outcome for growth of monetary aggregates was reasonably satisfactory, other aspects of policy were giving cause for concern. The PSBR rose to £9.2bn. compared with £5.2bn. in 1977/8. The rate of inflation, as measured by the GDP deflator, had fallen from an average of 21.1 per cent per annum in 1976 and 1977 to 11.3 per cent in 1978, but bounced back to 14.5 per cent in 1979 (see Table 4.5 and Fig. 4.2).

## 7. Monetary Policy since 1979

### (a) *The Second Oil Price Shock and the Ending of Exchange Control*

The Conservative Government elected in May 1979 inherited from its predecessor a rising rate of inflation combined with moderate monetary growth. The government had agreed to implement the recommendations of the Clegg Commission on public sector pay which resulted in pay increases of 15–25 per cent. In his June Budget the new Chancellor, Howe, introduced a higher uniform rate of VAT at 15 per cent, compared with the old standard rate of 8 per cent, which was rapidly reflected in higher prices. There was a second sharp rise in oil prices from October 1978 to June 1979 as a result of OPEC II. The second oil-price shock did not have such an inflationary impact on the British economy as its predecessor in 1973–4. Since Britain was now self-sufficient in oil, the rise in oil prices was associated with a rise rather than a decline in sterling and the impact of higher energy costs on import prices was therefore cushioned. Britain was, however, to feel the full impact of the world recession which followed the second major rise in oil prices.

In the budget of June 1979 monetary policy was tightened as the target range for £M3 was set at 7–11 per cent for the remainder of 1979/80 compared with the target of 8–12 per cent set by the previous Labour Government. MLR, which had been raised to 14 per cent in February 1979 and subsequently reduced to 12 per cent in April, was raised again to 14 per cent in June, followed by a further increase to a record 17 per cent in November. The exchange rate strengthened in response to the tightening of interest rates, as indicated by the rise in the sterling index from 80.6 in the fourth quarter of 1978 to 88.6 a year later[16] (see Tables 4.6 and 4.7 and Fig. 4.5). The Corset reintroduced in June 1978 remained in effect throughout 1979/80. For the first time sizeable Supplementary Special Deposits were paid as a result of the interest-bearing eligible liabilities of banks (IBELS) growing faster than the prescribed maximum rate. Banks responded to the pressure of the Corset by increasing lending which did not appear on their balance sheets. The most widely used method of by-passing the Corset took the form of the rediscounting of bills which had been accepted by banks. The growth of bills held outside the banking system was known as the 'bill leak' and reached £2,700m. in the second quarter of 1980. Although the growth of £M3 in 1979/80 which turned out at 10 per cent, was within the target range of 7–11 per cent, it was substantially distorted by the operation of the Corset. Excessive monetary growth was effectively massaged by the Corset, as the market

---

[16] Maynard (1988) points out that the tightening of monetary policy and the rise in the exchange rate under the new Conservative Government started well before the 1980 Budget.

TABLE 4.7. *Monetary targets for £M3 1976/7–1986/7*

| Targets for £M3: Date Set | Projections and out-turns (Annual percentage changes) | | | | | | | | | | | | |
|---|---|---|---|---|---|---|---|---|---|---|---|---|---|
| | 1976/7 | 1977/8 | 1978/9 | 1979/80 | 1980/1 | 1981/2 | 1982/3 | 1983/4 | 1984/5 | 1985/6 | 1986/7 | 1987/88 | 1988/89 |
| July 1976 | 9–13 | | | | | | | | | | | | |
| March 1977 | | 9–13 | | | | | | | | | | | |
| April 1978 | | | 8–12 | | | | | | | | | | |
| June 1979 | | | | 7–11 | | | | | | | | | |
| March 1980 | | | | | 7–11 | (6–10) | (5–9) | (4–8) | | | | | |
| March 1981 | | | | | | 6–10 | (5–9) | (4–8) | | | | | |
| March 1982 | | | | | | | 8–12 | (7–11) | (6–10) | | | | |
| March 1983 | | | | | | | | 7–11 | (6–10) | (5–9) | | | |
| March 1984 | | | | | | | | | 6–10 | (5–9) | (4–8) | (3–7) | (2–6) |
| March 1985 | | | | | | | | | | 5–9 | (4–8) | (3–7) | (2–6) |
| March 1986 | | | | | | | | | | | 11–15 | | |
| Out-turn | 7.2 | 16.4 | 11.3 | 16.2 | 19.4 | 12.8 | 11.2 | 9.4 | 11.9 | 16.9 | 19.0 | | |

*Sources: National Institute Economic Review and OECD, Economic Outlook.*

increased its holdings of liquid assets, which were not included in the broad monetary aggregate (Bank of England, 1982*a*).

The channelling of lending away from the banking system, known as disintermediation, in contrast to the reintermediation resulting from Competition and Credit Control, led to an understatement of monetary growth. However, the days of the Corset were numbered following the Conservative Government's decision to abolish exchange controls in October 1979. This granted to UK residents the same freedom as had been available to non-residents since the return to convertibility in 1958. Once controls had been abolished UK residents could borrow from and hold deposits with banks located abroad. Since the Corset applied only to British-based banks, UK residents could readily arrange loans from overseas banks or from the overseas branches of British banks. The control of bank lending through the Corset was rendered ineffective and this was recognized by its abolition in June 1980.

The Conservative Government was determined to reduce the rate of inflation which had resumed an upward trend as the rate of increase of the GDP deflator rose from 11.3 per cent in 1978 to 14.5 per cent in 1979. They were also concerned about the growth of public borrowing. Although the ratio of the PSBR to GDP had fallen back to 3.75 per cent in 1977, after averaging 8.3 per cent in 1975–6, it rose again to 6.5 per cent in 1979, which was a cyclical peak when some decline might have been expected. A reduction in the PSBR was seen as the key factor in reducing the rate of monetary growth which was required for bringing down the rate of inflation (Walters, 1986). (see Tables 4.5 and 4.6 and Fig. 4.4.)

(b)  *The Medium Term Financial Strategy of 1980*

The Medium Term Financial Strategy (MTFS) introduced in the Budget of March 1980 set out to achieve a progressive reduction in the rate of growth of the money supply over a four-year period backed up by a decline in the ratio of the PSBR to GDP. The objective of reducing inflation through reduced monetary growth over the medium term became the dominant feature of macroeconomic policy. Emphasis was placed upon £M3 as the chosen monetary aggregate and fiscal policy was seen as providing essential support for monetary policy. In the subordination of short-run demand management to medium-term control of the price level, and in the dominance of monetary over fiscal policy, the 1980 MTFS was at the opposite extreme to the *Radcliffe Report*. The MTFS implicitly assumed the controllability of £M3 and that the chosen monetary aggregate was stably related to nominal income on account of the predictability of the velocity of circulation. Here again the MTFS contrasted strongly with the views of the Radcliffe Committee.

The strategy emphasized the importance of announcing a path for monetary growth which would serve to generate expectations of a decline in the rate of inflation during the period of the strategy. This assumed that the private sector would come to share the authorities' belief in the connection between the growth of £M3 and the rate of inflation. In addition the announced path for monetary growth served as a discipline for the authorities. The credibility of their strategy would depend upon their resolve in adhering to the announced targets. The authorities therefore surrendered a large measure of discretion in seeking to establish the credibility of their policy in order to influence the expectations of the private sector about the course of inflation. In this respect the MTFS was a considerable development of the one-year monetary targeting introduced by the Labour Government in 1976. A reduction in government borrowing would be needed to prevent upward pressure on interest rates as monetary growth slowed, since rising interest rates would 'crowd-out' private sector investment.

In its reply to the questionnaire prepared by the Treasury and Civil Service Committee (1980) the Treasury emphasized the need for the new policy to be viewed in a medium-term context, contrasting this with shorter run objectives of demand management policies in the 1950s and 1960s. Policy objectives were to be stated in terms of achieving intermediate financial targets rather than ultimate real goal variables, such as the level of output and employment. Incomes policy which had figured prominently in the counter-inflation policy of the previous Labour administration was considered to have been largely ineffective in the medium term and to have been discredited by the wage explosion of 1978–9. In addition it conflicted with the commitment to free-market principles of the Conservative Government. The new strategy was based on a close co-ordination between the PSBR and the growth of £M3 so reinforcing the counterpart approach to the money supply, which the Bank had emphasized in the 1970s. Thus £M3 emerged with increased significance as an intermediate target despite the breakdown of demand functions for broad money in the 1970s and problems of monetary control under CCC.

The Medium Term Financial Strategy unveiled by Chancellor Howe in March 1980 set a target for the growth of £M3 of 7–11 per cent for 1980/1, falling gradually by 1 per cent per annum to 4–8 per cent in 1983/4 (see Table 4.7). The declining rate of monetary growth was to be matched by a parallel decline in the ratio of the PSBR to GDP, which was projected to decline from 3.75 per cent in 1980/1 to 3 per cent in 1981/2, to 1.5 per cent in 1983/4. The decline in the PSBR would help to reduce the rate of monetary growth, since the Treasury claimed a close medium-term connection between the PSBR and the growth of £M3.

£M3 behaved very differently from what the Chancellor had envisaged in his Budget. Its rate of growth accelerated following the abolition of the Corset which was announced in the Budget and became effective in June. The ending of the Corset meant that banks could compete freely for interest-bearing deposits through bidding up the rates of interest payable on wholesale deposits and certificates of deposit. Lending which under the Corset had been diverted from banks' balance sheets through the 'bill leak' now reappeared, swelling both lending and deposits. The result of such reintermediation was an upsurge in the growth of £M3 which grew by 19.4 per cent in 1980/1 against a target range of 7–11 per cent. While the growth of broad money suggested that monetary policy was too lax, other indicators pointed in a quite different direction.[17]

MLR, raised sharply in 1979 to a record 17 per cent in November was held at this level until July 1980. There was a positive interest differential in favour of sterling which was associated with a rise of 25 per cent in the effective exchange rate in both 1979 and 1980. The growth of M1 was checked by the high level of interest rates growth, slowing to only 4.1 per cent in 1980. There was also a sharp slow-down in the growth of M0 (see Figs. 4.1 and 4.5). The rise in the exchange rate was not

---

[17] On the evidence for the tightness of monetary policy, see Walters (1986) and Buiter and Miller (1981b), and for assessments of monetary policy in the 1980s, see Allsop (1985a) and Laidler (1985).

wholly attributable to the tightness of monetary policy. An additional factor was the impact of the second oil price shock at a time when Britain was approaching self-sufficiency in oil production. However a separation between the two forces operating on the exchange rate cannot readily be made.

The strengthening of sterling coincided with a sharp rise in domestic costs. Wage bargainers did not heed the government's warning about absolute priority being given to reducing inflation. The increase in average earnings shot up from 10.1 per cent in 1978 to 18.8 per cent in 1980. The rise in labour costs combined with the strengthening of the nominal exchange rate implied a steeper appreciation of the real exchange rate. There was an estimated rise in UK relative unit labour costs of 40 per cent between 1978 and 1981 which undermined the competitiveness of British industry. The degree of overvaluation of sterling in the second half of 1980 was unprecedented in the post-war period and well in excess of the overvaluation resulting from the return to the gold standard in 1925.

The output measure of GDP declined by 3.3 per cent from its cyclical peak in 1979 to 1981, which was the trough of the recession (see Table 4.5 and Fig. 4.2). Over-appreciation of the exchange rate was the main cause of the severity of the downturn, which also reflected the international recession. This episode confirmed the importance of the exchange rate as the principal channel through which monetary policy influences the economy.

(c) *The Control of the Money Supply*

The unsatisfactory performance of the government's chosen monetary aggregate in 1980 added urgency to the ongoing debate on techniques of monetary control. Monetarists, in particular B. Griffiths, urged the introduction of monetary base control. Under this scheme the Bank of England would determine the wide monetary base (M0) consisting of currency in the hands of the public and bank reserves, leaving the determination of the money supply to the textbook bank money multiplier discussed in the Introduction. The Bank of England favoured the flow-of-funds approach to the money supply. It was particularly concerned that the introduction of a strict form of base control would lead to extreme fluctuations in interest rates which could have disturbing effects on the financial system (Bank of England, 1979). Despite Friedman's powerful support for monetary base control in his evidence to the Treasury and Civil Service Committee,[18] such a scheme was not introduced, but the Bank of England announced some changes in technique in March 1980, which became effective in the following August.[19]

The Bank was to allow market forces a greater role in the determination of interest rates, but would not surrender control over short-term rates. It announced that the long-established practice of creating a shortage of cash in the money market by overissuing Treasury bills and then providing relief to the discount houses on terms of its own choosing would be discontinued. The Bank was to intervene in the bill market to maintain very short-term interest rates within an

[18] Treasury and Civil Service Committee (1980) Memorandum by M. Friedman.
[19] The debate on monetary base control is discussed in D. Savage (1980), Gowland (1982), and Artis and Lewis (1981). This approach to the money supply is used in Fischer (1987). The case for the money supply being endogenous is argued in Dow and Saville (1988).

unpublished band and would influence interest rates through operations in the bill market rather than by lending at the discount window (Bank of England, 1980, 1981a, 1981b). When the new operating techniques came into effect in August, MLR was suspended in recognition of the increased influence of market forces in the money market. The base lending rate of the clearing banks replaced MLR as the main indicator of short-term rates, although the Bank retained the right to reintroduce an administered MLR should circumstances require it.

Reserve ratios were redefined under the new arrangements, the 12½ per cent Reserve Asset Ratio (RAR) and the 1½ per cent cash ratio were abolished. All banks were required to hold ½ per cent of eligible liabilities at the Bank of England, but this ratio was not to be used for purposes of monetary control. Thus the reserves held by commercial banks became effectively non-mandatory, but the Bank still reserved the right to call for Special Deposits. The new system worked out rather differently in practice from what was intended at the time of its introduction for reasons which will be explained later on (Bank of England, 1982b).

(d) *Recasting the MTFS*

The authorities recognized that £M3 was giving misleading signals about the stance of monetary policy in the summer of 1980. Despite the excessive growth of £M3 in relation to its target set, MLR was reduced by 1 per cent to 16 per cent in July, followed by a reduction to 14 per cent in November and to 12 per cent in the March 1981 Budget. The exchange rate responded to the cut in interest rates as the sterling–dollar rate fell by 21.3 per cent from Q4 1980 to Q1 1981 and the effective rate fell by 10.4 per cent (see Fig. 4.5). The rapidity of the decline caused the Bank of England some concern, since too sharp a decline in sterling would threaten its main objective of reducing inflation. The base lending rate of the clearing banks which had effectively replaced MLR as a measure of short-term interest rates went up from 12 per cent in September to 16 per cent in October. Having achieved its purpose of stemming the decline in sterling, the Bank allowed interest rates to resume their downward course as base rates came down gradually to a trough of 8 per cent by November 1982, while the effective exchange rate remained fairly steady. Thus even at an early stage of the MTFS, the authorities were setting interest rates with as much regard for the exchange rate as for monetary aggregates. Interest rates were raised when sterling was weak, and reduced when it was firm.

This relaxation of monetary stance was accompanied by a tightening of fiscal policy. The March 1981 Budget set a target for the PSBR of £10.5bn. for 1981/2 which was a sharp reduction on the out-turn of £12.7bn. during 1980/1. While monetary policy was relaxed to correct the overvaluation of the exchange rate, fiscal policy was tightened to confirm the anti-inflationary aims of the authorities. Such restrictive measures in a recession were unprecedented in British economic policy since the war and were reminiscent of the budgetary contraction introduced by the National Government in the depression of 1932.

During 1981/2 £M3 again overshot its target range rising by 12.8 per cent, but the margin of error was lower than in the previous year. Hence in the April 1982 Budget the government's financial strategy was recast in a more flexible and relaxed form. The target range for monetary growth was raised to 8–12 per cent in

1982/3 and to 7–11 per cent in 1983/4. There was also a rise in the projected ratio of the PSBR to money GDP for 1982/3 from 2.25 per cent to 3.5 per cent. Targets were to be set for narrow money (M1), broad money (£M3), and an even broader aggregate (PSL2), which included deposits with building societies as well as banks. Monetary conditions were to be assessed in the light of the behaviour of three aggregates and the exchange rate. Thus the revised version of the MTFS marked an important change of emphasis whereby policy became more pragmatic and less mechanical, but it was still directed towards the reduction of inflation (Bank of England, 1983).

The rate of growth of money GDP declined from 17.2 per cent in 1980 to 8.8 per cent in 1982, while the inflation rate, measured by the GDP deflator, fell back from 19.8 per cent to 7.5 per cent over the same two years. Deflationary policies within the United Kingdom checked inflation. In addition, contractionary macroeconomic policies in other industrial countries pushed the world economy into recession, bringing about a sharp decline in commodity prices.

The growth of £M3 in 1982/3 turned out to be 11.2 per cent, falling for the first time within its target range of 8–12 per cent, while both M1 and PSL2 grew close to their upper limits. In the March 1983 Budget the target growth rate for all three monetary aggregates set a year earlier at 7.11 per cent was confirmed. The out-turn was that £M3 rose by 9.4 per cent, but both M1 and PSL2 grew slightly in excess of the targeted upper limit.

The Bank of England was able to regulate the growth of £M3 through selling gilt-edged to the non-bank private sector in excess of the PSBR. This offset the growth of credit to the private sector. The demand for credit had proved unresponsive to increases in interest rates and the Bank of England concluded that credit demand was relatively price inelastic (Goodhart, 1984). The authorities preferred to achieve monetary targets by overfunding rather than by forcing interest rates to the levels which might be necessary to curtail the demand for credit. There were however difficulties in the tactics used by the Bank of England. Excess sales of gilts drained the banking system of liquidity, which needed to be offset by open-market purchases of Treasury bills. This implied that the Bank of England dominated the setting of short-term interest rates, contrary to the intentions of the changes in money-market arrangements introduced in 1981. Furthermore, the running down of the market's holdings of Treasury bills meant that the Bank's operations in the bill market came to depend increasingly upon purchases of commercial bills. Critics claimed that the Bank, by selling gilts and buying bills, was distorting the yield curve, by raising long-term rates of interest relative to short-term rates. This could have given rise to arbitrage operations, not unlike the 'round tripping' which occurred under the initial phases of Competition and Credit Control.[20]

(e) *The Introduction of M0 and Pressures on the Exchange Rate*

Lawson became Chancellor in the Conservative Government re-elected in June 1983, in succession to Howe, and a new version of the MTFS was introduced in the

---

[20] For further discussion of overfunding, see Bank of England (1982c) and Goodhart (1989).

1984 Budget (see Table 4.7). The rate of growth of £M3 was set at 6–10 per cent for 1984/5 and projected to decline by 1 per cent per annum over a five-year period to 1988/9. The targeting of both M1 and PSL2 which had exceeded their target range in 1983/4 was discontinued. M0 or the wide monetary base, consisting largely of currency in the hands of the public, was introduced as a new measure of narrow money, with a target range of 4–8 per cent in 1984/5 reducing to 0–4 per cent in 1988/9. The change of target did not herald a switch to monetary base control, and the Bank did not alter its tactics in the money market. The slower rate of growth projected for M0 than for broad money took account of the well-established upward trend in its income velocity on account of economies in the public's holdings of notes and coin (see Fig. 4.1). In the event £M3 grew at 11.9 per cent, still in excess of its upper limit, despite heavy use of overfunding by the Bank of England and M0 also ended up just in excess of its target range.

The main feature of monetary policy during 1984/5 were the two periods of weakness of the pound in the summer of 1984 and early in 1985 (see Fig. 4.5). The Bank responded to the decline in sterling by raising base rates sharply and then reducing them gradually as pressure on the pound abated. This followed the pattern set in the autumn of 1981 and also in the winter of 1982–3.[21]

A contributory factor to the pressure on sterling in 1984/5 was the overshooting of the PSBR, which came out at 3.1 per cent of money GDP against a target of 2.25 per cent. The main reason for the overshoot was the prolonged miners' strike, which served to undermine confidence in the pound in addition to its impact on the government's finances. In the 1985 Budget the Chancellor aimed to put the MTFS back on course by correcting the rise in the PSBR. He announced that the PSBR in 1985/6 would be 2 per cent of money GDP £7bn. in contrast to the out-turn of £10.2bn. in 1984/5. The target range for £M3 was confirmed at 5–9 per cent in 1985/6 falling to 2–6 per cent in 1988/9, and the previously announced path for M0 was also confirmed.

### (f) *The Abandonment of Targets for Broad Money*

The exchange rate strengthened in 1985 in response to both the fiscal tightening in the Budget and the maintenance of a favourable interest differential between sterling and the dollar (see Fig. 4.5). Declining interest rates in the United States enabled the Bank of England to bring down base rates gradually from the crisis level of 14 per cent maintained from January to March to counter the decline in the exchange rate. Judged by the behaviour of both the exchange rate and the level of real interest rates of about 5 per cent, monetary policy could be judged to be fairly tight. However, the growth of the broad monetary aggregate pointed to another conclusion. The growth of £M3 far outstripped its modest target range of 5–9 per cent rising by a massive 16.9 per cent (see Figs. 4.1 and Table 4.7). Faced with the prospect that attempts to curb the growth of broad money by raising interest rates would also push up the exchange rate, the authorities gave priority to the exchange rate over the monetary target. Despite rapid monetary growth, interest rates were gradually reduced from 14 per cent in March to 11½ per cent by the end of July. In

---

[21] The sterling crises of July 1984 and of Jan. 1985 are described in D. Smith (1987), ch. 8.

October the Chancellor announced the suspension of the target for £M3 for the remainder of the financial year.

A contributory factor to the explosive growth of £M3 had been the decision in the 1985 Budget to follow a policy of full funding for the PSBR and to discontinue overfunding. The decision to end overfunding meant that the rate of growth of broad money would be more closely related to the underlying growth of bank lending of about 20 per cent per annum.[22] In view of the reluctance of the authorities to raise interest rates to the level necessary to curtail the demand for bank credit, there was no real alternative to the abandonment of the targeting of £M3.

The authorities were inclined to attribute the rapid growth of both broad money and the demand for bank credit to structural change arising from increased competition and innovation in financial markets, in particular the entry of banks into the rapidly growing market for mortgages. These changes led to a breakdown in the relationship between broad money and nominal GDP, making the targeting of £M3 unsatisfactory (see Fig. 4.1; Bank of England, 1984c, 1986). The suspension of the target for £M3 in October 1985 was followed by the announcement of a one-year target range of 11–15 per cent for its growth in 1986/7 in the 1986 Budget. Since £M3 continued to rise at nearly 20 per cent per annum, as bank lending grew rapidly, no target was set for the growth of broad money in the March 1987 Budget. The remaining monetary aggregate, M0, behaved rather better, its growth of 4.1 per cent barely exceeding the lower limit of its target range of 3–7 per cent in 1985/6, and the target range was set at 2–6 per cent for 1986/7. Also in contrast to the rapid growth of £M3, the PSBR undershot its target of 2 per cent of GDP in 1985/6 with an out-turn of 1.6 per cent.

### (g) *Targeting of the Exchange Rate and Domestic Recovery*

During 1986 and 1987 monetary policy was dominated by exchange rate considerations. The extreme overvaluation of the dollar, which reached a peak in the spring of 1985, to be followed by a period of sustained dollar weakness led to growing interest among policy makers in the stabilization of the major currencies. This was reflected in the discussions in September 1985 between finance ministers at the Plaza in New York on international co-operation over exchange rates, which was followed by the Louvre Accord in the spring of 1987. There was also international co-operation over the speedy reduction of interest rates following the Wall Street crash of October 1987 (Goodhart, 1989).

During 1987 the authorities held sterling within a narrow range about a rate of 3 Deutschmarks to the pound, which implied a gradually rising sterling–dollar rate on account of the continuing weakness of the dollar. This policy was in the spirit of the Louvre Accord on exchange-rate stability and could also be interpreted as a preparation for participation by Britain in the Exchange Rate Mechanism (ERM) of the European Monetary System. There was an interest differential of about 3–4 per cent in favour of sterling against both the dollar and the Deutschmark leading to upward pressure on the exchange rate. The Bank of England responded by holding sterling down, through purchases of foreign exchange as reflected in a massive

---

[22] For a survey of the finance of the PSBR, see Bank of England (1984b).

increase in the official reserves which reached a peak of £25bn. in April. The Bank also discouraged the inflow of capital by reducing interest rates, followed by further reductions in the wake of the collapse of equity prices in October, to cushion the impact of a possible deflationary shock. Base rates came down gradually from 11 per cent in October 1986 to 8.50 per cent in December 1987, followed by further reductions to 7.5 per cent in May 1988.

The decline in short-term interest rates did not take proper account of the vigour of the domestic recovery. The authorities may have attached excessive weight to other targets and to have overlooked the state of the economy. The growth of M0 at 3.5 per cent in 1986/7 was in the mid-point of its target range and the PSBR was smaller than projected. In the absence of a targeted broad monetary aggregate the authorities placed increasing weight on the expected path for the growth of money GDP. This turned out fairly well in 1986/7, but was followed by an overshoot in 1987/8 when money GDP rose by 9.8 per cent compared with an anticipated 7.5 per cent. During 1987/8 M0 rose at the upper limit of its target range, while £M3, now known simply as M3, continued to grow at more than 20 per cent per annum (see Fig. 4.1).

The strength of the economic recovery during 1987 and 1988 took the authorities by surprise with real GDP rising at 4 per cent per annum (see Table 4.5). It was not until June 1988 that the Bank of England reversed the previous policy of reducing interest rates. Base rates went up from 7½ per cent early in June to 13 per cent by end of November. The authorities had finally resolved the conflict between holding down the exchange rate and containing inflation by reaffirming their counter-inflationary policy. They had, however, by their previous policy of lowering interest rates encouraged a massive expansion of credit, which had contributed to the strong recovery of domestic demand. Even M0 grew more rapidly in 1988, rising at nearly 7 per cent per annum in excess of its target range of 1–5 per cent, while the rate of growth of money GDP at 10 per cent per annum in 1988/9 was well in excess of the growth rate of 5.75 per cent projected in the 1988 Budget.

The factors accounting for the rapid growth of broad money and credit in the 1980s are not fully understood (Bank of England, 1986). A major influence appears to have been the increased competitiveness of the banking system.[23] Banks entered the mortgage market and lent freely to the personal sector for house purchase. They competed for funds by setting interest rates payable on deposits at competitive levels. The liability management techniques, which had been developed in the 1970s for borrowing and lending to companies were now extended to the finance of the personal sector, leading to a rise in both the liquid assets and liabilities of households. Bank deposits became a more attractive form in which to hold wealth as even small depositors received interest rates which approximated those ruling in money markets. At the same time real interest rates became positive in the 1980s as inflation declined more rapidly than nominal interest rates (see Fig. 4.3). Banks became close competitors with building societies both in bidding for deposits and in lending on mortgages. M4, which includes building society deposits, became a better measure of broad money than £M3 which excluded them. The effect of such competition was to narrow the margin between borrowing and lending rates, so

---

[23] There is a brief summary of the issues in OECD (1987) and see also Goodhart (1986), Podolski (1986), and Rose (1986).

reducing the cost of credit to the personal sector. Even more important in explaining the growth of household indebtedness was the greater availability of credit following the abolition of hire-purchase restrictions in 1982 and the ending of the rationing of mortgages which was also due to competition between banks and building societies. However, removing restrictions on borrowing by the personal sector has made it more sensitive to the cost of credit as household debt has increased. Also during the 1980s stockbuilding and fixed investment have shown greater sensitivity to interest rates (Burns, 1988).

The authorities attributed the rapid expansion of £M3 in the mid-1980s to structural changes in the credit market. They were less willing to recognize that their policy of reducing interest rates during 1987 and early in 1988 in the interests of exchange-rate policy was a major contributor to credit expansion during this period. In retrospect it would appear that the credit growth in 1986–8 led to overstimulation of the economy resulting in a massive balance of payments deficit and a resurgence of inflation in 1989. It may be concluded that monetary policy was too tight in 1980–1 and too relaxed in 1987–8. Monetary policy has had to bear the main burden of correcting the subsequent overheating of the economy, since fiscal fine tuning remained out of favour with the government. Rising short-term interest rates bore the full weight of restraining domestic demand, since credit restrictions were generally agreed to be of limited use in a highly competitive and deregulated financial system.[24] Monetary policy, which started the decade as a formal exercise in monetary targeting, ended as discretionary policy relying upon adjustments in short-term interest rates with little support from fiscal policy (Bank of England, 1987).

## 8. Conclusion

This chapter has traced the course of monetary policy from 1945 to 1988. There has been a general trend throughout the period for the burdens placed on monetary policy to increase. This trend has partly reflected the evolution of economic ideas as Keynesian demand management has been displaced by a more Monetarist approach to policy making. It has also been a consequence of the floating of sterling in 1972, which greatly increased the scope for monetary policy to influence domestic activity via the sterling prices of traded goods and services. Growing international capital mobility since the 1950s resulted in monetary policy having a reduced impact under fixed exchange rates, but having a major effect with a floating rate. The increasing weight placed on monetary measures by policy makers has also reflected the greater significance attached to the control of inflation, compared with the attainment of real goals, such as output and employment. The move towards a nominal framework for policy has been accompanied by a switch in emphasis from a short-term to a medium-term perspective. The contrast between the Radcliffe Report, with its emphasis on short-run demand management, and the Medium Term Financial Strategy, which concentrates on medium-term objectives set in a nominal framework, illustrates this point.[25]

---

[24] The case for introducing credit controls is examined in Shields (1988).
[25] Burns (1988) emphasizes the nominal income framework of the MTFS and seeks to diminish the role of £M3 in sharp contrast to the 1980 version of the MTFS.

Monetary targeting evolved from the DCE targets introduced on the recommendation of the IMF in 1967 and 1969 and then discontinued. One-year monetary targets introduced by the Labour Government in 1976, after negotiations with the IMF, prepared the way for the medium-term targeting of the PSBR and £M3 in the 1980 MTFS. Failure to achieve targets for broad money did not undermine the creditibility of the MTFS, because of progress made in achieving the final objective of bringing down the rate of inflation.

During the 1960s monetary and fiscal policy were not closely co-ordinated. The adoption of targets for monetary aggregates led to emphasis being placed on the co-ordination between monetary and fiscal policy. Such co-ordination was implicit in the counterpart approach to the determination of £M3 which was developed by the Bank of England and the Treasury.

The striking improvement in the attainment of objectives for the PSBR from 1985/6 increased confidence in sterling and gave greater scope for the reduction in interest rates. Unfortunately the authorities used the freedom too generously, so stirring up a credit boom in 1987 and 1988. The vigorous recovery produced symptoms of a widening balance of payments deficit and rising inflationary expectations, which were reminiscent of the stop–go cycles of the 1950s and 1960s.

# 5

# Trade and the Balance of Payments

## J. FOREMAN-PECK

The balance of payments and the exchange rate repeatedly made headline news in the years after 1945. Underlying the persistent problems with foreign payments were the changing character of world trade and the transformation of domestic politics. The bulk of nineteenth-century international trade had entailed the exchange of manufactures for primary produce. Growing affluence in the Western world after 1945 and accelerated technical progress swelled the trading of manufactures to account for the major part of international exchange of goods. In this increasingly sophisticated world market, British industry was far less comfortable. With some exceptions the Commonwealth nations, intent on industrializing, had less to gain from links with Britain after the war than in the first four decades of the twentieth century. The United Kingdom gradually shifted her pattern of specialization, as the principal market and source of supply for her goods became Western Europe. Entry into the European Community in 1973 was only one stage in a slow but long established process of reorientation of trade and politics.

British governments of the 1950s and 1960s had acquired the commitment to keep down unemployment to an undefined minimum by demand management. Inflationary pressures generated by these policies caused periodic balance of payments crises. Abandoning the par value exchange rate in 1972 merely substituted higher inflation and a falling exchange rate for balance of payments problems. Floating exchange rates failed to be the panacea that many observers of the 1960s believed. As the balance of payments began to bear the full burden of the Common Agricultural Policy and the impact of competition from Common Market industries, the exchange rate swung down and then up in response to the 1979 oil price rise, North Sea oil, and a tightening of monetary policy. British manufacturing industry, which had begun declining absolutely after 1975, contracted as unemployment rose. The exchange rate made a major contribution to these fortunes. After allowing the dollar–sterling rate to fall to an all-time low in the mid-1980s, policy shifted towards an exchange-rate target as a defence against inflation.

The channels through which the exchange rate and the balance of payments interacted with the rest of the economy were many and varied. The first section therefore outlines the fundamental trade linkages and discusses their measurement. The following section concentrates on the proximate causes of trends in, and the structure of, the British balance of trade. The third section considers actual and potential trade policy, asking whether output and employment could have been higher had different policies been pursued. Basic exchange rate concepts are summarized in the fourth section. Section 5 is a brief narrative history of the balance of payments and the exchange rate. The sixth section points to the changing views about the way the economy worked and thus also to the opportunities for policy.

Finally the impact of the oil price shocks of 1973–4 and 1979 on the exchange rate
and the domestic economy are examined.


## 5.1 Basic Trade Concepts

Fig. 5.1 represents the United Kingdom's 'trade block', distinguishing policy instruments in oval boxes from target variables in rectangular. On a number of occasions
since 1945 governments employed tariffs to raise import prices (the 1964–6 import
surcharge), and subsidies to lower export or import competing prices (under the
Common Agricultural Policy). They did so because they wished to boost exports or
to cut back on imports. In principle a government could subsidize exports and so
raise domestic output and employment, if the consequences of financing the subsidy
were ignored. Orderly Marketing Agreements (OMAs), quotas on import volumes,
and voluntary export restraints (VERs) were other policy instruments, all directed
at imports, which are discussed later in the chapter. Governments adopted these
policies sometimes because rising output and employment drew imports into the
economy, while diverting exports to the home market. These trade changes then
caused a deterioration in the balance of payments.

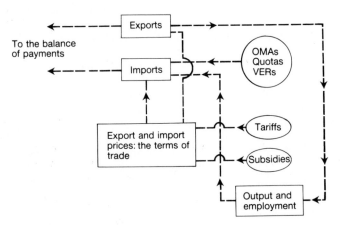

FIG. 5.1.   *The trade block*

*Note*:   Oval boxes indicate policy instruments.


Evidence of this deterioration was and is provided by the trade statistics to which
governments and the market reacted quickly. Unfortunately the numbers recorded
in the trade account were not perfectly accurate measures, especially of exports. In
1969 British exports were found to have been under-recorded by about 2 per cent,
amounting to an estimated £130m. in 1968. Over the affected period 1964–8, the
allowance for under-recording was not sufficient to turn the current balance positive
in any deficit year however. Changes in official statistics complicate matters further.
Statistics of retained imports (as against total imports) were no longer published
after 1963 and therefore these could only be inferred from re-export statistics,
which in turn were discontinued after 1969. As their name suggests, British invisible

exports, earnings from services, were even less easy to measure, official data having to rely on sample surveys.

Whether or not the statistics tell the true story, an upturn in economic activity then feeds through the 'trade block' into 'the balance of payments block' (Fig. 5.2). In particular the balance of trade, one of the three components of the current account of the balance of payments, is affected. In addition to the balance of trade, there is the balance of profits, interests, and dividends, which for the United Kingdom has been positive and increasing in peacetime at least since the beginning of the nineteenth century. The third category that contributes to the current account is the balance of transfers, such as the net foreign exchange cost of money sent home by immigrants and payments by the government for the European Community's Common Agricultural Policy.

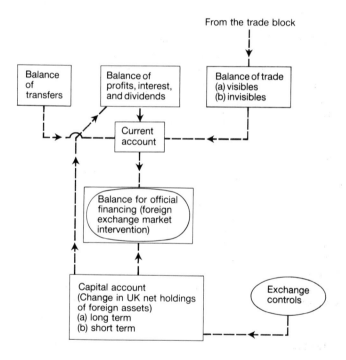

FIG. 5.2.  *The balance of payments block*

At the bottom of Fig. 5.2 the capital account records changes in the stock of foreign assets and liabilities of the United Kingdom. Long-term capital movements are subdivided into direct investment (that is investment by multinational companies), and portfolio investment such as the purchase of foreign shares or government bonds. Outward investment is a debit for the balance of payments because British investors have to buy foreign exchange and sell sterling. The reverse is true for the acquisition of British assets by persons living outside the country; inward investment is a credit. Earnings from the accumulation of past net balances on the capital account feed back to the current account through the balance of profits, interest, and dividends, as shown by the arrow on the far left in the figure.

The sum of net long-term capital movements and the current account has been employed as an indicator of the state of the balance of payments. Short-term capital flows have been extremely volatile, determined by expectations about the future course of the exchange rate or government policy, among other influences. Sterling balances, introduced in Chapter 2, the holdings of working balances of sterling by private traders, foreign banks, and foreign governments, were likely to be sold whenever the future of the British economy or the British balance of payments looked unhealthy enough to endanger the value and earning power of these assets. These expectations were not necessarily correct, and therefore a measure of the United Kingdom's international economic relations such as this indicator, which abstracts from the erratic influences of short term-capital, is desirable, although the feasibility of distinguishing different types of capital investment is questionable.

The final element of the balance of payments, which ensures that the sum of the components is zero, is the balance for official financing.[1] Every acquisition of foreign goods, services, and assets must be financed somehow and for a given exchange rate, the public sector must have paid for what the private sector has not. When the government was prepared to allow the demands and supplies of foreign currency from international economic transactions to be entirely market-determined, there was no change in the level of foreign exchange reserves and the balance for official financing was accordingly zero. Otherwise, a balance of payments deficit meant that foreign exchange reserves were being depleted or foreign official loans were financing the deficit. A policy variable directly impinging upon the balance of payments was exchange control. Exchange controls may influence the entire balance of payments but for most of our period only the capital account was affected. When the government allowed the exchange rate to be largely determined by market forces, as between 1979 and 1981, the balance of payments influenced the exchange rate (in the macroeconomy block, Fig. 5.3) and then the exchange rate determined the balance of payments through export and import prices and the balance of trade. When, as was more usual, the government controlled the exchange rate to achieve other objectives, the direct link between the balance of payments and the exchange rate was broken by offsetting changes in the balance for official financing.

### 5.2 The Trend and Structure of Foreign Trade

#### *The International Trading Environment*

At first sight the international economic environment between the ending of the Korean War and the OPEC oil embargoes at the end of 1973 was extremely favourable for the United Kingdom. World trade grew at an unprecedented rate, both as an accompaniment to the long post-war boom and as trade and currency

---

[1] In fact the components of the balance of payments only sum to zero in the absence of measurement errors, or when the 'balancing items' are zero. Substantial measurement errors persisted throughout the period. In 1988 the £12.3bn. discrepancy in the balance of payments was almost enough to double or to wipe out the recorded £14.6bn. deficit for the year.

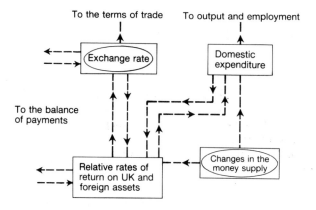

FIG. 5.3. *The macroeconomy block*

restrictions, accumulated in the years between the World Wars and through the financial strains of war, were abandoned. Improved transport, motorways, larger ports, containerization, and roll-on/roll-off systems cut the costs of moving goods between countries. Jet travel and marked reductions in telecommunications costs thanks to satellites, optical fibres, and less spectacular innovations, made much easier the communication on which trade is based. The nineteenth-century predominant pattern of exchanging manufactured goods for food and raw materials was largely supplanted by a remarkable expansion of trade in manufactures between industrial countries.

Conditions deteriorated in the decade after 1973. Trade growth slowed to an average of 3 per cent per annum for all merchandise exports and 4.5 per cent per annum for manufactures, compared with 9 per cent and 11 per cent per annum respectively in the preceeding ten years (GATT, 1985, p. 4). The recession of 1980–3 saw total merchandise export growth drop to an average of 0.5 per cent per annum, including a fall of 3 per cent in 1982. Far less severe was the earlier recession associated with the first oil crisis. Between 1974 and 1975 world merchandise exports also fell by nearly 3 per cent, but strongly recovered the following year. In this less promising period after 1973, Britain's international circumstances changed in directions that would have been regarded as favourable in the 1950s and 1960s. With entry into the Common Market in 1973, the United Kingdom gained access to the rapidly growing economies of Western Europe on better terms than had formerly been available. By the end of the 1970s, North Sea Oil was already heading Britain towards the unique position of an industrial country self-sufficient in oil.

### The Loss of Market Share

Despite advantages of first a booming world economy, followed by entry to the Common Market and the tapping of North Sea oil, British trade performance was generally weak and the balance of payments and the exchange rate were regarded for most of the period as an unfortunate constraint upon economic policy. As Fig. 5.4 shows, the share of British exports in world trade declined for nearly three decades, with only a temporary reversal in 1967, when the pound was devalued against the dollar by 14.7 per cent. Initially this trend could be explained as an inevitable consequence of the recovery of Britain's most severely war-damaged industrial competitors. By the end of the 1950s any such explanation for the continuing loss of market share lacked credibility. Had British exports of manufactures (which accounted for most of UK exports) grown at the same rate as world exports of manufactures, row 1 of Table 5.1 indicates that sales would have decelerated in the second half of the 1950s and accelerated strongly in the 1960s. In fact export growth increased in each successive sub-period (line 5) because competitiveness did not fall so markedly between 1955–9 as it had in 1950–5. That is because the recovery of Britain's industrial competitors took place mainly in the first half of the fifties.

TABLE 5.1. *Attribution of percentage changes in the volume of UK exports of manufactures 1950–1971*

|                        | 1950–5 | 1955–9 | 1963–7 | 1967–71 |
|------------------------|--------|--------|--------|---------|
| World market growth    | +38.5  | +26.3  | +45.8  | +57.78  |
| Area                   |        |        | −2.2   | −4.35   |
| Commodity composition  | −6.4   | −4.9   | +0.71  | +0.072  |
| Market share           | −29.6  | −12.5  | −33.0  | −9.32   |
| Actual increase        | 2.6    | 8.8    | 11.3   | 44.15   |

*Sources*:   Calculated from Maizels (1963) and Batchelor, Major, and Morgan (1980).

*Note*:   Columns may not sum because of rounding errors.

In each period the United Kingdom producers lost potential exports by concentrating their efforts on countries (line 2) that either had below-average growth rates or had adopted import-substitution policies. As Chapter 2 demonstrated, British trade at the beginning of the period was to a great extent conducted with the Commonwealth and the sterling area. Unlike all other major Western European countries, this distributed British exports relatively evenly around world markets, with no single country, even in 1972, taking as much as 10 per cent of her exports. By contrast, 13 per cent of West German exports were sold to France and 10 per cent to the Netherlands. France sent over one-fifth of her total exports to Germany and more than one-tenth each to Belgium and Italy. Despite adverse export market trends, Table 5.1 shows clearly that both area and (favourable) commodity patterns played only a small role in the United Kingdom's loss of world markets in the first three sub-periods.[2] The principal contribution came from a loss of competitiveness reflected in a falling market share (line 4), holding constant the effects of area and commodity. Competitiveness was markedly increased by the 1967 devaluation and the subsequent macroeconomic measures taken to ensure that the exchange rate change was effective.

Unlike Britain, the six countries of the EEC in the period 1967–71 experienced very substantial positive area effects, with negative market competitiveness and

Although Table 5.1 does not distinguish area from commodity effects in the first two periods, a similar exercise by Wells (1964) for 1955–9 supports this proposition.

commodity effects (Batchelor, Major, and Morgan 1980). EEC trade grew primarily between member countries because of market integration. If the EEC had been classified as one country, and only extra-EEC trade had been counted as international trade (by analogy, say, with the United States), then the growth of 'world' trade would have been slower and Britain's loss of measured market share would almost certainly have been reversed between 1967 and 1971; the 1967 devaluation would have appeared even more effective.

Other, poorer, nations were industrializing and competing in products, especially textiles, which were important British exports. Perhaps then this relative decline was merely the 'cost of an early start', which some economic historians consider had already been a problem for the British economy between 1870 and 1914. Beenstock (1983) identified these costs as a more general difficulty for all advanced industrial countries by the 1970s in the face of the export growth of the newly industrializing economies, Brazil, and the South East Asian 'gang of four', Singapore, Hong Kong, Taiwan, and South Korea. The new industrializers, Beenstock contends, forced up commodity prices relative to prices of the now cheaper manufactured goods. Because manufacturers are typically capital-intensive, this price change reduced the share of the returns to capital (profits) in industrial countries' incomes and raised the wage share. Deindustrialization followed in developed countries, together with 'mismatch unemployment', as labour adjusted only sluggishly to changed employment opportunities. As industrial production became more efficient in LDCs, capital was diverted from less productive uses in developed countries and enhanced the externally owned debt of the newly industrializing countries.

A comparison with the course of West Germany's share of world trade suggests this explanation will not do for Britain's experience. Fig 5.4 shows German export share continuing to rise throughout the period except when world trade patterns were particularly distorted by the oil price hikes of 1973 and 1979, and long after any conceivable post-war recovery effect must have been exhausted.[3] It is easier to identify the symptoms than the causes of the British loss of competitiveness, but even that is by no means simple. British prices (the GDP deflator), rose relative to those in the rest of the world. The British real exchange rate, the purchasing power of sterling relative to other currencies, therefore also increased on trend during the fixed exchange rate period, reaching a local maximum in 1966 (Fig. 5.5). Devaluation the following year entirely counterbalanced this sustained rise, but the trend quickly resumed until the pound was floated in 1972. British goods in general then were apparently becoming less price competitive throughout the 1950s until 1967. The same was true for Western Europe as a whole between 1955 and 1972 (Saunders, 1975, p. 12). 'Apparently', because the measured rate of inflation for exports was probably more upward biased than for imports. Exports are principally manufactured goods in which quality improvement is generally more rapid than in primary products. Official price indices do not usually correct for such quality changes. For that reason the deterioration of British quality competitiveness, broadly interpreted, is concealed. Other evidence is available though. Waiting times for delivery were often long, encouraging both foreign and domestic customers to switch to other suppliers. As world incomes rose, the propensity to buy British

---

[3] The exception to this generalization about war recovery is the Olson (1982) effect. Possibly the social regeneration which stemmed from the destruction of traditional social institutions provided a much longer lasting boost to economic activity.

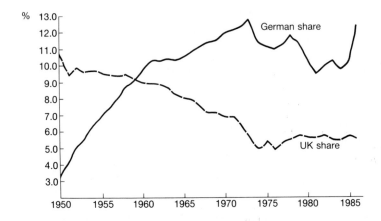

FIG. 5.4. *The share of world merchandise trade of the United Kingdom and Germany (calculated from IMF International Financial Statistics)*

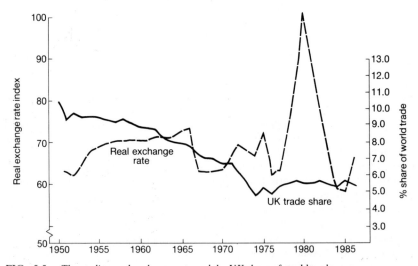

FIG. 5.5. *The sterling real exchange rate and the UK share of world trade*

goods fell (Thirlwall, 1986). That most likely reflected a failure to maintain British quality competitiveness, since manufactured goods are continually being improved and modified.

Even if British goods were becoming more expensive for a given quality relative to those produced elsewhere, that was not necessarily harmful to the balance of payments. An improvement in the terms of trade, a rise in export prices relative to import prices, such as occurred in the 1950s, meant that British resources could earn more foreign goods through producing for export than formerly. On the other hand, given that the demand for British exports and the British demand for imports were responsive to price changes, export volumes fell relative to what they would otherwise have been, and import volumes increased. With a fixed foreign exchange value of the currency the impact on the current account of the balance of payments might have been favourable none the less, at least in the short run, before the full price responsiveness effects worked their way through the markets. Higher sterling export prices with, say, a fixed dollar rate of exchange, will earn more dollars as long as there is only a smaller proportionate decline in foreign demand. Cheaper imported goods priced in dollars require a smaller dollar expenditure, as long as the demand for these dollar imports is not price elastic. Unfortunately, the failure of British industry to supply the competitive mix of price and quality *did* exert pressure on the balance of payments through losing foreign and domestic market shares. So long as import controls were maintained, the actual demand for imports could not be price elastic and the current account was protected from the underlying tendencies of the British economy. Once controls were removed, as they were by the end of the 1950s, the demand for imports, principally imports of finished manufactures, proved extremely price elastic and balance of payments problems became more pressing.

This cause of the balance of payments difficulties was long unrecognized because most statistical measures of the responsiveness of import price elasticities derived from time series data underestimated the effects that would follow from relative price changes and tariff reductions. The impact of tariff cuts was greater than expected because the market saw them as permanent, because they were well publicized and because they often involved the reduction or abolition from near-prohibitive levels. Moreover many studies considered imports in excessively broad groupings and employed inappropriate relative price indices (which for example failed to indicate tariff change effects).[4] Compared with those obtained from time series econometrics, Scott's (1963) disaggregated study of UK imports calculated much higher price elasticities for UK manufactured imports, which appear to accord better with subsequent post-war experience.

Consumers were getting what they wanted: cheaper foreign goods of given quality than could be bought on the British market. Against this gain must be weighed the fact that British manufacturing, failing the market test at the prevailing exchange rate, was contracting relatively during the 1950s and 1960s and absolutely during the 1970s and 1980s, measured by the number of people employed. Had British industrial performance been better, more jobs would have been lost from manufacturing (Rowthorne and Wells, 1987), productivity growth potential in that sector was so high relative to the growth of demand for manufactures. The problem was rather the low level of manufacturing output, an issue which will be considered later in the discussion of North Sea oil.

Lack of competitiveness lost Britain markets at home and abroad. But rising

---

[4] Considering a group of 'semi-manufactures' adds together unwrought nonferrous metals, which show substantial price variations but which are rather price inelastic, with other categories having the opposite characteristics (Barker, 1976, pp. 170–1). Even in the mid-1920s British tariff experience suggested high import price elasticity of demand for motor vehicles (Foreman-Peck, 1979), but it was not until the later 1950s and 1960s that the consequence of this elasticity was fully exposed.

import penetration was a universal experience of industrial countries, a consequence of trade liberalization encouraging an expanding division of labour. By the 1970s world trade/GNP ratios, so far as they can be measured, had returned to the levels attained in 1913 (Grassman, 1980). Since trade between EEC states was by then becoming even freer than it had been before the First World War, higher ratios were attained subsequently. The British problem was that, although from the 1960s and especially in the 1970s, the proportion of national income and output exported increased (Table 5.2), it did not rise fast enough to match the British desire to import. Between 1974 and 1985 manufactured consumer good imports more than doubled. Import penetration, measured by the ratio of import value to apparent consumption, rose from 19 to 36 per cent. The increase was particularly rapid between 1979 and 1982. Larger retailers were more import-dependent but they were not obviously the initiators of this trend. A questionnaire in the mid-1980s asking retailers why they preferred foreign sources, yielded the most common reply (40%) of 'greater variety'—the products they wanted were just not available in the United Kingdom (Morgan, 1988).

TABLE 5.2. *The percentage composition of United Kingdom and German merchandise exports 1935–1983*
(selected product groups)

|  | 1935–8 | 1948 | 1953 | 1963 | 1973 | 1983 |
|---|---|---|---|---|---|---|
| *United Kingdom* | | | | | | |
| Textiles | 23.0 | 11.2 | 12.6 | 6.2 | 4.7 | 2.1 |
| Non-electrical machinery | 9.0 | 14.0 | 15.4 | 21.0 | 19.4 | 17.0 |
| Transport equipment | 6.8 | 14.2 | 14.4 | 15.4 | 12.5 | 9.0 |
| Iron and steel | 6.5 | 4.1 | 5.3 | 5.0 | 3.5 | 2.2 |
| Chemicals | 6.3 | 6.8 | 6.9 | 9.0 | 10.4 | 11.4 |
| Electrical machinery | 3.7 | 6.6 | 6.7 | 7.8 | 6.5 | 5.4 |
| Scientific instruments etc. | 0.6 | 1.0 | 1.0 | 1.8 | 2.8 | 2.4 |
| Minerals, fuels, lubricants | 9.0 | 3.3 | 5.7 | 4.0 | 3.0 | 21.7 |
| Manufactures as a proportion of total exports | 74.4 | 85.2 | 81.3 | 82.5 | 83.9 | 65.9 |
| Merchandise exports as a % of GNP | 9.8 | 15.1 | 17.2 | 15.4 | 19.1 | 23.2 |
| *Germany* | | | | | | |
| Textiles | | | 4.5 | 3.6 | 4.5 | 3.2 |
| Non-electrical machinery | | | 21.0 | 22.6 | 21.7 | 18.5 |
| Vehicles | | | 7.7 | 16.0 | 16.2 | 18.6 |
| Iron and steel | | | 7.6 | 7.8 | 7.4 | 4.7 |
| Minerals, fuels, lubricants | | | 11.1 | 5.6 | 2.5 | 3.4 |
| Chemicals | | | 10.9 | 11.3 | 11.8 | 13.1 |
| Electrical machinery | | | 6.3 | 8.0 | 8.8 | 7.3 |
| Instruments | | | 2.4 | 3.5 | 2.8 | 2.1 |
| Total exports/GNP | | | 15.9 | 15.6 | 23.3 | 31.2 |
| Merchandise exports as a % of GNP | | | 11.12 | 15.3 | 19.6 | 25.7 |

*Source*: UK Annual Abstracts of Statistics, UN Yearbooks of International Trade Statistics.

*Multinational Companies*

At the same time that import penetration was rising, so also was foreign ownership of British manufacturing industry. Employment in foreign owned manufacturing subsidiaries apparently doubled between 1953 and 1963, reaching about 7 per cent of the total by the second date. As a proportion of net manufacturing output, foreign companies' production was 10 per cent in 1963 and 17.7 per cent in 1988.

Multinational companies had already a well-established tradition in the United Kingdom, but two elements gave added impetus to their expansion and changed the nature of their activity after 1945. First, increasing affluence boosted the demand for the manufactured consumer goods in which these firms so often specialized. Second, much early foreign direct investment had been a way of leaping over import restrictions or, to a lesser extent, avoiding transport costs. Unable to sell exports to Britain foreigners chose to establish plants. These 'horizontal' multinationals substituted for trade. With the liberalization of trade, such strategies became unnecessary. Instead, beginning with the formation of Ford Europe in 1968, multinational companies extended their internal division of labour by specializing national plants in particular processes. Ford's Bridgend factory manufactured engines for much of Europe, while the components were assembled on the continent and the finished cars, with Welsh engines, were exported back to Britain. This intra-firm trade by 'vertical' multinationals allowed the companies to utilize scale economies in increasingly integrated supranational markets (Casson, 1986).

Although foreign investment grew rapidly in Britain, the EEC proved an even stronger attraction for US multinationals. Between 1960 and 1970, US investment in the UK relative to US investment in both the EEC and the UK fell from 60 per cent to almost 40 per cent. By 1976 the ratio had declined to 32 per cent. Thereafter the relative attractiveness of the UK increased somewhat. Allowing for some lags, the pattern is consistent with the vertical investment for an integrated European market outweighing any horizontal investment. The partial recovery of the ratio after 1976 was a lagged reaction to the British admission to the European Community in 1973 (Blair, 1987).

Most foreign direct investment originated in the United States, but other countries' investment grew more rapidly, often in a rather different pattern. Not until 1969 was the first Japanese manufacturing subsidiary, Universal Fasteners, installed in the United Kingdom. Throughout the period Japanese foreign direct investment was concentrated in banking, insurance, and export merchanting activities. The Japanese appreciated the British talent for individualistic innovation rather than their ability to work in groups. They therefore acquired and built up assets in sectors where small units were viable (Dunning, 1986). Only with the rising yen of the 1980s did the Japanese come to see Britain as an attractive manufactures export platform for the Common Market.

By the late 1960s foreign direct investment had sufficiently penetrated the economy to give rise to some concern. The economic and strategic implications of foreign ownership of three-quarters of the breakfast-cereal and vacuum-cleaner industries may have been insignificant, but that was less obviously true of office machinery (computers), of nickel, or perhaps even of tractors. Foreign control of key technologies might conceivably have turned the United Kingdom into a 'branch plant economy'. In such an economy new technology is generated in another country and the deployment of this technology is potentially controlled by foreign governments whose interests do not necessarily coincide with those of the host state. By the early 1980s one-half of the motor industry's sales were those of foreign-owned companies, as were more than two-fifths of sales of office machinery and data processing, more than one-third of chemicals, almost one-third of instrument engineering, and one-quarter of mechanical engineering.

As British employment and industrial capacity declined during the 1970s and 1980s, fears about possible harmful effects of inward foreign direct investment gave way to vigorous efforts to woo multinational plants by official organizations such as the Invest in Britain Bureau. Foreign companies had consistently showed higher returns and productivity than the average domestic company in the same sector (Steuer et al., 1973). Now this was more likely to be interpreted as due to superior management techniques from which Britain could learn, than evidence of skill in exploiting buyers. Foreign management were able to conduct their industrial relations more harmoniously than indigenous teams (Buckley and Enderwick, 1985); the British were now inclined to welcome this improvement in performance.

Much government aid had been aimed at attracting foreign enterprise to regions of high unemployment. Possibly such areas might be especially vulnerable to multinational bargaining for state support. In fact the prosperous south-east depended most on multinational companies for employment in the early 1980s; foreign-owned companies accounted for one-quarter of manufacturing value added (a proportion matched by Wales and East Anglia) and one-fifth of employment. Repatriation of profits and royalty or service payments on such a volume of investment could strain the balance of payments. The evidence shows that payments to the United Kingdom during the 1960s were double payments from the UK overseas. Yet it was the outward foreign direct investment, generating these earnings for the UK, that attracted more adverse official attention by the 1960s for balance of payments reasons. The Reddaway report judged that every £100 invested abroad yielded £9 annual income to the nation. This proved insufficient to repel government restrictions on new overseas investment. Only in 1979 were all controls on outward investment finally removed. Artis and Taylor (1989) found the effect on direct investment of abolition of controls small compared with portfolio investment.

### The Commodity Structure of Trade

What Britain exported and imported reflected the pattern of opportunities offered by the domestic economy relative to the rest of the world. Changes in her commodity structure of trade therefore provide evidence about the sources of the loss of competitiveness and the impact of the major external shocks to the economy. British foreign trade was traditionally highly specialized especially in textile exports—with their concomitant demands for raw material imports. By comparison Germany showed a more balanced commodity structure of exports at the beginning of the twentieth century (Foreman-Peck, 1983, pp. 79–81), but became specialized to approximately the same, now reduced, degree as the United Kingdom (Table 5.2).[5]

---

[5] Commodity concentration may be measured by the H (Hirschman–Herfindahl) index which is the sum of the squared shares of exports in the total. The numbers for Table 5.2 are:

While commodity concentration may maximize the gains from trade in an unchanging world economy, it may also render the exporter vulnerable to unexpected shifts in market demand. Table 5.2 shows that the two most radical transformations of the structure of British exports were those associated with the reallocation of resources during the Second World War and immediately afterwards, and the adjustment necessitated by North Sea oil. Over the war period the low productivity retailing sector, which largely supplied non-tradeable services, was scoured for labour for the armed services. At the end of the war much of this labour did not return to retailing. Engineering employment expanded markedly, a change reflected in the increasing importance of exports of transport equipment, and electrical and non-electrical machinery. Rationing of scarce iron and steel to favour exports in the late 1940s and heavy taxation of consumer durables sold on the home market made a major contribution to this reallocation. The origins of the best selling Land Rover/Range Rover can be directly traced to the impact of these policies on the motor industry.[6] In passenger cars the United Kingdom achieved the most remarkable rise in world export market share between 1937 and 1950 (Maizels, 1963). Household durables and chemicals, both sectors with considerable growth potential, also increased their shares of world exports, but Switzerland and the United States, performed even better in these commodities. The share of textiles, where British long-term prospects for successfully competing with Japan and the newly industrializing nations were not favourable, fell sharply between 1935/8 and 1948. By historical standards, the industrial transformation indicated by the trade data was very substantial for such a short period.

Equally radical was the change between 1973 and 1983 in manufacturing as a proportion of total exports, a fall from over four-fifths to two-thirds. Most of this contraction can be traced to the reaction to North Sea oil which came on stream in 1976. The oil was more expensive than imports at world prices before 1973 but did save an enormous import bill. Inevitably Britain's existing pattern of international specialization was disturbed. The direct contribution of oil and gas to GDP reached 4.4 per cent by 1980 (Hall and Atkinson, 1983). The balance of payments impact of £7.5bn. by 1980 changed the relative competitiveness of British and foreign goods by driving up the exchange rate. On the import side (Table 5.3) this de-industrialization, and technical developments, reduced raw material requirements from 12.4 per cent to 2.3 per cent of imports. The European Community's Common Agricultural Policy, and low income elasticities of demand cut food imports from 19.5 per

| | 1900 | 1935/8 | 1953 | 1963 | 1973 | 1983 |
|---|---|---|---|---|---|---|
| United Kingdom | 0.205 | 0.083 | 0.076 | 0.090 | 0.073 | 0.101 |
| Germany | 0.036 | n/a | 0.086 | 0.107 | 0.104 | 0.096 |

[6] Before the war the Rover Company had found a small market niche in staid cars for the British middle class, which were virtually impossible to sell outside the country. The threat of being unable to resume production encouraged the directors quickly to develop a product that could be used on the farm both as a tractor-substitute and as a car. Because of the steel shortage the body was to be made of aluminium. The Rover Company was small and time was short, and therefore no investment was made in body shell pressings; instead plates were to be bolted over a frame and the body shape was designed accordingly. The resulting product, the Land Rover, proved an extraordinarily saleable export. In the following three decades more were manufactured than the entire Rover car output in the first 80 years of the twentieth century.

TABLE 5.3. *The percentage composition of United Kingdom imports 1935–1983*

|                          | 1935–8 (av.) | 1948 | 1953 | 1963 | 1973 | 1983 |
|--------------------------|--------------|------|------|------|------|------|
| Food beverages and tobacco | 43.4 | 41.2 | 38.6 | 34.8 | 19.5 | 6.4 |
| Basic materials          | 24.4 | 29.2 | 29.9 | 20.5 | 12.4 | 2.3 |
| Minerals fuels and lubricants | 4.6 | 7.5 | 9.3 | 11.7 | 10.9 | 10.7 |
| Manufactures             | 19.8 | 17.4 | 18.5 | 32.5 | 56.2 | 68.0 |
| (finished manufactures)  |      |      | (6.1) | (13.5) | (29.2) |      |
| Imports % of GNP         | 18.6 | 19.8 | 22.5 | 17.7 | 25.0 | 25.3 |

*Source*:  Mitchell (1988).

cent to 6.4 per cent and manufactured imports rose from 52.2 per cent to 68 per cent of the total between 1973 and 1983.[7] Each of these shifts on the import side began earlier though. Imports of raw materials grew only slowly after 1965 because the expansion of some domestic supplies, such as aluminium from the smelter in Anglesey and pulp, from the mill in Fort William, substituted for them.

An indication of the influences upon the commodity structure of trade, albeit one that ignores policy measures such as import controls and government export subsidies, is offered by the Hecksher Ohlin theory (Ethier, 1983). According to this theory, market forces will encourage economies to specialize in the production for export of goods and services which require a great deal of resources that are relatively abundant in those individual economies. In return, economies will import products which are intensive in resources that are relatively scarce. Given the different national endowments of resources, international trade compensates for the inability of these resources to be moved between nations to permit their optimum combination in production by moving the goods they make instead.

Viewed in this light it seems not to matter in what particular group of products a nation specializes; one commodity structure is no more preferable than another. But that conclusion is not necessarily correct, once the possibility is conceded that the market does not always allocate resources ideally. Certain types of product or resources might present greater or lesser opportunities for future income generation and the market may be unable to capitalize all these opportunities in asset prices. Capitalization of the benefits from investment in humans is impossible because people cannot be bought and sold. New products are likely to constitute the most rapidly growing sector of trade between high income countries and these goods and services typically are research- or skill-intensive. Temporary monopoly rents may well raise the rate of return on such products. A country that lacks suitable means of overcoming the inadequacies of market organization will underinvest in the research and skills that form the basis of the sectors with the potential for fastest expansion.

[7] The years chosen for comparison are those when the Korean War ended and the long post-war boom began (1953), the last full year of the 13 years of Conservative rule (1963), the end of the post-war boom with the first oil crisis (1973), and the end of the depression caused by tight monetary policy and the first oil crisis (1983). There are decadal intervals between benchmark years which display changes of comparable pace.

There is some reason to believe that between 1880 and 1935 British industry was indeed handicapped by underinvestment in skills. Those industries that employed more unskilled labour and capital in their production processes showed a higher propensity to export, and industries that employed more skilled labour exported less (Crafts and Thomas, 1986). Towards the end of the period covered by the present chapter this pattern had changed. By 1979 the interindustry distribution of exports showed that sectors with higher proportions of employees with professional and technical competence and with higher earnings, exported more (A. D. Smith *et al.*, 1982). British industry had gone some way to rectifying earlier deficiencies in investment in human capital, but the world economy had changed even faster. In the intervening period both the skill-intensity and the research and development intensity of British imports increased faster than those of exports (Katrak, 1982).

Britain's comparative advantage, her low opportunity costs relative to the rest of the world, may have been deteriorating in products that used skilled labour, or research and development, so that exports were discouraged. Education and management institutions may have been ineffective in encouraging investment in the appropriate human capital and motivating workers, relative to those in other countries. Such institutional deficiencies would constrain the innovation which is crucial to ensure that appropriate skills are available to maintain the economy's competitiveness. Human capital requirement will be continually changing in a growing economy. Institutions need to be able to cope with retraining and reallocation, and attitudes of management and labour force must be flexible if skills are not always to be partly obsolete by the time they are available.

A country which innovates first will establish an export potential which will gradually be eroded as other economies imitate. The initial 100 per cent export share of the new product will decline but another innovating product or technique may come to the leader country's rescue. An economy that maintains a fixed commitment to a particular sector must be continually innovating, otherwise the sector's lead will be lost and the economy's comparative advantage will shift to another industry. Table 5.2 shows that German export shares were rather more stable than British.[*] Germany's stronger merchandise export performance between 1953 and 1983 should be associated with more rapidly changing category shares at a high level of disaggregation, as a measure of the ability to reallocate resources to new products as well as to innovate. In fact Germany showed less 'flexibility' than the United Kingdom in 1963–7 and 1967–71 even with a fine commodity classification (Batchelor, Major, and Morgan, 1980, p. 62). Japan and Canada, which increased their market shares in world exports of manufactures the most, scored highly on this measure.

Technical innovations very specific to particular types of products explain the paradox that the trade data appears to show countries exporting and importing similar goods from each other. Comparative advantage was no longer a characteristic of broad groupings. Obviously the magnitude of this intra-industry trade depends upon how finely the products are classified. Even with very precise product specifications however, by the 1970s the nature of Britain's specialization had become

[*] One approach to measuring variability is to sum the absolute values of the changes in the category percentages. Batchelor, Major, and Morgan (1980) sum all the increases of more than 0.1 per cent in a country's export share on the grounds that the decreases must exactly offset the increases.

hard to define. In metalworking machine tools, the British trade statistics distinguished nearly 50 categories. More than half a million pounds of trade between the United Kingdom and Germany took place in each of eighteen types and in fifteen of these there were both substantial exports to Germany and imports from her (Saunders, 1975, p. 28). Milling machines, automatic chucking lathes, and grinding machines alone made up one-fifth of the trade in each direction.

Pairwise international comparisons of industrial productivity give some indications of the causes of export performance, bearing in mind that it is not the absolute productivity of an industry but the productivity of an industry relative to others in the same country that determines the pattern of international specialization. During the 1960s and 1970s labour productivity in the manufacturing industry showed that, whereas US industries were able to utilize scale economies at the plant level, British industries were not, presumably because of industrial relations problems (Davies and Caves, 1987). Industries which undertook more research and development were more productive, as were industries more exposed to international competition. More concentrated industries were less productive, larger markets encouraged larger plants and higher prices reduced market size. These observations are consistent with a model in which trading advantage goes to firms with larger markets, by permitting greater utilization of scale economies, and spreading overheads such as research and development. British industry could not expect favourable effects from British entry to the Common Market unless they learned how to manage larger plants; only then could British firms gain from a domestic market the size of the United States, with, among other benefits to the consumer, an increase in competitive pressure which increases efficiency and reduces prices.

*Invisible Trade and International Transfers*

Before the Second World War the balance of payments of the United Kingdom had been buoyed up by large net earnings of invisibles and little in the way of transfers abroad (Table 5.4). This surplus was greater than that earned in 1963 and more than covered the considerable deficit on merchandise trade, which was smaller both in 1963 and 1953 than the average for 1935–8.

Shipping maintained or enhanced its contribution to the balance of payments over the war period. 1953 debits were three times the pre-war average whereas credits increased by considerably more. This favourable position was not to last. The British mercantile marine, which in 1960 had consisted of 2,950 ships of over 500 tons, comprised only 693 vessels in 1985. Average tonnage of these ships was rising so that total gross tonnage did not decline on trend until after 1975. But in the following ten years the tonnage fell by almost two-thirds to 12,208m. tons, one-third below the 1960 figure. High British wages relative to labour productivity encouraged ship-owners to replace British seamen by those from countries where average wages were much lower. A legal obligation that British registered shipping should be manned by a substantial proportion of British seamen sealed the fate of the industry, which the transport demands of the 1982 Falklands War highlighted. Civil aviation generated a surplus on invisibles but one quite inadequate to balance the deficit on sea transport from the 1970s. Foreign travel also showed a deficit by

TABLE 5.4. *UK invisible balance of trade, selected items, 1935–1983*
(£M)

| | 1935–8 (average) | 1953 | 1963 | 1973 | 1983 |
|---|---|---|---|---|---|
| Shipping: debits | 79.25 | 242 | 671 | 2,174 | 4,099 |
| | +22.75 | +134 | −11 | −122 | −1,076 |
| credits | 102.0 | 376 | 660 | 2,052 | 3,023 |
| Interest profits and dividends: debits | 34.75 | 211 | 405 | 1,502 | 10,525 |
| | +193.25 | +75 | +387 | +1,396 | +1,948 |
| credits | 228 | 286 | 782 | 2,898 | 12,473 |
| Government: debits | 21.75 | 218 | 429 | 941 | 1,302 |
| | −14.25 | −56 | −389 | −798 | −832 |
| credits | 7.5 | 162 | 40 | 143 | 470 |
| Financial and other services: debits | | 218 | 273 | 727 | 3,549 |
| | | +123 | +233 | +1,204 | +5,771 |
| credits | | 341 | 506 | 1,330 | 9,320 |
| Invisible balance | +339.75 | +195 | +162 | +1,460 | +3,632 |
| Visible balance | −266.25 | −219 | −49 | −2,295 | −716 |
| Total current balance | −27.75 | +179 | +113 | −835 | +2,916 |

*Source:* Annual Abstract of Statistics.

the 1970s. Financial and other services were growing, with nearly a £5.5bn. balance in 1983. These counterbalanced the merchandise deficit.

In 1973 UK exports of services were nearly 11 per cent of GDP whereas Germany's exports were just under 5 per cent. Although Germany continued to run a deficit on trade in services into the 1980s, as a proportion of GDP it was falling. By contrast, over the period from 1973 to 1984, the British surplus as a proportion of GDP fell. Invisibles appear to have been more price elastic than visible trade. Exports of goods rose much more strongly than services. Consequently Britain's changing pattern of trade cannot be primarily attributed to the development of a mature economy in which employment moves from manufactures to services because that is the allocation which high-income consumers demand in an advanced technology economy. Even British competitiveness in services was deteriorating.

The big change in the immediate post-war period came in government invisibles transactions, where non-Empire military commitments, principally in West Germany, placed an increasing strain on the balance of payments at a time when net invisible earnings from shipping were disappearing. The difficulties of bearing the costs of maintaining a rather modest military presence abroad has sometimes been represented as a symptom of national decline.[9] That view fails to take into account the increasing burden of a high technology military commitment overseas on a scale which had not been sustained in peacetime in the heyday of the Victorian economy and empire. Indian taxes, not British, paid for the British Army in India during the nineteenth century and therefore no British demand for foreign exchange was generated by these forces.

With accession to the Common Market in 1973, an additional major invisible debit was added to the balance of payments, transfers under the European Community's Common Agricultural Policy (CAP). Agricultural spending was the most important sector of the EC budget, accounting for two-thirds of expenditure in 1972 and in 1983, and more in the intervening period. The principal beneficiaries were therefore those countries with the largest agricultural sectors. The EC's budgetary method placed the greatest burden upon countries which imported much of their food and/or raised a high VAT revenue. Two estimates for 1978 of the costs of CAP transfers for Britain, were $1,500m. and $1,700m., say 0.5 per cent of GNP. With the third lowest GDP per head in the later 1970s, the United Kingdom was paying among the highest net contributions.

Government transfers, over and above a general government deficit of £1bn. amounted to a net payment of £1.9bn. in 1983, more than five times the 1973 balance. If the onset of these payments had not coincided with the windfall gain of North Sea oil and a tight monetary policy, a considerable depreciation of the exchange rate could have been expected.

---

[9] In 1967 Philip Larkin, bemoaning military expenditure cuts, wrote:

> Next year we shall be living in a country
> That brought its soldiers home for lack of money.
> The statues will be standing in the same
> Tree-muffled squares, and look nearly the same.
> Our children will not know it's a different country.
> All we can hope to leave them now is money.

## 5.3 Trade Policy

*Protection in the 1950s*

Domestic industry can be selectively protected from foreign competition by taxes (tariffs) or quotas on imports, by subsidies, or by discriminatory regulations or conditions, such as unique domestic electricity supply voltage in the case of electrical appliances. If a government is concerned with general protection, then in most instances the choice of a different exchange rate will do the trick more effectively, encouraging exports as well as reducing import competition. During the 1950s the principal motivation for the British Government's protectionist policies was support for the balance of payments. The question then arises why they chose protection and how well it worked.

During the 1930s international trade and prosperity had been reduced by tariff and quota wars in which countries retaliated against foreign restrictions on their exports by raising similar barriers against imports from the perpetrators. It was to avoid a repetition of these events and to rescue the international economy from the web of tariffs, quotas, and prohibitions that the Americans in 1945 proposed an International Trade Organisation. In the course of eventually abortive negotiations to establish this body, a recommendation emerged for discussions about reductions in trade barriers according to a code of conduct embodied in the General Agreement on Tariffs and Trade (GATT). Bilateral or multilateral negotiations between countries were based upon simultaneous attempts to match lists of concessions which nations were prepared to make, with tariff cuts that were being requested. When concessions were agreed between a pair of countries, they had to be extended to all participants in the GATT round. The first round began in 1947, achieving concessions principally from the United States. By the mid-1950s American tariff reductions were estimated to have cut duties by 50 per cent of 1934 rates.

Using the admittedly crude index of tariff revenue to import volume, British trade policy relied much more on quantitative restrictions than tariffs in the early part of the period. Throughout the three decades after 1950, customs duties amounted to only between 2 and 3 per cent of expenditure on imports.[10] Quantitative controls have the advantage for a government of allowing a more exact influence over the volume of foreign goods marketed than do tariffs. In view of the primary balance of payments justification for these restrictions, that was important. But they also impose greater restrictions on consumers and in that respect are more objectionable. The policy question is whether, given the particular difficulties created for the British and the world economy by the dollar shortage, better solutions were available. Every effort was made to boost exports to the dollar area but this was insufficient, given domestic policy objectives. As long as these objectives were inviolate, it is hard to see what the alternatives were to controls in the early 1950s. The pound had already been markedly devalued against the dollar in 1949 and the dollar shortage had not disappeared. The British economy and those of other countries needed time to recover from the war and to adjust to changed post-war conditions. Merely altering a price, the exchange rate, would not immediately

---

[10] Deardoff and Stern (1983) show that at least from the late 1960s taxes on capital and labour had a far greater distortionary effect than taxes on trade.

and painlessly have achieved this end. The controls were, in any case, soon removed. One-third of imports were subject to direct controls in 1954. By 1958 only dollar imports, amounting to one-tenth of the total, were restricted.

Protection of the balance of payments from the burden of food imports was the justification for state support for agriculture. Relative price movements, changes in techniques, and direct grants by the government had contributed to an approximate increase of 50 per cent in agricultural output between the mid-1930s and the mid-1950s (Scott, 1963, p. 22). Imports had therefore been greatly reduced. When other forms of government and private investment expenditure were cut during the stop phases of the stop–go cycle, agricultural subsidies remained untrimmed. In 1955/6 the government spent about £140m. upon price guarantees, nearly £60m. upon production grants and almost £8m. upon research and development. This form of agricultural policy had been chosen to avoid raising a tariff barrier against cheap Commonwealth food imports.

That support continued throughout the post-war period until the Common Agricultural Policy may be explained by the unusual electoral position of the industry, which allowed it great power in rural constituencies, and by the lobbying efficiency of the National Farmers' Union. The method of support was of considerable interest, being described by one expert as the only rational agricultural policy in existence (D. G. Johnson, 1965). In order that consumers should not suffer from higher food prices because of guaranteed prices to farmers, the United Kingdom operated a 'deficiency system'. Every year the government agreed the level of prices they would guarantee and if world prices fell below these targets then the difference was paid as a subsidy to the farmers. From the viewpoint of the Treasury the system offered the disadvantage of requiring them to pay an open-ended subsidy for which they could not easily plan. Increasingly the subsidy was therefore limited to standard quantities of commodities.

*Trade Liberalization Strategies*

British policy in the 1950s favoured freer trade in general, especially with Western Europe, but objected strongly to participating in supranational administrative European groupings such as the European Coal and Steel Community. Belgium, the Netherlands, and Luxemburg proposed the creation of institutions necessary for a European Common Market. When the Foreign Ministers of France, West Germany, and Italy also agreed that this might be a desirable direction in which to move, the Spaak committee was set up to prepare the ground and the United Kingdom was invited to participate. The British representatives at the Spaak committee meetings of 1955 advocated a European free trade area but the six signatories of the European Coal and Steel Community preferred a customs union. The difference between the two arrangements is that a customs union harmonizes remaining tariffs against the outside world. Obviously a common external tariff would have created problems for the Commonwealth, with whom 40 per cent of Britain's trade was conducted. At the end of 1955 Britain left the Spaak committee.

As an alternative, the British put their weight behind an OEEC proposal for a free trade area which included the Common Market. The British wanted to exclude agriculture from the proposals because they did not wish to jeopardize their low-cost Commonwealth supplies. Failure of these negotiations in 1958 decided the UK,

Norway, Sweden, Denmark, Austria, and Switzerland to begin negotiations the following year for a free trade area. On 4 January 1960, the Stockholm Convention establishing the European Free Trade Area was signed. EFTA was always intended only as an intermediate step towards European integration. It was prompted by the expected coming into force of the Treaty of Rome, creating the EEC on 1 January 1959 and by the transformation of French politics with General de Gaulle's return to power in 1958 which led directly to the French veto on an Industrial Free Trade Area proposal in November (Macmillan, 1972, p. 45). British fears that she would be excluded from Europe by a high EEC external tariff barrier turned out to be unwarranted. The French announced that tariff cuts under the Treaty of Rome would be extended to all OEEC and GATT members.

Although the form of the European Free Trade Area suited British interests, the size and economic power of the partners made it very much a second-best solution. Tariff cutting proceeded apace. Most of the British industries producing commodities showing some effects of EFTA were not greatly affected because their total trade with EFTA was relatively small (EFTA, 1969). The formation of the free trade area by 1965 had only a marginal effect on total UK imports but UK exports were about 2 per cent higher. Of greater economic significance for British trade was President Kennedy's signing of the 1962 Trade Expansion Act which allowed him to negotiate 50 per cent tariff cuts. The motivation for this legislation was the desire to support Britain's 1961 application to join the Common Market in order to create a Western European bastion against Communism. As a means of pushing Britain into Europe the policy failed but the trade liberalization of the Kennedy GATT Round may have raised British imports by as much as 15 per cent (Batchelor, Major, and Morgan, 1980).

*Pressures for Protection in the 1960s*

While international political pressures, economic growth, and the cold war favoured liberalizing trade in manufactures, growing import penetration and a deteriorating balance of payments encouraged protection in Britain. Faced with a balance of payments crisis, the newly elected Labour Government in October 1964 imposed a 15 per-cent import surcharge on manufactures and semi-manufactures. Because Britain's EFTA partners objected strongly, and so did the GATT, the surcharge was reduced to 10 per cent six months later. In November 1966 the surcharge was removed and the following year an alternative policy for righting the balance of payments was tried, devaluation.

When the surcharge was removed, there was a 13 per-cent rise in the volume of formerly restricted imports the following year. The tariff had certainly proved effective (see for example Thirlwall, 1986, p. 157). But that is not to say it was desirable. Removal of the tariff approximately coincided with the beginning of the decline in manufacturing output as a proportion of total output. This ratio had been slightly higher at the beginning of the 1950s under the stimulus of the rearmament boom. Subsequently, it had shown a tendency to decline during recessions, and rise during upswings, reflecting increasing returns in manufacturing relative to other sectors. After the mid-1960s the ratio fell from around 35 per cent to about 25 per cent in 1985. Manufacturing output in 1984 was lower than it had been in 1969.

In an open economy, sectors in which the economy has a comparative disadvantage may be expected to decline, and that seems to have been the state of manufacturing. The question is whether policy, such as the import surcharge, should or could have prevented or limited some of that decline, or whether comparative advantage itself was influenced by policy. If the source of the distortion was the incorrect views of speculators about the underlying health of the British economy—and the volatility of international capital later demonstrated for most countries in the 1970s and 1980s is consistent with this position—then the optimum policy was to tax the capital movements in some way. However in the absence of such a tax, an import surcharge might have been better than no action at all, so long as retaliation could be prevented—clearly a problem.

That devaluation proved more acceptable to the international community probably stemmed from the policy's legitimation by an international institution, the International Monetary Fund. For tariffs no such institution existed; indeed GATT did the opposite, but GATT could be and was circumvented by the use of non-tariff barriers to trade. 'Voluntary Export Restraints' for cotton textiles were set up by the United Kingdom in 1959 because the gains from trade were not apparent to the British cotton textile industry. Between 1950 and 1970 cotton textile employment fell from a quarter of a million to 76,000 in the face of exports from newly industrializing developing countries. Most of the industry's energies were devoted not to modernizing (labour productivity in spinning fell between 1950 and 1955) but to lobbying the government for protection (Singleton, 1986). Although formally the industry was successful, the quotas did not prove particularly restrictive of imports, and the winds of foreign competition failed to invigorate either. Because the limitations were 'voluntary', they did not violate the rules of GATT, but clearly the agreements were only reached either because they were ineffective, a form of political window dressing for the importing government, or because the exporting countries feared they would lose out in some way if they did not concede to the 'requests'.

Textile producers in low wage developing countries had a comparative advantage relative to producers in all high income industrialized economies because of the labour-intensity of the processes. All industrial nations' governments were therefore lobbied by their textile industries for protection. In 1962 the Long Term Arrangement on the Cotton Textile Trade (an Orderly Marketing Agreement) committed the industrial countries, including the United Kingdom, to eliminate their import restrictions but in return their domestic industries were to be given time to adjust by a reduction of imports below what they would have been in a free market. Adjustment took rather longer than expected in this original agreement, which was extended until 1974. Thereafter the agreement was replaced by the similar Multi-Fibre Arrangement to which the EEC countries were signatories. The continued decline of the British industry at least suggests that a shock, which the absence of such an agreement would have caused, might have been no less conducive to modernization.

### Joining the Common Market

Customs unions, like voluntary export restraints and orderly market agreements, were not prohibited by the United Kingdom's treaty obligations under the GATT. The Common Market (or the European Community) was more than a customs union, among other reasons because it involved substantial financial transfers between member governments under the Common Agricultural Policy. For the Prime Minister, Harold Macmillan, the attraction of the Common Market was none the less that it was a customs union. He judged that British industrialists believed that membership of such an enormous market was essential to be able to compete with the United States or Russia. Contrary to French protestations, the Commonwealth could not be a single economic unit and therefore was no alternative (Macmillan, 1973, p. 22).

The French vetoed the British application to join the EEC in 1963 nominally because the British were unwilling to abandon special economic links with the United States and to accept the Common Agricultural Policy (CAP) fully by 1969. Some French objections to British membership were less sophisticated. The French Minister of Agriculture is reported as saying, 'Avec les six, il y a cinq poules et un coq. Si vous joignez avec des autres pays il y aura peut-être sept ou huit poules, mais il y aura deux coqs' (Macmillan, 1973 p. 365). Macmillan thought that the General's objections, which were always the stumbling block, were fuelled by his London experience as leader of the Free French during the Second World War. Harold Wilson tried again for EEC entry in 1967 without asking for the range of concessions of the previous applications. An equitable sharing of the CAP burden however remained on the agenda—quite reasonably, it seems, with the benefit of hindsight—as did the safeguarding of some Commonwealth interests. De Gaulle once more succeeded in blocking the application on grounds of the vulnerability of the sterling system (Swann, 1978).

British entry into the EEC clearly had to wait until General de Gaulle ceased to be a political force. 'Les événements de Mai 1968' and the April 1969 referendum ultimately smoothed the British path with the resignation of de Gaulle. Even so if progress was to be made, Britain and France had to find a rapprochement, which the Heath–Pompidou meeting of May 1971 achieved. The interest for commercial policy in entry to the EEC was the length of the transition period over which British tariffs with the Six would be eliminated (five years 1973–7) and the Common External Tariff adopted (four years 1974–7). A similar adjustment period was allowed for agriculture: the full CAP was to be implemented only gradually over a five year period from 1973. Reducing trade barriers between the United Kingdom and other members of the European Community expanded British imports and exports. By encouraging specialization in production of goods and services in which Britain had a comparative advantage, this trade creation effect should have been beneficial. Only if those whose jobs disappeared in the face of stronger import competition failed to find comparable work in other sectors could this aspect of EEC membership have proved harmful.

The adoption of the common external tariff was a different matter. Goods formerly bought from Commonwealth states were likely to be made more expensive, stimulating British buyers to switch their purchases to EEC sources even though the opportunity cost of these products may have been higher. All studies of the impact of the Common Market have shown these trade-diversion effects were outweighed by trade creation.

In practice isolating the trade effects on Britain of the Common Market has proved difficult because of the trend towards increased trade with Western Europe which began well before the British joined the Common Market (as had the trend towards a higher market share of imported manufactures). It is therefore difficult to separate this underlying tendency from the trade effects of joining the customs unions. Winters's (1987) calculations are the most reliable so far but the magnitude of the effects attributed to the Common Market may indicate a failure fully to make the required separation. Winters estimates that over half of actual British imports in 1979 from every member of the original Six, were attributable to accession. British imports from Germany alone rose by £3.75bn. Relative to what they would have been if Britain had not joined the Common Market, UK sales on the home market fell by a massive £12bn. This trade creation represents a net saving of resources, assuming no increase in unemployment, because UK consumers could buy these goods cheaper, duty free, than those produced in Britain. Winters calculates that as a result of joining the EEC, UK imports of manufactures from her new partners increased approximately by £8bn., home sales fell by £4.5bn. and exports to non-partners fell by £1.5bn. Britain's trade balance was worsened and her output of manufactures reduced, by at least 1.5 per cent of GDP.

On the one hand the costs of consuming manufactured goods were cut, on the other hand unemployment had increased, probably by more than if Britain had not joined the Community. Competition, as earlier in textiles, did not necessarily encourage better economic performance at least in the short term, and resources did not shift instantaneously between sectors. That does not suggest EC entry was undesirable; only that more effective supply-side policies should have been implemented to cope with these rigidities.

EC membership did not create access for British goods to all EC markets nor were EC exports invariably allowed into the United Kingdom. Western European state procurement was almost always from national producers under longstanding agreements that gave little incentive for efficiency. State enterprise was usually granted a legal monopoly which sufficed to keep out foreign goods. Even when foreign products were formally permitted, regulations for certifying they were suitable for the national market generally constituted a major barrier.

Telecommunications, with a state monopoly network operator, exemplified this system. National 'carriers' of telecommunications services had very considerable buying power for expensive and complex main telephone exchanges, for transmission equipment, for telephones and for private automatic branch exchanges. The carrier specified the design of equipment and certified that it was conformed with. When the United Kingdom abandoned this arrangement by turning a section of a government department, the Post Office, into a profit-orientated corporation, British Telecom, in 1981, imports of telecommunications equipment soared, both absolutely and relative to exports. How much demand had been suppressed and diverted in earlier years was indicated by the deterioration of the telecommunications balance of trade. Had other European telecommunications liberalized at the same time, the deficit would have been smaller, but the profits of the principal British companies showed few signs of sagging (they themselves were major importers), and British buyers gained much cheaper and more varied products.

The second principal economic effect of EEC membership has already been mentioned in the discussion of international transfers. In contrast to the British system of agricultural support, the Common Agricultural Policy raised food prices to target or 'threshold' levels by a variable import levy, in order to enhance farm incomes. In addition the European Community would buy farm produce for stockpiling or disposal at lower prices overseas, so as to maintain a 5–10 per cent lower support price. The resulting 'butter mountains' and 'wine lakes' incensed the

British press, both because of the higher prices they caused and because finance for these hoards came from the European taxpayer. Compared with free trade in agriculture in 1984 the CAP made European taxpayers 18bn. ECUs worse off, producers 47bn. ECUs better off and consumers 43bn. ECUs worse off (Harvey and Thomson, 1985). A nation that consumed and paid taxes but did not produce as much agricultural output as average, such as Britain, was inevitably heavily penalized.

### 5.4 Basic Exchange Rate Concepts

The 'macroeconomy block' (Fig. 5.3) interacted with trade and the balance of payments in a number of ways. The impact of an upturn in economic activity, a rise in domestic expenditure, has already been considered. In the present chapter, the concern is primarily with three policy instruments in the block: the exchange rate, interest rates (or returns on UK assets), and the money supply. Before 1972, policy was directed to supporting a virtually fixed exchange rate until changes in parity could not be avoided (in 1949 and 1967). After 1972, policy varied between smoothing fluctuations, aiming at a target range, and allowing a free float. Each of these objectives, except the free float, required that the Bank of England intervene in the foreign exchange market to buy or sell sterling, drawing upon or adding to the Bank's foreign exchange reserves. Usually other measures were implemented at the same time, such as altering exchange rates or domestic expenditure. Raising interest rates attracted 'hot money' or short-term capital. The resulting stronger private demand for sterling, from the capital account, reduced the support necessary from official financing.

Exchange-rate policy should not be separated from economic policy as a whole or from the achievement of other objectives, including full employment. The exchange rate itself and the means used to control it generally interacted strongly with these other objectives. A desire to maintain both a high level of employment and a fixed exchange rate generated the 'stop–go' cycle of the 1950s and 1960s. The appreciation of sterling between 1979 and 1980 was intended to reduce inflation but also had pronounced effects on domestic industry and employment.

Why governments pursued their exchange-rate policies and what effects they had can only be understood when we know what implicit exchange-rate theory the government held and what theory was actually relevant. The same applies to the balance of payments when the exchange rate was fixed. A theory appropriate to the British economy with strict controls on the international movement of capital (as in the late 1940s) is likely to be unsuited to a period, like that of the 1980s, with very high capital mobility. In the first case, and through the 1950s, a theory of the exchange rate or balance of payments in which the current account was the principal determinant, exemplified by Keynesian models, made good sense. As international activities increased in importance and restrictions were eased, a theory such as the monetary theory of the balance of payment, which placed much greater emphasis on the capital account, was appropriate.

Monetary and portfolio balance theories focused on the difference between short and long-run exchange rates. The long-run exchange rate is most plausibly determined by relative prices in each pair of countries. This 'purchasing power parity' theory predicts that, with free international movement of goods, the prices of tradeable goods of different countries must ultimately move in line with each other, otherwise unexploited opportunities for profit would persist. To the extent that these goods are substitutes for each other, a divergence of price trends with an unchanged exchange rate would make it possible to buy products in the country with the lower price level and sell them in the country with the higher. This arbitrage process would eventually eliminate the price difference.

In the short run, as long as capital movements were unrestricted, the strongest effect on the exchange rate and the balance of payments was the demand to hold different volumes and mixes of assets denominated in different currencies. For capital assets, there is a strong tendency for interest parity to hold; the interest differential on comparable assets of two countries must equal the expected percentage changes in the exchange rate, for otherwise there would be profits to be had from buying assets in the high return economy and selling them in the low. The forward exchange market, where foreign exchange for delivery at specified future dates is bought and sold, is an institutional means by which expectations about future exchange rate changes are expressed.[11]

Under the par value regime with high capital mobility, expectations of a depreciation had to be met either by raising interest rates, with adverse effects on the domestic economy, by depleting foreign exchange reserves, by foreign borrowing, by cutting spending, or by devaluation which fulfilled the market's expectations. Reducing domestic expenditure and/or the money supply growth would affect both the capital account through interest rates and eventually the current account through a reduced domestic demand for imports; the 'stop' of the 'stop–go' cycle. During the 1960s when academic and government opinion believed fiscal policy more effective than in the 1980s, a commonly recommended policy was to use fiscal policy to control the level of unemployment and inflation, and monetary policy to control interest rates and the balance of payments.

How independent monetary policy could be under fixed exchange rates or an exchange-rate target depended upon the extent of capital mobility. A monetary contraction brings upward pressure on the exchange rate (less domestic expenditure on imports, higher interest rates) and requires that the Bank of England sell sterling and buy foreign exchange to prevent the exchange rate rising above the upper limit of the target range. But selling sterling increases the money supply, counteracting the initial contraction. How much offsetting intervention is necessary turns upon the volume of international capital that is available to move and upon the expectations of those who control that capital. Whether there is a net monetary contraction depends upon the balance between the initial contraction and the exchange market intervention. The greater the international mobility of capital, the more sterling has to be sold. The intervention can be 'sterilized'; that is government debt can be sold to absorb the sterling support providing that the assets can be generated from the government budget deficit or the national debt.

The extreme case of perfect capital mobility has rather striking implications. Devaluation will be quite ineffective in the long run. Devaluation causes a once-and-for-all rise in reserves (more competitive exports sell better and bring in more foreign currency, the demand for imports is reduced) and in prices (higher import

---

[11] Expected percentage exchange rate changes, as determined by the forward market, are linked to interest rates by 'covered interest parity'. Uncovered interest parity is the link between international interest rate differentials and the expected percentage exchange rate change, as indicated by the expected future current (or spot) exchange rate. This last variable is not necessarily identical with the corresponding forward rate.

prices raise the cost of living and of manufacture) but has no long run effect on the balance of payments. If devaluation has been forced by excessively expansionary monetary policy, without a change in monetary policy, further devaluations would be necessary (because the temporary improvement in the balance of trade will expand the domestic money supply and raise prices, thereby eventually worsening the balance of trade). In view of the downward slide of sterling for most of the period covered by this chapter, this scenario will be examined in more detail later. An 'unnecessary' devaluation has the same effect as a necessary devaluation. Only when devaluation is accompanied by a reduction in the growth of domestic credit does the policy yield some return in the form of a less draconian effect on unemployment. With a reduction in monetary growth alone, the fall in demand will throw people out of work until wages and prices adjust to the new environment. A devaluation changes a price and signals a new direction for employment in import substitution and in supplying foreign markets.

## 5.5 The Balance of Payments and the Exchange Rate 1951–1986

*'Stop–Go': The Balance of Payments as a Constraint upon Policy*

What was to be the post-war regime of par value exchange rates had been agreed at the 1944 Bretton Woods conference in New Hampshire, which had also established an international supervisory institution, the International Monetary Fund. IMF member countries were to set a par value for their currencies in terms of gold or the US dollar. Once fixed, par values might only be changed to correct a 'fundamental disequilibrium' in the balance of payments. Reserves for the support of the fixed exchange rate could be supplemented by the Fund's resources, themselves contributed by member countries. Beyond a certain amount, access to these reserves was conditional upon the borrowing economy pursuing policies which the IMF judged would support the currency at an acceptable exchange rate.

In fact for the first ten years of its life, currency controls rendered the IMF of little relevance. Not until the end of 1958 did sterling completely fulfil the terms of the IMF agreement, by ensuring there was only one form of current account sterling, freely convertible into any foreign currency and freely transferable between all non-residents. But the British government was committed to maintaining a fixed exchange rate and this proved to be a constraint upon policy from the beginning. The first 'stop' of the stop–go cycle was reached in 1951. The strains of rearmament provoked a crisis within the Labour Government and as the terms of trade deteriorated, rumours of devaluation caused a loss of foreign exchange reserves. The new Conservative Government of 1951 therefore introduced drastic import cuts, higher interest rates, hire purchase restrictions, and steps to limit fixed investment.

From the viewpoint of the government in power, 'stop–go' was entirely rational, given the fixed exchange rate. A government had to keep unemployment down but to deflate whenever necessary to maintain the exchange rate. The Conservative governments of the 1950s were luckier than the preceding Labour governments. Declining defence expenditure and favourable movements of the terms of trade gave a free boost to the UK balance of payments and incomes throughout the 1950s. Nearly half the turn-round in the balance of payments in 1952 was due to these terms of trade improvement rather than to policy. Expansion was resumed in 1953 and continued until 1955 when the current account and the balance for official financing were in deficit. At the beginning of that year a move had been made towards *de facto* convertibility (sterling to be freely exchangeable for all other currencies) which further threatened reserves. Policy therefore shifted to deflation, after the Conservatives had been re-elected.

The Suez expedition at the end of 1956 provoked another external crisis and, a year later, there was another run on the pound. Mr Thorneycroft, then Chancellor of the Exchequer, judged that the 1957 crisis stemmed from domestic inflation. In September Thorneycroft announced the need to control the money supply, government current and capital expenditure, and bank advances. In January Mr Thorneycroft resigned, apparently over the priority to be given to price stability as a policy objective.

An expansionary budget in 1959 led up to an election in which the Conservatives were again successful. But before 1960 was out, the balance of payments was again swinging into deficit so that the 1961 balance for official financing was the largest for the post-war period until then. The early months of 1963 showed the Labour Party ahead of the Conservatives in the polls and pressure mounted within the Conservative Party to replace Mr Macmillan as Prime Minister. An expansionary budget in 1963 helped to turn the balance of payments into deficit before the end of the year (the 1963 balance for official financing required £58m. be drawn from official reserves). The election of 15 October 1964 was preceded by widespread discussion of the worsening balance of payments.

Almost the entire lifetime of the Labour governments between 1964 and 1970 was dominated by the same issue. Until 1969 each year showed a negative balance for official financing of sizes unprecedented before 1964 and the current account was only positive in 1966. In order to avoid a devaluation, the government announced a 15 percent surcharge on imports of manufactured goods on 26 October, a policy apparently offset by the autumn 1964 budget which provoked enough uncertainty so that a run on sterling began. This drain on reserves was checked by extra credits from foreign central banks but speculative crises recurred in 1965. A series of the severest restrictions introduced by the Labour government to date were announced in July 1965. These convinced many commentators that the government had abandoned the optimistic growth targets of the National Plan, two months before it was published, in favour of defending the exchange rate whatever the cost in unemployment. After an election successful for the Labour Government a second major speculative crisis began in July 1966. A six-and-a-half week seamen's strike began in May, but the publication of the first quarter deficit and June's gold losses showing there was little chance of a balance of payments improvement without a change of policy, were more telling. The Prime Minister, Harold Wilson, however, strongly resisted any suggestion of devaluation, attacking the newspapers for 'selling Britain short at home or abroad'. A deflationary package of 20 July announced public expenditure cuts and higher consumer taxes, together with a statutory six-month freeze of wages, salaries, and dividends.

Early in 1967 confidence was sufficiently restored that nearly all central bank assistance had been repaid. Common Market negotiations then encouraged the view that the United Kingdom would have to devalue before entering. The Arab–Israeli Six-Day War and the oil embargo did not deter the government, worried by forecasts of three-quarters of a million unemployed in the winter, from the reflationary relaxation of hire-purchase controls. A dock strike disrupted Britain's foreign trade, which, in any case, showed a persistent tendency to be in deficit. Rather than subject the economy to intensive IMF supervision, which was the condition of another loan, the cabinet on the morning of 16 November chose devaluation. Failure to answer a Parliamentary question that afternoon about a fresh foreign loan precipitated an enormous outflow of foreign funds from London. When the next evening the Treasury announced a devaluation from $2.80 to $2.40, few countries followed suit, in contrast to the 1949 devaluation.

Some public expenditure cuts were implemented but the similar speculative runs on sterling recurred, for imports proved more buoyant than the government had expected. With unemployment at 2.4 per cent the government was loathe to cut back spending to any great extent until 1968. By the beginning of 1969 devaluation had turned the current balance positive. When the government changed in 1970 there was a substantial balance of payments surplus. Very clearly no boom had been engineered to coincide with the 1970 election.

In the face of rising unemployment in 1971 the Conservative Government announced their intention of permanently ending the 'stop–go' cycle. It was neither necessary nor desirable to distort the domestic economy in order to maintain the exchange rate, the Chancellor announced in the 1972 budget. Despite a current account surplus in the second quarter and the June increase in the Bank Rate, in the face of speculative pressure, the pound was floated in that month, depreciating by about 7 per cent against a trade weighted basket of other currencies.

## The Floating Exchange-Rate Regime

The 1972 float allowed a test of the frequently advanced claim that British economic growth had been unjustifiably constrained by the par value regime. Unfortunately it was only a partial test because the OPEC oil price increases of October 1973 and the subsequent embargoes spoiled the experiment. The world economy slumped. Most of the deterioration in the balance of payments in 1973 was attributable to the shift in the terms of trade rather than the pressure of home demand. Non-oil commodity prices rose by 62 per cent in 1973, the largest recorded annual increase. Import and export volumes grew by almost equal amounts between the second halves of 1972 and 1973.

The general election of March 1974, during the miners' strike, was won by the Labour Party, which pursued generally expansionary policies in its first year. British inflation soared above the rates of other major industrial countries but the sterling–dollar exchange rate did not immediately fall to compensate for the decline in competitiveness. 'Petro-dollars' recycled to London supported the exchange rate. Unable to spend all their newly acquired income, a number of oil producers chose to invest in the West. Current account oil deficits were offset by capital account improvements against the dollar and the yen at least. Against the Deutsch-mark the decline was continuous and precipitous until 1979.

The slide against the dollar began in 1975 when the current account deficit as a proportion of national income reached a post-war low (Fig. 5.6). The British Government applied to the IMF for funds to support the exchange rate, just as they had when the rate was nominally fixed, and the rate temporarily stabilized. However many of the government's advisers felt that the rate was too high, and that the

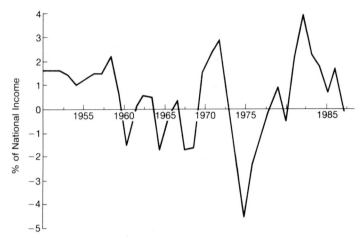

FIG. 5.6.   *Current account/surplus or deficit as a proportion of national income*

market was wrong (Keegan and Pennant-Rea, 1979, pp. 160–1). Then in March 1976 sterling again began to fall against the dollar. The IMF believed that public expenditure was too high. From this premiss they deduced that the public sector borrowing requirement was excessive, that growth in the money supply was too fast and that inflation was too high. Continuing runs on the sterling balances forced the British Government to seek loans from other central banks, loans which were not offered without strings. In September the government was driven to apply to the IMF. The pound fell to $1.55 in October and minimum lending rate reached 15 per cent before the IMF team arrived in Britain.

£5bn. cuts were demanded by the IMF. The British Government conceded £2bn. The IMF loan was agreed in December 1976 and the dollar–sterling rate recovered in 1977. By 1978 North Sea oil was buoying up the sterling–dollar rate. The following year sterling was appreciating against the yen and the Deutschmark as well, in response to Mrs Thatcher's tight money policy and the combination of North Sea oil with higher oil prices. According to one estimate, every 1 per-cent reduction in the rate of monetary growth at first raised the exchange rate by 2.3 per cent (Buiter and Miller, 1981a). Profits in British industry collapsed and unemployment rose.

In 1981 the previous meteoric rise of the dollar–sterling rate was matched by an equally precipitous fall. The last quarter average rate in 1980 was $2.387 which then fell to $1.15 in the first quarter of 1985. The declines against the yen and the Deutschmark were less extreme. The exchange rate index against all currencies declined by about 28 per cent over the same period, having risen by approximately 25 per cent over the preceding two years. A considerable part of the movement in the dollar–sterling rate must therefore be understood in terms of American, rather than British, conditions. The US real effective exchange rate rose by about one-third between 1980 and 1984 at a time when the Federal Government budget deficit and the US current-account deficit were increasing. Imports were drawn in rapidly as the American economy recovered from recession. Under other circumstances the dollar would have fallen, but the capital account inflows more than offset the current account deterioration. Tight Federal Reserve monetary policy pulled up US interest rates and gave foreigners an incentive to buy US assets.

From 1982, when the dollar real effective rate had returned to the 1975 levels, the world debt crisis discouraged US banks from making loans. High American interest rates were also the last straw for some industrializing debtor economies. In August 1982 Mexico announced a ninety-day suspension of external debt payments. Commercial banks in the developed world ceased lending to newly industrialized economies, which were therefore obliged to make massive net financial transfers to the West for the repayment and servicing of post-foreign borrowing. The IMF stepped in to organize a package that would prevent Mexico formally defaulting and insisted on Western commercial bank participation. Japanese investment in the US also supported the dollar. Japanese net portfolio investment overseas was reported as having increased in 1984 by more than $23bn. over the previous year.

Over the same period OPEC failed to maintain the real price of oil that had been achieved in 1979–81. As a 'petro-currency', which had appreciated when oil prices had risen, sterling could expect to fall as the price of Venezuelan oil in US dollars fell by more than 17 per cent between 1982 and 1985, while US finished-goods prices rose by nearly 5 per cent. The remarkable collapse in oil prices however came in 1986 when they more than halved. By then British economic policy had changed to reduce the havoc this could wreak on the exchange rate. Dissatisfied with the policy of targeting the money supply measure M3, on the stated grounds that the public were using deposits more for saving relative to transactions, the authorities in 1985 opted to control the monetary base, M0, which included only claims on the government and Bank of England. At the same time the authorities were believed to be operating with an effective exchange-rate target of between 78 and 82 on a base of 1975 = 100. Broad money (M3) began to grow rapidly in 1985/6. World stock markets boomed until the crash of October 1987. To almost universal surprise, the crash did little to suppress demand, so that coupled with an expansionary 1988 budget, inflation and imports rose. By the beginning of 1989 the current-account deficit was equivalent to 4 per cent of GDP. Rather than allowing the exchange rate to fall, eventually to choke off the trade deficit, fear of the inflationary consequences of higher import prices made Chancellor Lawson prefer high interest rates to constrain demand and to restore the trade balance by that path.

## 5.6 The Balance of Payments and Exchange-Rate Policy

Clearly the most dramatic exchange-rate policy decisions of the par value regime were the devaluations of 1949 and 1967. An evaluation of these two events therefore forms part of the subject matter of this section. But the years of post-war reconstruction also saw two major exchange-rate policy decisions, which were largely determined outside the country. The convertibility crisis of 1947 has been discussed in Chapter 2. Here the impact of Marshall Aid is assessed. For the floating rate period after 1972 the central policy issue is whether the wide swings in the exchange rate could have been reduced. This section therefore examines causes and remedies for this volatility, paying particular attention to the impact of the oil-price shocks of 1973 and 1979.

*Marshall Aid and the Foreign Exchange Constraint*

Structural adjustment after the war, a network of controls on the allocation of raw materials, of imports, and, for most of the period, on capital, made the current account appear the principal external constraint upon economic policy in the late 1940s. Post-war reconstruction would be accelerated by American capital good imports, yet exporting sufficient to earn the necessary foreign exchange was problematic. Under these conditions Marshall Aid, or the European Recovery Programme (ERP), made a greater contribution to post-war recovery than suggested by the relatively small proportion of British national income it constituted. Between 1 July 1948 and 30 June 1949 the flows under the European Recovery Programme amounted to 2.4 per cent of British GNP (Milward, 1984). The significance of these resources was the additional imports they provided. 11.5 per cent of British imports were funded by Marshall Aid in 1949 and 7.5 per cent in 1950. Would 1949 British imports otherwise have been lower by the amount of Marshall Aid, only 88.5 per cent of their actual level? In current prices that would still have exceeded the volume of imports in 1947. If 1949 imports had been 11.5 per cent lower, by how much would British incomes have been cut? Perhaps 1947 income levels were unsustainable, because foreign-exchange reserves were being lost in that year, and even that level of output needed further foreign support if it was to be maintained.

If all imports were essential, the reciprocal of the marginal propensity to import measures the import constraint upon income. Where * indicates the level of the variable in the absence of Marshall Aid $(A)$, $M$, imports in 1949, $m$, the marginal propensity to import (about 0.24 in the late 1940s) and $Y$, output and income in 1949, from the national income/import relation:

$$M - M^* = m(Y - Y^*) \tag{1}$$

But
$$\frac{A}{Y} = 0.024 = \frac{M - M^*}{Y} \tag{2}$$

Dividing (1) by $Y$

$$\frac{M - M^*}{Y} = \frac{m(Y - Y^*)}{Y} \tag{3}$$

Rearranging (3) and substituting for $(M - M^*)/Y$ from (2)

$$\frac{Y - Y^*}{Y} = .024 \times \frac{1}{m} = 10\%$$

1949 GNP was about 10 per cent higher in real terms than in the absence of Marshall Aid, when GNP would have been a little below the level of 1946.

Suppose now the model is extended to distinguish between dollar and non-dollar imports, with only the former being a constraint. The marginal propensity to import from North America was as low as the government could make it. If recovery was constrained by the inability to import from North America then more dollars would have been more effective in shifting this constraint than the first calculation implies. In the foregoing calculation $1/m$ becomes nearer 8 (for 1947–8) than 4 and 1949 GNP then appears 20 per cent higher in real terms because of the ERP.

Next consider the repercussions on the rest of the world. If each European country was in a similar position to the United Kingdom, their higher incomes would have allowed them to import more British, as well as more American, goods. However in the second scenario non-dollar imports were not a constraint. More British non-dollar exports would therefore merely have added to inflationary pressures in the United Kingdom. They would not have hastened recovery unless there was a non-dollar import constraint as well.

On the basis of the simplest of current-account Keynesian models, appropriate when capital controls were so restrictive, the ERP appears to have been of greater importance for post-war recovery than the share in GNP indicates at first sight.


### Devaluations under the Par Value Regime

Like Marshall Aid, both the 1949 and the 1967 devaluations 'worked', at least in the sense that the current account was turned round and capital flowed into the country in their aftermaths. Neither 'worked' in the sense of permanently resolving the British balance of payments problem. Moreover, the very possibility of devaluation may have been destabilizing or expensive in terms of the need either to keep foreign-exchange reserves or to borrow abroad, or because of the loss of control over the level of domestic economic activity. Speculation about devaluation recurred in 1960 for instance when there was a possibility that the Deutschmark was out of alignment with sterling. Then speculators were presented with a one-way bet. If sterling was to be devalued, it was best to sell immediately and reap the gains by buying back afterwards. If sterling was not devalued, speculators would not lose from selling. Of course the long-term inflation rate in the UK relative to Germany also created the conditions under which speculators could take this safe bet. The question then is whether periodic devaluation was no more painful than tighter monetary or fiscal policies, or than a successful supply-side policy designed to improve competitiveness.

The 1949 devaluation in an economy with controls that restricted the mobility of capital presents features which might invalidate assumptions based on long-run theories with perfect capital mobility. However the evidence may be interpreted as consistent with such theories, depending upon the credibility of the length of the reaction lags. The size of the devaluation was so large that some have maintained that it was determined by a desire to render further devaluations, seen by certain officials as a national humiliation, unnecessary. In fact the devaluation should be understood as an essential post-war adjustment, an appreciation of the dollar, because many countries followed the United Kingdom in devaluing against the US currency. Whereas the devaluation against the dollar amounted to 30.5 per cent, the trade-weighted devaluation was only 9 per cent. Recession in the United States caused an accelerating drain on British foreign exchange reserves between the first and second quarters of 1949. Cairncross claims that the extent of the devaluation on 18 September 1949, from \$4.03 to \$2.80, was determined by world economic conditions and the loss of reserves. An earlier devaluation could have been successful with a rate of \$3.00 or \$3.20 (Cairncross and Eichengreen, 1983, p. 132). Despite no substantial reduction in the level of domestic demand to switch resources into export and import-substituting industries, by the end of 1949 three-fifths of the summer's lost reserves had been recovered and the remainder were recouped by April 1950. In that sense, devaluation appeared successful.

Whether this recovery had much to do with devaluation is doubtful though. More likely the resurgence of the US economy was principally responsible. Then the outbreak of the Korean War in 1950 altered international demand and further obscured the impact of devaluation. The relative price change of devaluation did seem to switch the pattern of trade in the required direction. The ratio of UK exports to the dollar area to exports to the sterling area, rose from 19.5 per cent to 28.2 per cent between 1948/9 and 1952/4. The ratio of UK imports from the dollar area to imports from the sterling area fell from 60 to 44.6 per cent over the same period, although in both cases it must be admitted that other influences may have been responsible. Given the importance of labour costs in production, it is through labour-market pressures that prices may be likely to change: devaluation raises the cost of imported food, which could encourage higher wage demands, in turn increasing domestic prices and affecting the competitiveness of domestically produced goods, both exports and import substitutes. Between 1949 and 1950 import prices rose by 17 per cent while export prices increased by only 5 per cent. Yet retail prices went up by only 2 per cent, food prices by 4.5 per cent, and hourly earnings by 3.5 per cent, despite no significant tightening of fiscal policy.

Public investment cuts probably prevented expenditure rising as fast as it might have done but the total still increased (Dow, 1964, 218–19). With relatively static expectations of inflation, enforced by an incomes policy, the price impact might have taken longer to work through the economy than in the less restricted economy of the 1960s and 1970s. Over the five years from the devaluation, UK prices (the GDP deflator) rose by 16.4 per cent compared with 13.3 per cent in the United States. What is more difficult to assess is by how much British prices would have risen in the absence of devaluation. The rearmament boom of 1950 was inflationary but Britain was in any case one of the more inflationary countries of Western Europe throughout the period after 1945.

As with the 1949 devaluation, domestic wages and prices rose more slowly after the 1967 devaluation than did import prices. The 1967 rise in costs of foreign exchange as a result of the 14.3 per cent devaluation against the dollar was 13.9 per cent, when currencies were weighted by UK import shares, and this increase fed through to import prices in the first year after devaluation. The wage reaction was more limited because for most consumer goods, prices rose only by about 5 per cent, leaving room for increased competitiveness. Food, rent, and public service components of the cost of living index were not sharply increased by devaluation. Moreover, an incomes policy, introduced in March 1968, delayed the adjustment of labour earnings to the higher cost of living. The immediate impact of the policy was less successful than price and wage data might suggest because demand was not reduced to allow resources to transfer to supplying the foreign rather than the domestic sector. Indeed the government had expanded rather than contracted demand just before devaluation. Not until the following year was demand cut back, a stance which was broadly maintained until mid-1971. None the less the ending of the period of wage restraint in 1970 saw a rapid rise in real earnings and industrial unrest.

Devaluation and deflation undoubtedly enhanced the foreign exchange position between 1968 and 1971 but improved competitiveness was dissipated. Artis and Currie (1981) estimated that the effects of a sterling devaluation were almost completely offset by increases in domestic prices and wages over a period of five years. Inspection of Fig. 5.5 does indeed suggest devaluation only temporarily restored British competitiveness. The structural supply-side problems or the excessive demand expansion and inappropriately optimistic policy targets were not changed at the same time and devaluation alone was not sufficient to transform Britain's long-term balance of payments problem.

*Exchange-Rate Volatility and the Floating Rate Regime*

The par value regime had provided a series of target exchange rates supported by the concerted efforts of the world's principal central banks through arrangements such as the 1961 Basle Agreement and General Arrangements to Borrow. It constrained governments from pursuing excessively inflationary policies and encouraged international trade and specialization by ensuring general exchange rate stability. British inflation in the 1970s would probably not have proceeded so far if the balance of payments had still been regarded as a constraint. The cost to the general taxpayer of these benefits was the reserves used to support the exchange rate.

With the introduction of floating rates, governments were less restricted in their fiscal and monetary policies and speculators had no target rates upon which to focus, except those of the market. Even with perfect foresight, after the occurrence of unforeseen events such as oil price rises, exchange-rate volatility is endemic in a floating exchange-rate regime (Dornbusch, 1976). The exchange rate overshoots the long-run equilibrium because of the slower speed of adjustment of goods markets than of financial markets. An unexpected reduction in the money supply as in 1979 raised the long-run exchange rate by cutting the British relative to the foreign price level. In the short run, domestic interest rates rose because money was scarcer, foreign funds were attracted until the exchange rate rose above the long-run level and was expected to fall. The expectation of the fall in the exchange rate then exactly counterbalanced the gains from the higher British interest rates and the exchange rate was on a dynamic equilibrium path. If goods prices changed immediately when the money supply did, nominal domestic interest rates would not have altered (although real rates would) and the exchange rate would have jumped immediately to the long-run equilibrium; there would have been no 'overshooting'.

The deviations from purchasing power parity, reflected in real exchange rate movements, shown in Fig. 5.3 between 1975 and 1979, and 1979 and 1983 are rather too long lasting to be explained by this mechanism alone however. A more plausible explanation must abandon the assumption of 'rational expectations', that speculators were fully aware of the underlying structure of the economy and acted accordingly, despite making mistakes. Institutional reasons for doubting the full 'rationality' of the foreign exchange market include the time horizons of the dealers. As the pound fell towards parity with the dollar in 1985, it was obvious that in terms of the relative purchasing power of the two currencies, the pound was undervalued and must eventually rise against the dollar. Foreign exchange dealers had to close their accounts and show a profit every month or at least over a fairly short period. They must have known the pound would rise eventually but whether it would rise during their accounting period depended less upon undervaluation than upon what other dealers thought would happen over the period. Dealers therefore were loathe to buy pounds in expectation of a rise for some time after the currency had become severely undervalued. The Bank of England may have known better than the market in the short-term but the volume of money moving over the exchange was usually too great for the Bank to offset.

In the relatively stable exchange-rate environment of the 1950s and 1960s, market views about the long-term trend of competitiveness of the British economy, and therefore the exchange rate prospects were probably correct. In the 1970s, with the major oil price shocks, the development of North Sea oil, massive transfers to the European Community, the removal of remaining restrictions on outward invest-ment in 1979, and the pursuit of widely divergent national economic policies, judging appropriate exchange rates was far more difficult. These shocks to the international monetary system were so violent that a par value system for the whole world would have had difficulty committing the reserves necessary to survive. But currency blocks were feasible by the late 1970s, as the European Monetary System (EMS) demonstrated.

The EMS, established in March 1979, replicated some of the features of Bretton Woods on a smaller scale. Each member's currency was assigned a central rate against other EEC currencies and a permissible band of fluctuation around this rate. An intervention mechanism provided for consultation and participation by all Community members in maintaining or changing parities. A system of credits for financing payments imbalances between members was managed by the European Monetary Cooperation Fund. Exchange rates between members have been more stable than have those of the United Kingdom, which chose to remain outside. Had Britain joined the system in 1979 it is possible that the extremity of exchange-rate behaviour in the years since then and 1985 would have been mitigated. Collective and co-ordinated intervention by all EMS central banks could have been more effective than any independent national support policy. The costs of not modifying exchange-rate behaviour were less those of the effects of the variability of the rate on manufacturing industry (which seem to have been negligible (*Bank of England Quarterly Bulletin*, 1984)) than those of the persistent deviation of the rate from the long-term equilibrium.

*Oil Shocks and the Exchange Rate*

World oil price shocks and North Sea oil played a major role in the swings of the exchange rate, creating considerable problems for exchange-rate policy and for the manufacturing industry. One estimate with a macroeconomic model indicated that more than half of the 45 per cent rise in the dollar purchasing power of sterling between 1977 and 1981 was due to North Sea oil and the increase in the real price of oil (Bond and Knobl, 1982). The oil shock of 1973/4 might have been expected to expand the manufacturing sector, relative to what it would otherwise have been, in order to produce the extra exports necessary to pay for the more expensive oil imports. In fact the 'recycling' of petro-dollars sent the wrong signals to the real economy until late 1975. Unable to spend all their windfall gains, a number of oil producing nations lent considerable sums in London, which held up the sterling exchange rate. British imports did not become much more expensive, British exports did not become greatly cheaper in world markets, and the manufacturing sector continued a relative decline which became absolute in 1976.

In that year North Sea oil production began; within five years it exceeded home consumption, and comparative advantage dictated a contraction of manufacturing. Industries which had devoted resources to exporting in order to buy imports of oil were no longer obliged to do so. Reduced demands for foreign exchange for imported oil pushed up the exchange rate, thereby ensuring manufacturing became less profitable and importing more so. The current balance, which had been negative between 1973 and 1977, turned positive in 1978 and, after a negative figure in 1979 (when there was a larger net capital inflow), yielded positive balances totalling over £17bn. in the four years 1980–3. This was achieved by recession reducing the demand for imports.

Compared with the addition to official reserves (including the UK's reserve position in the IMF) of £9.6bn. in 1977, official attempts to prevent sterling rising in 1979 and 1980 were weak; the increase in official reserves over those two years was £1.3bn. Appreciation of sterling between 1979 and 1980 was beyond the government's control as long as they adhered to the Medium Term Financial Strategy, which made the money supply a target. What is less clear is whether abandoning the target and selling sterling on the foreign exchange market could have prevented much of the rise. In view of the increased output that North Sea oil constituted and that underlay the rise in the exchange rate, a fiscal or monetary expansion need not have greatly driven up domestic prices.

The United Kingdom could have benefited from North Sea oil by an appreciation of the exchange rate in a fully employed economy (Forsyth and Kay, 1980). Foreign goods were made cheaper in terms of British goods. The problem was that the shift in the terms of trade, which the oil price rises and the tapping of North Sea oil caused, not only had a price effect but also an asymmetrical income effect. When the terms of trade moved against the United Kingdom between 1973 and 1975, the increased demand for British goods and services boosted employment even though the pure price effect made the economy worse off. Conversely the favourable movement in the terms of trade between 1977 and 1981 reduced the demand for British exports and so contracted employment. Even though the price effects of the second shift was roughly sufficient to offset the consequences of the first, the employment effects were very different. Structural adjustment over the war and post-war period had been undertaken in an economy with a high pressure of demand which made the directions in which resources should move relatively obvious. In 1979–81, just at the time when fiscal policy could have been effective in holding up demand, both government and their advisers had lost faith in its efficacy.

## 5.7 Summary and Conclusion

After the Second World War the world economy began a sustained expansion at an unprecedented pace. Britain's high dependence upon foreign trade placed her in a position to benefit especially from this growth. Until the mid-1950s the less war-damaged British economy was in addition able to take advantage of the weakened state of her industrial competitors, Germany and Japan. Rearmament for the Korean War contributed to the dissipation of the lead but in any case loss of world export market share was inevitable if, as was desirable, other countries rapidly industrialized. The grounds for concern were not the market share but the frequent balance of payments crises which might have been avoided had British goods and services been more competitive at home and abroad. A radical transformation of the structure of British exports, towards more rapidly growing sectors such as motor vehicles based on relatively advanced technology and a redirection towards Western Europe, was accompanied by a positive association between skilled labour or human capital and the export intensity of an industry, which had not been apparent between 1880 and 1948. However research intensity was not a positive influence upon exports in the 1970s which, given British endowments in research at the time, may be indicative of institutional failure. Exports of 'invisibles' such as shipping and financial services had been major sources of foreign income in the nineteenth century. The contribution of shipping earnings declined from the 1970s and financial services increased in importance. There was little evidence of a shift towards services in the composition of British exports as the manufacturing sector declined. North Sea oil from the mid-1970s reduced the need to export manufactures or to supply them for the home market.

Trade liberalization stimulated a strong upward trend in imports of manufactures throughout the period. The propensity to consume imported manufactures had returned to the levels prevailing before the First World War by about the mid-1970s. Membership of the Common Market encouraged a further import penetration because of the absence of visible barriers to trade between member countries. Both balance of payments problems and industrial decline generated pressures for a return to protection. The import surcharge of 1964–7 proved politically awkward and devaluation had to be chosen instead. Restrictions on textile imports from less developed countries failed to halt the decline of the British cotton industry or to encourage modernization. Whether tighter restrictions on other imports would have encouraged industrial regeneration may therefore be doubted.

Immediately after the Second World War the shortage of dollars to service war debts and finance imports for reconstruction was an overriding problem. By shifting this import constraint, the European Recovery Programme increased British national income by more than the share of the transfers in GNP at first sight suggested. Throughout the 1950s and 1960s the balance of payments was widely regarded as an unwarranted constraint upon economic policy and economic growth. Two devaluations, in 1949 and 1967, were forced by balance of payments crises. Both devaluations were successful in turning round the balance of payments position but the trend of deteriorating competitiveness was resumed almost immediately. When the government in 1972 decided to discard the 'par value' exchange rate regime in order to remove the balance of payments constraint upon policy, it soon became apparent that the balance of payments had in fact been a constraint upon inflation. During 1976 the British government was forced to seek support from the International Monetary Fund for exchange-rate finance even though no obligation was recognized to maintain a particular external value of sterling. By the time of the 1979 oil shock, North Sea oil had transformed the endowments of the British economy so that the world price rise enhanced British wealth instead of reducing it, as in 1973/4. Together with a tightening of monetary policy at the same time, this shock caused a rapid appreciation of sterling which reduced employment in manufacturing and raised unemployment. Although the gains from North Sea oil were to be taken by an appreciation of the exchange rate, some fiscal expansion to maintain employment during the transition period would have avoided dissipation of the benefits in higher levels of unemployment and deindustrialization.

As the exchange rate fell after 1981, the adverse consequences of the appreciation were only very slowly reversed. The slow recovery of the British economy thereafter was not helped by the curious behaviour of the US dollar in response to an easy US fiscal policy and tight monetary policy. By the mid-1980s sterling was clearly undervalued, almost at parity with the dollar. British economic policy shifted somewhat, away from money supply targets and towards the exchange rate. In the face of the oil price slide of 1986 this proved helpful but towards the end of 1988 high interest rates became necessary to prevent a fall in the exchange rate as inflation picked up.

# 6

# Inflation*

## N. W. C. WOODWARD

### I. Introduction

One of the most conspicuous features of the post-war economy has been the continuous upward rise in the general price level. Over the period from 1950 to 1984 the Retail Price Index rose in every year at an average rate of 7 per cent. This is in marked contrast to earlier nineteenth- and twentieth-century peacetime experience, when there was little or no tendency for aggregate prices to rise (Lipsey, 1960). It is also evident that up until the 1970s there was a trend towards rising inflation. The 1950s and the first half of the 1960s were years of 'creeping inflation' in which the inflation rate rarely rose above 5 per cent. However, towards the end of the 1960s there was a marked acceleration until by the end of the 1970s the underlying rate had reached double figures. The outcome was that by the 1980s inflation control had come to dominate economic policy with the result that there was a change in emphasis from the maintenance of full employment to the adoption of strict financial control.

There is room for disagreement about the significance of this inflation. It could be argued, for example, that growth performance during the post-war years was comparable with, if not better than, that during earlier periods when inflation was lower. However, this is a rather complacent view. For one thing inflation has been unpopular and on more than one occasion may have cost a national government a general election[1] (Mosley, 1984). Judging from the experience of the mid-1970s, inflation has also been a potent factor influencing the distribution of income and wealth (Piachaud, 1978; Foster, 1976). Furthermore, it has had some important consequences for economic performance. The balance of payments problems of the 1960s, for example, were at least partly due to a loss of price competitiveness (Llewellyn and Potter, 1982). Similarly the slow-down in economic growth and the rise in unemployment during the 1970s was related to the acceleration of inflation (Maddison, 1982; Boltho, 1982b; Brown and Darby, 1985).

It is the aim of this chapter to account for the inflationary trends over the years since 1950. We start by outlining why economies may be exposed to inflation. This is followed by an overview of British experience during the twentieth century. We turn then to matters of explanation. In particular, we raise the questions why inflation was relatively mild during the 1950s through to the mid-1960s and why the position deteriorated subsequently? Finally, we look at the disinflation of the 1980s.

---

* The author would like to thank Nick Crafts and Baron Duckham for comments on an earlier draft of this chapter.
[1] The 1970 General Election is the most obvious example, although the inflation issue also probably played an important role in 1979.

At the outset it should be emphasized that the history of post-war inflation has been a controversial subject. According to one classification there have been two main explanations (Laidler and Parkin, 1975). First, there are those of the monetarists. They view the inflationary process as a demand-side phenomenon, one that is triggered off and sustained by excessive monetary growth. Their basic position has been that the inflation of the post-war period was due to misguided financial policies on the part of both British and overseas governments. Taking an almost contrary view is the sociological school. They believe that the fundamental causes of the post-war inflationary problems have come from the supply-side through a variety of institutional, political, and social changes which have placed continuous upward pressure upon costs.

The position taken in this chapter is more eclectic. In common with the monetarists inflation is seen ultimately as a monetary phenomenon, and it is argued that that at least part of the rise in inflation from the late 1960s can be attributed to demand pressures. However, it will also be claimed that supply-side factors have played an important, if not crucial, role in the process.

## II. Causes of Inflation

### II.1 Core, Demand, and Supply Inflation

Let us start by briefly reviewing what economic theory has to tell us about the causes of inflation. In looking at this we shall use the 'Core-Augmented Phillips Curve'. This approach has been adopted in many modern treatments of inflation (see, for example, Lipsey 1983; Eckstein, 1981; R. J. Gordon, 1984) and is the implicit model used in the historical analysis which follows. Its most distinctive characteristic is that the rate of inflation is viewed as the sum of three components: Demand, Supply, and Core Inflation.

Core inflation represents the underlying inflation in any period and emerges because, even in the absence of special demand or supply disturbances, there is an automatic tendency for costs and prices to rise each year as part of a continuous wage–price spiral. According to conventional theory the rate of core inflation is strongly influenced by the inflationary expectations of the community. This is rationalised on the grounds that, because many wage and price contracts are fixed for discrete periods, there is an incentive for firms and wage negotiators to look forward, to anticipate future cost and price increases in order to protect their real wage and profit positions against future inflationary upsurges.

Unfortunately our knowledge of how inflationary expectations are formed is somewhat rudimentary. Nevertheless there is a fairly widespread consensus that they are strongly influenced by recent inflationary experience, although they may also be conditioned by a variety of other factors including the stance of government policy, both past and present. This implies that whenever the economy is exposed to a temporary demand or supply disturbance there is a danger that this will have a more permanent effect upon inflation by raising inflationary expectations.

Demand inflation, our second component, represents that part of the inflation which is due to excess demand pressures in the economy. In principle such excess spending might emerge for one of a number of reasons: an investment boom, an export surge, or a more expansionary monetary or fiscal policy. Such impulses will then put upward pressure on prices through a number of channels. The first possibility is that the excess spending will directly push up prices. Except in a few auction markets, however, this mechanism is relatively unimportant at least in the short run, because firms invariably respond to higher demand pressures by expanding their production and running down their stocks rather than by raising their prices. A more important channel, therefore, is through the impact of demand upon unit wage costs.[2] As economic activity increases there will be a general increase in the demand for labour, which will encourage producers to increase overtime working, to lower their hiring standards, and to raise their relative wages in an attempt to attract labour, all of which will raise labour costs. Furthermore, where wages are fixed by collective bargaining the higher levels of product demand will raise trade-union bargaining power and lead to higher wage settlements.[3] Finally, where the exchange rate floats, the excess demand pressures will spill over into an additional demand for imported goods and materials, which in turn will depreciate the currency. To the extent that foreign goods are priced in overseas currencies this will automatically raise the price of imports, which will then feed through, both directly and indirectly, onto domestic prices.

The concepts of Core and Demand inflation are illustrated in Fig. 6.1, with the aid of a series of Expectations-Augmented Phillips Curves.

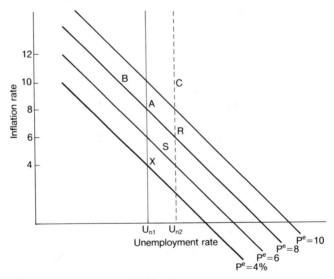

FIG. 6.1.   *Expectations-Augmented Phillips Curve*

These are drawn on the assumption that the actual rate of inflation is determined by the expected rate of inflation and by the pressure of demand. The latter is proxied

[2] Unit labour costs refer to labour costs per unit of output. Such costs will be positively associated with nominal wage movements and negatively with productivity improvements. The latter, of course, reduce costs by raising efficiency.

[3] In Britain collective bargaining between employers and trade unions is the dominant form of wage-fixing with approximately three-quarters of employees covered by such agreements.

by the extent to which unemployment is above or below the full-employment–unemployment rate or, as it is also known, the Non-Accelerating Inflation Rate of Unemployment (NAIRU). It follows that when, for example, the expected inflation rate is 8 per cent and unemployment is fixed at NAIRU (Un1) then there will be no excess demand pressures in the economy and the inflation will settle at the core rate of 8 per cent. When, however, the pressure of demand rises so that unemployment falls below NAIRU the economy will move in a north-west direction to a point such as B, where inflation is 10 per cent and demand inflation 2 per cent.

There is also a presumption in the model that in the long run the economy will automatically move towards NAIRU. For example, if the economy was at B the actual rate of inflation would have risen above that expected. In response to this, and to the excess demand pressures in the economy, the wage–price spiral will accelerate. As long as the authorities do not accommodate this rise in inflation (see below) then the level of real spending will fall and unemployment will rise, pushing it back towards NAIRU.

Just as expansionary pressures tend to raise inflation so deflationary demand policies can be used to reduce it. However, such policies inevitably result in macroeconomic costs in the form of lost output and a temporary rise in unemployment. The main reason for this is that when a government reduces the growth of nominal spending, inflation will be slow to respond, so that a reduction in real spending and output (or at least its growth) will take place and this will raise unemployment above NAIRU. After a while, however, the inflation rate will respond to the economic slack and the level of real spending will rise again (or grow more quickly), thus gradually returning the economy to NAIRU (Gordon, 1984; Dornbusch and Fischer, 1984). In terms of Fig. 6.1, therefore, the economy will move in a clockwise direction from (say) A through to R, S, and eventually X.

Economists sometimes measure the costs of such policies in terms of the 'sacrifice ratio'. This is equal to the ratio of the cumulative output lost (or the cumulative rise in unemployment) to the permanent reduction in inflation. Its size will depend upon how quickly inflation responds when the disinflation is initiated, which, in turn, will be influenced by the responsiveness of wage inflation to the level of unemployment (i.e. the slope of the Phillips Curve) and upon the speed with which inflationary expectations adjust downwards. It follows that if inflation is slow to respond the authorities will need to introduce supplementary policies if they are to reduce the size of the sacrifice ratio.

No doubt there are a number of policies that could be adopted to effect this. One possibility is for the authorities to introduce a temporary incomes policy at the same time as they initiate the deflation. In principle this will maintain the level of real spending while reducing the level of nominal expenditure. It also became fashionable in the 1970s to argue that the key to an efficient disinflation was for the authorities to maintain a credible policy stance—to emphasize their determination to bring down inflation in the hope that this would bring about a rapid downward adjustment in inflationary expectations (Fellner, 1979 and 1980). Similarly, it has been argued that if the authorities appreciate the exchange rate at the same time as they introduce the policy this will have an immediate effect upon inflation and improve the credibility of the policy (R. J. Gordon, 1982a).

The third component of inflation, supply inflation, is caused by an increase in production costs, that increase having come about independently of the current level of domestic demand.[4] This latter qualification is necessary because, as we have seen, a demand inflation will be associated with increased costs. Yet the ultimate cause of the cost increase was an excessive level of spending. It follows that to qualify as an autonomous supply inflation the increase should have been caused by some structural or external disturbance unrelated to the pressure of domestic demand.

Supply inflation can take a variety of forms, two of which deserve special mention. First there is wage-push. This, as the name suggests, occurs when institutional, structural, or other autonomous labour-market disturbances exert an upward pressure on prices through unit wage increases. In the view of many eclectic economists Britain has been relatively susceptible to such inflation. It has been argued, for example, that Britain enjoys a limited degree of social cohesion which has made her prone to conflicts over the prevailing distribution of income; that her economic performance has been poor and this has made it more difficult to satisfy material aspirations; that wage bargaining is both decentralized and unsynchronized and that this has given rise to the problems of leap-frogging and competitive bargaining.[5]

It has also been argued that an upsurge in wage-push pressures will tend to raise NAIRU on the grounds that they will have to be neutralized by a rise in unemployment if the wage–price spiral is not to accelerate (Layard, 1986). For example, in Fig. 6.1. if wage-push pressures added two points to the existing inflation rate then the authorities would be obliged to raise unemployment to Un2 because it is only at this level that the expected and actual rates of inflation are equal. Un2 then becomes the new NAIRU. This implies, therefore, that in the long term rising unemployment may reflect the same pressures which, in the short run, result in an upsurge in inflation. Indeed it is the contention of the following chapter that autonomous wage-push pressures have been one of the most important causes of the rise in unemployment since the late 1960s.

The other type of supply inflation is import-push. This occurs when there is a rise in the price of imported goods and primary commodities. As we shall see, on occasions the latter have been an important source of inflation in Britain. In part this has been due to the occasional volatility of primary commodity prices. But it also reflects Britain's high dependence upon imported sources of foodstuffs and industrial materials.

Whether or not an import push will have a sustained impact upon inflation is difficult to predict a priori. Invariably an import shock is a once-and-for-all disturbance so unless any complications set in it should only have a short-term effect upon the inflation rate; once the import costs have been passed on the inflation rate will fall back to its previous level. Nevertheless the impact may be more complicated.

---

[4] This type of disturbance is known by other names, such as supply side and cost. The widely used term 'cost-push' is also appropriate in as much as it refers to an autonomous shock.

[5] 'Decentralized' refers to the fact that bargaining takes place at the company or plant level as opposed to centralized bargaining which is conducted on an industrial, national, or perhaps regional basis. 'Unsynchronized' refers to the tendency for wage settlements to be concluded throughout the year rather than being compressed into one or two months. 'Leap-frogging' refers to the wage–wage spiral which emerges when one group obtains a higher rate of increase than one in a comparable position, which, in turn, encourages the latter to push for a restoration of its relative position.

One possible reason for this, of course, is that the import-push may raise inflationary expectations. Another possibility is that trade unions may attempt to restore the real wage position of their members—a phenomenon referred to as 'real wage resistance' (Hicks, 1975). In this case the adverse import shock will raise domestic prices, which will then lead to compensatory wage settlements thus accelerating the wage–price spiral. However, it should be emphasized that it is not inevitable that there will be a permanent rise in the inflation rate. The international experience of the 1970s suggests that the impact of an import-push is related to a variety of social and institutional factors. For example, evidence suggests that countries with corporate wage-bargaining systems and with relatively high levels of social consensus were able to adapt more successfully to the shocks at that time.[6] In this respect Britain, with decentralized bargaining, powerful work-place trade unions, and a relatively low degree of social cohesion was bound to face severe adjustment difficulties (Sachs, 1979; McCallum, 1983; Bruno and Sachs, 1985; Bean et al., 1986).

An import-push, as with any supply-shock, also poses a dilemma for the authorities in as much as it will tend to raise both unemployment and inflation in the short term, thus taking the economy to a point such as C in Fig. 6.1. Faced with this problem the authorities can adopt one of two broad strategies, neither of which they will relish. First, they might introduce an accommodating policy by expanding the level of nominal spending. This, of course, will reduce unemployment but will very probably raise the long-term rate of inflation, either by raising inflationary expectations or by encouraging trade unions to resist the inevitable fall in living standards. Alternatively, they might adopt an extinguishing policy by reducing nominal demand. This, by contrast, will eliminate the additional inflationary pressures, but it will also raise unemployment above NAIRU at least temporarily (Gordon, 1984).

## II.2 *The Role of Money and Exchange Rates*

We turn now to the role of money in the inflationary process. Although fairly controversial at one time, virtually all economists, regardless of their persuasion, would now accept the minimalist position that a sustained increase in prices would be impossible without an expansion of the money supply. This position is largely supported by the available empirical evidence which shows that when we correlate the rate of monetary growth against the inflation rate, either for a cross-section of countries or for different time periods within a country, a fairly strong positive association emerges. This has generally been taken to support the contention that over long periods monetary growth is a necessary condition for inflation. Nevertheless the year-to-year association between the two variables tends to be much weaker, and this suggests that over short periods inflation may be influenced by a variety of factors of which monetary growth is only one (Artis and Lewis, 1985; Chouraqui and Price, 1985; Pratten, 1985).

There are two ways in which monetary growth may influence inflation. The first

---

[6] It also suggests in fact that low trade union density countries with highly decentralized bargaining systems, such as the United States and Japan, were also able to adapt quite successfully to the shocks of the 1970s (see Calmfors and Driffill, 1988, and R. B. Freeman, 1988).

possibility is that the inflationary process may be triggered off by the adoption of an expansionary monetary policy. Assuming that the monetary expansion is not offset by a change in the demand for money the easy credit conditions will increase the level of nominal spending faster than the capacity to produce, thus generating a demand inflation. It should be noted, however, that in the short term this link between monetary impulses and inflation will be more powerful when the exchange rate floats. This is simply because a monetary expansion, by lowering interest rates, will result in a rapid depreciation of the currency which, in turn, will raise the price of imported goods and services. An implication of this is that with the adoption of floating in 1972 the British economy became more susceptible to inflationary impulses from monetary sources.

The other way in which monetary factors may be important is that the inflation is caused by non-monetary factors but that the authorities then validate it through an accommodating monetary policy. This refers to the practice of expanding the money supply in line with increases in its demand. By fairly general agreement the pursuit of this policy under inflationary conditions will perpetuate the process. For example, the economy might be exposed to a steady core inflation, which, other things equal, is bound to raise the demand for money. If the authorities then expand the money supply to meet this increased demand the core inflation will be sustained. However, if the authorities adopt a non-accommodating stance the economy will face a liquidity squeeze. This will throw the economy into recession until eventually the inflationary pressures are choked off. To that extent a sustained increase in prices is possible if, and only if, the money supply is allowed to expand.

We have already referred to the fact that inflation is more responsive to monetary changes under floating exchange rates. There are, however, other ways in which the exchange-rate regime may influence inflation. First, there is the extent to which domestic prices are influenced by those in other industrialized countries. The main presumption here is that when the exchange rate is fixed the domestic inflation rate will be strongly influenced by that overseas (Ball and Burns, 1975; Budd and Dicks, 1982). This can be rationalized on the grounds that the inflexibility of the exchange rate, combined with highly elastic demand conditions, will force producers in the export and import-competing sectors to keep their prices more or less in line with those in international markets.[7] However, it would be wrong to take this argument too far. For one thing it is evident from the experience of the 1980s that domestic prices can move out of line with those in international markets, at least in the short term. In any case relative improvements in non-price competitiveness or currency devaluations may allow a country to raise its prices faster than those in international markets. In addition, many of the goods and services included in official price indexes are not traded on international markets so that their prices are largely exempt from international pressures. Nevertheless despite these qualifications we would expect that under a fixed exchange rate system, such as the Bretton Woods adjustable-peg, the rate of inflation would be quite strongly influenced by world developments.

Under a floating system, by contrast, things tend to be rather different because relative price changes will be automatically offset by exchange-rate movements. For

[7] This is just another way of stating that prices must move towards Purchasing Power Parity. For an introductory discussion see Begg (1984), and Fischer and Dornbusch (1984).

example, if there is a rise in the price of tradable goods on international markets this will have only a limited effect upon domestic prices because the improvement in competitiveness will automatically be eliminated by an appreciation. Similarly, under inflationary domestic conditions producers can allow their prices to rise more rapidly than those overseas because the rise in relative prices will be automatically compensated by a depreciation. The implication, therefore, is that domestic inflation will be largely insulated from international disturbances, although it becomes more sensitive to internal ones.[8]

The other way in which the exchange-rate system is important concerns the freedom that it bestows upon governments to pursue inflationary financial policies. The main presumption now is that under a fixed system a government cannot sustain a highly expansionary policy because this will automatically generate a balance of payments deficit. Such a deficit, moreover, can be financed for only a relatively short period and will eventually oblige the authorities to introduce deflationary policies to correct the imbalance. Under floating, by contrast, this balance of payments constraint is absent. A government can pursue an expansionary policy in the knowledge that a depreciation will automatically eliminate any deficits.

Thus our expectation would be that under the Bretton Woods system individual governments were prevented from pursuing highly expansionary policies and that this acted as a check to inflation world-wide. On balance this view would seem to be correct and is supported by the fact that when the system broke down in the early 1970s a number of countries used their new found freedom to pursue inflationary policies (Budd and Dicks, 1982). However, the view that the Bretton Woods system imposed a high degree of discipline upon governments needs to be qualified in two ways. First, under the rules of the game, a country could exercise the devaluation option if it was faced with persistent balance of payments difficulties, and a number of countries took advantage of this as a means of pursuing permissive demand policies. Second, the United States, as the major reserve currency country, could pursue an expansionary policy in the knowledge that she could sustain a deficit.

## III. Twentieth-Century Experience

Let us now examine the pattern of inflation over the twentieth century. Figures 6.2 and 6.3 respectively show the Retail Price Index (and its forerunner the Cost-of-Living Index), and its annual rate of change, the inflation rate. The Retail Price Index, of course, is only one of a number of series available, the Wholesale Price Index and the GDP Deflator being the most widely used alternatives. These indexes measure different things and there is no presumption that the Retail Price Index is the best. Nevertheless the choice of an index is something of a secondary issue, because, as Table 6.1 shows, the various series are quite closely correlated. One of the main conclusions to emerge is that the twentieth century has been one of relatively high inflation. In 1985 the price index was more than 30 times higher than in 1900. This represents a compound rate of increase of more than 4 per cent per

[8] It should be noted that this only applies to a rise in the price of industrial products. A rise in the price of imported materials will not automatically result in an appreciation, so that the economy will not be insulated.

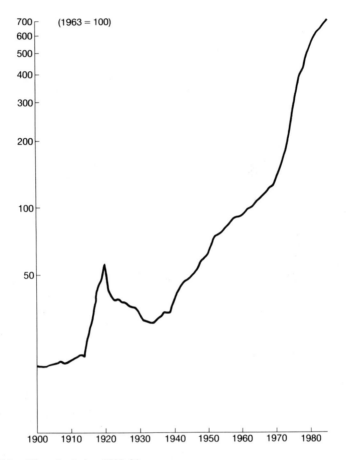

FIG. 6.2.  *The price index: 1900–86*
Sources:  Bain and Bacon (1988); *Economic Trends,* annual supplement (1988).

year which is higher than during earlier centuries. Indeed the available evidence
suggests that from the end of the thirteenth century to the beginning of the present
one, there were only two periods when sustained price increases took place. The
first of these, the so-called Sixteenth Century Price Revolution, occurred between
the 1480s and 1640s and with an average of increase of less than 2 per cent was a
period of 'creeping inflation'.

The second took place during the second half of the eighteenth and early part of
the nineteenth centuries and was even more modest. Even at its peak during the
Revolutionary and Napoleonic Wars it only averaged 3.3 per cent (Deane, 1979).

Nevertheless the inflation record has varied quite considerably during the twentieth century. First, it can be seen that in the years leading up to the First World
War prices were virtually stable; the price index rose by less than 10 per cent, and in
some years it actually declined, so that taking the years 1900–14 as a whole the
inflation rate averaged only 0.7 per cent. This low rate of inflation was, no doubt,
due to a number of favourable circumstances. Probably more than anything else,

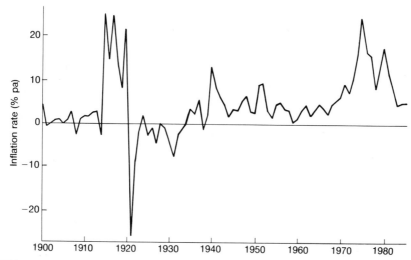

FIG. 6.3.   *The inflation rate: 1900–86*
*Sources*:   As figure 6.1.

TABLE 6.1.   *Average inflation rates: 1900–1984*[a]

|  | Retail prices | Wholesale prices | GDP deflator |
|---|---|---|---|
| 1900–14 | 0.7 | 1.2 | 0.5[b] |
| 1915–20 | 16.5 | 20.7 | 18.8 |
| 1921–38 | −1.5 | −2.8 | −1.7 |
| 1939–45 | 6.3 | 8.8 | 6.8 |
| 1945–50 | 4.3 | 9.1 | 4.7 |
| 1950–67 | 3.8 | 3.8 | 3.9 |
| 1968–73 | 7.5 | 6.5 | 8.1 |
| 1974–80 | 15.9 | 15.7 | 16.2 |
| 1980–7 | 6.9 | 6.2 | 6.7 |

[a] Estimated as compound growth rate.
[b] 1900–13.

*Sources*:   *Economic Trends*, annual supplement (1986); Mitchell (1975).

however, it reflects the fact that Britain was on the Gold Standard, so that her price movements were strongly influenced by those in competitor countries, which at this time were extremely modest.

With the outbreak of the First World War the Gold Standard was suspended (until 1925) and between then and the end of the post-war boom in 1920 Britain went through a period of unprecedented inflation. In fact over the years 1915–20 the price index more than doubled and inflation rose to an average of 18 per cent. This inflation was primarily a consequence of the way in which the war was financed. Inevitably the war resulted in a large increase in public expenditure with the result that between 1914 and 1918 government expenditure increased by more than 600 per cent in nominal terms. To finance this however, the authorities introduced only relatively modest increases in taxation and were thus forced to rely primarily upon borrowing. This then resulted in a large increase in nominal spending and the emergence of excess demand pressures (Deane, 1979; Peden, 1985).

With the cessation of hostilities there was a rapid reduction in public expenditure. Nevertheless, high inflation continued through to 1920. Again the explanation comes from the demand side. Specifically, the authorities made the mistake of embarking on a rapid programme of decontrol, which had the effect of releasing pent-up consumer and investment demand, previously contained by wartime restrictions. The outcome was a major spending boom, and, when this ran up against capacity restraints, a continuation of the demand inflation (Aldcroft, 1986).

In 1920 the post-war boom came to an end and the economy moved from a situation of inflation to one of deflation. As Fig. 6.1 shows, between then and 1938 the trend in the aggregate price index was downwards, although this was interrupted in the recovery from the 1929–32 Depression. Taking the 1921–38 period as a whole we find that prices fell or were stable in 14 of the 18 years, falling at an average rate of 1.5 per cent.

Viewed from the 1990s the most remarkable feature of this period was the rapid switch from high inflation in 1920 to deflation in 1921. This transformation came about as a result of a number of developments. On the domestic front an obvious influence was the slump of 1920/1. This was extremely severe and inevitably put downward pressure upon domestic prices and wages. This process, however, was assisted by the widespread use of sliding-scale agreements in industry and to the fact that inflationary expectations, conditioned by a long history of price stability, or even deflation, before the Great War, adjusted downwards rapidly. These pressures were then reinforced by favourable developments on the international front. With the emergence of world recession in 1920 there was a fall in world export prices and this, together with the appreciation of sterling in 1920–1, gave British manufacturers an additional incentive to cut their costs and lower their prices. At the same time it resulted in a fall in the price of imported goods and materials.

The continuation of these deflationary trends for the remainder of the inter-war period reflects the persistence of a number of these forces. First, of course, the period was one in which the pressure of demand remained relatively low (Matthews et al., 1982). Another influence, important during the 1920s to the abandonment of the Gold Standard in 1931, was the overvaluation of sterling. Finally, we should mention that for most of the period the deflation was sustained by falling import prices, so much so that between 1921 and 1938 they declined by 30 per cent.

The return to wartime conditions in 1939 saw the re-emergence of inflationary conditions with the result that prices rose by 13 per cent in 1940 (Fig. 6.2). However, for most of the Second World War the government adopted a resolute approach towards controlling inflation. In this they were largely successful; inflation was brought down to 2 per cent in 1944 and 4 per cent in 1945, and taking the 1939–45 period as a whole the rate averaged 6.3 per cent, well below the figure for the First World War. In part this success was achieved through a more stringent financial policy, the most conspicuous difference being that there was much less dependence upon borrowing and a more concerted effort to reduce consumption through increased taxation, although the introduction of consumer rationing inevitably raised the savings ratio. Nevertheless despite the improved financial management excess demand pressures were never completely eliminated, so that the containment also reflects the use of a number of other measures, including price controls, subsidies, standardization schemes, and quality controls, which deliberately aimed to cut costs and suppress inflationary pressures.

Mention should also be made of the fact that during the war wage inflation remained extremely modest. Between 1940 and 1945 average weekly wage rates increased at an average rate of 5 per cent and for most of the war lagged behind price increases. Furthermore this was achieved without the use of a formal incomes policy and in spite of an overfull employment position which placed labour in a powerful bargaining position. This suggests that the trade unions deliberately exercised wage restraint, something which reflects their general sympathy with the war as well as the widespread inclusion of trade union officials in the wartime administration.

During the Reconstruction period inflationary pressures remained a problem due, in part, to rising import prices but also to the continuation of excess demand pressures within the economy. Moreover, because of the need to rebuild export production, price stability remained an important goal of economic policy. In this respect performance was again moderately successful. Between 1945 and 1950 the inflation rate fluctuated between 3 and 7 per cent, averaging 4.3 per cent. At no time was there a return to the excesses of 1919–20.

The relative success of the inflation policy after 1945 can be attributed to a number of developments, but in the first instance the most important was the retention of the wartime controls. Thus, in the early post-war years controls were deliberately used to contain demand pressures and to prevent the prices of a number of key commodities from rising rapidly. However, from 1947 onwards the direction of policy changed: the controls were gradually relaxed, and had more or less disappeared with the change in government in 1951, while fiscal policy came to play a more active role in regulating the level of aggregate demand and damping down excess demand pressures. The Labour Government also used its close relationship with the trade union movement to encourage the latter to exercise wage restraint. It is difficult to judge how successful this was in the early years because demand pressures were exceptional. However, 1948 saw the introduction of the first post-war voluntary incomes policy, and there cannot be any doubt that this was extremely effective between then and 1950, and ensured that wage increases were kept well below the increase in retail prices. Nevertheless this policy was to set the pattern for the remaining post-war experiments, and in October 1950, partly as a consequence of the 1949 devaluation, broke down.

Finally, we have the years from 1950 to 1987, the period that is the subject of this chapter. The first thing apparent about this period is that it was one of fairly rapid inflation: retail prices rose in every year (the lowest rate of increase was recorded in 1959 when it was 0.6 per cent), at an annual average rate 7.2 per cent. This record is better than during the First World War. Nevertheless it is well above the average for the other two peacetime periods, and inferior to that of the Second World War and Reconstruction years. Thus the inflation, although not unique, has been unusual by previous historical standards.

However, this does not do full justice to the complexity of the period (Table 6.1). For this reason it is useful to break down the post-war years into four phases: 1950–67, 1968–73, 1974–80 and 1980–7. The first of these was a period of 'creeping inflation', with inflation averaging 3.8 per cent, remarkably low considering the high pressure of demand in the economy. The record, however, started to deteriorate in the late 1960s, so that our second period represents a transitional phase between the relatively low inflation of the 1950s and 1960s and the high inflation of the 1970s. During these years inflation fluctuated between 5 and 9 per cent, with an average of just under 7 per cent. The third sub-period, with a rise in the inflation rate to 15 per cent, witnessed a marked deterioration. Moreover, this rise took place against the background of a fall in economic growth and increased unemployment. The final phase, that from 1981 to 1987 is notable as one of disinflation: 18 per cent in 1980 down to a core rate of roughly 5 per cent between 1983 to 1987 (although in 1988 there were signs that inflation was rising again). These former years, of course, coincide with the counter-inflationary strategy of the Thatcher Government.

In remaining sections of this chapter we will examine these four sub-periods in more detail. In particular, we shall attempt to provide explanations for why performance deteriorated between the 1960s and 1970s, and how the disinflation was effected in the 1980s.

### IV. The 1950s to Mid-1960s

During our first sub-period (1950–67) the economy moved through four inflation cycles. The first of these saw inflation fluctuate between a low point of 2.9 per cent (1950) and a peak of 9.4 (1952). During the second it moved from 1.7 (1954) to a peak of 5.0 per cent (1956), in the third between 0.6 (1959) and 4.2 per cent (1962), and in the fourth between 2.0 (1963) and 4.8 per cent (1967). The pattern that emerges, therefore, is one of fairly modest fluctuations around a core of about 3 per cent. Two questions thus arise: Why did the inflation rate fluctuate? Why was the core rate low, at least as judged by later standards?

The inflation fluctuations were largely the result of changes in the pressure of demand, which were themselves closely associated with the 'stop–go' cycle. These cycles occurred because over these years a commitment to full employment, together with a trade-off between unemployment and the current account of the balance of payments, induced governments to alternate between periods of expansion and contraction (Chapter 3). In doing this, however, they generated a series of inflation cycles, with inflation rising and falling as the economy moved around its NAIRU.

The inflation cycles are illustrated in Fig. 6.4, which suggests that as a generalization the economy tended to move in a clockwise direction with three distinct stages. The first was a period of expansion with rising inflation and falling unemployment (1950/1, 1954/5, 1959/61, and 1963/5). Such expansions were usually checked by a series of contractionary measures. As a consequence the economy would move into a second phase, with a duration of approximately one year, in which both inflation and unemployment rose simultaneously (1951/2, 1955/6, and 1961/2). These 'stag-flations' occurred because inflation invariably responded to the deflationary measures with a longer time-lag than unemployment. Finally, as price movements responded to the lower pressure of demand there would be a disinflationary phase with falling inflation and rising unemployment (1956/9, 1962/3, and 1965/7).

Nevertheless there are certain discrepancies from this general pattern. It is

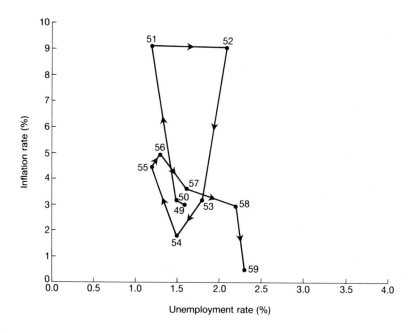

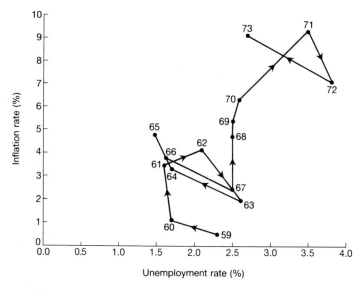

FIG. 6.4.  *Inflation and unemployment*
Source:  *Economic Trends*, annual supplement (1986).

noticeable, for example, that between 1963 and 1967 there was no stagflation. This is attributable to the introduction of a wage freeze in 1966, which brought inflation down more rapidly than would otherwise have been possible under the deflationary measures introduced at that time.

It is also apparent that the first cycle does not conform very closely; it was associated with much greater fluctuations in the inflation rate and during the disinflationary years (1952/4) there was a fall in both inflation and unemployment. In large part these differences were the consequence of the Korean War which broke out in the summer of 1950. The war had both demand and supply-side effects. On the demand side it resulted in a temporary increase in public expenditure and export demand. On the supply side it generated a world-wide increase in the demand for raw materials which inevitably raised primary commodity prices. The result was that between 1949 and 1951 import prices rose by 51 per cent. This, together with an upsurge in wage costs, pushed inflation up from 3 per cent in 1950 to 9.0 in 1951 and 9.4 in 1952.

Nevertheless the impact of the Korean War was short-lived so that by 1953 inflation was back down to 3 per cent. This experience, moreover, was in marked contrast to the mid-1970s, when there was a more or less comparable increase in import prices but an upward shift in the inflation rate. In large part, the difference is attributable to the fact that in the early 1950s the commodity price increase was subsequently reversed. Thus in 1952 world commodity prices fell by 11 per cent and in 1953 by a further 5 per cent so that by 1953 the commodity price index was only 8 per cent above that of 1949. In the immediate years following 1973, however, no such reversal took place; commodity prices continued to rise, although at a slower rate.

Another possible reason for the difference is that the import-push of the early 1970s, unlike that of the 1950s, had been preceded by a gradual rise in the inflation rate. It was much more likely, therefore, that the supply-shocks of the 1970s would have an upward effect upon inflationary expectations. It has also been argued that the supply-shocks of the 1970s took place against the background of an unsettled labour market and changed labour attitudes, and this increased the likelihood that the impact of the disturbance would be more prolonged (Allsopp, 1982).

Turning to the second question, that of why the average inflation rate remained low over the period, the moderation seems to have been due to a number of favourable circumstances (see also Maddison, 1982). In the first instance it can plausibly be argued that the low rate of core inflation was in large part a consequence of the nature of the inflation cycle, and, in particular, to the fact that periods of rising inflation were both short-lived and relatively mild. Thus between 1950 and 1967 there was only one episode, that of 1959–63, in which the inflation rate rose in more than two consecutive years. And after the Korean boom the largest upward movement in the price index in any year was two per cent (1954–5 and 1960–1), and during the first two phases of the inflation cycle only four per cent (1959–62). Both of these features, it is suggested, made it less likely that there would be any significant upward shift of inflationary expectations.

One reason why the upward movements in inflation after 1952 were modest and short-lived is that there were no further major episodes of import-push. Between 1953 and 1967 primary commodity prices fluctuated largely in response to changes in the level of economic activity among the industrialized countries as a whole. But, because the pressure of demand never became excessive or increased rapidly, they moved within a fairly modest range. Thus the maximum increase between any two years was 4 per cent. Moreover, the upward and downward movements tended to cancel one another out, so that the annual compound rate of increase was only 0.5 per cent.

On the demand side, sustained and rapid increases in the inflation rate were checked because over the period British governments were committed to maintaining the exchange rate at the 1949 parity of $2.80. This obliged them to pursue a fairly restrictive policy stance (Matthews, 1968); it discouraged them from adopting highly expansionary policies and on those occasions when demand management became overzealous, as in 1962–3, the commitment to the exchange rate obliged them to reverse their position.[9] That, however, is not to deny that policy may have been a mildly inflationary factor. Governments at this time set themselves ambitious employment targets and, despite the balance of payments constraint, this encouraged them to maintain a level of demand which on balance was marginally excessive. The resulting loss of competitiveness finally obliged them to devalue in 1967 (Laidler, 1976).

Another favourable influence was the low rate of inflation in the other industrialized countries. As Fig. 6.5 shows between 1950 and 1967 it averaged only 2.7 per cent, and, if increases in the price of tradable goods are considered, the rate of world inflation was even lower (Ball and Burns, 1976). As we have argued earlier, this low rate of inflation abroad was bound to place an upper limit on movements in domestic wages and prices.

There is room for dispute as to why world inflation was modest at this time; it was

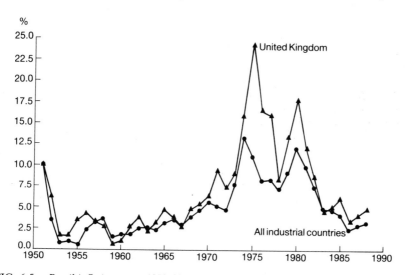

FIG. 6.5.   *Retail inflation rates: 1950–85*
*Source: International Financial Statistics Yearbook, various issues.*

[9] The 1962–3 experience refers to the so-called Maudling Experiment, when the Chancellor at that time, Reginald Maudling, deliberately embarked on an expansionary policy in an attempt to stimulate investment and hence economic growth.

probably the outcome of a number of favourable developments. But, in view of its importance among the industrialized countries, we should single out the role of the United States. Contemporary estimates suggest that for most of the period from the mid-1950s to the mid-1960s there was a significant element of spare capacity in the American economy (R. J. Gordon, 1980). This was primarily attributable to the cautious financial policies of the Eisenhower Administration, which, in turn, resulted in modest rates of monetary expansion, not only in the United States but in the world economy as a whole.

Finally, in the view of some economic historians the moderate inflation of these years was also due to the relative unimportance of autonomous wage pressures, and this is reflected not only by the low rates of wage inflation, but also by the low rate of unemployment and comparatively high profitability.[10] It has been suggested at the international level that this wage moderation was the outcome of a number of developments which reduced social tensions within the industrialized countries, including the rapid growth of real incomes, the impact of the Cold War in consolidating Western societies, and the increased social cohesion promoted by the improvement in state welfare provisions (Maddison, 1982). Another explanation, nearer to home, is that of Flanagan, Soskice, and Ulman (1983). They argue—and their case is well supported with documentary evidence—that the wage moderation was part of a conscious attempt on the part of the trade unions to exercise restraint; that there was a tacit agreement between the unions and the government that the former would exercise restraint in exchange for non-intervention in wage bargaining and industrial relations. This implicit agreement offered advantages to both parties. For governments it combined the possibility of combining consensus policies with low inflation and high employment. For the unions it brought the prospect of continued independence from state interference and, in as much as wage moderation brought about high employment, raised their membership.

None of this is to deny that autonomous wage pressures played no role in the inflation or that they became more important over the period (Brown and Darby, 1986). During the 1950s and 1960s a number of structural changes took place which may have increased the importance of wage-push pressures. It is noticeable, for example, that in response to inflation annual wage settlements became more frequent in industry, and that these and other structural changes (see below) may have increased the inflationary bias of the economy.[11] It is also the case that during the 1960s governments became more willing to experiment with incomes policy in the belief that wage inflation had become less responsive to demand pressures (Blackaby, 1978a). The late 1950s also witnessed the first demands for trade union reform (Elliot, 1978). The 'implicit contract', therefore, was largely a feature of the 1950s.

---

[10] The point here may not be immediately obvious. It is, that, in the face of demand restraint and competitive pressures in the international sector, employers will not be able fully to pass on autonomous wage increases, so that the economy will be exposed to a profits squeeze which will discourage them from expanding their employment.

[11] It is sometimes argued that there is a tendency for inflationary pressures to grow with the frequency of wage negotiations because trade union negotiators have to be seen to have secured some increase. Such annual wage settlements became more prevalent during the 1940s and 1950s and were presumably a reaction to inflation.

## V. The Late 1960s to Early 1970s

Our second sub-period (1968–73) in many respects is the most interesting. The main feature of the period is that it was one of deteriorating economic performance. In 1967 inflation was 2.4 per cent. It then rose gradually to a peak of 9.4 per cent in 1971, after which it fell back slightly in response to the 1970–1 recession and then to the Heath Government's incomes policy of 1972–4. This rise in inflation, moreover, took place against the background of a rise in unemployment (Fig. 6.4). In 1967 unemployment stood at 1.6 per cent. It then rose to a peak of 3.7 in 1972 as a result of the recession, only to fall back to 2.6 during the subsequent boom.

Why then did inflation rise over these years? The first possibility is that it was the product of excess demand pressures. This, however, is something that we can discount immediately because the main indicators suggest that, if anything, the period was one of weakening demand. We have, for example, just noted that unemployment, which has often been taken as an indicator of demand pressure, was rising for most of this period. No doubt part of the rise in unemployment was due to an increase in frictional unemployment, although this was not recognized by policy-makers at the time (Chapter 7). Nevertheless there is no evidence that the NAIRU rose faster than the actual unemployment rate. Furthermore, other indicators, such as the vacancy rate and the proportion of firms complaining of a lack of orders, point in a similar direction (Matthews et al., 1982).

At the international level, there were two disturbances which were clearly important. First, there was the devaluation of November 1967. This, of course, was bound to have an immediate impact upon domestic costs by raising the price of imported materials and foodstuffs, and to a lesser extent finished goods. The result was that there was a rapid rise in import prices from almost zero in 1967 to 12 per cent in 1968. Nevertheless the effects were short-lived because by 1969 the increase was back down to 3 per cent. On top of this the late 1960s was a period of rising inflation throughout the Western economies. This is confirmed in Fig. 6.5 which shows that between 1967 and 1970 the rate of inflation in the industrialized countries rose from 2.9 to 5.6 per cent. In as much as this was reflected in an acceleration in the price of tradable goods it was bound to put upward pressure on British inflation. In the event British prices rose rather faster owing to the special influence of the devaluation.

This increase in world inflation has been the cause of some dispute. Some commentators have argued quite convincingly that it was at least partly due to an upsurge in labour militancy. Nevertheless it was also the consequence of a more expansionary domestic policy in the United States. This had been initiated by the Kennedy tax cuts of 1964 and was then followed by an increase in government expenditure in the second half of the 1960s as a result of the Vietnam War and the social programme of the Johnson Administration. As the higher levels of expenditure were largely financed through borrowing, both monetary and fiscal policy became expansionary so that from 1965 the American economy began to overheat (R. J. Gordon, 1980). One consequence of this was that the US inflation rate rose from an average of 2.0 per cent between 1957 and 1967 to one of 5.2 between 1967 and 1973.

The other important aspect of the inflation in these years concerns the wage explosion of the late 1960s and early 1970s. As Fig. 6.6 illustrates in the late 1960s wage inflation was running in the region of 7 to 8 per cent. By the early 1970s, however, it had risen to between 12 and 13 per cent. This wage explosion, moreover, was associated with an apparent upsurge in labour militancy. For example, over this period there was a rapid increase in trade union membership from 42.7 per cent of the labour force in 1968 to 47.2 in 1972. At the same time there was a significant increase in strike activity, and as Table 6.2 confirms, this was reflected in all the main strike indicators. These impressions, moreover, are strengthened by two other measures of labour militancy. First, there was a significant widening of the trade union wage differential (Layard *et al.*, 1978). Second, there was a continued rise in the share of labour in national income (Brown and Darby, 1986).

FIG. 6.6.   *Wage inflation: 1950–1985*
*Source:   Economic Trends*, annual supplement (1986).

What were the causes of this upsurge in wage inflation? This again is a contentious issue. The usual interpretation is that it was the product of autonomous wage pressures. Nevertheless, some economists, especially those associated with the monetarist school, have tried to minimize, and in some cases completely deny, the

TABLE 6.2.   *Indicators of net strike activity*[a]

|  | 1960–8 | 1969–73 |
| --- | --- | --- |
| Number of strikes (000s) | 1415 | 2723 |
| Number of workers involved |  |  |
| (i) Thousands | 1189.3 | 1446.4 |
| (ii) As per cent of employees | 5.3 | 6.5 |
| Number of working days lost |  |  |
| (i) Thousands | 2872 | 9881 |
| (ii) As per cent of potential |  |  |
| working time | 0.05 | 0.20 |

[a] Net—excluding mining.
*Source:*   Durcan *et al.* (1983).

supply-side origins of the wage explosion (Ward and Zis, 1974; Zis, 1975). Basically their explanation is that the wage explosion and labour unrest ultimately was a response to the demand and monetary conditions in Britain and in the United States earlier in the decade. These excess demand pressures, it is argued, through the impact of devaluation and the rising price of world manufactures, resulted in an acceleration in price inflation in Britain. However, inflationary expectations did not immediately adjust upwards with the result that wage increases lagged behind those of prices. The resulting decline in real wage growth then created a sense of frustration and grievance which was then manifested in an upsurge in strikes and wage inflation.

This explanation of the wage explosion, however, is not completely convincing. For one thing it would lead us to anticipate that, given the severity of the wage explosion, it should have been preceded by a rapid increase in the rate of price inflation (Soskice, 1978). But as Fig. 6.5 shows this was not the case. Price inflation undoubtedly rose between 1967 and 1969 but the increase was fairly modest. Furthermore, the empirical evidence, for what it is worth, does not suggest that the wage explosion was preceded by a rise in inflationary expectations as the explanation predicts (Williamson and Wood, 1976).

Nevertheless, given the present state of our knowledge, it remains difficult to account for the upsurge in inflationary wage pressures at this time, and any explanation can only be extremely tentative. Not that there has been any shortage of explanations; indeed the wage inflation has attracted a widespread literature. On the basis of this it is tempting to view it as the product of two sets of disturbances. First, there were a number of structural changes which had taken place over the post-war period and which had increased the potential inflationary bias of the labour market by changing attitudes, expectations, and bargaining power. Then, during the late 1960s, there were a number specific developments which may have acted as a direct stimulus to the wage explosion. These more or less account for the timing of the events (Soskice, 1978; R. Jones, 1987).

Part of the explanation for the upsurge in wage-push is that it was a consequence of the long post-war boom. By the late 1960s the British economy had enjoyed low levels of unemployment for almost 30 years. The period had also been one in which governments had been committed to full-employment policies. This then brought about a change in attitudes towards inflation in that wage negotiators became less concerned about the possible employment consequences of inflationary wage settlements. No doubt this was strengthened over time as memories of the high unemployment of the inter-war years faded and as the proportion of the labour force which had acquired their work experience in this period declined (Boltho, 1982b; Phelps-Brown, 1983).

At the same time under the pressure of full employment, wage bargaining in the private sector became decentralized. Whereas at the beginning of the period wage bargaining was largely conducted at the industry level between official trade-union representatives and employer's associations, by the late 1960s it was increasingly being conducted between shop stewards and local management at the plant or company level (Royal Commission on Trade Unions, 1968; Clegg, 1979). Moreover, this decentralization had some important implications for wage inflation. First, with the shift in bargaining to the shop-floor there was less opportunity for the trade unions to influence wage settlements and thus bring about restraint in wage bargaining; wage negotiations were now more likely to be influenced by the median union voter, who was less concerned with the possible impact of wage pressures on unemployment. Second, with the growth of decentralization the strike became a more powerful weapon, simply because when firms negotiate individually they run the risk of losing part of their market share to competitors not involved in the dispute. Third, decentralization increased the likelihood of leapfrogging and overbidding.[12]

In similar vein it has also been argued that the upsurge in the wage inflation was in part due to the emergence of, or growth of, an 'aspirations gap' (i.e. the difference between the feasible and actual growth of real wages) which put pressure on trade-union negotiators to push for higher wage settlements. This aspirations gap was itself the outcome of a number of developments. Rapid economic growth during the post-war years raised expectations about possible future living standards, while other changes, such as the growth of advertising, the spread of television, and motor car ownership, increased demands for relative advancement among lower income groups (Phelps-Brown, 1975; Panic, 1978). This gap may also have been aggravated from the mid-1960s by a slow-down in the growth of take-home pay. This slow-down was associated less with the devaluation than with the rise in direct taxation which had been the main source of finance for the more ambitious social programme of the Labour Government (Jackson et al., 1972).

Whatever the underlying causes of the structural changes, the result was that by the mid-1960s, if not before, there was a good deal of dissatisfaction with the operation of the labour market. This led to attempts to reform industrial relations and the introduction of a third formal incomes policy. However, during the late 1960s the economy was exposed to two disturbances which played a part in the subsequent wage explosion. First there was the 'Continental Wage Explosion' which was marked by an upsurge in wage inflation and labour militancy in a number of European countries. This, it is alleged, originated in France following the student and social unrest in May 1968. It then spread through a 'demonstration effect' to Italy, West Germany, Britain, and some of the smaller countries between 1969 and 1970 (Phelps-Brown, 1983).

But then second, and probably more important, the Labour Government's incomes policy broke down. This had been introduced in 1965 but had started to collapse with the withdrawal of trade union support in 1968. The effect of this policy, however, had been to upset the traditional pattern of relativities, because it had been applied more stringently to the public-sector workers. The relative deterioration in their position became a source of grievance with the result that between 1969 and 1971 there were some bitter disputes in the public sector. It seems likely, moreover, that the higher level of wage settlements in the public sector had upward influence upon the overall level of wage increases (Godley, 1977; Flanagan et al., 1983).

## VI. The 1970s

As a result of the disturbances of the late 1960s and early 1970s the underlying inflation rate had risen to somewhere between 8 and 9 per cent. However, a further deterioration in economic performance was to take place. This began with a rapid rise in inflation to a post-war peak of 24 per cent in 1975, despite a further rise in

---

[12] 'Overbidding' refers to a situation where trade union negotiators push for high wage settlements in order to ensure that the group which they represent does not fall behind in the pay league. Obviously such overbidding increases the inflationary bias.

unemployment (Fig. 6.7). At this point, not surprisingly, counter-inflation measures came to dominate economic policy, and with some success; by 1978 inflation had been brought back down to 8 per cent. Yet the respite was short-lived and between 1978 and 1980 inflation re-accelerated to 18 per cent, at which stage the policies of the Thatcher Government began to make more significant in-roads into the problem. In this section, therefore, we need to explain why inflation rose so rapidly in the mid-1970s and, more briefly, how it was subsequently brought down and why it temporarily re-accelerated.

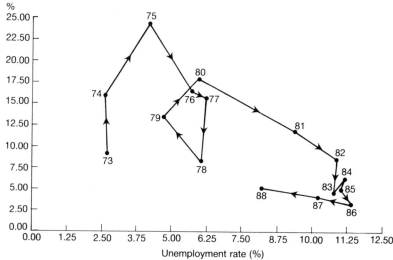

FIG. 6.7.   *Inflation and unemployment: 1973–88*
*Sources*:   *Economic Trends* (1986); *Employment Gazette* (various issues).

The rise in inflation during the mid-1970s was the outcome of both demand and supply factors. On the demand side the main influence was the policy of the 1970–4 Heath Government. The government had assumed office committed to a continuation of the tight policies of the previous administration. In large part this was motivated by a desire to reduce inflation, although the government also fell back on the largely unsuccessful expedient of holding back increases in public sector pay. However, in 1971/2, in an attempt to reduce unemployment and stimulate economic growth, this policy was put into reverse. The new strategy was initiated by a number of expansionary fiscal changes. At the same time the monetary stance became significantly more expansionary, in part because of the monetary reforms of 1971 (Fig. 6.8). Coupled with this reflation two other measures were introduced. First, in an attempt to contain inflationary pressures emerging from the expansion, another formal incomes policy was introduced. Second, the government made the commitment to float the exchange rate if the expansion appeared to be threatened by balance of payments difficulties. In the event the inevitable happened and in the summer of 1972, some nine months before the collapse of Bretton Woods, sterling was floated following a confidence crisis (Stewart, 1978).

In later years the 'Heath–Barber Boom', with some justification, was severely criticized. Not only was the economy given a major stimulus, but that stimulus was applied over an extremely short period. The outcome was that in 1973 the economy

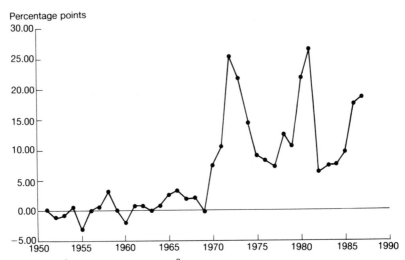

FIG. 6.8.   *M3 excess monetary growth*[a]

[a]Growth of M3 less growth of real GDP.

*Source*:   *Economic Trends* annual supplement (1986).

exhibited all the signs of overheating: the pound began to depreciate, skill shortages appeared, and in some areas there were complaints about generalized manpower shortages. The only reason that inflation did not emerge as a major problem in that year is that it was temporarily suppressed by the prices and incomes policy, which broke down in the winter of 1973/4. Nevertheless the authorities belatedly recognized their mistake and during the course of 1973 some mildly deflationary measures were introduced.

It seems likely, therefore, that in 1974/5 Britain was heading for another period of stagflation. These problems, however, were aggravated by a series of supply-side disturbances. First, there was a rise in the price of primary commodities. This began in 1971, after which it accelerated until mid-1974. Moreover, the extent of the rise appears to be unprecedented. Writing in 1975 and using *The Economist*'s Commodity Price Index, Cooper and Lawrence report that over the preceding 115 years there had been no single year when prices had risen more rapidly than in 1972–3 (63 per cent) and no three-year period compared with 1971–4 (159 per cent).

The 1971–4 'Primary Commodity Boom' was the outcome of a number of disturbances. The increase in material prices was largely the result of an unusually synchronized boom among the industrialized countries (McCracken *et al.*, 1977). Food prices, however, although influenced by the buoyant demand conditions, were forced up primarily through a variety of supply-side disturbances. For example, 1972 was a year of harvest failures in the USSR, South-East Asia, and elsewhere; in 1972/3 there was a decline in the Peruvian anchovy catch which raised the price of animal foodstuffs; over the same period the supply of a number of commodities was adversely affected by official acreage controls (Bosworth and Lawrence, 1982).

The other supply-shock of these years, of course, was the first oil price increase of 1973/4 when the price of oil was raised by almost 400 per cent. The immediate cause of this was the retaliation taken by the Organisation of Petroleum Exporting

Countries (OPEC) against the pro-Israeli stance of some Western countries during the Yom-Kippur war in the autumn of 1973. Nevertheless, it was very likely, even in the absence of the war, that some increase in oil prices would have taken place at about this time. One reason for suggesting this is that the world upturn in 1972/3 had increased the demand for oil and created a seller's market. Another, and possibly more important reason, is that during the early 1970s the OPEC countries began to act less as a loose organization and more like a cartel. This enabled them to exploit their potential market power more effectively (Bosworth and Lawrence, 1982).

Although it is difficult to estimate quantitatively the inflationary impact of the oil price increase (OPEC 1), given the magnitude of the shock, it was bound to be substantial especially once the indirect effects have been taken into account. The shock, moreover, has also been identified as a major contractionary (or stagflationary) factor in the recession of 1973–5. There are a number of reasons for this. First, the rise in oil prices brought about a significant redistribution of world income from the industrialized to the oil-exporting countries. Unfortunately the latter were unable to spend all of their increased earnings, thus raising the level of world saving. At the same time it exposed a number of the industrialized countries to inflation and balance of payments problems, which forced them to adopt restrictive monetary and fiscal policies. Finally, the oil shock, by raising inflation and by creating uncertainty, reduced consumer and investment spending (Allsopp and Mayes, 1985).

As if the Primary Commodity Boom and OPEC 1 were not enough, 1974–5 witnessed another wage explosion which eclipsed even that of 1969–72 (Fig. 6.6). In 1973 wage inflation was contained to 13 per cent largely because of the incomes policy. But when this broke down in 1974, it rose to 20 per cent and to 26 per cent in 1975. However, given the disturbances and the unsettled nature of the labour market at this time, increases of this magnitude were predictable. It reflected a number of influences. First, in 1974, if not 1975, demand pressures remained high within the labour market, and may well have encouraged trade unions to resist a cut in living standards. At the same time the supply-shocks, coming on top of the rise in inflation in the late 1960s and early 1970s, undoubtedly raised inflationary expectations. Given the convention of annual wage settlements in Britain these disturbances were bound to show through as soon as the incomes policy was relaxed.

These pressures were then supplemented by two special factors. First, there cannot be much doubt that the miners' dispute in the winter of 1973/4, with all its widespread publicity, set an inflationary tone to wage bargaining. Of even greater significance was the 'threshold' clause in Stage III of the Heath Government's incomes policy. To make the policy more palatable this had index-linked earnings to prices once inflation had risen to 7 per cent. Unfortunately the threshold had been introduced before the oil price shock and, for some inexplicable reason, was retained until November 1974, by which time it had automatically accelerated the wage–price spiral.

The rapid inflation in 1974–5 was also a reflection of the Labour Government's demand policy which would be described as partially accommodating. Rather than reduce inflation through a tight demand stance the government chose to introduce a series of supply-side instruments which included price controls, subsidies, and voluntary wage restraint. Its reluctance to introduce an extinguishing demand policy was, in part, determined by its desire to maintain a low rate of unemployment, but was also probably influenced by the experience of 1970/1, which implied that inflation had become less sensitive to such pressures. Whatever the reasons, the failure to adopt deflationary policies ensured that inflation continued to rise into 1975, even though in most other industrial countries it peaked in the previous year. And this, together with the system of wage bargaining, helps to explain why the inflationary effects and the adjustment problems associated with the supply-shocks appear to have been worse in Britain than in most other Western countries.

By the beginning of 1975, therefore, inflation had assumed crisis proportions and forced the government to strengthen its counter-inflation policy. Its main initiative was the 'Social Contract'. This had been introduced with the change of government in 1974 and represented an agreement with the trade unions that in exchange for progressive legislation the latter would exercise wage restraint.[13] In 1974 the policy proved to be largely ineffective, in part because of the threshold arrangements. In the summer of 1975, however, at the initiative of the government the TUC agreed to strengthen its part of the bargain and in the following two years supported a maximum weekly increase in pay of £6.00 (1975–6) and (for 1976–7) 5 per cent. In the event the policy proved to be remarkably successful at least in the short term. Earnings growth was reduced from a peak of 26 per cent in 1975 to 15 in 1976 to 10 in 1977, with the result that price inflation fell in each year between 1975 and 1978. As a result there can be little doubt that in the short run the Social Contract proved to be an effective way of reducing the sacrifice ratio, although its long-term benefits are more questionable.

Over the same period the incomes policy was supported by the introduction of tighter financial policies, although these were partly a reaction to the 1976 sterling crisis. As a result 1975–6 saw the introduction of monetary targets, the extension of cash limits for the control of public expenditure, and a more restrictive monetary and fiscal stance (Allsopp and Mayes, 1985). These measures, moreover, were successful in that from the beginning of 1977 the depreciation of sterling, which had taken place more or less continuously since 1972, was arrested.

Largely as a result of this restrictive stance the 1974–9 Labour Administration has been portrayed as the first post-war government to renege the commitment to full employment. To some extent this position is substantiated by a doubling of the unemployment rate. But it is also somewhat misleading. For one thing the view that there was a strong commitment to full employment before 1974 has been exaggerated. This had already been indicated by the willingness of the 1964–70 Labour Government to allow unemployment to rise in the face of balance of payments difficulties. But second, it is undoubtedly the case that between 1974 and 1979 the government was reluctant to pursue an all-out deflationary policy in the interests of containing inflation. This is reflected in the fact that over this period the stance of monetary policy, judging at least from real interest rates and excess monetary growth (Fig. 6.8), remained fairly accommodating.

This policy must be judged to have been fairly successful at least up until 1978. But it then started to go wrong as inflation accelerated rapidly until 1980. This re-acceleration in part might be attributed to less stringent financial conditions, although it is doubtful if these played anything other than a minor role. Undoubtedly

---

[13] The most conspicuous legislative example was the reform of the 1971 Industrial Relations Act. This was secured in the 1974 and 1976 Trade Union and Labour Relations Acts.

the main proximate cause was another wage explosion following the breakdown of the Social Contract in the autumn of 1977. At this time the TUC refused to endorse any further limits on wage increases. The government, therefore, was obliged to adopt a policy of exhortation backed up with the threat of cash limits in the public sector and sanctions in the private sector. It is doubtful, however, whether this was very effective in that from a rate of 10 per cent in 1977 wage inflation rose to over 18 per cent in 1980. Associated with this there was a marked rise in strike activity especially amongst public-sector workers in the winter of 1978–9.

Two other supply-shocks were important at this time. The first arose from an increase in Value Added Tax in June 1979. This was part of a supply-side strategy of shifting the burden of taxation away from direct to indirect sources, and reducing the marginal rate of tax, with the aim of improving economic incentives. Whatever the merits of this switch it had an immediate, although short-term effect upon prices, directly adding as much as 4 per cent to inflation in 1979–80. The other disturbance arose from another significant rise in the price of oil (OPEC 2). The principal cause of this was the Iranian Revolution of January 1979, which reduced the supply of oil coming onto the world market. As at this time the world economy was expanding, albeit at a relatively modest rate, the inevitable outcome was an oil shortage. This, moreover, was aggravated by an increase in the speculative demand for oil as consumer countries tried to beat possible shortfalls and price increases (Bosworth and Lawrence, 1982). The result was that between 1978 and 1981 the price of oil rose by over 150 per cent. However, on this occasion, in contrast to that of 1974, the government reacted passively, making no attempt to offset the oil price shock through supply-side measures. The result was that OPEC 2 had a temporary though appreciable impact upon prices in 1979–80, adding perhaps as much as 3 per cent to the inflation rate.

## VII. The Disinflation of the 1980s

With the election of the Conservative Government in May 1979 far-reaching changes in the nature of economic management took place. One important indication of this was the official attitude towards inflation and unemployment. Whereas previous administrations had shown a commitment to both high employment and price stability the Thatcher Government would pledge itself solely to the reduction of inflation. This demotion of high employment as an immediate goal of economic policy was justified on the grounds that in the long run unemployment was largely determined by microeconomic conditions and so was not amenable to control through demand management (Lawson, 1984). Inflation, however, was predominantly determined by financial conditions and these were something over which governments had some control.

In framing its counter-inflationary strategy the Thatcher Government adopted a strong ideological position. As regards its financial policies it was, of course, influenced by the monetarists. The government, however, also seems to have been attracted towards the so-called Supply-Side Economics which came into vogue in the late 1970s and early 1980s, especially in the United States. The essence of this was that income and corporate tax reductions, through their effect upon incentives, would have a favourable influence upon economic performance including the reduction of inflation (M. J. Evans, 1982). Nevertheless the Thatcher Government was never committed to tax cuts to the extent that it was prepared to make them the central element in their strategy. Instead it gradually developed a more broadly based strategy for improving the supply-side performance of the economy. This included industrial relations reform, privatization measures, a more active competition policy, and additional support for the small firm sector (Riddell, 1985).

There are a number of other aspects of the government's policy that are worth outlining. First, the strong emphasis upon inflation control was based upon the belief that inflation had been a cause of poor economic performance, especially low growth and high unemployment. This belief presumably was based on the familiar arguments that inflation disguises relative price movements and hence reduces the efficiency of a market economy (Friedman, 1977); that it is associated with uncertainty and low investment; that it encourages saving at the expense of consumption; and that it may result in a loss of international price competitiveness (Britton, 1983).

Judging from Ministerial pronouncements, the government also seemed to take an orthodox monetarist position when explaining the acceleration of inflation in the 1970s. To simplify somewhat, the rapid increase in inflation in the mid-1970s was viewed primarily as a demand disturbance, itself caused by rapid monetary growth earlier in the decade. After this the high underlying inflation was sustained by high wage settlements, themselves the product of adverse inflationary expectations. Yet the whole process was accommodated by excessive monetary growth.

It was for this reason that the central element of the government's counter-inflationary strategy was a progressive reduction in the growth of the money supply. With the change in government in May 1979, therefore, the first moves were taken to reduce the demand for bank credit by raising interest rates. By the end of the year short-term interest rates had been pushed up to a record 17 per cent where they stayed until the early part of 1980, after which the general direction was downwards. Over the same period fiscal policy became an instrument of monetary policy. In particular, it became an explicit goal to reduce the size of the Public Sector Borrowing Requirement (PSBR), the main attraction of this being that it would reduce the dependence upon residual finance from the banking sector and hence allow the authorities to achieve more accurate monetary control.

The outcome was that fiscal policy became extremely restrictive in the early 1980s. For example, one set of authors has estimated that, on the assumption of 2 per cent growth rate, the cyclically adjusted budget moved from a surplus of 1.2 per cent of GDP in the second quarter of 1979 to one of 5.6 per cent three years later (Biswas et al., 1985). It is more difficult to measure the stance of monetary policy and, in any case, the money supply figures are extremely difficult to interpret at this time, in part, because of the abolition of the 'Corset' and partly because of the unusually high level of distress borrowing. Nevertheless the impression gained by most commentators is that monetary policy was extremely tight. One reflection of this is that real short and long-term interest rate rose respectively from $-2.5$ and $-3.2$ per cent in 1979 to 5.8 and 6.8 per cent in 1982 (Allsopp and Mayes, 1985).

The cornerstone of the government's counter-inflationary strategy, therefore, was an old-fashioned deflation. But as with all deflationary policies there was a distinct possibility, because of wage inertia, that the short-term burden of adjustment would fall principally upon output and employment. Nevertheless the government seems to have been fairly confident that a disinflation could be effected rapidly and without significant transitional costs. This view seems to have been based upon the belief that the main handicap to a rapid disinflation was adverse inflationary expectations, but that these could be 'unwound' rapidly by the adoption of a credible policy stance. This position, however, seemed to many outside the government to be extremely optimistic. For one thing the experience from the mid-1960s seemed to imply that wage inflation had become fairly unresponsive to demand pressures. Another and more serious problem was that it is difficult for governments to establish credibility when wage negotiators recognize that it is often in the interests of governments to pursue expansionary policies that undermine their commitment to financial restraint (Backus and Driffil, 1986; Blackburn and Christensen, 1989). Indeed the 'stop–go' policies of the post-war period would seemed to have confirmed this.

Nevertheless the government adopted a number of other measures as a means of establishing the credibility of their policy. First, it became explicit policy that sterling be allowed to float more cleanly than hitherto. One effect of this was that, largely in response to the higher interest rates, there was a 22 per cent rise in the nominal exchange rate in 1979–80 with an associated significant loss of international price competitiveness (Buiter and Miller, 1981b, 1983). These developments in all probability had an extremely favourable impact upon inflation. The appreciation tended to reduce the price of imported materials, while at the same time the loss of price competitiveness forced producers within manufacturing to adopt a tougher position in wage bargaining. It is likely, moreover, that the appreciation by speeding up the disinflation improved the credibility of the policy and had a favourable impact upon inflationary expectations.

A second measure, which was also designed to improve the credibility of the strategy, was the extension of monetary targets through the introduction of the Medium Term Financial Strategy in 1980. This established targets for both monetary growth and the PSBR for periods of up to four years. Clearly one of the main aims of this was to illustrate the government's determination to adopt a more stringent financial policy in the hope that this would influence inflationary expectations. It is doubtful, however, whether it was very successful and may even have been counter-productive. For one thing it is doubtful whether financial conditions had ever played a direct part in influencing wage negotiations. For another the authorities failed to meet their targets especially in the early 1980s, and the publicity which this attracted may possibly have done more harm than good.

Another way in which the government apparently aimed to improve the credibility of its policy was through publicizing the policy. Thus prominent Cabinet Ministers, especially the Prime Minister, would periodically announce in fairly forceful terms that the government was determined to reduce inflation and that there would be no reverse of the counter-inflationary policy. Obviously the aim of this was to influence wage settlements and to undermine the belief that the authorities would adopt inflationary financial policies in the face of rising unemployment. Whether or not these announcements had the desired effect is difficult to prove. Nevertheless the impression gained is that this was an effective measure, which became increasingly so the longer the authorities maintained their restrictive posture.

There is one other aspect of the policy that we should mention. That concerns the unwillingness of the government to resort to a formal incomes policy as a way of reducing inflation or minimizing the sacrifice ratio. The justification for this was that incomes policies were unworkable except perhaps in the short term, and that they distorted the workings of the labour market. By the late 1970s this view was relatively uncontroversial; most British economists accepted that the traditional 'Norm with Exceptions' approach, which had been the basic format of British incomes policies in the 1960s and 1970s, had not worked well and that more fundamental reforms to the wage bargaining system were required (Blackaby, 1979). Nevertheless it would be wrong to argue that the government was indifferent to wage determination. In the early 1980s they introduced a series of industrial relations measures (Chapter 13) which deliberately set out to improve the bargaining position of employers and were expected to exert downward pressure on wage settlements. Similarly within the public sector the cash limits included an allowance for increases in pay, and, although there was no obligation for wage settlements to settle at or below the implicit norm, increases above that were bound to have adverse effects upon employment and to encourage restraint.

The strategy met with both success and failure. The main achievement, of course, was the speed of the disinflation after the initial hiccup. As Fig. 6.5 shows, because of the disturbances at the end of the 1970s, it is difficult to gauge what the underlying inflation rate was when the policy was initiated in 1979. Nevertheless after the supply-shocks of 1979–80 had worked their way through there was a rapid disinflation from a peak of 18 per cent in 1980 to an average of just below 5 between 1983 and 1987. Such rates had not been achieved since the late 1960s and brought Britain back into line with that in the other industrialized countries.

The main proximate cause of this disinflation was a rapid deceleration in wage costs (Fig. 6.6). Between 1980 and 1982 the growth of average earnings fell from 18 to 9 per cent, after which they stabilized at around 7 per cent. This decceleration was more rapid than many economists had predicted and contradicted the contention that wage inflation had become completely unresponsive to demand pressures. No doubt it also reflected the operation of a number of forces including the design of the counter-inflationary strategy. There cannot be much doubt, however, that the severity of the downturn, which was comparable with the Great Depression of 1929–32, by threatening innumerable firms and plants with closure, was a potent factor influencing attitudes and leading to lower wage settlements. At the same time the reduction in wage costs was assisted by a significant improvement in productivity growth. This again would seem to have been partly attributable to the severity of the downturn, which exposed the company sector to a profits squeeze and weakened trade union resistance to change and thus brought about an improvement in working practices (Buiter and Miller, 1983).

At more or less the same time the disinflation was speeded up by a fall in primary commodity prices (Beckerman, 1985; Beckerman and Jenkinson, 1986). For example, between 1980 and 1982 the UNCTAD primary commodity price index showed a decline of 28 per cent, after which it remained fairly stable. Oil prices also fell at this time. They rose by 12 per cent between 1980 and 1981, but between 1981 and 1985 they fell by 22 per cent. This fall in primary commodity prices largely reflected the emergence of a world-wide recession between 1979 and 1981. This was itself a reaction to the counter-inflationary policy in the United States and to OPEC 2, which, by reigniting inflationary pressures in the industrialized countries, had encouraged them to adopt extinguishing policies.

Despite the rapid disinflation after 1980, however, the Thatcher experiment clearly contradicted the contention that the strategy could be carried out without a significant loss of output or a rise in unemployment. Thus between 1979 and 1981 real GDP fell by 4.8 per cent and industrial production by 9.8. Over the same period unemployment (on the old measure) rose from 5 per cent in 1979 to 10.5 per cent in 1982. Thereafter there was a slow-down in the rate of increase with unemployment peaking at over 13 per cent in 1986. Although in part this deterioration was due to the world recession, there cannot be any doubt that an important cause was the profit squeeze which was itself the product of the deflationary strategy at a time when the economy was exposed to the inflationary supply-shocks of 1979–80 (Worswick, 1984). Nevertheless, as Table 6.3 shows, the sacrifice ratio was not obviously inferior to that of the other Western countries which adopted disinflationary policies at about this time.

TABLE 6.3. *Unemployment sacrifice ratio: 1981–1988*

| Country | Ratio | Country | Ratio |
|---|---|---|---|
| Australia | 7.65 | France | 1.41 |
| Netherlands | 5.03 | Italy | 1.02 |
| Germany | 4.17 | Switzerland | 0.81 |
| Spain | 3.70 | Norway | 0.68 |
| Ireland | 2.41 | Japan | 0.66 |
| Austria | 2.29 | Luxembourg | 0.52 |
| Canada | 2.18 | Portugal | 0.44 |
| Greece | 2.08 | Sweden | 0.27 |
| Belgium | 1.98 | Finland | 0.25 |
| U.K | 1.54 | U.S.A | −0.09 |
| New Zealand | 1.53 | Denmark | −0.11 |

*Source*: Dornbusch (1989).

Faced with this rise in unemployment the government did not react in the traditional manner by reflating the economy. And indeed at the height of the recession in 1981 fiscal policy was actually tightened. Although this rejection of Keynesianism should not be exaggerated, the strategy adopted was very much at variance with that of the Labour Government in the mid-1970s which, as we have seen, was reluctant to deflate. This change in direction, of course, was due to a combination of factors. We have already pointed to the different ideological position of the government and to the fact that its policy was seen as an investment in credibility (Begg, 1987). But probably more than anything else the ability and willingness of the government to persist with this policy stance reflects the underlying dissatisfaction of the electorate with the policies of the 1970s, coupled with the general unpopularity of inflation.

The other disappointing aspect of performance was the failure of inflation, particularly wage inflation, to fall after 1983 despite the high levels of unemployment (Fig. 6.7). Indeed in response to demand pressures, wage increases started to accelerate after 1987. This obviously implies that in the mid- to late 1980s wage settlements were not very sensitive to the level of unemployment. The reasons for this are not altogether clear. One possibility is that with the development of decentralized bargaining, wage negotiators had become more sensitive to the wage-employment prospects of those in employment and less to those unemployed (Lindbeck and Snower, 1985). This would help explain why wage inflation fell rapidly between 1980 and 1983, when unemployment increased significantly, and why it subsequently stabilized and even rose in response to the improvement in the employment situation. It has also been argued that NAIRU has risen over the period due to a change in the composition of employment. The basis of this contention is that with the severity of unemployment in the early 1980s a fairly high proportion of those affected became subject to long-duration unemployment. This effectively removed those concerned from the labour market either by discouraging them from searching for employment or by reducing their attractiveness to employers (Nickell, 1986). But the result was that the unemployment rate significantly over-stated the excess supply pressures in the labour market.


## VIII. Conclusions

At the beginning of this chapter it was argued that the rise in inflation in the late 1960s and 1970s was an important development during the post-war period and that it was more than coincidence that it was associated with a deterioration in other aspects of macroeconomic performance. Certainly this inflation was subsequently reduced. But this was achieved through deflationary measures that raised unemployment, and to some extent the emergence of high unemployment from the mid-1970s should be regarded as a manifestation of the same pressures which had resulted in an upsurge in inflation. In accounting for this rise in inflation the explanation advanced has been similar to that proposed in the well-known OECD Report of the mid-1970s (McCracken *et al.*, 1977). This viewed the deterioration as the outcome of a large number of interrelated disturbances. For simplicity these can be summarized under four headings: external developments, policy mistakes, supply-shocks, and structural changes.

Of the external developments the most important was the unwillingness of the British Government to maintain its commitment to a fixed exchange rate in the early 1970s. This removed an important financial discipline upon the conduct of domestic policy, something of which British Governments took advantage for most of the decade. Nevertheless the abandonment of the commitment to a fixed exchange rate should be regarded as part of a long-term process which began with the abandonment of the Gold Standard in 1931 and continued with the ratification of the Bretton Woods system in 1944 (Deane, 1979). A significant feature of the latter was that it allowed a country to devalue its currency, an option which Britain exercised twice, and to pursue expansionary policies in the knowledge that Balance of Payments difficulties could be removed without the need to take restrictive measures. In practice the system also allowed the United States to run Balance of Payments deficits, a privilege not extended to other countries except for short periods. Although for most of the Bretton Woods period the American Government did not take advantage of this, its policy became more expansionary in the late 1960s and it became a source of rising inflation in the world economy.

Policy mistakes, however, were not confined to the US Government. On the domestic front the Maudling Experiment of 1962/3, which preceded the 1967 devaluation, the Heath–Barber Boom with the decision to float sterling, the inclusion of the threshold clauses in Stage III of the Heath Government's incomes policy and the increase in VAT in 1979 are all conspicuous examples of policy mistakes which contributed to the rise of inflation. More controversially, it has also been argued that the failure of the Labour Government to move decisively in the aftermath of OPEC 1 was a policy error which made subsequent adjustment more difficult.

The view that the high inflation of the 1970s was primarily the outcome of misguided government policy is one, of course, which is most closely associated with the monetarists, who have argued that the rise in inflation was the direct consequence of higher monetary growth. The evidence clearly supports the contention that monetary conditions were easier in the 1970s than before (Fig. 6.8), and it is also certainly correct that a less permissive monetary policy would have resulted in lower inflation, although quite possibly at the expense of higher unemployment. For all that, however, it is also doubtful whether a more restrained and less erratic monetary policy would have totally prevented inflation from rising during the 1970s.

One important reason for this was that the economy became more exposed to autonomous supply-side disturbances. First, there was an unusual number of severe import shocks: the Primary Commodity Boom of 1972–3, OPEC 1, and OPEC 2. These, moreover, were superimposed on a labour market that had become more prone to autonomous wage pressures, that was sensitive to import shocks and in which wage settlements had apparently become less sensitive to demand pressures. These autonomous wage-push pressures reflect long-term structural changes. Numerous institutional, social, and economic changes took place over the post-war period and, given the present state of our knowledge, it is difficult to ascertain what has been relevant and what has not. But, for example, rising material aspirations, more egalitarian attitudes and the emergence of decentralized bargaining all spring to mind as potentially important developments. Furthermore Britain was handicapped by the destabilizing impact of incomes policies and by a poor relative growth performance.

# 7

# Unemployment*

## S. N. BROADBERRY

### I. Introduction

The rate of unemployment in Britain since 1870 is shown in Fig. 7.1. Viewed in this long-run historical perspective, post-Second World War unemployment trends are very striking. A 20-year period from the end of the war to the mid-1960s was characterized by low and stable unemployment. During this period many optimistic social and economic commentators believed that the problem of unemployment had been solved, and that full employment had been secured for ever. However, this optimism was rudely shattered with the rising trend of unemployment from the late 1960s. Indeed, the late 1970s and the early 1980s saw a return to the unemployment rates of the 1920s and 1930s. Although unemployment has fallen since 1986, there has been no return to the full employment of the 1950s and 1960s. In this chapter, then, we shall seek to understand why unemployment was so low in the 1950s and 1960s, and why it rose so sharply during the 1970s and 1980s.

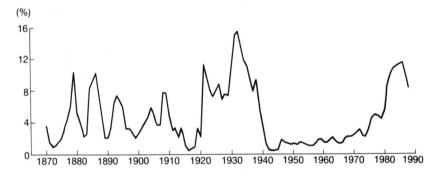

FIG. 7.1.  *Unemployment rate 1870–1988*

One basic difference between the rising unemployment of the 1930s and that of the 1970s is that the former was accompanied by falling prices, while the latter was accompanied by rapid inflation. Put crudely, this difference reflects the fact that unemployment in the 1930s was rooted in falling aggregate demand, which tended to reduce prices as output fell and unemployment rose, while the unemployment of the 1970s was rooted in restrictions of aggregate supply, which put upward pressure

* I am grateful to the editors for many helpful comments, and to Tim Jenkinson for allowing me access to unpublished work. Any remaining errors are my responsibility.

on prices as output fell and unemployment rose. The further increase of unemployment in the early 1980s resulted from government policy to deflate aggregate demand as a way of reducing inflation. A relaxation of policy from the mid-1980s has seen some reduction of unemployment, accompanied by a rekindling of inflationary pressures.

However, before we seek to explain the pattern of unemployment we should first of all clarify what we mean by unemployment, and why it matters. On the issue of what we mean by unemployment, we note that the rate of unemployment is the number of people without a job expressed as a percentage of the total registered labour force (Parkin and Bade, 1986, p. 86). This is thus a stock concept, which can be related to flows into and out of unemployment. The unemployment rate can rise because more people become unemployed (i.e. inflows rise) or because less unemployed people find jobs (i.e. outflows fall). In the latter case, the duration of unemployment will rise. In post-war Britain variations in the unemployment rate have been principally due to variations in duration rather than to variations in the number of people of losing their jobs (Creedy, 1981, p. 8).

Most people take it for granted that a rise in the unemployment rate is a bad thing. This arises from the notion that unemployment is involuntary, and that the unemployed would like a job at the going wage. If people are voluntarily unemployed, they have chosen leisure over income, so that a reduction in the unemployment rate would not necessarily raise social welfare. Thus we shall need to consider the possibility that some unemployment represents a choice of leisure over income. However, as we shall make clear later on, we do not believe that such an approach is at all satisfactory as an explanation of the rising trend in unemployment since the mid-1960s.

Thus we regard most unemployment as economically inefficient, representing involuntarily foregone production. In addition, there has been a long tradition in the social sciences which emphasizes the psychological, social, and political evils of unemployment. We refer the interested reader to Sinfield (1981) for an introduction to the literature, and here confine ourselves to a brief statement of the issues. From the emergence of mass unemployment in the 1930s, social psychologists have charted the reaction of individuals to unemployment, noting a pattern of shock–optimism–pessimism–fatalism. After the initial shock of losing his job, the worker remains optimistic as he begins to search for a job. However, after a while, when he fails to obtain a job, he becomes pessimistic, worried, and distressed. Finally, the individual becomes fatalistic, with an attitude of despair (Sinfield, 1981, p. 37).

From the political point of view, too, mass unemployment has been blamed for pathological trends such as the rise of political extremism, which threatens the democratic system. Clearly the 1930s provide some evidence here, and again in the 1970s and 1980s a common reaction to rising unemployment has been a polarization of political life (Sinfield, 1981, ch. 5; Garraty, 1978).

In addition unemployment has been linked to many social trends. Rising crime, violence, drug and alcohol abuse, and even suicide, have all been blamed on the high unemployment of the 1970s and 1980s, and the boredom, frustration, and bitterness of the unemployed.

## II. Unemployment Experience

### 1. *The Labour Force*

The definition of the labour force used here is employees in employment, plus the armed forces and self-employed, plus the unemployed. The aggregate figures for the UK are plotted in Fig. 7.2. Clearly there is a rising trend, but with some fluctuations. Before we discuss the post-war situation in more detail it will be helpful to introduce a historical perspective, comparing labour force growth since 1945 with the experience of the previous century. Matthews *et al.* (1982) show that the post-war growth of the labour force has been considerably slower than in the preceding century. This can be explained essentially by demographic factors. After 1914 population growth slowed down as fertility fell by more than mortality. However, the labour force continued to grow steadily between the wars as the proportion of children in the population fell. After 1945 the fall in the birth rate stopped and the proportion of children in the population began to rise. In addition, the proportion of the elderly in the population began to rise.

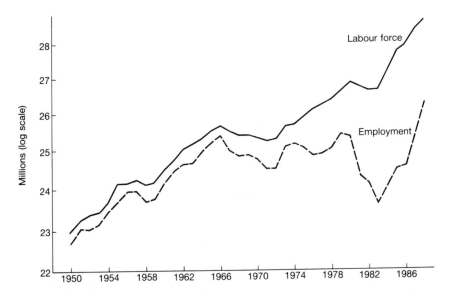

FIG. 7.2. *Employment and the labour force*

Turning to the situation since the Second World War we can identify a period of growth in the labour force until 1966, followed by a period of stagnation to 1974, in turn followed by a recovery of growth. These trends can be related to demographic factors and activity rates. Much of this section draws on the discussion in Prest and Coppock (1984, ch. 5). The slow-down of labour force growth from 1966 can be attributed to slower population growth and adverse age distribution trends on the demographic side, and to a rapid extension of education in the 15–24 age groups on the participation side. From the mid-1970s we see a recovery in the labour-force growth rate primarily as a result of the post-war 'baby-boom' having a favourable effect on the age distribution.

Activity rates have behaved rather differently for men and women. For men there has been a downward trend in activity rates, with young men spending longer in education and older men retiring earlier. These trends are the results of rising income and greater social provision.

While male activity rates have been declining through the post-war period, female activity rates have risen sharply, mainly due to a rise in activity rates for married women aged 25–64. This represents an acceleration of a trend that began at the turn of the century. It can be explained by a combination of supply and demand factors. On the demand side, the huge rise in the demand for labour during and after the Second World War must have increased job opportunities for women. On the supply side, there has been a fall in family size and substantial labour-saving technical progress in housework, which has given women more time to spend in the labour market. However, we must be careful here, since rising incomes will also lead to an increased demand for leisure, which would tend to reduce women's participation rates.

So far we have said nothing about the stagnation in the labour force during 1981–3, which we have not treated as a separate phase. For this represents what is known as the 'discouraged worker' effect during the recession of those years. The idea is that in recessions, when jobs are scarce and wages low, marginal workers become discouraged from seeking a job, and withdraw from the labour force in some way, for example to continue with education, retrain, or retire. Thus the labour force contracts with a recession. However, in addition to the discouraged worker effect, there is also an 'added worker' effect, which works in the opposite direction. If primary or permanent workers are made redundant during a recession, household income may be maintained by 'secondary' or temporary workers taking jobs. The procyclical movement of the labour force apparent from Fig. 7.2 suggests that the discouraged worker effect outweighs the added worker effect during the post-war period.

To what extent has the growth of the labour force been responsible for rising unemployment? Foster (1974) suggests that although in the long run more people entering the labour force means more demand as well as more labour supply, there can be short-run problems of integrating a large cohort into the workforce, since new workers need to be combined with experienced workers. Thus it is possible to have excess supply of inexperienced workers with excess demand for experienced labour. Foster offers this as an explanation for rising unemployment from the mid-1960s. This does not seem a very promising argument, since as we saw from Fig. 7.2, the labour force fell from a peak in 1966. However, the argument may be more plausible as an explanation of the rising labour force from the mid-1970s, as the post-war baby-boom generation entered the labour market.

## 2. Employment

The definition of employment used here includes the armed forces and the self-employed. Aggregate employment is shown in Fig. 7.2. After an upward trend to 1966, employment fluctuated around the 25-million level before taking a sharp plunge during the recession from 1979. After a sustained recovery from 1983, employment only surpassed the 1966 peak level in 1988.

As with the labour force, the aggregate figures mask some divergent trends between males and females. Both male and female employment rose steadily to the mid-1960s, after which female employment continued to grow while male employment fell. Only with the sharp recession from 1979 did female employment fall significantly. Another significant difference between male and female employment is the much higher proportion of women who work on a part-time basis.

There have also been large changes in the distribution of employment between sectors. During the mid-1950s manufacturing accounted for about 42.5 per cent of employment, but this had fallen to only 27 per cent by 1983 (Prest and Coppock, 1984, p. 248). Indeed, since 1966 employment in manufacturing has fallen in absolute as well as relative terms. However, as Matthews *et al.* (1982) note, the size of the manufacturing sector was artificially swollen by the Second World War, so to some extent the decline in manufacturing employment can be seen as a return to the pre-war 'norm'. The decline in manufacturing employment has been accompanied by a rise in service sector employment, particularly in insurance, banking, finance, and business services, and in professional and scientific services.

Another way of breaking down employment is between the public and private sectors. Public sector employment has increased its share of total employment over the post-war period, rising from 24 per cent in 1961 to 30 per cent in 1980 (Prest and Coppock, 1984, p. 248). This trend has been reversed slightly since 1980 with privatization and cutbacks in government expenditure. These trends can be explained in terms of shifts in demand and productivity growth differentials. The latter is particularly important in explaining the relative growth of service-sector employment, since productivity growth has been much higher in the manufacturing sector, thus reducing labour demand in manufacturing.

Junankar (1981) relates unemployment to structural change, measured by changes in the size of manufacturing output against GDP. However, no analytical framework is offered. The inference is that structural change has been too fast during the 1970s and 1980s. Yet this is surely unsatisfactory. The decline of British manufacturing during this period is more plausibly seen as a failure to bring about structural change quickly enough in the face of rapid changes in demand.

### 3. *Unemployment*

Since the Second World War, with the universal extension of the unemployment insurance system, we have a quantitative picture of unemployment trends across the whole economy. This contrasts with previous periods, for which we have to infer total unemployment from series of varying reliability based on trade union figures or unemployment insurance data of incomplete coverage (Garside, 1980). Thus there are problems of comparability between periods. Nevertheless, most historians agree on the general picture of unemployment that can be drawn from Feinstein's (1972) estimates, shown in Fig. 7.1.

Unemployment before 1914 is usually seen as highly volatile, with large sectors of the economy subject to intermittent, casual employment conditions. Equally clearly, there is general agreement that the inter-war period was characterized by an underlying high level of unemployment, with peak levels higher than anything seen before 1914. With a return to full employment during the Second World War, the 1950s and 1960s are characterized by a very low and stable rate of unemployment. It is this post-war boom that stands out as exceptional in a historical context. The rising unemployment of the 1970s and early 1980s has led to a return of the unemployment levels of the 1930s. Despite falling unemployment during the mid-1980s, there has been no return to the full employment of the 1950s and 1960s.

Finally on the aggregate unemployment figures, within the post-war period there have been a number of subtle changes in the way unemployment is measured. For example, the treatment of students, school-leavers, those on training schemes, married women, pensioners, etc., can make a significant difference to the recorded rate of unemployment. Again, however, there is surely no doubt that the broad trend shown in Fig. 7.1 is correct. The only question is whether the rise in unemployment during the 1970s and 1980s has been under-recorded by excluding those on special employment schemes.

In this section we consider the distribution of unemployment between regions, industries, occupations, and age and sex groups. Dealing first with the regional distribution of unemployment, Table 7.1 gives unemployment rates by regions over the period 1929 to 1986.[1] Although the regional classifications have changed in detail over time, it seems clear that there has been a narrowing of the differential between the relatively prosperous south and the depressed north. During the high unemployment of the 1930s, the North, Wales, and Scotland had unemployment rates about three times higher than the South-East. The proportionate differential was similar during the boom of the 1950s and 1960s. By the 1980s, however, the difference was less than a factor of two. Also, by the 1980s the previously prosperous West Midlands and North-West were experiencing high rates of unemployment comparable with the North, Wales, and Scotland.

TABLE 7.1. *Regional unemployment rates*

| | 1929 | 1937 | 1951 | 1964 | 1973 | 1979 | 1986 |
|---|---|---|---|---|---|---|---|
| South-East | 4.5 | 5.4 | 0.9 | 1.0 | 1.3 | 2.9 | 8.3 |
| East Anglia | 4.5 | 5.4 | 0.9 | 1.0 | 1.6 | 3.7 | 8.6 |
| South-West | 6.8 | 6.8 | 1.2 | 1.5 | 2.1 | 4.6 | 9.6 |
| West Midlands | 9.1 | 6.6 | 0.4 | 0.9 | 1.7 | 4.7 | 12.7 |
| East Midlands | 9.1 | 6.6 | 0.7 | 1.1 | 1.8 | 3.8 | 10.2 |
| Yorks & Humber | 12.6 | 12.0 | 0.7 | 1.1 | 2.3 | 4.7 | 12.6 |
| North-West | 12.6 | 12.8 | 1.2 | 2.1 | 2.9 | 5.9 | 14.1 |
| North | 12.6 | 16.7 | 2.2 | 3.3 | 3.9 | 7.3 | 15.3 |
| Wales | 18.2 | 20.7 | 2.7 | 2.6 | 3.0 | 6.3 | 13.9 |
| Scotland | 11.0 | 14.0 | 2.5 | 3.6 | 3.8 | 6.8 | 14.0 |
| Northern Ireland | 13.8 | 21.7 | 6.1 | 6.6 | 4.9 | 9.7 | 18.6 |
| United Kingdom | 9.7 | 10.1 | 1.3 | 1.7 | 2.0 | 4.7 | 11.3 |

*Sources*: Beck (1951); Ministry of Labour *Gazette* (1951); *Economic Trends*.

One reason for this narrowing differential is post-war regional policy, which resulted in firms moving to previously depressed regions to take advantage of capital grants and tax incentives. However, we should be careful not to overstate

[1] This section draws on Aldcroft (1984), ch. 1.

the importance of regional policy, since there were other factors at work. In particular, with the rise in the relative importance of services, one would expect less geographical dispersion of unemployment rates (Aldcroft, 1984, p. 14). A severe contraction in a geographically concentrated manufacturing industry will no longer have an immediate dramatic effect on the overall unemployment rate in the region since the manufacturing sector is no longer such a large employer. Furthermore, redundancy payments will help to dampen the knock-on effects to other businesses within the region.

Although the dispersion of unemployment between regions has narrowed over the post-war period, a new spatial dimension to unemployment has emerged, with high rates of unemployment in inner city areas (Prest and Coppock, 1984, p. 256). In particular, there has been a movement of manufacturing employment out of the inner-city areas to outer-city areas, small towns, and rural areas. This has happened in all regions.

A second aspect of the distribution of unemployment is variation across industries. Compared with the situation between the wars, unemployment has been more evenly dispersed among industries during the post-war period. Between the wars the unemployment rate in the old staples of coal-mining, shipbuilding, cotton, and iron and steel was sometimes as much as seven or eight times as high as in the new industries such as chemicals, cars and aircraft, gas, water and electricity, and electrical engineering.[2] In the post-war period, although the unemployment rate has generally been higher in manufacturing than in services, within manufacturing unemployment has been fairly evenly spread. For example, in 1975, when the rate of unemployment for the economy as a whole was 4.7 per cent, the highest rate in manufacturing was 9.0 per cent for leather, leather goods, and fur, and the lowest rate was 2.8 per cent for instrument engineering.[3]

A third feature of the unemployment distribution is occupational differences. Here we know that the less skilled have a much larger probability of experiencing unemployment than the skilled. Evidence suggests that the position of semi-skilled and manual workers has deteriorated over the post-war period, particularly since the 1970s, when unemployment among these groups has risen especially fast (Aldcroft, 1984, p. 16).

Fourth, let us consider demographic aspects. We have already noted the different employment and labour-force experiences of men and women, so it is not surprising to find lower unemployment rates among women in the post-war period. This was also true between the wars, as the figures of Beck (1951) demonstrate. This remains true over all age groups. However, for both men and women, unemployment rates vary considerably by wage group. Prime-age men and women have lower unemployment rates than younger (under 25) and older (over 55) groups. Youth unemployment (under 20) has become particularly serious during the 1970s and 1980s, and appears to be due to a cutback in recruitment during recession and a rise in the cost of hiring young workers relative to the cost of hiring adults (Prest and Coppock, 1984, p. 254). This relatively high youth unemployment during the 1970s and 1980s is in marked contrast to the situation in the 1930s, when juvenile unemployment

[2] Using figures on the insured unemployment in Department of Employment and Productivity (1971), Table 164.
[3] Department of Employment *Gazette*, 1975. Note that the official unemployment rate given here has subsequently been revised downwards.

was relatively low. Garside (1977) attributes this low juvenile unemployment of the 1930s to the relative cheapness of juvenile labour at the time, although Benjamin and Kochin (1979a) argue that it was a result of the unavailability of unemployment benefits for this group of workers.

The relatively high unemployment among older workers during the post-war period is a continuation of a trend which also existed during the inter-war period. This high rate of unemployment among older workers is caused by long duration rather than by any greater probability of job loss. This reflects a reluctance of firms to hire older workers, since many older workers are less flexible, more prone to illness and disability, and are likely to command a wage in excess of their declining productivity (Prest and Coppock, 1984, pp. 254–5).

The rising duration of unemployment in the 1970s and 1980s has seen a rise in the problem of long-term unemployment of twelve months or more. This also occurred in the 1930s, as noted by Crafts (1987). This is of particular concern since a long spell of unemployment leads to loss of skills and loss of confidence on the part of workers, who are no longer really part of the effective labour force. On the part of employers, a long spell of unemployment is seen as a signal of unsuitability for employment. Thus the probability of re-employment falls markedly with long unemployment. Cross (1982) calls this a 'hysteresis' effect, since it implies that a reversal of the forces causing the rise in unemployment will not lead to a reduction of unemployment.

## III. The Causes of Unemployment

### 1. Inflation, Unemployment, and Labour Market Equilibrium

A great deal of economic analysis explores the relationship between unemployment and inflation. The basic idea is that there is a natural rate of unemployment where the supply and demand for labour are in equilibrium. If the government raises aggregate demand in an attempt to lower unemployment below this natural rate, then inflation accelerates.

To see this, consider the process outlined in Fig. 7.3. Suppose the economy is initially at a state of rest with zero inflation at the natural rate of unemployment $U^*$. Suppose the government raises aggregate demand to lower unemployment to $U_1$. The economy moves along the Phillips Curve $PC_1$ with inflation rising to $\overset{\circ}{P}_1$. Consider the position in the labour market. Workers' expectations of inflation are zero, given by the rate of inflation at the beginning of the period. However, inflation actually rises to $\overset{\circ}{P}_1$, so that the nominal price level will be higher at the end of the period. Thus nominal wages will also be higher. With constant inflationary expectations, workers will perceive the higher nominal wage rate as a higher real wage rate, and thus will be less likely to quit their jobs, while those previously unemployed will be more likely to accept job offers. Thus at the end of the period unemployment is $U_1$ and inflation is $\overset{\circ}{P}_1$.

However, in the long run expectations of inflation will adjust. If again workers expect inflation next period to be equal to inflation last period, expected inflation rises to $\overset{\circ}{P}_1$ at the beginning of the second period, and the Phillips Curve shifts out to

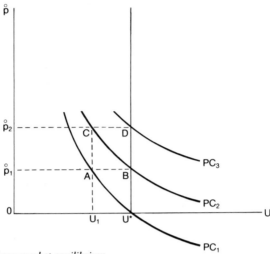

FIG. 7.3.   *Labour market equilibrium*

$PC_2$. Workers then correctly see that the higher nominal wage is not a higher real wage and search longer between jobs, so that unemployment rises back to $U^*$. A similar analysis would take the economy to C and D as aggregate demand expanded and expectations adjusted again. Thus unemployment can only be held below the natural rate at the cost of accelerating inflation.

The natural rate, then, is best regarded as the rate of unemployment below which there will be accelerating inflation. Hence Layard and Nickell (1985) use the term non-accelerating inflation rate of unemployment or NAIRU. This name is preferred to the natural rate, since there need not be anything natural about it. This is particularly important in a non-competitive economy, where, for example, trade unions may restrict the supply of labour.

## 2. *The Determinants of the NAIRU*

The NAIRU is most easily understood using a diagram from Layard (1986), reproduced here as Fig. 7.4. At any time there is a limit to the living standards workers can have, which Layard calls the 'feasible' real wage. This feasible real wage can be thought of as the inverse of the normal price mark-up (of prices over wages) of firms. Firms have to make a profit, so if workers succeed in obtaining an increase in money wages, firms must raise prices. But then there is inflation and the higher money wages negotiated by unions do not translate into higher real wages. The feasible real wage is a horizontal line in Fig. 7.4 because the normal price mark-up is assumed not to vary with unemployment.

Workers have a 'target' real wage, which is not necessarily the same as the feasible real wage. But if the target is greater than the feasible real wage, inflation will result. Workers press for higher money wages, and firms respond by increasing prices. A rise in unemployment is then needed to moderate the target real wage and stop inflation from accelerating. This effect is represented by the downward-sloping

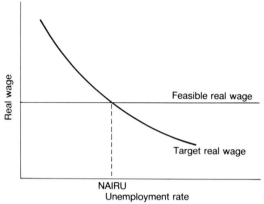

FIG. 7.4.  *The NAIRU*

target real wage curve, indicating that as unemployment rises, workers, fearful for their jobs, reduce their wage aspirations.

The NAIRU is given by the intersection of the feasible and target real wage curves. Where the two curves meet, the target real wage is consistent with the real wage that is feasible, so there will be no pressure for inflation to accelerate. Note that the NAIRU could rise because of a fall in the feasible real wage (caused for example by a rise in the price of imported raw materials), or because of a rise in the target real wage (caused for example by trade union militancy). Note also that unemployment could rise because of a rise in the NAIRU or because of a rise in unemployment above the NAIRU (caused for example by a deflationary aggregate demand policy).

It should be noted that in this approach, the traditional macroeconomist's distinction between Keynesian unemployment (due to insufficient aggregate demand) and classical unemployment (due to excessive wages) disappears. For as we shall see, although much of the rise in unemployment during the late 1970s and early 1980s can be seen as a result of a deflation of aggregate demand, this deflationary policy must in turn be seen as a response to inflationary pressures arising from the excessive target wages of workers.

### 3. *A Quantitative Summary*

The basic facts that we seek to explain are the low rate of unemployment during the post-war boom of the 1950s and 1960s and the rising unemployment of the 1970s and early 1980s. To a large extent the reasons for the low unemployment of the 1950s and 1960s can be taken to be the absence of the factors which explain the higher unemployment of the 1970s and 1980s. This is not entirely satisfactory, however, because as we saw from Fig. 7.1, the post-war boom was exceptional in a historical context. Thus we shall also examine the factors underlying the post-war boom in the next section. For the remainder of this section, however, we shall take the major problem to be explaining the rise in unemployment from the late 1960s. Here we examine the broad trends in the variables which have commonly been used to explain this rise in unemployment.

In Figs. 7.5 to 7.7 we plot the major variables that have been used to explain fluctuations in unemployment during this period. We begin by considering in Fig. 7.5 factors which may have caused the NAIRU to rise through a rise in the target real wage. A popular explanation has focused on the role of the social security system. Many authors have claimed that much of the rising unemployment of the 1970s and early 1980s can be interpreted as a rise in voluntary unemployment as a result of generous unemployment benefits.[4] A rise in the ratio of unemployment benefits to wages (known as the replacement ratio) causes workers to become more choosy about the jobs they are prepared to take, and thus raises the target wage. For any given level of vacancies, there will be a higher level of unemployment, as unemployed workers spend longer searching for an acceptable job.

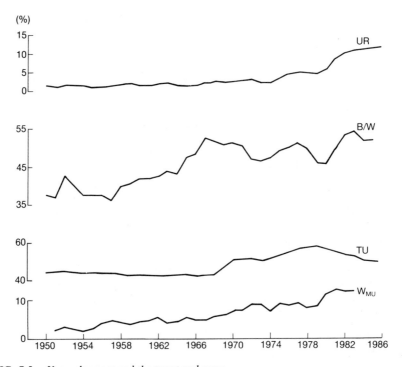

FIG. 7.5.  *Unemployment and the target real wage*

Most labour economists agree that the provision of a high level of benefits will tend to raise the unemployment rate, but it is also generally agreed that the elasticity of unemployment with respect to benefits is fairly low (Narendranathan *et al.*, 1986). Thus it seems likely that the rise in the replacement ratio (B/W) during the 1960s, which can be seen in Fig. 7.5, accounts for a small rise in the rate of unemployment. However, since the replacement ratio has not been on a rising trend since the late 1960s, this does not seem a promising explanation for the sharp rise in unemployment during the late 1970s and early 1980s. Indeed, during the late 1970s the replacement ratio actually fell. It is interesting to note at this point that

[4] See particularly Minford (1983).

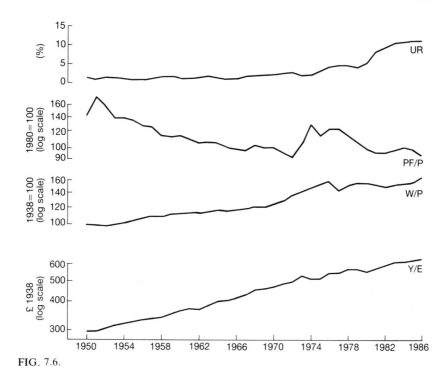

FIG. 7.6.

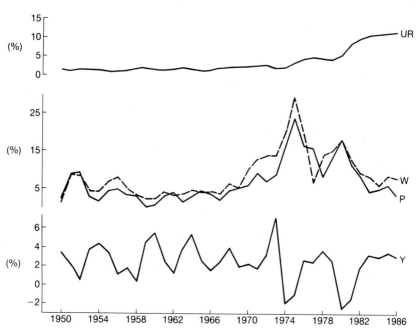

FIG. 7.7.

Benjamin and Kochin (1979*b*) also blame the high unemployment of the inter-war period on a high replacement ratio. However, as Metcalf *et al.* (1982) point out, since the replacement ratio was of the same order of magnitude in the 1930s and the 1950s, the benefit system cannot explain the difference between high unemployment during the 1930s and low unemployment during the 1950s.

In Fig. 7.5 we also plot two measures of trade union power, another factor which has been blamed for raising the target real wage and hence the NAIRU. There has been a long tradition, formalized by Hines (1964) that wage inflation was linked to trade-union power. The simple proxy for union power used by Hines was the proportion of the labour force unionized. This is shown in Fig. 7.5 as the variable TU. The large rise in TU from the late 1960s suggests there may be some role for union power in the accelerating inflationary pressure of this period. More recently, Layard and Nickell (1985) argue that the trade union wage mark-up (of union over non-union wages) is a better measure of union power. Unlike the proportion of the labour force unionized, the union wage mark-up ($W_{MU}$) has continued to rise during the 1980s.

We now turn to factors which may have caused the NAIRU to rise through a fall in the feasible real wage. One obvious candidate here is the real import price (PF/P) shown in Fig. 7.6. After falling steadily from the Korean War peak, the real import price received a sudden jolt with the oil shock of 1973–4, when the price of oil was quadrupled. However, the second oil shock of 1979–80, when the price of oil was further doubled, does not show up here, as by this time Britain was a net exporter of oil. A second factor affecting the feasible real wage is employers' labour taxes. We do not graph this variable as Layard and Nickell are only able to pin down the trend, but not the absolute level. The employers' labour tax rate has risen throughout the period, but with the sharpest increases occurring during 1965–6 and 1975–8. Another factor affecting the feasible real wage is the slowdown of productivity growth during the 1970s after the long boom of the 1960s. This is seen as a factor behind the rising NAIRU because of workers' refusal to adjust real wage aspirations to the lower productivity growth. Thus in Fig. 7.6 the trend in real wage (W/P) growth accelerates during the 1970s just as the trend in labour productivity (Y/E) growth turns down. This illustrates an important caveat to the Layard and Nickell view, where workers pressing for higher wages leads only to higher inflation because firms raise prices to offset the higher wages. Unemployment then rises only because the government deflates demand to reduce inflation. In an open economy, it may not be possible for firms to raise prices sufficiently to offset the higher wages because of competition from foreign firms which do not face higher wages. Then the higher real wage may lead to a fall in labour demand as in the standard case of classical unemployment.

However, there seems little doubt that the main effect of the rising target real wage and falling feasible real wage of the 1970s was the acceleration of inflation. It was this acceleration of inflation which finally led the government to reduce aggregate demand, which brought inflation down only at the cost of a huge rise in unemployment. Thus in Fig. 7.7 we plot the rate of price inflation ($\dot{P}$) and the rate of growth of aggregate demand ($\dot{Y}$). In addition we plot the rate of wage inflation ($\dot{W}$) along with the rate of price inflation to illustrate the frustration of the attempt by workers to get a bigger share of the national income.

## IV.  Unemployment in the 1950s and 1960s: The Post-War Boom

During the 1950s and early 1960s, unemployment rates of between 1 and 2 per cent were regarded as normal. Seen from this perspective, when unemployment began to rise from the late 1960s, it is natural that economists at the time sought merely to explain why unemployment was rising. However, seen from a historical perspective, unemployment during the 1950s and 1960s seems abnormally low and stable, and we also need to explain this fact. Thus in this section we ask what were the factors underlying the post-war boom?

To a large extent this low unemployment of the 1950s and 1960s was a feature of the world economy as a whole. How, then, do we explain the long boom after the Second World War compared with the long slump after the First World War? For a long time it was believed that the difference was the adoption of Keynesian full employment policies after the Second World War. However, this myth was exploded by the apparently uncontrollable rise in unemployment from the late 1960s. Furthermore, as Matthews (1968) noted, governments acted to restrain rather than boost demand in the post-1945 period. The major reason for the higher level of aggregate demand during the post-war period was a higher level of investment.

One way in which it is possible to reserve a role for demand management here is via the creation of a general environment conducive to investment. There is surely something to be said for this view, for the differences between international economic relations between the wars and after the Second World War could hardly be more stark. After the First World War there was chaos in the international monetary system with huge debt and reparations problems, dramatic inflations, currency realignments, and eventually an attempt to restore the gold standard. Furthermore, world trade was hampered by tariffs, quotas, and bilateral agreements. After the Second World War a conscious effort was made to avoid these non-cooperative aspects of inter-war international economic relations with the establishment of the International Monetary Fund (IMF) and the multilateral General Agreement on Tariffs and Trade (GATT). It is worth noting that the end of the post-war boom has coincided with the abandonment of the fixed exchange rate and a retreat from free trade.

Such an environment on the demand side was surely conducive to full employment. However, inflexibilities on the supply side may still have hindered the achievement of this objective. Hence we also need to consider the situation within the British labour market. Flanagan et al. (1983) argue that the reason for the low unemployment of the 1950s and 1960s was the existence of an 'implicit' incomes policy between unions, employers, and governments. This made it possible for governments to maintain a high and stable level of demand without this leading to accelerating inflation through a wage explosion.

Indeed, Flanagan et al. stress in particular the 'implicit' agreement during the period 1951–64 between the Conservative Governments and the Trades Union Congress (TUC). In return for wage restraint on the part of the TUC, it is argued, the Conservative Governments of the time refrained from anti-union legislation, formal incomes policy (with a brief and not very serious exception in 1961–2), and high unemployment. This tacit agreement can be seen in historical context as a reaction to the experience of the 1920s and 1930s, when industrial relations were conducted in an atmosphere of conflict and bitterness. The Conservatives were anxious to distance themselves from memories of the anti-union legislation and mass unemployment of the inter-war period. The TUC for its part recognized that if governments were to keep out of matters such as union activity on the shop floor, restrictive practices, and immunities, there would have to be some restraint on wage claims. This notion of a cooperative solution to the wage bargaining problem of the 1950s and 1960s fits together naturally with the characterization of the inter-war period as a non-cooperative solution in Broadberry (1986). Broadberry (1987) traces the roots of this post-war cooperation to the war experience itself.

Relating the experience of the 1950s and 1960s to our theoretical model, a world boom together with favourable terms of trade meant that the feasible real wage grew at a rate that was relatively fast by historical standards. In addition, with the experience of the 1930s very much in mind, trade unions acted to keep the target real wage in line with the feasible real wage, so that the NAIRU was relatively low. Governments, for their part, managed demand so as to keep the actual unemployment rate close to the NAIRU. Thus the British economy experienced rapid growth with full employment. However, from the late 1960s, many of the favourable features of the post-war environment began to disappear.

## V. Unemployment in the 1970s and 1980s: Crisis

### 1. Estimates of the NAIRU

The principles behind the calculation of the NAIRU from an econometric model of the labour market are discussed in Appendix 7.1. Layard and Nickell (1985) find that their estimates of the NAIRU rise from under 2 per cent during the 1950s and early 1960s to nearly 11 per cent by the early 1980s. The figures are given in Table 7.2 for males only.[5] During the period 1956–66 the actual unemployment rate was equal to the NAIRU, so that inflation remained low and stable. The low NAIRU was the result of the world boom and the implicit agreement between unions and government on wage restraint. From 1968 to 1974, with the breakdown of wage restraint and falling productivity growth, the NAIRU rose. Since the actual unemployment rate did not rise by as much, actual unemployment remained below the NAIRU and inflation accelerated. From 1975 to 1979, although actual unemployment rose, the NAIRU continued to rise further with union militancy, stagnation of productivity growth, and adjustment to the oil price shock of 1973–4, so that inflationary pressure remained. This inflationary pressure was originally dampened down by incomes policy, but only temporarily. Finally, in the face of continued target wage growth and a further jolt to the price of oil, the NAIRU rose further during 1980–3, but with the deflationary policy of the Thatcher Government the actual unemployment rate rose above the NAIRU, and inflation was reduced.

In Table 7.3 we give a breakdown of the reasons for the rise in the male unemployment rate, obtained from the Layard and Nickell study. The benefit replacement ratio, the union wage mark-up, mismatch, and incomes policy all

---

[5] We have already noted that female employment and unemployment behaved differently.

TABLE 7.2. *Estimates of the NAIRU*
(for males only, % points)

|  | 1956–66 | 1967–74 | 1975–9 | 1980–3 |
|---|---|---|---|---|
| NAIRU | 1.96 | 4.12 | 7.80 | 10.72 |
| Actual male unemployment rate | 1.96 | 3.78 | 6.79 | 13.79 |

*Source*: Layard and Nickell (1985), Table 7.

TABLE 7.3. *Breakdown of the change in the male
unemployment rate 1956–1983*
(% points)

|  | 1956–66 to 1967–74 | 1967–74 to 1975–79 | 1975–79 to 1980–83 |
|---|---|---|---|
| Benefit replacement ratio | 0.54 | −0.09 | −0.10 |
| Union wage mark-up | 0.84 | 0.86 | 0.57 |
| Mismatch | 0.14 | 0.18 | 0.44 |
| Incomes policy | – | −0.31 | 0.43 |
| Real import prices | −0.36 | 1.01 | −0.67 |
| Employers' labour taxes | 0.42 | 0.67 | 0.78 |
| Demand factors | 0.47 | 0.82 | 5.14 |
| Total | 2.05 | 3.14 | 6.59 |
| Actual change | 1.82 | 3.01 | 7.00 |

*Source*: Layard and Nickell (1985), Table 6.

represent factors affecting the target real wage, while real import prices and employers' labour taxes affect the feasible real wage. Finally, demand factors affect the extent to which unemployment deviates from the NAIRU.

Dealing with the target real wage, the benefit replacement ratio has a small positive effect on unemployment during the late 1960s and early 1970s, but since that date any effect has been negative since the replacement ratio has fallen. The union wage mark-up has increased unemployment throughout the period. In addition, mismatch or frictional unemployment has risen slightly, thus suggesting a minor role for structural change. Finally, incomes policy had an effect of dampening down wage inflation during the period 1975–9, but this was more than offset by catch-up effects during 1980–3.

Turning to the feasible real wage, real import prices had their strongest effect during the 1970s, with the oil price shocks and the explosion of commodity prices. During the rest of the period, the downward trend in real import prices acted to increase the feasible real wage and thus lower the NAIRU. Employers' labour taxes exerted downward pressure on the feasible real wage throughout the period, especially from the late 1960s. However, the single most important factor behind the surge in unemployment after 1979 was the deflation of demand as a counter-inflation policy. The sharp rise in unemployment from 1979 can thus be seen to a large extent as the cost of the reduction of inflation. A similar policy has been followed in many OECD countries with similar results.

Given the relatively short run of annual time series data available, the precise magnitude of these estimates should be treated with some caution. The results should thus be seen as illustrative rather than definitive. In particular, one short-coming of the Layard and Nickell estimates is the absence of a separate term for productivity growth, which plays such an important role in the estimates of Grubb *et al*. (1982). We suspect that this is due to collinearity between aggregate demand and productivity, so that the productivity growth slowdown effect is subsumed within the demand factors in the Layard and Nickell estimates.

## 2. *International Comparisons*

Table 7.4 shows unemployment rates standardized by the OECD to enable inter-national comparisons to be made. There is no clear trend of rising unemployment in the USA or Japan, and of the other major economies, Britain's experience is closer to that of France and Germany. Italy, Belgium, and the Netherlands also exhibit rising unemployment trends of similar magnitude, while the performance of the Scandinavian countries appears considerably better.

TABLE 7.4. *OECD standardized unemployment rates*

|             | 1960 | 1968 | 1974 | 1980 | 1983 | 1986 |
|-------------|------|------|------|------|------|------|
| UK          | 1.3  | 2.1  | 2.1  | 5.6  | 11.2 | 11.1 |
| USA         | 5.4  | 3.5  | 5.5  | 7.0  | 9.5  | 6.9  |
| Japan       | 1.7  | 1.2  | 1.4  | 2.0  | 2.6  | 2.8  |
| France      | 1.1  | 2.6  | 2.8  | 6.3  | 8.3  | 10.3 |
| Germany     | 1.0  | 1.2  | 2.1  | 3.3  | 8.2  | 8.2  |
| Italy       | 5.5  | 5.6  | 5.3  | 7.5  | 9.3  | 10.5 |
| Belgium     | 3.3  | 2.9  | 2.4  | 7.7  | 12.9 | 11.6 |
| Netherlands | 0.7  | 1.4  | 2.7  | 6.0  | 13.7 | 11.8 |
| Sweden      | 1.7  | 2.2  | 2.0  | 2.0  | 3.5  | 2.7  |
| Norway      | 1.2  | 1.1  | 1.5  | 1.7  | 3.3  | 2.0  |
| Denmark     | 1.9  | 1.2  | 3.5  | 6.5  | 11.4 | 7.0  |

*Source*:   OECD Main Economic Indicators.

One way of illuminating these cross-country differences is to examine the flexibility of labour market institutions, as in Bean *et al*. (1987). One variable of interest is the unionization rate since we may expect a less competitive, highly unionized economy to adjust less effectively to changed conditions, or even to be the source of economic disturbances such as inflationary wage claims. Britain's poor performance with respect to the USA and Japan appears explicable in this way, but there remains the problem of the good performance in highly unionized Scandinavia. The difference here seems to be with the scope of labour market institutions, or what is sometimes called the degree of corporatism. The Scandinavian economies have highly centralized labour market institutions, which can organize a centralized response to changed conditions and prevent small interest groups from trying to gain at each other's expense.

### 3. *A Summary*

We round off this section with a chronological summary of trends in unemployment since the 1950s. A longer account of the interaction between inflation and unemployment over this period is given in Chapter 6.

#### (a) *The 1950s and Early 1960s*

During the 1950s and the early 1960s, unemployment remained close to the NAIRU, which was itself below 2 per cent. The small fluctuations in unemployment and inflation can be associated with the stop–go cycle, while the low level of the NAIRU can be attributed to the world boom and the post-war agreement between the Conservative Governments and the TUC.

#### (b) *The Late 1960s and Early 1970s*

During the late 1960s and the early 1970s, target real wage growth began to accelerate with increasing union militancy just as the growth of the feasible real wage began to falter. Let us pause to consider some of the factors behind this rising militancy. First, the guarantee of full employment was beginning to be taken for granted by union negotiators, who were thus freed from concern about the threat to employment from high wage settlements. Second, this trend was reinforced by the disappearance from the labour market of older workers whose formative years had been during the mass unemployment of the 1920s and 1930s, and who were thus less likely to take full employment for granted. Third, the development of a decentralized wage bargaining system weakened the authority of the TUC, on whom the post-war agreement with the government for wage restraint depended. Fourth, there was a wage explosion in Continental Europe following social unrest in 1968 which had a demonstration effect on British wage bargaining. Finally, there was the breakdown of the incomes policy which had been introduced in 1965, but which by 1968 had led to serious relativity-related unrest.

The key factor behind the decelerating feasible real wage growth was faltering productivity growth. As with the wage explosion this trend was not confined to Britain, and marked the end of the post-war world boom. However, aspirations were slow to adjust. This became clear with the devaluation of 1967, which could only hope to resolve Britain's competitiveness if the higher import prices were not matched by higher wages, since higher wage costs would have to be passed on in higher prices. Since real wage growth accelerated at this time, it seems clear that the real wage flexibility necessary for the success of devaluation was lacking. Faced with a rising NAIRU as target real wage growth accelerated and feasible real wage growth decelerated, governments responded by trying to prevent actual unemployment from rising too much. This was done by adopting expansionary monetary and fiscal policies. With actual unemployment below the NAIRU, inflation began to accelerate.

#### (c) *The Mid- and Late 1970s*

During the mid- and late 1970s, the NAIRU continued to rise with persistent upward pressure on target real wage growth, and renewed downward pressure on feasible real wage growth. The target real wage growth remained high with continuing union militancy, which is reflected in rising union density, and high levels of the trade-union wage mark-up and also of strike activity. The breakdown of the Heath Government incomes policy during the winter of 1973–4 gave an added boost to inflationary wage claims. Similarly there was an inflationary boost when the Labour Government's social contract broke down with the 'winter of discontent' during 1978–9.

The feasible real wage continued to stagnate with continued slow productivity growth. In addition there was now further downward pressure on feasible real wage growth from real import prices, especially since the quadrupling of the price of oil during 1973–4. With the NAIRU continuing to rise, governments continued to try to hold the actual unemployment rate below the NAIRU, eschewing deflationary measures. Attempts were made to dampen down inflationary pressures with incomes policies. However, such measures could at best hope to hold back inflationary wage claims for a short while. Without reining back demand, incomes policies can be seen as an example of 'King Canute economics' (Hartley, 1977, p. 78).

After a sterling crisis in 1976, IMF support was made conditional on the adoption of targets for monetary growth, but the Labour Government placed its faith in incomes policy rather than deflationary monetary policy as the main plank of its counter-inflation strategy.

### (d) The Early 1980s

During the early 1980s, the NAIRU continued to rise, although the bulk of the rise in unemployment can be seen as the result of deflationary demand policies which raised the actual unemployment rate above the NAIRU. The target real wage continued to rise as unions further increased their wage mark-up over non-union wages. Although the second oil shock after the Iranian revolution in 1979 did not lead to a rise in the real import price, as Britain was by this time a net exporter of oil, it did nonetheless represent an increase in energy costs for firms which put downward pressure on the feasible real wage, particularly in energy-intensive sectors.

The centrepiece of the government counter-inflation policy was control of money supply growth. The adoption of monetary targets was inherited from the outgoing Labour Government, but the policy was seized on with new vigour by the Conservatives. In addition, targets were announced for the Public Sector Borrowing Requirement (PSBR). The exchange rate was allowed to float more freely and an incomes policy was specifically ruled out. As monetary conditions tightened, the exchange rate appreciated, competitiveness worsened, and unemployment rose dramatically.

### (e) The Mid-1980s

For the period since 1983, we do not have the Layard and Nickell estimates of the NAIRU. However, estimates of the NAIRU from a similar model have been produced by Jenkinson (1987) who finds a reduction in the NAIRU over the period 1983–7 from 13.7 per cent to 11.0 per cent.[6] It seems likely that this reduction in the

---

[6] These estimates were kindly made available by Tim Jenkinson.

NAIRU is largely the result of improvements on the feasible real wage side, since wage increases have remained relatively high.

In fact, it may be that these two factors are related, with workers prepared to accept changes in work practices leading to productivity improvements, in return for wage increases. As Matthews and Minford (1987) note, trade-union reforms have meant that a ballot majority is now required for strike action. Since most workers benefit from a high-wage-for-high-productivity deal, it is difficult for a union to oppose such deals. The prospect of lower wages for higher employment, as with American 'give-back' deals thus seems remote. This is an example of how labour markets may operate in favour of 'insiders' (those with secure jobs in the union sector) and against 'outsiders'. However, as Layard and Nickell (1987) note, such a view is difficult to distinguish from 'hysteresis', due to the effective withdrawal of the long-term unemployed from the labour force. As the duration of unemployment has risen with the unemployment rate, the number of long-term unemployed has increased, and as they have effectively withdrawn from the labour force, they have not exerted downward pressure on wages.

The productivity 'miracle' of the 1980s, which underpins feasible real wage growth, has received much attention, with economists and politicians anxious to know whether it represents a new sustainable trend of higher growth or a one-off shift to a new higher level of productivity. The problem is complicated by the dramatic changes in capacity utilization that have taken place. Nevertheless, as noted in Chapter 9, it seems unlikely that all of the improvement can be regarded as simply a one-off change. Thus the rising feasible real wage does appear to be at least partly sustainable.

Note, however, that as the actual unemployment rate has fallen below the NAIRU during 1987–8, inflation has once again begun to accelerate, and the government has reacted by tightening monetary policy. This has been necessary despite the fact that unemployment is still much higher than during the boom of the 1950s and 1960s. Thus we note that the Thatcher Government has not managed to break completely with the mould of the past in terms of the trade off between inflation and unemployment. As the ghost of 'stop–go' returns, the goal of achieving full employment without accelerating inflation seems as far away as ever.


## VI. Government Policy

In this section we briefly review government policy towards the issue of unemployment. Many of the issues are discussed in detail in other chapters, so we confine ourselves here to a broad outline. Just as we can identify a change in the scale of unemployment from the late 1960s, so too we can identify a change in government policy at about the same time. Tomlinson (1985) calls the period from the Second World War to the mid-1960s the 'New Regime', and the subsequent period the 'New Regime in Decline'. The New Regime can be seen as embodying a commitment to full employment, from which governments have been retreating since the late 1960s.

## 1. *Policy in the Full Employment Era*

It is normally agreed that during the Second World War a Keynesian revolution took place in economic policy-making. Recently this issue has stirred up much controversy, with Tomlinson (1984) even going so far as to claim that there never was a Keynesian revolution in the true sense of the word, since although budgetary policy was used to control aggregate demand during and after the war, the problem was one of excess demand rather than deficient demand, and the real test of Keynesianism is the use of budget deficits to raise demand. Tomlinson is also sceptical about the role of economic theory in changing economic policy-making. There is surely an element of truth about this, but it is hard not to be struck by the difference between unemployment policy between the wars and a document such as the 1944 White Paper on Employment Policy, which baldly stated 'The Government accept as one of their primary aims and responsibilities the maintenance of a high and stable level of employment after the war' (Ministry of Reconstruction, 1944).

However, the White Paper was rather vague and confused on how the high level of employment was to be secured via budgetary policy. As Winch (1972) points out, the suggestions of contra-cyclical public investment programmes and variations in national insurance contributions were both outside the normal budgetary framework. And furthermore, tentative proposals for varying the tax rate with the trade cycle were followed by a statement that this did not mean planning for a budget deficit in slump years (pp. 270–1).

In the light of the low level of unemployment actually achieved during the 1950s and 1960s, it is interesting to note that the architects of Keynesian demand management during the 1940s were not simply naïve optimists. Indeed, as Winch notes, Beveridge's estimate of the minimum achievable rate of unemployment in peacetime was a modest 3 per cent, compared to the 1 per cent actually achieved.[7] Furthermore, the early Keynesians were not unaware of the difficulties of securing full employment without government–union cooperation on wages policy.[8] The breakdown of the post-war cooperation since the late 1960s has led to the resurgence of this problem.

The 1950s and 1960s are often known as the 'stop–go' era. This refers to alternative periods of expansion of demand in response to rising unemployment and contraction of demand in response to rising inflation or a deteriorating balance of payments position. Viewed from the perspective of the 1980s, however, the fluctuations in unemployment at this time were very small.

With aggregate unemployment generally under 2 per cent, the focus of policy shifted to the distribution of unemployment. In particular, regional policy was used in an attempt to even-out the regional imbalances that had persisted between the wars. In contrast to the inter-war period, when the emphasis had been on labour mobility (moving workers to the jobs), the post-war period saw a much greater emphasis on capital mobility (jobs to the workers). As we noted earlier, there has been a narrowing of regional unemployment rate differentials during the post-war period. This surely reflects to some extent the success of regional policy.

Another feature of labour market policy during the full employment era was the emergence of a specific policy on training. During the 1950s, government attitudes

---

[7] See Jones (1987) for a recent discussion of these issues.
[8] See, for example, Beveridge (1944), pp. 198–201.

were to leave training to industry. During the 1960s, however, concern about the consequences of skill shortages for economic growth led governments to intervene. The Industrial Training Act of 1964 set up Industrial Training Boards to oversee all aspects of training in individual industries and the facilities in Government Training Centres were steadily expanded (Blackaby, 1978a, ch. 13). Viewed from an international perspective, however, British policy on human capital formation has been very inadequate, as noted recently by Daly et al. (1985).

Other specific labour-market policies at this time dealt with problems which have subsequently disappeared or changed substantially in nature. First, Britain actively recruited migrant workers from the Commonwealth in the immediate post-war years, as the post-war boom created a shortage of labour. In 1975 the foreign-born population of the United Kingdom was about 3m., or 5.5 per cent of the population (Boltho, 1982, Table 6.5). As unemployment began to rise from the mid-1960s, however, restrictions on immigration were tightened as the emphasis shifted from increasing to reducing the labour supply.

Another interesting feature of labour-market policy at this time was the attempt to influence the distribution of employment between the manufacturing and service sectors. The Selective Employment Tax (SET), introduced in 1966, taxed service sector employment and subsidized manufacturing employment. This reflected the desire of the government to stimulate the growth of the manufacturing sector, which was seen as the engine of growth. In fact, soon after its introduction SET became irrelevant as aggregate unemployment rose and the problem became one of finding jobs in any sector. SET was finally abolished in 1973 (Blackaby, 1978a, ch. 4).

## 2. Policy during the Retreat from Full Employment

As unemployment began to rise from the late 1960s, the belief that demand management could cure unemployment began to evaporate in policy-making circles. Perhaps the final attempt at the Keynesian cure came with the expansion of demand during 1973. The sharp rise in inflation that followed this episode convinced many of the failure of Keynesian policies. The emphasis began to switch to controlling inflationary pressures. This change of attitude is well illustrated by Prime Minister James Callaghan's address to the 1976 Labour Party Conference, 'We used to think that you could spend your way out of a recession and increase employment by cutting taxes and boosting government spending. I tell you in all candour that that option no longer exists. It only worked, on each occasion since the war, by injecting a bigger dose of inflation into the economy, followed by a higher level of unemployment at the next step. That's the history of the last twenty years.'[9]

The policy of restricting demand to control inflation was begun by the Callaghan Government, but was continued even more intensively by the Thatcher Government elected in 1979. The use of demand management as a tool of employment policy has thus been totally abandoned by policy-makers. This view is stated explicitly in the 1985 White Paper on Employment, which stresses price stability and the removal of barriers to labour and capital mobility as prerequisites for a return to full employment. In the Labour party a 'new realism' has seen the leadership distancing itself from many of the traditional socialist policies which have proved

---

[9] Labour Party (1976), p. 188, quoted in Tomlinson (1985), p. 119, with extensive discussion.

unpopular with the electorate during the 1980s. For example, as Coates and Hillard (1987) note, the Deputy Leader Roy Hattersley emphasizes new incentives rather than controls.

In addition, regional policy has been scaled down during the 1970s and 1980s, as regional imbalances have narrowed. Policy on training, however, has been strengthened, and expanded into a general policy on manpower, with the creation of the Manpower Services Commission in 1972 (Blackaby, 1978a, p. 609). During the 1970s and 1980s the Manpower Services Commission has been responsible for many job-creation schemes. Policies can be divided into those that attempt to lower the supply of labour and those that attempt to raise the demand for labour.

Employment subsidies can be seen as an attempt to raise the demand for labour by lowering the cost of labour to the employer. The problem with employment subsidies is that firms may simply substitute subsidized for unsubsidized labour, or may receive the subsidy for employment which they would have provided anyway. Even if subsidized firms do take on new labour, competition from their output may result in a loss of employment in unsubsidized firms (Prest and Coppock, 1984, p. 262).

Profit-sharing can be seen principally as a measure to increase the demand for labour. The rationale for this, set out in the 1986 Green Paper on Profit Related Pay, is to increase wage flexibility and thus reduce employment fluctuations. The basic idea is that in a recession wages fall with profits and thus firms need not shed labour. In addition, it is argued that since workers have a direct stake in the performance of the firm, incentives for work effort are improved.

Measures that work on the supply side include schemes to encourage early retirement, work-sharing, and hours reduction. The problem with all these measures is the issue of who bears the cost. If work-sharing is introduced without income-sharing, unit labour costs rise, which results in higher inflation if the higher costs are passed on in the form of higher prices. If the firm is unable to raise prices because of competitive forces, it is likely to reduce rather than increase employment (Prest and Coppock, 1984, pp. 263–4). Another special employment measure (SEM) which has the effect of reducing labour supply in the short run, but improving its quality in the long run, is the series of youth training schemes, introduced to combat the huge rise in youth unemployment during the late 1970s. By the end of 1983 these measures covered about 400,000 young workers (p. 262).

Finally, there has been an attempt at trade union reform to increase labour market flexibility. Under the Thatcher regime, legal immunity has been weakened, but as we noted earlier, the trade union wage mark-up has continued to rise during the 1980s.

## VII. Conclusion

Unemployment in Britain since the Second World War can be split into two periods. Before the mid-1960s there was an era of full employment, when unemployment was both low and stable. From the mid-1960s however, unemployment has risen strongly upward, so that by the beginning of the 1980s unemployment rates were broadly comparable to the rates suffered during the 1930s. Despite recent reductions, unemployment has remained well above the level of the 1950s and 1960s. The low unemployment of the 1950s and 1960s can be seen primarily as the result of a world boom, although labour-market conditions in Britain were also favourable. Cooperation between government and unions on wages policy made it possible to achieve a high level of employment without accelerating inflation. The major reason for the rise in unemployment from the late 1960s was the refusal by governments to validate the inflationary pressures from import price increases and wage demands in excess of productivity improvements. Policy-makers began to see inflation as the major economic problem, and policies to reduce inflation by restricting the growth of demand caused unemployment to rise very sharply from the late 1970s.

### APPENDIX 7   1. Calculating the NAIRU

To see how we can obtain estimates of the NAIRU from an econometric model of the Labour market, let us consider the simple model of Grubb, Jackman, and Layard (1982). All variables are in natural logarithms. Wage inflation ($\dot{w}$) is related to expected price inflation ($\dot{p}^e$), unemployment ($u$), and a target growth of the wage ($g^e$):

$$\dot{w} = \dot{p}^e - au + g^e \tag{1}$$

The price level ($p$) is a weighted average of domestic and import costs:

$$p = (1 - \beta)(w - x) + \beta(p + \mu) \tag{2}$$

where $x$ is the trend output per head and $\mu$ is the relative mark-up of import prices over domestic prices. The coefficient $\beta$ represents the share of imports in income. Taking first differences of equation (2), we have:

$$\dot{p} = \dot{w} - \dot{x} + \left(\frac{\beta}{1 - \beta}\right)\dot{\mu} \tag{3}$$

For labour market equilibrium we require actual and expected inflation to be equal, or $\dot{p} = \dot{p}^e$. Then substituting (3) into (1) and solving for $u$ yields:

$$u^* = \frac{1}{a}(g^e - \dot{x}) + \frac{\beta}{a(1 - \beta)}\dot{\mu} \tag{4}$$

The NAIRU, $u^*$, thus rises if the target wage is higher than permitted by productivity growth, or if import prices rise by more than domestic prices.

Layard and Nickell (1985) work with a three-equation model for labour demand, price determination, and wage determination. The algebra is more complex but the principle is the same. The system must be solved for the equilibrium rate of unemployment, or NAIRU.

# 8

# Supply-Side Management

## M. W. KIRBY

### 1. Introduction

To the student of post-war economic history the term 'supply-side management' was, until recently, an unfamiliar one. It does not appear in conventional textbook accounts of the period and it is only in the last decade that it has been accorded a secure place in the literature of applied economics (Bartlett and Roth, 1984). In one major sense this is hardly surprising. In an era dominated by the Keynesian paradigm in its policy guise of aggregate demand management, the generation and maintenance of full employment income by means of fiscal policy was given pride of place. Macroeconomic countercyclical policies were the order of the day for British governments in the 1950s and 1960s and the preoccupation with short-term stabilization served to divert attention away from consideration of the long-term growth prospects of the economy as a whole. Supply-side management—the framing of appropriate policies to increase the supply of productive factors (labour and capital inputs being the most important) and the efficiency with which they are combined—went by default. To caricature the period would be to suggest that economic policy was founded on the assumption that 'if demand is right, supply will look after itself' (Skidelsky, 1977*a*). In the 1930s, in conditions of mass unemployment and severely circumscribed international trade, such a view was understandable and it certainly helps to explain the relatively shallow microeconomic foundations of the *General Theory*. Yet it would be wholly wrong to conclude that post-war British governments were indifferent to supply-side issues. It is salutary to remember, for example, that Sir Stafford Cripps, before his elevation to the Exchequer in 1947, briefly held office as Minister of Economic Affairs with specific responsibility for 'planning'. In the early 1960s the creation by the Conservative Government of the National Economic Development Council (NEDC), following the 'great reappraisal' of 1960, was recognition of the structural weakness of British industry, the adverse consequences of 'stop–go' economic policies, and the need to enhance the economy's long-term growth prospects by introducing measures of indicative planning. In 1964 the incoming Labour Government established the Department of Economic Affairs (DEA) charged with the task of drawing up a National Plan to contain target rates of growth for output, exports, and incomes, and this was followed in the 1970s by a renewed commitment to a centralized industrial strategy, albeit of a less ambitious nature than the earlier experiments in indicative planning. All of these initiatives were inspired by the desire to increase the potential output of the economy and they were by no means the only governmental measures on the side of supply. Other examples would include the introduction of investment incentives for industry in 1945, the creation of the Monopolies and Restrictive

Practices Commission in 1948, the Restrictive Trade Practices Act of 1956, the Industrial Training Act of 1964, and the founding of the Industrial Reorganisation Corporation (IRC) in 1966. Although much has been made of the lack of continuity in the management of supply in the light of the Treasury's continuing concern with balance of payments and exchange-rate problems, and the tendency for incoming governments to abolish or downgrade the institutional innovations of their predecessors (Morris and Stout, 1985), there is a strong case for emphasizing the elements of evolution and continuity in supply-side measures. Policies for industrial restructuring, for example, have featured in every decade since 1945 and their origins go back to the 'rationalization' measures of the inter-war years (Kirby, 1987). Similarly the phenomenon of tripartism, an integral component of the planning and strategy experiments of the 1960s and 1970s, can be traced back at least as far as the Board of Trade Working Parties on individual industrial sectors, which were established after 1946 (Middlemas, 1979), and this applies also to government underwriting of high technology ventures. In all of these respects the similarities in policy content between Labour and Conservative administrations up to the late 1970s were greater than the differences. This, of course, is not to deny the critical importance of *perceptions* of policy on the part of its intended recipients, notably those engaged in industry outside the Home Counties, as they responded in an atmosphere of uncertainty to the prospect of major changes in the direction of policy in the light of party political rhetoric and expressed intentions (Clare Group, 1982; Morris and Stout 1985). The fact remains, however, that the whole of the period from 1945 to 1979 was characterized by an ongoing, if uneven commitment to interventionist supply-side policies.

In the years since 1979 supply-side management has undergone fundamental change as a result of the election of a Conservative administration deeply antipathetic to the trend of previous policies. Considerable emphasis has been placed upon the creation of an economic environment conducive to the efficient and flexible operation of markets. Thus restraints have been placed upon the growth of public expenditure in order to release resources for a private enterprise sector responsive to the incentive effects of heightened competition and reduced taxation levels. The rationale for such policies is grounded in the belief that conventional demand management and a rising trend in public expenditure, in stimulating inflation, have weakened the microeconomic base, and that existing supply-side measures have either been ineffectual or have contributed to inefficiency by undermining market disciplines at the level of individual households, firms, and industries. Although a fairly broad spectrum of established supply-side policies was retained after 1979 there can be little doubt that the Thatcher Government's free-market rhetoric has been perceived as marking a major discontinuity in the course and direction of economic policy.

Before proceeding to examine the record of supply-side management since 1945 one important qualification should be made. It is simply that supply-side policy cannot be considered in a vacuum. Monetary variables, for example, and those macroeconomic policies designed to deal specifically with external trade and payments can have significant effects on current and potential output. Indeed, demand management itself can be viewed as a supply-side policy insofar as it helped to create a climate of business expectations favourable to growth (R. C. O. Matthews, 1968). Similarly, prices and incomes policies designed to contain inflationary pressure can have important supply-side implications if their aim is to curb trade union power or to secure productivity improvements. Even policies which are at first sight narrowly supply oriented may not be designed to promote the growth of output *per se*. Whilst post-war regional policy, for example, has had the economic rationale of limiting inflationary pressure by attempting to secure the employment of underutilized capacity, social considerations and motives of political expendiency have loomed large. Similarly, with regard to post-war competition policy, its origins are to be found in the 1944 White Paper on *Employment Policy* (Ministry of Reconstruction, 1944), which drew attention to the possibility that governmental attempts to stimulate aggregate demand might be frustrated by the restrictive practices of large-scale firms and collusive selling organizations. What this means is that it is extremely difficult to define the limits of supply-side management. Economic policies which affect the growth of output may well be the product of concern with 'non-supply' issues and may even be inimical to economic growth. Conversely, some policies which appear to be overtly supply-oriented may derive much of their rationale from political and social considerations.

## 2. Supply-Side Policy in the 1940s

At a superficial level there is an excellent case for claiming that the post-war Labour Government had both the means and the motives to engage in an active and purposeful strategy for supply-side management. After 1940 the logistic demands of a booming war economy had placed the state at the centre of economic affairs, as evidenced by the panoply of direct controls in existence by the summer of 1945. In addition to broad fiscal and monetary controls the state wielded considerable authority over the determination of prices, consumption, and investment levels, the allocation of raw materials and labour, and the absolute size of the foreign-trade sector. All of these powers were integral elements of the war economy and together with the exercise of direct ministerial control over large sections of industry, they had determined the nature and extent of quantitative production programmes (Wiles, 1952). In inheriting these controls the Labour Government was in possession of unprecedented powers for the management of a peacetime economy. In terms of motives it is possible to identify at least three factors which seemed to point towards supply-side intervention. At the most general level the war had been instrumental in altering public perceptions of the legitimate role of the state in economic affairs (Addison, 1975). This was exemplified by the *Employment Policy* White Paper which committed post-war governments to the maintenance of a 'high and stable level of employment'. The concern expressed about the pricing policies of monopolistic producers was a clear reference to the pre-war trend towards cartelization in British industry, and although the White Paper offered no policy prescriptions in this respect it did point to the need for some kind of governmental surveillance of commercial practices. The dangers of inflationary pressure were also addressed in the context of the labour market. Again, no policy guidelines were offered but the call for 'moderation in wage matters' and for labour mobility underlined the need for restraint on the part of trade unions in the collective bargaining process (A. Booth, 1983*a*; Peden, 1983; Rollings, 1985).

A further motivating factor was provided by the collectivist traditions of the Labour Party based upon the commitment to nationalization enshrined in clause IV of the 1918 constitution. Free markets were rejected because they promoted the unequal distribution of income and wealth, and the experience of the inter-war years had provided ample evidence of the manifest failure of capitalism to sustain employment levels. The war economy had subordinated markets to a centrally coordinated productive system which had worked efficiently and equitably. Political dogma therefore combined with practical experience to justify the case for 'ordered planning under national control' (Labour Party, 1943). Finally, the sheer magnitude of Britain's post-war economic problems appeared as justification enough for an active supply-side strategy. Industry had to be reconverted to peacetime needs, physical damage repaired, and new resources made available to compensate for wartime disinvestment and lack of maintenance of plant and equipment. If the official wartime pledges on employment policy and the creation of a welfare state were to be redeemed this would impose additional burdens on the country's limited resources over and above those arising from the minimum task of restoring living standards to their pre-war level. Above all, the prospect of a high and rising balance of payments deficit cried out for an ongoing commitment to the business of exporting which could only be sustained by extensive government controls over the allocation of resources.

In the event the Labour Government did not engage in a long-term strategy aimed at regenerating the British economy from the supply side. In view of the near-bankruptcy of the economy it was, perhaps, inevitable that ministers should become increasingly obsessed by the need for short-term stabilization, notably with regard to the balance of payments. Sir Stafford Cripps may have thought in terms of 'central and coordinated production' (Cairncross, 1985), but the government's most elaborate statement of the planning process, set out in the *Economic Survey for 1947* (HM Treasury, 1947), did not provide an effective blueprint for supply-side management. Production targets were set for a limited number of strategically important industries, and 'economic budgets' for national income and expenditure and manpower for a period of one year were supplemented by sectoral analyses of such problem issues as the balance of payments, capital investment, and the availability of raw materials. Yet as Alec Cairncross has pointed out the *Survey* failed to describe how supplies of scarce resources were to be balanced, or how future output was to be estimated. Thus the planning exercise lacked consistency, and this weakness was compounded by the lack of any reference to the price mechanism and still more by the complete neglect of the machinery for implementation. In short, the Labour Government was unable to reconcile its desire to 'plan from the ground up' with the aspirations of a democratic society in which freedom of choice was accorded high priority (Rogow and Shore, 1955). An exercise in long-term planning was undertaken in 1948 but the resulting 'Long-Term Programme' (HM Treasury, 1948) was extremely circumspect in approach, emphasizing future uncertainties in a general context of imperfect information, and also the 'very special circumstances' in which compulsory powers could be used to curtail individual freedom. As Cairncross has observed, after 1947 the idea of planning became increasingly divorced from the allocation of resources as the management of supply gave way to demand management by means of fiscal policy (Cairncross, 1985).

By the end of its period of office full employment, the control of inflation, and equilibrium in the balance of payments were the principal policy objectives of the Labour Government and the very fact of their successful attainment after 1945 served to weaken its resolve to pursue a centralized supply-side strategy. Even in relation to nationalization it cannot be claimed that the government's programme was motivated primarily by supply-side considerations. Political and moral aspirations were intermingled with technical and economic objectives in varying degrees, and in any event the presumption of greater efficiency under a regime of state ownership could only be validated in the long term. At the opposite end of the industrial policy spectrum the establishment of the Monopolies and Restrictive Practices Commission in 1948 was an indication of a growing concern with rigidities in the industrial structure but again its potential contribution to greater economic efficiency could not be immediately ascertained in view of the general lack of knowledge of the power and extent of producers' associations.

Attempts to limit trade-union bargaining power in an extremely buoyant labour market proceeded by means of ministerial exhortations for voluntary wage restraint. This approach achieved considerable success in the 18-month period from March 1948 when the annual rate of increase of hourly wage rates fell from just under 9 per cent to 2.8 per cent. In the year after devaluation in September 1949 it fell to 1 per cent, although the policy began to crumble rapidly after the summer of 1950 in the wake of a substantial rise in the retail price index (MacDonald, 1960). As for industrial productivity the Labour Government devoted much time and effort to highlighting the 'efficiency gap' between British and American industry. Economic ministers in general, and Sir Stafford Cripps in particular, addressed innumerable meetings of employers and trade unionists on this theme. Official Working Parties were established in 17 manufacturing trades to examine ways in which efficiency might be raised, but the attempt to extend this experiment in 'cooperation with industry' by the creation of tripartite Development Councils failed: only three were established (in Jewellery and Silverware, Clothing, and Furniture) and by 1953 only one (Furniture) remained in existence (Leyland, 1952; P. D. Henderson, 1952). Finally, the Labour Government attempted to encourage greater industrial investment as an aid to economic reconstruction. Two institutions were established—the Industrial and Commercial Finance Corporation and the Finance Corporation for Industry—to help mobilize capital resources, in the former case for small-scale firms subject to the so-called Macmillan Gap, and in the latter for larger firms requiring 'bridging' finance without recourse to established financial channels. Both organizations were based upon pre-war precedents and their limited scope fell far short of the proposed National Investment Bank which had featured in the Labour Party's 1945 election manifesto (Grove, 1962; Ward-Perkins, 1952). A genuinely new policy initiative was the introduction of initial allowances in 1945. This was a scheme of accelerated depreciation designed to boost investment by delaying taxation. Insofar as it produced a gain in interest charges the scheme created a 'liquidity effect' thereby encouraging firms to re-equip or expand productive capacity on the basis of internal financing. The allowances were doubled in 1949 but they were suspended with effect from April 1952 in the aftermath of a budget distorted by the exigencies of rearmament financing (Dow, 1964).

## 3. Supply-Side Policy in the 1950s

The last section highlighted the rise to prominence of short-term macroeconomic prerogatives as the determining factor in the formulation of economic policy in the later 1940s. This trend was confirmed in the 1950s so that by the end of the decade it was an accepted orthodoxy that the principal economic task of government was 'to regulate demand and keep the economy in external balance' (Brittan, 1971). In practice this meant that governments were concerned to maintain full employment, price stability, the exchange value of the pound, and a surplus on the balance of payments. It is of course commonplace to point out that to 'steer' the economy in such a way as to achieve these objectives simultaneously was extraordinarily difficult, if not impossible, in the light of their incompatibility (Feinstein, 1983), but equally noteworthy is the fact that collectively these objectives represented a commitment to short-term stabilization focusing on the Treasury's annual budget statement. Throughout the 1950s, therefore, consideration of the economy's long-term growth prospects, of the expansion of productive potential, and the strengthening of the microeconomic base, barely featured in economic management.

In retrospect the neglect of supply-side issues was understandable. The full employment commitment, for example, was increasingly perceived to be the acid test of electoral popularity for governments and faith in their employment-creating abilities was all the more potent in view of the undiminished strength of collective memories of the inter-war period with its mass unemployment and commensurate levels of social distress (Tomlinson, 1985). The commitment to maintain the exchange value of sterling, moreover, cannot be dismissed simply as the product of an irrational concern with a particular macroeconomic symbol. Sterling convertibility was regarded as vitally necessary to sustain Britain's position as a major trading and commercial nation with an important role in the management of the international economy (Livingstone, 1966; Strange, 1971). This ambition was as much the product of political as of economic considerations and it marks the 1950s as a decade in which British governments persistently failed to match the country's commitments to its resources. The disparity between ambition and reality inevitably manifested itself in recurring balance of payments crises, leading to the infamous stop–go cycle of economic activity which began to emerge in the mid-1950s. The effects have yet to be quantified but it is a reasonable presumption that the uncertainties induced by the cycle had adverse consequences for long-term investment programmes in a wide spectrum of industries, from capital goods to consumer durables (Brittan, 1971; Bacon and Eltis, 1978; Pollard, 1982).

Reference has already been made to the introduction of initial allowances in 1945 in order to stimulate industrial investment. After their suspension in 1952 they were restored in the following year by the Conservative Chancellor of the Exchequer, R. A. Butler, who then proceeded to devise a new policy instrument—the investment allowance for plant and machinery combining the liquidity advantages of the old measure with a subsidy in the form of full tax remission against the value of the allowance. These new allowances were introduced in 1954, but after a balance of payments crisis in the following year they too were withdrawn and replaced by initial allowances. In 1957 the latter were increased but in 1959 investment allowances were reintroduced. In the decade 1950–60 allowances for capital investment were changed on six occasions. What had been conceived originally as an overt supply-side measure was quickly transformed into an instrument of short-term stabilization. In evidence before the Radcliffe Committee the directors of large industrial companies expressed the unanimous view that in planning long-term investment the fluctuating regime of official incentives was ignored. Smaller companies intent upon expansion, however, could not afford to be so complacent and it seems likely that it was at this level that the elements of uncertainty induced by stabilization policies was most damaging to business confidence. When it is considered that there was a considerable delay between incurring capital expenditure and receipt of the financial benefit, and that firms making low profits were unlikely to have a tax liability in excess of the value of the investment allowance it seems legitimate to conclude that the fluctuating regime of incentives was an ineffective means of stimulating investment-led growth. This was tacitly conceded by the Conservative Government in 1961 when it was announced that investment allowances would no longer be used as an instrument of demand management (Dow, 1964).

In the context of the 1950s two further areas of government policy which had some bearing on supply-side management should be noted. The first was one of the few supply-side measures of the decade and it took the form of legislation to curb restrictive practices in industry. The second—government support for research and development (R and D) expenditure—can hardly be classed as a deliberative industrial policy insofar as it was determined by military defence priorities, but it certainly had major implications for the composition of industrial output. The Labour Government's Monopolies and Restrictive Practices Act of 1948 had been founded on a pragmatic approach to the issue of industrial structure. Monopoly and collusion were not condemned as inherent evils, but as the Monopolies and Restrictive Practices Commission proceeded with its inquiries the extent to which industry was subject to restrictive agreements was revealed. Public opinion began to move decisively against restrictionism and in 1956 the Conservative Government responded to this new mood by establishing a judicial body, the Restrictive Practices Court, with powers to enforce the abandonment of restrictive agreements. As one authority has pointed out, the effect on cartels was 'devastating' (Allen, 1968) and there can be no doubt that the Court was instrumental in securing the virtual elimination of overt price fixing in the industrial sector. On the other hand, the emergence of alternative forms of market control makes it impossible to arrive at an accurate assessment of the Court's effectiveness in stimulating industrial efficiency. Certainly there can be no presumption that information agreements, or indeed mergers, were consistent with the achievement of scale economies (Meeks, 1977; Swann et al., 1974).

On the subject of R and D it was a notable British achievement that throughout the 1950s expenditures in this area were the highest in Western Europe. The 1939 figure of £6m. had risen to £30m. by 1945 with a further increase to £187m. in 1955. By the mid-1950s more than 60 per cent of R and D expenditure was being directed towards defence-related projects and less than one-third funded by private industry. Clearly the UK was not neglecting R and D, but by West German and Japanese standards resources were being allocated in a distinctive way, with an extremely high concentration in the aircraft industry and other areas of high technology with particular reference to military electronics and the nuclear power programme in its civil and military aspects. Although UK industry achieved some outstanding successes in these areas, especially in the light of the immense competitive and financial advantages enjoyed by the USA (Saul, 1979), the counterpart of the British effort was the relatively low proportion of R and D expenditure devoted to the more mundane areas of machinery and vehicles, precisely the sectors of manufacturing industry in which West Germany and Japan were to have their most important export successes. Despite the impressive British performance in such fields as radar and aeroengines it would appear that the overall returns were low, and to make matters worse such high prestige activities, in attracting the most talented scientists and engineers, deprived conventional manufacturing industry of scarce manpower resources (Peck, 1968; C. Freeman, 1978). To the extent, therefore, that the pattern of R and D expenditure was determined in large measure by non-market considerations it encouraged rigidities in the industrial structure. Most insidious of all, it created at the popular level a climate of irrationality which tended to encourage a naïve form of nationalism 'not significantly different from the loyal support of local sports teams' (Wright, 1979).

## 4. The 'Great Reappraisal': Supply-Side Policy in the 1960s

By the early 1960s considerable disquiet was being expressed in political and academic circles about the course and direction of UK economic policy. Although demand management *per se* was not under attack the manner of its implementation, in accentuating the short-run cyclical pattern of economic activity, was certainly viewed as deficient (Dow, 1964). 'Stop–go' became a stock phrase in economic journalism as a convenient and critical shorthand for the record of demand management, but it very soon became associated in the public mind with other failings in UK economic performance, notably with regard to inflation, the balance of payments, and economic growth. It was inflationary pressure, itself the product of the full employment commitment, which was a prime cause of the successive balance of payments and exchange-rate crises which underpinned the stop–go cycle, while the UK's failure to match the growth performance of its principal overseas competitors had serious implications for relative living standards, and also for the long-term stability of the external account. All of these factors were inter-linked and together they pointed to the need for a new perspective on the management of the economy. It was in this context that a renewed interest in supply-side issues began to emerge, markedly different to that adopted by the post-war Labour Government with its unpopular regime of physical controls. The new approach, far from being rooted in British experience, derived its inspiration from France and the indicative planning exercises of the 1950s which it was assumed had played a key role in a rapid and successful programme of economic reconstruction (Leruez, 1978). Industrialists themselves were among the initiators of the supply-side debate for it was at the 1960 conference of the Federation of British Industries that a report was prepared which pointed forcefully to the deleterious effects on business confidence and investment of stop–go policies and called for discussions between government and the business community 'to assess plans and demands in particular industries for five or even ten years ahead' (cited in Brittan, 1971). The view was also expressed that a higher growth rate could of itself alleviate balance of payments problems and secure stable prices. Other noteworthy contributions in this area were the 1960 Political and Economic Planning (PEP) publication *Growth in the British Economy* and a conference in the following year under the auspices of PEP and the National Institute of Economic and Social Research, which extolled the virtues of French planning. Their collective impact was all the greater at a time of balance of payments difficulties. The accompanying sterling crisis necessitated deflationary measures which abruptly curtailed the demand for motor vehicles and other consumer durable products. In February 1962, therefore, the Conservative Government responded to the new climate of opinion by establishing the National Economic Development Council (NEDC) as an independent body composed of government, business and trade union, and 'independent' representatives with a remit to examine the growth potential of the economy, identify supply constraints, and to secure agreement for their removal.

The creation of an institution committed to long-range planning, and serviced by its own expert staff in the National Economic Development Office (NEDO), was part of what has been termed the 'great reappraisal' in British foreign and economic policy at the outset of the 1960s. The decision to seek entry to the EEC in 1961 covers both categories, whilst the movement towards a formal incomes policy (in itself part of the 'planning' experiment), the attempt in 1961 to clarify the financial position of nationalized industries, and the innovation of 'regulators' (variations in purchase tax between budgets and surcharges on employers' National Insurance contributions), all fall into the latter category (Brittan, 1971). Together these initiatives were an indication of considerable unease with existing economic policies and, apart from the introduction of 'regulators', which were designed to refine and improve the techniques of demand management, they all pointed to a growing interest in longer term issues.

Whilst it is true that the decision to embark upon an experiment in planning derived considerable impetus from French experience in the 1950s it is important to note that the British version differed markedly from its foreign counterpart. In the first instance the French planning machinery was fully integrated into the structure of government and, most important of all, the planning process itself carried with it elements of *dirigisime* (such as state control of the capital issues market) which would have been politically unacceptable in the UK. These differences were exemplified by the first official statement to be produced by the NEDC—*Growth of the United Kingdom Economy to 1966* (NEDC, 1963b). Its focal point was an annual target rate of 4 per cent for the growth of output in the specified period. The implications of this for the UK national accounts were then analysed quantitatively in the light of consultations with a range of industrial sectors comprising about 40 per cent of GNP. These consultations were carried out hurriedly but they did serve to highlight potential obstacles to the achievement of a growth rate significantly higher than the average for the 1950s. Thus, attention was paid to such issues as the rate of savings, export prospects, the availability of skilled labour, and the potential for productivity growth. A further publication, *Conditions Favourable to Faster Growth* (NEDC, 1963a), set out cautiously and pragmatically details of the policies which might be used to stimulate growth. These included manpower training, measures for regional development, taxation reforms, and, most controversially, the control of incomes. Governmental acceptance of the NEDC approach was underlined by the Treasury's adoption, albeit reluctantly, of the 4 per-cent growth target and the fact that this second publication provided the basis for the Chancellor's reflationary budget in 1963.

There can be little doubt that as originally conceived the Conservative Government's experiment in indicative planning represented a significant discontinuity in economic policy. The adoption of a specific growth target and the creation of a forum to discuss the means of achievement were the result of official and unofficial perceptions of the limitations of short-term stabilization policies. In short, the

NEDC, in providing a link between government and industry, and in disseminating the results of its deliberations, was expected to create an atmosphere of confidence in the official commitment to sustained economic growth. Industrial investment would be encouraged—all the more so if businessmen, taking their cue from government, began to plan ahead in a more systematic way. The decision taken at the end of 1963 to establish separate Economic Development Committees (EDCs) to analyse growth prospects in individual industries was a further step along the road of government–industry coordination in devising long-term policies (Middlemas, 1983).

In assessing the contribution of the NEDC to the reappraisal of the goals of economic policy before the election of the Labour administration in October 1964 it is difficult to resist the conclusion that it was of little more than symbolic importance. Certainly none of the growth targets set out by the Council were achieved and although the reflationary budget of 1963 indicated that the Treasury was prepared to borrow abroad or run down the reserves to meet a balance of payments deficit caused by stockholding (Blackaby, 1978a), the fact remains that during the course of 1964, with a record balance of payments deficit in prospect, the NEDC was reduced to a position of impotence (R. Bailey, 1968). The 1964 budget was only mildly deflationary but there is no evidence to suggest that the government was prepared to sustain its so-called dash for growth in the event of prolonged deterioration in the reserve position. To that extent the psychological value of the NEDC experiment was severely weakened. Indeed, it is possible to argue that the NEDC growth objective was itself destabilizing—formulated in the trough of a stop–go cycle and implemented, via the 1963 budget, at a time of strongly rising home demand (Opie, 1972).

It has been suggested that the Labour party was 'taken aback' by the Conservative Government's decision to adopt a measure of indicative planning (Budd, 1978; Hare, 1985). If this is so then the party soon rallied with its electorally attractive emphasis on science and technology and the claim that the Conservatives' planning commitment was 'a cynical and utterly unacceptable substitute for the lifelong sincerity and solidarity of the Labour Party on this crucial issue' (Labour Party, 1964). These themes were prominent in the general election campaign of 1964 when Labour politicians proclaimed that a Labour Government would engage in 'purposive' and 'effective' planning which would have 'teeth in it somewhere'. Reality, however, was to fall very short of electioneering slogans: it would have astonished the party leadership in 1964 to learn that a Labour Government would preside over the death of indicative planning in Britain.

One of the first acts of the Labour Government was to establish a new ministry, the Department of Economic Affairs (DEA), unemcumbered by detailed executive functions, and principally concerned with planning and the coordination of economic policy to ensure the efficient use of physical resources in the long term. The rationale for this administrative innovation was twofold, first to provide a counterweight to the Treasury in the policy-making process, and second to serve as a focal point for the new government's planning endeavours. The latter took the form of a National Plan which was published in September 1965, only 11 months after the General Election. It stated, positively and unequivocally that:

The Plan is designed to achieve a 25 per cent increase in national output between 1964 and 1970. This objective has been chosen in the light of past trends in national output and output per head and a realistic view of the scope for improving upon these trends. It involves achieving a 4 per cent annual growth rate of output well before 1970 and an annual average of 3.8 per cent between 1964 and 1970. (DEA, 1965)

The intention, therefore, was to match the growth target in the NEDC planning experiment of 1963. No doubt this was politically expedient, but in a number of respects the National Plan was a deeply flawed supply-side initiative. In the first instance it had been prepared far too hurriedly. The consultations with industry to provide sectoral estimates of output, exports, and investment on the basis of a 25 per-cent growth target in the prescribed period were severely devalued because the relevant questionnaire was founded on unwarranted assumptions. The coverage of individual industrial sectors, moreover, was uneven with information being colla-ted by EDCs, trade associations, 'representative' bodies, the NEDO, and relevant government departments. Discussions to achieve consistency in the overall Plan between these various bodies was attenuated and, in the view of one critical observer, they were not helped by the fact that

In far too many cases what purported to be the plans and expectations of an industry were in fact the views of a relatively small sample of companies written up by the officials of the trade association and accepted by a more or less representative committee of the association. For many companies the concept of a 25 per cent growth rate had no very clear meaning in terms of their own activities. (Bailey, 1968)

Most reprehensible, however, was the fact that no attention was paid to the possibility of different growth paths in response to alterations in the target rate of growth as a result of changing circumstances. Yet as the Plan stated in its very first section, the 'central challenge' was to achieve higher growth and at the same time produce an external surplus. In other words, the Plan was 'a mixture of a goal and a constraint' and it presented no clear view as to how the latter was to be removed—except that accelerated growth in itself would tend to produce external equilibrium (Opie, 1972). These weaknesses were revealed dramatically in the summer of 1966 when the Plan was summarily abandoned in the aftermath of a traditional, if unusually severe, sterling crisis. In the final analysis a Labour Government deeply hostile to the Treasury's preoccupation with short-term stabilization felt bound to conform to the requirements of orthodoxy by defending the existing exchange rate with all the deflationary means at its disposal. In retrospect it is difficult to regard the government's attempt at indicative planning as anything other than a fiasco—a 'music-hall joke' which destroyed the credibility of the DEA as a newly created ministry with specific responsibility for strengthening the supply side of the economy. Given the external constraints which British governments felt obliged to accept in the 1960s 'the successful assertion of positive growth policies, often involving valuable long-term industrial investment but at a damaging short-term cost in demand terms was not possible' (Wilson, 1974). In that setting it seems likely that a far more sophisticated National Plan would also have come to grief.

Before examining other long-term initiatives on the supply side that were intro-duced after 1960 there is one further aspect of economic policy directly related to economic planning that needs to be highlighted. Inflationary pressure had been mounting during the course of the 1950s and by the end of the decade the principal cause was identified as excessive wage increases. Inflationary wage settlements could be viewed as an important element in the stop–go cycle insofar as they tended to undermine the balance of payments. In this respect they imposed real costs on the supply side of the economy by reducing the incentive to invest, thereby increasing the natural rate of unemployment. In 1956 the then Conservative Government had embarked upon a campaign for wage restraint by exhortation and in the following two years went as far as to overrule a pay award to Health Service workers and a conciliation offer to London busmen. In 1957 an official Council on Prices, Productivity and Incomes (the Cohen Council) was established to monitor the pace of wage inflation and to establish criteria for the assessment of pay claims. The Council subsequently modified its original view that inflationary pay increases should be pre-empted by a wages freeze and higher unemployment, and the government itself proved incapable of reconciling the need for wage restraint with industrial peace (Knowles, 1962). Yet this brief and largely ineffectual flurry of activity in the area of incomes policy was a sign of things to come.

In July 1961, in the midst of a balance of payments crisis, the Conservative Government introduced a non-statutory pay pause which was followed in October 1962 by the creation of a National Incomes Commission (NIC) responsible for devising a 'norm' for annual wage increases and reviewing any wage settlements that the government chose to refer to it. Lacking compulsory powers the NIC was expected to induce wage restraint via its educative effects on public opinion. Indeed, the 3–3.5 per-cent norm or 'guiding light' that the NIC set was determined in part by the NEDC planning exercise with its target rate for the annual growth of productivity per head of 3.2 per cent. Neither of these initiatives can be viewed as successful in achieving their objectives: the effects of the pay pause were extremely variable, even in the public sector where it was applied most vigorously, while the impact of the NIC was greatly reduced by its limited terms of reference and the fact that from the time of its inception unemployment, rather than inflation, was coming to be the dominant concern of government. In a major sense the NIC was a functional, if ineffective, substitute for the control of incomes within the context of the NEDC planning exercise. From the outset the TUC maintained an unbroken hostility to the incorporation of wages as a legitimate issue for discussion within the NEDC framework, although the 1963 TUC Report did endorse the NEDC view that 'there would be a need for policies to ensure that money incomes, wages, salaries, profits as a whole rise substantially less rapidly than in the past' (Blackaby, 1978a). It was this reference to all incomes, together with political loyalties, which enabled the succeeding Labour Government to inaugurate its own incomes policy under DEA auspices and in conformity with the general objectives of the National Plan.

Within two months of the general election the TUC and employers' organizations had been persuaded to sign a joint Declaration of Intent to 'keep under review the general movement of prices and money incomes of all kinds', and early in 1965 a new institution—the National Board for Prices and Incomes (NBPI)—was established to fulfil the same educative role as the now defunct NIC. Further progress was achieved in March when the TUC accepted a 3–3.5 per-cent norm for annual wage increases. At this stage the policy was a voluntary one but as the wage rate index accelerated in the first half of 1965, and as pressure on the exchange rate mounted, the government sought to achieve a more effective form of wage restraint by obtaining TUC acceptance of an 'early warning' system for wage increases together with the vetting of all major wage claims by a committee of the TUC General Council. These initiatives were also found wanting and during the sterling crisis of

July 1966 a statutory pay freeze was imposed. This lasted for six months and it was followed in January 1967 by a period of 'severe restraint' characterized by a 'nil norm'. 'Exceptional cases' for wage increases could only be justified by reference to productivity agreements, narrowly defined, comparability, and the distribution of manpower. This phase of incomes policy, which ended in June 1967, was followed by an attempt to use the machinery of the NBPI to delay wage claims and wherever possible achieve genuine productivity agreements.

By the autumn of 1969 incomes policy was defunct and discredited in the eyes of the government. Indeed, in a dramatic reversal of approach, the Prime Minister, heavily influenced by the report of the Donovan Commission on trade unions (Donovan Commission, 1968), which had drawn attention to the problem of shop-floor militancy, was personally committed to the reform of trade union law as a means of containing wage inflation. Nevertheless, when judged by results in reducing the level of wage settlements during the period of their operation, the various phases of incomes policy did achieve a measure of success. During the period of freeze and severe restraint, for example, earnings rose by only 2 per cent a year compared with a rate of 8 per cent in the preceding phase, and taking the whole of the period during which incomes policy was operational (from the fourth quarter of 1964 to the second quarter of 1969), whilst the average annual rise of earnings of 6.5 per cent was only a marginal reduction from the 7.5 per cent recorded in the two years prior to the autumn of 1964, this must be set against the fact that the latter half of the 1960s was subject to considerable pressure for rises in money incomes in response to steadily declining real post-tax earnings and the devaluation of sterling in 1967. In the absence of an incomes policy, therefore, it is reasonable to presume that wage inflation would have been higher. Having said that, the sharp acceleration in the rate of increase in money earnings to 12 per cent per annum in the three-year period after the termination of the policy was sufficient to match the reduction obtained during its operation. This is indeed the conclusion of several studies of the effectiveness of incomes policies in the post-war years—that despite successes in operational phases their net effect on the rate of wage inflation was nil (Parkin and Sumner, 1972; Henry and Ormerod, 1978). It should also be emphasized that the Labour Government's approach to incomes policy could not be regarded as part of a well-conceived supply-side strategy. The proclaimed link with planning was extremely tenuous in practice, even before the demise of the National Plan and, more to the point, the successive attempts to relate the growth of earnings to productivity were a failure, abjectly so after 1967 (Clegg, 1971). In both its voluntary and statutory phases the policy failed to resolve the problem of exceptional treatment for specific groups of workers, and the obsession with norms failed to take account of increases in earnings arising from payments-by-results schemes affecting up to 9m. workers. Evasion was also difficult to check when it was a comparatively simple matter for trade unionists, with the active connivance of management, to engage in unnecessary or even fictitious overtime, or secure higher rates of pay for the same work by enhanced job grading. More specifically on the supply side, incomes policy was rarely, if ever, directed towards achieving desired changes in the allocation of manpower (Blackaby, 1978a), whilst in a broader setting the 'moral legitimation' of the policy went by default in the absence of public debate on 'the ethical validity of existing income distribution' (Fox, 1985).

If the 1960s were noteworthy for two short-lived experiments in indicative planning, of much greater significance for supply-side management in the longer term was the introduction during the course of the decade of deliberative and detailed policies to improve the efficiency of the industrial sector. Such policies were certainly relevant to planning insofar as they were expected to accelerate economic growth, but their widespread introduction can be explained by other, albeit related, considerations, notably the desire to raise the level of exports, to improve the international competitiveness of British industry, and to override market forces when they were obstructing or delaying the achievement of desired objectives. The policies themselves can be categorized under a twofold classification, one *supportive*, the other *innovative*. Under the Conservative administration good examples in the former category are the Cotton Industry Act of 1959, designed to promote 'modernization' and reduce surplus capacity in the domestic industry in the face of Far Eastern competition, and the offer in 1963 of aid to the shipbuilding industry in the form of financial incentives for shipowners to place orders in UK yards. As for the latter category the decision in 1964 to extend the scope of the work of the National Research Development Corporation (a body formed in 1948 to expedite the process of innovation where it was deemed to be in the national interest) and to endow the Department of Scientific and Industrial Research with extra funding for industrial research purposes was a clear indication of the official desire to strengthen the technological base of British industry. In a similar vein the acceptance of the Robbins Report (Robbins, 1963) recommending a substantial increase in the provision of higher education, and the establishment of the first of a series of Industrial Training Boards in 1964 financed by compulsory levies on firms was a reflection of growing awareness of the need to raise the quality of the labour force in the face of the long-standing British neglect of scientific and technical education. Measures of this kind, in conjunction with the NEDC experiment, have led several commentators to conclude that there was a great deal of continuity in supply-side policy across the divide of the 1964 general election (Brittan, 1971; Young and Lowe, 1974). The Labour Government's claim, therefore, that it was engaging in more 'purposive physical intervention' must rest upon differences in emphasis and scale. This clearly applies to the National Plan but it is also true of deliberative industrial policy. Here, the Labour Government not only continued the *ad hoc* interventionist tradition established by its predecessor, but also introduced a range of new policy instruments and institutional devices. If at one end of the scale the government attempted to raise productivity and industrial investment by public and private exhortation, at the other end it established the Industrial Reorganisation Corporation (IRC) in 1966, as a 'merger broker' with the ambitious tasks of promoting 'industrial efficiency and profitability' and the growth of the economy as a whole. There was little new in the business of exhortation, but after 1964 the persistence of ministerial appeals for greater exports, investment, and productivity began to match that of the Labour Government in office after 1945. This applies also to the provision of advice and seminars where the newly created Ministry of Technology (MinTech) played a key role in ensuring the dissemination of technical information to industry through such established bodies as the National Engineering Laboratory and the National Physical Laboratory, and new creations such as the National Computing Centre, founded in 1966 to encourage computer applications in industry. As for financial inducements, among the very few non-discriminatory measures the most important was the replacement of investment allowances by grants in 1966. The aim here was to reduce the inherent uncertainty of the allowance system by shortening the payment lag and by offering the prospect of a cash payment. Elsewhere, financial provision for industry was highly discriminatory. This was exemplified by the Industrial Expansion Act of 1968 whereby the government acquired an equity shareholding in International Computers Ltd. (ICL) and agreed to fund R and D expenditures amounting to £13.5m. over a period of four years. In the case of shipbuilding government guarantees were again offered to shipowners placing orders in UK yards, and the Shipbuilding Industry Board (SIB), established in 1967, was permitted to borrow substantial funds from the Exchequer in order to secure rationalization through amalgamations. Nationalization of the 14 largest firms in the steel industry in 1967 also provided the occasion for public subventions and technical modernization. There are many other examples in this category—in the aircraft industry, for example, and in textiles and aluminium smelting. Collectively, they mark a dramatic increase in the pace of microeconomic intervention, and also in the trend towards selectivity in industrial policy (Graham, 1972; Young and Lowe, 1974).

Perhaps the most ambitious initiative, and certainly the most controversial, was the establishment of the IRC. As indicated above this body had an extremely wide remit, but the focal point of its activities was the arrangement of mergers and for this purpose it was endowed with 'pump-priming' funds amounting to £150m. In a very real sense the IRC owed its origin to the prevailing view that British industry in general was organized on too small a scale to meet the challenge of foreign competition and that market forces could not be relied upon to produce desirable structural changes. It was also a product of the demise of indicative planning and hence the perceived need for 'purposeful' intervention at the level of the individual firm. Exhortation and financial inducements were regarded as valuable in themselves as part of the armoury of industrial policy, but they were likely to improve industrial performance only in the longer term, and even then to an uncertain extent.

In the event, the IRC proved to be a cautious organization, anxious to maintain its independence from government, and to avoid giving rise to the suspicion that it was a vehicle for 'back door' nationalization. In this it was largely successful, and in the 50 mergers over which it presided its judgments were accepted as professional and soundly based. In the final years of its existence the IRC began to adopt an increasingly sceptical view of the benefits of mergers, preferring instead to highlight the need for improvements in managerial standards (itself a precondition for successful mergers) and, with government encouragement, to act as a quasi-merchant bank with the object of stimulating selective investment (Hague and Wilkinson, 1983).

Thus the 1960s marked a significant break with the previous decade in terms of supply-side management. From the late 1950s onwards there had been growing dissatisfaction with Britain's economic performance in general and that of the industrial sector in particular. With the emergence of chronic balance of payments problems and exchange-rate crises the prevailing Conservative policy of 'holding the ring' for industry was rapidly undermined leading to the 'great reappraisal' of 1960. After the failure of indicative planning in 1966 it was inevitable that a Labour Government which had proclaimed the virtues of the 'white heat of the technological revolution' should seek to influence industrial performance directly. Strengthening the microeconmic base would raise the potential output of the economy, thereby stimulating aggregate supply: inflationary pressure would be reduced and balance of payments and exchange-rate problems would diminish as economic growth accelerated.

## 5. The 1970s: Supply-Side Management and the Concept of Industrial Strategy

Viewed as a distinctive period in the evolution of supply-side management the 1970s represent a high peak of physical intervention, notably with regard to the industrial sector. Indicative planning may have been discredited but this did not prevent the 1974 Labour Government from reinvoking the spirit if not the substance of planning with its officially designated 'industrial strategy' launched under NEDC auspices in 1975. The industrial strategy itself was in many ways a logical progression from the deliberative policies initiated by the 1970 Conservative Government. Yet at the outset of the decade electioneering rhetoric and political action seemed to point towards a radical break with the interventionist trend of the 1960s. It is instructive to note that the Conservative Government was elected to office in 1970 on the basis of its 'Selsdon Park' programme of 'disengagement', and whilst it is true that the adoption of such a programme was motivated in part by opportunistic electoral considerations it did tap deeper philosophical roots within the party, in particular the liberal tradition of a freely competitive market economy leading to allocative efficiency (Walkland, 1984). In practical terms this entailed the application of efficiency criteria to the nationalized sector (including elements of privatization and 'hiving off'), the rejection of prices and incomes policies as inconsistent with market disciplines, the downgrading or abolition of 'socialist' institutional devices such as the NBPI and the IRC, and finally, in a memorable phrase, the non-subsidization of 'lame-duck' industries and firms. In short, the supply side of the economy was to be reinvigorated by a new spirit of competition leading to greater industrial efficiency. This, it was hoped, would enable the UK to meet the challenge of EEC entry.

After the election the NBPI and the IRC were indeed abolished, as were the SIB and a number of other advisory boards established in the 1960s, including 6 out of 22 EDCs. Hiving off and privatization began with the sale of state-owned public houses and travel agents, and the disposal of brick-making works owned by the British Steel Corporation. Investment grants were replaced by allowances in October 1970 and the new 'lame ducks' policy was applied to the Birmingham Small Arms Company in 1971 when it was left to the banks to resolve a severe cash crisis. Yet well before the end of 1971 a combination of political and economic factors was threatening to destroy the disengagement experiment. The catalyst was undoubtedly the bankruptcy of Rolls Royce as a result of losses incurred in the development of a new generation of civil jet engines. Faced by the prospect of large-scale unemployment in Lancashire and Central Scotland, and a severe impairment of the country's defence capability, the government decided to nationalize the company and to provide substantial funding in order to complete the development of the RB211 engine. The official response to the collapse of one of the most important manufacturing concerns in the country, employing more than 80,000 workers, was to argue that the financial rescue was an exceptional case, fully consistent with the disengagement policy in view of the close relationship between the aircraft industry and the state. The credibility of this position, however, was fatally weakened by the bankruptcy of Upper Clyde Shipbuilders in the summer of 1971. The government's initial response was to refuse to underwrite the company's liquidity requirements but all four of its yards were maintained in operation by new owners who again, as in the case of Rolls Royce, received large public subsidies. Confirmation of the government's 'U-turn' was provided by the official rescue operation mounted during the course of 1971–2 on behalf of the Belfast shipbuilding concern, Harland and Wolff, which was also in danger of bankruptcy (Young and Lowe, 1974; Mottershead, 1978).

Thus, a powerful mixture of political, social, and economic factors, reinforced in the case of Rolls Royce by military considerations, led to a fundamental reappraisal of the course and direction of economic policy at the micro level. In the final analysis the 'lame ducks' philosophy was subordinated to the ongoing political requirements of the full employment commitment (Dell, 1973; M. Holmes, 1982). In all of these respects the Industry Act of 1972 was of more than symbolic importance. This act was a significant contribution to the development of regional policy but in the present context it was especially noteworthy because of its extensive provisions for selective financial assistance for industry on a UK-wide basis. It even went as far as to offer grants in exchange for state shareholdings in recipient companies, a procedure which drew the critical and accurate comment from the CBI that the legislation was firmly in accord with the detailed interventionist stance of the previous Labour Government. This view could only have been reinforced by the simultaneous creation of new advisory agencies such as the Department of Trade and Industry's Industrial Development Unit, Industrial Development Advisory Board, and Industrial Development Executive (M. C. Fleming, 1980).

The Conservative Government indulged in an equally spectacular *volte-face* in its approach to incomes policy. As noted above it had abolished the NBPI, assuming that the threat of bankruptcy would curtail inflationary wage settlements in private industry. The attempt to bring the trade unions 'within the law' under the terms of the Industrial Relations Act of 1971 could also be regarded as a means of securing wage restraint. Both of these strategies were soon undermined, the first by the government's rejection of market disciplines, and the second by the non-cooperation of the trade union movement. By themselves these developments were sufficient to generate renewed interest in incomes policy but the most important precipitating factor was the government's decision in 1972 to reflate the economy in an attempt to increase the rate of economic growth: incomes policy would help to prevent domestic inflation, and the balance of payments position would be safeguarded by a floating exchange rate. In November 1972, therefore, after attempts to negotiate voluntary restraint with the TUC and CBI had failed, a statutory prices and incomes policy was introduced. It passed through three phases. Stage I, which lasted until March 1973, imposed a standstill on wages, dividends, rents, and the majority of prices, and Stage II, which was in operation until September 1973, limited annual pay increases to £1 per week with an addition of 4 per cent of an employer's pay bill per employee in the preceding year. The final Stage III, inaugurated in November 1973, was intended to be more flexible. The limit for pay increases was raised to £2.25 per week with an annual maximum of £350 (compared with £250 under Stage II), and for the first time provision was made for productivity agreements and extra payments for working 'unsocial hours'. In the former case lessons had been learnt from the experience of the NBPI after 1967 and the conditions to prevent abuse were stringent. Most controversial, however, was the introduction of indexation agreements whereby wage increases would be triggered automatically if the price level rose above a designated threshold. This was an attempt to reduce the allowance for future inflation which trade union negotiators habitually attempted to incorporate in wage settlements.

By any standards the Conservative Government's incomes policy must be judged a failure. Whilst it is likely that Stage I produced a slower rate of increase in average earnings than would have been the case in the absence of the policy (especially at a time of rising import prices and falling unemployment), the remaining stages witnessed the beginnings of a wage/price spiral. The key element in Stage III was the commitment to indexation and since the price index that was chosen fully reflected import prices, as the world economy boomed during the course of 1973, threshold payments were triggered off at regular intervals. The *coup de grace* for the policy, however, was administered by the miners who broke through the pay code even though the flexible arrangements incorporated in Stage III (in particular, the provision for 'unsocial hours') had been specifically designed to pre-empt a wages confrontation in the coal industry. In attempting to learn from the mistakes of its predecessor in office, the Conservative Government had produced an incomes policy which despite its evolution through 'stages' was too inflexible in the context of a labour relations system geared to the maintenance of relativities, the principle of comparability, and the sustained growth of money wages. The bodies established to administer the policy—the Pay Board and the Price Commission—'were obliged to follow codes which were defined far more tightly than previous pay and prices policies, and were also statutory instruments open to interpretation by the courts'. In effect, the quasi-judicial approach enshrined in the pay code 'strove to close or limit every possible loophole' thus creating the conditions for the very confrontation with the miners that the government had sought to avoid (Clegg, 1979). It was a lesson which the succeeding Labour Government did not fail to learn.

On returning to office in 1974 the Labour Government lost no time in announcing its intention of regenerating British industry. At that time the contraction of the manufacturing sector of the economy in terms of employment was a growing cause for concern and this 'deindustrialization' of the UK economy was ascribed principally to the historically low level of industrial investment (Blackaby, 1978b). In a White Paper, published in August 1974, it was announced that

The Government propose to create a new instrument to secure where necessary large-scale substantial investment to offset the effects of the short-term pull of market forces. These new powers of initiative are better exercised through a new agency than dealt with directly by the Government, and for this purpose it is proposed to set up a National Enterprise Board (NEB). (Department of Industry, 1974)

At first sight this looked to be an attempt to rectify one of the principal deficiencies of microeconomic intervention after 1964, namely the threatened non-compliance of private industry with the Labour Government's planning objectives (Shanks, 1977). This impression was heightened by the statement that the NEB's 'main strength in manufacturing will come through the extension of public ownership into profitable manufacturing industry by acquisition of individual firms'. The White Paper also introduced the concept of 'planning agreements' to be negotiated between government and industry to ensure the latter's compliance with official objectives. All of these proposals were incorporated in the Industry Act of 1975. This legislation fell far short of the highly interventionist programme originally envisaged by the Labour Party's National Executive Committee (Holland, 1972, 1975): the £1,000m. allocated to the NEB was viewed as too small for the stated tasks of maintaining productive employment, industrial efficiency, and international competitiveness. Planning agreements, moreover, were to be voluntary and in the whole of the period to 1979 only two were negotiated—one with the National Coal Board and the other with the financially weak Chrysler car company. As for the NEB, the suspicion expressed by some sections of political opinion that, like the IRC, it too was a vehicle for 'back-door' nationalization, proved to be wholly unfounded. By 1979 the bulk of its resources had been used for subventions to Rolls Royce (£95m.) and the ailing British Leyland Motor Corporation (£569m.), the latter having been nationalized in 1975 within the terms of the 1972 Industry Act (Fleming, 1980). This in turn produced criticisms that the NEB was merely an institutional device for dealing with the problems of 'lame duck' firms. In one sense this was obviously true but it is difficult to envisage any government in the 1970s accepting with equanimity the catastrophic effects on regional and local unemployment if, say, British Leyland—the sole remaining volume car manufacturer in UK ownership—had been allowed to succumb to market forces. It should also be borne in mind that although automobile products and aeroengines were the NEB's primary concerns as a state holding company, by the end of the 1970s it had diversified its interests to include such 'high technology' sectors as computers and electronics. It had major shareholdings in ICL and Ferranti, and had founded three new firms—INMOS to produce semiconductors, NEXOS electronic office equipment, and INSAC computer software. That the NEB did not emerge as a more impressive instrument of microeconomic intervention can be readily explained by reference to domestic political constraints, in particular the government's weak position in the House of Commons (the Conservative Party was pledged to abolish the NEB), and secondly the external constraint imposed by the conservatism of overseas financial institutions and markets in rejecting any policy innovation which smacked of full-blooded socialism. Thus, like the IRC, the NEB tried for the most part to avoid 'public controversies believing in the long run it was more important to act sensibly and produce worthwhile results than indulge in a political free-for-all' (Marks, 1980).

With the playing down of the role of the NEB and planning agreements the emphasis of government policy began to change in favour of the kind of selective supply-side intervention favoured by its predecessor in office after 1971 (Coates, 1980). In November 1975 the change in direction was signalled by the publication of the official document *An Approach to Industrial Strategy* (HM Treasury/Department of Industry, 1975) which announced in grandiose terms that economic policy was to be directed to transforming Britain into 'a high-output, high wage economy . . . by improving our performance and productive potential'. The strategy itself was to be coordinated by the NEDC (thereby avoiding the charge that it had been imposed from above by ministers), and the original structure of EDCs was to be augmented by the creation of Sector Working Parties (SWPs), organized on the tripartite model, and charged with the task of devising medium-term policies to raise productive potential and competitive standards in key growth sectors (A. Lord, 1976). The emphasis, therefore, was on 'picking winners' and by 1980, 39 SWPs had been formed, encompassing 40 per cent of total manufacturing output, with particular concentrations in engineering, chemicals, and textiles. Contemporaneous with the EDC initiative was the growth of selective assistance schemes under the terms of sections 7 and 8 of the Conservative Government's 1972 Industry Act and section 8 of the 1965 Science and Technology Act. The key measures here were the Accelerated Projects Scheme (APS) of 1975–6, subsequently replaced by the Selective Investment Scheme (SIS), the Product and Process Development Scheme (PPDS) of 1977, the Microprocessor Application Project (MAP) of 1978, and the Microelectronics Industry Support Programme (MISP), also launched in 1978. Whilst the APS, SIS, and the PPDS were aimed at conventional manufacturing industry with a broad preference for the engineering sector, the MAP and MISP were the product of an appreciation of the importance of the new 'heartland' technology of the silicon chip where the speed of change both in relation to the technology itself and the pattern of markets was so rapid that it was felt that a substantial effort was required of government to achieve the widest possible dissemination of new knowledge and the application of microprocessors in industry. This was to be achieved by a combination of publicity, seminars, training programmes, and the provision of finance for innovation (M. C. Fleming, 1980; Kirby, 1984).

By 1979 the SWPs had generated a considerable amount of activity, concentrating on recommendations for raising productivity levels, improving the quality of production by the provision of investment funds and manpower training, and extending the range of market opportunities by paying specific attention to selling techniques and the availability of export finance. A number of selective investment schemes had also been introduced, all of them designed to strengthen the supply side of the economy. Yet despite the efforts expended it seems that the overall results were meagre. The SWPs, for example, had 'no teeth' and their role, like that of the EDCs, was confined to exhortation to implement agreed strategies for improved industrial performance at the level of the individual firm. The dissemination process was imperfect: many small-scale firms were unaware of the existence of SWP reports, and their larger counterparts tended to resist replicating at plant level the management–trade union relationship which was the hallmark of the SWP/EDC structure. It also appears that whilst agreement could be reached within SWPs on the need to present a common front in challenging foreign producers, the competitive process in the domestic market encouraged overt resistance to the exchange of sensitive commercial and technical information (Forester, 1979; Grant, 1982).

It is hardly surprising therefore that by the late 1970s the case for an active supply-side policy focusing on a conscious industrial strategy was under severe attack. It is possible to discern at least five strands in the anti-strategic stance: few of them are self-contained and together they constituted a powerful critique of interventionist supply-side policies. Even at the most superficial level the telling point was made that despite the basic continuity of deliberative policies and their tendency to become increasingly interventionist over time, the secular rate of unemployment had risen continually from the mid-1950s. It was thus a credible argument that 'more of the same' could not reverse this apparently inexorable trend. Second, there was the central fact of a century-long process of relative economic decline with political, social, cultural, economic, and technical factors intermingled in varying degrees (Olson, 1982). Many commentators offered diagnoses of the so-called

British disease in the 1970s, notably Sir Henry Phelps-Brown whose conclusion that a cure could only be effected by difficult and far-reaching changes in deeply embedded social customs and practices merely served to underline the lack of proportion between ends envisaged and the kind of 'strategic' supply-side policies implemented in the 1960s and 1970s (Phelps-Brown, 1977). In a similar vein it was argued that although some advocates of deliberative supply-side policies displayed an awareness of the need to raise managerial standards in British industry they persistently underestimated the dimensions of the problem—the long-standing preference for pragmatism, historically weak provision for management and technical education, and the legacy of complacency inherited from the days of imperial commerce. All of these factors combined to produce 'a self-perpetuating state of inadequacy' of sufficient magnitude to render abortive an increase in the flow of investment and R and D expenditures to promote greater competitiveness and productivity (Carter, 1981a).

Fourth, the whole concept of an 'industrial strategy' was attacked on the grounds that it neglected the principle of comparative advantage in international trade and ignored the problem of future uncertainty in a rapidly changing world. In this setting a policy of 'picking winners' was not only doomed to failure but was also positively harmful insofar as the presumed 'winners' tended to be located in areas where the technology was both risky and expensive. Finally, it was claimed that the strategic perspective was the product of an unwarranted belief in the country's 'manifest industrial destiny'—that it was right and proper that Britain should constantly strive towards an industrial structure which reflected the current world technological frontier. As several commentators observed, 'In so far as such attitudes prevail a more assertive industrial strategy is likely to give rise to a succession of dubious or wasteful projects' (Clare Group, 1982). The recent historical record provided ample justification for such a view, with the civil nuclear power programme and the Concorde project as outstanding examples of a peculiarly British kind of 'bipartisan technological chauvinism' (P. D. Henderson, 1977; Burn, 1978).

Before proceeding to assess the policy response of the Conservative Government after 1979 to these strictures there is one final aspect of the Labour Government's interventionist stance that requires examination. This concerns attitudes towards incomes policy. During its period of opposition after 1970 the Labour Party, disillusioned by the experience of incomes policy in the 1960s, and anxious to restore a close working relationship with the TUC after the abortive attempt to legislate for trade union reform in 1969, devised the concept of the 'social contract' whereby a future Labour Government would secure voluntary wage restraint by passing legislation designed to strengthen trade unionism. There was a particular commitment to the repeal of the Conservative Government's Industrial Relations Act, but the social contract was expected to embrace price controls in the nationalized sector, food subsidies, rent controls, tax concessions, and higher pensions. In this way it was hoped that the rise in money incomes would conform to the growth of output. In the period 1975–7 the policy was implemented with some measure of success. During this time the TUC adhered to a voluntary incomes policy in circumstances of unprecedented inflationary pressure. For the year from July 1975 pay increases were restricted to a 'norm' of £6 per week with no increase for those earning in excess of £8,500 per annum, and in the second stage from July 1976 weekly increases in the range £2.50—£4.00 were permitted with a maximum limit of

5 per cent. In 1976 average earnings rose by 13.9 per cent, slightly more than the 12.9 per cent increase in the retail price index (RPI), but in the following year the rise in earnings was limited to 8.5 per cent whilst the RPI rose by 17.6 per cent. Throughout this period sterling was under considerable pressure and in these circumstances the government's attempts to limit pay increases to 10 per cent for the year from July 1977 began to encounter stiff resistance, notably in the public sector. An official limit of 5 per cent for 1978 proved unacceptable to public-sector unions determined to recoup their position *vis-à-vis* private industry and the entire policy collapsed in the so-called winter of discontent in 1978–9 when local authority employees engaged in aggressive strike action in defiance of the 5 per-cent norm. This episode in the development of incomes policy raised several important issues. In the first instance it was an excellent example of the blurring of the distinction between a voluntary and a statutory policy insofar as public sector employees were subject to more rigorous pay restraint than their private-sector counterparts (Dawkins, 1980). Second, the flat rate pay increases permitted under the first and second stages were not conducive to the efficient allocation of labour (Brittan and Lilley, 1977; Metcalf, 1977). They also eroded differentials, paid little or no regard to productivity movements, and in failing to resolve the problem of 'special cases' created tensions and resentments which ultimately produced severe labour unrest. Finally, the period of the social contract raised an acute political issue, namely the extent to which the Labour Government secured wage restraint by enacting specific items of legislation desired by the TUC. To some this was merely a recognition of the reality of trade-union power and influence, but to others on the right of the political spectrum it represented the exercise of undue influence by a sectional interest group within British society. From this latter perspective, therefore, the period of the social contract was profoundly anti-democratic and, despite its 'voluntary' nature, thoroughly inconsistent with allocative efficiency in the labour market.

## 6. Conclusion: The 1980s Supply-Side Revolution

In surveying the record of supply-side management between the 'great reappraisal' of 1960 and the end of the 1970s the most outstanding feature is the fundamental continuity of policy as successive Conservative and Labour administrations attempted to rejuvenate microeconomic performance by expanding the range of deliberative policies for industrial support against a general background of planning in the 1960s and the officially designated industrial strategy after 1975. The disengagement experiment of 1970 was swiftly terminated for reasons of political and economic expediency to be followed by the 1972 Industry Act, one of the most powerful weapons of discriminatory intervention ever to be devised within the framework of supply-side management. As for the Conservative Government after 1979 it is also possible to point to elements of continuity in supply-side management. The selective investment and assistance clauses of the 1972 Act, for example, remained in force, as did the inherited commitments to the PPDS and MAP. The diffusion of information technology was accorded high priority and substantial public funding was provided for this under the 'Support for Innovation' scheme launched in 1982. The counterparts, moreover, of a lessening emphasis on regional policy *per se* were the Cabinet's decision in 1980 that the first manufacturing facility to be constructed by

INMOS should be located in South Wales, and the scale of financial inducements offered to the Japanese Nissan Company in a successful attempt to persuade the firm to establish a major vehicle assembly plant within the UK. Similarly, the creation of the British Technology Group by the merger of the NEB and NRDC in 1981 did not lead to a reduction in the level of public funding for British Leyland or Rolls Royce. On the contrary, the vehicle, aerospace, steel, and shipbuilding industries received major subventions after 1979. To some observers this retention of a fairly broad spectrum of established policy instruments suggested that there was little that was 'consistent and explicit' in the new government's approach to supply-side management and that 'the case for new initiatives must rest not on the notion of reversing a barely discernible trend towards disengagement and reliance on the market, but on a belief that long-established and broadly agreed British policies are in some way inadequate or misdirected' (Clare Group, 1982; NEDO, 1982). The perception of continuity, however, must be based upon retrospective observation and it is now clear that this view was somewhat premature—not least because it pays scant regard to the need to make a careful distinction between policy in operation and the genuine uncertainties induced by political debate and the desire of all parties to differentiate their approach to economic management in the light of electoral considerations (G. Chandler, 1984).

There can be no doubt that the Conservative Government came to office in 1979 determined to inaugurate a new era of supply-side management in the belief that previous policies had retarded economic growth by stifling the invigorating effects of market forces (Walters, 1986). Political ideology was a key element in this view, in particular the Hayekian belief in the intrinsic merits of the liberal market order in the face of collectivist ideals which served to undermine individual initiative. Such considerations had influenced the Selsdon Park programme of 1970, but the so-called supply-side revolution derived its major impetus from the perceived failure of demand management policies to combine full employment with price stability. New developments in the discipline of economics were a further important influence in precipitating the end of the Keynesian consensus on economic policy. The very term 'supply-side economics' was coined in the mid-1970s in the USA where it came to be synonymous with reductions in taxation 'not to stimulate aggregate demand, but to alter relative prices in favour of work, saving and investment' (Bartlett, 1985). Another critical development, predating the emergence of supply-side economics, was the rise of the monetarist school of thought. This derived its validity from the quantity theory of money which pointed to excessive growth of the money supply as the prime cause of inflation. Finally, there was the innovation of the theory of rational expectations which purported to demonstrate the ineffectiveness of demand management in a situation where markets clear automatically and all unemployment is essentially voluntary. The policy implications of these developments were twofold—first to 'roll back the frontiers of the state' in economic affairs, and second to enhance the role of market forces in order to encourage allocative efficiency. In practice this entailed the introduction of a medium-term financial strategy aimed at reining back the growth of public expenditure and reducing inflationary pressure via lower interest rates, thereby creating a macroeconomic environment conducive to the efficient functioning of the market economy. The subsidies payable to nationalized industries were reduced, as was the overall level of expenditure on industrial support programmes for the private sector. A new emphasis was placed upon revitalized competition policy, not least in the service sector, and the monopoly powers of specific public corporations were reduced. In a similar vein the government sought to reduce trade-union bargaining power: incomes policies were rejected in the belief that they introduced rigidities into the labour market and, with the experience of the social contract in mind, endowed union leaders with excessive political influence. Trade-union legal privileges were also curtailed and an attempt made to enhance the quality of the labour force and to alleviate specific skill shortages by the introduction of new measures for industrial training. A new emphasis was placed on encouraging the formation of small firms in the belief that they had a valuable role to play in stimulating structural diversity and in offsetting the risk aversion of large-scale firms by encouraging the development of a Victorian-style 'enterprise culture'. In this respect too, substantial reductions in direct taxation were clearly identified as a long-term objective consistent with the view that tax incentives were an essential component of a flourishing market economy. Finally, an increasingly ambitious programme of privatization was implemented. This was motivated in part by budgetary considerations, but it was also a product of the belief in the innate superiority of private enterprise over state-run bureaucracies. The common denominator underlying these attitudes and policies was a profound scepticism concerning the legitimate role of the state in economic affairs, and the rejection of an approach to supply-side management which could be labelled 'strategic' or 'planned'. The record of post-war economic history was viewed as at best a testament to the ineffectiveness of such policies and at worst as confirmation of their damaging effects in accelerating relative economic decline (Lomax, 1982).

It is too early to pass a final verdict on this 'revolution' in supply-side management. Indeed, an interim judgement would suggest that the government's free market rhetoric has been severely constrained by political and economic realities: the doctrine of monetarism has been jettisoned and, as noted above, conventional industrial support programmes have been maintained, albeit with lower levels of funding. To that extent it is possible to argue that there has been a revolution in the style rather than the substance of supply-side management (Thompson, 1986). But this is a rather subtle academic view which takes no account of public perceptions of economic policy and the manner of its political presentation. The essential point to note is that in marked contrast to its predecessors in office in the 1960s and 1970s the present Conservative administration has adopted an approach to economic affairs which denies the consensual proposition that broadly based agreements for regenerating the supply side of the economy in accordance with an overall growth objective are either desirable or necessary. In this respect, the downgrading in status and curtailment of the functions of the NEDC in 1987 was of more than symbolic importance in that the centrist policies associated with it are viewed as having subsidized inefficiency and contributed to declining competitiveness by undermining the disciplines of the market. To critics of the record of economic management before 1979 even the most cursory examination reveals a depressing sequence of proven strategic and administrative errors on the supply side. But to present this experience as a rational justification for a new experiment in 'disengagement' is to luxuriate in a form of cynicism which assumes that there is no room for improvement in deliberative policies and that decision-makers are incapable of learning from their mistakes. It may well be that intensified government intervention on the supply side would lead to resource misallocations resulting in a waste of public money, but given the present acute difficulties of the industrial sector and the ample evidence which points to the persistent inability of British businessmen to respond to market signals (Aldington, 1985) it is difficult to disagree with the view of a former Economic Director of the NEDO that 'Only the government can be relied upon to concern itself with the survival of a modern and relevant industrial base' (Stout, 1981). Perfection is rarely attainable and unless it is assumed that market solutions are always optimal, or that inaction is preferable to action, it seems unreasonable to apply more stringent tests to the evaluation of economic management than to other areas of human endeavour.

# 9

# Economic Growth*

## N. F. R. CRAFTS

## A. Introduction

By the late 1950s there was widespread concern at Britain's failure to grow as fast as other advanced countries. In the subsequent 30 years our relatively poor performance in terms of output and productivity growth has been the subject of repeated analysis and many remedies have been proposed both by governments and academics. Not only did Britain lag behind in the years of the long post-war boom which ended in 1973, but in the difficult years of the later 1970s we remained near the bottom of the growth league in a world where living standards were rising much more slowly. This experience is not only important in providing a context for Thatcherite economic reforms but also provides some benchmarks with which to judge their success.

Table 9.1 puts British economic growth in a comparative perspective as well as setting the post-war years against the experience of earlier eras. The estimates are based on historical national accounts statistics with output measured in constant prices. Strictly speaking the table describes trends in labour productivity but it also offers a good guide to comparative growth in real income per person which follows a similar pattern. The periodization is chosen to show trends between years of relatively full utilization of resources with a view to minimizing distortions arising from short-term economic fluctuations, except for the use of 1987 figures which are the latest available.

Table 9.1 reveals very clearly the long-standing peacetime tendency to slower

TABLE 9.1. *Growth rates of real output per worker employed* (% per annum)

|  | UK | USA | France | Germany | Japan |
|---|---|---|---|---|---|
| 1873–99 | 1.2 | 1.9 | 1.3 | 1.5 | 1.1 |
| 1899–1913 | 0.5 | 1.3 | 1.6 | 1.5 | 1.8 |
| 1913–24 | 0.3 | 1.7 | 0.8 | −0.9 | 3.2 |
| 1924–37 | 1.0 | 1.4 | 1.4 | 3.0 | 2.7 |
| 1937–51 | 1.0 | 2.3 | 1.7 | 1.0 | −1.3 |
| 1951–64 | 2.3 | 2.5 | 4.3 | 5.1 | 7.6 |
| 1964–73 | 2.6 | 1.6 | 4.6 | 4.4 | 8.4 |
| 1973–9 | 1.2 | −0.2 | 2.8 | 2.9 | 2.9 |
| 1979–87 | 2.1 | 0.6 | 1.8 | 1.5 | 2.9 |

*Sources*: Matthews *et al.* (1982, p. 31) and OECD (1988).

* I am grateful to many people for helpful comments on an earlier version including especially S. Broadberry and P. Seabright. The mistakes are my responsibility.

growth in labour productivity than our competitors. Note also that the years 1951–73 represent both the UK's highest output per worker growth *and* the period when the largest gap existed between ourselves and the fastest growing countries. The table also reflects the general slowdown in productivity growth after 1973 and the UK's move up the comparative league table since 1979.

The years of slower growth saw not only a decline in real income per head relative to other countries but also a large reduction in our share of world exports of manufactures and, from the end of the 1960s, a deindustrialization of employment which became pronounced after 1979. In 1970 US dollars the UK advanced from a per capita GDP of 2094 in 1950 to 3981 in 1979; by contrast in the same period Germany went from 1374 to 4946, France from 1693 to 4981, and Japan from 585 to 4419 (Maddison, 1982, p. 8). From a share in manufactured exports of 25.4 per cent in 1950 the UK fell to 11.2 per cent in 1969 and 7.6 per cent in 1984 (House of Lords, 1985). Employment in UK manufacturing declined from 8.2m. (36.9 per cent of total employment) in 1969 to 7.2m. (32.1 per cent) in 1979 and 5.3m. (25.2 per cent) in 1985 (Department of Employment Gazette, 1986). With these figures in mind it is interesting to look at labour productivity in manufacturing.

Table 9.2 reveals a persistent tendency for American productivity to be over twice the British level. A similar calculation for 1937 gives a ratio of 2.25 (Rostas, 1948, p. 47) and suggests a rise in the American lead during World War Two. Much more striking, however, is that for three decades European productivity advance steadily exceeded our own, especially in Germany. Reconstruction aided German productivity growth in the 1950s but not thereafter while in the 20 years from 1959 to 1979 Germany had moved from parity with the UK to a lead of over 60 per cent. The recent acceleration in British manufacturing productivity growth, combined with much slower German productivity growth, has, however reduced the gap back to what it was around 1974.

TABLE 9.2. *Output per person-hour in manufacturing, 1951–1988: comparisons with the UK in selected years*

|      | UK  | USA | France | Germany |
|------|-----|-----|--------|---------|
| 1951 | 100 | 270 | 71     | 68      |
| 1964 | 100 | 268 | 90     | 117     |
| 1973 | 100 | 234 | 101    | 133     |
| 1979 | 100 | 243 | 129    | 163     |
| 1988 | 100 | 224 | 122    | 138     |

*Source*:  Van Ark (1990).

Looking at the whole economy rather than just manufacturing and adjusting for hours worked gives a rather different picture of comparative productivity levels, as Table 9.3 shows. The overtaking of Britain by European countries in the 1960s still stands out, however. It is also worth noting the much superior performance of the American economy in the years 1870 to 1950 and the still inferior Japanese productivity level in the 1980s resulting from the relatively underdeveloped state of sectors other than exportable manufactures.

TABLE 9.3. *Real GDP per hour worked: comparisons with the UK in selected years*

|      | UK  | USA | France | Germany | Japan |
|------|-----|-----|--------|---------|-------|
| 1870 | 100 | 97  | 48     | 50      | 17    |
| 1890 | 100 | 113 | 49     | 55      | 19    |
| 1913 | 100 | 135 | 60     | 65      | 23    |
| 1929 | 100 | 158 | 70     | 65      | 30    |
| 1938 | 100 | 154 | 82     | 73      | 35    |
| 1950 | 100 | 185 | 70     | 54      | 24    |
| 1960 | 100 | 188 | 84     | 84      | 33    |
| 1973 | 100 | 156 | 105    | 100     | 62    |
| 1979 | 100 | 150 | 114    | 113     | 70    |
| 1986 | 100 | 133 | 119    | 105     | 68    |

*Source*: Feinstein (1988), p. 4, amended in accordance with Maddison (1989), table 7.3.

This generally rather gloomy statistical record has prompted a number of questions and has given birth to a wide range of supposed explanations, some of which, as we shall see, are not very persuasive. The most obvious questions are the following:

(1) Why has the UK been relatively so slow-growing until recently?
(2) Does the post-1979 growth performance indicate that there has been such a substantial payoff from the 'Thatcher Experiment' that relative economic decline has been permanently reversed?

These questions have already produced a great deal of work by economists. For economic historians there are additional important issues which arise in the following questions.

(3) What were the effects on post-war growth of the legacy of the inter-war and wartime periods?
(4) Were the reasons for relatively slow growth the same after the Second World War as in the preceding 70 or so years?

It is easy to imagine in the light of Table 9.1 that the UK had been in long-term decline for over a century since the days of our pioneering leadership in the Industrial Revolution and that this arises from continuing, longstanding features of our society and economy. Part of the historian's task is to evaluate such commonly held views.

## B. Accounting for British Economic Growth

A more sophisticated description of the growth of output and productivity can be obtained using 'Growth Accounting'. This technique has come to be widely used in the past quarter-century and formed the basis of a seminal study by Matthews *et al.* (1982) of British economic growth. The methodology decomposes the rate of economic growth into contributions from the inputs of capital and labour and from total factor productivity growth as in equation (1)

$$\triangle Y/Y = \alpha \triangle K/K + \beta \triangle L/L + \triangle TFP/TFP \qquad (1)$$

where $\alpha$ and $\beta$ are coefficients representing the elasticity of output growth to capital and labour growth respectively and TFP $= Y/(\alpha K + \beta L)$. For the post-war years values of $\alpha = 0.3$ and $\beta = 0.7$ would be appropriate. If capital and labour are measured very accurately, it will be possible to allow for changes in their quality and TFP growth will reflect improvements in technology and elimination of inefficiencies in the use of resources. In practice, depending on data availability and the range of the comparisons being made some or all of the improvements in factor input quality is likely to be captured in TFP growth. Table 9.4 gives a long run and comparative perspective on the sources of growth based on the growth accounting approach.

It is clear from Table 9.4 that the years 1950–73 represent a period of particularly high TFP growth both for Britain and the other countries. This period also saw much higher investment and capital stock growth. TFP growth has slowed significantly since 1973 in all countries including Japan and Britain's shortfall has been much less. During 1950–73 when Britain experienced much slower growth than Germany, France, or Japan, compared with those countries slower TFP growth accounted for 52, 75, and 29 per cent respectively of the gap in growth rates, and capital accumulation was responsible for 31, 7, and 31 per cent respectively. Britain's competitors undoubtedly had more scope for productivity increases after the war from reallocation of resources away from agriculture and the catching up of American technology during reconstruction and Table 9.4 shows that these factors played a significant part in their faster TFP growth, in particular in the Japanese case.

## C. Hypotheses to Explain Slower Economic Growth in the UK

In this and the following section the chief emphasis will be on the first of the questions raised in the first section. In effect we shall be reviewing propositions concerning the factors which lie behind the proximate sources of growth of equation (1). Before proceeding to the detailed arguments, however, it may be helpful to note the following preliminary points.

(i) As equation (1) implies, growth of capital per worker (through investment) and of output per unit of total input (through greater efficiency and technological progress) determine the growth of real output per worker and theories seeking to explain poor British growth performance can be thought of as possible reasons for slow progress in either or both of these growth determinants.

(ii) In making comparisons of growth between countries it is important to try and distinguish to what extent the reasons for slower UK growth lie in domestic failure as opposed to circumstances beyond our control. (For example, continental Europe started the post-war period with greater scope to contract small-scale agriculture and a bigger backlog in technology than Britain.)

(iii) Examination of the growth of output and productivity in different sectors of the British economy indicates that a poor performance relative to Germany was pervasive (Panic, 1976). We might therefore expect to find some general forces at work and this has encouraged many writers towards a macro level approach.

TABLE 9.4. *Sources of GDP growth*
(% per year)

| | UK | | | USA | | | France | | |
|---|---|---|---|---|---|---|---|---|---|
| | 1913–50 | 1950–73 | 1973–84 | 1913–50 | 1950–73 | 1973–84 | 1913–50 | 1950–73 | 1973–84 |
| Capital quantity | 0.34 | 0.99 | 0.77 | 0.54 | 1.02 | 0.85 | 0.31 | 1.10 | 1.20 |
| Labour quantity | −0.20 | −0.11 | −0.93 | 0.25 | 0.85 | 0.95 | −0.67 | 0.01 | −0.86 |
| Capital quality | 0.45 | 0.52 | 0.38 | 0.45 | 0.51 | 0.43 | 0.45 | 0.56 | 0.43 |
| Labour quality | 0.32 | 0.09 | 0.20 | 0.35 | 0.29 | 0.36 | 0.36 | 0.35 | 0.48 |
| TFP | 0.38 | 1.53 | 0.64 | 0.99 | 1.05 | −0.27 | 0.61 | 3.11 | 0.93 |
| Catch up | 0.00 | 0.14 | 0.29 | 0.00 | 0.00 | 0.00 | 0.00 | 0.52 | 0.49 |
| Structural change | −0.04 | 0.10 | −0.26 | 0.29 | 0.12 | −0.07 | 0.09 | 0.46 | −0.12 |
| GDP growth | 1.29 | 3.02 | 1.06 | 2.78 | 3.72 | 2.32 | 1.06 | 5.13 | 2.18 |

| | Germany | | | Japan | | |
|---|---|---|---|---|---|---|
| | 1913–50 | 1950–73 | 1973–84 | 1913–50 | 1950–73 | 1973–84 |
| Capital quantity | 0.13 | 1.88 | 1.03 | 0.54 | 2.88 | 2.17 |
| Labour quantity | −0.02 | 0.29 | −0.90 | −0.20 | 1.99 | 0.18 |
| Capital quality | 0.45 | 0.53 | 0.35 | 0.45 | 0.58 | 0.38 |
| Labour quality | 0.22 | 0.18 | 0.07 | 0.61 | 0.52 | 0.41 |
| TFP | 0.52 | 3.04 | 1.13 | 0.84 | 3.40 | 0.64 |
| Catch up | 0.00 | 0.68 | 0.40 | 0.00 | 1.02 | 0.44 |
| Structural change | 0.20 | 0.36 | 0.05 | 0.62 | 1.22 | 0.21 |
| GDP growth | 1.30 | 5.92 | 1.68 | 2.24 | 9.37 | 3.78 |

*Source:* Maddison (1987), p. 679; for Germany and Japan I have included Maddison's 'capacity use effect' and 'labour hoarding' in capital and labour quantity respectively. Maddison's estimates are based on growth accounting as in equation (1) with weights of $\alpha = 0.3$ and $\beta = 0.7$.

(iv)    Table 1 shows that the UK has a long history of relatively slow growth, and readers familiar with pre-1945 economic history will be aware of many criticisms of economic performance both before and after World War One. It does not necessarily follow, however, that the same explanations apply throughout or even that the reasons for slow growth since 1945 have deep historical roots.

Over the past 25 years or so economists have puzzled over what is so different about Britain. Among the most prominent hypotheses at one time or another have been the following.

(1) *Balance of Payments Constraint.* This argument takes as its starting point the demand side of the economy and can be found in a number of variants, for example Beckerman (1965, ch. 2) and Thirlwall (1986, ch. 11). The suggestion is that the growth of demand for exports constrains domestic growth through the requirement for balance in external payments. This balance condition means that

$$\frac{\Delta Y}{Y} h \times e_m = \Delta \frac{Y}{Y} RW \times e_x \tag{2}$$

$$\text{and} \quad \frac{\Delta Y}{Y} h = \frac{\Delta Y / Y_{RW} \cdot e_x}{e_m} \tag{3}$$

(where $h$ is the home country, RW is the rest of the world and $e_x$ and $e_m$ are the income elasticities of demand for exports and imports of the home country respectively) if the balance of payments cannot be brought into equilibrium by changes in competitiveness (the real exchange rate). It has frequently been argued that the elasticities facing Britain are much less favourable than those for other economies (Thirlwall, 1979, p. 51). This constraint on the demand side would put a ceiling on growth in the basic case; in a more elaborate argument there would also be an adverse effect on productivity growth arising from 'dynamic economies of scale' (see below) which in subsequent periods could tighten the balance of payments constraint still further. It should be noted, however, that if the real exchange rate is free to vary (i.e. balance of payments difficulties can be solved by a rising relative price of imports) then the consequences of unfavourable demand conditions should be felt on growth of real incomes (through the terms of trade) rather than of real domestic product. Moreover, the chief obstacle to adjustment of the real exchange rate is usually expected to be from the resistance of trade unions to reductions in real wages leading to depreciation of the nominal currency being offset by rising money wages (and thus labour costs). Thus in terms of output growth the problem would stem from a combination of trade conditions and labour market institutions.

(2) *Fiscal Policy.* There are two rather different versions of this type of argument. The older variant relates to the 'stop–go' demand management policies and was cogently presented by Dow (1964). He claimed that the government's attempts to stabilize the growth of aggregate demand had in fact destabilized the economy with somewhat adverse effects on investment. More important he advocated that policies for the management of demand needed to be given a role in the long-term improvement of productive potential by being used in conjunction with indicative planning to create favourable expectations of sales growth, and thus a high rate of capital accumulation (1964, ch. 16; see ch. 3).

A decade later the emphasis switched to an argument that government expenditure was 'crowding out' private-sector investment and thus inhibiting growth. The best known theory is that of Bacon and Eltis (1978) which discussed the roles of the 'non-marketed' and 'marketed' sectors of the economy; they argued that the surplus of output over consumption in the marketed sector was potentially available for net exports, investment in the marketed sector, or could be siphoned off for use in the non-marketed sector and that after 1960 government claims had taken increasingly more of the marketed sector's production. Since in practice they saw workers as able to pass on any taxes aimed at cutting real wages and consumption to profits and thus investment they regarded the process as very damaging for long run growth. In the notation of equation (4), $I_n + C_n$ grew at the expense of $I_m$, where we have

$$Y_m - C_m \equiv I_n + C_n + NX_m + I_m \qquad (4)$$

where the subscripts $m$ and $n$ refer to the marketed and non-marketed sectors.

Obviously the Bacon and Eltis hypothesis is much closer to Thatcherite diagnoses of the reasons for slow growth whilst Dow's views were very much those of the incoming Wilson Government in 1964. There is, however, a more important difference to be noted. At bottom the Bacon and Eltis view stresses the power of trade unions to resist inroads on real wages whilst demanding increasing welfare provisions as the underlying problem—much as the Thirlwall diagnosis of balance of payments constraint sees real wage rigidity as preventing export-led growth. By contrast, the 1960s optimism of Dow was that long-run demand management and indicative planning would raise domestic productive potential and international competitiveness through faster investment and associated technological progress without foundering on trade union wage pressures.

(3) *Verdoorn's Law and the Structure of Employment.* One of the most influential items in the post-war debate on growth was Kaldor's inaugural lecture (1966). In it he drew attention to the apparent existence of the following relationship in the manufacturing sector

$$p_m = a + be_m \qquad (5)$$

(where $p_m$ is the rate of growth of output per worker, $e_m$ is the rate of growth of employment, and $b > 0$.) Equation (5) is known as Verdoorn's Law and it implies that output growth brings with it productivity growth in manufacturing. In Kaldor's formulation this resulted from dynamic economies of scale. If this claim is valid, then several insights into slow British economic growth follow.

(i) There could be reason to suppose that early British industrialization, which by the post-World War Two period had left very little labour in agriculture, had exhausted much of the economy's ability further to expand manufacturing employment and thus had reduced our post-1945 growth potential relative to other countries. (The argument would go well beyond that of Maddison (1987), as reported in Table 9.4, who merely accounted for a static reallocation effect from previously under-employed labour.)

(ii) Linked to the growth of North Sea Oil which raised the exchange rate and tended to retard manufacturing employment growth via reducing the price to us of manufactured imports, Verdoorn's Law could help explain relatively poor productivity growth in the 1970s.

(iii) Most important, the possibility is opened up of cumulative causation (virtuous/vicious circle) accounts of relatively slow British growth. Thus slow expansion of the economy, perhaps due to the balance of payments constraint, retards productivity growth which in turn reduces the prospect of loosening the constraint through increased competitiveness etc.

(4) *Supply-Side Problems.* The first three hypotheses considered stress aspects of the macroeconomic environment which made it difficult to achieve fast growth. Recently, however, critics have pointed much more to weaknesses at the microeconomic level which have independently had adverse effects on the supply side of the economy—this change of emphasis is well reflected in Walters (1986, ch. 9). Such complaints are by no means new, of course, and can also be found in discussions of the late nineteenth century and inter-war economies.

Among the factors which have often been blamed for poor productivity growth and, linked to this, a low rate of investment with disappointing profitability are obstructive industrial relations and restrictive practices by trade unions, inadequately trained and technologically unqualified management, low rates of skill acquisition by workers, badly directed research and development, and distortions arising from the tax system. The upshot is argued to be a slow rate of adoption of new methods and a failure to reap the full potential of technological change reflected in the growing productivity gap between British industry and that of other countries characteristic especially of the 1960s and 1970s.

Put in terms of basic economics these arguments imply widespread 'market failure' in the sense of failing to achieve an efficient allocation of resources. Included in this would be that market forces operating through new entry and takeover were not able to prevent an inadequate productivity performance. The textbooks would see government action as potentially able to remedy such problems but the critics tend to regard the state as, if anything, exacerbating resource misallocation. Olson (1983) has argued that there is a general tendency for stable democracies to develop a large number of special interest groups whose activities retard the resource reallocations necessary for full exploitation of improved technological possibilities unless they have been disrupted by a period of war, foreign occupation, or totalitarian government. Britain is seen by him post-1945 as particularly prone to this 'sclerosis' problem.

The ideas contained in these four prominent hypotheses have had their reflection in government policies. Evidently Thatcherite administrations since 1979 have acted as if they were accepting the diagnosis of 'supply-side problems' and have sought in particular to reduce tax and trade-union obstacles to growth. That trade union reform might ameliorate the workings of the labour market and thus lessen the severity of the balance of payments constraint and the profits squeeze has been widely recognized since the Donovan Commission of 1968, if not earlier and, of course, the Wilson Government's National Economic Plan sought a way of managing demand along the lines Dow proposed. (These policy initiatives have been analysed in detail in Chapter 3). The dashes for growth under Chancellors Maudling (in 1963/4) and Barber (in 1972/4) can be understood in terms of attempts to defeat the balance of payments constraint supplemented by policies to restrain the workings of the labour market based essentially on an analysis close to the first hypothesis discussed. (These episodes were considered in full in Chapter 5.)

## D. Empirical Evaluation of Hypotheses to Explain Slow Growth

It is now time to return to the historical evidence related to British economic growth to examine the plausibility of the arguments listed above. The late 1980s provides a useful vantage point for this exercise in that it permits a perspective from a date well beyond the fast growth era prior to 1973 and at a point when Thatcherite policies have had a fair time to make an impact. Our review of the evidence is arranged in the order of the hypotheses listed in the previous section.

(1) *Balance of Payments Constraint.* During the fast-growth years 1951–73 when Britain was outperformed so decisively by rival economies it is certainly true that our exports grew much less quickly than those of countries like Germany and Japan, as Table 9.5 shows. Thirlwall drew from this experience support for the idea that British growth was balance of payments constrained and argued that in practice relative price effects were small so that equation (3) could be restated as the 'law', 'that except where the balance of payments equilibrium growth rate exceeds the maximum feasible capacity growth rate, the rate of growth of a country will approximate to the ratio of its rate of growth of exports and its income elasticity of demand for imports' (1979, p. 50). Table 9.5 reports this equilibrium growth rate for $\triangle Y/Y$ as estimate (a) and comparisons with the actual growth of output seem to support Thirlwall's claims. Moreover the initial evidence of econometric estimates for the income elasticity of demand for exports by Houthakker and Magee (1969) further reinforced this position, and using equation (3) gives estimates for the equilibrium growth rate consistent with balance of payments equilibrium labelled (b) in Table 9.5. The UK was seen to be constrained by an income elasticity of demand for exports of only 0.86 compared with Germany at 2.08 and Japan at 3.55, while import elasticities were 1.51, 1.89, and 1.23 respectively.

TABLE 9.5.  *Thirlwall's law, 1951–1973*

|         | Equilibrium $\triangle Y/Y$ | | | Actual | |
|---------|------|------|------|-------------------|-------------------|
|         | (a)  | (b)  | (c)  | $\triangle Y/Y$ | $\triangle X/X$ |
| UK      | 2.7  | 2.8  | 7.1  | 2.7  | 4.1  |
| USA     | 3.4  | 3.2  | 6.6  | 3.7  | 5.1  |
| France  | 5.0  | 4.6  | 6.2  | 5.0  | 8.1  |
| Germany | 5.7  | 5.4  | 5.9  | 5.7  | 10.8 |
| Japan   | 12.5 | 14.1 | 8.0  | 9.5  | 15.4 |

*Sources*:  Derived from OECD (1988), Thirlwall (1979), and Balassa
(1979); for discussion of differences between estimates (a),
(b), and (c) see text.

These estimates of income elasticities of demand for exports appear to be unreliable, however, as they do not make adequate allowance for the possible intervention of supply factors nor do they control for non-price (quality) influences on demand, although it is widely believed that British exports were increasingly affected by relatively poor performance in terms of delivery dates, reliability, etc. It is notable that Britain's exports were not relatively concentrated in goods where demand was only growing slowly—weak export performance seems to be associated rather with losses of market share. Moreover there is evidence that trade performance is strongly affected by trends in research and development and that poor British achievement in this area had a significantly adverse impact on export growth (Mayes and Buxton, 1988). This led Balassa (1979) to calculate an income elasticity of demand for exports for each country based on what would have been the case had they maintained their market shares. This seems to be a more acceptable methodology, potentially getting round the difficulties of the Houthakker–Magee figures. Balassa's estimates suggest that the income elasticities of demand for exports for the UK, Germany, and Japan were 2.20, 2.27, and 2.00 respectively and give the estimates for equilibrium $\triangle Y/Y$ reported as estimate (c) in Table 9.5. Using Balassa's estimates then leads to the implication that British growth was less constrained by demand elasticities than French or German growth and only slightly more constrained than Japanese growth.

Recent research on the labour market also relates to the question of the balance of payments constraint. In general, the evidence seems to suggest that real wages are quite slow to adjust to new market conditions but are not completely rigid so that in the medium term it is possible for the real exchange rate to adjust. Indeed real wage flexibility in post-war Britain was probably a little greater than before World War One (Hatton, 1988). It is the case, however, that British labour market institutions appear to adjust more slowly to shocks than those of more 'corporatist' economies such as Sweden (Bean et al., 1986).

Thus the evidence for a balance of payments constraint bearing particularly tightly on British growth as a result of exogenous demand factors and rigid real wages is not compelling. In particular, it seems likely that demand conditions were broadly as favourable as for other economies but that Britain failed to take advantage of fast growth in world trade through declining competitiveness. This suggests that the solution to Britain's apparent balance of payments constraint may well have involved domestic productivity improvements and the remedying of supply-side failures at home.

(2) Fiscal Policy. The evidence to support the hypotheses put forward in this category is also not very persuasive. It is arguable whether government demand management in the Keynesian years actually did make for greater instability (see Chapter 3) but in any event detailed study demonstrated that the UK experienced decidedly milder economic fluctuations than the fast growing economies (NEDO, 1976b, pp. 25–6) and, in the absence of a solution to the balance of payments problem, the experiment of the National Plan was short-lived and unsuccessful (see Chapter 5).

Table 9.6 places the Bacon and Eltis 'crowding out' argument in long-run perspective. This offers a rather different picture from that obtained by concentrating on the 1960s and early 1970s. In particular, the following points should be noted:

(i) In the long run the rise of government financed (non-market sector) consumption appears to come at the expense of marketed sector consumption whilst marketed sector investment holds up well. (As compared with the pre-war years marketed sector investment has been able to advance markedly against marketed sector consumption). This is a much less damaging outcome than was discussed by Bacon and Eltis.

(ii) The Thatcherites, despite their instinctive sympathy for reversing the rise of the non-marketed sector, have not succeeded in so doing. The recovery

TABLE 9.6. *The long-run relationship of the marketed and non-marketed sectors* (% of marketed output)

|  | 1924 | 1937 | 1955 | 1965 | 1974 | 1979 | 1987 |
|---|---|---|---|---|---|---|---|
| Marketed sector consumption | 81.4 | 76.4 | 56.7 | 53.0 | 51.2 | 47.0 | 46.3 |
| Marketed sector investment | 6.5 | 9.4 | 14.0 | 17.3 | 19.0 | 19.7 | 17.3 |
| Balance of trade | −3.0 | −5.0 | −1.8 | −0.9 | −6.1 | 0.2 | −0.2 |
| Government financed consumption | 9.3 | 9.8 | 20.3 | 18.8 | 22.1 | 21.8 | 25.0 |
| Government purchases of materials & investment | 5.8 | 9.5 | 10.7 | 11.7 | 13.8 | 11.3 | 11.2 |

*Sources*: Derived from Feinstein (1972), Bacon and Eltis (1978), and Central Statistical Office (1988).

in total factor productivity growth and relatively good growth in the 1980s have occurred regardless of this.

(iii) The squeeze on profits, which was marked in the mid-1970s, has been reversed. Thus net trading surplus as a percentage of value-added averaged 27 per cent in 1985–7, which was much the same as the 1960s level, compared with 18.6 per cent in 1974–6 (Central Statistical Office, 1988).

Thus the Bacon and Eltis hypothesis appears much less plausible now than at the time it was originally put forward. The reason for this may possibly be found in the workings of the labour market which writers such as Layard and Nickell (1986) have uncovered in seeking to explain a rising NAIRU (see Chapter 7). Their model suggests that rising tax rates to fund the growth of the non-marketed sector will in the long run tend to raise unemployment rather than lower profitability, as also would greater trade-union wage militancy. This implies that in the long run there need be no impediment to investment and growth, although, because equilibrium is not reached very quickly, in the short run there could be adverse consequences from expansion of the non-marketed sector. The behaviour of profitability in the past twenty years tends to support this view.

(3) *Verdoorn's Law and the Structure of Employment*. The key empirical question concerns the validity of the claim that expanding the manufacturing sector gives productivity gains arising from extra technical progress and learning effects. For practical investigation variants of equation (5) have been employed notably using the identity

$$q_m \equiv p_m + e_m \tag{6}$$

(where $q_m$ is the rate of growth of output in manufacturing) to obtain

$$q_m = a + (b + 1)e_m \tag{7}$$

McCombie (1983) estimates (7) for a cross-section of 11 advanced countries for 1950–65 and finds $b = 0.39$ in line with Kaldor's prediction. However, Chatterji and Wickens (1983) who investigated time series of equation (5) for six countries for 1960–80 found $b$ significantly greater than zero only in the United States.

Verdoorn's Law on this evidence might apply to the early post-war period but not more recently. In fact, it seems quite probable that even the 1950–65 result is spurious and occurs simply because in the period of rapid catching up of American technology after the war those countries who were most able to benefit from this process enjoyed rapid growth of employment and output and productivity without there being any causal connection running from greater employment growth to productivity growth.

Time series evidence for the UK has been examined in some detail in Chatterji and Wickens (1982). They conclude that British manufacturing is characterized by Okun's Law rather than Verdoorn's Law, that is that there has been a short-run cyclical relationship between employment growth and labour productivity but no long run one. This point is clarified in Fig. 9.1.

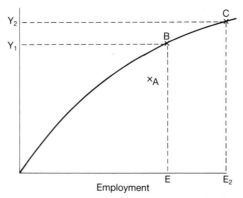

FIG 9.1.  *The relationship between employment and output in the short and medium term*

OBC is a typical production function showing output rising with employment but with employment having diminishing marginal productivity. With all factors fully employed and a given capital stock and technology an increase in employment from $E_1$ to $E_2$ rises output from $Y_1$ to $Y_2$. In a recession, however, firms typically hold onto much labour in the short term (because of union agreements, hiring and firing costs, etc.) although it is underemployed. In recovery, output rises rapidly as the underemployment is eliminated. Over the cycle output varies proportionately more than employment and labour productivity varies directly with output and employment (Okun's Law). The economy moves from point B to A and back again. Any test of Verdoorn's Law must avoid contamination by allowing for this Okun effect. When this is controlled for, Chatterji and Wickens conclude that for Britain (and other countries) after 1960 the Verdoorn dynamic economies of scale do not exist.

Thus it would seem unwise to see the contraction in manufacturing employment since 1968 (or much more rapidly since 1979) as of itself an explanation for unsatisfactory productivity performance in British manufacturing; nor should blame be put on the legacy of a small agricultural labour force. It would also appear in the light both of this evidence and the earlier discussion in this section that the dashes for growth of Chancellors Maudling and Barber were ill-advised in that they could not have been expected to lead to a virtuous circle of rising productivity, greater competitiveness, a relaxation of the balance of payments constraint, higher growth, rising productivity, etc. Given that productivity increases could not be readily induced in manufacturing by expansionary demand management and the lack of success in sustaining incomes policies it is not surprising that both episodes led to big balance of payments deficits without permanently raising the growth rate (see Chapter 3, 5).

(4) *Supply-Side Problems*. Tables 9.2 and 9.4 showed that levels of productivity in the UK have been disappointing relative to those of other countries. Further examination of details of the productivity gap which developed in the post-war period is suggestive of reasons for lagging productivity growth and can offer insights into the importance of alleged supply-side failures in the economy. Studies have been carried out at the sectoral and the company level; these have mostly concentrated on manufacturing which in 1977 accounted for 61.4 per cent of the production sector's total productivity shortfall relative to Germany (A. D. Smith *et al.*, 1982, p. 28).

Davies and Caves (1987) investigated the factors which in cross-sections of sectors of manufacturing in 1967/8 and 1977 were associated with *relatively* good or bad productivity in a UK industry compared with its American counterpart using regression analysis. This technique can reveal the effects of variables which differed between sectors (such as the degree of trade-union membership) but not those which were economy-wide (such as income taxation). Davies and Caves's results suggest that the most important factors leading to relatively lagging UK labour productivity were trying to operate large plants but failing to gain advantages from them, lower capital per worker, a less educated workforce, high unionization, and relatively bellicose workers (in 1967/8 only—a period of high strike activity in the UK), and lower research and development. Table 9.7 gives an indication of the extent to which 'avoidable failure' accounted for the UK productivity lag in 1967/8. It is suggestive of failures in supply-side policy and company management which if remedied during the 1950s and 1960s might have significantly raised the British productivity growth rate.

Two international comparisons of productivity in companies are particularly

TABLE 9.7. *Predicted improvements in relative net output/head from achieving best practice standards throughout British manufacturing in 1967/8*
(%)

| | |
|---|---|
| Eliminating capital shortfall | 9.1 |
| Removing substandard educational background of workforce | 8.5 |
| No adverse trade union problems | 6.7 |
| Correcting plant size | 5.5 |
| Making good R & D shortfall | 4.7 |

*Note*: 'Best practice' is regarded as achieving one standard deviation better than the mean actually achieved—thus, for example, 'removing substandard educational background' would imply all sectors having workers with as many years of schooling relative to their American counterparts as the sector one standard deviation above the average in 1967/8. The predicted effect on productivity comes from the authors' regression analysis.

*Source*: Adapted from Davies and Caves (1987), table 7.4; for precise definitions of variables consult the original.

noteworthy, those of Pratten (1976) relating to 1972 and of Daly *et al.* (1985) for 1983/4. Pratten's findings are summarized in Table 9.8 and relate to international companies with operations in both countries based on interviews with management and unions. Several interesting points arise from these results. In particular, the large role played by behavioural factors, essentially stemming from labour relations, is of significance as is the relatively small part played by differences in capital per worker in the UK–Germany comparison. It is also clear that North Americans have a big advantage over Europeans in the length of their production runs presumably based on a large and relatively homogeneous home market. The finding on behavioural factors is consistent with the outcome of 25 studies covering six sectors at various times in the post-war period listed by Pratten and Atkinson (1976, p. 574) 23 of which report inefficient labour usage, in 14 cases from restrictive practices and in 21 cases reflecting management failure according to the authors. Daly *et al.* in their comparison of the UK and Germany agree that lack of modern machinery is not a major factor in lower UK productivity. They stress the lack of qualifications of foremen and associated with this poor maintenance of machinery, inadequate quality control, excess breakdowns, etc. and conclude that 'the most important overall implication of the study is that lack of technical expertise and training . . . is the stumbling block' (1985, p. 59). Thus, the regression findings of Davies and Caves are to a considerable extent echoed in company level studies.

TABLE 9.8. *Labour productivity comparisons in international companies: reasons for productivity differentials* (1972)

| | German advantage over UK (%) | North American advantage over UK(%) |
|---|---|---|
| *'Economic' causes* | | |
| Length of production runs | 5½ | 20½ |
| Plant and machinery | 5 | 6 |
| Other[a] | 2 | 6 |
| *'Behavioural' causes* | | |
| Strikes and restrictive practices | 3½ | 5 |
| Manning and efficiency | 8½ | 6 |
| Total differential[b] | 27 | 50 |

[a] Other economic causes include differences in product mix, capacity utilization, and quality of materials.
[b] The contributions to the total differential are multiplicative not additive.

It should be remembered, however, that these attempts to 'account' for productivity gaps are not wholly persuasive. In particular, they do not deal with interactions between variables—for example deficient plant size or investment could itself reflect industrial relations problems or poor management. The consistency of these various findings is well-reflected in the major study by Prais (1981) who reviewed performance in ten industries in the 1960s and 1970s. In six of them he found increases in productivity had been retarded by problems of negotiating appropriate manning levels with trade unions when technological improvements became possible (brewing, tobacco, motor vehicles, tyres, metal boxes, and newspapers) and in the other four (manufactured foods, machine tools, typewriters, and furniture) the chief retarding factors were found to lie in inadequate training and skills-acquisition for the labour force. It is important that Prais also showed (1981, ch. 7) that large plants in Britain in the 1970s were extremely strike-prone relative to small plants domestically or equally large plants abroad and this provides a major reason for Davies and Caves's finding that Britain does badly in industries where large plant-size is normal in other countries.

The inhibitions on productivity performance coming from industrial relations appear to have intensified during the 1960s and 1970s. In particular, attempts at trade union reform following the 1968 Donovan Commission Report appear to have been counterproductive. The main thrust of developments in this period was towards greater formalization of bargaining structures but in the environment of the 1970s this appears to have reduced rather than enhanced managerial freedom and in a cross-section of industries was correlated with slower productivity growth (Batstone, 1988, pp. 142–3). At the end of the 1970s econometric evidence suggests that in large firms with a closed shop, union presence had a substantial negative effect on labour productivity and the rising trade union density of the 1970s (see Chapter 11) was probably not conducive to rapid productivity growth (Metcalf, 1988a, pp. 8–11).

The nature of industrial relations in Britain and some important contrasts with the post-war position in other countries in this regard are perhaps the most promising way of building on Olson's sclerosis hypothesis. Batstone (1986) points out that it is important to examine not just the long-run stability of democratic institutions but also the 'scope' of unions and 'sophistication' of unions and employers. Unions with narrow scope represent the interests of small sub-groups of workers and can be expected to be more obstructive of productivity improvements than all-encompassing unions, which would have more reason to fear the costs of such actions. Sophistication involves the ability to co-ordinate interests and to develop and implement strategy. Batstone argues that the post-war UK persistently experienced narrow scope and low sophistication in its industrial relations and that this explains the particularly debilitating form of its sclerosis. As Table 9.9 shows, there does appear to be a correlation worth further research, although the post-1973 experience is less supportive.

Thus it seems quite likely that overmanning and problems arising from the structure of industrial relations adversely affected not only British productivity levels but also the rate of growth of productivity. Similar outcomes are likely with regard to research and development and education, which also were highlighted in Table 9.7. Measured as a proportion of GDP British expenditure on R and D until the mid-1970s was second only to the United States. Unfortunately this relatively high level of spending appears to a significant effect to have been misdirected. Government support was unduly concentrated on high technology and the aircraft industry (C. Freeman, 1982, p. 189; Pavitt, 1976, p. 114), while industry-financed R and D grew much more slowly relative to profits or output than in Germany or Japan during the 1960s and 1970s (Patel and Pavitt, 1987, pp. 72–3). NEDO

N. F. R. CRAFTS

TABLE 9.9. *Industrial relations and productivity*
*growth, 1950–1973*
(growth of GDP/person-hour)

|  | High sclerosis |  |  |
|---|---|---|---|
| *Broad scope, high sophistication* |  | *Narrow scope, low sophistication* |  |
| Netherlands | 4.4 | Canada | 3.0 |
| Norway | 4.2 | USA | 2.6 |
| Sweden | 4.2 | UK | 3.1 |
| Belgium | 4.4 | Australia | 2.6 |
|  | Low sclerosis |  |  |
| *Broad scope, high sophistication* |  | *Broad scope, low sophistication* |  |
| Austria | 5.9 | Japan | 8.0 |
| Finland | 5.2 | France | 5.1 |
| West Germany | 6.0 | Italy | 5.8 |

*Source*:   Adapted from Batstone (1986), table 1.

concluded that 'The UK puts emphasis on science and in particular "big science" . . . at the expense of engineering. The sectoral distribution of R and D effort appears inappropriate to patterns of world demand and export growth' (1983, p. 2). The outcome in terms of patented inventions, a key indicator, shows a decline relative to key rivals; thus in 1958 Britain had 23.4 per cent, Germany 25.6 per cent, and Japan 1.9 per cent of all patents granted to foreign applicants in the United States but by 1979 the percentages were 10.1, 23.9, and 27.7 respectively (Pavitt and Soete, 1982).

Neither the Butler reforms of the 1940s nor the comprehensive school movement of the 1960s improved the availability of technical education at school. Moreover, growth of vocational qualifications among the labour force was relatively slow in Britain even though years of schooling increased at a similar rate to elsewhere and in the late 1970s Britain was spending much less on vocational training with the result that whilst over 60 per cent of the German manufacturing workforce had at least intermediate qualifications less than 30 per cent were similarly qualified in the UK (Sanderson, 1988). This was indeed a longstanding weakness which was well documented in Ministry of Labour reports as early as the mid-1950s (Sheldrake and Vickerstaff, 1987, pp. 29–31).

The discussion in this section has emphasized possible explanations for the UK's poor productivity growth. This may seem slightly surprising in view of a widely held and longstanding belief that the UK has invested too little. Certainly the share of investment in national income in the post-war period has been some 5 percentage points less than the average of European countries. Nevertheless, the sources of growth analysis of the second section suggested that only a relatively small part of the shortfall in British growth in 1951–73 came from slower capital accumulation where this was regarded as a separate source of growth.[1]

[1] In practice, however, it may not be appropriate to regard capital accumulation as an independent factor in long-run economic growth. There is an automatic tendency for the rate

An exploration of the evidence on investment in manufacturing in Britain and Germany bears out this emphasis with more detail. As Table 9.10 shows, as far as manufacturing is concerned the UK invested a fairly similar proportion of output to Germany. In each economy over 1954–72 the rate of growth of the capital stock slightly exceeded the rate of growth of output but the difference in the growth of output per worker was almost entirely due to TFP growth (1.4 out of 1.7 percentage points per year) (Panic, 1976, pp. 4, 20, 38, 64). The UK experienced a lower level of output per unit of capital and thus its investment translated into a much lower rate of growth of capital (3.9 per cent per year compared with 7.4 per cent in Germany in 1954–72, Panic, 1976, p. 20). It is also important to note the role played by low capital productivity in the existence of a low rate of profit even prior to the difficulties of macroeconomic adjustment in the 1970s. This is shown in Table 9.10 based on the identity

$$\frac{\pi}{K} \equiv \frac{\pi}{Y} \cdot \frac{Y}{K} \tag{9}$$

(where $\pi$ is profits). Both the Wilson Committee and NEDO (1975) concluded that there was no reason to regard the cost or availability of external finance as a greater obstacle to investment in Britain than elsewhere; 'the major constraints on investment in recent years have been the related factors of the depressed and fluctuating level of demand, poor capital to output ratios and the low rate of return anticipated on new investment' (Great Britain, 1980, p. 258).

It would appear therefore that low rates of capital accumulation reflected a lower rate of growth of demand for capital in Britain rather than difficulties relating to the supply of funds. The lower rate of growth of demand for capital was closely linked to a lower productivity. Investment received a lower rate of return and produced a lower capital stock growth because of poor capital productivity; in 1958–72 the increase in net output per unit of investment in Germany was 1.9 times the British level (CBI, 1977) and in 1973–9 1.7 times (OECD, 1988). In addition the inefficient use of labour discussed earlier in this section has tended to lower the level of capital per person.

Low productivity from additions to the capital stock relative to German achievements emerges as a key feature of the above picture. In part this seems to have arisen because of the industrial relations and educational deficiencies already reviewed but some additional reasons should be noted.

(1)    There is evidence that the capital market was not all that successful in monitoring management and eliminating inferior performance through mergers and takeovers. Although Franks and Harris (1986) show that

of growth of the capital stock to equal that of output growth, as equation (8) reminds us

$$\frac{\triangle K}{K} \equiv \frac{I}{K} \equiv \frac{I/Y}{K/Y} \tag{8}$$

$K/Y$ is the capital-to-output ratio and thus when capital grows faster than output the rate of growth of the capital stock is falling (and vice versa) because the investment ratio is divided by a larger number. (Thus a higher investment rate does not in the long run lead to a faster growth rate of the capital stock.) In addition, evidence on the determinants of investment in the UK indicates that firms aim for a fairly constant capital-to-output ratio (the investment function is a flexible accelerator) modified in the short run by fluctuations in interest rates and unforeseen changes in aggregate demand (Bean, 1981).

TABLE 9.10. *Investment, profits, and capital productivity in British and German manufacturing* (%)

| | United Kingdom | | | | Germany | | | |
|---|---|---|---|---|---|---|---|---|
| | 1964 | 1973 | 1979 | 1987 | 1964 | 1973 | 1979 | 1985 |
| Investment/output | 12.4 | 11.2 | 13.2 | 11.5 | 13.7 | 11.6 | 11.2 | 12.7 |
| Profits/output | 31.0 | 26.9 | 22.4 | 33.7 | 35.2 | 31.2 | 28.8 | 30.3 |
| Output/capital | 39.1 | 34.6 | 29.0 | 29.8 | 52.2 | 52.9 | 50.0 | 48.2 |
| Profits/capital | 12.1 | 9.3 | 6.5 | 10.0 | 18.4 | 16.5 | 14.4 | 14.6 |

*Sources:* Derived form T. P. Hill (1979) and OECD (1986).

the stock market predicted improved profits on the announcement of successful bids, Meeks (1977) found that post-merger performance in the period 1954–72 was on average characterized by reduced profits and productive efficiency, while Singh (1975) showed that the risk of being a takeover victim was much more a function of size than profitability.

(2) The overall performance of the nationalized industry sector, especially in the 1970s, must be regarded as disappointing as far as productivity growth is concerned (see Chapter 12 and Pryke (1981) ).

(3) Throughout the period studies have expressed doubts concerning the recruitment and education of managers. Thus Swords-Isherwood concluded 'the educational background of the average British manager is inferior to that of his equivalent in other major industrial countries . . . a mix of elite, academically specialised, non-technical education, and the right social background remain the sure road to success in British management' (1980, pp. 88–9), findings which are very similar to those in the 1950s of the Acton Society Trust (1956). When Dunning compared the productivity of American and British managed companies operating in the UK, he found that the American companies were superior in each of ten industrial groups by 34 per cent on average in 1950 and 32.8 per cent in 1954 (1958, p. 181).

It is plausible to suggest therefore that the chief reasons for relatively slow British economic growth in the post-war period lie in institutional, supply-side weaknesses. In turn this suggests either that economic policy may be directly to blame or that there was a failure to develop appropriate policy initiatives. Certainly policy-makers expressed strong desires for faster growth especially from the early 1960s on and to a considerable extent the diagnosis presented above was already a familiar one by the end of that decade.

For example, as early as 1948, concern over lagging British productivity led to the setting up of the Anglo-American Council on Productivity which in the following five years produced a stream of well-publicized reports on various industries. These detailed studies were generally highly critical of the poor quality of British management and the restrictive practices of trade unions. Significant weaknesses in education and training were highlighted in the famous manifesto of the National Economic Development Council (1963a) and the shortcomings of research and development were laid bare in the much discussed Brookings report on the British economy (Caves, 1968, ch. 12). By the late 1960s widespread anxiety over the growth-inhibiting consequences of British industrial relations was echoed by the Donovan Commission.

Nevertheless, as Chapter 5 has related, supply-side policy did relatively little to combat the sources of low productivity growth discussed in this section despite the many permutations explored during the 1950s through the 1970s. The main thrusts were to be found rather in subsidizing investment, supporting declining industries, and promoting mergers.


## E. The Historical Context of Post-War Growth

In this section our focus will be on the historical background to post-war British economic growth as we take up the related questions of the impact of the legacy of the past on recent growth performance and of the extent to which the obstacles to faster growth have changed over time.

It is widely believed, although not always for well thought out reasons, that the failures of the post-war economy are deeply rooted in the past, presenting successive governments both with an unenviable legacy and a most daunting task in any attempt to remedy Britain's relative economic decline; thus Eatwell argues that 'The weakness of the British economy . . . is the cumulative product . . . of the entire history of Britain since the end of the nineteenth century, when it first became evident that Britain was unable, or unwilling, to adapt to a competitive world in which her pre-eminence could no longer be taken from granted' (1982, p. 50). Certainly complaints about the poor quality of industrial management, trade union obstacles to productivity advance, the inappropriate and inadequate education system, and slowness to develop and apply advanced technology were already commonplace at the start of the century—as they have been in recent decades. Nevertheless much remains to be done to convince a sceptic that there were powerful strands of continuity underlying unsatisfactory growth in different periods or that it really was extremely difficult to escape from the unfortunate legacy of an early start in industrialization.

The disappointing years of the 1950s through to the early 1970s were a period when investment at home as a share of GDP was roughly double that of any previous era and when TFP growth was three times that of the inter-war years. (Matthews *et al.*, 1982, Table 4.7). Indeed, the economic growth of the West in the twentieth century has been characterized by the potential for much greater productivity growth than was possible in the eighteenth or nineteenth centuries. It is important to recognize that during the industrial revolution Britain never achieved TFP growth of more than 0.7 per cent per year and that the nineteenth century peak rate was only briefly above 1.0 per cent (Crafts, 1985, p. 81). Moreover, this early productivity growth was concentrated in relatively few sectors (such as cotton, iron and steel, and railways) and resulted much more from trial and error innovation than from scientific education and research and development expenditures. By the turn of this century the United States was pioneering a new and much higher growth path based on the large corporation, electrification, mass production, use of scientifically trained manpower, and investment in research. The result was a dramatic rise in United States TFP growth from an average of 0.5 per cent per year in 1855–1905 to 1.5 per cent in 1905–27 (David, 1977, p. 186). In the early twentieth century Britain was unable to achieve a similar acceleration in productivity growth and it occupied a position in the international economy based on the exports of 'low-tech' Victorian staples quite different from that of the United States as it assumed the status of most advanced economy (Crafts and Thomas, 1986).

There are reasons to believe that British growth and productivity performance prior to World War One should be regarded as something of a failure, although the new economic historians of 15–20 years ago quite rightly exposed some of the then popular criticisms as unacceptable. Indeed the productivity estimates of Table 9.3 provide a prima facie case for doubting McCloskey's famous claim that the late Victorian economy was a case of 'an economy not stagnating but growing as rapidly as permitted by the growth of its resources and the effective exploitation of the available technology' (1970, p. 459). Certainly quantitative investigation has shown that in several important cases (e.g. ring-spinning, basic steel) alleged failures rapidly to adopt new techniques were in fact correct decisions under British cost conditions and it has also been demonstrated that the London capital market was not biased in favour of foreign investment (Sandberg, 1981; Edelstein, 1982) but at the same time research has shown up a number of major shortcomings, notably the following.

(a)   There are reasons to be sceptical of the effectiveness of British education, training, and research in an age where these factors mattered much more than earlier in the achievement of rapid productivity growth. In particular, despite improvements in technical education notably from the spread of technical colleges there was a much lower standard of technical training for most workers than in Germany while the public school's contributions to technological knowledge among the employers were weak and few managers had technical qualifications (Sanderson, 1988). Moreover, the supply of qualified engineers in England was only a third of the French or German levels (Ahlstrom, 1982, p. 14) and expenditure on R and D, although rising, was still less than £1m. per year in 1910 (Sanderson, 1972*b*). Britain's share of patents granted in the United States as a percentage of all foreign patents fell from 36.2 per cent in 1890 to 23.3 per cent in 1913 (Pavitt and Soete, 1982).

(b)   Business historians repeatedly point out unfavourable comparisons between British firms and their continental or American counterparts, particularly in respect of slowness to move to exploit the advantage of large-scale corporate capitalism (A. D. Chandler, 1980), hostility or indifference to new methods (Coleman and MacLeod, 1986), and failure to achieve full management (as opposed to union) control over work practices particularly in engineering and related sectors such as motorcars, shipbuilding, and iron and steel, so that 'second-best' levels of capital intensivity and plant size became rational to adopt initially and hard to change subsequently (Lewchuk, 1987; Zeitlin, 1987).

(c)   The economy suffered from weaknesses in the capital market associated with problems of inadequate information and lax requirements for disclosure and auditing. As a result there was no effective takeover mechanism to eliminate bad management (Hannah, 1974) and an inadequate new issues market to develop sectors like electricity (W. P. Kennedy, 1987, ch. 5). Although in itself less good at allocating funds than a perfect capital market, the German reliance on investment banking with direct involvement of bankers in industrial activities may have been much more effective both in monitoring management and financing high-risk, high pay-off projects (Tilly, 1986).

The period from World War One to 1950, although not a time of complete regeneration of the economy, did see progress on the supply side. Expenditure on research and development in the UK of less than £1m. per year in 1910 rose to perhaps £10m. by the late 1930s (Sanderson, 1972*b*), manufacturing became organized more on a corporate basis (Hannah, 1983) and the number of students reading science and technology was five times larger in 1938 than in 1913 (Sanderson, 1972*a*). By the late 1940s our problems lay not in doing too little research and development but in the allocation of the funds. The 1948 Companies Act by requiring much more disclosure of information led to the development for the first time of the takeover mechanism as a serious check on managerial incompetence. The structure of the manufacturing sector moved towards 'new' industries; by 1937 chemicals, vehicles and electrical engineering accounted for 21.1 per cent of output compared with only 8.8 per cent in 1900 (Matthews *et al.*, 1982, pp. 255–7). The rate of TFP growth in manufacturing rose from 0.6 per cent per year in 1873–1913 to 1.9 per cent in 1924–37, virtually the same as in 1951–64 (Matthews *et al.*, 1982., Table 8.3) and the post-depression years of 1932–7 saw growth of real GDP at 4 per cent per year despite the parlous state of the world economy.

These encouraging signs of progress are not the complete picture, of course, and other aspects of the development of the economy in the inter-war years are much less favourable to subsequent growth. For example, the growth of the 1930s was much stimulated by policies with good short-term impacts on recovery but dubious long-term consequences such as tariffs and rearmament. In response to hard times and in the absence of anti-trust laws, industry became highly collusive (Gribbin, 1978). No adequate solution was found to the shortfall in technical education even in the 1944 Education Act (Sanderson, 1988) and managers continued to be poorly qualified. Of those entering management in large companies in the late 1930s only 15 per cent had any professional qualifications (Acton Society Trust, 1956). Moreover, top management continued to be recruited from a narrow social elite—the average wealth left by fathers of the chairmen of the top 200 corporations in 1920–39 was £43,000, compared with only £5,300 in the 1960s (Rubinstein, 1986*b*, p. 187). It is also clear that even in large organizations conservative management practices prevailed as reflected in company structures, training for executives, and recruitment of directors so that a recent survey of business histories concludes that 'even large companies retained a cosy amateurishness' (Gourvish, 1987, p. 34). Evidence of the seriousness of continuing problems in the quality of management together with the unresolved difficulty of 'narrow scope' union opposition to productivity improvement is clear in the Anglo-American Council on Productivity reports discussed above in the fourth section.

Certainly many industries seem to have failed to keep pace with best practice techniques and work organization abroad including coal, cotton, motor vehicles, shipbuilding, and steel (Kirby, 1977; Porter, 1979; Lewchuk, 1987; Tolliday, 1987) and, as Table 9.3 shows, our relative position in terms of productivity performance in 1938 was distinctly worse than in 1913.

With its low rates of investment and its poor record in human capital formation, its family capitalism, and weak technological progress capability, the Victorian economy would have struggled even more than Britain actually did post-1945. The adaptations and changes that had occurred were mostly in the right direction. Nevertheless there were 'traditional weaknesses' in education and training and in industrial relations and these problems have mattered more in the economic environment since 1945. Doubts also exist throughout concerning the quality of British management which, as noted, capital market imperfections allowed to persist and which, more surprisingly, do not seem to have been particularly effectively dealt with by the much more aggressive climate of mergers and takeovers of the 1950s and 1960s.

The 'traditional weaknesses' might, in principle, seem to be suitable areas for government to provide effective remedies. In both cases, however, it can be argued that history had produced, in Olson's phrase, 'sclerotic tendencies' which mitigated against successful policy responses. Thus, trade unions entered the post-1945 economy in a position of unprecedented potential strength with their legal immunities intact, their membership levels very high, and the labour market at an extremely low level of unemployment (see Chapter 13). Faced with this situation governments sought cooperative solutions with the TUC to a possible inflationary crisis. For instance, in return for a tacit incomes policy, the Conservatives in the 1950s forswore deflation, labour legislation, and explicit incomes policy. In the long term this approach failed as the locus of bargaining switched to the plant level and shop stewards became more important in exploiting the latent bargaining power of workers. For as long as cooperation was pursued as a solution to the changed bargaining power of organized labour there was a major constraint on attempts at reforming industrial relations in pursuit of a system of collective bargaining more conducive to productivity growth (Flanagan *et al.*, 1983, pp. 374–407). For example, as Metcalf notes (1988*b*, pp. 8–9) the Donovan reforms of the 1970s took place against a background of record state handouts to 'lame ducks' and of incomes policies which precluded much potential bargaining about work practices and accordingly they were undermined as instigators of productivity advance.

In the field of education and training politicians were hindered from taking a more active role by the weakness of the central bureaucracy in the face both of a historical decentralization of power within the educational world and of vested interests on both sides of industry (Finegold and Soskice, 1988). Thus initiatives such as the 1964 Industrial Training Act, which established Industrial Training Boards financed by levies were seriously flawed in failing to challenge trade-union control over apprenticeships or to establish training in transferable skills (Vickerstaff, 1985) while entry to apprenticeship was restrictive and training within it was unreliable (Liepmann, 1960).

It is possible therefore to argue that the past had a somewhat unfavourable impact on post-war economic growth in terms of bequeathing a legacy which contained both supply-side weaknesses and obstacles in the way of amelioration of those deficiencies. To an extent it is possible then to sympathize with Olson's sclerosis version of an early-start hypothesis of poor growth post-1945. By contrast, the earlier discussion in the fourth section should be read as indicating that the Kaldor/Thirlwall hypotheses, which can also be seen as early-start arguments in which the unfavourable legacy is in terms of an inability to exploit Verdoorn's Law and an adverse export demand situation produces a vicious circle of balance of payments constrained growth, are not very convincing ways of linking slow post-war growth to our earlier economic history.

## F. The Thatcher Experiment and Growth in the 1980s

Tables 9.1 to 9.3 established that in terms of productivity advance British performance in the 1980s has been both an improvement on the 1970s and creditable with regard to international comparisons. More sophisticated calculations for manufacturing alone allowing for the important Okun's Law effect bear out these conclusions: Muellbauer (1986, p. xiii) found trend TFP growth of 2.76 per cent per year from the second half of 1980 through early 1986, slightly higher even than the 2.63 per cent he estimated for the 1959–72 period. (An industrial breakdown of achieved and forecast labour productivity growth is shown in Table 9.11.) Darby and Wren-Lewis (1988) find a constant *underlying* trend for manufacturing from the 1960s through the 1980s and argue that productivity behaviour in the 1970s and early 1980s was distorted by errors in forecasting demand growth and their subsequent correction. For the whole economy, including the much larger services sector, it should be noted that productivity growth during the boom years of 1984–8 at 1.8 per cent per year was rather less than the average of 2.4 per cent in 1951–73.

TABLE 9.11. *Changes in real output per worker in UK manufacturing*
(%per annum)

|                          | 1954–75 | 1975–80 | 1980–84 | 1984–90 |
| ------------------------ | ------- | ------- | ------- | ------- |
| Food, drink, & tobacco   | 2.2     | 2.8     | 4.5     | 3.1     |
| Chemicals                | 4.4     | 0.4     | 6.1     | 4.3     |
| Metals                   | 1.0     | −1.9    | 13.4    | 3.6     |
| Engineering              | 2.1     | −0.3    | 4.5     | 3.9     |
| Mechanical               | 2.4     | −1.6    | 0.8     | 3.5     |
| Electrical               | 3.1     | 3.2     | 8.1     | 5.0     |
| Motor vehicles           | 2.3     | −2.0    | 4.1     | 3.1     |
| Textiles & clothing      | 2.5     | 0.6     | 7.3     | 2.2     |
| All manufacturing        | 2.5     | 1.0     | 5.6     | 3.7     |

*Source*: Warwick University Institute for Employment Research (1986).

The Conservative Governments of the 1980s have departed substantially from the earlier post-war consensus on economic policy, and political events (Falklands War, Labour Party splits) have permitted a lengthy experiment. The Thatcherites can be seen as having abandoned earlier efforts at cooperative solutions to the control of inflation by means of implicit or explicit incomes policies and the commitment to full employment and thus as having more freedom to manoeuvre in seeking to reform industrial relations in order to give management an opportunity to control restrictive practices and to obtain faster productivity growth. Important new supply-side policies have included the moves towards privatization of national-ized industries, reducing income tax rates for high earners, the reform of trade union law, and especially recently, initiatives to strengthen education and training. It does appear to be the case that tighter financial controls on nationalized industries together with the prospect of privatization and weaker trade unions have brought about an improvement in productivity growth (see Chapter 12). For example, TFP growth in British Steel and British Coal was −2.5 per cent and −1.4 per cent per year respectively in 1968–78 but 4.6 per cent and 0.6 per cent respectively in 1979–83 and 9.0 per cent and 5.6 per cent respectively in 1983–7 (Kay and Bishop, 1988).

This section reviews what is known more generally about the sources of produc-tivity growth in the Thatcher period thus returning to the second of the questions posed in the first section. A close look at 1980s experience can be useful for two reasons; first, it can provide further evidence in connection with the reasons for earlier slow growth and, second, it can offer some guidance as to the extent and sustainability of the improved performance of recent years and thus inform a provisional verdict on the gains which may have resulted from the Conservatives' new supply-side approach.

Three rather obvious points can be made straightaway with regard to the hypotheses to explain slow growth in the pre-Thatcher years discussed in the fourth section.

(1)  The 1980s has not seen a rolling-back of the share of the non-marketed sector in marketed sector output, as Table 9.6 demonstrates. The Thatcherite escape from the Bacon and Eltis problem has come from a return to normal profit levels in industry, which, as Chapter 7 argues, have resulted from the restraints on real wage pressures provided by high unemployment and faster productivity growth.

(2)  The improved productivity performance has not come from a Verdoorn's Law effect through expansion of manufacturing output and employment, nor has it been associated with a rise in manufacturing investment which in 1987 was still about 10 per cent lower than in 1979. As Table 9.10 shows, although profitability has recovered in the 1980s this has not been based on an improved output-to-capital ratio to any great extent and it appears that in capital (as opposed to labour) productivity the UK lags further behind Germany than it did in 1973. By 1988 the proportion of manufacturing firms operating at full capacity was higher even than 1973.

(3)  The relatively rapid growth of the British economy in recent years has been accompanied by a move into substantial deficit in the balance of payments. This is a result of increased demand for imports rather than a declining share of world trade and comes against a background of reduced world trade growth in the 1980s as compared to the 1960s. It remains to be seen whether the economy can now adjust its real exchange rate (competitiveness) in order to permit faster growth in the UK than elsewhere to coexist with external balance.

There are, in fact, several competing (but not mutually exclusive) hypotheses to explain the recent revival in labour productivity growth, particularly in manufacturing. Muellbauer (1986, p. iv) lists closure of below average productivity plants, improved industrial relations, and faster technological change as prime candidates. In addition, he points out that official statistics may mismeasure growth of the capital stock following the rise in energy prices—in effect, some capital assumed to be scrapped in the 1980s may already have gone in the 1970s such that the growth of capital was then held back more than the figures suggest. To the (unknown) extent that this is the case, the improvement of the 1980s over the 1970s reflects the repercussions of OPEC activity rather than a gain from Thatcherism.

The early 1980s was a period of substantial closures in manufacturing as over 5,000 plants were shut between 1979 and 1982 compared with a net increase of over 13,000 plants between 1973 and 1979; the net losses were particularly of large plants with employment in establishments of 1,500 or more employees falling by 1m. between 1979 and 1984 (Oulton, 1987, p. 53). It appears likely that these closures will have helped to extricate companies from their worst industrial relations problems (cf. Prais, 1981) and will have helped adjustments within sectors toward optimal plant size (cf. Davies and Caves, 1987, and Table 9.7). The recovery of manufacturing since 1982 has seen a continuing (slower) contraction in the number of large plants while very small plants have risen steeply in number. These developments are probably favourable for long-run productivity growth and tend to support part of the fourth section's diagnoses of weaknesses leading to earlier productivity problems. Since, however, large plants on average have rather higher output per worker than small ones, closures per se do not seem to explain rising overall labour productivity levels in the short run in the early 1980s (Oulton, 1987, p. 55).

Surveys of working arrangements and industrial relations in the 1980s have confirmed a very considerable increase in flexibility and success in eliminating restrictive practices in a labour market and legal situation more favourable to management. It seems probable, therefore, that there has been a positive short-term impact in catching up already achieved European productivity levels through reductions in overmanning (cf. Pratten, 1976, and Tables 9.7 and 9.8). This is borne out by the well-known cases of steel and motor vehicles as well as the leap in productivity growth in some sectors to levels well above anything achievable in the steady-state, which comes over to an extent in Table 9.11. The implication of this would be to confirm that productivity growth in earlier periods was retarded by inability to extract maximum advantage from available improvements in technique. Thus after 1980 60 per cent of wage settlements had at least one productivity enhancing concession (Metcalf, 1988b, pp. 16–17); in the three years to 1987 ACAS found that over 25 per cent of respondents to their survey had succeeded in introducing one or more types of flexibility in crafts and skills use (1988, p. 19) and a mid-1980s survey found only a third of managers were constrained in their organization of work compared with just under a half at the time of Donovan (Daniel, 1987, p. 168). ACAS concluded that their results were 'consistent with the view . . . that in recent years, the presence of trade unions has not appeared to inhibit the introduction of new working practices' (1988, p. 30).

Although for the moment at least the conduct of industrial relations has changed, it is less clear that there has been a reform of the underlying structure which Batstone's work, reported in Table 9.9, described as 'narrow in scope and low in sophistication'. Thus multi-unionism has not decreased significantly, union presence in manufacturing is virtually the same as in the late 1970s and the number of shop stewards has risen slightly. Batstone concluded that in these respects 'there has been no transformation of the pattern of workplace industrial relations . . . the role which trade unions play . . . is still probably greater than . . . at the time of Donovan' (1988, p. 180). Given this background and the very high correlation across industry between declines in employment at the start of the decade and productivity growth over the first half of the 1980s, it is probable that fear rather than a new cooperation has been the factor which has enabled the realization of productivity gains frustrated by the climate of the 1960s and 1970s and the success in reducing Germany's productivity lead (Metcalf, 1988b, pp. 22–32). This argument can be refined using the econometric investigations of bargaining models summarized in Wadhwani (1989). This research based both on Workplace Industrial Relations Surveys and on company accounts data suggests an early 1980s surge in productivity growth in unionized firms resulting not from union legislation per se but from changes in bargaining power contingent on a harsher macroeconomic climate reflected in severe pressure on profitability and rising unemployment leading to new bargaining equilibria with fewer restrictive practices. By 1985–8, however, unionized firms' productivity growth had returned to the levels prevailing in the non-unionized sector.

The Conservative Government has placed much faith in the incentive effects of lowering income tax rates at the top end, from an 83 per cent marginal rate on earned income in 1978/9 to 40 per cent in 1988/9. Dilnot and Kell (1988) in a careful examination of trends in tax revenue have suggested, however, that, although there probably has been a favourable behavioural response, the effect is not large. They calculate an upper bound impact of £1.2bn. on tax revenue in 1985/6.

Other weaknesses contributing to relatively low productivity growth in Britain identified in the fourth section appear still to remain in the late 1980s. A recent Select Committee report found that defence still dominates the UK's research and development effort, that skilled scientific manpower for other needs is in short supply, and that of the five leading industrial nations the UK now devotes the lowest share of GDP to R and D (House of Lords, 1986, pp. 21, 24, 39). The deterioration in levels of R and D expenditure per worker in Britain relative to other countries evident before 1979 has continued as Table 9.12 shows. By 1985 the share of Western European country patents in the USA accruing to the UK had fallen further to 15.8 per cent compared with 17.3 per cent in 1979 (Patel and Pavitt, 1988).

TABLE 9.12. *R and D expenditure per employed person* ($1980)

|  | 1965 | 1970 | 1975 | 1980 | 1985 |
|---|---|---|---|---|---|
| United Kingdom | 290 | 314 | 322 | 381 | 464 |
| United States | 670 | 670 | 606 | 636 | 810 |
| France | 247 | 291 | 326 | 382 | 536 |
| Germany | 200 | 318 | 395 | 492 | 612 |
| Japan | 111 | 206 | 270 | 353 | 544 |

*Sources:* Englander and Mittelstadt (1988).

On the other hand, it should be noted that the Department of Trade and Industry following a thorough policy review in 1984/5 appears to have developed a more effective programme of support for R and D, concentrating now on improving information flows, and that DTI spending on support for science and technology is expected by 1989/90 to be 47 per cent of its total expenditure compared with 6 per cent in 1979/80 (Barber and White, 1987, p. 44). Where management skills are concerned, the UK still lags as far behind other countries in training managers and a recent report concluded that a tenfold increase in management education was required (NEDO, 1987, p. 13).

Although the Thatcher years have seen considerable progress in combating one of the 'traditional weaknesses' of the British supply side, namely industrial relations obstacles to productivity enhancement, there appears to have been little significant achievement on the second area of weakness, education and training. The main thrust of new provision has been and will continue to be YTS for teenagers but so far this has been ineffective as a means of increasing the skills base of the economy and eradicating failings in shopfloor personnel, highlighted by Daly *et al.* (1985) in comparing Britain with Germany, as the survey by Deakin and Pratten (1987) shows. Thus of trainees coming out of YTS in April 1986 to January 1988 76.8 per cent had not obtained any qualification (I. Jones, 1988, p. 65). By 1988 CBI reports of skill shortages were similar to 1970s levels. In the important engineering sector, craft and technician qualifications awarded in Britain rose from 27,000 in 1975 to 30,000 in 1987 but in France and Germany in the same period the increase was from 66,000 to 98,000 and 103,000 to 134,000 respectively and restrictions associated with apprenticeship still flourish (Steedman, 1988). Indeed it can be argued that, although the government has been able to force the pace of reform through the Manpower Services Commission, thus obviating many of the earlier institutional obstacles to change, it has not developed a coherent stance on the education of 'non-academic' adolescents and it has so far achieved very little to improve the level of training among adult members of the labour force (Finegold and Soskice, 1988). At the same time employer attitudes to training appear grounded still in complacency and ignorance (Coopers and Lybrands Associates, 1985, pp. 4–5) and it follows that any sizeable change in the average quality of the British labour force is going to be very slow to materialize.

In sum, the evidence gives some support to the emphasis in the fourth section on supply-side failings as major reasons for slow British growth in the post-war period. There is reason to believe also that useful progress has been made in the Thatcher years in remedying some of our earlier deficiencies but perhaps only two cheers are appropriate at the moment. As the Warwick estimates in Table 9.11 suggest, it seems probable that productivity growth above the levels of the earlier post-war period can be maintained but that the rapid advance of the early 1980s may partly have been once and for all, so that it is not fully sustainable.

It is important, nonetheless, to recognize and to give credit to the difference in the thrust of supply-side policy in the 1980s compared with the 1930s, in the aftermath of an equally severe recession. Broadly speaking, policy in the 1930s strove to reduce the competitive pressures on enterprises whereas in the 1980s the opposite has been the case. Thus in the 1930s foreign investment was restricted, cartels were encouraged, and tariffs were increased while in the 1980s foreign exchange restrictions were lifted, competition policy was maintained, privatization was initiated and Britain remained a member of the European Community. Pressures on manufacturers in particular to pursue higher productivity were intensified by the high exchange rate policy of the early 1980s whereas Britain's departure from the Gold Standard in 1931 led to a period of lower real exchange rates (Dimsdale, 1981).

Similarly, policy towards lame ducks was substantially different; for example, during the 1930s government attempts to promote rationalization of coal and steel were undermined by concerns over their impact on unemployment and as a result productivity suffered (Supple, 1987; Tolliday, 1987) while in the 1980s the unemployment consequences of raising efficiency and eliminating excess capacity in those same industries were accepted.

## Concluding Comments

At this point it is opportune to pull together and recapitulate some of the findings of earlier sections before raising a few more general implications of the material covered in this chapter.

The major arguments of the chapter have been the following.

(1) The chief reason for the relatively slow rate of growth of the UK in the post-war years has been poor productivity growth.

(2) Neither the Kaldor hypothesis that the UK was handicapped by its structure of employment and unable to exploit Verdoorn's Law in manufacturing nor the Bacon and Eltis claim that the growth of the non-marketed sector was a major disadvantage are convincing explanations for slow growth in the long run.

(3) The relatively severe balance of payments constraint suggested by Thirlwall is likely to reflect domestic supply-side problems. Adjustment of the real exchange rate may well be painful in its inflationary consequences but in practice it was probably not the balance of payments which was the binding constraint on growth performance or the initiator of a vicious circle.

(4) The important obstacles to faster productivity growth lay on the supply side of the economy and brought about a relatively slow reduction of overmanning and reduced the benefits from new technical possibilities in production. Growth was hampered by weak management, poor industrial relations, ineffective research and development, and low levels of vocational training.

(5) Supply-side policy in the pre-Thatcherite period was poorly directed and was not particularly successful in ameliorating productivity performance. Rather than remedying these weaknesses both Labour and Conservative Governments were seduced into ill-advised dashes for growth, supporting declining industries, over-enthusiastic encouragement of mergers, and subsidies to investment.

(6) The Thatcherite 'productivity miracle' has at best dealt with only a part of the supply-side problem by creating conditions in which improvement has been achieved with regard to restrictive practices and overmanning. A more fundamental reform of industrial relations, together with significant advances in training of both shopfloor and management and an enhanced research and development effort are all still to be achieved if Britain is fully to eradicate the causes of poor productivity performance.

(7) There is indeed a long history of supply-side problems in the UK contributing to relatively slow growth over the last century or so. It is important, however, to recognize that in many respects the post-war world was very different from that of the Victorians. By the 1950s there was much more research spending, the capital market had been significantly improved by new companies laws and more was invested in education and training. Equally, the post-war settlement together with much more powerful trade unions brought new obstacles to productivity improvement as governments sought to avoid confrontation

with organized labour. Perhaps the most persistent weaknesses have been in education and training (including the quality of industrial management) and in industrial relations.

These points have a bearing on more general issues relating to economic growth which serious students may wish to consider.

(8) The undisputed growth failure of the post-war economy should encourage scepticism of attempts to exonerate earlier economic performance. Also, however, it draws attention to the important question of why institutional arrangements failed; for example, it is important to ask why markets were bad at eradicating low-quality management or why entry of new firms could not obviate the restrictive practices of 'narrow scope' industrial relations.

(9) It follows that the microeconomics of the growth process matter much more than economists steeped in the growth models of the 1950s and 1960s were brought up to believe. Accordingly, future research will need to give more attention to questions of entry to and exit from markets and will need to take more seriously the historical evolution and strategic aspects of individual industries.

(10) As far as economic policy is concerned the main message that comes across is that recognizing obstacles to better productivity performance is much easier than removing them. Little in this chapter would be a great surprise to the members of the Anglo-American Productivity teams of nearly 40 years ago, but repeated diagnosis has not led to anything like a complete cure. Quite why this should be deserves further investigation.

# 10

# Regional Problems and Policies

## H. W. ARMSTRONG

### I Introduction

The United Kingdom now contains some of the most depressed regions in western Europe. This is clearly illustrated in Fig. 10.1 which shows unemployment rates in European Community regions in 1985. Nine of the eleven United Kingdom regions have unemployment rates in excess of the Community average of 9.9 per cent. Even the South East and East Anglia, the most prosperous of the regions of the United Kingdom, can be seen to have unemployment rates which compare unfavourably with their German, French, and Italian counterparts.

The severity of UK regional problems by comparison with our European Community neighbours is cause for considerable concern. So too is the enormous range of unemployment rates *within* the United Kingdom. In July 1986, for example, the unemployment rate in Northern Ireland (19.1 per cent) was more than twice that in the South East (8.7 per cent). Figures for individual towns and local areas show an even greater variation. In July 1986 Crawley enjoyed the lowest unemployment rate in the United Kingdom (5.1 per cent) while Strabane in Northern Ireland suffered a 38.7 per cent unemployment rate, more than seven times the Crawley figure (*Employment Gazette*, September 1986).[1]

The geographical pattern of unemployment in the United Kingdom has been surprisingly stable over many years. Table 10.1 ranks regions in terms of their unemployment rates in July 1932 and July 1986. Regions near the top of the list in 1986 are the same regions near the top in 1932, although the particular ordering of each region has changed slightly.

The unemployment rate is, of course, widely known to be an imperfect indicator of regional problems (J. S. Lord, 1981). Many unemployed persons, for example, do not *register* as such because they are not entitled to unemployment benefits. This problem of 'hidden' unemployment is particularly widespread among married women. Moreover, in recent years there have been a large number of changes to the eligibility criteria which determine just who is recorded as unemployed. This has made it even more difficult to use unemployment rates as indicators of regional disadvantage.

Regional policy has, in the past, been criticized for concentrating too much upon regional *unemployment* disparities. Some have argued that other measures of regional disadvantage are preferable—such as regional earnings differentials, or differences in the incidence of ill-health or housing provision. It should be noted,

---

[1] These figures refer to travel-to-work areas as defined by the Department of Employment.

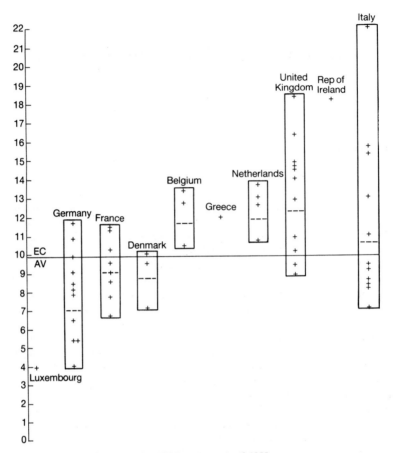

FIG. 10.1.   *Unemployment rates in EEC regions, April 1985*

*Note*:   Each cross represents a separate region; each broken line represents the national average unemployment rate. Comparable figures for Spain and Portugal are not available.

*Source*:   Eurostat, *Regions* (October 1985).

however, that other indicators of the regional problem, such as migration rates or per capita income, tell much the same story as unemployment rates (Armstrong and Taylor, 1985*a*).

The persistence of severe regional disparities over a period in excess of 50 years, during which there have been repeated regional policy initiatives, may seem a damning indictment of British regional policy. Nothing could be further from the truth. Despite appearances to the contrary, regional policy can claim considerable success. Without it the depressed regions would have been in much worse shape than they currently are. It is obvious, however, that regional policy has not been successful enough.

In this chapter the root causes of the malaise in the depressed regions will be examined. It has become fashionable to suggest that the high unemployment of the

TABLE 10.1. *Regional unemployment rates, 1932 and 1986*
(%)

| July 1932 | | July 1986 | |
|---|---|---|---|
| Region | Unemployment rate | Region | Unemployment rate |
| Wales | 38.4 | N. Ireland | 19.1 |
| North East | 30.8 | North | 16.9 |
| Scotland | 29.1 | North West | 14.5 |
| N. Ireland | 29.0 | Scotland | 14.3 |
| North West | 25.9 | Wales | 14.2 |
| Midlands | 21.1 | West Midlands | 14.0 |
| South West | 16.3 | East Midlands | 11.3 |
| South East | 12.8 | South West | 9.9 |
| London | 12.6 | South East | 8.7 |
| | | (Greater London) | (9.6) |
| United Kingdom | 22.8 | United Kingdom | 11.9 |

*Note*: 1932 and 1986 unemployment rates are not directly comparable. Regional boundaries are not identical in the two years. The 1932 unemployment rates refer to numbers of persons (insured and uninsured) registered as unemployed as a percentage of *insured employees* at mid-1932. The 1986 unemployment rates are those registered as unemployed and claiming benefits as a percentage of mid-1985 employees in employment plus unemployed.

*Sources*: *Historical Abstract of Labour Statistics*, Tables 110 and 162; *Employment Gazette* (September 1986).

1980s represents a return to conditions reminiscent of the 1930s. Such a comparison is misleading. Though superficially similar, the problems faced today by the depressed regions are very different from those faced in the 1930s. Profound changes in economic and social conditions have occurred in the post-war period. These complex changes, and the continuously evolving regional policy which grew out of them, form the subject matter of the chapter.

The chapter begins with the regional policy inherited by the nation in 1945. This regional policy was the product of experimental schemes in the 1930s and the wartime experience of centralized planning and control. The next section looks in detail at the major forces which have moulded and shaped the regions in the post-war years. This is followed, in the next two sections, by a review of regional policies in the years since 1945. The following section considers how successful British regional policy has been in creating jobs and inducing firms to move to the depressed regions. The chapter concludes on a positive note and attempts to signpost a route forward for regional policy in Britain.

## II The Legacy of the 1930s and the Second World War

The origins of British regional policy reach back into the inter-war years. The experience gained during those years was to profoundly affect the types of regional policy which emerged after 1945. No discussion of post-war regional policy in Britain would be complete without an examination of the pre-1945 experience.

*Worker Transfer Policy*

The creation of the Industrial Transference Board (ITB) in 1928 can be regarded as the beginning of regional policy in Britain. Rapidly rising unemployment, particularly in a number of coal-mining areas, lay behind the decision to set up the ITB. The recommendations of the Board (Industrial Transference Board, 1928) led to a system of financial subsidies designed to induce unemployed workers and their families to move to the more prosperous areas. Subsidies were quickly extended from coal-miners to other groups of workers.

Government policy was not confined solely to attempts to stimulate migration. Training Centres were also established, and Employment Exchanges were encouraged to help to find work for the unemployed in the more prosperous regions. Later, Transfer Instructional Centres were set up 'to rehabilitate men who had lost physical fitness and industrial "morale"through prolonged unemployment' (Dennison, 1939, p. 176).

The rationale for worker transfer policy was a simple one. Prevailing orthodoxy of the day regarded unemployment as a failure of the market mechanism. If unemployed persons could be induced to migrate to the expanding industries in the South East and Midlands the smooth operation of the market mechanism would be restored. Providing help for the unemployed in their home regions could play no part in this philosophy for 'as an essential condition for the growth of the will to move, nothing should be done which might tend to anchor men to their home district by holding out an illusory prospect of employment. We therefore reject as unsound policy relief works in depressed areas' (Industrial Transference Board, 1928, p. 18).

Worker transfer policy was operated continuously from 1928. The initial Industrial Transfer Schemes were replaced by the specially designed wartime General Transfer Scheme on 1 June 1940. Figure 10.2 shows the numbers of assisted migrants between 1928 and 1945. Prior to the war some 30,000 persons received assistance each year. During the cyclical upturns of 1929 and 1936 the numbers topped 45,000. These numbers are greatly in excess of anything achieved by post-1945 worker transfer schemes (for which 1972 was the best year when 19,000 migrants received assistance). Closer inspection, however, reveals that the pre-war transfer schemes were a failure, and this accounts for their gradual fall from grace after 1936 (Pitfield, 1978). The numbers assisted formed only a tiny proportion of all migrants between 1928 and 1939 (A. J. Brown, 1972). With over 3m. unemployed, assisted migration can have had only a negligible impact on the problem. It must also be remembered that many of those assisted would probably have migrated anyway, and that between one-third and one-half of those assisted subsequently became disillusioned and returned home.

Though ultimately unsuccessful the experience obtained from the transfer schemes proved valuable. Two main lessons were learned. First, the numbers of unemployed persons who can reasonably be expected to migrate is very small. There are several reasons for this. To begin with, 'psychic' costs of migration (particularly those resulting from separation from one's family) greatly exceed money costs (Sjaastad, 1962). Yet the transfer schemes met only part of the money costs of migration. In addition, the unemployed are among the least mobile of all groups in society. The longer a person is unemployed the less likely he is to migrate. Finally it is now known that migration is drastically reduced during recessions (Brant, 1984; Ogilvy,

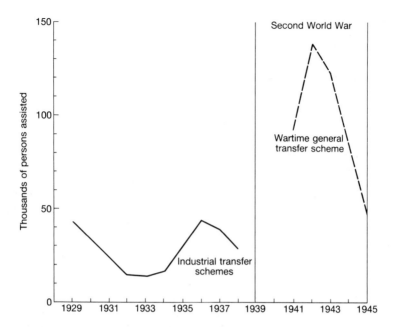

FIG. 10.2.    *Worker transfer policy in Britain, 1929–1946*

*Notes*:    1.  Figures for the Industrial Transfer schemes include all adults and juveniles assisted and
transfered through Employment Exchanges. They exclude Household and Family removals
schemes and assisted transfers not undertaken through Employment Exchanges.
2.  Figures for the General Transfer Scheme are based on numbers receiving lodging allowances
at 31 December each year.

*Sources*:    Pitfield (1978); Department of Employment (unpublished).

1982). Migration is a risky business when unemployment is high in all regions.
More migrants become discouraged and return to the depressed regions in a
recession (Vanderkamp, 1972; Bell and Kirwan, 1979). The implication is clear that
migration schemes fail at the time they are most needed—during recessions.

The second lesson learned from the pre-war experience with transfer schemes
was that such schemes can actually make regional problems worse. Migration is
highly selective. Migrants tend to be young, skilled, highly educated, and already
holding down a job (Kottis, 1972). These are the very last people a depressed
region can afford to lose if it is to have a long-term future.

The pre-war transfer policy was a manifest failure. By 1934 it was already proving
difficult to find suitable potential migrants to assist (Dennison, 1939). The Second
World War did nothing to alter this perception of failure. The high numbers of
assisted transfers during the war itself (see Fig. 10.2) merely reflect the compulsory
nature of wartime worker transfer policy.

At no time since 1945 has any government suggested that transfer schemes alone
could solve regional problems. The wartime coalition government stated firmly that
'the government do not rely primarily on large-scale labour transfers for a solution
of the unemployment problems of particular areas' (Ministry of Reconstruction,
1944, p. 15). This opinion is shared by the present government which has stated
that 'wage adjustment and labour mobility cannot be relied upon to correct

regional imbalances in employment opportunities' (Department of Trade and Industry, 1983b, p. 3).

## The Special Areas

As optimism in the ability of transfer policy to solve regional problems in the 1930s waned, attempts to create jobs in the depressed areas themselves became more fashionable. The 1934 Special Areas Act is a landmark in British regional policy. It was the first ever serious attempt to 'take work to the workers'.

Four Special Areas were created—South Wales, Central Scotland, the North East, and West Cumberland. These had been pin-pointed by a series of commissioned studies (Ministry of Labour, 1934). The two Commissioners appointed to administer the policy were given few powers initially. Only £2m. was set aside for their use and they were prevented from helping either private companies or from undertaking major public works programmes. The result was inevitable. Between 1934 and 1935 63 per cent of expenditure in England and Wales was on sewage schemes, back-to-the-land smallholding schemes, and public health initiatives (see Table 10.2).

The limitations of the 1934 Act quickly became apparent and additional powers were gradually added to the Special Areas armoury. In 1936 *loans for small businesses* were introduced.[2] 1936 also witnessed the successful introduction of *industrial (or 'trading') estates* at Team Valley (North East) and Treforest (S. Wales). Most important of all, however, was the 1937 Special Areas (Amendment) Act. This sanctioned the giving of *loans to large companies*. It also allowed the introduction of *tax incentives* (in the form of rates, income tax, and National Defence Tax remissions). Finally, as the Second World War approached, the depressed areas began to reap the benefits of the *preferential placing of government contracts*. Between April 1936 and August 1937, for example, £32m. of armaments orders were placed with Special Areas firms.

The Special Areas policy was not a success. It took the war to put the depressed areas back to work. Moreover, between 1934 and 1939 only 113 out of 2,870 new factories in Britain (3.9 per cent of the total) opened in the Special Areas (McCrone, 1969). The majority of new factories continued to be London-based. There was a general recognition, however, that the Special Areas legislation had come too late and had not been vigorously pursued from the start. In better times and with greater determination it might have succeeded.

Despite its weaknesses, the Special Areas policy could point to one or two notable successes. The industrial estates proved to be worthwhile from the start. By 1939 some 12,000 workers had found jobs on the estates. Many firms on the industrial estates were founded by refugees (A. J. Brown, 1972) and their success helped to dispel the myth of the inherent unsuitability of the depressed areas for modern firms.

Perhaps the most important legacy of the Special Areas policy was that the policy instruments which were to be used in post-war years—loans, factory building, industrial estates, tax incentives, and preferential government contracts—were tried and tested between 1934 and 1939.

---

[2] 1936 also witnessed a private initiative by Lord Nuffield who made £2m. available for loans and equity participation in larger companies in the Special Areas.

TABLE 10.2. *Financial commitments made by the Special Areas Commissioner in England and Wales by 31 December 1935*

| (a) *Industry* | £000 | |
|---|---|---|
| Harbour/quays | 404 | |
| Site clearance and improvement | 155 | |
| Trading estates company | 100 | |
| Development councils | 25 | |
| Miscellaneous | 5 | |
| | | 689 |
| (b) *Health* | | |
| Hospitals | 503 | |
| Maternity/child welfare centres, etc. | 17 | |
| District nurses/ambulances | 27 | |
| Baths | 75 | |
| Water supply | 76 | |
| Sewerage and sewage disposal | 643 | |
| Miscellaneous | 3 | |
| | | 1,344 |
| (c) *Housing* | | 101 |
| (d) *Agriculture* | | |
| Small holdings schemes | 949 | |
| Group holdings schemes | 29 | |
| Assisted allotment schemes | 1 | |
| | | 979 |
| (e) *Other* (e.g. voluntary schemes, clubs, centres, of which schoolchildren holiday camps = £175,000) | | |
| | | 331 |
| Total | | 3,443 |

*Source*: Commissioner for Special Areas (1936), pp. 101–2.

*The Wartime Experience*

The Second World War led to fundamental changes in attitudes towards unemployment in general, and regional problems in particular. The immediate dramatic effort of the war itself was to eliminate regional unemployment problems. Unemployment in Britain fell by half from 1.25m. in 1939 to 645,000 in 1940. By 1944 only 79,000 people were unemployed (Ministry of Labour and National Service, 1947, p. 53). Many of these people were virtually unemployable.

The depressed regions not only benefited from the general rapid expansion in demand for goods and services, but also from the essential nature of coal, shipbuilding, iron, and steel industries during wartime. The principal problem during the war was not unemployment, but labour shortages. Over 5m. men and women were eventually drawn out of the labour force and into the armed forces. The depressed areas had the surplus labour resources and were also well placed to benefit from the dispersal of strategic industries from London and the cities of the Midlands. Between 1939 and 1945 the government built 130 new factories for strategic industries in the depressed areas (Board of Trade, 1948). The war not only put the unemployed back to work, it also drew into employment many women who had previously not considered working. This is shown in Table 10.3 which gives the numbers employed in each region in July 1945 as a percentage of those employed in July 1939. Notice how, as a result of the demands of the war, the numbers of men employed fell in all regions, whilst the numbers of women employed increased in all regions. Increases in female employment were highest, however, in those regions such as the North and Wales where few women had worked prior to 1939. By June 1945 no region had an unemployment rate greater than 2.5 per cent (Board of Trade, 1948, Appendix 4).

TABLE 10.3. *Numbers of insured employees
in each region in July 1945 as a percentage
of insured employees in July 1939*

| Region | Males | Females | Total |
|---|---|---|---|
| London and SE | 63 | 106 | 76 |
| Eastern | 74 | 146 | 90 |
| Southern | 76 | 174 | 96 |
| South Western | 76 | 154 | 93 |
| Midlands | 78 | 121 | 90 |
| North Midlands | 77 | 118 | 88 |
| E. and W. Ridings | 75 | 111 | 85 |
| North Western | 73 | 107 | 85 |
| Northern | 79 | 165 | 94 |
| Scotland | 74 | 121 | 87 |
| Wales | 79 | 218 | 97 |
| Great Britain | 73 | 121 | 86 |

*Source*:   Minstry of Labour and National Service (1947), p. 129.

The war was eventually to result in much more than transient full employment in the depressed areas. There emerged a determination not to return to the bad times of the 1930s. The confidence and experience gained with wartime controls on the economy was to lead to industrial location controls being retained as part of post-war regional policy. In addition, the war left a legacy of new factories in the depressed areas. These were subsequently turned over to private companies and were to play an important role in regional policy in the immediate post-war period.

### The Barlow Report and the White Paper on Employment Policy

The radical change in attitudes during the war is epitomized by the Barlow Report (Royal Commission on the Distribution of the Industrial Population, 1940) and the White Paper on Employment Policy (Ministry of Reconstruction, 1944). The Barlow Report has been described as 'a landmark in the development of thought on regional problems in Britain . . . In several respects it was ahead of its time' (McCrone, 1969, p. 104). Its greatest contribution was the development of a cogent *economic* case for regional policy. To the Barlow Commission, regional policy was vital to the national interest. The problems of the big cities (congestion, pollution, and deprivation) and the wasted labour resources in the depressed areas were seen as opposite sides of the same coin. Disperse industry and population away from London and Birmingham and you would solve both problems simultaneously. To these powerful arguments the war itself added another—the need to disperse industry for strategic reasons. Many of the detailed proposals of the Barlow Report (e.g. stronger urban planning controls, new towns, industrial estates, and location controls on companies) were adopted after the war.

The 1944 Employment Policy White Paper was a document every bit as far-reaching as the Barlow Report. It contains the famous commitment to full employment. This commitment was crucial to the success of post-war regional policy. By committing governments to the pursuit of full employment when the war was over the White Paper paved the way for a more successful attack on regional problems. The White Paper also set out the broad guidelines for post-war regional policy—location controls and financial incentives to get firms to move to the depressed areas, and training facilities for workers already there.

As the post-war era dawned in 1945, Britain inherited a regional policy legacy which was to serve it well. To the hard-won experience of the transfer policies and Special Areas programmes of the 1930s had been added the wartime experience of planning and controls. This experience was coupled with a vigorous determination to avoid a return to high unemployment. The scene was set for a serious attempt to eliminate regional problems.

### III The Changing Nature of Post-War Regional Problems

Regional policy over the years since 1945 has had to operate in a dynamic, changing world. Some of the problems faced in the depressed regions have changed, some have disappeared, while newer types of problem are constantly emerging.

In examining post-war regional problems it is important to keep two facts firmly in mind. First, during the major part of the post-war period until the late 1970s, the United Kingdom enjoyed historically unprecedented prosperity. Aggregate demand was high and national unemployment rates low. The depressed regions shared in this prosperity and the regional problems we will discuss in this section, though certainly a cause for concern, were until recently small by comparison with pre-war problems. Second, in examining post-war regional problems it is important to remember that for long periods (especially in the late 1940s, and again in the 1960s and 1970s) government was strenuously trying to eliminate regional problems. The problems we observe are not therefore as bad as they otherwise would have been.


*Regional Problems 1945–58*

The immediate aftermath of the Second World War was, of course, dominated by the need to convert from a wartime to a peacetime economy. This conversion carried with it a considerable threat to the former depressed regions, which had benefited from the high level of demand in the wartime economy, and whose heavy industries had been so important to the war effort.

The most immediate threat was posed by the demobilization of large numbers of working-age men and women. Some 4.5m. persons were demobilized by the end of 1946 and a further 3.5m. workers were released over the same period from firms making armaments and supplies for the armed forces. The reallocation of labour on such a vast scale inevitably caused some increase in unemployment as Fig. 10.3 shows. By June 1947 the national rate of unemployment stood at 3 per cent while the newly designated Development Areas were experiencing 4.5 per cent unemployment.

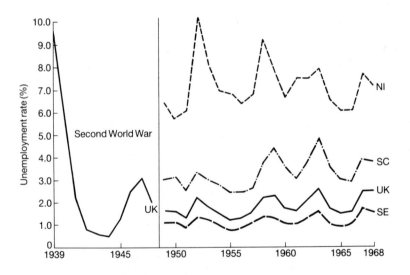

FIG. 10.3.   *UK unemployment rates, 1939–1968*

*Notes:*  1. Figures include both male and female unemployed.
2. Figures before and after 1948 are not strictly comparable. Prior to 1948 figures comprise *insured* workers unemployed. After 1948 unemployment insurance became compulsory.
3. Because of regional boundary changes 'SE' refers to London and the South East together with E. Anglia from 1949–64. Thereafter the figures refer to the South East region (as defined from 1 April 1965).

*Source:*   *Historical Abstract of British Labour Statistics*, Tables 161 and 168.

It is surprising that unemployment did not rise further. Three factors, however, combined to cushion the effects of peace on the depressed regions.

(a) *The post-war boom*: The end of the war led to a surge in previously suppressed demand for consumer goods. The capital goods industries and construction sector were also under pressure to make good war damage and to allow companies to recover from underinvestment during the war. Continued high aggregate demand benefited all regions.

(b) *Reduction in the workforce*: As the war ended many people simply left the workforce. This was particularly the case with women workers. The employment of women reached a peak of 735,400 in 1945. By mid-1947 this had fallen to 636,400. The exodus of women and older workers from the workforce helped to cushion the effect of demobilization on unemployment. Of course, not all women drawn into employment during the war chose to leave their jobs afterwards. Between 1939 and 1947 female employment in the Development Areas rose by 165,600 (Board of Trade, 1948).

(c) *Regional policy*: This was extremely actively pursued in the immediate post-war period and helped to maintain prosperity in the depressed areas.

As the 1940s gave way to the 1950s it became apparent that there was to be no immediate return to the high unemployment and severe regional problems of the 1930s. UK unemployment rates remained remarkably low throughout the 1950s and regional problems were correspondingly muted (Fig. 10.3). Successive governments enjoyed the luxury of not needing to worry too much about regional problems. Some regional problems did, of course, remain. Northern Ireland, as Fig. 10.3 shows, continued to exhibit all of the characteristics of a severely disadvantaged region. Other depressed regions (e.g. Scotland) had unemployment rates not greatly in excess of the national average. The lack of serious regional problems throughout the early and mid-1950s reflected the healthy state of demand for the products of the basic staple industries (coal, iron and steel, textiles, etc.) upon which the less prosperous areas were still heavily dependent.

Regional disparities throughout the 1950s and early 1960s exhibit a clear cyclical pattern. The downturns of 1952 and 1958, though quite mild by historical standards, tended to lead to sharper rises in unemployment in the depressed areas than in the South East. This is revealed by Fig. 10.3 and also by Table 10.4, which shows that a 1 per-cent rise in the UK unemployment rate during this period was associated with a rise of 2.24 per cent in Northern Ireland, 1.74 per cent in the North West, but only 0.64 per cent in the South East and East Anglia. Such cyclical sensitivity in the depressed areas is now known to be partly, but not entirely, the result of over-dependence on certain industries which are hardest hit in recessions (Brechling, 1967; Taylor and Bradley, 1983).

The presence of persistent, though minor, regional problems in the 1950s is revealed not only in unemployment rates but also in other ways. The depressed regions continued to lose emigrants throughout the 1950s and the more prosperous regions gained from net in-migration (Table 10.5). The net movements of people out of the depressed areas remained extremely small, however. Even in Northern Ireland net out-migration averaged only 0.7 of 1 per cent of the population between 1951 and 1961 (Table 10.5). Indeed, as is also clear from Table 10.5, the rate of

TABLE 10.4. *Increase in regional unemployment rate associated with a 1% rise in UK unemployment, 1949–1964*

| | |
|---|---|
| South East and East Anglia | 0.64 |
| West Midlands | 0.67 |
| East Mids. and Yorks./Humbs. | 0.96 |
| Wales | 1.37 |
| Scotland | 1.40 |
| North | 1.40 |
| North West | 1.74 |
| Northern Ireland | 2.24 |

*Note*: These figures represent the coefficient $\alpha_1$ in the fitted equation

$$Ur = \alpha_0 + \alpha_1 \, UK + \alpha_3 t + \varepsilon$$

Where $Ur$ = regional unemployment rate; UK = United Kingdom unemployment rate; and t = time trend where 1949 = 1 and 1964 = 16.

*Source*: *British Labour Statistics Historical Abstract*, Table 168.

TABLE 10.5. *Components of regional population change, 1951–1961*

| Region | 1951–6 | | 1956–61 | |
|---|---|---|---|---|
| | Net migration | Natural increase | Net migration | Natural increase |
| South East[a] | +0.1 | +0.4 | +0.4 | +0.5 |
| E. Midlands | +0.1 | +0.5 | +0.2 | +0.6 |
| W. Midlands | 0.0 | +0.6 | +0.2 | +0.7 |
| South West | +0.1 | +0.3 | +0.6 | +0.4 |
| Yorkshire/Humberside | −0.2 | +0.5 | −0.3 | +0.5 |
| North West | −0.2 | +0.3 | −0.2 | +0.4 |
| North | −0.3 | +0.6 | −0.2 | +0.7 |
| Wales | −0.2 | +0.3 | −0.2 | +0.3 |
| Scotland | −0.6 | +0.6 | −0.6 | +0.7 |
| N. Ireland | − | − | 1951–61[−0.7 | +1.1] |

[a] Including East Anglia.

*Note*: Figures are *average annual* changes expressed as a percentage of the regional population.

*Source*: McCrone (1969), Table III, p. 156.

natural increase in population continuously exceeded the net out-migration rates in the depressed regions in the 1950s. Population therefore continued to grow in all regions, depressed and prosperous alike.

## The Re-Emergence of Serious Regional Problems 1958–9

The 1958/9 recession marks a turning-point for post-war regional problems. The traditional industries of the depressed areas—coal, steel, textiles, and shipbuilding—

had shared in the national prosperity and had enjoyed great success in export markets in the aftermath of the Second World War. In 1958, however, a combination of circumstances was to bring regional problems once more back onto the agenda of the government. The long period of post-war prosperity for the traditional industries finally came to an end. The backlog of work to be done was gradually overcome and fierce foreign competition began to emerge. These forces, combined with the 1958/9 world recession, had serious effects on the mining, shipbuilding, and textile industries as Fig. 10.4 shows.

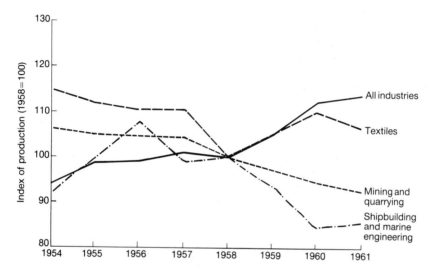

FIG. 10.4.   *Changes in production for selected industries 1954–1961 (1958 = 100)*
Source:   *Annual Abstract of Statistics.*

The result of this combination of circumstances was a sharp worsening of regional disparities. After a short lag the government responded by strengthening regional policy. The 1958/9 recession, however, proved to be only the beginning of much worse problems. From that date until the present time governments have faced a long and difficult struggle to prevent regional problems from becoming more and more severe. In doing so, they have had to cope with substantial and far-reaching changes in the economies of the depressed regions. It is to these changes which we now turn.

## The Evolution of the Regional Economies 1959–86

The British economy of 1986 differs enormously from its 1950s counterpart. During the intervening years a series of changes with major implications for the depressed regions have occurred. The most important of these have been the decline of manufacturing and rapid growth of the service sector; the more rapid growth of employment in smaller towns and rural areas; the emergence of severe problems in inner-city areas; the effects of EEC entry and the oil crisis on the depressed areas; and the implications of a massive recession between 1979 and 1981. Each of these will be considered in turn.

## The Decline of Manufacturing and the Rise of the Service Sector

The decline of industries such as textiles and shipbuilding in the late 1950s fore-shadowed a decline in manufacturing as a whole. Employment in manufacturing industry in Britain reached a peak in 1965 and has been in decline ever since (Fig. 10.5). Output in manufacturing continued to increase until 1973, stabilized between 1973 and 1979, and then fell sharply between 1979 and 1981. Employment losses have been spread over a wide range of manufacturing industries and have not been confined to 'traditional' industries. By contrast, as Fig. 10.6 shows, service employment has grown rapidly, faltering only during the 1979–81 downturn. Growth has been particularly rapid in certain services (e.g. hotels and catering) and employment has actually fallen in others (e.g. transport, postal, and telecommunications services).

The shift from manufacturing to services has had extremely important implications for the depressed regions. Regions heavily dependent on manufacturing have experienced severe adjustment problems. The regions which appear to have been particularly badly hit have been the West Midlands, the North West and Yorkshire/Humberside. By contrast, in the South East over 71 per cent of employees are in service industries. The heavy dependence on manufacturing industries may go some way towards explaining the emergence in recent years of the West Midlands as a depressed region when formerly it had been quite prosperous.

Significant though the decline of manufacturing has been, it is important not to oversimplify the forces which have operated in the depressed areas. The East Midlands, for example, has a heavy dependence on manufacturing and yet has not experienced the same scale of problems faced in the West Midlands. More complex processes are clearly at work than simply a shift from manufacturing to service jobs. One general conclusion is, however, valid. Realistically, we cannot expect to return to the kind of large scale employment in manufacturing enjoyed in the 1960s.

## The Urban–Rural Shift in Employment Opportunities

A striking feature of the period since 1960 has been the emergence of a pronounced 'urban–rural' shift in job opportunities in Britain. London and the conurbations have lost jobs on a large scale whilst simultaneously, as Table 10.6 shows, the smaller cities, the towns, and the rural areas have enjoyed rapid employment growth. Part of this urban–rural shift is the result of companies physically moving out of the cities. Most, however, is the result of *in situ* differences in rates of growth of employment.

The urban–rural shift in job opportunities has, as Table 10.6 indicates, been most pronounced for manufacturing industries. A similar, but less severe phenomenon is also clearly revealed for services.

Table 10.7 sheds more light on the phenomenon of the 'urban–rural' shift. It shows that the processes at work have continued in the period since 1975, with

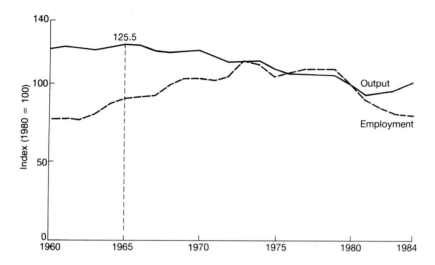

FIG. 10.5. *Indices of national output and employment in manufacturing 1960–1984*
*Source*: *Economic Trends* (various issues).

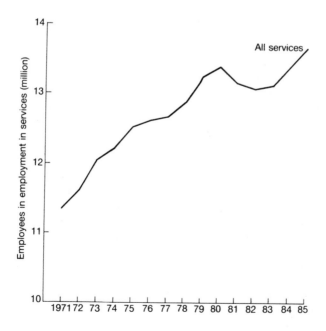

FIG. 10.6. *Employment in all services in Great Britain, 1971–1985*
*Source*: *Employment Gazette* (April 1984), Historical Supplement 1; *Employment Gazette* (1986).

TABLE 10.6. *Percentage change in employment by type of area: Great Britain, 1959–1975*

| Area | Manufacturing | Services | All industries |
|------|--------------:|---------:|---------------:|
| London | −37.8 | 1.9 | −11.4 |
| Conurbations | −15.9 | 5.9 | −4.7 |
| Free-standing cities | 4.8 | 16.0 | 12.5 |
| Industrial towns | 16.3 | 21.1 | 22.0 |
| County towns | 28.8 | 15.2 | 18.0 |
| Rural areas | 77.2 | 11.4 | 14.0 |

*Source*: Fothergill and Gudgin (1982), pp. 16, 22, 44.

TABLE 10.7. *Percentage change in employment by type of area: England and Wales, 1974–1981*

| Area | Manufacturing | Commercial offices | Retailing | Warehousing |
|------|--------------:|-------------------:|----------:|------------:|
| London | −25.6 | 3.2 | −4.8 | −9.7 |
| Conurbations | −30.5 | 9.5 | −9.0 | −6.7 |
| Free-standing cities | −23.0 | 25.0 | −5.2 | 5.0 |
| Industrial towns | −20.6 | 24.6 | 1.2 | 17.3 |
| County towns | −18.0 | 22.3 | 3.9 | 22.5 |
| Rural areas | −9.7 | 28.3 | 5.7 | 22.7 |

*Source*: Crawford *et al.* (1985), p. 22.

absolute job losses in manufacturing now being recorded in all areas but with the conurbations continuing to experience the most severe problems. Table 10.7 also reveals that the big cities are continuing to perform badly in terms of their service industries and have even lost jobs in certain service sectors.

The precise causes of the 'urban–rural' shift in job opportunities are poorly understood. There is evidence to suggest that the poor performance of the large conurbations is not the result of their having an industrial structure dominated by slow-growing industries, or having more of the larger manufacturing companies which have done so badly in recent years. Nor do high local authority tax bills in the big cities seem to be to blame. Debate instead has concentrated on two possible explanations of the decline in employment in the big cities. First, production costs may be significantly higher in the conurbations. Labour costs, and site and factory rents are substantially higher there than in smaller towns and rural areas. Second, the mere *unavailability* of good-quality premises and factory sites may hinder production in the big cities. Premises are often cramped and poorly designed. This latter explanation has found most favour among researchers trying to identify the causes of the 'urban–rural' shift (Fothergill *et al.*, 1984).

Whatever the precise causes of the urban–rural shift, its implications for regional problems have been far-reaching. For those left behind in the central areas of the large conurbations the evaporation of job opportunities has had severe implications. The urban–rural shift may also help to account for the fact that regions such as the South-West, East Anglia, and the East Midlands have grown quite rapidly. These regions contain no large conurbations. By contrast, the North West (containing Greater Manchester and Merseyside) and the West Midlands (containing Birmingham) have done badly. It would appear that the presence of a large conurbation is no longer the great asset for a region which it once was.

### The Crisis in the Inner Cities

The urban–rural shift in job opportunities has been one, but by no means the only, force behind the gathering inner-city crisis in Britain. The inner-city crisis is not confined to Britain. Other countries too have experienced a similar phenomenon.

The major British conurbations continuously expanded in population until the early 1960s. The share of the national population living in the conurbations has fallen in the years since then (Evans and Eversley, 1980). Population decline has been most marked in the inner areas of these cities. Between 1971 and 1981, for example, the population of inner London fell by 17.6 per cent (Redfirn, 1985).

As has already been shown, this population decline has been accompanied by severe job losses, particularly in manufacturing. The results of a quarter of a century of decline are now plain to see. The inner cities have become synonymous with high unemployment, crime, social deprivation, and poor housing. Table 10.8 shows some of the main characteristics of the inner-city areas and contrasts them with the more favoured outer areas of the cities. The inner areas are characterized by declining population, a high proportion of ethnic minorities, many single-parent families, high unemployment, widespread private rented accommodation (often of poor quality), and low rates of car ownership.

The problems of the inner-city areas are an issue more properly the concern of urban policy than of regional policy, and are therefore largely beyond the scope of this chapter. Nevertheless, the emergence of a new type of severely disadvantaged geographical area in Britain—the inner city—has very important implications for regional policy. To begin with, it must be acknowledged that regional policy itself may have exacerbated the inner-city crisis, particularly in London and Birmingham. Regional policy has for many years deliberately sought to tempt manufacturing firms away from London and Birmingham. It is not surprising, therefore, to find strong pressure on the government to curtail regional policy and to close off what has been a major source of firms for the assisted areas.

Recognition of the severity of the inner-city crisis is itself now having an effect on the depressed regions. The government finds itself fighting deprivation on several different fronts—in the depressed industrial areas of the 'north', in the depressed rural areas where depopulation has taken its toll, and now in the inner-city areas. The resulting diversion of financial resources can only weaken the efforts to help what were traditionally regarded as Britain's main problem regions—the depressed industrial areas of the 'north'.

### The European Community and Regional Problems

Britain entered the European Community (EC) in 1973. The full long-term effects of EC entry on the British economy have still to reveal themselves. It is clear however, that the effects of EC membership have been far-reaching. Whilst it is

TABLE 10.8. *Characteristics of inner and outer wards of major English cities, 1981*

| Cities in metropolitan counties | | Percentage change in population 1971–81 | Percentage of persons in households with a new commonwealth head of household | Percentage of children under 16 in single-parent households | Percentage of economically active men aged 16–64 out of work | Percentage of households: | | With a car available |
|---|---|---|---|---|---|---|---|---|
| | | | | | | Rented from private landlord | With 1 or more persons per room | |
| Birmingham | – inner | −17.6 | 36.6 | 8.9 | 25.4 | 21.4 | 10.6 | 38.3 |
| | – outer | −4.5 | 6.1 | 7.5 | 16.6 | 9.4 | 4.5 | 52.2 |
| Sheffield | – inner | −19.5 | 6.3 | 8.2 | 19.0 | 16.7 | 4.2 | 37.0 |
| | – outer | −1.5 | 1.9 | 4.6 | 12.6 | 7.9 | 3.0 | 51.2 |
| Liverpool | – inner | −26.6 | 3.0 | 11.2 | 31.0 | 29.6 | 6.8 | 25.3 |
| | – outer | −9.5 | 0.9 | 6.7 | 21.0 | 14.4 | 4.9 | 45.3 |
| Manchester | – inner | −24.5 | 18.3 | 12.6 | 28.3 | 19.3 | 8.1 | 29.9 |
| | – outer | −13.7 | 3.0 | 8.8 | 17.6 | 15.9 | 4.6 | 43.8 |
| Leeds | – inner | −14.6 | 15.2 | 11.0 | 22.2 | 23.0 | 5.3 | 34.9 |
| | – outer | −7.4 | 2.4 | 8.0 | 13.3 | 9.0 | 3.5 | 49.3 |
| Coventry | – inner | −11.1 | 15.8 | 7.2 | 19.3 | 14.6 | 6.7 | 51.8 |
| | – outer | −3.2 | 4.7 | 7.3 | 17.3 | 8.0 | 4.8 | 61.7 |
| Bradford | – inner | −12.7 | 34.8 | 6.6 | 23.9 | 18.4 | 12.2 | 31.9 |
| | – outer | 0.2 | 7.2 | 7.1 | 14.7 | 9.4 | 5.1 | 50.4 |
| Wolverhampton | – inner | −8.4 | 34.6 | 6.0 | 24.3 | 15.9 | 9.0 | 44.8 |
| | – outer | −4.2 | 8.0 | 6.8 | 17.4 | 5.3 | 4.7 | 59.0 |
| Sunderland | – inner | −15.1 | 1.3 | 6.6 | 19.9 | 14.7 | 3.8 | 44.6 |
| | – outer | −6.4 | 0.3 | 6.7 | 24.3 | 5.7 | 6.0 | 40.8 |
| Newcastle-upon-Tyne | – inner | −18.0 | 7.1 | 9.0 | 21.7 | 30.5 | 4.3 | 32.4 |
| | – outer | −11.0 | 1.3 | 8.7 | 20.7 | 12.0 | 5.7 | 36.9 |
| London | – inner | −17.6 | 18.8 | 12.7 | 14.4 | 29.9 | 7.1 | 41.3 |
| | – outer | −5.0 | 11.7 | 6.5 | 8.0 | 15.0 | 4.2 | 64.0 |
| GB (average) | | 0.6 | 4.1 | 0.6 | 11.6 | 13.2 | 4.3 | 60.5 |

*Source:* Redfirn (1985). Table 2.

difficult to disentangle the effects of EC membership from other changes (e.g. the oil crisis), it has become increasingly obvious that the EC has affected regional problems in Britain.

The EC is basically a common market onto which a number of common policies (such as agriculture policy) have been grafted. A common market is a free-trade area in which free movement of capital and labour is also encouraged. In the longer term the EC is seeking full economic and monetary union. This would involve a unified monetary system; stabilized exchange rates between member states; and the major weapons of tax, spending, and monetary policy powers being lodged with Brussels rather than with the individual member states.

EC membership affects the depressed regions of Britain in a number of different ways (Armstrong, 1978; Armstrong and Taylor, 1985a). The first and most obvious effect arises from entry to a customs union. The removal of tariffs (particularly on manufactured goods) against our partners in the EC, together with the imposition of a Common External Tariff against the rest of the world has led to trade creation and trade diversion effects. Trade creation arises because free trade means cheaper goods, and cheaper goods mean greater demand. Trade diversion arises because consumers in Britain find it more attractive to buy goods from EC producers (since tariffs have been removed) than from the rest of the world (whose goods now face the Common External Tariff). The result of these changes has been a re-orientation of our trade toward the EC. Between 1973 and 1984, for example, the *share* of all UK exports going to the EC rose from 31 per cent to 39 per cent of the total. The share of imports into the UK from the rest of the EC rose rose from 39 per cent to 50 per cent over the same period. Between 1973 and 1984 exports of manufactured goods to the rest of the EC rose 60 per cent (by volume) while imports from the rest of the EC rose 300 per cent (Dearden, 1986).

The regional implications of this re-orientation of trade towards the EC are very significant. The resulting free trade leads to specialization along the lines of comparative advantage. Those regions heavily dependent on industries out-competed by our EC rivals suffer job losses. Those regions containing industries in which Britain has a comparative advantage enjoy job gains. Good or bad, *all* regions have had to live with this process of major structural change and adjustment.

The structural changes resulting from the removal of tariffs are only the first step in a much longer process of economic integration in the EC. It is widely believed that economic integration (culminating in full economic and monetary union) will tend to widen further the gap between rich and poor regions in Europe. A striking feature of the regional problem in Europe is the way in which the depressed regions tend to be the *peripheral* regions of the EC. Regions at the geographical centre of Europe— the 'golden triangle'—are best placed to exploit the advantages of the customs union. These central regions, which exclude most of Britain, enjoy much easier access to the 321m. market of the EC (Keeble *et al.*, 1982). They also enjoy the agglo-meration and external economies which arise from close proximity to the major industrial, financial, and population centres of the EC. Success feeds upon success. In an integrating EC these well-established core regions can be expected to continue to exploit their advantages and to draw towards themselves both capital and labour, draining the economies of the peripheral regions. Member states such as Britain or the Republic of Ireland which have many depressed regions may find it hard to halt this process—particularly if their governments are stripped of powers to devalue their currencies or to operate defensive fiscal and monetary policies (McCrone, 1971).

Finally, it should be noted that EC policies can, in a variety of ways, cause problems for the depressed regions of Europe. An excellent example of this is the Common Agriculture Policy. This has tended to favour the farmers of the more prosperous northern regions of Europe—those producing cereals, dairy produce, beef, and sugar beet. Hill farmers and those in poorer Mediterranean regions have benefited much less (see Commission of the European Communities, 1981a). EC policies designed to improve capital mobility have had similar adverse effects, for member states have resorted to the widespread use of financial subsidies to 'competitively bid' for mobile investment projects. This tends to undermine the effectiveness of subsidies to firms investing in depressed regions.

EC membership has not been an unmitigated disaster for the depressed regions of Britain. The EC offers the prospect of greater prosperity for all, and the EC has set up its own fund to help depressed regions. EC entry has, however, led to a whole series of complex and difficult adjustments which the depressed regions have had to face and which they have not yet come to terms with. These effects will be with us for many decades to come.

*The Oil Crisis, North Sea Oil, and Regional Problems*

Two developments in the world oil industry in the 1970s and 1980s have had extremely important implications for the British economy as a whole and for the depressed regions. The first and most important of these was the world oil crisis. This resulted from major oil price increases in 1973/4 and again in 1979/80 engineered by the oil cartel OPEC. The disruptive effects of these sudden price movements in such a key commodity were felt by many countries. The depressed regions of Britain were adversely affected by the oil crisis in a number of ways. As consumers of oil, producers in the depressed regions were directly affected by the oil price rises. More important, however, were the effects of the oil crisis on the British economy. Britain shared in the slow-down in trade and higher unemployment rates induced by the oil crisis. This was true both before 1979 and, with a vengeance, after 1979. Rising unemployment always poses more severe problems for the depressed regions than for the rest of the country and regional disparities always widen during recessions. By striking at the national economy the oil price increases simultaneously delivered a blow to the already weak economies of the depressed areas.

The impact of buoyant world oil prices on the depressed regions is complicated by the fact that although Britain was almost wholly a consumer of oil at the time of the first price rise, by 1979 Britain had also become a substantial producer. Moreover, the closest regions to the North Sea oilfields are Scotland and the North. These two regions in recent years have therefore been in the paradoxical position of suffering job losses as a result of a national recession whilst simultaneously enjoying job gains from North Sea-related activity.

It is important to keep the North Sea oil industry in perspective. As Table 10.9 shows, oil output has in recent years averaged only 5 per cent of national GDP (reaching a peak of 6.5 per cent in 1984). Offshore activities have created about

TABLE 10.9. *The development of North Sea oil production*

| Year | Production (m. tons) | Price (US$ per barrel) | Oil as % GDP | Year | Government revenues (£b.) |
|------|------|------|------|------|------|
| 1977 | 38 | 13.6 | 1.5 | | |
| 1978 | 53 | 13.6 | 1.7 | 1978/9 | 0.6 |
| 1979 | 77 | 20.7 | 2.9 | 1979/80 | 2.3 |
| 1980 | 79 | 34.7 | 3.9 | 1980/1 | 3.9 |
| 1981 | 88 | 37.0 | 4.8 | 1981/2 | 6.5 |
| 1982 | 100 | 32.9 | 5.2 | 1982/3 | 7.8 |
| 1983 | 111 | 29.9 | 5.6 | 1983/4 | 8.8 |
| 1984 | 121 | 29.6 | 6.5 | 1984/5 | 12.0 |
| 1985 | 122 | 27.6 | 5.8 | 1985/6 | 12.2 |

*Source*: Hall *et al*. (1986).

25,000 jobs (0.1 per cent of the British workforce) while on-shore jobs associated with the oil industry (e.g. support services, oilrig and ship construction) have probably pushed the total employment figure to 100,000. These are significant but by no means enormous figures. Most of the oil-related jobs have benefited Scotland, and within Scotland the Grampian Region (which includes Aberdeen) has been the principal beneficiary (Table 10.10). It should also be noted that the government has been a major beneficiary, with oil taxes netting £12.2bn. in 1985/6. These, together with the important beneficial effects of oil on the balance of trade, have helped the national economy and with it the depressed regions.

TABLE 10.10. *Employment in companies wholly related to the North Sea oil industry* (thousands)

| | 1977 | 1983 | 1985 |
|------|------|------|------|
| *Scotland* | *28.6* | *66.8* | *63.8* |
| Central/Lothian | 0.6 | 0.6 | 0.5 |
| Fife | 0.8 | 1.4 | 1.3 |
| Grampian | 15.7 | 48.0 | 52.4 |
| Highlands | 7.1 | 8.6 | 3.4 |
| Strathclyde | 1.9 | 3.5 | 2.4 |
| Tayside | 1.8 | 2.5 | 1.8 |
| Islands | 0.8 | 2.2 | 2.0 |

*Source*: *Scottish Economic Bulletin* (June 1986), p. 35.

The effects of the oil crisis and the opening up of the North Sea oilfields have therefore been complex. The direct effects of North Sea oil developments have been relatively small except for certain limited areas. Much more significant have been the macroeconomic effects of the oil crisis and the relative freedom of action conferred on the government by the existence of North Sea oil output. Oil continues to spring surprises with implications for the depressed areas.

## The 1979–81 Recession

The single most important event in recent years as far as the depressed regions are concerned was the 1979–81 recession. This was by far and away the most severe of all of the post-war recessions in Britain. Between 1979 and 1981 the national unemployment rate increased from 5.0 per cent to 10.2 per cent. The period since the worst of the recession has been one of persistently high unemployment.

The causes of this massive recession are the source of some debate. 1979 was the year of a major oil price increase which triggered a world-wide downturn. British government policies after 1979—notably a restrictionist fiscal and monetary policy stance and the rapid appreciation of the sterling exchange rate—also contributed to the recession. Manufacturing industry was particularly badly hit. Between 1979 and 1984 the numbers of employees in employment in manufacturing fell by 30.0 per cent in the North, by 32.8 per cent in Wales, by 27.7 per cent in the West Midlands and by 17.3 per cent in the South East (*Regional Trends*, 1985, Table 7.2).

The 1979–81 recession, and the long drawn-out period of high unemployment which followed it, have had extremely serious implications for regional problems in Britain. As Table 10.11 shows, the result of the recession, as in all previous recessions, was to widen the gap between the more prosperous and less prosperous areas. Because the 1979–81 recession was so much worse than previous post-war recessions, the resulting widening of the gap was that much more severe. As a result, we now face the most serious set of regional problems experienced in the whole of the post-war period. It must be borne in mind, however, that the 1979–81 recession was merely the last in a whole series of changes, dating back to the early 1960s, which have tended to make life more difficult for the depressed regions. The government's response to these growing problems forms the subject matter of the remainder of this chapter.

## IV The Phases of Post-War Regional Policy

The post-war history of regional policy in Britain is not one of sustained, consistent effort. The vigour with which regional policies have been pursued has waxed and waned. The changes in commitment to solving regional problems have sometimes been sudden and of surprising magnitude.

A useful first step in analysing regional policy is to attempt to divide the post-war period into distinct 'phases', each characterized by weak or strong commitment to regional policy and each with its own distinctive 'package' of policy instruments in operation. Any attempt to divide post-war regional policy into clear phases is inevitably controversial. Changes in government commitment to regional policy are rarely immediately obvious or instantaneous. Disagreement on the precise timing of turning-points always occurs. Nevertheless, the broad pattern of phases shown below is a valid one.[3]

[3] This classification is based upon one developed by Moore *et al.* (1977).

TABLE 10.11. *Differences between regional and UK unemployment rates, 1979 and 1986*

| Region | Difference between each regions' unemployment rate and the UK unemployment rate | |
|---|---|---|
| | July 1979 | July 1986 |
| N. Ireland | 4.9 | 7.2 |
| North | 2.8 | 5.0 |
| North West | 1.1 | 2.6 |
| Scotland | 2.0 | 2.4 |
| Wales | 1.8 | 2.3 |
| West Midlands | −0.1 | 2.1 |
| Yorkshire/Humberside | 0.1 | 1.9 |
| East Midlands | −0.9 | −0.6 |
| South West | 0.2 | −2.0 |
| East Anglia | −1.0 | −3.0 |
| South East | −1.7 | −3.2 |

*Note*: During this period the UK unemployment rate rose from 5.0% to 11.9%.

*Sources*: *Regional Trends* (1985), Table 7.20; *Employment Gazette* (October 1986), Table 2.3.

## Phase I: Active Regional Policy 1945–50

This phase represents the first major onslaught on regional problems and was instituted by the Distribution of Industry Act, 1945. The initial set of policy instruments handed to the Board of Trade was essentially a legacy from the pre-war Special Areas policy—factory building and loans to firms on industrial estates; limited grants and loans for other companies; derelict land reclamation; and the provision of basic public services. To these in 1947 was added a new and powerful weapon—the Industrial Development Certificate (IDC) system. This imposed direct controls on new factories and extensions of over 5000 sq.ft. The scheme drew upon the experience with industrial controls gained during the Second World War. The policy 'package' was supplemented by the extremely successful conversion of some 13m. sq.ft. of wartime munitions and other factories to industrial use.

The wide range of policy instruments available, the determination of the government, and the broad geographical extent of the Development Areas eligible for assistance resulted in a surge in government expenditure on regional policy, as Fig. 10.7 shows.

## Phase II: Passive Regional Policy 1950–9

The initial active phase of post-war regional policy reached its peak in 1947. The emergence of a major balance of payments crisis in 1947 forced the government to make public expenditure cuts, and one of the programmes to suffer was regional

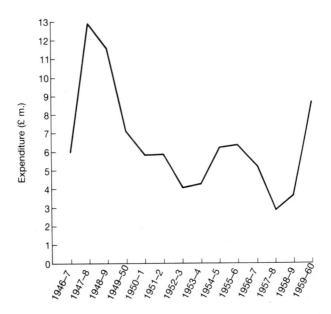

FIG. 10.7.    *Regional policy expenditure under the Distribution of Industry Acts*
*1945/6–1959/60*
*Source*:   McCrone (1969), Table III.

policy. The replacement of the Labour Government by a Conservative one in 1951 completed the downgrading of regional policy which had already begun. The regional policy legislation and policy instruments were kept in place. They were simply not pursued with the same vigour. Factory building was reduced; the building of advance factories was ended; and expenditure on subsidies to firms was cut back (see Fig. 10.7).

*Phase III: Transition 1959–63*

The re-emergence of severe regional problems in 1958 stimulated a re-awakening of regional policy. The initial response of the government was to breathe new life into the Distribution of Industry Acts which still remained on the statute books. Expenditure on regional policy was increased. IDCs were made more difficult to obtain in the South East and Midlands, and in 1958 assistance was extended to a number of high unemployment areas not previously part of the Development Areas.

As the full scale of the new regional problems became apparent, more funda-mental reform was decided upon. The Distribution of Industry Acts were replaced by a new Local Employment Act in 1960. All of the previous policy instruments were retained. To them were added grants to enable firms to build their own factories. Assistance was also extended to non-manufacturing companies. One retrograde step was the abolition of broad Development Areas and their replacement by a mosaic of Development Districts which could be quickly designated or de-designated. The outcome of all of these changes was that expenditure on regional policy doubled between 1960 and 1962.

### Phase IV: Active Regional Policy 1963–70

The period 1963–70 marks the most prolonged, most intensive, and most successful attack ever launched on regional problems in Britain. Between 1962/3 and 1969/70 there was a *sixteen*-fold increase in spending on regional policy (in real terms). Fig. 10.8 charts this enormous increase in spending. IDC controls were also very strictly applied during this period.

During this active period of regional policy almost all of the inherited policy instruments were retained. In addition, however, a whole series of radical and innovatory policies were brought in. The most important of these were:

| | |
|---|---|
| 1963 | Standard rates of investment grants and factory building grants. |
| 1963 | 'Accelerated' depreciation—the first major post-war 'tax break' policy for assisted area firms. |
| 1964 | Regional planning machinery established. |
| 1964 | Industrial Training Boards and Training Centres. |
| 1965 | Office Development Permits to control office expansion in London and Birmingham. |
| 1965 | Highlands and Islands Development Board. |
| 1966 | Large automatic investment grants. Land reclamation grants. The creation of five broad Development Areas covering almost half of Britain. |
| 1967 | Regional Employment Premium—a labour subsidy. |
| 1967 | Special Development Areas enjoying higher rates of assistance. |
| 1967 | Intermediate Areas designated and given assistance. |

### Phase V: Transition 1970–5

The early 1970s mark what, in retrospect, has proved to be a major turning point for regional policy in Britain. Expenditure on regional policy continued at a high level (see figure 10.8). After a brief period between 1970 and 1972 when major investment grants were withdrawn, the 1972 Industry Act instituted major new types of help for the regions (notably Regional Development Grants and Regional Selective Assistance for firms).

Unfortunately, despite the government's efforts the tide had already begun to turn against regional policy. Employment in manufacturing in Britain peaked in 1965 and thereafter fell continuously. The early 1970s saw the first oil crisis and a worsening macroeconomic situation. The deteriorating national economic situation undermined regional policy. A policy based on encouraging manufacturing firms to invest in the assisted areas cannot succeed if manufacturing is everywhere in decline and if aggregate investment is low. The first indication of the decline was in IDC controls, which were steadily relaxed in the late 1960s and early 1970s. By 1975 the decline in the effectiveness of regional policy had become visible to all.

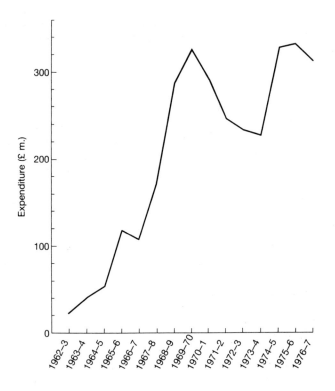

FIG. 10.8.   *Expenditure on regional policy in Britain, 1962/3–1976/7 at constant 1970/1*
            *prices*

*Note*:   This series includes expenditures under the Local Employment Acts; Regional Employment
          Premium and Selective Employment Tax; 1966 Industry Act investment grants; Regional
          Development Grants; Regional Selective Assistance; and incorporates tax changes.

*Source*:   McCallum (1979), Table 1.5.


*Phase VI: Decline 1975–84*

After 1975 there was a period of continuous decline for regional policy. Between
1975 and 1979 attempts were made to staunch this decline. The dispersal of civil
service jobs proved quite successful in the late 1970s. 1975 saw the introduction of a
European Regional Development Fund. 1976 witnessed the creation of Development Agencies in Scotland and Wales and the launching of the Development Board
for Rural Wales. On the other hand, the abolition of the Regional Employment
Premium in 1976, the rapid erosion of IDC controls, and the general economic
malaise all weakened regional policy further.

From 1979 onwards the pace of decline quickened. The severe 1979–81 recession
dealt a death blow to the traditional regional policy aimed at encouraging manufacturing firms to relocate in the assisted areas. In addition, the government proceeded
to dismantle large parts of regional policy. Office Development Permits were

terminated in 1979. IDCs were ended in 1981. Rates of subsidy for firms were reduced and the geographical extent of the assisted areas was dramatically cut between 1979 and 1982.

The result of all of these changes was a rapid reduction of regional policy expenditures (see Fig. 10.9).

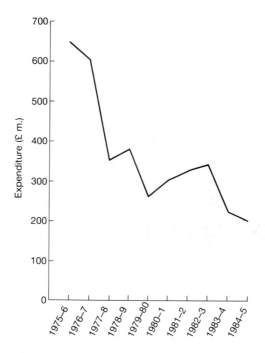

FIG. 10.9.    *Expenditure by the British Government on regional policy 1975/6–1984/5 (at constant 1975 prices)*

*Notes*:    1.   These figures include all regional policy schemes controlled by the Department of Trade and Industry (including factory building by English Estates). They do not include expenditures by the regional agencies and boards in Wales and Scotland, or by the European Regional Development Fund.
            2.   GDP deflator used throughout.

*Sources*:   *Annual Reports* of Industry Acts (various); *Economic Trends* (various issues).

*Phase VII: Transition 1984–*

Although the period since 1984 has witnessed a continued fall in government expenditure (in real terms) on regional policy, and although this is projected to continue, 1984 nevertheless marks yet another turning point for regional policy. In 1984 two major sets of reforms to regional policy were introduced. The first set of reforms concerned Department of Trade and Industry schemes. These reforms mark a major change of tack for regional policy, and probably spell the end of 'traditional' regional policy based upon large *automatic* investment grants designed to attract *manufacturing* firms to the assisted areas. Automatic investment grants have been cut back and selective assistance increased. Assistance to service industries has been greatly increased. There are strong suggestions that in future more help will be given to small firms and for innovation in the assisted areas. Finally, the map of eligible assisted areas has begun to grow again with the addition of parts of the now-depressed West Midlands.

These reforms, taken together with the second set of reforms introduced by the EC in 1984 to strengthen the activities of the European Regional Development Fund, mark a significant change of direction. This change of direction has not yet been backed by more government money, but is nevertheless a significant change. Regional policy is once more in transition.

## V  The Changing Nature of Regional Policy

Regional policy in Britain has suffered greatly from the lack of consistent effort by successive governments. The picture revealed in the previous section is one of marked variation in commitment. The rise and fall of expenditure on regional policy has been accompanied by frequent changes in the policy instruments themselves. The vast majority of the changes made to the policy instruments affected details of the policies without changing their fundamental nature. The broad characteristic features of what may be termed 'traditional' regional policy were never seriously challenged between 1945 and 1984. It is only in recent years that fundamental change has begun to occur.

For most of the post-war period it was the minutiae of regional policy that attracted government attention. Rates of grant were frequently changed, as were floorspace limits for IDCs, rates of labour subsidy, and eligibility criteria for regional policy schemes.[4] There was a constant drawing and redrawing of the boundaries of the assisted areas. Some of these myriad changes were very desirable. Many however were for ideological reasons or for short-term political gain. In retrospect, most can be seen to have merely confused potential investors and to have raised doubts among businessmen as to how long the promised assistance could be expected to continue to flow.

### The Characteristics of 'Traditional' Regional Policy

The 'traditional' regional policy which predominated between 1945 and 1984 was characterized by seven main features:

#### 1. 'Work to the Workers'
The lessons of the failure of worker transfer policies between 1928 and 1939 were not forgotten. Post-war regional policy has concentrated on taking 'work to the workers', rather than on encouraging large-scale out-migration from the assisted areas.

Successive governments have learned well the lessons of the 1930s. Large-scale labour migration would simply make matters worse for 'it tends to be the young,

---

[4] See Armstrong and Taylor (1985a), Appendix, for a full chronology of changes.

the more skilled and the more enterprising who are ready to move in search of work, leaving the less-favoured localities with a still more dependent population and a workforce even less able to climb out of disadvantage' (Department of Trade and Industry, 1983*b*, p. 3).

## 2. *The Emphasis on Manufacturing Industry*

Post-war regional policy in Britain has been characterized by an overwhelming bias in favour of manufacturing industry. Service industries have not been entirely ignored, but until recently have played only a minor role in the regional policy effort.

The traditional bias in favour of manufacturing is not surprising. The main depressed regions in Britain have been *industrial* regions. Their problems were initially caused by the run-down of mining and manufacturing industries such as textiles, shipbuilding, iron, and steel. They inherited a labour force rich in industrial skills upon which incoming firms could be expected to draw. The real mystery is not the bias in manufacturing, but the length of time it took to redress this bias once manufacturing employment began to decline in the late 1960s.

Although services have long played a small role in the regional policy effort, serious attempts to swing regional policy more towards the service sector date from 1972 when certain types of services were made eligible for Regional Selective Assistance.[5] Subsidies for services were increased in 1976. Moreover, services were eligible for European Regional Development Fund assistance from the very beginning of the Fund in 1975.

In reality the amount of financial assistance given to services in the depressed regions grew very slowly during the 1970s. Only since 1984, when services for the first time became eligible to receive large Regional Development Grants has the proportion of regional assistance given to services increased substantially.

The provision of regional policy assistance to services is inherently more difficult than for manufacturing. A much higher proportion of services are oriented towards *local* rather than national or international markets. Giving financial help to a newsagent or a garage would simply cause another local newsagent or garage to suffer. Jobs created in one company would simply be at the expense of other local jobs. On the other hand, some services genuinely serve national or international customers. This is particularly true of those serving tourists (e.g. craft shops, hotels, etc.). It is also true of many business and financial services which contribute to 'invisibles' earnings on the nation's balance of payments account.

The great difficulty in providing regional policy subsidies to services is in distinguishing between 'local' and 'non-local' services. This is by no means as simple as it may first appear because many service companies (e.g. hotels) simultaneously serve both local and non-local clients. Moreover, the proportions of 'local' and 'non-local' clients vary from hotel to hotel.

The whole question of which services to assist and which to exclude becomes even more complex when we turn to business services. Should assistance be given to services used by local industries (e.g. market consultancy, accountants)? A case can be made for helping services which are purely locally oriented but which

---

[5] Although they continued to be excluded from Regional Development Grants—the major instrument in the government's arsenal of policy instruments.

enhance the efficiency of local industry—such as consultants and research and development organizations. But should this argument be used to justify giving help to lawyers, accountants, and financial institutions? The dividing line is very unclear. It is obvious, therefore, that assistance to services must be given on a highly selective basis, with each case carefully considered on its merits. This poses severe problems for British regional policy, which is highly centralized. Selectivity and discretion require careful scrutiny and detailed local knowledge. It remains to be seen whether British regional policy has the ability to make the correct choices of which companies to assist.

### 3. *The Emphasis on 'Mobile' Manufacturing Plants*

For most of the post-war period the principal target of British regional policy has been the mobile manufacturing plant. Location controls and investment subsidies have been designed to encourage manufacturing companies to set up plants in an assisted area rather than in some other location. Sometimes these plants have represented entirely new capacity for the company. In other cases the new plants have been at the expense of factories closed down in the non-assisted areas. In a significant minority of cases the new plants have been set up by foreign-owned multinational companies.

As Table 10.12 shows, the emphasis on mobile manufacturing plants was particularly marked during the heyday of regional policy in the 1960s. During the 1970s the influx of mobile manufacturing plants slowed dramatically. The 1980s have seen a further substantial fall. It should be noted, however, that the decline in importance of immigrant plants in the 1970s and 1980s was not the result of a deliberate change in emphasis in regional policy. It resulted from a worsening national economic situation and the evaporation of the pool of new investment upon which regional policy draws. Regional policy in the 1970s and 1980s has continued to set out its stall to attract mobile manufacturing plants. There are simply a lot fewer around.

Traditional British regional policy has used a combination of 'stick and carrot' measures to induce mobile manufacturing plants to locate in the assisted areas. The

TABLE 10.12. *Numbers of manufacturing jobs created in immigrant and indigenous firms, 1960–1981* (thousands)

|  | Immigrant firms | Indigenous firms | All firms |
|---|---|---|---|
| 1960–71 | 197 | 139 | 336 |
| 1971–81 | 56 | 21 | 268 |
| 1960–81 | 253 | 351 | 604 |

*Notes:* 1. Gross jobs estimates do not allow for subsequent job losses in these firms through plant closures and contractions.
2. These estimates exclude multiplier effects on service industries (estimated to have led to an additional 180,000 job by 1981).

*Source:* Moore *et al.* (1986), p. 10.

'stick' has been location control policy in the form of IDCs. The 'carrot' has been a range of investment subsidies and, between 1967 and 1976, subsidies on the use of labour. Indigenous firms were not excluded from these subsidies and many did indeed benefit, as Table 10.12 shows. Immigrant plants were, however, the cornerstone of traditional regional policy and the drying up of the pool of potential 'movers' in the South East and Midlands is the principal reason for the decline of regional policy since 1975.

The emphasis placed on immigrant firms by traditional regional policy has left the policy in considerable disarray in the 1980s. It has also had a number of other unfortunate implications. Many companies responded in the 1960s and early 1970s by establishing branch plants in the assisted areas whilst retaining headquarters functions and main parent plants in the South East and Midlands. These branch plants were frequently the first to be closed down when the economic climate worsened. They have also proved to be very poorly integrated with the rest of the assisted area economies. The emphasis in mobile manufacturing plants has, in addition, left the government in a difficult 'competitive bidding' situation, particularly with our EC neighbours. Regional incentives are used to bid vigorously for multinational investment projects (e.g. the vehicle assembly plants of Nissan at Washington, and Ford at Bridgend). Lucrative subsidies must be offered because our Continental neighbours are also using their own regional incentives to competitively bid for the same projects.

The many criticisms of the traditional bias in favour of mobile manufacturing plants should not blind us to the real success of the policy during the 1960s when many tens of thousands of jobs were created in the assisted areas. The realization has, however, gradually dawned that we are unlikely ever to return to the sort of conditions so favourable to attracting mobile plants. The result has been a gradually growing awareness of the need to provide greater help for indigenous firms in the assisted areas. Particular attention has been focused on helping small and medium-sized enterprises and on stimulating new small-firms formation in the assisted areas. The assisted areas have a poor record of new business starts, and have underdeveloped small-firms sectors (Storey, 1982).

Most of the initiatives designed to encourage small firms and new firm formation have been national in character and not part of *regional* policy. The European Regional Development Fund, the regional development agencies in Scotland and Wales, and more recently the local councils (see Armstrong and Fildes, 1988) have pioneered methods for helping small firms in the assisted areas. Department of Trade and Industry policies are also now beginning to move in this direction. Unfortunately, the traditional instruments of regional policy—location controls and large standard investment grants—are poorly designed for small, indigenous firms. The experience of regional agencies and local councils suggests that flexible 'packages' of help comprising advice, the provision of suitable small factory units, small loans and grants, and equity participation are best suited to small firms. Each package of help must be carefully tailored to the needs of the small firm and support must be sustained on a continuing basis. This sort of approach is very different from traditional regional policy and is, moreover, very difficult for a *national* government to provide. It requires the participation of local and regional-level organisations.

### 4. *Location Controls and Investment Subsidies*

Location controls and investment subsidies have formed the backbone of traditional regional policy since 1945. Location controls have always been a controversial regional policy instrument. Controls on business of any kind sit uneasily with the 'indicative' planning favoured by Western democracies. Those who believe that businessmen should be free to select their own plant locations point to the risks of controls leading to inefficient locations being chosen. In practice, there is no evidence of lower productivities in assisted area manufacturing plants by comparison with their non-assisted area counterparts.

A more serious concern with controls is that they may have resulted in projects refused an IDC in the South East or Midlands being abandoned altogether or relocated abroad. Evidence suggests that 13 per cent of projects refused an IDC between 1958 and 1971 were subsequently abandoned and 1 per cent were relocated abroad. Interestingly, 50 per cent of projects initially refused an IDC were subsequently modified (i.e. reduced in size or relocated elsewhere in the *non*-assisted areas) so as to be able to obtain an IDC (Commission of the European Communities, 1981*b*).

Despite these problems, IDCs proved to be a valuable and effective policy instrument. They were very cheap to operate, since no subsidy was involved. They also proved very flexible since the vigour with which they were applied could be altered at short notice. Most important of all, IDCs proved a useful method for forcing companies to make contact with the Department of Trade and Industry. This enabled the Department to use its formidable powers of persuasion and to bring the size of the available regional subsidies to the attention of company managers. Location controls were therefore used jointly with investment subsidies as an extremely effective 'double act'.

Investment subsidies themselves have been the subject of a series of major controversies. An investment subsidy represents a subsidy on the use of one particular factor of production, capital. As such, they are likely to have two major effects on companies receiving them, both likely to cause job losses: (i) the now relatively cheaper (subsidized) capital will tend to be substituted for the relatively expensive (unsubsidized) labour, and (ii) since an investment subsidy is a subsidy on *new* capital, it is likely to be used to retool the factory. Most modern plant and machinery is labour-saving.

There is little doubt that the large regional investment grants have caused substantial job losses in some industries. Moore *et al.* (1986), for example, estimate that regional subsidies led to a loss of 28,000 jobs in the chemicals industry between 1966 and 1976 as more capital-intensive production methods were introduced.

Superficially, therefore, it is surprising that traditional regional policy has relied so heavily on investment subsidies rather than on labour subsidies for assisted area firms. Labour subsidies, in the form of the Regional Employment Premium were tried alongside investment subsidies between 1967 and 1976. They were abandoned partly because of their ineffectiveness and partly because of opposition from the EC which regarded them as a threat to free competition.

There are several reasons for favouring investment subsidies in preference to labour subsidies. First, the fear that investment subsidies would lead to a massive substitution of capital for labour is an exaggerated one. Most modern manufacturing is quite rigidly constrained in the capital/labour ratios used in production, and the scope for large-scale substitution of capital for labour *once the plant is in place* is limited (Buck and Atkins, 1976; Tooze, 1976). In addition, the ability to substitute capital for labour depends on the availability of capital and this too can sometimes be constrained. Moreover, it must also be remembered that factor subsidies give rise to *output effects* as well as substitution effects. An investment grant should allow a company to cut product price, thereby stimulating demand for its product (O'Donnell and Swales, 1977, 1979). Extra labour will be required to produce this extra output. Job gains as a result of this output effect may well exceed job losses as a result of capital being substituted for labour.

The second main argument in favour of investment subsidies concerns the retooling with state-of-the-art machinery, much of which is labour-saving. Although this may cause initial job losses in the assisted areas, it is surely no bad thing to have assisted area firms equipped with the most up-to-date machinery. Far from being a disadvantage, this effect of investment subsidies is a great bonus.

The final, and most telling argument of all in favour of investment subsidies and against labour subsidies concerns the long-term future of the assisted areas. An investment subsidy is a once-for-all subsidy which encourages the most modern and rapidly growing manufacturing industries to set up in the assisted areas. A labour subsidy is a *continuing* hand-out, week in week out, for existing industries. Investment subsidies are therefore a vote for the future and for change. Labour subsidies are a vote for the status quo and for the preservation of the past. They run the risk of maintaining inefficient industries which it would be better to let go to the wall.

Investment subsidies have therefore won the debate with labour subsidies. There is little chance of replacing them with labour subsidies. In recent years there have been attempts to reduce some of the waste involved in the existing investment grants system. One of the problems involved in giving large *automatic* investment grants to eligible projects is that the money is sometimes given to firms which would have located anyway in the assisted areas. Since 1984 attempts have been made to prevent money going to such cases. These efforts to tidy up the investment grant system do not disguise the fact that investment subsidies remain a key element in the regional policy armoury and are likely to remain so.

Somewhat more controversial is the issue of how best to give investment subsidies. Traditional regional policy has relied heavily on *cash grants* and *low-interest loans*. Since 1966 the major expenditure item in regional policy has been investment grants (except for a brief period 1970–2). These grants have been for the costs of plant, machinery, and new factory buildings. The use of large, automatic investment grants at standard rates has had the great virtue of being simple for businessmen to understand and very 'visible'.

In conclusion, a convincing case can be made for investment subsidies and it is not surprising that they remain at the heart of British regional policy. Location controls are not much use when times are bad, but have nevertheless proved extremely effective in the past. Traditional British regional policy has been rather staid and unenterprising. No attempt, for example, has been made as in other countries to subsidize energy costs (e.g. electricity prices) or transport costs (e.g. rail freight rates) in the assisted areas. Nor have direct price or operating cost subsidies been tried.

## 5. *The Delimitation of Broad Assisted Areas*

Successive governments have found tinkering with the map of the assisted areas an irresistible temptation. Areas have been designated and de-designated with bewildering speed. Although many of the changes have been substantial, over most of the post-war period a single basic philosophy has been followed. The assisted areas have, except for a brief period in the early 1960s, been broad geographical areas. The maps of eligible assisted areas have been drawn to include not only the high unemployment 'blackspots' but also the nearby more prosperous towns and cities together with wide swathes of adjacent rural areas. In July 1979, for example, the assisted areas encompassed 43 per cent of the working population of Britain.

The broad geographical scope of the assisted areas is interesting. The great danger, of course, is that regional assistance will be thinly spread and lose its impact. Two main alternative methods for designating assisted areas exist. The first involves deliberately restricting the eligible areas to localities suffering hard-core unemployment problems. This was tried between 1960 and 1965 when a multitude of small Development Districts replaced the former broad Development Areas. In 1961 the Development Districts were reduced until they covered only 7.2 per cent of the population of Britain. By 1965, however, they had expanded so much that they once more covered broad geographical areas. The period 1979–82 also saw a rapid cut-back in the areas eligible for regional assistance (from 43 per cent of the working population in 1979 to 28 per cent in 1982). The process has now been reversed, however, and the assisted areas currently encompass 35 per cent of the working population. Broad Development Areas have been preferred to fragmented Development Districts because whilst reducing the assisted areas to the hardest-hit localities ensures that the money goes to the worst places, these localities are rarely the ones with the best growth prospects. To be successful regional policy needs to include areas of good growth potential alongside the localities in severe decline.

The second main alternative to the designation of broad assisted areas is to ignore the hardest-hit localities and instead to target the regional assistance on a small number of 'growth poles'. These are normally cities and industrial complexes with excellent growth prospects. The problem with this approach is that it rests upon the paradoxical proposition that intra-regional disparities must be allowed to widen in order that inter-regional disparties be eliminated. Support for growth pole policy has long antecedents in Britain and has figured prominently in some parts of regional policy. The Highlands and Islands Development Board (HIDB), for example, has pursued growth pole policies in the north of Scotland for many years. Traditional regional policy in Britain, however, with its heavy reliance on automatic investment grants (the precise destination of which are outside the government's control) has proved ill-designed for the pursuit of growth pole policies.

## 6. *The Lack of Formal Regional Planning*

British regional policy has been characterized by the almost complete absence of formal regional planning. This sets British regional policy apart from many other countries. One reason for the lack of regional planning has been the total failure of *national* planning in Britain. Ideally, plans for the development of each region should be an integral part of the national plan of a country. Regional planning has also been handicapped by lack of regional governments in Britain. Regional governments would provide the impetus for regional planning together with the resources and personnel required in the planning process.

The only serious attempt to introduce regional planning in Britain coincided with the *National Plan* of 1965. An incoming Labour Government created a new ministry, the Department of Economic Affairs. Ten Economic Planning Regions were established in Britain each with its own Regional Economic Planning Council and Regional Economic Planning Board. The Councils were staffed by appointees drawn from the ranks of the 'great and the good' of each region. The Boards were staffed by civil servants drawn from the regional offices of the various government ministries.

The 1965 *National Plan* was the lynchpin of the new regional planning system. The National Plan was introduced at a time of unprecedented prosperity for Britain. The country faced problems that would be the envy of the present government— labour shortages and excess aggregate demand. The various regional planning documents reflected these preoccupations. The *National Plan* was overtaken by events almost as soon as it was published. The onset of severe balance of payments problems led to macropolicy changes which destroyed its chances of success. National planning quickly became discredited. The demise of the Department of Economic Affairs (DEA) in 1970 fundamentally undermined the whole process. The regional Councils and Boards survived the demise of the DEA. Regional Planning was, however, meaningless in the absence of a National Plan. The Councils also suffered from having only limited advisory powers and from the lack of credibility arising from the non-elected nature of their membership. They proved extremely ineffective and were finally abolished in 1980.

In recent years longer-term planning for the depressed regions has re-emerged from a surprising quarter. Under the European Regional Development Fund regulations member states wishing to receive EC aid must submit regular Regional Development Programmes. These documents require a statement of long-term objectives for regional policy and are planning documents of a sort. They still fall a long way short of formal regional planning but have, nevertheless, forced the British government to take a longer view of regional policy than it normally has done. They have also forced the government to take the coordination of different aspects of the policy seriously.

## 7. Central Government Control of Regional Policy

Traditional regional policy in Britain has been almost completely monopolized by the national government. All the major policy instruments have been controlled by the Department of Trade and Industry, operating through a network of regional offices and the Scottish and Welsh Offices. Training and worker transfer policies have been controlled by the Department of Employment. Infrastructure investment in the region (e.g. new roads) has also been run largely from the centre. Local authorities in Britain do have a long tradition of providing sites and factory premises for firms but this has been on a fairly limited scale until recently.

The highly centralized nature of traditional British regional policy stands in marked contrast to many federal countries where state and provincial governments usually play a major role in industrial development initiatives. The near-monopoly of regional policy enjoyed by the national government began to weaken in 1965. The Highlands and Islands Development Board established in 1965 was given very wide powers to stimulate economic revival in the north and west of Scotland. The

HIDB proved to be a forerunner of a number of new agencies. It was joined in 1976 by the Scottish Development Agency, the Welsh Development Agency, and Mid-Wales Development. There is now strong pressure for similar agencies in English regions.

The various agencies and boards in Scotland and Wales share a number of common features. To begin with, they are largely dependent on the national government for funds (in the form of Grants-in-Aid), although income from their own investments has risen steadily. They enjoy wide powers to help industrial development and they offer a great variety of types of assistance: advice to firms; sites and factory premises; grants; loans; and equity participation. They are also heavily involved in redeveloping urban areas and reclaiming derelict land.

The emergence and rapid expansion of development agencies in Scotland and Wales has been accompanied by the rapid growth of local authority involvement in economic development initiatives throughout Britain (Association of District Councils, 1984). Local authorities have greatly increased their expenditure on assistance to industry since 1979 (Armstrong and Fildes, 1988). It is now clear that the national government no longer has a monopoly on spatially discriminating industrial policy—regional agencies and local councils are now also actively involved.

The predominant position of the national government has also been weakened by the emergence of an EC regional policy. Britain entered the EC in 1973. This immediately gave Britain's depressed regions access to financial assistance from several sources. The European Investment Bank provides loans for industrial and infrastructure projects in the depressed regions. The European Social Fund supports training and worker transfer schemes. The European Coal and Steel Community assists the retraining of redundant coal and steel workers and also makes 'conversion' loans to companies hiring redundant coal and steel workers. Finally, the European Agricultural Guidance and Guarantee Fund helps farmers in the poorer agricultural areas. Entry to the EC in 1973 also brought the British Government's own regional policy under the umbrella of the Community's competition policy regulations. This places member states' own regional policies under a series of constraints and rules designed to try to prevent regional subsidies being used to competitively bid for multinational investment projects (Deacon, 1982).

Further EC involvement in regional policy in Britain occurred in 1975 with the establishment of the European Regional Development Fund (ERDF). This fund gives grants to services, industry, and infrastructure projects in the assisted areas. The ERDF has grown and developed very rapidly (Armstrong, 1983, 1986).

*Recent Changes in Regional Policy in Britain*

The 'traditional' regional policy set out above had already begun to decline prior to 1979. Between 1979 and 1984 the pace of decline accelerated rapidly. Expenditure on regional policy continued to fall quickly (in real terms). Location controls were completely abandoned and, between 1979 and 1982, the eligible assisted areas were ruthlessly pruned. Most serious of all, however, was the 1979–81 recession. This was so severe that it led to high unemployment in all regions and almost eliminated the pool of mobile manufacturing plants upon which traditional regional policy relied.

Two major sets of reforms in 1984, one concerning Department of Trade and Industry policies and the other concerning the European Regional Development Fund (see Armstrong and Taylor, 1985b), mark a major turning-point for British regional policy. Table 10.13 sets out the main reforms. Seven fundamental changes are now in progress:

(i) Service industries have now joined manufacturing as major recipients of regional assistance. All participants—DTI, ERDF, regional agencies, and local authorities—are now helping service firms.

(ii) There is a major switch from *automatic* grants to selective and discretionary assistance to firms underway.

(iii) Indigenous development is now favoured instead of immigrant firms. Attention is now switching rapidly towards small and medium-sized companies and towards encouraging new firm formation.

(iv) There has been a burgeoning of different *types* of assistance for companies. Location controls have gone. Investment subsidies remain important. In addition, however, the various organizations involved in regional policy now offer financial advice, business and technical advice, flexible loans and guarantees, equity participation, operating cost subsidies, and specially designed factory units and sites. The emphasis is now on 'tailored' packages of help individually put together for companies. Help is often now ongoing instead of just at the start of a project.

(v) The geographical extent of the assisted areas, having been greatly reduced between 1979 and 1982, is once more beginning to expand. The expansion, however, has been in the West Midlands (see Fig. 10.10). This reflects the emergence of severe problems in the West Midlands.

(vi) The erosion of the national governments' dominant position looks set to continue further. EC, local and regional-level expenditures are likely to continue to increase. British regional policy is now truly multijurisdictional.

(vii) Whilst formal regional planning remains as discredited as ever, the advent of the ERDF has forced the government to take a longer-term view of regional policy than it has previously done. The need to coordinate the activities of the various governments and agencies is also now an issue of some importance.

It is too soon yet to see the precise nature of the new regional policy now emerging. One thing is, however, clear. There can be no return to the 'traditional' type of regional policy which has dominated the post-war era.


## VI The Effectiveness of Regional Policy

Estimating the effectiveness of regional policy has proved to be an extraordinarily difficult task. The primary objective of British regional policy has always been the reduction of regional differences in *unemployment*. When judged in terms of its ability to reduce unemployment disparities regional policy would appear to have been an abject failure. Regional unemployment differences are currently wider than at almost any other time in the whole post-war period.

TABLE 10.13. *The 1984 reforms to Department of Trade and Industry schemes and the European Regional Development Fund*

(a) *Department of Trade and Industry Schemes*

  1 *Expenditure*. Cuts of 300m. (on a budget of around 700m.) planned for 1987/8. In addition a switch in emphasis from Regional Development Grants to Regional Selective Assistance is planned.

  2 *Assisted Areas*. Special Development Areas (which enjoyed a 20% rate of RDG) abolished. Development Areas cut. Intermediate Areas redesignated and expanded to include parts of the W. Midlands.

  3 *Regional Development Grants*

  (a) Inclusion of certain eligible *service* industries for the first time.
  (b) Assisted projects must result in *new* or *expanded* productive capacity or alter the nature of the production *process* (thus eliminating grants towards purely replacement investment).
  (c) Rate of RDG in Development Areas to be 15% (remains zero in Intermediate Areas). To help small firms and services (with low investment outlays), as an alternative to the 15% investment grant, RDG now offers a grant of 3,000 per net job created.
  (d) Larger firms (over 200 employees) have a cost per net new job limit of £10,000 imposed. RDG must not exceed this figure.

  4 *Regional Selective Assistance*. As before. Available in Intermediate Areas as well as Developed Areas.

(b) *European Regional Development Fund*

  1 Replacement of fixed national 'shares' of ERDF (the UK share was 23.8% prior to the 1984 reforms) by a set of 'indicative ranges' within which member states shares must fall (over a three-year period). The UK 'indicative range' was initially set at 21–42%—28.56% of ERDF expenditures.

  2 Simpler procedures and improved rates of investment grant in some cases.

  3 A rapid switch from project-by-project assistance to *programme* assistance. A programme is an integrated set of schemes and packages of assistance designed to meet specific goals and to run for several years.

  4 Improved help for small firms and indigenous development of regions.

  5 An increase in Integrated Development Operations targeted on deprived urban areas.

*Sources*:  Council Regulation (European Economic Community) no. 1787/84 of 19 June 1984 on the European Regional Development Fund, *Official Journal of the European Communities*, OJ L169, vol. 27 Brussels (28 June 1984); Department of Trade and Industry, *Press Notice No. 681* (28 November 1984).

To conclude from the current unemployment situation that regional policy had failed would, however, do post-war regional policy a great injustice. Current regional unemployment disparities tend to disguise the real successes of post-war regional policy for two main reasons:

  (a) had there been no regional policy, unemployment rates in the depressed regions would have been considerably worse than they are now.
  (b) regional policy has created many jobs in the assisted areas. Not all of these

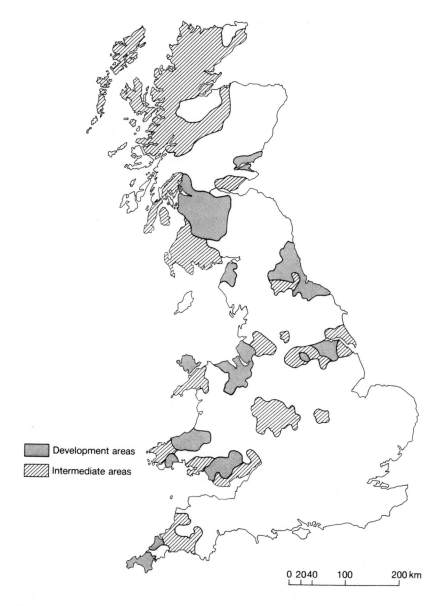

FIG. 10.10.   *The British assisted areas November 1984*
*Source*:   Department of Trade and Industry.

jobs, however, have been filled from the ranks of the unemployed. Some
of the extra jobs attributable to regional policy have been taken by people
who would otherwise have migrated. They chose instead to stay and work
in the depressed regions. Other jobs created by regional policy have been
filled by people who were not *registered* as unemployed (e.g. many married

women) and who have been attracted into the workforce by new jobs coming into the assisted areas.

A successful regional policy therefore tends to cut out-migration and increase activity rates[6] as well as reducing unemployment. There is not a direct one-to-one relationship between extra jobs created by regional policy and reductions in unemployment.

Because the true success of regional policy is not revealed by changes in unemployment it is necessary to look elsewhere for measures of the full benefit enjoyed in the assisted areas. Research has concentrated on the effects of regional policy on *employment, investment*, and the *movement of manufacturing establishments* to the assisted areas.

### The Effects of Regional Policy on Employment in the Assisted Areas

The number of extra jobs in the assisted areas attributable to regional policy is probably the most important indicator of whether the policy has been successful or not. The most serious difficulty facing those seeking to measure the employment-creating effects of regional policy in the assisted areas is that it is hard to know precisely what would have happened to employment in the absence of regional policy. The number of jobs attributable to regional policy is given as the difference between actual employment and what the employment count would *otherwise* have been. The latter, 'policy-off', situation is a hypothetical one and therefore extremely difficult to estimate.

The most widely used technique for estimating the number of jobs created in assisted areas by regional policy has been that pioneered by Moore and Rhodes (1973). This technique has been repeatedly refined and updated. The most recent set of estimates (Moore *et al.*, 1986) refers to the period 1950–81. Data constraints prevent the estimates of the employment effects of regional policy 1945–50. The Moore *et al.* technique uses a two-stage procedure.

### (i) Effects of Regional Policy on the Indigenous Sector of the Assisted Areas

The 'indigenous' sector of the assisted areas is defined by *excluding* all companies which have opened in the assisted areas since 1945. Fig. 10.11 shows how the effects of regional policy are estimated. The A* series is obtained by taking *actual* manufacturing employment in the assisted areas and adjusting the figures to allow for the effects of industry 'mix'. The assisted areas tend to have a rather high proportion of declining manufacturing industries (declining in employment terms). Employment in the assisted areas would be expected to decline more quickly than elsewhere because of this poor industry mix. The A* series is an employment series which has been adjusted to allow for this dependence on 'poor performers'. This ensures that regional policy does not get the blame for job losses which are the result of a poor industry structure in the assisted areas.

The T series in Fig. 10.11 is derived by looking at what happened to employment

---

[6] The activity rate is the proportion of the population of working age (15–65 for men and 15–60 for women) either in work or seeking work.

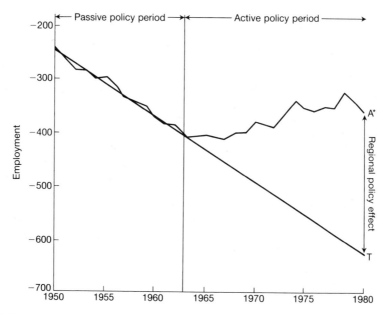

FIG. 10.11. *Estimating the effects of regional policy on the main assisted area regions, 1950–81*

*Source*: Moore *et al*, (1986), Fig. 4.3.

in the assisted areas between 1950 and 1963 when regional policy was almost non-existent. As Fig. 10.11 shows, manufacturing employment (even after allowing for the effects of a poor industrial base) was falling in the assisted areas in the 1950s. By projecting this downward trend forward to 1981 the T series shows what employment *would have been* in 1981 had regional policy not been re-activated after 1963.

The final step in estimating the effect of regional policy on employment in the indigenous sector is a simple one. The difference between A* (actual employment—adjusted for industry mix), and T (what employment would have been had there been no regional policy) is the figure required. Moore *et al*. (1986) estimate that this figure in 1981 was 277,000 jobs. Regional policy, therefore, between 1963 and 1981 led to 277,000 new jobs in the assisted areas. It should be noted that these are *surviving* (or 'net') jobs in 1981. Regional policy also created many other jobs (particularly in the 1960s) which were subsequently lost through plant closures and redundancies. If these 'non-surviving' jobs are added to those surviving, we get a *gross* job creation figure at 1981 of 351,000. This represents a sizeable achievement.

## (ii) *Effects of Regional Policy on the Immigrant*
   *Sector of the Assisted Areas*

The immigrant sector comprises those firms coming into the assisted areas in post-war years. Estimating the number of firms attracted into the assisted areas by regional policy is a tricky task. A certain volume of movement between regions occurs quite naturally. There is also a distinct cyclical effect—the number of plants set up in assisted areas always falls in a recession and rises during an upturn. This is because companies have more money to invest during cyclical upturns.

There is little doubt that regional policy has had a strong impact on the movements of manufacturing plants in the post-war period. There was a surge in the number of manufacturing plants setting up in the assisted areas in 1945–50 and again in 1963–75. This is precisely when regional policy was most active.

Moore *et al.* (1986) estimate the effect of regional policy on the movement of manufacturing plants into the assisted areas by means of statistical regression techniques.[7] The chosen techniques allow not only for the effect of regional policy but also for other factors which influence the movement of plants. Their results suggest that incoming firms created 253,000 extra jobs between 1960 and 1981, 173,000 of which survived subsequent closures and lay-offs.

In total, therefore, some 604,000 jobs in manufacturing appear to have been created in the assisted areas between 1960 and 1981, 450,000 of which survived subsequent closures and lay-offs.

These jobs, however, are only the *manufacturing* jobs created. To these must be added extra jobs in services resulting from the multiplier effects generated by a more buoyant manufacturing sector. Some 180,000 *extra* service jobs were sustained by the manufacturing industry brought in by regional policy. The final score in terms of *surviving* manufacturing and service jobs in 1981 is therefore 630,000. Most of these jobs were created during the heyday of regional policy in the 1960s and early 1970s.

*The Effects of Regional Policy on Investment and the Movement of Manufacturing Establishments*

Further support for the success of regional policy has been provided by research concentrating on investment and on the movement of manufacturing plants (as distinct from employment in those plants).

The techniques pioneered by Moore and Rhodes have been applied to investment data for the various regions of Britain. The results strongly support the view that regional policy in the 1960s and early 1970s gave a strong boost to manufacturing investment in the assisted areas (Rees and Miall, 1979; Marquand, 1980).

In addition to the regression techniques used by Moore *et al.* (1986) to examine industrial movement, which were discussed earlier, there have been other rather different techniques used to look at the effect of regional policy on industrial movement (see Ashcroft and Taylor, 1979; Twomey and Taylor, 1985). Between 1960 and 1977 some 974 plant relocations resulted from regional policy (Twomey and Taylor, 1985). Interestingly, not all of these plants moved to assisted areas. Some plants seem to have been driven out of London and Birmingham as a result of

---

[7] The preferred regression equation was:

$$MDA_t = a_1 + a_2MU + a_3II_{t-1} + a_4IDC_{t-1} + a_5REP_{t-1} + \varepsilon_t$$

where MDA = numbers of moves to British Development Areas in year $t$
$MU_t$ = male unemployment rate in year $t$ (this picks up business cycle variations in industrial movement)
$II_{t-1}$ = value of regional investment subsidies
$IDC_{t-1}$ = IDC refusal rate
$REP_{t-1}$ = value of regional labour subsidies (Regional Employment Premium)
$\varepsilon_t$ = error term.

being refused an IDC, and have moved not to an assisted area but to East Anglia and the East Midlands. Most relocating plants, however, did go to the assisted areas.

Estimates of the effects of regional policy on industrial movement have been the subject of considerable controversy. Differences in the statistical models used have given quite widely varying results in terms of the numbers of moves attributable to regional policy. Differences of opinions also exist on precisely which policy instruments have been most effective in persuading firms to move to assisted areas. All of the studies agree on the effectiveness of the investment subsidies. There is, however, some disagreement on how effective the Regional Employment Premium was. Moore *et al.* (1986), for example, give it an important role. Others (e.g. Twomey and Taylor, 1985) regard IDCs as having been much more effective. What all of the studies *do* agree upon however, is that regional policy during the 1960s and early 1970s was a very effective policy for encouraging manufacturing firms to relocate in the assisted areas. This effectiveness[8] however, has been undermined by the depressed state of the national economy in recent years.

### Conclusion

This chapter has examined regional problems and regional policy in Britain during the post-war period. For over 40 years Britain has been involved in a long struggle to try to reduce the disparities in economic welfare between its regions.This struggle has now entered a critical phase. Regional problems have worsened dramatically in recent years. This rapid worsening of the scale of regional problems has coincided with a serious malaise in regional policy. The gradual decline in 'traditional' regional policy during the 1970s has rapidly accelerated in the period since 1979. Traditional policies based on using location controls and investment subsidies to attract 'mobile' manufacturing plants to the assisted areas were very successful in the 1960s and early 1970s. They are now largely ineffective.

To make matters worse, it has become much harder to make a strong case for having regional policy. When unemployment is high in *all* regions it is hard to argue for special treatment for some areas and not for others.

It is vital that we end the current malaise in regional policy. Regional unemployment remains what it always was—a waste of a valuable resource. The unused labour resources in the assisted areas are a vital, skilled national resource. To bring them into employment again would yield output gains from which the whole country could benefit. Regional problems are also socially and politically divisive. The 'north–south' divide is a very real one now. Moreover, the over-concentration of industry and people in the South East is both strategically and environmentally

---

[8] 'Effectiveness' has been defined here in terms of the numbers of jobs created by regional policy. In recent years attempts have been made to estimate the *cost effectiveness* of regional policy in terms of the cost to the government per job created. It has, for example, been estimated that between 1960 and 1980 the regional policy cost per job created was £35,000 (Moore *et al.*, 1986). This compares favourably with other types of government policy (e.g., public works). Such cost-per-job estimates are theoretically unsound and should not be used as an aid to policy-making. They refer only to the costs to the *Exchequer* and not to the true *social* costs of regional policy.

undesirable—not least for those living in the South East. It also represents an inflationary 'time bomb' for Britain.

There is an urgent need for a new regional policy initiative. There can be no simple return to 'traditional' regional policy based upon attracting mobile manufacturing plants to the assisted areas. Manufacturing employment is in long-term decline. There are, however, other options (see Armstrong and Taylor, 1986). A stimulus to the national economy, however small, would be of great benefit to the assisted areas for, as we have seen, when UK unemployment falls unemployment in the assisted areas falls faster. Much more could be done to help small firms, services, innovation, and indigenous development in the assisted areas. More could also be done to coordinate the activities of the various government agencies now helping industry in the assisted areas. The government should, in addition, ensure that, wherever feasible, *all* government spending programmes such as health and defence discriminate in favour of assisted area firms. Finally, the recent large cuts in the regional policy budget should be reversed. Unless changes such as these are soon introduced there is a risk that the hard-earned gains of post-war regional policy will be thrown away.

# 11

# Industrial Organization
# and Competition Policy

## J. G. WALSHE

The structure of British industry has gradually evolved over the centuries. That structure did not rapidly emerge with the growth of manufacturing concerns in the nineteenth century; and to explain industrial structure purely in terms of the formation of giant corporations during the present century would be highly misleading. So the evolution of industrial organisation has been a long, unevenly paced, irregularly disturbed process; and, in the short run, it is impossible to undo the work of centuries and start again. The structure we have is here to stay in the foreseeable future. Nevertheless, it may still be profitable to analyse how firms and industries are structured. First, it may be possible to advance our understanding of how industrial organization is likely to evolve and influence future developments to our advantage. Second, even if there is little to be done about the prospective pattern of industry it may yet be feasible to adjust for any unwelcome effects of that system on employment, the growth of incomes, technical progressiveness, and trade.

Other chapters in this book take up the story of industrial organization from the point of view of general supply-side management and the nationalized industries. The first task of this chapter will be to describe the general structure of British industry; particular trends in the evolution of that structure over the past half century will also be traced. Second, the major factors explaining change in the structure will be explored and an attempt will be made to outline the principal effects of change. The third part of the chapter will appraise the results of competition policies introduced by successive administrations since 1945. Finally, some recent trends in company strategy will be sketched and the implications for competition policy broadly assessed.

## Trends in Industrial Structure

There are no systematic data covering structural change over the whole of UK industry. Information on manufacturing industry is now fairly exhaustive but coverage of the service sector of the economy, which produces about three-fifths of private-sector output, is sadly lacking. It may be that this statistical shortcoming is relatively unimportant, and can be made good by recourse to casual empiricism; or that the readily available data is a useful proxy for development in the economy as a whole. However, it is as well to remember throughout that our sources are patchy and irregular. Trends in market concentration will be discussed first; the aggregate concentration of plants and firms will be described in the following section.

(i) *Market Concentration*

In the first decade of this century the structure of British industry was relatively fragmented. That is to say, most firms and the plants which they operated did not produce a significant share of domestic production. There were exceptions where amalgamations had secured almost complete monopolization before the First World War: in certain chemicals (salt, alkali, borax) and cotton textiles trades, for example, and in cigarettes, seed crushing, wallpaper, and cement (Pollard, 1983). However, apart from these relatively isolated instances, the great staple industries of coal-mining, iron and steel, cotton and wool textiles, shipbuilding and engineering, remained in the hands of numerous independent, competitive firms (Allen, 1966). Hannah (1983) suggests that in 1880 the largest 100 firms probably accounted for less than 10 per cent of manufacturing output.

In subsequent decades waves of merger and amalgamation (often with official support during the 1920s and 1930s) reinforced monopolies in chemicals and seed crushing, while promoting new near-monopolies in soap, margarine, sugar, matches, glass bottles, whisky distilling, and yeast (Pollard, 1983). Jervis (1971) and Utton (1972) have assembled lists of the more important mergers at the turn of the century and, again, during the inter-war period. The remarkable feature of many of these mergers was that large numbers of firms joined together at one time—for example, no less than 46 firms went into the formation of the British Cotton and Wool Dyers Association in 1890, 33 firms merged in the British Portland Cement Manufacturers in 1912, while Imperial Chemical Industries brought together 37 firms in 1926. Company reports at the time of the mergers invariably referred to the need to eliminate ruinous price competition and excess capacity so that some, but not all, of these mergers were followed by attempts to restructure the production side of the industries concerned. Many of the attempts to institute price stability were less than successful; consequently there were further attempts to mop up newly emerging companies in the 1920s and, when that strategy in turn failed, to organize trade association management of prices and output (Utton, 1972). Nevertheless, although merger movements before 1939 were often spectacular in scope, their impact was fairly limited. Leak and Maizels (1945) estimated that there were only 33 trades in manufacturing (out of a total of 302 surveyed, and contributing only 7 per cent of manufacturing employment), where the leading three firms controlled more than 70 per cent of employment. Utton (1972) suggests that in less than a third of these trades had merger played a dominant part in building up market share.

By the time of the 1935 Census of Production almost two-thirds of employment in manufacturing industry was in plants of less than 500 employees. At the same time, as Table 11.1A shows, some 60 per cent of manufacturing employment was in firms of less than 500 employees. Also, the average size of plant was very small. On the basis of Factory Inspectors' reports Sargant Florence (1953) estimated that the mean size of plant was only 23.5 persons in 1938, having advanced from 16.5 persons in 1904. The picture in the service industries was rather more variable. Many of the utilities and transport concerns were publicly owned or had been concentrated into giant regional concerns; but finance, insurance, construction, personal services, the professions, retail and wholesale distribution, and the entertainment industries were populated by many thousands of separate concerns. Some idea of the sea-change which occurred after 1935 is given by Table 11.1B. By 1984,

TABLE 11.1A. *Employment in manufacturing, 1935*

| Employment size | Firms N | % | Employment N (000s) | % |
|---|---|---|---|---|
| 1–10 | 132,338 | 76 | 536.8 | 9 |
| 11–99 | 31,214 | 18 | 1119.6 | 20 |
| 100–499 | 8,299 | 5 | 1735.2 | 31 |
| 500–999 | 1,002 | 1 | 688.5 | 12 |
| 1,000+ | 649 | | 1614.2 | 28 |
| | 173,502 | 100 | 5694.3 | 100 |

TABLE 11.1B. *Employment in manufacturing, 1984*

| Employment size | Enterprises N | % | Employment N (000s) | % |
|---|---|---|---|---|
| 1–99 | 114,186 | 96 | 1131 | 23 |
| 100–499 | 3,904 | 3 | 796 | 17 |
| 500–999 | 524 | ½ | 358 | 7 |
| 1,000+ | 558 | ½ | 2543 | 53 |
| | 119,172 | 100 | 4828 | 100 |

*Sources*: Leak and Maizels (1945); Business Statistics Office (1987).

firms with over 500 employees still accounted for only 1 per cent of manufacturing firms, but they now controlled some 60 per cent of employment.

While the first four decades of the century saw little change in the structural position, it would be wrong to infer from this that the competitive circumstances of British industry had not altered. Movements to curtail competition either by amalgamations, or by cartel arrangements to determine output shares, or by looser trade association agreements on prices and conditions of sale, have had different origins at different points in time. At the turn of the century, for example, the cheapening of transport, and the elimination of quality differences as mechanization prevailed over craft production, removed the basis for many thriving local monopolies and provided the impetus for attempts to control competition. During the First World War the stimulus to combination derived from the panoply of controls on production, wartime shortages of materials, and the emergence of government as an important customer for the main staple industries. In the late 1920s with the onset of world recession, and the gradual loss of export markets as protectionism spread, the major industries sought to alleviate their condition by agreements on price and output.

When these experiments met with scant success, as in cotton (Jervis, 1971), it became obvious that surplus capacity would need to be removed before 'weak selling' could be eliminated. Rationalizations of industrial capacity were sought alongside more general schemes to control competition. While it is true to say that comparatively little actual surplus capacity was removed by the 'rationalization movement' (Buxton and Aldcroft, 1979), one by one the main industries moved out of a pro-competitive climate. The Coal Mines Act of 1930 which encouraged price and output control was supplemented in 1936 by central selling arrangements. The Spindles Act of 1936 gave the organized cotton spinners enabling powers to reduce capacity. The British Iron and Steel Federation had by 1939 established control over prices, output, and investment in virtually the entire industry (Gribbin, 1978). In transport and agriculture state-sponsored schemes to limit unfettered competition were introduced, while in shipbuilding Shipbuilders Security Limited was formed to supervise amalgamations and the scrapping of surplus plant (Allen, 1966). In many trades the explicit allocation of production quotas obtained: for example, in the Sulphate of Ammonia Federation, the National Benzol Company, the Nitrate Producers Association, and the Cable Makers Association (Pollard, 1983).

In the background, encouraging these attempts to control competition, stood the government. Apart from specific industry-based schemes, backed by statutory instruments and legislation, Government provided a more general commitment. For example, free trade was formally abandoned in 1932. Henceforth, using the bargaining device of a protective tariff, industries could negotiate for more 'orderly' marketing by foreign exporters in the UK market. Again, the Finance Act of 1935 included incentives to contribute to approved schemes for the reduction of surplus capacity. Although the general strategy pursued by government failed to equate productive capacity with demand, nevertheless, by the second half of the 1930s a considerable change in the competitive climate had been effected.

Thus by 1939 a substantial segment of British industry had become, for all intents and purposes, controlled by trade associations. The wartime control of foreign trade and domestic output was thus embroidered upon a peacetime network of formal and informal price and output restrictions. Independent 'competition' gave way to licensing systems covering factory space, manpower, and materials. As Barnett has observed (1986, p. 59):

Nor was there any internal competition in the British home market, for all production and distribution was subject to a comprehensive array of government controls, allocations and rationing . . . British firms producing war supplies under government contract were working on the basis of 'cost-plus': that is, their actual production costs with a fixed profit rate added; so there was no spur to efficiency or cost cutting.

Many of the wartime controls were retained well into the 1950s. For example, the organization of material allocations which covered over 90 per cent of industrial raw materials in wartime still covered almost two-thirds of materials in 1952 (Dow, 1964). Allocation systems were organized with the help of existing trade associations; they were often under the barest nominal control of central departments of State; and materials shares were devised usually on the basis of what different firms had used before the war. There were also more informal controls over investment in plant and machinery and vehicles, particularly with respect to the division of sales between home and export markets in the engineering industry.

The history of structural change in the 1950s and 1960s may best be understood as a shaking loose from the circumstances of wartime and post-war controls. The abandonment of controls and the introduction of pro-competitive policies, leading to the abolition of restrictive agreements between members of trade associations, was designed to promote two kinds of change. First, the more efficient firms could grow at the expense of less efficient concerns. Second, as the intensification of the competitive process proved too fierce for some market participants they could either succumb and exit, or be acquired by successful companies.

The general trends in industrial structure discussed above may be illustrated with some data. Table 11.2 assembles a variety of sources on industry and market concentration over the last half century. As might be expected from the foregoing discussion, the average level of industrial concentration in the 1930s was relatively low—for the 42 broad industries covered in column 1 five-firm employment concentration cannot have been higher than about 44 per cent (assuming, improbably, equal shares for the three firms sharing 26.3 per cent of employment in 1935) and was, very likely, in the range 30–40 per cent. The notion of an industry, however, was fairly remote from that of a market and would usually include several principal products which might be more highly concentrated. Even so, the 1935 Census of Production covered returns from almost 10,000 firms with employees of 100 or more (see Table 11.1 above). Leak and Maizels (1945) convey an impression of UK industry divided into roughly three sectors. First, a collection of monopolies or near-monopolies, responsible for less than one-tenth of net output in 1935; this group contained such exotica as hair clippers, plumbago crucibles, cream of tartar, rubber accelerators, tennis balls (uncovered), parachutes, and guano. Second, a group of fairly concentrated trades in the modern sector of industry such as rayon, dyestuffs, rubber tyres, photographic apparatus, electrical wires, and motor cars, where three-firm employment concentration lay between about 50 and 85 per cent (contributing some two-fifths of manufacturing net output in 1935). Third, there was the vast bulk of industry in the older trades of iron and steel, shipbuilding, cotton, wool, brewing, furniture, leather, clothing, building, and so on, where three-firm employment concentration was less than one-third and in many cases was under 10 per cent.

This broad structural picture changed hardly at all in wartime and, again, concentration only increased slowly during the 1950s. Evely and Little (1960) described the early 1950s structure of industry in terms similar to those employed by Leak and Maizels for 1935. Trades which could be thought of as virtually monopolistic accounted for barely more than 10 per cent of employment; those possessing an 'essentially competitive' structure accounted for a quarter of employment; and over three-fifths of total employment was provided by trades that were 'betwixt and between'. There seems to have been a break in the mid-1950s, or near the end of the 1950s, and which continued throughout the 1960s, whereby a substantial restructuring of product markets took place, resulting in increased average levels of concentration. As P. E. Hart and Clarke (1980) observe, this sustained increase must be attributed to the average tendency for all industries to increase concentration, rather than to a tendency whereby high concentration trades grew relatively to low concentration trades. However, after 1970–5 the increase in concentration was on average very minor and the typical market during the later 1970s and early 1980s seems, if anything, to have experienced a decline in concentration. These trends are somewhat altered if competition from imports is allowed for (cols. 4 and 7 of Table 11.2). Adjustments which assume that all of imports are competitive with domestic products, and are not in any way controlled by the leading firms, indicate that the rate of market concentration increase started to falter in the late 1960s rather than the early 1970s.

It must be stressed that Table 11.2 shows average levels of concentration. Many product markets particularly in the leather goods, furniture, and clothing industries are very much more fragmented with five-firm concentration ratios of below 20 per

TABLE 11.2. *Changes in industrial and market concentration
in the UK 1935–1983*
(%)

| Year | (1) | (2) | (3) | (4) | (5) | (6) | (7) |
|------|-----|-----|-----|-----|-----|-----|-----|
| 1935 | 26.3 |      |      |      |      |      |      |
| 1951 | 29.3 |      |      |      |      |      |      |
| 1958 | 32.4 | 55.4 | 56.5 | 52.3 |      |      |      |
| 1963 | 37.4 | 58.6 | 60.1 | 55.4 |      |      |      |
| 1968 | 41.0 | 63.4 | 64.8 | 58.8 |      |      |      |
| 1970 |      |      |      |      | 46.2 |      |      |
| 1975 |      |      | 65.0 | 56.4 | 47.9 |      |      |
| 1977 |      |      | 64.8 | 54.8 |      |      |      |
| 1979 |      |      |      |      | 46.8 | 52.1 | 41.8 |
| 1981 |      |      |      |      |      | 51.5 | 40.8 |
| 1983 |      |      |      |      |      | 50.6 | 39.0 |

*Notes*:  (1) Average, unweighted 3-firm employment concentration ratios for 3-digit
industries (N = 42).
  (2) Average, unweighted 5-firm sales concentration ratios for 4-digit industries
(N = 144).
  (3) Average, unweighted 5-firm sales concentration ratios for 4-digit industries
(N = 121).
  (4) Column (3) adjusted for imports (assumed not to be controlled by the top five
firms).
  (5) Average, unweighted 5-firm gross output concentration ratios for 3-digit
industries (N = 93).
  (6) Average, unweighted 5-firm gross output concentration ratios for 3-digit
industries (N = 199).
  (7) Column (6) adjusted for imports.

*Sources*:  R. Clarke (1985), cols. 1–2; Utton and Morgan (1983), cols. 3–4; Mann and
Scholefield (1986), cols. 5–7.

cent. Conversely, there is a significant group of product markets with five-firm
concentration ratios in excess of 90 per cent; in many of these there are only one or
two significant producers and high concentration has persisted over several decades
(Evely and Little, 1960; Walshe, 1974; R. Clarke, 1985): for example, sugar
refining, gin and whisky distilling, cigarettes, cans and metal boxes, cement, cars
and certain car component markets, aircraft and airframes, and several product
markets in the chemical industry. Thus there is a fair degree of dispersion around
the 'typical' product market in which five leading firms share 50–60 per cent of
domestic sales.

### (ii) *Plant and Aggregate Concentration*

Markets and industries are an obvious central focus for our discussion; however,
the more markets approximate to monopoly conditions the more that interest must
by definition shift to the firm rather than the market, as a resource allocator.
Moreover, to the extent that a great number of individual firms diversify into two
or more product markets, and obtain large absolute size, it is appropriate to assess
them in relation to the aggregate of all markets rather than each market singly.

Their very size, as well as their residence in a number of unrelated product markets, excites questions about the implications for efficiency and the competitive process. For example, does their large size render them subject to decreasing returns to scale? Do they restrict output below socially optimal levels? Have these giant firms invented a new competitive process, a struggle for corporate control, while soft-pedalling on traditional product market rivalries? (Utton, 1982). Should the internal capital market of these firms now be the central concern of industrial organization studies? How exactly do they organize themselves internally: by product markets. or by functions such as marketing, production, finance, and research?

To appreciate the force of these questions requires a statistical framework. Table 11.3 sets out the few facts we have about aggregate and plant concentration. They convey a striking impression of rapid advance in aggregate concentration, defined as the share of the hundred largest enterprises in manufacturing net output—which roughly doubled over the half century before 1970, and almost complete constancy in plant concentration over a similar period. After 1970 aggregate concentration in manufacturing promised briefly to continue the upward trend established in the 1950s and 1960s but has, in the event, stabilized at little more than the level

TABLE 11.3. *Trends in aggregate and plant concentration* (%)

| Year | (1) | (2) | (3) |
|------|------|------|------|
| 1909 | 16 | | |
| 1924 | 22 | | |
| 1930 | | 10.8 | |
| 1935 | 24 | 11.2 | |
| 1948 | | 9.0 | |
| 1949 | 22 | | |
| 1951 | | 9.4 | |
| 1953 | 27 | | |
| 1954 | | 10.1 | |
| 1958 | 32 | 10.5 | |
| 1963 | 37 | 11.1 | |
| 1968 | 41 | 10.8 | |
| 1970 | 40/41 | | 39.8 |
| 1974 | | | 42.2 |
| 1978 | | | 41.1 |
| 1982 | | | 41.1 |

*Notes:* (1) Share of the hundred largest enterprises in manufacturing net output, UK. Early years are approximations; upper figure for 1970 includes steel and lower excludes it.
(2) Share of the hundred largest manufacturing establishments in net output, UK. The figure for 1930 is an approximation; that for 1958 is based on sales rather than net output.
(3) Share of the hundred largest enterprises in manufacturing net output; UK.

*Sources:* Prais (1976); Mann and Scholefield (1986).

achieved in 1968. Hughes and Kumar (1984), who measure aggregate concentration in both the financial and manufacturing sectors, agree with this finding although they place the concentration plateau in the middle rather than the early 1970s.


(iii) *A Summary*

A reasonably clear picture has emerged. The earlier decades of the century were relatively uneventful in terms of ownership concentration. There were spasmodic bursts of merger activity, which established a sizeable handful of long-standing monopolies and near-monopolies. But the pre-1939 industrial scene was most notable for the degree of explicit and covert collusion on price and output policies by legally separate enterprises. Hence, neither market nor aggregate (and certainly not plant) concentration increased remarkably. Wartime controls helped to ossify the industrial structure and may even have reduced aggregate concentration by bringing into play the greater adaptability of small firms in a period of capital starvation (Prais, 1976).[1] The 1950s and 1960s saw a rapid and sustained increase in ownership concentration both in individual markets and in the aggregate of markets. From the standpoint of the mid-1980s those two decades appear to show the economy in a state of disequilibrium as it lurched away from a structure based on minimum rivalry and sought a structure adapted to the rigours of domestic and international competition. By the mid-1970s this process had been worked through and stability was restored. Henceforth the structure changed only minimally, the most striking features being a further slight reduction in market concentration as import competition grew in importance; and a decrease in aggregate concentration in the private sector as the more concentrated manufacturing sector declined relative to the less concentrated services sector. In addition, one or two of the top one hundred enterprises disappeared each year with merger activity;[2] and as medium-sized concerns grew they occasionally forced their way into prominence.

[1] Hannah and Kay (1977) and Hannah (1983) tell a rather different story. They perceive quite dramatic increases in concentration during the 1920s mainly owing to merger activity, and an equally steep decline in concentration over 1930–48. This latter trend is said to have returned concentration roughly to the level of 1919 and was supposedly the result of rapid internal growth by medium-sized concerns. However, P. E. Hart (1979) has argued that the measure of concentration used by Hannah and Kay, based on stock market valuations of the surviving publicly quoted companies, leads to serious bias in their findings. On balance, the picture of mild concentration increase in the inter-war period, with virtual stability during wartime, is the one preferred here.

[2] Hannah (1983) has an interesting table showing what happened to the top 100 manufacturing firms at various dates throughout the century. There was a tendency for the number of firms leaving the top 100 to decline as the decades proceeded.

|  | Survived in top 100 | Acquired by another in top 100 | Exit to lower rank |
|---|---|---|---|
| Top 100: 1919 by 1930 | 52 | 17 | 31 |
| Top 100: 1930 by 1948 | 71 | 5 | 24 |
| Top 100: 1948 by 1957 | 71 | 3 | 26 |
| Top 100: 1957 by 1969 | 68 | 22 | 10 |

Some products, unheard of in the 1950s, had swiftly assumed significance (video recorders, word processors), while others had withered on the vine (incandescent gas mantles). But these were just evidence of normal turnover in products and enterprises; the structure had either reached a state of equilibrium, or was marking time before another precipitate leap in a direction yet to be determined.

## Explaining Structural Change

The profound change in industrial organization during the 1955–75 period deserves a fuller discussion. In particular, what precisely accounted for the rapid and sustained increase in concentration? There are two main approaches to the explanation of structural change in industry. First, there is a purely statistical approach whereby the growth in concentration, whether it be product or aggregate concentration, is divided up between internal and external growth. Thus, firms may either grow by the transfer mechanism of internal expansion, displacing less efficient firms, responding most readily to new tastes, and installing new processes more rapidly than their competitors. Or, alternatively, firms may grow by acquiring other going concerns, either voluntarily or after a protracted fight to the death. External growth is highly visible; whereas internal growth, which may be caused by random variations in the growth rates of firms, is less spectacular but no less real. Second, structural change may be explained by looking behind the statistical story at the real economic factors promoting increased concentration. This approach asks why firms have sought larger absolute or relative market size. Were there powerful economic forces making for the structural changes witnessed in the 1950s and 1960s, or were they mere happenstance? We will review the literature on each of these approaches in turn.

## (i) *External and Internal Growth*

The measurement of the contribution of mergers to observed increases in concentration is fraught with difficulties (Hannah and Kay, 1977). Thus, the studies reported in Table 11.4 have had to grapple with several methodological problems which a bald listing of results does not expose. However, on the basis of these studies (and others for a non-random selection of high concentration trades: Evely and Little, 1960; Walshe, 1974) it is reasonably clear that mergers and acquisitions played a major role in increasing concentration during the 1950s and 1960s. A cautious observer might propose that at least half of the increase in concentration can safely be attributed to acquisition activity.

That still leaves a substantial residual change in concentration to be explained by internal growth, that is, the differential rates of growth experienced by market incumbents without the benefit of acquisitions. Concentration may increase when large firms grow internally, on average, more rapidly than small firms; but it is also possible to show that, even if firms of all sizes have the same average expectation of internal growth, concentration can increase over time. Table 11.5 sets out an example of such a process. The assumption employed is that the chances of growing, remaining at the same size, or declining, are independent of the size of

TABLE 11.4. *Some studies of the contribution of mergers to concentration increases*

| | Aaronovitch & Sawyer (1975) | Hart, Utton & Walshe (1973) | Hart & Clarke (1980) | Hannah & Kay (1977) | Hannah & Kay (1977) | Utton (1971) | Hannah & Kay (1977) | Prais (1980) |
|---|---|---|---|---|---|---|---|---|
| | (1) | (2) | (3) | (4) | (5) | (6) | (7) | (8) |
| Time period Coverage | 1958–67 Large quoted firms in manufacturing and distribution | 1958–63 Random sample of 30 manufacturing industries | 1958–68 Random sample of 27 products | 1957–69 Manufacturing companies | 1969–73 Manufacturing companies | 1954–65 Large companies | 1919–30 Manufacturing companies | 1950–72 Manufacturing companies |
| Percentage of concentration increase attributed to merger | 62% | One third of industries were *merger intensive* and over four-fifths of CR5 increase could be attributed to those industries. | 14 out of 27 products were *merger intensive*. Mergers responsible for about half of the average increase in product concentration. | Between 103% and 127% depending upon measure used. [a] | Concentration did not change. Acquisitions may have had small effect on concentration. in the absence of other changes. | From two-fifths to one half of increase in concentration. | Between 68% and 88% depending upon the measure used. | Mergers probably accounted for a third to a half of rise in aggregate concentration since the 1950s. |

[a] Concentration would have declined in the absence of acquisitions.

*Notes:* The separate studies used several different measures of concentration; for full details consult the sources. See also Curry and George (1983) for an extended summary of studies.

*Sources:* Sawyer (1985); Hannah & Kay (1981); Prais (1980).

TABLE 11.5. *An illustration of the effect of dispersion of growth rates on the size distribution of firms*

| Period | Size of firm | | | | | | | | |
|---|---|---|---|---|---|---|---|---|---|
|  | 1 | 2 | 4 | 8 | 16 | 32 | 64 | 128 | 256 |
| 0 |  |  |  |  | 81 |  |  |  |  |
| 1 |  |  |  | 27 | 27 | 27 |  |  |  |
| 2 |  |  | 9 | 18 | 27 | 18 | 9 |  |  |
| 3 |  | 3 | 9 | 18 | 21 | 18 | 9 | 3 |  |
| 4 | 1 | 4 | 10 | 16 | 19 | 16 | 10 | 4 | 1 |

*Note*: I am indebted to Mr Sawyer for permission to use this example.
*Source*: Sawyer (1985).

firm. It is thus assumed that all firms have an equal chance of the same proportionate growth but that, in the event, one-third decline by 50 per cent in the subsequent period, one-third remain the same size, and one-third grow by 100 per cent. Consequently, the distribution of firm sizes gradually disperses until in time period 4 a fairly skewed distribution of firm size is obtained. The 5-firm concentration ratio (CR5: the share of sales produced by the largest five firms) for time period 0 is 6.2 per cent, while at the end of period 4 the CR5 is 32 per cent. As Sawyer observes of this example:

In this process large firms grow at the same average rate as small firms, and that would leave the share of the originally large firms constant. But some small firms overtake previously large firms, boosting the share of the large firms when the group of large firms is reconstituted to include the faster-growing former small firms and exclude the slow-growing formerly large firms.

This tendency for concentration to increase purely because of random variations in growth rates between firms has been labelled 'spontaneous drift' (Prais, 1976). A model of spontaneous drift can be shown on reasonable assumptions to generate a theoretical increase in the share of the 100 largest enterprises in manufacturing net output, which approximately coincides with the actual series shown in col. 1 of Table 3 (Prais, 1976). Therefore, it is possible to be fairly sceptical about studies showing a significant contribution by mergers to concentration increases in the UK, and no little controversy has raged around the various findings on offer (Hart, 1981; Hannah and Kay, 1981). From our point of view it is interesting to reflect that the stability of concentration measures over the 1970s and 1980s probably owes something to a tendency for smaller firms to grow systematically faster than larger firms in the size distribution.

### (ii) *Motives for Growth*

The ultimate objectives of firms seeking larger relative size may be thought of as the real factors driving structural change. First, firms may have sought to obtain scale economies at the plant level, based on the division of labour and indivisibilities in the operation of machines. This may have resulted in the building of plants which were very large in relation to the size of national markets (Utton, 1970). Because national markets vary in size (so that a plant supplying 75 per cent of the UK washing-machine market might, for example, satisfy less than 5 per cent of the US market) it should be possible to compare the rank orderings of industry by concentration level in different countries to test for the importance of scale economies. George and Ward (1975) have examined this possibility in a comparison of the UK with the US and a number of European countries. They found that: '. . . the concentration ranking of industries tends to be similar in both countries' (the UK and the US) while in addition, '. . . the ranking of industries by concentration level tends to be similar in a number of countries'. It is interesting to contrast this finding with an attempt to summarize the literature on estimates of minimum efficient plant scale (Department of Prices and Consumer Protection, 1979). This showed that in the 45 markets for which estimates were possible, minimum efficient size could be obtained with a plant producing less than 10 per cent of market sales in 19 cases (over two-fifths of the sample). In less than one-fifth of cases (including turbo generators, tractors, cars, and aircraft) was a market share in excess of 50 per cent required to obtain minimum efficient plant size.

Second, scale economies at the level of the firm, or multi-plant economies, may be important. As Prais (1976) has argued, there is little force in the plant scale hypothesis as a major explanation for increasing aggregate concentration because the 100 largest plants in the UK have been responsible for a virtually static share of total output (see Table 11.3 above). However, the 100 largest UK firms in 1972 owned an average of 72 plants each and those plants on average employed only 430 persons (Prais, 1976). The largest firms may have gained economies from multi-plant working of several kinds:

- large multi-unit firms can employ expensive management specialists and spread those costs, and the costs of other overhead items, over many operations;
- large firms may reap financial economies from superior bargaining strength when purchasing materials;
- firms in heavy transport cost industries can economize on those costs by building several plants of small size.

As Utton observes (1970) empirical assessments of the importance of these factors are few and unconvincing. Prais (1976) regards the transport cost factor as being of mild significance in the UK context; and the other marketing factors are not thought to have contributed much to the increase in aggregate concentration over 1909–72.

Third, there was Galbraith's (1952) view that only large, oligopolistic firms had the resources and incentive to invest in and exploit the research-intensive technologies of the twentieth century. This view received little empirical support in the UK context. The early work of Jewkes et al. (1958) on the sources of 60 modern inventions concluded that firms in a competitive environment were just as likely to introduce new products and processes as those in heavily concentrated industrial sectors. More recent and comprehensive research by Pavitt et al. (1987), found that although firms with less than 1,000 employees accounted for only 3.3 per cent of research and development spending in 1975 they were, nevertheless, responsible for 34.9 per cent of identified significant innovations between 1970 and 1979. We shall return to this theme below in discussing the possible welfare effects of increasing oligopolization.

Fourth, Kay and King (1978) and Prais (1976) have stressed that financial factors promoted increases in aggregate concentration. For example, financial intermediaries such as pension funds and insurance institutions held a majority share of the equity in UK quoted companies. These intermediaries chose to deal mainly in large blocks of shares issued by larger companies; that tended in turn to create conditions of favourable access to finance for the larger companies.[3] Prais was also alert to the significance of the divorce of management from control. The median holding by the board of directors of the 100 largest manufacturing companies was only one half per cent of their ordinary voting capital at the time Prais wrote:

The precariousness of control that is a feature of the present system makes it more vulnerable to take-over operations . . . The process has therefore to some extent become cumulatively reinforcing (a greater size of company leads to lower boardroom ownership, which leads to precarious control, which leads to take-overs, which lead to even larger companies . . .) and that is partly why merger activity has accelerated in the last two decades. (Prais, 1976).

Fifth, one of the real factors behind observed structural change in industry was the desire to establish control over market output, investment, and prices. This motive may have been particularly strong after the break up of wartime and post-war cartels based on trade associations. As wartime cartels were formally abandoned in the 1950s and 1960s under the impact of competition policy (see below) the leading concerns in each industry may have sought to re-establish control either by informally continuing to regulate price and output—for example, by means of information agreements—or, where competition threatened to become established, by selective acquisition of rival capacity. While this proposition may be an interesting one to subject to empirical testing, observers have been aware that acquisition of rivals need not have been the only strategic response to the new competitive climate. As Allen noted: 'It has been said that minimum price agreements are giving place to an exchange of actual prices, quota schemes to arrangements to notify turnover, contract allocation to "bid filing", and collective price maintenance to an exchange of list prices. None of these new devices is registrable, under the 1956 Act, although they may well have powerful effects on competition and prices' (Allen, 1966, p. 75).

One study (O'Brien et al., 1979) attempted to examine the impact of competition policy on the rate of acquisition in 27 industries over 1951–72. The period studied therefore covered both the years before the 1956 Restrictive Trade Practices Act, which was instrumental in causing the abandonment of many cartels, and a substantial time after the Act. Six industries were chosen as a control group, unaffected by policy, against which to contrast the rate of acquisition activity (measured in two ways: the ratio of expenditure on acquisitions to total assets, and the proportion of firms in an industry acquiring or being acquired) observed in the remaining policy-affected industries. The authors found that the control group (chemicals, construction, hotels, brewing, tobacco, machine tools, vehicle distribution, and printing and publishing):

---

[3] Prais mentions the treatment of interest on debentures in company taxation, and low real interest rates on debentures, as two other factors providing an artificial incentive to acquire other going concerns. Low real interest rates on debentures meant that companies could expand company debt, and acquire victim companies, at very little cost. The tax treatment of debenture interest payments, which viewed them as a cost before calculating profit and therefore not subject to corporation tax, encouraged expansion of this kind of company instrument. See Prais (1976), pp. 103–6.

had the highest proportion of both acquirers and acquired firms in all three periods, and since this group contains the industries unaffected by policy there is no sign that competition policy had a significant effect in driving firms into merger . . . It was interesting to discover, in addition, that once general trends in the economy had been allowed for, there was no significant change in the expenditure of the three groups affected by competition policy over the period of time covered by our study. The same was true of the acquisition proportions. (O'Brien et al., 1979, p. 140)

It may first be objected that it is simply not possible to construct a suitable control group for the UK: the effect of competition policy on cartel arrangements would have been felt in all industries, so all-pervasive was the change in the competitive climate. Thus, even if the machine tool industry (one of the control group industries) was not directly affected by a Restrictive Trade Practices Court judgement its suppliers and customers would have been. Under such circumstances the industry could not hope to remain isolated from upstream and downstream realignments affecting its ability to negotiate terms and conditions of trade. Second, this research still does not adequately model the desire to monopolize or oligopolize by means of merger. The advent of a new competition policy may have signalled to firms that there was an intensification of the competitive climate. As a result firms may have sought defensive mergers. But a defensive merger would not have been the only strategic response available to firms. For example, they could resort to a variety of covert or non-registrable activities to achieve roughly the same objectives as were obtained before the tightening of competition policy.

Finally, there has been much econometric work seeking to explain levels of concentration and changes in concentration. This work has been lucidly summarized by Curry and George (1983) and will serve to highlight the foregoing discussion. Curry and George reviewed 11 cross-sectional studies on the determinants of levels of concentration using UK and US data. Ten of these studies found that plant scale economies were a significant determinant of concentration. Other factors found to be of some importance were the number of plants per firm (statistically significant in four studies) and initial capital requirements (with the right, positive, sign in four studies). Although the plant scale determinant was always found to be statistically significant, taken alone this factor did not explain much of the observed variation in concentration levels in most of the studies. The same source reported 17 studies on changes in concentration. Thirteen of these found that industry growth was inversely related to concentration change (seven estimates of this effect being statistically significant). But by far the most interesting finding was that concentration change was inversely related to the initial level of concentration; ten studies included this variable in the specification, nine of which discovered an inverse relationship (with eight estimates statistically significant). Although some may dismiss this feature of the results as no more than confirmation of the law of gravity, it may have implications for the formation of government policy on industrial organization. Will all high-concentration product markets, which may loosely be interpreted as oligopolistic, eventually be invaded by new competitors or displaced by new products? If so, should not policy be relatively passive, both in relation to monopolies and tactical attempts to buttress monopoly (that is, mergers)? What if this finding was true in both directions, that is, low concentration trades tended to show high concentration change? Should policy remain vigilant in these instances?

(iii) *A Summary*

Few of the explanations for structural change over the 1950–80 period are very persuasive. We may be reasonably confident that the desire to obtain economies of multi-plant operation, and the desire to acquire large size so as to more readily exploit inventions, were not powerful factors for change. On the other hand, the need to secure large market size in order to achieve minimum efficient scale, and a variety of financial factors, appeared to play a not inconsiderable part in the history of structural change. Finally, a striking feature of the period was the occasionally hectic scramble for rival firms. Whether acquisition activity was prompted by an aggressive desire to exploit market power, or was a purely defensive response to the loss of cartel arrangements, still awaits conclusive research. The immediate task to address is an assessment of the effects of structural change in British industry. As we have suggested above, if high concentration is a transitory phenomenon, competition policy might need to be relatively passive. Moreover, to the extent that structural change brings economic benefits—in the form of incomes growth, technical progressiveness, and an improved allocation of resources—policy may need positively to encourage industry restructuring.

## The Impact of Structural Change

The simplest approach to this assessment is to divide the remarks roughly into two sections: one on the process of structural change, dwelling in particular on the effects which mergers have had on industry; and one on the effects of monopoly and near-monopoly.

(i) *Mergers and Acquisitions*

The disappearance of minor figures from the industrial landscape—Thomas Ramsden's Stone Trough brewery in South Yorkshire, Eccles Caravans, McMichael's televisions, Fulford Trumps animal feeds—has often been the occasion for regret. For example, how can consumers be compensated for the loss of a frothy pint of Stone Trough's Old Ram? This sort of question is unfortunately answered rather imperfectly in appraising the effects of mergers. Table 11.6 sets out some of the available data on the numbers of mergers which have taken place in the last quarter of a century and their economic characteristics. After a period of decline in the mid-1970s the number of acquisitions caught by the Business Monitor series (which excludes financial sector acquisitions) appeared to stabilize at around 400–500 per annum and then accelerated upwards. By the mid-1980s the index of real expenditure had climbed above the previous peaks of activity in 1968 and 1972. To put the sums spent into some kind of perspective, the cash sum paid for acquisitions in 1986 was about 26 per cent of private sector gross domestic fixed capital formation. Table 11.6 is the longest series of reasonably comparable data on merger activity in the post-war period.

However, Hannah (1983) has contrived a useful impression of broad trends over the period 1940–80 by collating several sources, all with different coverages. The

TABLE 11.6. *Merger activity, industrial and commercial companies, UK, 1963–1988*

| Year | Number of aquisitions (1) Number | Index of real amount paid (2) Index | Qualifying merger panel cases (3) Number | Merger panel cases | | |
|------|------|------|------|------|------|------|
| | | | | Horizontal (4) % | Vertical (5) % | Conglomerate (6) % |
| 1963 | 888 | 100 | — | — | — | — |
| 1964 | 940 | 134 | — | — | — | — |
| 1965 | 1000 | 146 | 48 | 84 | 9 | 7 |
| 1966 | 807 | 140 | 63 | 85 | 8 | 7 |
| 1967 | 763 | 216 | 96 | 92 | 4 | 4 |
| 1968 | 946 | 362 | 133 | 91 | 2 | 7 |
| 1969 | 846 | 201 | 126 | 91 | 0 | 9 |
| 1970 | 793 | 238 | 80 | 78 | 0 | 22 |
| 1971 | 884 | 164 | 110 | 66 | 4 | 30 |
| 1972 | 1212 | 357 | 114 | 40 | 10 | 50 |
| 1973 | 1205 | 213 | 134 | 76 | 2 | 22 |
| 1974 | 504 | 141 | 141 | 65 | 2 | 33 |
| 1975 | 315 | 64 | 160 | 77 | 4 | 19 |
| 1976 | 353 | 79 | 163 | 66 | 7 | 27 |
| 1977 | 482 | 117 | 194 | 57 | 11 | 32 |
| 1978 | 567 | 146 | 229 | 67 | 10 | 23 |
| 1979 | 534 | 187 | 257 | 68 | 4 | 28 |
| 1980 | 469 | 155 | 182 | 68 | 1 | 31 |
| 1981 | 452 | 107 | 164 | 71 | 2 | 27 |
| 1982 | 463 | 178 | 190 | 64 | 4 | 32 |
| 1983 | 447 | 150 | 192 | 73 | 1 | 26 |
| 1984 | 568 | 294 | 259 | 79 | 1 | 20 |
| 1985 | 474 | 309 | 192 | 42 | 4 | 54 |
| 1986 | 696 | 475 | 313 | 74 | 1 | 25 |
| 1987 | 1125 | 408 | 321 | 80 | 1 | 19 |
| 1988 | 1224 | 503(e) | 306 | 45 | 1 | 54 |

*Notes:*   (i) Col. (2) is the expenditure on acquisitions, adjusted for changes in the FT 500 Ordinary Share Index, and indexed. The 1988 figure is based on data for the first three quarters.

    (ii) Merger Panel data for 1965 are part year only. The data are the percent value of assets acquired. Merger Panel cases are those caught by the criteria laid down in various competition policy Acts (see below).

    (iii) From 1969 onwards the first two columns' data are based on the financial press; prior to 1969 company accounts were the source employed.

*Sources:*   DTI (1989a); DPCP (1978); OFT (1987); Scouller (1987).

summary picture is presented in Table 11.7. Given that the 1970s data was probably an understatement of the true position (press reports were the data sources rather than, as in the 1960s, company accounts) it is quite clear that the final 20 years of this period saw an exceptional restructuring of industrial ownership.[4]

[4] The number of mergers in the 1960s by far surpasses that estimated by Hannah for any decade after 1880. Only the 1920s spate of mergers, including the joining together of ICI, begins to approach in scale the events of the 1960s. See Hannah (1983), pp. 175–8 for more detailed figures.

TABLE 11.7. *Merger activity, 1940–1980*

|  | Firm exits by merger (number) | Values at 1961 share prices of firm exits (£ millions) | Merger values as proportion of total investment spending (percentage) |
|---|---|---|---|
| 1940–9 | 788 | — | — |
| 1950–9 | 1,867 | 1,507 | 10 |
| 1960–9 | 5,635 | 4,709 | 28 |
| 1970–9 | 3,166 | 2,736 | 12 |

*Source*: Hannah (1980).

Table 11.6 shows that much of the merger activity screened by the Mergers Panel[5] has sought to extend market control. There are isolated years when the proportion of asset values acquired in conglomerate mergers rises to about half of the cases screened (1972 and 1985) but, on the whole, about two-thirds to three-quarters of the asset values were acquired in horizontal mergers. Merger Panel cases were never more than half the number of mergers in the Business Monitor series and usually very much less than half. Hughes's (1989) verdict on the available merger data was: 'horizontal activity has remained the dominant form even though its position has slipped compared with the peak years of the late 1960s and early 1970s.'

A broad impression of the consequences of merger activity for changes in the structure of industry has already been obtained (see above, Table 11.4). The consequences for the conduct and performance of industry depend to a considerable extent upon the motives for merger. In view of the discussion above it is clearly possible that many mergers were sought in order to extend control over market decisions on prices and outputs. Cowling (1982) is fairly unequivocal that, in most of the industries he researched, mergers were primarily sought with monopolization in view. Scouller (1987) has taken a broader view of merger motives: mergers may have been sought for efficiency reasons, but the sheer diversity of probable motives is likely to confound the search for a link between acquisitions and improved economic performance.

Business historians have analysed this problem in the following way: if mergers created technical opportunities to expand plant or firm size and obtain scale economies then, *ceteris paribus*, costs should have declined and profits increased. A larger market share will also have ensured that more of the gains from innovation accrued to the firm and, therefore, there will have been greater incentives to invest in research. In general, the greater the market share and larger the absolute size of firm the smaller the risk which would arise from the actions of competitors; hence, firms would be more willing to take on the risks inherent in new products and processes. Thus, a range of static and dynamic efficiency benefits should have

[5] The Mergers Panel, which is convened and chaired by the Office of Fair Trading, is an interdepartmental body of officials which screens merger candidates. It takes papers, prepared for it by an OFT secretariat, which set out the competition (and other issues) which appear to be raised by a merger bid. Information may be sought from raider and victim companies in compiling the facts of each case. The Mergers Panel feeds the results of its deliberations to the Director General of the OFT, who then advises the Secretary of State for Trade and Industry on the grounds for and against referring a merger to the Monopolies and Mergers Commission.

showed up either in profit margins or the revenues generated from the firm's risk capital—both of which changes should be reflected in the rate of profit on net assets employed. Meeks and Meeks (1981) have shown that all of the accounting measures usually employed to assess the effects of mergers on performance—the profit/sales margin, the rate of return on equity, and the rate of return on net assets—are biased in various ways, some of which can be allowed for in empirical work. Perhaps the most serious from our point of view is that all the measures designed to elicit information about efficiency benefits will be biased upwards to the extent that they reflect post-merger changes in bargaining or market power. In a way this is a helpful bias: if it is discovered that mergers have not, by and large, led to improved performance then, given that the measures are biased upwards, we may be quite confident that mergers actually entailed a deterioration in performance.

The impact of merger activity on individual British industries may only be glimpsed here. Industries such as brewing were radically altered. There were about 700 brewers active in 1945 and 358 breweries (owned by 247 firms) still operated in 1960. In the 11 years after 1960 about 150 companies ceased to trade as a result of mergers and takeovers, and 147 breweries were closed down. Further takeovers and closures followed until, in 1975, there were only 155 breweries owned by 87 firms. The market share of the seven national companies meanwhile increased from 45 per cent in 1960 to approximately 80 per cent in 1975 (Dunn, 1979). Scores of local brews have disappeared as the national concerns used capacity at their large-scale breweries to service newly acquired tied public houses. On the other hand, the efficiency gains arising from rationalization in brewing were extremely modest (Cowling et al., 1980). By the early 1980s the British brewing industry had become heavily concentrated and had invested in relatively large plants. The median size of British brewery was about the same as that in US industry; but productivity, measured in terms of beer produced per employee, was only about one-quarter to one-third of the level obtaining in the US (Prais, 1981).

Table 11.8 displays the findings of several aggregate studies of merger efficiency benefits. Only one of these (Cowling et al., 1980) sought to measure efficiency benefits by other than accounting data, and Sturgess and Wheale (1984) are the sole representative of a large literature which measures merger effects using stock market and dividend data.[6] If it is accepted that the Table 11.8 studies are a fair representation of the research in this field, then it is quite clear that rational stock market operators ought to have regarded merger intensive companies as poor investments; for the evidence on pure efficiency gains arising from merger was, to say the least, discouraging. Only one of the eight studies cited offers comfort to those who believe that mergers have had desirable efficiency consequences.

However, there are four qualifications to append to this view. First, some mergers may have been undertaken precisely because there was a period of poor profitability ahead (Prais, 1980). Second, Prais has observed (1980, p. xvii):

---

[6] Those interested in this approach may consult Chiplin and Wright (1987) for a review of UK studies. Franks et al. (1988) have performed the most exhaustive work on share price data over 1955–85. They looked at share prices two years after a merger (rather than restricting their research, as has usually been the case, to price effects around the time of the merger) and found that for cash-paying raiders shares appreciated as fast (no faster) as before the merger; for equity-paying raiders shares underperformed by 9 per cent on the same measure. With all the admitted faults of accounting ratio research, as reported in the text, there is little in this share price research which merits an altered conclusion.

TABLE 11.8. *Some studies of post-merger performance*

| Author | Period | Findings |
|---|---|---|
| Newbould (1970) | 1967–8 | Surveyed 38 public companies: after 2 years 17 companies reported no benefits and for 21 no further benefits anticipated within 5 years. |
| Singh (1971) | 1955–60 | Compared ROCE (adjusted for industry change) pre and post-merger in sample of 77 firms. Profitability fell in over half cases left in sample in each of 3 post-merger years. |
| Utton (1974) | 1961–70 | 39 intensive acquirer's ROCE over 1966–70 compared to industry ROCE and ROCE of control group of internal growers over 1961–70. Over half acquirer's ROCE fell relative to industry in 1966 and 1967 and acquirer's ROCE consistently inferior to internal growers in the 1960s. |
| Meeks (1977) | 1964–72 | 213 acquiring companies pre-merger ROCE compared to merger year and 7 post-merger year's ROCE (all data standardized for average industry profitability): profitability declined in all 7 post-merger years. |
| Cowling *et al.* (1980) | 1965–75 | Total factor productivity measures and other data employed to assess merger activity: 'Efficiency gains from mergers are in general not found' and: 'In many cases efficiency has not improved, in some cases it has improved but no faster than one would have expected in the absence of merger.' |
| Cosh *et al.* (1980) | 1967–9 | Total acquisitions in public quoted sector (290) with 137 horizontal. Both control group and merging firms profitability fell 3 and 5 years after merger, but merging group's profitability fell by 1.5% less; results not statistically significant. |
| Kumar (1984) | 1967–9 | 354 mergers surveyed: 'Since, in general, profitability declined after merger, even under the assumption of unchanged monopoly power, this may be taken to suggest no efficiency gains, and indeed some deterioration.' |
| Sturgess & Wheale (1984) | 1961–70 | Reworked Utton's (1974) sample in terms of annual shareholder return:price change plus dividend for internal versus external growers. For 1966–70 found that internal growers' return exceeded external growers' return in 3 years out of 5. |

*Note:* ROCE: return on capital employed.

The second difficulty arises from the usually very skewed distribution of business risks: that is, typically there are only a very few large 'winners', but these are large enough to more than offset the very many small 'losers' . . . The various studies that have appeared showing that more than half the firms engaged in mergers have done less well than, for example, the average for their industry are therefore entirely compatible with the possibility that the group of mergers as a whole yielded a positive return.

Third, it may be that conglomerate mergers, which appeared to be increasing in importance throughout the period, provided better opportunities to exploit firm-specific skills of the acquirer. But it has to be observed that none of the studies in Table 11.7 which attempted to assess benefits from diversification mergers obtained encouraging results. Fourth, Cowling (1982) took the interesting long-term view that efficiency losses from the merger movement resulted from post-merger managerial chaos and the inflation of middle management overheads in loosely structured giant concerns. The post-merger problems of asserting managerial authority and retrieving profitability were compounded by outmoded Unitary-form managerial structures (where the combined company would have one production operation, one marketing function, one finance function, and so on) with each company function fighting its corner in capital allocation decisions. As many of these enterprises have now adopted Multi-divisional form structures, where capital allocation decisions have been centralized in one headquarters organization, it is conceivable that firms have re-established control over profit flows within the organization. Two studies, one by Cable and Steer (1978) in the UK, which showed that the adoption of optimal organizational form made a positive difference of 6–9 per cent in profitability, and one by Teece (1981) in the US have lent considerable statistical support to Cowling's view. But it must be conceded that, whatever the support for this longer-term narrative, in the short to medium-term there is much evidence that mergers have contributed to a deterioration in industrial efficiency.[7]

## (ii) *Monopolization*

Research on the effects of monopolization has aimed to elicit the static and dynamic efficiency benefits, if any, arising from concentrated industrial structures. That research suffers from an evident shortcoming: have accounting measures of efficiency assessed the superior efficiency of monopolists, or have they measured the monopolist's ability to exploit market power? There is a burgeoning literature which takes the latter view and attempts empirical quantification of the social costs of monopoly. The essence of the work in this field may be seen by referring to Fig. 11.1. It was supposed that initially firms were in a competitive equilibrium with constant costs. Price was set equal to marginal cost: so price was set at $F$ and the industry produced output quantity $B$. Then, a few firms colluded or one firm achieved monopoly power, perhaps after a costly struggle with bankrupted or peripheralized competitors. One view, associated initially with Harberger (1954), was that price increased to, say, $G$ and quantity fell to $D$. Price rose to $G$ rather than profit-maximising $H$ presumably because of imperfect collusion or the threat of new entry. The industry now made monopoly profits of $GDEF$ providing costs

---

[7] The picture in the USA is very similar. For a recent review of evidence see Ravenscroft and Scherer (1988).

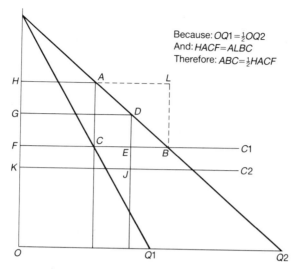

FIG. 11.1. *Exemplifying monopoly welfare loss*

did not change. *BE* was no longer produced even though consumers were willing to cover the costs of producing *BE*. Thus, *DBE* was the familiar welfare loss triangle representing a complete write-off in welfare terms since nobody, not even the monopolist, obtained benefit from the misallocation of resources implied. It might have been possible to set off against *DBE* welfare gains of the order of *FEJK* if it were possible, as a result of monopolization, to obtain plant or multi-plant economies of scale equal to $C_1 - C_2$. But such gains were not inevitable. Indeed, monopoly may have induced management sloth and costs may have risen, eating away at *GDEF*.

An alternative view (Cowling *et al.*, 1980) was that *DBE* substantially understated the welfare loss from monopolization: to assume that prices only increased to *G* under monopoly was to assume away the exercise of monopoly power. The standard profit-maximization postulate determined that price and quantity would be set where marginal cost equalled marginal revenue. Since the marginal revenue schedule exactly bisects the area under the demand curve the monopolist could exercise market power and produce output *A* at a price of *H* making profits of *HACF*. The welfare loss triangle was thus equal to *ABC* which could be deduced to be precisely half of *HACF*. Moreover, it was possible to go further than this and suppose that part of actual costs would be expenditure intended to sustain the monopoly position, such as advertising expenditure, and these costs were in fact an additional welfare loss. It was arguable that the 'battle' costs incurred by those firms who lost out in the struggle to become the monopolist should be added in to the calculation of welfare loss.

Using the Harberger assumptions for the top 103 firms in the UK in 1968/9 Cowling obtained estimated welfare losses equal to less than half of 1 per cent of the gross corporate product of those firms. When the assumption was employed that monopolists fully exercised their market power, which Cowling recognized to be an 'upper bound' assumption, welfare losses were estimated to range from

4–7 per cent of gross corporate product. As these firms were responsible for roughly one-third of GNP in 1968/9, and many firms outside the top 100 may be assumed to have exercised monopoly power, it was clear that losses from the exercise of monopoly power were not trivial.

If the annual welfare losses attributable *in theory* to monopoly may have been such as to compare with the annual rate of per-capita incomes growth in the UK during the post-war period, it is obviously important to establish whether monopolization or high concentration has in fact led to the *exercise* of monopoly power. In practice, the empirical work in this field has sought to determine whether profits—usually in relation to total revenues or value added—were related to various concentration measures. Clarke (1985) has provided a useful summary of the UK research which is partially reproduced here in Table 11.9. Clarke described these results as rather more mixed than similar studies for the US and concluded that 'The available evidence, therefore, does not show a clear pattern in the concentration–profitability relationship, and hence gives no general support for the market concentration doctrine' (Clarke, 1985, p. 112). He also points out that this might be because the UK data is very poor; or it might be because there simply was no general relationship. It is worth remarking, however, before we uncritically accept Clarke's verdict on this research, that the four studies showing a statistically significant effect of concentration on profits all show that the effect was positive. Although many of these studies had problems in matching profits data to industries the data is of the highest quality in the reports of the Monopolies and Mergers Commission (MMC). Utton (1986) used these reports to assess the relationship between monopolization and profits in 49 markets. He disaggregated his sample into three groups: dominant firms, concentrated oligopolies, and loose oligopolies, and expressed the average rate of return earned by firms in these markets relative to the average for quoted manufacturing companies. His results are reported in Table 11.10. They are very persuasive: dominant firms (with more than 50 per cent of a market, where the second ranked firm had a share less than half that of the leader) were able to earn at least twice the industry average rate of profit.

Relatively high rates of profit earned by dominant firms need not solely, or even partly, indicate the exercise of monopoly power—on the contrary, high returns might be regarded as evidence of continuously superior productive and marketing efficiency. That would certainly be the view of, for example, Littlechild (1989) who took a sceptical view of the type of econometric results reported in Table 11.9. First, he believed that when more variables were included to explain profits the explanatory power of the concentration variable declined. His second misgiving was less obvious: the largest firms in almost all industries were more productive than smaller firms in the same industries—so that the Table 11.9 studies merely reveal that high concentration trades typically had more larger firms than low concentration trades. While it would be wrong to dismiss much careful statistical work without equally careful work showing contrary results it is as well that such theoretical qualifications are borne in mind. We shall return to this theme in a later section.

Before concluding this section it may be remarked that the full flavour of monopoly welfare loss is rarely conveyed by data from financial accounts. The reduction of variety in consumption goods has already been noted. Second, the aberrant conduct of monopolists in defending their profits may be surveyed in

TABLE 11.9. *Some studies of the profits–concentration relationship in the UK*

| Author | Period | Concentration | Other statistically significant variables | $\bar{R}^2$ or $R^2$ |
|---|---|---|---|---|
| Shepherd (1972) | 1958–63 | (+) | Market growth; market size | 0.114 |
| Phillips (1972) | 1951 | + | Advertising intensity; plant size (perverse sign) | 0.260 |
| Holtermann (1973) | 1963 | (−) | Capital intensity; advertising instensity; growth; capital expenditure | 0.454 |
| Khalilzadeh-Shirazi (1974) | 1963 | (+) | Capital intensity; plant size; advertising dummy; exports | 0.544 |
| Cowling & Waterson (1976) | 1963–8 | + | None | 0.096 |
| Hart & Morgan (1977) | 1968 | (+) | Capital/labour ratio; advertising intensity | 0.432 |
| Hitiris (1978) | 1963, 1968 | + | Effective protection; capital intensity; growth | 0.380 |
| Lyons (1981) | 1968 | + | Advertising intensity; export intensity; domestic production and intra-industry trade measures | 0.312 |
| Geroski (1981) | 1968 | nonlinear | Advertising intensity; exports; imports; growth | 0.394 |
| R. Clarke (1984) | 1970–6 | (−) | Advertising intensity; capital intensity; growth; sector dummies | 0.655 |

*Notes:* Only selected results are quoted.
( ) denotes *not* significant on 5% one-tail test.

*Source:* adapted from Clarke (1985).

TABLE 11.10. *Relative profitability of leading firms in three types of oligopoly*

| Group | Number of markets | Average market share of leader | Average profit relative |
|---|---|---|---|
| Dominant firm | 19 | 72.9 | 2.03 |
| Concentrated oligopoly | 21 | 39.6 | 1.53 |
| Loose oligopoly | 9 | 26.1 | 1.16 |
| Total | 49 | 50.1 | 1.66 |

*Note*:  The average profit relative is the average rate of return on capital employed relative to the average for quoted manufacturing companies.

*Source*:  Utton (1986).

reports of the MMC. For example, the major ice cream producers have in the past refused to allow competitor products to be stored in refrigerator cabinets supplied to retailers (Monopolies and Mergers Commission, 1979). Such behaviour might be regarded as merely petty. But occasionally rivalry has been more vigorous: for instance, the systematic smashing of competitor dispensing machines, sited in gentlemen's lavatories, in the contraceptive sheaths market (MMC, 1975). Perhaps we had here a case of the 'invisible hand' being shoved aside by the mailed fist.

A summary of the empirical work encountered so far in this section might propose that monopoly power has been exercised in the UK, and that the welfare losses associated with monopolization may have been quite considerable. However, there are two important provisos to set against that finding. First, the research reported has only accounted for the static welfare losses of monopoly; it may be that the gains from monopolization in a ceaselessly growing dynamic economy outweigh the static losses. Second, nothing is forever. High concentration may be a transitory phenomenon: a monopolist in a product market may be supplanted by fresh entrants as competitors are attracted by the substantial profits to be made. Indeed, the decline in average product concentration observed in the UK during the 1980s may be confirmation of this long-term view. We shall consider these two points in the remainder of this section.

The theoretical underpinnings of the proposition that high concentration promotes innovation (Schumpeter, 1942) are that the negligible prospects of price competition reduce risk and permit a longer time horizon for research; that in oligopolistic settings price competition is eschewed but non-price competition swells to fill the vacuum; that a large market share implies a greater gain from a proportionate decrease in costs or increase in revenues; and that market dominance reduces the risk of imitation by competitors. While all of these arguments imply that monopolists have strong incentives to pump resources into research and development (R & D) they do not guarantee a flow of invention in monopolized market settings; nor do they ensure that, once invented, a new product or process will be rapidly adopted, that is, that innovation will occur. The incentives to delay the introduction of a new invention may be quite strong in an uncertain industrial environment; they will be especially strong where the discounted time stream of revenues from a new product are less than those of the existing product. For example, this might explain the lack of enthusiasm in industry for long-life light bulbs.

Much of the evidence on the innovation–concentration relationship is of US origin. Several excellent summaries of the evidence exist (e.g. Kamien and Schwartz, 1982) which tend to suggest that high concentration has not promoted relatively high innovation output. For example, Williamson (1965) found that the share of innovations contributed by the largest four firms appeared to decline as concentration increased (the critical CR4 ratio seemed to be about 50 per cent). A fair overall verdict is that 'The standard hypothesis tested is that R & D activity increased with monopoly power. Little support for the hypothesis has been found. Instead a new hypothesis has emerged that a market structure intermediate between monopoly and perfect competition would promote the highest rate of inventive activity' (Kamien & Schwartz, 1982, pp. 103–4). The UK Review of Monopolies and Mergers Policy (Department of Prices and Consumer Protection, 1978) anticipated this broad conclusion:

No one particular market structure has exclusive claim to be the most conducive environment for innovation: the evidence, although limited, tends toward some perhaps moderate degree of concentration. Taken as a whole it suggests that a variety of firm sizes and market structures provides the best balance between stimulating a flow of research and invention and the subsequent development of this in terms of innovation.

Finally, it may be expected that monopolies 'wither away'. However, there are reasons for suspecting that dominant market positions can persist over long periods of time. First, as Williamson (1972) has argued, some firms establish a market lead through superior management ability, and even when that management has passed on, lesser entrepreneurs find it difficult to mount an attack on the inherited position. Second, the phenomenon of 'spontaneous drift' discussed earlier will place larger firms in control of even larger market shares over time. Third, cost differences, perhaps associated with learning effects, may prove an insuperable entry barrier to new market aspirants. Fourth, single dominant firms more readily perceive the effect of new entry on their market share and therefore react more fiercely to that threat than, say a group of oligopolists, to whom new entry does not pose the same apparent problems. There are obvious counter-arguments to these propositions (Littlechild, 1986): smaller firms have great incentives to capture monopoly profits; the height of entry barriers can be overstated, especially in respect of larger diversifying concerns; and so on. Our view on these competing positions is thus in need of an empirical framework.

Utton (1986) has compiled some evidence on the persistence of UK monopolies over time. His sample of 19 products was biased to the extent that it depended largely on Monopolies and Mergers Commission reports; as this meant that he included mainly markets dominated by single firms he was by definition excluding from the sample markets where significant market share erosion has taken place. Nevertheless, he found that in 12 product markets out of 19 the dominant market share declined over time, and these declines were sustained, in some cases, in the face of attempts by the dominant firm to bolster its share with acquisitions of smaller concerns (Wallpaper Manufacturers, Imperial Group in cigarettes, Blue Circle in cement, and Dunlop in tyres). Only in seven cases did market share increase or remain stable (safety glass, breakfast cereals, flat glass, clutches, plasterboard, cellulosic fibres, and contraceptive sheaths). Market share erosion took some considerable time to occur, 30 or 40 years in most cases; and at the end of the period surveyed, all but six dominant firms still had a share greater than 50 per cent.

Utton's findings may be contrasted with those of Walshe (1974) who surveyed a sample of 35 trades characterized by Evely and Little (1960) as being high concentration trades in 1951. Twenty-five of these trades saw an increase in concentration between 1951 and a variety of dates in the late 1960s; for three trades there had been a decline in concentration and in a further seven cases no change in concentration could be safely surmised. Thus, an interesting joint finding emerges: although in many cases the market position of a single dominant firm may not prove indefinitely durable, it is typically the case that high concentration is maintained over long periods of time. In some cases, such as wallpaper and razors, the change in fortunes of the dominant firm signalled a transition from a near-monopoly to a duopoly. In others, although dominance was eroded this was accompanied by a fall in the total number of firms and a more equal sharing of the market spoils. Thus, it would be reasonable to conclude that although monopoly has shown some tendency to erode over time, this has not been coupled with a significant loosening of overall market structure.

### (iii)  *A Summary*

The effects of high and increasing concentration may, therefore, be summarised in terms of five propositions, here stated without the qualifications arising in the foregoing discussion:

- mergers have not contributed materially to an improvement in industrial performance;
- monopolistic structures have had the potential to impose serious welfare losses on society;
- the evidence suggests that monopoly power was exploited in the UK so that potential welfare losses were to some extent real;
- there was very little evidence to suggest that there was an offset to those losses from the effect of concentrated market structure on technical progressiveness;
- there was some evidence to suggest that monopolies gradually diminished over time, but little to counter the impression that high concentration, once obtained, proved remarkably durable.

The narrative so far has, first, described the industrial structure and changes in that structure over the last half century. Second, an attempt has been made to understand why change has occurred and what might be the broad economic effects of the structural position observed. We turn now to consider government policies devised in response to structural change in industry.

### Competition Policy

Post-war British governments have not had the benefit of all the research reported above when framing their competition policies. This must be recalled when reflecting upon the way in which policy formulation has developed over the period. Events were reacted to in a more or less fire-fighting style, often with considerable delay.

Indeed, lags in the production of policy-making information usually meant that fires could be extinguished, but only after the industrial fabric had been irretrievably damaged. The least peccable administration in this respect was the first post-war government. During wartime considerable debate had taken place about a variety of post-war reconstruction themes, notably the emerging welfare state and commitment to full employment (C. Barnett, 1986). Beveridge (1944) had suggested a largely macroeconomic rationale for an active policy in regard to monopolies and trade associations. The analysis was essentially Keynesian in tracing a path from oligopolization of markets, to exploitation of market power by increasing prices, to excessive cash wage demands, to increasing real wages and, therefore, to declining employment:

The response of industries already strongly organized to the setting up of a high demand for their services might take the form of endeavouring to exploit the demand by raising prices, rather than of meeting demand by increased production. It is essential that a full employment policy should be protected against such risks of exploitation. (Beveridge, 1944, pp. 203–4).

Thus, as Kirby (1984) observed British competition policy had its origins in macroeconomic policy concerning the level of output and employment rather than microeconomic concerns with the allocation of resources between industries. As Fig. 11.1 shows, monopolization theoretically results in too few resources being devoted to monopoly products and, in a world of limited resources, too great a share of resources being devoted to competitively produced outputs. The immediate post-war government could be forgiven for neglecting this theoretical finding as largely irrelevant; after all, a competitively organized industry at that time would have been regarded as an object of singular curiosity.

The concern was felt, however, that the grip of the trade associations on economic affairs was too pervasive: 'It is highly probable that by the end of the nineteen-forties the area covered by monopoly and restrictive practices was larger than before the war, and the power of the organisations had certainly increased. By that time it is likely that restrictive practices of some kind had become characteristic of a very large part, perhaps the greater part, of British industry' (Allen, 1966). Restrictions imposed by trade associations would be designed to limit output and keep up prices; they would also have the effect of slowing down the transfer of output to the most efficient producers, to the detriment of international competitiveness and, ultimately, economic growth. Table 11.11 summarizes the legislative instruments used to control a variety of perceived defects in the organization of UK industry over 1948–80. It is best to organize comment on policy developments under three main headings, namely restrictive practices, mergers, and monopolies.

### (i) Restrictive Practices

When Adam Smith asserted that 'people of the same trade seldom meet together, even for merriment or diversion, but the conversation ends in a conspiracy against the public or in some contrivance to raise prices' (Smith, 1970) he probably had in mind such groups as the coal-mine owners of the Newcastle Vend agreeing on quotas and prices for the London market (Marshall, 1920). He might not have foreseen that 50–60 per cent of manufacturing output would be affected by restrictive agreements in 1956 (Gribbin, 1978), or that over 80 per cent of those agreements

TABLE 11.11. *The development of UK competition policy*

---

1948 *Monopolies and Restrictive Practices (Inquiry and Control) Act*

Establishment of the Monopolies and Restrictive Practices Commission to investigate markets for goods where one-third or more controlled by one firm or a group of firms acting together.

1956 *Restrictive Trade Practices Act*

Agreements between two or more firms to restrict the trade in goods to third parties made *registrable*. Register of Restrictive Agreements administered by a Registrar responsible for referring agreements to Restrictive Practices Court. Court to decide whether or not restriction was against the 'public interest'.

1964 *Resale Prices Act*

*Individual* resale price maintenance unlawful (therefore same as concerted restrictive agreements).

1965 *Monopolies and Mergers Act*

Mergers involving a market share of 33% or more, and/or assets of £5m. or more could be referred to the Monopolies and Mergers Commission (MMC). Commission decides whether or not merger operates against the public interest and recommends accordingly.

1968 *Restrictive Trade Practices Act*

Information agreements (exempt from the 1956 Act) made registrable. Provision for exemption of agreements judged by the Minister to be of national importance.

1973 *Fair Trading Act*

Focal point of policy to be new Office of Fair Trading under control of the Director General of Fair Trading (DGFT) who assumed the duties of the Registrar (of restrictive agreements) and also had (previously Ministerial) power to refer a dominant firm to the MMC. Merger references still ultimately Ministerial. Share of market criterion for merger and dominant firm references reduced from one third to one quarter.

1976 *Restrictive Trade Practices (Services) Order*

Services made subject to competition policy. Consumer Protection Advisory Commitee established which could investigate specific practices (e.g. terms of sale, packaging, debt collection methods).

1980 *Competition Act*

'Anti-competitive Practices' may be referred to the MMC, which decides whether or not practice operates against public interest. Minister may refer public bodies (e.g. nationalised industries, water undertakings) to MMC to assess efficiency, costs, standards of service and possible abuses of market position. MMC to decide whether conduct is against public interest and make recommendations accordingly.

---

contained clauses aimed at maintaining industry price structures and levels (Clarke, 1985).

As Allen (1979) recalled, the official perception of competition policy in the 1940s was far from liberal:

As a temporary civil servant at the Board of Trade during the early 1940s, I recall the shocked surprise with which most of the older permanent officials greeted the initial proposals of the enthusiasts who held that Britain's future industrial efficiency depended on restraining monopolistic practices. It was, of course, natural that they should cast a cold eye on the proposals, since many of them had been actively engaged before the war in promoting cartelisation of the staple industries.

In fact, government waited until 1956 to introduce general competition legislation even though the extent of collusive agreements in British industry was known during wartime. It has to be supposed that the authorities needed the clinching evidence of the 17 reports of the Monopolies and Restrictive Practices Commission produced between 1948 and 1956 before they would act to make restrictive practices illegal. Those reports demonstrated that practices such as exclusive dealing arrangements, quota schemes, and the collective enforcement of resale price maintenance were widespread in British industry. However, such practices were not, even then, made illegal by the 1956 Act. Agreements were made registrable and, after registration, were the subject of a court case where a judge and two lay people pronounced on whether or not the practices contained in the agreement were against the 'public interest'. A judicial cost-benefit appraisal of the detriments and benefits of an agreement was debated in open court with the defendants appealing to seven specific 'gateways' (such as protection from injury, or employment benefits). The defendants also had to show that, on balance, the agreement was in the public interest. Thus, essentially, the tribunal-like proceedings of the Commission were superseded by a formal court procedure with the important practical difference that, as court precedent was being established, other registered agreements waiting to be heard might be adversely affected.

That is what effectively happened. Seven of the first eight cases heard were 'struck down'; that is, made illegal. When it became apparent in the Yarn Spinners Agreement that the unemployment protection 'gateway' was not likely to prove successful a great many firms abandoned all hope of winning a defended case and decided to abolish or vary their agreements (Stevens and Yamey, 1965). Consequently, by 1966 83 per cent of 2,550 registered agreements had been varied or discontinued with relatively few court cases having been decided. By 1978 the court had had 487 goods agreements referred to it, but 436 of these had not been defended; of the remaining 51 cases defended by firms only 12 had been upheld and 39 had been struck down by court order (DPCP, 1979).

The court procedure was a fairly costly method of establishing whether such a small proportion of agreements ought to be allowed to continue. It was perhaps for this reason that subsequent restrictive practices legislation, including the 1968 and 1976 Acts, contained devices whereby not all registrable agreements needed to go through an expensive court procedure. The 1968 Act, which was designed to screen information agreements[8] (perhaps employed to circumvent the provisions of the 1956 Act) gave the Secretary of State power to exempt trades deemed to be of national importance. Presumably the drafters of this clause had in mind such industries as petrochemicals where ignorance about the intentions of competitors might occasion very costly investment mistakes. Again, the 1976 legislation on services included a provision, known as the Section 21(2) procedure, whereby the Director General of Fair Trading (DGFT) could make a representation to the Secretary of State for a direction to discharge him from sending a case to court if restrictions 'are not of such significance as to call for investigation by the Court'

---

[8] Information agreements were arrangements whereby members of associations, instead of formally agreeing to observe given price levels, provided a central secretariat with information on actual prices, costs, and outputs. This information would then be circulated to members.

(OFT, 1987). Some 732 (or 63 per cent) of the 1,153 services agreements registered up to the end of 1985 had been dealt with by the Section 21(2) procedure.

The empirical work on whether or not restrictive practices legislation made much of an impact on competitive practices in industry all related to goods agreements. Heath's (1961) sample of 159 agreements disclosed the important fact that a majority of firms were seeking to replace struck-down price agreements with information agreements. Allen (1966) has listed such devices: the 'open price' agreement which sought to obtain uniformity of prices in a trade; 'bid filing' which entailed notifying a central agency of tender prices after a contract had been allocated; the dissemination of turnover figures to replace quota schemes; an exchange of list prices instead of collective resale price maintenance. In only a third of the sample did respondents to Heath's questionnaire feel that competition had increased after termination. A later study by Swann et al. (1974) suggested more encouraging effects over the medium term. Out of a sample of 40 industries 34 agreements had been terminated and between 50 and 60 per cent of these industries had provided some evidence of intensified competitiveness after termination. On the other hand, in half the terminated cases an information agreement on prices had been substituted and, by and large, the impression was that this device had successfully diluted the impact of termination on price competition. The study by O'Brien et al. (1979) attempted to contrast the experience of struck-down and abandoned agreement industries with a control sample of industries (chemicals, construction, hotels, brewing, tobacco, machine tools, vehicle distribution, and printing and publishing). This work may not have successfully controlled for all relevant factors. Nevertheless, one of the results is worth quoting (1979, pp. 142–3):

Our tests do not indicate that profitability has been seriously impaired, or its instability increased, by the operation of competition policy . . . firms that were parties to restrictive agreements experienced relative stagnation in their sales during the periods when cartels were in operation, and their performance actually improved with the ending of the agreements.

It is all too easy to be pessimistic about the impact (or lack of it) made by restrictive practices legislation. A summary might propose that the early Acts were largely circumvented, while a lack of commitment on the part of the authorities appeared to have substantially diluted the effect of the later legislation. It might further be added that, as the gains from non-disclosure of an agreement were so great in relation to the penalties (in practice, the only material penalty arose if an affected party decided to bring a private action for damages: Borrie, 1987), there may have been large numbers of undisclosed agreements. However, that is the worst-case scenario. Many of the mergers sought in the 1960s may also be characterized not as defensive but as aggressively designed to make possible the more rapid closure of obsolete capacity kept open by price agreements. The leaner firms left after the shake-out still had to compete and, after 1968, the recourse to information agreements was blocked. The evidence over the long run suggests that for the most part firms sought various accommodations with the new competitive circumstances, including diversifying into adjacent and unrelated industries.

(ii) *Mergers*

In common with the legislation on restrictive practices (1956) and information agreements (1968) legislation on mergers (1965) was introduced some years after the need for it had been signalled by increasing acquisition activity. Table 11.11 gives some of the detail of legislative control over 1965–80 (as well as a market share criterion for referral there was an assets test whereby non-horizontal mergers could be referred). It is important to note that the Monopolies and Mergers Commission (MMC) had to establish that the merger 'does' or 'may be expected' to operate against the public interest. Thus, the Commission observed (MMC, 1987):

(i)   it was not sufficient that a merger 'might' have operated against the public interest—almost any merger might have done so;

(ii)  the parties to a merger did not have to show that a merger will be in the public interest.

Hence, a merger could have been neutral with respect to the public interest and still be allowed to proceed. The definition of the 'public interest' spelt out in Section 84(1) of the 1973 Act, was therefore crucial. The MMC in considering a merger had, *inter alia*, to have regard to the desirability of:

-  maintaining and promoting effective competition;
-  promoting consumers' interests in respect of (a) price, (b) quality, and (c) variety;
-  facilitating through competition (a) cost reductions, (b) new techniques, and (c) new entry;
-  seeking a balanced distribution of industry and employment;
-  promoting competitive activity in export markets.

Only a moment's reflection is required to see how the MMC may have encountered intellectual difficulty in applying these criteria—for example, it might be possible to achieve cost reductions by sacrificing product variety, or by closing down an uneconomic plant in a depressed area.

Table 11.6 shows that in practice for much of the 1965–88 period such conflicts of priorities must have dominated OFT Merger Panel discussions. Horizontal mergers were by far the most important category of merger, qualifying for screening by the Merger Panel, (numbers of actual Merger Panel cases are not made public). Table 11.12 shows that horizontal mergers have been of roughly similar importance in the cases actually referred to the MMC for investigation. The record of MMC findings must be interpreted with care. Table 11.12 reveals that only about two-fifths of the 73 cases pronounced upon by the MMC over 1965–87 were found to be against the public interest, a result which is rather unexpected in view of the biased nature of the sample: all such proposals were filtered by the Mergers Panel and the sample cannot have been in any sense random. If the MMC findings were to be consistent with the broad thrust of the findings in Table 11.8 one might have projected that at least two-thirds of mergers would be expected to operate against the public interest—particularly in view of the quantitative importance of horizontal mergers in the caseload sent to the MMC. The Mergers Panel will have carefully considered whether effective competition was likely to be curtailed in horizontal merger cases. The inference that on over half the occasions when the Mergers Panel supposed there was a risk that effective competition would be curtailed they were in fact quite wrong seems to stretch credibility. The reflection that about one-quarter of cases were abandoned upon referral, and may have been found to be against the public interest, does not make the results of MMC investigations seem any more credible. In any case, many abandonments will have taken place for reasons unconnected

TABLE 11.12. *Outcome of merger referrals 1965–1987*

| Type of merger | | | Public interest finding | | |
|---|---|---|---|---|---|
| | Referred | Abandoned | Against | Not against | Against |
| Horizontal | 68 | 15 | 23 | 30 | 43 |
| Vertical | 6 | 1 | 1 | 4 | 20 |
| Conglomerate | 28 | 13 | 5 | 10 | 33 |
| Total | 102 | 29 | 29 | 44 | 40 |

*Note*: The col. 1 classification of cases follows the OFT system whereby any element of horizontality or verticality in a merger will ensure that a merger is classified to that row. For example, Guinness/Distillers (1986, abandoned) was classified as horizontal because of the overlap in the whisky market even though the companies concerned may have viewed the merger as conglomerate.

*Sources*: DPCP (1987) and Annual Reports of the Director General of Fair Trading.

with the likelihood that an adverse MMC finding was forthcoming. As Pickering (1983) has observed 'Companies that withdrew following a reference have tended to explain that a full MMC enquiry would be costly in management time and would cause several months uncertainty for both the companies concerned. Other observers . . . suggest that some withdrawals have indicated a recognition that the case for the merger was not strong or a concern that information might be published that would be damaging to the bidder.' Such *ex post* rationalizations might be greeted with scepticism, but it is likely that many abandonments were based on straightforward commercial calculations where the costs of referral (certain) exceeded the (putative) benefits of merger.

The defence of the MMC's record was that the law it had to work with was too demanding. It was impossible in most cases to firmly 'expect' a public interest detriment—even where a merger created a dominant market share of, say, 80 per cent, there was still a chance of new entry from imports, or a powerful conglomerate, if that dominant position were to be abused by raising prices. This view therefore favoured either forcing merging concerns to prove that corporate marriage was positively in the public interest, or completely scrapping MMC investigations into horizontal mergers and making such ventures *per se* illegal. The second kind of defence proposed for the MMC was that it faithfully attempted a cost-benefit appraisal and found that, in most cases, while there may have been detriments these were expected to be quantitatively small in relation to cost efficiencies. As Williamson (1968, 1977) has shown it was possible for the welfare effects of quite dramatic price increases post-merger (of the order of 20 per cent) to be offset by very modest cost savings (perhaps as little as 3–4 per cent). The MMC could, therefore, be forgiven for taking the view that proposed cost savings were likely to overshadow uncertain losses arising from declining competitiveness.

However, as both Clarke (1985) and Utton (1975, 1982) have argued, it was not sensible to expect the MMC to conduct a thorough cost-benefit analysis within the maximum six-month (currently three-month) period allowable. It was simply too difficult to obtain precise measures of potential cost savings and dynamic benefits, or to speculate about the impact of declining competitiveness upon:

- the prices, quality, and variety of goods produced by merging firms;

- the prices, quality, and variety of goods produced by non-merging firms in the same product market;
- and the precedent which a merger created for prices at issue in subsequent mergers within the market, or industry, or elsewhere in the economy.

Thus, Williamson's so-called piecemeal approach to the economic analysis of mergers raised difficulties which it was unfair to expect the MMC to have resolved adequately. Certainly, it would be unwise to accept that, for all of the merger cases found not to be against the public interest, no subsequent detriment in fact occurred.

While the MMC procedure may have resulted in an unacceptably large number of horizontal merger references escaping censure there is no knowing how many referrable horizontal mergers are deterred by the possibility of a reference and the attendant costs. It is known, however, that many hundreds of horizontal mergers were allowed to proceed without a reference; that is, in the preliminary judgment of the OFT and the Mergers Panel, they were not likely to raise public interest issues. Over the period 1965–88 less than 3 per cent of referrable mergers were sent to the MMC by the Secretary of State after a recommendation by the Mergers Panel. We may sum up the *ex post* probabilities here by noting that if two firms wished to merge and thereby increase their market share above 25 per cent they faced a 2–3 per cent chance of being referred to the MMC; and, if they were referred, they had a 40–5 per cent chance of not being allowed to proceed. So there was one chance in (about) 80 of the UK legislation preventing a horizontal merger taking place while as Table 11.8 suggests the chances were that, in almost three cases out of four, mergers may have led to deteriorating economic performance.

It became clear in the 1980s that firms wishing to merge could increase the odds against their referral to the MMC by various 'plea bargaining' devices (Borrie, 1987). Thus, in the case of the Hanson Trust and United Biscuits bids for the Imperial Group, and in the case of the Guinness and Argyll Group bids for Distillers during 1986, plea bargaining arose. In both instances, one of the bids for the victim company was originally referred to the MMC on competition grounds and then abandoned; and, in both cases, the bidders resubmitted their bids having eliminated the anti-competitive features of the initial proposals in the markets for snacks and blended whisky. The Secretary of State then decided not to refer the proposals to the MMC (OFT, 1987). Negotiating the divestment of the horizontal components of a merger package may be described as another aspect of 'rent-seeking' behaviour (Hay, 1985). British merger legislation, which was without clear rules for what was and what was not allowable, and which gave a large amount of discretion to officials in the OFT, the MMC and, ultimately, the Secretary of State, inevitably promoted such behaviour. Any gains from mergers were, of course, net of the costs of rent-seeking behaviour.

The general drift of the above discussion is clear. The UK operated a fairly benign merger policy in the face of accumulating evidence which suggested that most mergers did not promote industrial efficiency. Indeed, in contrast to the empirical work, there was an influential view that much merger activity betokened a competitive struggle in the 'market for corporate control' (Chiplin and Wright, 1987) which placed assets in the hands of the most efficient entrepreneurs. This and other related views will be returned to in a subsequent section.

(iii) *Monopolies*

British monopoly policy has assumed the *possibility* of static and dynamic market failure. In theory, output may be kept too low and prices too high above costs when effective competition is lacking. Under these circumstances firms may also under-invest in research and development, thus failing to innovate, cut costs, and promote economic growth. On the other hand, in industries characterized by heavy research start-up costs and an uncertain ability to retain the benefits of invention, competitive markets may be a disincentive to research and development. Moreover, some large firms which have dominant market shares may also enjoy substantial scale economies; reducing their market share would mean sacrificing static efficiency gains. Hence, UK monopoly policy has proceeded on the basis that to reduce or prevent monopo-lization were not in themselves desirable objectives: the ultimate policy aims were to obtain efficient production of goods and services, technical progressiveness, relatively low prices, growing exports, and so on. This pragmatic basis for monopoly policy was expounded by Hardie (1977) who also commended a natural justice argument for a relaxed attitude towards monopolies. That is, firms were encouraged to compete fiercely, and they did so; often, a dominant firm emerged from the competitive struggle; it was unreasonable to object that the rules were unfair and in need of revision when, after the race was run, there was only one winner.

Investigation of a monopoly position required that one firm had a 'technical' monopoly share of one-third or more of the domestic market; or that two or more firms jointly controlling one-third of the market were acting in concert ('complex' monopoly). The 1973 Act revised the reference criterion down to 25 per cent (see Table 11.11). Initially references were put forward on the basis of consumer and industrial complaints of monopoly abuse and after a general screening of industry. In the 1970s the latter evolved into an information system which took into account 'such matters as trade and consumer complaints, pricing behaviour and the level of advertising expenditure, the rate of merger activity as well as efficiency, profit per-formance and the extent of the contribution to inflationary pressures' (OFT, 1975).

The machinery of MMC investigation has been described by the Commission itself (MMC, 1987). First, a certain amount of survey work was performed to ascertain basic market facts and the preliminary views of interested parties. Then questionnaires were sent to the main parties to elicit information on pricing policies, profitability, ownership of subsidiaries, links with competitors and trade associations, and other related matters. These questionnaires were expected to be answered within 12 weeks, after which a 'public interest letter' prepared the main parties for a public interest hearing. The letter was usually accompanied by three annexes: one summarized all the relevant facts, a second recorded criticisms of monopoly abuse received, and a third set out the bearing of the two previous annexes on public interest issues. The main parties had two or three months to digest that material and prepare themselves for the public interest hearing where the MMC sought to discover conclusively whether the monopoly acted against the public interest. The report published (some two or three years after the start of proceedings) was thus the culmination of a sort of cost-benefit analysis; although, since the 'public interest' was defined to include only specific categories of cost and benefit, it was conceivable that some of the more speculative external effects of a monopoly position were neglected. Between 1950 and 1987 the MMC reported on 78 monopoly positions.[9] This may be compared to an estimate by the first Director General of Fair Trading that 'amongst the top one hundred industrial concerns in the UK there are at least five hundred product markets which qualify technically for reference to the Monopolies Commission' (Methven, 1975). The product reports published over 1983–8 examined the supply of cinema films, caravan sites in Northern Ireland, animal waste, tampons, postal franking machines, white salt, services at greyhound racing tracks, steel wire fencing, marine navigation radio receivers, specialized advertising services (with particular reference to magazine advertising aimed at campers, climbers, and walkers), pest control services, and gas piped to non-tariff customers. The picture conjured up of the average consumer by this motley collection from the foothills of British industry may not seem very familiar. The list represents an average of two reports per annum. As it would seem that monopoly policy was relatively dormant in the 1980s, it is appropriate to assess its past impact on the competitive climate in industry.

One of the earliest pieces of research on the MMC was the study by Sutherland (1969). He surmised that there was a major inconsistency between the findings in the Flat Glass report and the findings in the Colour Film and Cellulosic Fibres reports. While Pilkington's glass monopoly was not against the public interest the Kodak and Courtaulds monopolies were found contrary to the public interest: yet Pilkington's performance (the level and rate of change in prices, and the level of profits) compared unfavourably with that of Courtaulds, and was in one respect inferior to that of Kodak.[10] In other cases, Sutherland decided that the MMC acted consistently: for example, where the MMC had identified anti-competitive or discriminatory practices it had suggested remedies to alter those practices or reduce other entry barriers to the trade. Sutherland also found that, although the Commission made much of scale economy arguments for monopoly, the reports did not quantify the size of these benefits. The Commission was thought to be particularly lenient on high levels of monopoly profit and, overall, the MMC had 'a reasonably predictable set of attitudes towards different aspects of a monopoly situation. If my analysis is acceptable the monopolist is more likely than the economist to be satisfied with the way these attitudes affect the MMC's approach to a reference' (1969, p. 87). In a later review work Gribbin and Utton (1986) summarized the general findings of the MMC over 1958–85. They noted that out of 45 goods references surveyed only four monopoly positions were found, in themselves, to be against the public interest; in seven cases the Commission discovered no evidence of adverse conduct or performance; but in the remainder of cases some aspect of monopoly conduct had been singled out for criticism. The types of behaviour condemned by the Commission were restrictions on the sale of competing goods, restrictions on supply to outlets and supply of inputs to competitors, full-line forcing, tie-in sales and rental-only contracts (one case whereby a piece of machinery could not be bought outright). The seriousness of these restrictions seemed to consist in their acting to throttle emerging elements of competition. They were thus substantial entry barriers to that competition which would, it was hoped, erode monopoly profits.

---

[9] This figure excludes restrictive practice reports such as those concerned with restrictions on advertising, stockbroking, and veterinary services, and instances where no monopoly was found to exist.

[10] Because of non-observable differences in risk the MMC has always been in some difficulty in assessing what might be an acceptable return in a monopolistic setting.

Perhaps the most interesting finding by Gribbin and Utton was on the quantitative incidence of entry barriers. They divided the MMC reports on the supply of goods and services in 49 markets into three groups: a monopoly either consisted of a *dominant* firm, or a *concentrated oligopoly* (usually a duopoly or a triopoly), or a *'loose' oligopoly*. Each group of markets had a collection of entry barriers—these might be technical, legal, distributional, price, and other. It was found that the dominant firm group had an average of about 3 entry barriers per market, while the other two groups had about 2 barriers per market. To put this finding into perspective one needs to recall the data in Table 11.10, showing that dominant firms obtained profit rates over twice the relevant industrial average.

The work by Shaw and Simpson (1984, 1986) has reviewed what happened to market share, profitability, and entry barriers *after* the MMC reported on 19 markets investigated between 1959 and 1973. The briefest summary of their main findings is:

- there was a tendency for the market share of monopolists to decline but it was generally mild and reflected a trend observed in a group of control markets;
- where the authorities had attempted to reduce entry barriers, in a bare majority of cases (7 out of 13 industries) the dominant firm or oligopoly group maintained its position;
- however, as far as could be judged from consolidated company accounts, persistently high post-reference profitability was the exception rather than the rule.

It is only fair to add that these results derived not simply from the nature of the MMC's recommendations, but also from the extent to which those recommendations were actually implemented by government. In this connection, A. Graham (1972) observed that 'It was rare for the recommendations of the Monopolies Commission to be carried out by the government in anything like their original form'.

The research works cited allow us to provide a general overview of the impact of monopoly policy. The authorities largely refused to condemn monopoly structures *per se*, and were very reluctant to recommend structural remedies. In almost half the industries reported upon, however, they recommended that entry barriers should be reduced; in the remaining cases either barriers were non-existent or considered unimportant. The patchy evidence on post-reference structure, conduct, and performance indicates that policy has had a limited impact on performance alone. Some observers (e.g. Cable, 1980) regard this overall record as disappointing and conclude that the MMC should have been encouraged to recommend structural remedies. Others (e.g. Hardie, 1977) applaud the pragmatic tentativeness of the MMC. The latter group stressed the inevitable difficulty that the Commission had in interpreting profits data: were high profits an indication of monopoly abuse or superior efficiency? Were the fruits of superior efficiency always to be shared with consumers? Or would the lowering of prices have deterred fresh capital from entry? Were there not respectable arguments for heavy advertising expenditures and price discrimination which had nothing to do with the erection of entry barriers? The ideas of this group have been sufficiently influential in the post-war period for us to briefly outline their thinking.

## Rethinking Competition Policy

The notion that entry barriers pose formidable difficulties for firms wishing to enter monopolized markets has been current since Bain's early work on US data (J. S. Bain, 1956). No comparable empirical work has been performed for UK industry; rather, it has been assumed in several concentration–profitability studies (see Table 11.9 above) that any tendency for profits to increase as concentration increased could be explained by entry barriers. The entry barrier might be plant scale economies requiring, say, 80 per cent of the market before minimum efficient scale was obtained; or product differentiation achieved by means of heavy advertising expenditure; or massive initial capital costs; or control of a vital raw material source; or a variety of legal impediments to production. Whatever the origin of the barrier it could prove both durable and insuperable. It might be proposed that policy should act to dismantle barriers, for example, by discouraging heavy advertising[11] or by removing legal restrictions on entry. Where barriers cannot be removed, policy should directly reduce the gains obtained behind them.

However, a distinguished succession of US economists has striven to show that giant firms do not have the potential to inflict great damage from behind entry barriers. Galbraith (1952) suggested that countervailing power would spring up to challenge large corporations. Clark (1940, 1961) devised the concept of 'workable competition' to distinguish circumstances where imperfect competition could restrain prices and promote efficiency. Finally, Demsetz (1973, 1982) argued that, apart from certain legal monopolies granted by governments, barriers have never been a permanent defence against entry. The various barriers described above would allow only trivial differences in price to obtain between monopoly incumbents and potential entrants. Demsetz took the view that what was actually observed in the many statistically significant tests of the concentration–profitability relationship was not the permanent reality of entry barriers but the superior efficiency of the dominant firm compared to market minnows. In a test of this proposition on US data he found that the profits of the market leader differed from the returns earned by small share firms as concentration increased. If collusion behind barriers had improved the profits of all market participants, Demsetz reasoned, a similarity in profit rates should have been discovered.

Very little support for this view has been found in the UK context. Clarke et al. (1984, p. 488) concluded: 'We find no evidence for the UK that differences between small and large firm profitability tend to be larger in high concentration industries.' On the contrary, they found some evidence to suppose that profit differences between small and large firms were, if anything, less pronounced in concentrated industries. Utton (1986) similarly found that in 14 out of 21 cases where profit relatives could be computed for both market leader and follower, the follower had the higher profit relative. In a further test which grouped firms together into market leaders and market followers Utton found some weak support for Demsetz's proposition, but the difference between the profit relatives of the two groups (about 14 per cent) was not statistically significant.

A further attack on the theoretical underpinnings of competition policy was

[11] This was actually attempted by the MMC in the case of the report on Household Detergents. See MMC (1966).

provided by Baumol (1982). Perfectly competitive markets were the theoretical ideal of policy. They ensured that no single producer, or group of producers, sheltering behind entry barriers, could control market price and output to their advantage. Baumol's 'contestable markets' theory sought to show that large numbers of actual competitors were not required to produce this desirable result. The theory essentially rests on the presumption that entry into most industries is 'ultra-free'. First, it assumes that new entrants need not face start-up costs above those experienced by incumbents. Second, capital costs are not sunk costs so that, with efficient markets in second-hand capital goods, exit costs are not punitive. Providing these entry and exit conditions hold, markets will be ultra-free and contestable. Entry does not have to materialize; large numbers of competitors are not required: the mere threat of new entry will ensure that actual prices are kept below exploitation levels. The implications for competition policy are both novel and far-reaching. Structural remedies are ruled out; governments must concentrate on freeing up capital markets, eliminating legal obstacles to entry, and so on.

The theory of contestable markets was for a while remarkably fashionable in the UK (Davies and Davies, 1984; Button, 1985; Ferguson, 1985) but it is difficult to see why. As Shepherd (1984) argued, the theory rested on the most slender empirical basis. The assertion that there were well-developed second-hand capital goods markets was little more than entertaining, even in the transport industries usually employed to illustrate the theory. Other industries are difficult to envisage in a 'contestable' context. For example, consider the application of the theory to brewing. A giant conglomerate might be tempted to build a modern brewery having noted the attractive returns made by brewers. The new entrant would require retail outlets and if the firm were starting from scratch it would be a matter of winning business away from the 'free' trade (consisting of outlets not tied to existing brewers) and bidding for the occasional untied house which came onto the market—a long and arduous process. If, in the event, profits did not live up to expectations (probably because of competitive retaliation by other brewers) and the conglomerate wished to exit, it would have a purpose-built brewery and perhaps some public houses to sell. The only firms likely to want to acquire such assets would be brewers—that is, those firms which had seen off the attempted entry. In the circumstances, the conglomerate could be excused for doubting whether entry was 'ultra-free' in the Baumolian sense. Similar considerations apply in virtually every other trade. The practical application of contestability theory seemed, therefore, to be limited to a few special cases—such as airline transport.

While the first two strands of the new thinking were weakened by an appeal to facts the third offensive has been all the more powerful for the almost complete absence of a falsifiable proposition. Littlechild (1986) has been a leading exponent of the 'Austrian' view of the competitive process, borrowing frankly from Schumpeter (1942) and others. This view took issue with the static equilibrium theory informing competition policy. Static theory emphasized a given market demand function, a known technology, and economizing behaviour on the part of entrepreneurs. To maximize profits under static conditions the monopolist was required to set output constant at the point where marginal cost equalled marginal revenue (see Fig. 11.1). In reality, Austrians asserted, very little was known about demand for a ceaselessly changing menu of products. Neither was technology a fixed point; entrepreneurs were ever alert to the possibility that new production processes could usurp existing technology. Indeed, entrepreneurial ability consisted of recognizing new opportunities on the supply and demand side and risking capital to back those foresights—not in the ability to make precise marginal calculations. As Schumpeter remarked: 'Capitalism, then, is by nature a form or method of economic change and not only never is but never can be stationary' (Schumpeter, 1942). In the modern formulation of this view Littlechild (1986) stated: 'Firms are always in transition. Some have learned and grown, some are learning and growing, others have misjudged the situation and are shrinking.' Hence, there was little sense in competition policy seeking out the abusers of monopoly power because a perennial gale of creative destruction would in time see off monopolists. Data showing relatively high profitability in monopolized markets could be dismissed as a purely transitory phenomenon, or a rightful reward for efficiency. Market structure was endogenous to performance rather than, as in the received view, being itself the cause of unacceptable performance. As we have seen, the evidence for these views was unconvincing but, ultimately, the central proposition was incapable of falsification for it could always be claimed that the demise of a monopolist was imminent: that a monopolized product would eventually become insignificant in consumption; that patents were about to expire; or that technical change would make existing products obsolete and encourage new entry.

Taken together with contestability theory and Demsetz's work on entry barriers, Austrian thinking constituted the theoretical case for a new emphasis in competition policy. Policy was not to dwell on imagined structural defects; nor should it infer from performance data, such as high profits, that a monopoly position was being exploited. Policy should concentrate on exploitative conduct and in particular should seek to extirpate anti-competitive practices: those instances where there was irrefutable evidence of action by market leaders to deter entry or exploit consumers.

The 1980 Competition Act introduced new powers to investigate such practices. There were five reports by the MMC on anti-competitive practices between 1980 and the end of 1987. Although this rate of referral cannot be expected to have had a large demonstration effect on technical monopolists in the UK (only firms with a turnover in excess of £5m. and a market share of 25 per cent or more could be referred) there was a fair amount of work on anti-competitive practices performed by the OFT which did not entail onward referral to the MMC (OFT, 1986). In some cases the DGFT sought informal undertakings from companies to abandon restrictions; for example, the British Airports Authority at Gatwick agreed to change the manner in which it awarded a franchise for the operation of chauffeur-driven cars in 1984. Of the five cases reported on by the MMC all were found to contain anti-competitive elements. However, in two of the cases although the practice was anti-competitive it was found to be not necessarily against the public interest. Thus, as in the case of monopoly references, the presumption of the legislation was neutral as regards the costs and benefits of competitive distortions. Each case would be judged on its merits rather than adverse conduct being found, in itself, objectionable. The low rate of referral to the MMC may have meant that the DGFT had become highly expert at gaining informal concessions from companies. This would not be surprising as most firms may be presumed not to want to incur the expense of a hearing at the MMC. Alternatively, if the DGFT perceived that there was a 40 per cent chance that an anti-competitive practice would be found to be not against the public interest, then he may have taken the view that the machinery of referral should only be used very selectively.

In retrospect, post-war competition policy represented a substantial investment of legislative time and faith in the processes of unfettered competition. This investment was not wholly without returns as the previous sections have sought to show. However, a summary review might propose that the policy on restrictive practices was largely circumvented by mergers and a resort to unregistered agreements; that merger controls in fact prevented only a tiny proportion of acquisitions taking place; that monopoly policy screened only a small percentage of technical monopolies, with indifferent results, and in the 1980s that policy appears to have concentrated on a handful of peripheral markets; that, finally, the controls directed at anti-competitive practices have yet to bite. This would be a perhaps too pessimistic view of the return on investment. Nevertheless, it is difficult to be confident that the costs expended on competition policy have secured commensurate benefits. In a wider context it may be that policy has been reacting to a set of old problems, of wartime and even pre-war vintage, and that industry has transformed itself so considerably in the post-war period that the assumptions of policy are no longer valid. These working assumptions, that domestic markets are the focus of the competitive struggle, and that single product markets should be the ultimate object of analysis and policy action, may be somewhat dated. Why that is so will be discussed in the penultimate section.

### Newer Trends in Industrial Organisation

There are two themes to discuss in this section. First, it has been suggested that it is unwise to assess market structures solely by reference to the sales of domestic producers (see Table 11.2). It might also be somewhat limiting to restrict our scope to domestic markets. The major market incumbents may have regarded themselves as active in an international, indeed global, setting. If so, it is appropriate to examine the impact that their strategies have had on imports and exports; for the behaviour of a powerful UK firm in an overseas market will have implications not just for price and output in that market but also for the designs of foreign competitors in respect of the UK market. Second, the average number of plants owned by the top 100 manufacturing concerns was 72 in the early 1970s. Doubtless some of these were acquired by monoproduct firms seeking to obtain transport economies; but the universality of multi-plant operation could mainly be explained by gradual diversification of product ranges. If conglomerate activity was widespread, both domestically and internationally, perhaps this had implications for competition here and abroad. Were the strategic objectives of diversifying concerns such as to cause them to mitigate or intensify rivalrous behaviour? What do we know about the conduct and performance of such firms in the new market setting they helped to create?

We need, first, to establish whether these two trends, conglomeration and internationalization, were quantitatively significant. Utton's (1979) study of diversified concerns was confined to manufacturing industry; because manufacturing provided rather less than half of the income-earning opportunities in the private sector of the economy the results are only partial. It was found that the largest 200 manufacturing firms had on average 43 per cent of their employment outside their primary industry (within a primary industry there might be several technologically related product markets). It was also estimated that each firm operated equally in about four to five industries.[12] We may be reasonably sure that on the crude measure employed by Utton (the proportion of firms operating in more than one industry) diversification has increased throughout the post-war period. For example, Channon (1973), covering the 1950–70 period found that just less than one-third of his sample of companies were diversifiers. Luffman and Reid (1984), in a study based on 496 surviving companies, show that during the 1970s most companies adopted a policy of no change in their product range. However, a significant minority, about one-fifth, opted for a greater range of products, while a mere handful decided to reduce the diversity of their product range. In general, therefore, we may conclude that virtually all the leading concerns in UK industry were diversified and that each decade since 1950 saw a significant minority of enterprises extend the degree to which they were diversified.

We can be less confident about the extent to which markets were internationalized; but there is a wealth of suggestive data to form the basis of an impression. It seems likely that explicit marketing arrangements whereby competitive [13] imports into the UK were controlled affected only a negligible percentage of imports (Jones, 1987). These restrictions, in the form of voluntary export restraints and orderly marketing arrangements, mainly concerned part of the trades in textiles, numerically controlled machine tools, clothing, vehicles, footwear, cutlery, consumer electronics, and pottery. Such controls appear to have increased in scope after 1970 but in the 1980s they effectively managed only 7 per cent of UK imports. There may, of course, have been unpublicized restraints on import competition. For example, Utton (1986) notes the findings of the MMC concerning unregistered restrictions on the import of matches and cellulosic fibres in the 1950s. Again, in the 1980s, several output-sharing cartels operated by the leading European chemical companies—in polypropylene, PVC, and low density polyethylene—were eventually discovered, and punished, by the authorities (*Financial Times*, 1989).

We are on firmer ground in describing the structural features of the UK export trade. Export cartels probably controlled competition in less than 5 per cent of the UK export trade (OECD, 1984). Trade cartels have been very common in primary commodities throughout the twentieth century (Long, 1981); but apart from such industries as heavy electrical machinery, where the number of global competitors was fairly small, export cartels have tended not to cohere in non-primary trade. However, although explicit cartels were rare UK exporting activity has been concentrated in a few hands. First, in 1981 half of UK exports were contributed by 72 enterprises (DTI, 1983*a*). Second, around four-fifths of UK exports were sold by multi-national enterprises (MNEs). That is, in 1981 over half of UK exports were sold by UK MNEs while another 27 per cent were controlled by MNEs domiciled in overseas markets (DTI, 1983*a*). Third, a significant proportion of UK exports (30 per cent in 1981) were intra-MNE group exports transferred from one affiliate to

[12] Clarke and Davies (1983) suggest that 90 per cent of the increase in aggregate concentration over 1963–8 may be attributed to horizontal mergers. From this they conclude that the casual evidence of a few sensational conglomerate mergers may be misleading. However, much depends upon how a merger is classified. The General Electric–Associated Electrical merger of 1967 was classified primarily as horizontal but it included a substantial element of diversification (Cowling *et al.*, 1980).

[13] Where import competition is circumscribed by explicit restrictive agreements it is reasonably certain that there will be a positive effect on profit margins in the domestic trade (Turner, 1980).

another in international sourcing and marketing networks (OECD, 1984). Fourth, as Buckley and Casson (1976) show, there was a fairly close relationship between high concentration in the domestic market and foreign MNE penetration of domestic production. Fifth, P. Holmes's (1978) study of firms from the top 200 UK exporters revealed that over 60 per cent of his sample firms considered that they had a dozen or fewer major competitors in world markets. The broadest summary of this trade data would note that much of UK exporting was in the control of the very largest enterprises, the majority of which were MNEs operating in fairly high concentration markets both here and abroad.

The trends in diversification and market internationalization are somewhat caricatured here; the foregoing discussion is a poor substitute for a fully rounded analysis. But it does help us to focus on the implications for competition. These have often been thought to be pro-competitive (Littlechild, 1986; Chiplin and Wright, 1987): for example, because conglomerates have comparatively easy access to capital markets, and are able to fund early entry losses, they will not hesitate to move laterally into exploited, oligopolized markets. Also, their superior management skills will enable them, after a learning period, to operate at lower costs than their more specialized rivals. These alleged effects are as much a matter of speculation as the supposed anti-competitive effects. The latter are usually taken to be the potential for predatory pricing (sustained by monopoly or oligopoly products elsewhere in the conglomerate range) and 'mutual forbearance'.

The phenomenon of mutual forbearance (MF) is particularly interesting in the light of theoretical developments in industrial economics (Vickers, 1985). MF is said to arise when conglomerates encounter one another in several markets. Each conglomerate will have different competitive strengths in separate product and geographical markets and will, therefore, recognize the mutual ability to inflict losses on one another. Purely by way of illustration let us imagine that conglomerate 'A' could obtain a profitable slice of say, the washing powder market, were it to pull out all the competitive stops. But it does not do so, for to compete vigorously in washing powders would excite conglomerate 'B' to retaliate by giving 'A' a torrid time in the electric shower market. Both conglomerates therefore learn that to co-exist peacefully is ultimately more profitable. MF in international conglomerate activity will be reinforced by an MNE presence in several country markets for the same product. The greater the spread across product markets nationally and internationally, clearly, the greater the potential for MF: 'The MNEs that compete in one national market may face each other in many markets and therefore recognize their mutual dependence more fully' (Caves, 1982, p. 103). Hence, it is not without interest that Dicken's (1986) survey of the geographical distribution of affiliates owned by 9,481 MNEs in 1973 showed that about 45 per cent had affiliates in only one country, 35 per cent had affiliates in 2–5 countries, and about one-fifth of MNEs had affiliates in 6 or more countries.

Both Caves (1982) and Utton (1982) suggest that there is little hard evidence to support MF-type theories. Let us attempt to garner some impressions from relevant research. First, Graham (1978) has shown that the arrival of European MNEs in the US supports the view that they were set up as bargaining devices to enforce MF-type behaviour. Second, Kogut (1988) noted that a long line of research studies has confirmed that foreign direct investment flows, and the subsequent export of manufactured goods, are significantly correlated with the existence of entry barriers in the domestic market. Moreover, industry concentration ratios (reflecting entry barriers) tend to be high for the same industries in several different countries (Pryor, 1972). Taken together these results allow Kogut (1988) to conclude that 'As a result, a significant proportion of world competition—whether channelled through overseas subsidiaries or through exports—involves the penetration of markets by members of different national oligopolies. At times, the penetration is mutual.' Third, the most familiar case of MF behaviour in the UK concerned Courtaulds' operations in the cellulosic fibre market (MMC, 1968). A number of overseas fibre producers had refrained from undercutting Courtaulds in the UK market for fear of retaliation in their own domestic markets and in other product markets where they were in competition with Courtaulds. Courtaulds and its international competitors did not need to explicitly collude to arrive at this mutually profitable outcome. As Vickers (1985) has argued provided that firms positively value future earnings (that is, they do not employ too high a rate of discount) they will quickly learn to collude 'non-cooperatively' and thereby maximise joint, independently earned profits.

Fourth, the most interesting piece of work in this research field has been conducted by Doz and Prahalad (1988). They made the important point that the top four or five competitors in most industries (an exception was IBM in computers) were fairly well-matched in terms of production, R & D and marketing resources—but that these resource capabilities differed between markets. Their table illustrating this point is reproduced here as Table 11.13. Philips, for example, was present in three product markets with a range of strengths in different geographical regions. In two product markets it was matched by General Electric, an MNE with a similarly eclectic product range. While Philips had relatively superior competitive strength to General Electric in the European medical imaging systems market, General Electric had relatively superior strength to Philips in the North American lamps market. Differing relative market strengths made real the threat of retaliation: if price and other forms of competition affecting cash flows became vigorous in one market, a competitor could mount a very damaging counter-strike in another market. Because of these inevitable market vulnerabilities firms will not adopt suicidal strategies. As Cowling and Sugden (1987) put it 'Recognition of each other's retaliatory power means firms will tolerate each others presence in the market to the extent of avoiding situations which leave each and every one of the firms in a worse position.'

Finally, the car industry has provided the most complete picture of mutual market penetration by international oligopolies. Indeed, in the car industry 'networking' took a decisive step towards full integration of competitive concerns. Component sourcing, R & D, and manufacturing activities were co-ordinated to obtain integration economies without the costs of merger: and if the relationship soured exit costs were low (Solvell, 1988). Thus, joint ventures by US and Japanese car producers in the US and third markets, usually reinforced by equity swaps, were commonplace by the mid-1980s. For example, the Japanese firm Mazda and US Ford built a Mexican plant to produce small cars for the US market. Chrysler imported components and cars from Mitsubishi, in which it had a 24 per cent equity stake. Similar transnational relationships, without the formality of equity stakes being acquired, have been forged between Honda and British Leyland, and Nissan and Alfa Romeo. Solvell concluded that 'Every car manufacturer of some size is in one way or another involved in these [sourcing] networks. . . . The risks of not

TABLE 11.13. *Examples of global market presence by leading industrial competitors*

| | | North America | Europe | Japan | Latin America | Rest of World |
|---|---|---|---|---|---|---|
| Automobiles | General Motors | ++++ | +++ | + | ++ | +++ |
| | Ford | +++ | +++ | + | ++ | +++ |
| | Toyota | +++ | + | ++++ | ++ | +++ |
| | Nissan | ++ | + | +++ | | +++ |
| | Volkswagen | + | ++++ | + | +++ | ++ |
| Lamps | Philips | ++ | ++++ | ++ | +++ | ++ |
| | General Electric | ++++ | 0 | 0 | ++ | 0 |
| | GTE Sylvania | ++ | ++ | 0 | + | ++++ |
| | Siemens | +++ | ++++ | ++ | +++ | ++ |
| Medical imag-ing systems | General Electric | ++++ | ++ | ++ | +++ | ++++ |
| | Philips | +++ | ++++ | + | ++ | ++++ |
| | Toshiba | ++ | + | ++++ | ++ | ++ |
| Colour TV sets | Philips | ++ | ++++ | 0 | +++ | ++ |
| | Matsushita | 0 | + | ++++ | + | +++ |
| | RCA | ++++ | 0 | 0 | 0 | 0 |

*Legend:* ++++ dominant presence
+++ strong presence
++ average presence
+ weak presence
0 no significant presence

*Source:* Doz and Prahalad (1988).

being able to reap potential economies from these networks is in itself an incentive to participate. If it turns out to be an unfruitful venture, exit barriers are relatively low. If global scale advantages turn out to be significant, we expect these networks to be tightened through equity.'

Where does this leave UK competition policy? The above discussion does not have straightforward implications. First, little is known about the structure, conduct, and performance of conglomerate MNEs; and it would be unsafe to proceed very far into policy action without a firmer empirical framework. While awaiting that development, the authorities might reflect upon whether it is in the interest of the UK to do anything about MF behaviour. As Caves (1982) has argued, a country pursuing a vigorous antitrust policy may not gain in overall welfare terms by discouraging MF internationally. For example, there might be unacceptably high transitional costs of unemployed resources if really rivalrous competition were suddenly to break out among non-cooperatively colluding oligopolists.

## Conclusion

Perhaps it is too pessimistic to conclude that British competition policy since 1945 has always been a case of 'too little, too late'. The 1940s and 1950s saw a sweeping away of trade association and official controls on production and marketing of output. The industrial restructuring which followed in the 1960s and 1970s, considerably abetted by mergers and acquisitions, achieved a few modest results in improving efficiency. For example, ownership restructuring may have speeded up the transfer mechanism, the process whereby output shares inevitably accrue to the relatively dynamic enterprises in the economy. But there was little evidence to suggest that competition—the means by which gains in economic performance are shared between owners, managers, and consumers—rapidly, or even gradually, intensified. The main discernible effect was to enable many industries to regroup around one or two dominant firms. There is some support for the proposition that the resulting process of oligopolization and monopolization was the occasion of substantial, recurring welfare losses arising in the form of resource misallocation. More tentatively, gains in market power may have provided a cushion for managerial incompetence and induced managerial sloth, leading to general losses in industrial efficiency. These effects help to explain, along with other telling considerations discussed elsewhere, the decline in competitive position suffered by British industry at home and abroad: if you fail to compete, you will fail to be competitive.

That truism has not, so far, compelled a revision of British competition policy. After a promising, if dilatory, start in the immediate post-war period, policy was largely passive, allowing oligopolization to proceed unchecked. That decision on policy stance may be traced to a number of factors:

- *Cultural pragmatism*: the distrust of *per se* doctrines and the desire to see each case treated on its merits; this meant that, inevitably, policy implementation was costly and slow.
- *Market dogmatism*: the belief that the market, even if it was composed of only one or two incumbents, knew best how to allocate resources; and where markets had demonstrable deficiencies these could rarely be made good by non-market, official interventions.

- *Ignorance*: in the form of poor and dated statistical information on changes in market structure, conduct, and performance; policy was consistently reacting to events rather than anticipating them.
- *Powerlessness*: the conviction that many anti-competitive developments were taking place out of reach of the authorities; in particular, where events were international in scope the locus for policy action was unclear.

Whatever dominated in this mixture of factors the whole provided a powerful set of reasons for doing rather little to supervise organizational change or investigate potential monopoly abuse.

It is tempting to view the late 1980s policy statements as continuing this passive approach. The expressed intentions with regard to merger policy (DTI, 1988*a*) laid stress on the competition criterion for merger referrals: 'Mergers which significantly threaten competition will normally be referred to the MMC for a full examination.' However, most of the practical proposals in the policy document were devoted to legislative changes aimed at speeding up and expediting *non-referral*.[14] A second statement (DTI, 1988*b*), on the recasting of restrictive practices controls, may nevertheless have heralded a radical revision of policy. The authorities decided that the existing controls, which had been periodically extended and revamped since their inception in 1956, had several major weaknesses: they did not deter the formation of damaging agreements; they caught agreements which did not significantly restrict competition; agreements could be drafted to avoid the law; many industrial sectors were exempt; and the procedures were complex and costly. It was proposed to abandon the machinery of registration and court hearings. Instead, the intention was to prohibit all agreements with anti-competitive purposes or effects; each of the current exemptions from the law (for example, bookselling) would be freshly reappraised by a new non-judicial authority based on the OFT; the OFT would have strengthened enforcement powers and sanctions, including powers of entry to business premises and substantial fines.

It is as well to emphasize that these proposals were contained in a *review* of policy; they have yet to acquire the force of law. Much will depend on the actual wording of the clauses drafted into law, on the practical implementation of the controls, on the rights of appeal, on the penalties for non-compliance and, indeed, on the parallel development of competition policy in the European Community. Also, as we have seen above, much damaging behaviour arises not from explicit anti-competitive agreements but from structural features which are extraordinarily difficult to unscramble. Nevertheless, these proposals give some grounds for optimism that an active, pro-competitive competition policy will emerge in the final decade of the century.

---

[14] First, it is planned to introduce a non-mandatory pre-notification procedure which will help the OFT to give rapid clearance to uncontentious cases. Second, the DGFT will be empowered to negotiate divestments and undertakings in order to remove the threat to competition posed by certain mergers.

# 12

# Nationalized Industries

## J. DUNKERLEY AND P. G. HARE

## 1. Introduction

The nationalized industries have for a long time been an object of political and economic controversy. The post-war Labour Government came to power in 1945 with an extensive programme of nationalization as the major plank of its industrial policy, backed by enormous popular support. Much of this programme was implemented, but the government lost confidence in itself and the programme gradually slowed down. Under the Conservatives, who ousted Labour in 1951, only the highly controversial steel industry was returned to the private sector, everything else remaining in state hands, a clear reflection of the post-war consensus. Although still part of official Labour party policy ('Clause 4'), the 1960s Labour Government took no action on nationalization other than to re-nationalize the steel industry, an act that was this time also accepted, albeit reluctantly, by the Conservatives. In contrast, the 1970s Labour Government adopted a much more interventionist stance towards industry and either directly, or through the then National Enterprise Board, brought several more industries (or in some cases, single enterprises) into public ownership. Finally, the Conservative Government elected in 1979 (and re-elected with a greatly increased majority in 1983 and again in 1987) embarked on a large scale privatization programme. The programme started quite slowly and cautiously, but it gathered momentum and by the end of 1988 several of the large state industries had been transferred to the private sector, with several others in the queue awaiting early privatization.

It is apparent from this résumé of the course of nationalization in Britain that government policy has undergone some dramatic shifts and reappraisals, as has public opinion on state ownership. Not only that, but all governments since the war have had to manage the industries residing in the state sector and this too has generated much soul searching, the visible manifestations of which have been several White Papers on general issues and a number of reports on particular industries. There has also been considerable debate among economists, both about the correct way to apply economic theory to the problems of nationalized industries, and about wider issues of regulating industries possessing some degree of monopoly power. In view of the prevailing fashion for privatization—influenced at least as much by questions of ideology and politics as by any consensus among economists as to its desirability—the latter has recently assumed far greater importance than it had before.

Surprisingly, perhaps, despite all these changes, the basic institutional form of a nationalized industry—the public corporation—has continued unchanged and has scarcely even been debated seriously since it was established in the 1930s. In addition, the formal mechanics of nationalization have rarely been questioned, based on nationalization bills which typically discussed management arrangements briefly and arrangements for compensation and the transfer of assets in detail. Nationalization was commonly seen as solving an industry's problem, rather than as part of a wider framework of planning; however, the particular problem concerned here varied over time. Often there was little appreciation of the scale of resources needed to achieve real change and a tacit assumption that a mere change of ownership was sufficient. Given this, it is hardly surprising that nationalization often proved to be a disappointment both to government and the general public alike. The high hopes and expectations of the 1940s gave way first of all to a tougher, managerial approach to public-sector production, and ultimately to disillusion and privatization.

The chapter is arranged in the following way: the second section is concerned with the early post-war period and the wave of nationalizations implemented by the first Labour Government after the war. The third section takes the story up to 1979 when the most recent Labour Government was defeated in a general election, covering the 1950s and 1960s relatively briefly and concentrating on the more interventionist years of the 1970s. The next two sections break out of this chronological account to examine some general issues. Thus the fourth section reviews the management arrangements of the nationalized industries, including some of the White Papers referred to above, while the fifth discusses nationalized industry performance. The period since 1979, with privatization rather than further nationalization being the order of the day, is discussed in the next section. This is a particularly interesting period, not only because it has marked an unambiguous end to the post-war consensus referred to above, but because the apparent political success of the privatization programme posed an unwelcome though long-overdue challenge to established Labour Party orthodoxy about the role of the state in economic life. The last section of the chapter draws out a few wider issues from the earlier analysis, to do with approaches to economic management and the future of nationalization.

Needless to say, the topic of this chapter is an enormous one and we have space to do little more than scratch the surface. Inevitably most events and issues have had to be presented in a highly condensed, summary form, though wherever possible reference has been made to sources containing more detailed information to assist readers wishing to pursue the history and economic analysis of the nationalized industries in greater depth.

## 2. The Rise of the State Sector

The programme of nationalization of the Labour party was detailed in their policy document 'Let Us Face the Future' which drew up a list of the key industries to be nationalized. The clear majority they gained in the 1945 election gave them a mandate to carry through this programme. Thus the period of the Attlee administration saw the public ownership of the Bank of England, coal-mining, the supply of electricity and gas, the whole railway system and a section of road transport, civil aviation, telecommunications and the iron and steel industry. The early post-war period was one where the economy, but particularly coal-mining, the railways, and iron and steel, was suffering from the underinvestment of the war years. There were problems of industrial unrest, particularly in the coal industry. There was also a changed political attitude towards the role of the state in the economy. The composition of the public sector which emerged between 1945–51 results from the conjunction of these influences.

This section deals first with the background to this nationalization programme. The evolution of the public corporation in the inter-war years is described and illustrated. We then sketch the political climate of 1945, as it bears on the questions of nationalization. The latter part of the section is a brief account of the main industries nationalized, and the legislation that implemented the programme.

Public corporations were first set up in the inter-war years as a solution to market failure, so public ownership was not a new idea in 1945. Moreover, the experience already gained in the control of those industries greatly influenced the organizational and managerial structure that was adopted for the newly nationalized industries. Also, public acceptance of the concept of the public corporation was established both by the integrity and quality of service of the BBC, and by the perceived success of the LPTB. Finally, the design and execution of this nationalization programme were the responsibility of Herbert Morrison who had, as Minister of Transport in the 1929 Labour Government, prepared the London Passenger Transport Bill which was later passed by the National Government.

Certainly Morrison saw the public corporation as the best form of administration for a state enterprise. The appointment of a Board to oversee the operation of the industry was supposed to ensure that it would be free from direct ministerial intervention in the day-to-day running of the concern, whilst at the same time ensuring public accountability through the responsible minister, who reported to Parliament. The Boards were supposed to act in accordance with the 'public' interest' and not to any sectional or narrow interest. In this way Morrison can be said to have founded the notion of 'corporate socialism'. The implications of the public corporation model for the management of the nationalized industries are examined further in the fourth section. The three major public corporations set up in the inter-war years were the Central Electricity Board (CEB), the British Broadcasting Company (BBC) which later became the British Broadcasting Corporation, and the London Passenger Transport Board (LPTB).

The Electricity (Supply) Act set up the CEB in 1926 to supervise the generation of electricity and to construct a high tension national grid to take advantage of the natural monopoly structure of the market. The problems during the First World War had highlighted the importance of security of supply and because of the subsequent development of the industry, a public monopoly was seen as the best structure. The CEB was a supervisory body with a brief to remodel and standardize the supply from the various private generating companies. This belated rationalization of the industry meant that the country had an integrated system of electricity generation by 1939. There had long been widespread support in Parliament for the public ownership of the electricity supply industry, based not on political arguments but on the industry's economic structure (Kelf-Cohen, 1961, p. 98).

The provision of a broadcasting service was undertaken by the BBC with careful safeguards for the consumer of this new medium of communication. The first transmission by the BBC was in November 1922 although the licence to broadcast was formally issued until January of the following year, after lengthy negotiations.

There had been many suggestions about the economic structure of the new broad-casting service as detailed by Coase (1950) in his book on the industry. Initially a market solution was envisaged with cooperation between competing firms. The Marconi Company, which was the initial market leader, suggested a system of supplying instruments to the householder on hire, the market then being divided between the companies concerned according to region, with transmission on different wavelengths. The major influence in the setting up of the monopoly was the Post Office (Coase, 1950, p. 9). There is no doubt that a competitive broadcasting system would have been possible, but as the Post Office did not foresee the important future of broadcasting, they thought that the structure was of no particular impor-tance. This, together with the problems of allocating districts and wavelengths led to the recommendation for a single broadcasting company. The view that a state mono-poly was better for the listener was to come later. The original financing system of royalty payments on the sales of sets was investigated by the Sykes Committee appointed in 1923 who then recommended the introduction of the licence fee on receiving sets (Sykes, 1923, para. 47). The pressure to regard broadcasting as a 'public utility service' came mainly from Lord Reith, then J. C. W. Reith, in his book *Broadcast over Britain* (1924), and in his Memorandum of Evidence to the Crawford Committee in 1925 (Reith, 1926).

The LPTB was an *ad hoc* Board which came into being because of London's vast size and special problems. The passenger system of London had a history of amalgamation and cooperation and this was formalized into a state monopoly by Herbert Morrison in the London Passenger Transport Act 1933. The problem of congestion had been intensified in 1924 with an increase in the number of competing bus proprietors accompanying the end of wartime controls. The argument for public control here is not so much concerned with the efficient management of a natural monopoly as with finding an institutional structure that makes proper allowance for the externality of congestion. Such an externality means that private producers (in this case the various undertakings providing transport services in London) left to themselves in an unregulated market fail to take account of the congestion costs imposed on consumers in deciding on their levels of activity. The Board acquired a monopoly of passenger transport services (except for taxis and main-line railways), carried out substantial extensions to the underground railways (the Tube) during the 1930s and made a start on the abandonment of tramways and the extension of bus services. From the limited financial records that are available there is a lack of evidence of cross-subsidization from the established profitable services to, for example, the extended tube railway system (C. I. Savage, 1966, p. 164). Also there is little evidence that the reorganization benefited from econo-mies of scale: Savage, however, concluded that improvements were more likely to raise the quality of service rather than be passed on in lower fares.

The Second World War ended in a very different climate to the First World War, one of the significant changes being the acceptance both across the political spectrum and among the general public of an increase in state intervention in the economy. The general feeling of euphoria was expressed in the slogan 'Never again', which referred not only to the war itself, but also to the Depression of the 1930s and the accompanying economic hardship and social deprivation.

Everyone recognized the immense political and economic importance of stable prices and full employment in the early post-war period. The Conservative attitude towards controls such as rationing was that measures which had been introduced for temporary use in an emergency should not be continued unnecessarily. Their major concern was to protect free enterprise, but there was a recognition that there would be a major adjustment in the early post-war period brought about by demobilization and the revival of private demand, and that intervention by the state could reduce some of the dislocation caused by the change. In 1943 even Churchill stated that 'state enterprise had its part to play' (Barry, 1965, p. 371) but for the Conservatives this was only for certain industries. In particular, there was general agreement over government involvement in the reorganization of and reinvestment in the coal industry (see McCallum and Readman, 1947, p. 56).

The ideological basis for nationalization dated back to the ideas of Sidney Webb. The constitution he drafted was adopted by the Labour Party in 1918 and calls for 'the common ownership of the means of production' in its famous 'Clause Four'. However the basic principles or administrative details had not been developed by 1945, as is pointed out by Shinwell (1955, p. 172). He held the post of Minister of Fuel and Power in the Attlee cabinet in 1945. His handling of the coal crisis in 1947 is criticized by Cairncross (1985, ch. 13) as 'incompetent', showing a lack of understanding of market signals and of the significance of a shortage of coal to industry. The political will to intervene in the economy was not enough, nor was the reliance on the experience of wartime controls for the management of a peacetime economy. Peden describes the management in the period 1945–51 as 'a rough and ready affair' (1985, p. 150). The death of Keynes in 1946 left the government without its principal source of economic advice. Although his General Theory, published in 1936, was to form the basis of post-war demand management, the understanding of the necessary economic concepts by Ministers was limited, and the national income statistics available at that time were also quite poor (see Cairncross, 1985, ch. 3).

However the initial problems of the administration of the nationalization programme have to be seen in the context of the aims of the Labour Government and the enormous economic problems they inherited in 1945. The failure of the private sector to provide the investment for the efficient running of the coal industry and the railways in the period before the Second World War provided part of the background to this programme. The proposals in 'Let Us Face the Future' set out a list of industries for nationalization, the selection comprising those where public ownership was considered likely to promote efficiency. Although nationalization was politically popular, the detailed proposals were not drawn up purely to achieve political ends: economic efficiency and modernization were important goals and the programme has to be evaluated in this light.

Three of the nationalization Acts of 1946 passed through Parliament without any significant opposition: the nationalization of the Bank of England, formalizing the existing relationship between the Bank and the government; the transfer of telecommunications from Cable and Wireless Limited partly to the Post Office and partly to a Commonwealth Telecommunications Board; and the further nationalization of civil aviation through the formation of BOAC (British Overseas Airways Corporation) by the government.

The drafting, amending, and eventual passage of the main bills was to prove very costly in parliamentary time. The initial legislation, however, was still only able to outline the form of administration, with most consideration being given to the financial arrangements. The main opposition to the coal and railway bills came initially from vested interests rather than political sources as negotiations proceeded to improve the terms of compensation to the private shareholders. This is not so true of the later measures, which faced growing opposition in Parliament to the principle of public ownership as public opinion began to shift. The Coal Industry Nationalization Bill was the first to be drafted. It was published in December 1945 after only four months' preparation, and passed by Parliament in July 1946. The National Coal Board (NCB) finally took control over the industry in January 1947. It was the industry facing the most difficult economic problems in 1945 and the case for nationalization or quasi-nationalization was not seriously questioned (Rogow, 1955, p. 155). An acknowledgement of the need to restructure the industry dates back to the Sankey Commission set up in 1919 (Sankey, 1919). By a bare majority the Commission advocated nationalization as the only way of avoiding industrial relations strife (Supple, 1986, p. 233). In fact the government failed to carry through this recommendation but most informed opinion at the time saw some radical change in the structure and probably the ownership of the industry as being inevitable (Supple, 1984, p. 227).

A further attempt had been made to rationalize the structure of the industry in the 1930 Coal Mines Act. This provided for the compulsory formation of cartels to improve efficiency and to provide an improvement in working conditions. The measure was unsuccessfully opposed by a well-organized federation of coal-mine owners. They were fighting to protect their private interests in the profits of the mines and realized that the capacity of a more efficiently organized industry would be hopelessly in excess of any feasible market at that time (Supple, 1986, p. 238).

Industrial conflict was an important factor in the acceptance of the need for reforms in the industry. The demands for an improvement in working conditions had brought about the Sankey Inquiry, and were again at the forefront of considerations for the reform of the industry in 1945.

It was also considered that the huge capital investment required to allow the industry to compete with its European rivals was not a sufficiently attractive proposition for the private sector (Brady, 1950, p. 52). These difficulties of industrial conflict and underinvestment were recognized during the period of wartime controls and formed the subject of the Reid Report in 1945 (Reid, 1945). The report was a thorough analysis of the industry's technical weaknesses and it recommended modernization and large-scale production. It pointed out that this was only possible with a reorganization of the industry but it did not, however, directly advocate a change in ownership.

The organizational structure that was adopted for the nationalized coal industry was that recommended by the Reid Report, of 48 groupings which were in turn combined into eight divisions. It was recognized that the financial structure would have to be centralized to allow cross-subsidization between pits with differing natural resources, but that the administrative organization would benefit from a decentralized structure. This was to encourage competition in cost and productivity between pits. The complex bureaucratic structure that emerged has subsequently been blamed for the failure of the industry to achieve the improvements that were believed possible at the time of nationalization. Apart from dampening initiative and enterprise and generally slowing down the decision-making process, the lack of management skills meant that decisions were based on expediency rather than principle. There was no procedure laid down to plan the industry's future in terms of its relationship with other industries. Moreover, industrial relations failed to improve significantly as a result of poor communications with the workforce (Brady, 1950, pp. 125–30).

The nationalization of the electricity industry was similar to that of the coal industry in that there was a good deal of expert opinion in favour of reorganization. However, unlike coal, the electricity-supply industry had been in public control under the CEB since 1933 and the private sector of the industry, more than one-third of the total, was subject to a wide degree of public supervision. The measure which nationalized the industry was the Electricity Act of 1947 establishing the British Electricity Authority (BEA). It took over the supply functions of the CEB, transferring the generation and transmission system of the national grid to the new authority. Also it took over the generation and distribution networks of the various municipal authorities and private firms. It was not to engage in distribution itself, this being undertaken by the various Area Boards operating under the general direction of the BEA. The exception to this pattern was the publicly owned Hydro-Electric Board in the north of Scotland. This was established in 1943 to exploit for the highland Scottish regions the hydro-electric power which they generated. The wartime controls had illustrated the advantages of a joint generation and distribution network. The BEA was ultimately responsible for the financial management of the industry with each Area Board being required to balance its books. Cross-subsidization between the Areas was possible via the prices charged to individual Boards for the power supplied through the central Authority and also through the charges they had to pay into the central fund. This was arranged so that broadly equal tariffs could be charged in the more remote areas as in the more densely populated and more profitable areas. The Minister was still responsible for planning in terms of coordination with national economic policy and in relations with other industries.

For the nationalization of the gas industry the government had the advantage of both a recent report from the Hayworth Committee (Committee of Inquiry into the Gas Industry, 1945) (originally set up in 1944 by the Coalition Government), and the experience of drafting the previous two power industry bills, coal and electricity. The Gas Act was passed in 1948 and set up the Gas Council and the Area Gas Boards. The findings of the Hayworth Committee were that the existing structure of the industry would restrict any further improvement in the efficiency of gas supply. The background of the industry was similar to electricity with a mixture of public and private control. About 36 per cent of the supply came from municipal authorities, the remainder from private companies of various sizes, but the private companies were also subject to stringent statutory provisions. The main resistance to the Bill this time came not from the owners of the industry over the terms of compensation but from the Opposition parties in Parliament. The existing private structure was defended on the grounds of the strength of the industry but the main objection was to the further extension of nationalization.

It is interesting to compare the centralized control of the electricity industry to the essentially decentralized regional control of the eight Area Boards covered by the gas industry. Control was handed over to the most successful managers of the large private undertakings. Each Board was autonomous, able to prepare its own capital expenditure programme, to take account of local conditions, and to deal with local problems. During the 1950s this decentralized control facilitated the rebuilding of much of the plant and mains network. This fairly loose and decentralized structure was only altered with the formation of the British Gas Corporation by the Gas Act 1965. This centralized the supply of gas to take advantage of the discovery of natural gas in the North Sea.

By far the most ambitious of the proposed nationalization measures was the attempt to create an integrated transport system as part of a system of national planning. The task of doing so was given to the British Transport Commission (BTC) by the Transport Act 1947. This was to cover the transport of people and goods, and to take in the road, rail, and canal transport networks. The Transport Act took over the railway companies together with their subsidiaries (including shipping and hotels), wharves and docks, navigable canals and inland waterways, the LPTB, and road haulage and bus companies. The 1947 Act gave the BTC conflicting obligations: the pricing arrangements were not detailed but the overall aim was that the railways should break even taking one year with another, while at the same time there was a requirement to maintain services even if loss-making. The Commission's duty was to provide an efficient transport system but it was not made clear how modernization and technical improvements were to be achieved.

In 1945 the transport industry already had a background of public control: the railways had been regulated by public authorities since their inception; their prices were controlled and they were required to provide a reasonable transport service; the Railways Act 1922, provided for the reorganization of the railways by the compulsory amalgamation of 119 companies into four main-line companies; the LPTB controlled the transport of the Greater London region; the Road Traffic Act 1930 and the state regulation of the road haulage industry in 1933 were early attempts to coordinate road and rail transport.

The experience during the war showed that the railways could be run more efficiently under central control. Unfortunately, by 1945 they were in a poor physical condition. During the inter-war years the railways had suffered a decline in freight from manufacturing industry together with an increase in competition from road transport, which forced them to reduce their prices. The lower profits resulted in a net disinvestment in the industry over the period and consequently urgently required modernization was not carried out. Their intensive use under wartime control worsened this trend, with no investment and little maintenance. Government controls remained until vesting day 1947, thereby keeping the industry's prices out of line with the rising costs of materials and labour for a further two and a half years of peacetime. During this period the Labour Government placed a greater emphasis on their full employment policy, preferring the inflationary implications of financing these losses to the politically unpopular option of shedding labour and raising transport costs.

In the final drafting of the legislation, political and administrative considerations played an influential role, as compared to the requirements for creating a restructured and integrated transport industry (Gourvish, 1986, ch. 1). The BTC appointed Executive Boards which were agents of the Commission, with a separate Board for each mode of transport (rail, road, inland waterways) with little or no decentralized decision-making. The result of this administrative structure was an absence of coordination at regional level. In fact the regions as defined by the different Boards did not even coincide so that regional problems had to go to the headquarters in London to be resolved.

Iron and steel was the last of the industries to be nationalized by the Labour Government of 1945–51 and certainly proved to be the most controversial. The Iron and Steel Bill went before Parliament in 1948 but the Iron and Steel Corporation did not assume control of the industry until February 1951. In October of that same year, the new Conservative Government pledged to return the industry to private ownership. They passed the Iron and Steel Act 1953, but during the period 1953–67 the industry remained under constant threat of renationalization. It was not until the 1967 Act, when the Labour Party again had a sufficient majority in Parliament to carry through such a controversial bill, that the industry was effectively nationalized.

Iron and steel was added into Labour's 1945 nationalization plans as a central element of the Party's plan for industrial development. The proposal was strongly opposed in 1945, became a key issue in the debates around the 1951 election and remained at the centre of political controversy throughout this period. The debate centred around three main points. First whether the interests of such a key industry, if left in private hands, could be reconciled with the interests of the nation as a whole, given the importance of the industry both for exports and for domestic construction. Second there was the problem of who was to provide the capital for modernization and development of the industry. There was also concern over the degree of monopoly in the industry, which had been effectively organized since 1934 as a tight cartel run by the British Iron and Steel Federation.

In the early post-war period the industry did not have the problems of reorganization and inefficient production faced by other industries, and it also had a good industrial relations record. Output was expanding despite the difficulties of this period and the length of time needed for the development of new steel production capacity. The uncertainty created by the planned nationalization did not prevent considerable investment during the whole period 1945–67 and the industry therefore provided adequate expansion of capacity. That is not to say, however, that it would not have benefited from faster modernization to keep in line with the growing foreign competition from Germany, Japan, and America (Kelf-Cohen, 1973, pp. 94–7). The Iron and Steel Corporation set up in 1951 had a problem of defining the industry. It took over all the securities of the existing companies in the iron and steel industry so taking into its control many engineering plants as well as those making steel; a small private sector remained. However, unlike any of the previous measures the 1949 Act left the existing management structures substantially intact, acknowledging their prestige and management experience.

## 3. Nationalized Industries up to 1979

The defeat of the Labour Party in the general election of October 1951 brought to an end this first phase of nationalization. With the exception of the iron and steel industry and road transport the status of the public corporations remained essentially unaltered over the period of Conservative government from 1951–64. This section reviews the main problems and changes in the nationalized industries through the 1960s and 1970s. The period covers the nationalization of the aerospace and shipbuilding industries as well as the renationalization of iron and steel, the establishment of the National Enterprise Board, and the move into state ownership of several major private companies through financial rescue operations (e.g. British Leyland, Rolls Royce). For reasons of space, the following discussion focuses specifically on British Rail, the Post Office, the aerospace and shipbuilding industries, and British Leyland. The National Enterprise Board is discussed fully in Chapter 8.

Economically this period witnessed a significant change in the sectoral importance of manufacturing. Net output of the UK manufacturing sector grew more slowly than the output of the economy as a whole, and this relative sectoral decline has to be seen in an international context, that is in the comparative performance of UK firms. Despite the presence of some relatively high-performance industries they did not match the growth rates of their counterparts in other industrialized countries.

The financial deficits which characterized the nationalized industries during this period can in part be attributed to the failure of the industries to adjust to this structural shift in the economy. They were also partly due to the provision of certain services on social rather than strictly economic grounds. However, there were other factors contributing to these financial problems, issues which had been recognized even before Labour's post-war nationalization programme when public corporations were first set up in the inter-war years.

Herbert Morrison had outlined his view of the public corporation in his book 'Socialisation and Transport' (Morrison, 1933). He saw the public corporation of the LPTB as being financially independent. The bill creating the Board provided for a receiver to be appointed if it failed to meet its liabilities. Morrison was concerned about the effect on the industry of a state guarantee of a financial deficit. Without some threat to its financial survival, Morrison argued that a public corporation would suffer from slack management, that the public would demand uneconomic prices, and that the employees might demand big concessions as to the conditions of labour (1933, p. 273). He recognized that without the market mechanism these factors could be a source of economic inefficiency.

For the first decade or so the nationalized industries behaved with the independence of public corporations as envisaged in the Nationalization Acts. Even during that period, however, industry–government relations often encountered serious difficulties, especially over the investment proposals of the industries. But in the ensuing 15 years the industries became more and more financially dependent on the government.

The increasing deficits of *British Rail* (BR) in the early 1960s highlighted the problems of management and prompted the government to provide an economic framework by which the performance of industries could be judged. The White Paper entitled *Financial and Economic Obligations of the Nationalized Industries* (Cmnd. 1337, 1961) stated that the provision of services on social rather than economic grounds had to be separately identified and financed. A second White Paper followed in 1967, *Nationalized Industries: A Review of Economic and Financial Objectives* (Cmnd. 3437, 1967), which introduced pricing on a marginal cost basis and the systematic screening of investment projects for all the nationalized industries. The public corporations' reasonable financial performance during the 1960s was in part due to the initial success of this framework, along with the view that they should be run more like normal commercial undertakings. The regulatory framework is discussed in more detail in the fourth section below, while performance issues are reviewed in the fifth section.

The rising deficits of the railways together with the failure of the BTC to implement a successful modernization plan led to the setting up of the Select Committee on Nationalized Industries and a Special Advisory Group. Their report (HM Treasury, 1960) recommended the breakup of the BTC. The subsequent legislation, the Transport Act 1962, represented the end of Labour's attempts to integrate and co-ordinate internal transport as a whole. Faced with these deficits the Act adopted competition as official policy. The Act replaced the Commission with a separate Board for British Rail. The government brought in Dr Beeching from ICI to chair the new board, and to implement their new policy for the railways of covering their costs. In 1963 he published a major Report (Beeching, 1963) which represented the first comprehensive economic analysis of the railways.

The Report recommended extensive closures together with a rapid modernization of the core of the system. Between 1962 and 1966 there was a rapid move to implement the cuts and the result was a substantial improvement in productivity with employment levels cut by one third. The Report was overoptimistic about its ability to eliminate the railway deficits, at least partly because it continued to overestimate demand. The introduction of freightliners, which the report recommended, turned out to be less profitable than hoped but the continuing deficits were blamed on the failure to implement all the cuts that Beeching recommended. Criticism is perhaps unfair as the Report only represented the first step in the reform of the railway system. The cuts were not continued when Beeching left British Rail in 1965 after the election of a Labour Government. It was felt that the railways needed a period of stability and the new government gave its commitment to a large railway system.

The 1968 Transport Act returned to the principle of social provision of transport although it still acknowledged the importance of economic goals, and stressed the need for the efficient running of the railway system. It pointed out the need to identify unprofitable lines but also gave a commitment to paying subsidies. It did reduce BR activities on the freight side, selling off the unprofitable Freightliners and National Carriers that had failed to compete with road transport.

The problem of productivity has been a continuing one for BR, particularly on the freight side where it compares badly with European standards. Subsidies, together with low rates of investment, resulted in a lack of pressure on management and unions to tackle the industry's problems. The practice of single manning of fully braked freight wagons had been accepted in many European countries and was acknowledged as far back as 1966 by BR. The adoption of single manning, however, was delayed in the UK partly because of union resistance but also by the failure to introduce the new, fully braked freight trains. Productivity gains are now being made in this area, as in several others.

When the *Post Office* was established in the 1930s it was treated as a government department with its finances controlled directly by the Treasury. The growth and increasing diversity of its functions made it difficult for the Post Office to remain as a normal Civil Service Department so in 1955 it became responsible for balancing its income and expenditure, and in 1961 its finances were released from direct Treasury control. The Labour Government decided in 1966 to convert the Post Office into a public corporation. They produced the Post Office Bill in November 1968, which was enacted in July 1969.

The functions of the Post Office fell into two main areas: postal services and telecommunications. The very different nature of the two functions eventually led to their separation. The Post Office was split into two corporations in 1980. The Post Office retained postal services and British Telecom was established to conduct business in telecommunications. The postal services are characterized by a technology which is still very labour intensive and so highlights the importance of wage rates for the industry (75 per cent of costs approximately are represented by wages and salaries). In contrast, telecommunications technology is increasingly capital intensive, with increasing levels of automation in the system. Moreover, the markets for the two services have developed at enormously different rates since 1945.

The performance of the Post Office over the 1960s and 1970s was not especially strong, economically. At times prices were seriously out of line with costs, and costs were excessively high because far too many workers were employed. The management did not effect the changes necessary to improve productivity and the labour force resisted change. From international comparisons it would appear that there was scope for higher productivity. A policy declaration by the Post Office entitled *Reshaping Britain's Postal Services*, published in 1972 (POUNC, 1972) was an attempt to improve productivity. It proposed to introduce mechanization and cut the second mail delivery, thereby reducing employment by about 25,000 over a period of seven years.

The unions, however, resisted the implementation of the proposal to cut the second delivery and delayed the introduction of mechanization. The management can also be criticized for failing to overcome union objections, and for failing to exploit opportunities to gain or retain business over this period. The Post Office carried a relatively small amount of unaddressed advertising material which requires few extra delivery staff and no sorting. They also failed to offer discounts for posting large quantities of mail and for pre-sorted mail. It is in just these areas that the Post Office has increased its output more recently.

The telecommunications industry has faced a very different economic situation to that of the postal service. Over the decade 1968–78 output increased by around 130 per cent. The problem for the industry was one of meeting this increase in demand, a difficulty illustrated by the substantial increase in the waiting list for telephone connections which rose to around 120,000 in the 1970s. The development of electronic exchange equipment in the UK lagged behind that of the leading firm in America, American Telephone and Telegraph (AT&T). Electromechanical exchanges had high maintenance costs because of the wear in the mechanical switching equipment. The introduction of electronic switching offered considerable savings in maintenance costs. Also, the computerized control system of the American system incorporated an error-detecting and correcting facility which made possible further cost savings. In the UK it was not until 1980 that the Post Office began to use fully electronic switching equipment whereas by the end of 1978 30 per cent of AT&T's customers were being served by electronic exchanges.

The Post Office can be criticized for its poor management of the research projects launched in the 1960s and for failing to realize the importance of controlling switching by computer. They could also be criticized for not making licensing agreements once AT&T had established a technological lead in the market. The failure to develop satisfactory switching equipment meant that in order to meet the increase in demand for services the Post Office was forced to install a considerable amount of obsolete plant. They could not therefore produce the large savings in maintenance costs that had been planned.

However, technological progress in other areas has made a large contribution to the increase in telecommunication services productivity. Computerization has allowed British Telecom to expand the business considerably with a comparatively small increase in the number of clerical workers, and the introduction of the subscriber trunk dialling system and dialling of international calls has reduced the number of telephone operators. After a slow start, the Corporation was improving its performance quite rapidly by the time that privatization came onto the policy agenda at the end of the 1970s (see the sixth section).

The *shipbuilding and ship repairing industry* was nationalized by the Labour Government elected in 1974. The initial legislation was drawn up by Tony Benn in 1974–5 but the legal process of nationalization was not completed until 1977. The Conservative opposition fought long and hard on the issue of nationalization itself and of compensation to the private shipyard owners, forcing the Labour Government at one point to redraft the legislation because of a legal technicality. This delay was a poor beginning for British shipbuilders causing uncertainty in the industry and difficulties in recruiting top management, and particularly a chief executive with the skill and experience required.

The background to nationalization was a boom in world shipping from the early 1960s caused, to a large extent, by the increasing demand for oil by the world's industrial nations. This boom was not shared by the British industry, which rapidly lost market share because of high costs, lack of new designs, and a general unwillingness to adapt to the new market requirements (see Williams *et al.*, 1983, Case Study 2). Nevertheless, the impact of the first oil price increase was more severe for the shipbuilding industry than for almost any other single industrial activity. During the period of adjustment that followed there was a dramatic reduction in the number of new ships demanded worldwide coupled with effective competition from Korea and Japan from their large and sophisticated new yards.

In order to obtain orders for the newly nationalized industry there followed a period of subsidy by the government which proved to be highly controversial. The Labour Government negotiated, in conjunction with the shipbuilding corporation, two major contracts. Their policy was to maintain employment in the industry but the cost of gaining the orders in a very competitive world market has been considered excessive and misplaced. Public money might have been better spent on developing new technology rather than on supporting a declining industry. The first contract was with Poland for several bulk carriers, and cost the British taxpayer £72.5m., well above the original estimated cost of £28m. The second was with India for six cargo ships, and was paid for largely through £51m. of foreign aid from the British Government as well as a subsidy of between £2.5m. and £5m. to reduce the price of the ships to an internationally competitive price.

By 1979 the extent of the decline in the industry was becoming obvious, yard closures were accepted as necessary, and the levels of subsidy had to be brought down. There were also objections to the subsidies from the EEC which was trying to implement a 46 per cent reduction in the total European shipbuilding capacity. The approach of the election delayed any action by Labour and the difficult task of rationalizing this persistently loss-making industry was left to the new Conservative Government after the 1979 election.

The nationalization of most of Britain's aircraft manufacturing industry to form *British Aerospace* involved virtually the same story as far as legal arrangements and timing were concerned. However, the industry was and remains at the forefront of new technology in many areas, has shown rapid improvements in productivity, and a willingness to introduce a range of new products, both alone and in cooperation with European partners (e.g. the European Airbus–British Aerospace has specialized in manufacturing the wings for these planes). In addition, the company has a largely captive market—the British Government—for its defence-related products, while facing far stronger competition in the civilian sector. Consequently although British Aerospace has had difficulties of its own, they have been nothing like the problems experienced by British Shipbuilders since its formation.

*British Leyland* is one of the major manufacturing companies rescued during the 1970s by the National Enterprise Board. Because of the company's position in the economy as a leading exporter and its importance to employment it was provided with financial support in 1974 when it reported a loss of £300m. (for details, see Williams *et al.*, 1983).

British Leyland, or BL Ltd. as it became, came into existence in 1968 through the merger of British Motor Holdings (BMH) and Leyland Motor Corporation. The merger had many problems. The new company had too many product lines; most of the cars being produced were old models, and some of them no longer profitable; some of the plants were not integrated production units and production took place at too many sites. Apart from this structural weakness of the new company there were other factors contributing to its poor competitive position. There were deficiencies in the design of BMH's models and the company had a record of poor productivity and mediocre marketing.

BL's major domestic rival was Ford who had not only introduced successful new lines but also had a very different management attitude. Ford were constantly comparing their performance and products with those of their competitors. They were also first to understand the importance of cost-control analysis, of good managerial personnel, and of the role of market research to help to produce cars that the customer wanted to buy. The weakness of the British Leyland approach was shown by their deteriorating performance and their failure to develop any satisfactory new models.

From 1968 to 1973, when BL faced a relatively favourable economic environment, their performance was disappointing. Their market share (as measured by production as a proportion of new registrations in the UK) fell from 71 per cent in 1968 to 51 per cent in 1973. Their share of domestic sales dropped sharply because of greater competition from imports, but exports also declined. It was not just BL who were losing their markets. BL and the other British manufacturers were criticized for failing to supply orders on time and quality surveys showed that British cars compared unfavourably with those produced abroad.

From 1973 to 1975 there was a major contraction in the car market and BL's weighted output declined by over 20 per cent. Although BL cut employment levels, staff costs per employee continued to rise without a compensating improvement in productivity. However, now the company also faced an increase in prices of fuel and materials, and although prices were raised, there was a spectacular decline in profitability. In the autumn of 1975 they found that the banks were no longer prepared to provide extra cash. The government offered financial support through the NEB and a team under Lord Ryder was appointed to report on the corporation's position.

The Ryder Report (Ryder, 1975) did correctly criticize the administrative structure of BL and advocated more decentralized control. It also blamed persistent underinvestment as one of the main reasons for the corporation's difficulties and recommended a massive injection of funds into the company. However, the report failed to tackle directly the sensitive issue of low productivity, perhaps not wishing to give offence to BL's workers and their shop stewards. There is no doubt that by the mid-1970s productivity in the British motor vehicle industry as a whole was considerably lower than in the major foreign manufacturers. There was no agreement with the unions on revisions of manning levels, and industrial disputes continued to be a major problem for the corporation. The Report recommended that the corporation should invest £240m. per annum over the period 1974–5 to 1981–2, which represented an increase of 60 per cent over its rate of expenditure during the preceding five years. But despite the government money invested in the corporation it failed to hold its market share against the increasing foreign competition which produced cheaper, more reliable, and more attractively designed cars.

However, since the mid-1970s BL has developed a far more appealing and up-to-date range of models, has concentrated production in fewer sites, has cut costs, and has substantially overcome the long-running sore of labour relations difficulties. Even so, its market share in the volume car business has not yet (as of the late 1980s) recovered sufficiently for observers to feel that the company has an assured future.

## 4. Managing the Nationalized Industries

As we saw in the previous two sections, nationalized industries in Britain were established as public corporations by a whole series of Acts of Parliament, some of which were subsequently amended as reorganizations were seen to be necessary. The Acts established the organizational framework and management structure for each industry; they also set out the industry's objectives, usually in very broad terms such as to produce and supply a specified range of products at a reasonable cost, and with an obligation to set prices to cover costs over a period of years. (Some of this section is based on Hare, 1984).

Although ministers had some considerable powers of intervention in the affairs of the nationalized industries, the day-to-day management was largely in the hands of industry boards. Even so, many of the detailed aspects of regulation were not specified in the statutes, and practice evolved over time. Several channels developed through which ministers or the government as a whole sought to influence the behaviour of the nationalized industries. These channels included general macroeconomic policy (including wage/price policy), ministerial guidelines and directives, White Papers, and special reports. In this section, we outline the ways in which these channels of policy have operated since the war and the economic principles underlying official policy; we also discuss the industrial relations experience of the nationalized industries and the public corporation organisational form.

Other chapters in the volume deal with macroeconomic policy (see Chapters 3 and 4). It obviously affects the nationalized industries in a variety of ways. Fiscal policy influences the demand for the goods and services produced by the state sector via its effects on the overall level of aggregate demand. Monetary policy has a lesser effect, operating through interest rates and hence the costs of borrowing by the nationalized industries. In addition, movements in the exchange rate are likely to have some effect on nationalized industry costs. At various times there has been an official prices and/or incomes policy and nationalized industry wages and prices have sometimes been called upon to play a part in such policies; at other times, unofficial and informal wage and prices policies have been applied to this sector of the economy. The resulting price distortions have sometimes led the nationalized industries to present rather misleading signals to the rest of the economy, hence stimulating some misallocation of resources.

Ministerial guidelines and directives have taken a number of different forms. The original expectation about the management structure was that industry boards would be responsible for so-called operational management and the ministers and boards together would take decisions on strategic matters. However, this separation is virtually impossible to achieve in practice (see Dell, 1973 for some discussion on this point) since an industry's need for support from the minister over, say, major investment decisions is likely to make it compliant as well over lesser issues formally out of ministerial control. A further complication is the role played by other government departments, notably the Treasury, in the management process, as well as periodic supervision by House of Commons select committees. The net result of all this is that the effective balance of power between industry directors and their boards on the one hand and supervising ministers on the other has depended at least as much on the personalities involved as on the formal position. Partly for this reason, Departments supervising several nationalized industries in a related field, e.g. energy or transport, have not found it so easy to achieve coordination across the branch as one might have expected. However, there are other impediments to this, as we shall see later in this section.

Subject to these rather important qualifications, what ministers were supposed to do in relation to the nationalized industries they supervised can be summarized quite simply: approve investment programmes; approve individual large projects; and determine (in consultation with the Treasury and the industry board) external financing limits (EFLs—see later) for the current year, and medium term financial targets. What this means in practice will become clearer as our discussion proceeds.

When the state sector was expanded after the war, neither the Treasury nor the supervising ministries, nor indeed the newly formed industry boards, had well founded ideas about how the industries should function and be managed. As time went on, however, and practice developed, the Treasury increasingly saw the need to codify its views about the nationalized industries. This was done in three important White Papers issued by the Treasury in 1961, 1967, and most recently in 1978 (see HM Treasury 1961, 1967, and 1978).

As one would expect, all three papers discussed the objectives of the industries, the recommended approach to pricing and investment policy (important because it received so little attention during the original parliamentary debates on nationalization), and the appropriate forms of financial target. But the balance between these elements varied a good deal over time. While the 1961 Paper emphasized the financial performance and commercial operation of the industries, by 1967 attention had turned strongly towards more economic criteria: marginal cost pricing and investment decision-taking using discounted cash flow methods (DCF) and a test discount rate (TDR) set by the Treasury. Detailed accounts of the theory involved here are provided in Webb (1973, 1976) and Turvey (1971), but it is convenient to summarize the main ideas here.

The simplest approach is based on a single industry (partial equilibrium) model, price and output being determined in order to maximize social welfare: the latter is normally measured, in these models, as the sum of consumer and producer surplus. Figure 12.1 illustrates such a model and it is therefore useful to develop our argument in terms of that diagram. The nationalized industry, assumed to enjoy a statutory monopoly, faces the demand curve DD. Constant returns to scale have been assumed, so that the long-run cost curves are horizontal, as shown. Short-run marginal cost is constant until full capacity operation is reached, and then rises steeply. Finally, consumer surplus and producer surplus are the two shaded areas on the diagram, labelled CS and PS respectively.

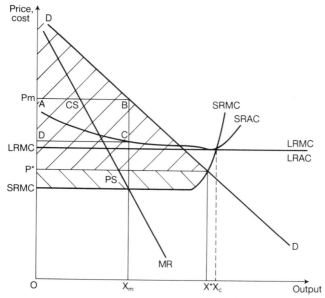

FIG. 12.1  *Simple model of a welfare maximizing nationalized industry*

In the short run, with *given* capacity it is clear that output, $X^*$, and the corresponding price, $p^*$ are the output–price combination which maximizes (CS + PS), as required. Hence

$$p^* = \text{SRMC}$$

is the *optimal pricing rule*.

The LRMC (and LRAC) includes the required return on capital; that is, the expected future returns on the project have to be positive in net present value terms at the test discount rate, to ensure allocative efficiency. The TDR is the rate of return which the Treasury requires from capital investments. The investment rule then is as follows:

> If $p^* > \text{LRMC}$, invest in additional capacity
> If $p^* < \text{LRMC}$, do not invest

What this means, essentially, is that if the price required to make the best use of existing capacity, $p^*$, is high enough (above LRMC), then investment is profitable; otherwise not. In Fig. 12.1, the position $(X^*, p^*)$ is one where investment is *not* profitable.

These are the main results for optimal policy in an industry not facing a financial target. If, however, a financial target is imposed and this requires the industry to earn greater profits than it would do at the optimum, then $(X^*, p^*)$ is no longer a feasible outcome. If the industry behaved as a profit-maximizing monopolist, it would produce at $(X_m, p_m)$, where SRMC = MR. The profits achieved at this point are, by definition, the highest possible (area ABCD). Assuming the required financial target to be less demanding than this, the industry will produce at an output level between $X_m$ and $X^*$, with a corresponding price between $p^*$ and $p_m$, in order just to satisfy the financial requirement. For a multi-product industry, the resulting departures from marginal cost pricing are not the same for each product, either absolutely or proportionately. Instead, the optimal departures are inversely proportional to the elasticities of demand for each product: this is the well-known Ramsey Rule. However, the 1967 White Paper never seriously considered what should happen if marginal cost pricing and financial targets turned out to be inconsistent, and hence never analysed these departures from MC pricing.

Contrary to this analysis, the White Papers expected that prices would be based on LRMC. This is not strictly welfare maximizing, but it might nevertheless be accepted as a reasonable policy if SRMC was expected to fluctuate widely and often, which would otherwise require frequent price changes; or if LRMC was expected to be easier to measure. However, this approach also requires some amendment to the investment rule, to give what is probably its more familiar interpretation. To sum up, the rules implied by the White Papers are as follows:

| | |
|---|---|
| Pricing rule | $p$ = LRMC |
| Investment rule | If $X > X_c$, invest in new capacity |
| | If $X < X_c$, do not invest. |

In the latter rule, $X_c$ is the current capacity level. To apply the rule in practice, given long investment lead times, $X$ should be the forecast level of demand at the price $p$, at an appropriate date in the future.

For economists, the 1967 Paper is easily the most interesting. However, the recommendation to set price equal to marginal cost wherever possible proved much harder to implement than had been expected. Identifying and estimating marginal costs appropriately turned out to be extremely difficult in many cases, especially in complex industries such as transport and communications. Nevertheless, the new thinking stimulated by the White Paper did begin to reduce the amount of cross-subsidization going on by forcing some movement away from relatively crude average cost pricing rules. In addition, it led to some improvements in the efficiency of the pricing structures through the widespread introduction of two-part tariffs and peak load pricing.

In many industries, both public and private, investment decisions (e.g. to build a new factory, electrify a railway line, replace or modernize a building) have commonly been made on non-economic grounds. Shortages and bottlenecks provide a natural stimulus to investment in order to provide some relief, but the desire to modernize, or often ill-defined perceptions of 'social need' have also justified investment. The 1967 White Paper sought to cut through this kind of argument by proposing a clear economic criterion, applicable to individual investment projects (along the lines outlined above).

Just as with the pricing rule, application of this criterion to the enormous range of practical situations proved to be extraordinarily difficult, in this case largely because of the problems involved in separating the effects of an individual project from the system as a whole. In addition, especially for the very largest projects (e.g. power stations, or a new railway line), the main influences on the returns to investment are the levels of demand 10–30 years ahead and the prices at which this demand is met. These depend on so many unknown factors, including possible changes in government policy, that any investment criterion has to accommodate enormous uncertainties. Although on paper the investment rule was clear and simple, there remained considerable room for debate about the proper treatment of inflation, depreciation and replacement investment, and taxes and subsidies. The discount rate was also subject to great controversy, but for the individual nationalized industries it was simply a number fixed periodically by the Treasury (initially 8 per cent, later 10 per cent). The new approach to investment opened up discussion about investment efficiency and probably stimulated some improvements in the industries' procedures, even when they were unable to use the new methods directly.

The 1967 White Paper also discussed the financial targets which the nationalized industries should be required to meet. Normally, the industries were expected at least to cover their costs and most were expected to earn a positive net return on capital employed. Although the Paper defended such targets for their role in ensuring managerial accountability and keeping down the industries' needs for public borrowing, it had nothing to say about their possible inconsistency with the pricing and investment rules discussed above. The inconsistency can occur in decreasing cost enterprises which set price equal to marginal cost. For then losses are inevitable; conversely, to avoid losses, some departure from marginal cost pricing may be required, as discussed above.

No such inconsistency faced the 1978 White Paper, since it once again placed greatest emphasis on the financial targets, while pricing and investment rules were somewhat relaxed. On pricing, the Paper merely required industries *to have regard* for marginal costs, as well as for other factors such as expected demand and the competitive position in setting their prices. On investment, a real rate of return of 5 per cent on the investment programme for an entire industry was the new requirement, with scarcely any discussion of the implications for individual projects.

In a period when inflation had become a more pressing issue than previously, it was not surprising that financial controls over the nationalized industries should be strengthened, though for a time their financial results were not very meaningful because of price distortions brought about by the government's stance on anti-inflation policy. The 1978 Paper envisaged two forms of financial control: cash limits (later known as external financing limits, or EFLs), and medium-term financial targets. The former are agreed annually for each industry, in consultation with its sponsoring department and the Treasury, as part of the government's programme for controlling public expenditure in general. As the cash limits applied to the nationalized industries, the EFLs constrain not the total expenditure by the industries (as would occur, for example, with non-revenue-earning departments like education), but their net contribution to the PSBR (Public Sector Borrowing

Requirement). Among other things, this approach could effectively constrain the industries' investment, since this is likely to be easier to cut back than most components of current spending in the short run. Such an impact would not only make it harder to achieve productivity gains in the future (see next section) but might also impair the industry's ability to meet medium-term financial targets. The latter targets were intended to cover three to five-year periods on a rolling basis, to give the industries a reasonably clear planning framework. By 1980, targets were agreed for most industries, and mainly took the form of a proposed return on net assets over the period concerned. However, the Post Office sought a specified return on turnover, while the financial situations of British Steel and British Leyland were then so uncertain that it was impossible to do more than seek to break even within a reasonable period. In practice, it was often unclear whether the targets should be regarded merely as statements of government or industry aspirations, or as plan targets with clear penalties for underfulfilment. These targets, as well as the other measures proposed in the 1978 White Paper and their comparison with the 1967 position, are critically discussed in Heald (1980).

As Heald argued, whereas the 1967 White Paper could be regarded as too ambitious, in attempting to specify a general framework for managing all the nationalized industries based on first-best welfare economics, the 1978 Paper was probably too cautious. Although it claimed to restore the 1967 framework, the elevation of financial controls and the downgrading of economic criteria actually took the control of nationalized industries back to the 'commercial' framework of the 1961 Paper. However, as we have seen, there are several different financial targets in use, principally the medium-term targets and the annual ones (EFLs), and the White Paper nowhere makes clear what the proper relationships between them should be. Moreover, within the specified 'minimal framework' it is not clear what objectives the nationalized industries either should or would pursue. Presumably most economists would not wish them merely to maximize profits, as statutory monopolies in many cases, but the guidelines are too vague to support much else.

Turning to *special reports*, these can be prepared by the management of the industries concerned, as with the Beeching Report on British Rail and the Ryder plan for British Leyland (both discussed in the preceding section), or by outside agencies like Parliamentary Select Committees, the National Board for Prices and Incomes (various reports in the 1960s), NEDO (a major study on productivity, published in 1976—see next section), and more recently the Monopolies and Mergers Commission (major report on the coal industry published in 1983). These reports serve a number of distinct functions. First, they usually set out a proposed or possible development strategy for the industry concerned; especially if this is accepted by the sponsoring ministry, this provides a framework within which specific investment proposals can be authorised. Second, the reports have often taken a view about the scale and structure of the industry, with implications for rationalization of parts of the business, shedding of surplus capacity and manpower, and associated measures. Third, they propose measures for raising productivity through better utilization of labour and capital, selective additional investment, and organizational changes to promote more effective management control.

In practice, these reports have succeeded in setting an agenda and in many cases correctly identifying the key problems for the industries discussed in them, and also for their supervising ministries, but the reports have rarely been implemented in full. Instead, partial implementation and subsequent revision or even abandonment of the original plans has been the norm, especially in the 1960s and 1970s. It is not hard to see why this was so. The reasons are partly political and partly economic. On the former, nationalized industries are typically large, politically 'visible' and in several cases concentrated in a small number of major centres, including marginal constituencies. Hence fears about the political repercussions of rapid, drastic change in the nationalized industries often resulted in delayed or very limited change. As we shall see in the sixth section, this has been much less true in the 1980s, when the Conservative Government sought to expose the state sector of industry to a more competitive environment. On the latter, and largely as a consequence of the previous political point, governments have been unwilling to place very strong financial pressure on state industries and this has clearly allowed them to continue with a variety of inefficient practices for longer than might otherwise have occurred.

Through all these channels, more or less imperfectly, nationalized industry policy and management have been influenced. However, throughout the period under consideration here, there has been astonishingly little debate about the basic organizational form adopted for state industry in the UK, namely the public corporation. Equally, the adoption of this form severely limited the role of the workforce in contributing to the management of these industries and had implications for industrial relations practices within them.

As noted in the introduction, the *public corporation* developed before the Second World War as a convenient management model for nationalized industries, being used first for the BBC, the CEB, and the LPTB. Tomlinson (1982, ch. 4) reviews the arguments for and against this form of organization in the context of a wider discussion of socialist policies towards industry, and we shall draw on his discussion in what follows.

First, it is important to consider the available alternatives. In the early debates, these were seen as absorption into the state, a nationalized industry then taking the form of a government department under direct ministerial control, or some form of workers' control/syndicalist model in which workers or their representatives played a significant role in enterprise/industry management.

The first of these alternatives, the statist solution, was anathema to most British socialists who sought, wherever possible, to distance new institutions from the central state bureaucracy. The second paid a great deal of attention to workers' interests and was rejected by many in the Labour Party for being too particularist on that account. The public corporation was a compromise which avoided both these difficulties, and which could, moreover, be presented as having a number of positive features of its own.

The features included public accountability through ministers and hence parliament; managerial decentralization; and in many cases, statutory monopoly in a specified field of business. Unfortunately, when examined more carefully, none of these offers quite what the early proponents of the public corporation model might have hoped. Public accountability refers to the view that the public corporation, rather than serving any particular interest, should be responsive to the general social interest as reflected in Parliament. Likewise, industry statutes commonly enjoined the nationalized industries to meet some financial target (usually fairly vaguely specified, such as to break even over a period of years) while supplying whatever was in the 'national interest'. The difficulty here is twofold. First, what *is* the social or national interest in relation to any given industry; and second how can parliamentary supervision ensure that this interest is served as well as possible? In practice, it rapidly became clear that the first question meant either that the industries should operate commercially (in which case, why nationalize?) or that they should also engage in socially desirable, uncommercial activity (in which case they could and did argue for open-ended subsidies).

In both cases, the notion of parliamentary supervision was completely mythical. Ministers, and especially MPs, lacked both the information and the energy to engage in the close and regular supervision that was sometimes encouraged. In effect, therefore, accountability to Parliament meant, for much of the time, accountability to no one. However, there have been various parliamentary select committees dealing with nationalized industries and these have sometimes produced useful reports on individual industries or the sector as a whole. Nevertheless, all this remains a far cry from the kind of supervision anticipated by early supporters of the public corporation.

Managerial decentralization and its associated problems were already referred to earlier in this section. On paper, the idea of giving industry boards responsibility for operational management and ministers more influence over strategic matters, especially concerning major investments, is appealing. However, hard experience quickly demonstrated its unworkability, because of the inevitable interconnections between the two types of decisions. As a result, the public corporation could be said to have achieved the worst of all worlds, in that it was more closely interwoven into the governmental machine than intended, yet still lacked a well-developed planning framework which might have enabled such integration to confer real economic benefits.

Finally, the effects of statutory monopoly on management structures and practices are worth discussing: it has been a neglected issue until recent developments concerning privatization (see the sixth section, below), but it has clearly had important, often detrimental effects on industry efficiency (see the next section). At first sight, the imposition of a statutory monopoly position appears to grant an industry considerable power in the market place (but hence the need for a suitable regulatory framework), but this apparent advantage is offset by several drawbacks, both for the industry itself and for society as a whole.

For society, the main drawback is that the lack of competition, especially if imports are restricted too, allows the industry to operate at higher cost levels than would otherwise have been possible. For the industry, the monopoly powers have proved to be a mixed blessing, because in most cases the relevant nationalized industry statutes have specified not only that the newly established industry should be the sole producer of, say, coal, but that coal, and coal-related products are what it must produce. Through a series of historical accidents, many nationalized industries do produce goods and services outside their normal production profile, usually by including various unrelated subsidiaries in the original nationalization bills. Once nationalized, however, they face major restrictions on their business policy: they have not been able to engage in takeovers and mergers (except with ministerial authority, e.g. the merger of BEA and BOAC to form British Airways in 1974); they cannot enter new lines of business by diversification, or abandon unprofitable business without ministerial permission; they cannot relocate production overseas;

and they have been unable to use the private capital market to finance modernization schemes. None of these limitations applies to private-sector firms and, as we shall see in the next section, their combined effect has had significant adverse effects on the economic performance of nationalized industries. As established in Britain since 1945, the public corporation has not been a resounding success.

In another important sphere, that of industrial relations, the problems of the public corporation are also apparent. After the war, the trade unions strongly supported the Labour Government's nationalization programme, but they soon discovered that the management arrangements—the public corporation model—scarcely differed from that of a large private sector company. Indeed, much of the organization and many of the managers were identical, which simply highlighted the lack of fundamental change within many of the industries concerned.

Trade unions in Britain have not traditionally been strong supporters of workers and their representatives participating directly in enterprise management. For instance, the Donovan Report (Donovan Commission, 1968), which recommended boards of directors with substantial union representation, was opposed not only by many employers but also by trade unions. So this omission from the public corporation model caused surprisingly little concern to most trade unionists. Instead, the unions expected to continue with something like the already established wage bargaining processes, but also expected that state ownership would be helpful in preserving jobs, as well as in modernizing those industries suffering from decades of underinvestment while in the private sector (e.g. the railways, the coal-mines).

According to Winchester (1983), these expectations were broadly fulfilled at least into the 1960s, the combination of centralized and formal collective bargaining machinery in the public sector and rapid growth of public spending in all areas providing a stable and sheltered bargaining context. However, by the early 1980s all this had changed, and the relationships between the government and major public-sector trade unions (including those operating in the nationalized industries) were seen as the main source of instability in British industrial relations. Three factors brought about this very significant change: problems of public/private wage relativities, pressures resulting from periodic incomes policies, and strengthening constraints on public expenditure. The last of these is clear from the 1978 White Paper on the nationalized industries, as we saw above.

The large size of many nationalized industries, and the failure fully to separate them off from the government bureaucracy, inevitably politicized the wage-bargaining process, to an extent which surprised trade unionists. Furthermore, Britain's relative economic decline with its associated rather slow growth, made public expenditure constraints inevitable, sooner or later, and this was bound to transform the public-sector industrial relations environment. Added to this was the fact that some nationalized industries were declining (e.g. coal, the railways), which could only exacerbate an already difficult situation.

For the unions, adjusting to the new, harsher climate of industrial relations involved a painful and at times expensive adjustment process. Perhaps the most dramatic instance is the coal industry, which in 1972 and 1974 inflicted serious defeats on the then Conservative Government (including, in the latter case, toppling the government and paving the way for a Labour Government) (for details, see McCormick, 1979). Yet a decade later, a bitterly fought, year-long strike was defeated by a much more determined government, and subsequently the industry began to put into effect a programme of adjustment and reconstruction, involving very large job losses, a programme which had been postponed for many years. Similar accounts could be given of the steel industry and to a lesser extent, the railways, though they still have further to go along the route to efficient modernization.

## 5. Performance of Nationalized Industries

Many of the nationalized industries began life in the public sector as industries with a long history of problems and weaknesses as a result of underinvestment and poor private-sector management (e.g. coal, rail), while others faced new opportunities as a result of expanding markets and rapid technological change (e.g. airlines, telecommunications). In both cases it is important to be able to assess their performance as it develops over time (part of what follows is based on Hare, 1984).

First, it is important to summarize the nationalized industries' overall position in the British economy. This is done in Table 12.1 (public corporations and nationalized industries being almost coextensive), which shows their share in GDP, employment, and fixed capital formation over the last few decades. In broad employment terms, the sector peaked (as a share in the economy) as long ago as 1961, since which time its share of employment has fallen, at first slowly and then much more rapidly. Investment in nationalized industries also peaked in the early 1960s (again as a share of total fixed investment in the economy), but its subsequent course has been more erratic until the recent rapid decline as a result of the government's privatization programme.

Against this general background to the nationalized sector, Table 12.2 presents a number of useful productivity measures for the main industries, with comparative data on UK manufacturing industry as a whole. The table shows data on total factor productivity (a measure that takes account of both capital and labour inputs) and labour productivity (a simpler and more reliable measure, but at the same time only a partial measure). The picture is quite mixed, though in many of the industries the 1960s was a good decade for productivity gains, the 1970s rather poor, and the most recent period much better once more. This general pattern is apparent in all three parts of Table 12.2.

Earlier in the chapter we commented on the achievements of the first public corporations. The rationalization of London transport by the LPTB in the 1930s provided a solution to the problem of congestion in London, and gains from the co-ordination of transport systems were seen in these non-market terms rather than as a reduction of fares resulting from an improvement in productivity. Likewise the public ownership of the coal industry provided the improvement in pay and conditions demanded by public opinion and provided the capital for the rationalization and an improvement in technology. It has never been in dispute that in this industry 'a degree of inefficiency was tolerated rather than face a formidable social problem' (Supple, 1986).

The first comprehensive report on the nationalized industries as a whole was produced by NEDO and published in 1976 (see NEDO, 1976b). This multi-volume study concentrated on the 15-year period 1960–75. It found that total output of the nationalized industries had been growing on average by 1.1 per cent per annum, well below the rate for all manufacturing industry which was then 2.7 per cent per annum. Some of the state industries, for example coal, steel, and parts of public

TABLE 12.1. *Public corporations in the British economy*

(a) *Analysis of gross domestic product (£bn.)*

| Year | 1948 | 1951 | 1961 | 1971 | 1977 | 1978 | 1979 | 1980 | 1981 | 1982 | 1983 | 1984 | 1985 | 1986 | 1987 |
|---|---|---|---|---|---|---|---|---|---|---|---|---|---|---|---|
| GDP public corporations | .8 | 1.2 | 2.4 | 4.9 | 14.5 | 16.5 | 18.1 | 21.6 | 24.4 | 26.8 | 28.1 | 25.9 | 23.0 | 25.2 | 21.2 |
| GDP[a] total | 10.3 | 12.6 | 24.2 | 49.4 | 129.0 | 148.1 | 172.1 | 199.4 | 217.7 | 238.0 | 260.9 | 278.7 | 305.3 | 323.8 | 354.5 |
| % public corporations of total | 7.4 | 9.5 | 9.8 | 10.0 | 11.3 | 11.1 | 10.5 | 10.8 | 11.2 | 11.3 | 10.7 | 9.3 | 7.5 | 7.8 | 6.0 |

a GDP income based

*Source:* CSO United Kingdom National Accounts (1988), Table 2.5 (and earlier issues).

(b) *Analysis of employment (thousands)*

| Year | 1956 | 1961 | 1971 | 1977 | 1978 | 1979 | 1980 | 1981 | 1982 | 1983 | 1984 | 1985 | 1986 | 1987 |
|---|---|---|---|---|---|---|---|---|---|---|---|---|---|---|
| Public corporations | 2084 | 2196 | 2009 | 2089 | 2061 | 2065 | 2038 | 1867 | 1756 | 1662 | 1610 | 1261 | 1199 | 996 |
| Total | 24509 | 25057 | 24398 | 24865 | 25014 | 25393 | 25327 | 24346 | 23908 | 23626 | 24235 | 24618 | 24756 | 25301 |
| % public corporations of total | 8.5 | 8.8 | 8.2 | 8.4 | 8.2 | 8.1 | 8.0 | 7.7 | 7.3 | 7.0 | 6.7 | 5.1 | 4.8 | 3.8 |

*Source:* CSO United Kingdom National Accounts (1988), Table 16.1 (and earlier issues).

(c) *Gross domestic fixed capital formation, at current prices (£m.)*

| Year | 1948 | 1951 | 1961 | 1971 | 1977 | 1978 | 1979 | 1980 | 1981 | 1982 | 1983 | 1984 | 1985 | 1986 | 1987 |
|---|---|---|---|---|---|---|---|---|---|---|---|---|---|---|---|
| GDFCF public corporations | 180 | 358 | 898 | 1862 | 4779 | 4944 | 5641 | 6653 | 6780 | 7114 | 7884 | 7305 | 5656 | 5545 | 4605 |
| GDFCF total | 1452 | 1913 | 4577 | 10515 | 27036 | 31060 | 36925 | 41561 | 41309 | 44763 | 48594 | 55108 | 60477 | 64227 | 70767 |
| % public corporations of total | 12.4 | 18.7 | 19.6 | 17.7 | 17.7 | 15.9 | 15.3 | 16.0 | 16.4 | 15.9 | 16.2 | 13.3 | 9.4 | 8.7 | 6.5 |

*Source:* CSO United Kingdom National Accounts (1988), Table 12.1 (and earlier issues).

TABLE 12.2 (a). *Productivity measures for nationalized industries*

*Percentage growth in total factor productivity (industry/enterprise data)*
*(annual trend percentage changes)*

| | 1948–53 | 1953–8 | 1958–63 | 1963–8 | 1958–68 | 1968–73 | 1973–8 | 1968–78 | 1978–85 |
|---|---|---|---|---|---|---|---|---|---|
| British Rail | 1.2 | −1.3 | 0.5 | 4.2 | | 2.4 | | | 2.8 |
| British Steel | | | | 3.0 | | 0.6 | −4.8 | −2.5 | 2.9 |
| Post Office | | | | | | | | | 1.9 |
| British Telecom | | | | 5.1 | | 5.1 | 10.7 | 7.8 | 0.5 |
| British Coal | 1.4 | −0.6 | 3.0 | 3.2 | 3.1 | −0.8 | −2.7 | −1.8 | 0 |
| Electricity | 3.0 | 4.3 | 5.1 | 1.2 | 3.1 | 0.8 | 1.4 | 0.7 | 1.4 |
| British Gas | 1.2 | 0.1 | 2.5 | 5.0 | 3.7 | | | | 1.2 |
| National Bus | | | | | | 0.8 | −2.7 | −1.4 | 0.1 |
| British Airways | 14.7 | 1.4 | 8.3 | 8.0 | 9.1[a] | 8.0 | 11.3 | 9.6 | 4.8 |
| UK manufacturing | 1.6 | 1.4 | 2.3 | 2.5 | 2.4 | 3.4 | 3.0 | 1.7 | |

[a] 1958–67.

*Sources:* Figures 1948–68 taken from Pryke (1971), p. 112; 1968–78 from Pryke (1981), p. 238; and 1978–85 from Molyneux and Thompson (1987), p. 59.

TABLE 12.2 (b). *Labour productivity—output per worker* (industry/
enterprise data) (annual trend percentage change)

|  | 1948–58 | 1958–68 | 1968–73 | 1973–8 | 1978–85 |
|---|---|---|---|---|---|
| British Rail | 0.3 | 4.3 | 2.7 | −1.2 | 3.9 |
| British Steel |  |  | 2.5 | −2.7 | 12.6 |
| Post Office |  |  | −1.4 | −1.2 | 2.3 |
| British Telecom |  |  | 7.7 | 8.6 | 5.8 |
| British Coal | 0.9 | 4.7 | 0 | −1.4 | 4.4 |
| Electricity | 4.6 | 8.0 | 8.7 | 1.9 | 3.9 |
| British Gas | 1.6 | 5.5 | 10.8 | 6.2 | 3.8 |
| National Bus | −0.6 | −1.4 | 1.9 | −3.0 | 2.1 |
| British Airways | 14.0 | 8.9 | 7.7 | 5.7 | 6.6 |
| UK manufacturing | 1.9 | 3.7 | 4.4 | 1.0 | 3.0 |

*Sources*: Figures 1948–68 from Pryke (1971), p. 104; 1968–85 from Molyneux and Thompson (1987), p. 58.

TABLE 12.2 (c). *Labour productivity—output per worker* (sectoral data)
(annual trend percentage change)

|  | 1980–1 | 1984–5 | 1985–6 | 1986–7 | 1987–88 | Average 1979–80 to 1987–8 |
|---|---|---|---|---|---|---|
| Nat. Industries | −1.8 | 5.5 | 8.1 | 8.3 | 6.8 | 4.1 |
| UK manufacturing | −5.3 | 4.7 | 1.8 | 4.7 | 7.4 | 3.7 |
| Whole economy | −3.7 | 1.2 | 2.8 | 3.6 | 4.4 | 2.2 |

*Source*: H.M Treasury (1989), Table 21.3.7.

transport, were declining steadily over this period (and continue to do so in many cases), while others, such as British Airways (two separate companies until 1974), telecommunications, electricity, and gas were expanding very rapidly, and it is hard to accept that the overall lack of dynamism in the state sector was inevitable.

Somewhat later, Pryke (1981) reviewed performance over the decade 1968–78. He found that productivity, measured as output per equivalent worker, actually fell in coal-mining, bus transport, the postal service, steel production, and British Leyland, while only gas, electricity, British Airways, and telecommunications were able to do better than the average for industry as a whole. This mixed performance may have reflected the real potential of the various industries, but equally well it could indicate that the management and control systems in operation were failing to exert enough pressure on the industries to reduce their costs. That possibility is supported by the fact that nationalized industry prices tended, on average, to increase at a faster rate than those for industry as a whole, while their profitability remained consistently below the industry average despite their price increases. This also implies that the returns to additional investment must have been low or even negative in some years, though the poor general situation masked an enormous diversity of outcomes, from substantial profits in gas and telecommunications to very large losses in steel and British Leyland.

In a critical survey of all the main nationalized industries, Redwood (1980) confirmed many of the problems identified in these earlier reviews, attributing the major problems to the complex and poorly functioning control framework for the sector. While supporting the strengthening of financial controls that followed the 1978 White Paper, he also emphasizes the need for greater clarity in specifying the aims, policies, and operating rules for the nationalized industry sector. In particular, he sets the scene for the privatization that was soon to get under way (see next section) by suggesting ways of dealing with each industry. Without going quite as far as wholesale privatization, he lists those industries in which he judges asset sales to be possible (either entire companies, or parts of the business which would be better managed as separate units); industries which could be self-financing subject to monopoly controls; industries needing reorganization under a cash limit regime; and industries where regulation by contract may be appropriate. Interestingly, the cautious agenda set out in this way has been overtaken by events, and in several cases the present government has gone further than Redwood then envisaged.

A somewhat more optimistic view of nationalized industry performance is taken in Molyneux and Thompson (1987). This shows that in the period 1978–85, productivity in the state sector rose rapidly, both in comparison to the state sector in previous periods, and in comparison to manufacturing as a whole. The industries remaining in the state sector also showed greater productivity gains than the newly privatized industries, putting into question the need for a change in ownership and highlighting the gains that are possible through changes in management style. Stronger financial controls since 1978, together with the threat or actual introduction of greater competition and/or partial or complete privatization must go a long way towards explaining this outcome. It should also be noted that nationalized industry's productivity is conventionally judged against manufacturing industry. This is an unfair measure as the state sector includes many service industries (railways, post office) which traditionally do not make the same productivity gains as the manufacturing sector.

One of the arguments for nationalization is that certain social objectives (e.g. providing public transport in remote areas) would not be met by the private sector. However, if state industries are to meet social as well as commercial objectives, then the associated costs and benefits need to be quantified to ensure that a proper level of subsidy is established. Unfortunately, it is clear from Molyneux and Thompson's analysis that scarcely any progress has been made in properly quantifying these costs and benefits. Almost equally bleak is the second issue about which the authors were highly critical. This is the failure of the state industries to make much progress in the direction of a more rational pricing structure, at least roughly based on sound economic principles (marginal cost pricing, etc.), despite much discussion and the White Papers. In practice, a good deal of the pricing structure is based on cost or demand patterns of long ago, and has often been overtaken by technological change and shifts in demand. As noted in the last section, debates about marginal cost pricing did lead to some improvements in pricing, but the most striking changes have actually been brought about by the recent introduction of competition in some industries.

For obvious reasons—mainly the lack of suitable comparators—not much work has been done on the direct comparison of public and private sector production. However, such comparisons are important, because they can help us to judge how far the problems of the nationalized industries are common to the whole economy, and how far they are peculiar to that sector. Pryke (1982) reports one such study in which he was able to compare public and private productivities. The chosen activities were civil aviation (British Airways and British Caledonian), short sea ship and hovercraft services (Sealink and European Ferries), and the sale of electrical and gas appliances and contracting (British Gas and the Electricity Boards, and Currys and Comet). In each case, Pryke found that 'public enterprise has performed relatively poorly in terms of its competitive position, has used labour and capital inefficiently and has been less profitable'. In his conclusion, Pryke argues that the basic problem is public ownership itself, which eliminates any possibility of bankruptcy or takeover and allows managers to have a comfortable life. Whether a similar comparison carried out today would be quite as damning is not clear. However, it is apparent that the plethora of critical studies on the nationalized industries that have appeared in recent years has helped to create the climate of opinion in which it became politically possible to reverse the process, and embark on a period of large-scale privatization. We examine this period in the next section.

## 6. The Thatcher Period

When the Conservative Party returned to power in the 1979 election, they brought with them a determination to scale down the public sector, and to improve the efficiency of what remained. Within the nationalized industries this commitment meant two things: increasing financial pressure on the nationalized industries and firms to force them to cut costs, and a programme of privatization. As HM Treasury (1986) makes clear, the results have been dramatic in both respects. On the effects of cost cutting, Table 12.3 shows how the borrowing requirements of the main nationalized industries have developed in the last five years (note that negative signs in the table refer to financial surpluses). Aside from 1984–5, which was adversely affected by the year-long coal strike (affecting the coal industry itself, electricity generation because it had to switch to higher cost fuels, and the railways because of the loss of coal traffic), the general tendency has been for losses to decline and profits to increase. These changes are very much in line with the improved performance reported in the last section.

On privatization about a quarter of the state sector of industry has now been transferred back to private ownership. Thus in 1979 the nationalized industries accounted for about 10 per cent of UK output and 14 per cent of fixed investment, employing nearly two million people; by 1985, they only accounted for around 7 per cent of output and 9 per cent of fixed investment, employing just over a million people (for details, see Table 12.1).

The privatization programme started off quite slowly and cautiously, but it gathered pace after the 1983 election, in which the Conservatives were confirmed in power with a greatly increased parliamentary majority. The programme has always been controversial, and the arguments for and against privatization have varied both over time and depending on the particular case under discussion. In addition, privatization has taken several distinct forms, and the whole debate about it has re-opened important questions about the nature and role of nationalization in the economy. Since, as we observed earlier, nationalization *per se* was for a long time

TABLE 12.3. *Major nationalized industries: external financing*
(£m)

| | 1981–2 | 1982–3 | 1983–4 | 1984–5 | 1985–6 | 1986–7 | 1987–8 | 1988–9 |
|---|---|---|---|---|---|---|---|---|
| Coal | 1226 | 951 | 1183 | 1720 | 429 | 902 | 918 | 750 |
| Electricity | −154 | −29 | −252 | 850 | −277 | −1101 | −1133 | −1122 |
| Post office | −12 | −61 | −62 | −100 | −75 | −93 | −80 | −97 |
| Steel | 766 | 568 | 318 | 523 | 411 | 22 | −290 | −318 |
| Rail | 960 | 848 | 811 | 1045 | 910 | 777 | 591 | 520 |
| Shipbuilding | 146 | 120 | 306 | 235 | 48 | 241 | 118 | 174 |
| Water[a] | 280 | 291 | 350 | 286 | 208 | 107 | 34 | 6 |
| Nationalized industries[b] | | | 2274 | 3827 | 1709 | 386 | 267 | 246 |
| Other public corporations | | | 966 | 1133 | 925 | 708 | 534 | 569 |
| Total public corporations | 3213 | 2689 | 3240 | 4960 | 2634 | 1094 | 801 | 815 |

[a] England and Wales
[b] Including others

*Source*:   Treasury (1986); Treasury (1989), Table 21.3.1.

seen as a 'solution' to the problems of various industries, this re-opening of discussion is a very welcome development.

To help organize our discussion of the recent and still continuing privatization programme, Table 12.4 lists the major state industries as of the late 1970s, together with the privatization measures, if any, that have been introduced in respect of each one. The list excludes a number of national and local development agencies and authorities, as well as several smaller companies about which there has been little or no question of privatization. However, it does include all the larger companies which have been affected by privatization in one way or another.

Privatization is a term that can be given several rather different meanings, depending on the context, and it can be introduced as a policy to achieve a number of objectives. Moreover, depending on the economic circumstances of various industries, its practical effects and hence its desirability can vary a good deal. Before looking at particular privatization exercises, therefore, we need to review these three issues: the meaning, objectives, and likely effects of privatization. Many of the points that we shall make are discussed more fully in Kay, Mayer, and Thompson (1986), as well as in Heald (1984), Beesley and Littlechild (1986); a more recent analysis is provided in Vickers and Yarrow (1988).

For nationalized industries, as opposed to other parts of the public sector that we do not discuss here, privatization can either mean the partial or complete transfer of ownership back to the private sector; or measures to enhance competition; or some combination of the two. The transfer of ownership has normally taken place via one or more public-share issues, though on occasion the chosen route has been a management buy-out. Competition can be enhanced by encouraging alternative suppliers to enter the market (which might involve relaxing a statutory monopoly), by relaxing various restrictions applying to the established suppliers or their customers, and in some cases by permitting imports.

TABLE 12.4. *Privatization since 1979*

| Name of corporation | Commencing date | Previous form | Privatization measures |
|---|---|---|---|
| Bank of England | March 1946 | Private company | None |
| British Aerospace | April 1977 | Private companies | Share issues 1981,1985 |
| British Airports Authority | April 1966 | Part of government department | Share issues 1987/8 |
| British Airways | April 1974 | Two state-owned companies, BOAC & BEA | Share issue, 1986 |
| BBC | 1927 | None | None, but financing issues discussed in recent Peacock Committee report |
| British Gas | January 1972 | Gas council and area boards | Share issues, 1986/88 new regulatory body |
| British Leyland | Effective nationalization, 1974, under NEB supervision | Private company | Jaguar—share issue, 1984 Rover Group sold, 1987 |
| BNOC | January 1976 | None | Oil production business formed into Britoil; share issues 1982, 1985 |
| British Petroleum | | Majority shareholding by British government | Share sales 1979, 1981, 1983, 1987 |
| British Rail | January 1963 | Part of BTC (1948–62) | None in main business; non-rail assets sold to private sector |
| British Shipbuilders | July 1977 | Private companies | Sold all but merchant shipbuilding activities; proposed completion 1989 |
| British Steel | July 1967 | Private companies | Share issue, 1988 |
| British Telecom | October 1981 | Part of post office | Share issue 1984/5 (instalments); new entry (Mercury) a regulatory body (OFTEL) |
| British Waterways | January 1963 | Part of BTC (1948–62) | None |
| Cable and Wireless | January 1947 | Domestic assets transferred to post office, April 1950 | Share issues, 1981 1983, 1985 |

(Table 12.4 *Contd.*)

| Name of corporation | Commencing date | Previous form | Privatization measures |
|---|---|---|---|
| Civil Aviation Authority | April 1972 | Various government departments & boards | None |
| Electricity Council (CEGB & area boards) | January 1958 | part of British Electricity Authority (1948–55), Central Elec. Auth. (1955–7) | 2nd reading of Privatization bill December 88; planned to commence 1990 |
| National Bus Company | January 1969 | Part of Transport Holding Company (1963–8), previously part of BTC. | Deregulation, 1980 split into separate companies. Majority sold to management; completed March 88 |
| National Coal Board | January 1947 | Private companies with government supervision | Planned privatization action mid 1990s. |
| National Freight Company | January 1969 | Same as National Bus Company | Management buy-out |
| North of Scotland Hydro-Electric Board | 1943 | None | White paper, 1988; privatization due in 1991 |
| Post Office | April 1961 | Government department | Girobank privatization plans |
| Regional water authorities | April 1974 | Part of local authority | Privatization in 1990 |
| Rolls Royce | Effective nation-alization 1973, subsequently under NEB supervision | Private company | 1987 proceeds to BL (now Rover Group) |
| Scottish transport group | January 1969 | Same as National Bus Company | Deregulation, 1980 |
| South of Scotland Electricity Board | April 1955 | Part of British Electricity Authority (1949–55) | White paper 1988, privatization due in 1991 |

*Sources*:   Blue Book (various years); recent White Papers;
        Maurice (1968), Davis (1984), Mayer & Meadowcroft (1985).

The basic objective of the privatization measures introduced in Britain has been stated as that of raising the efficiency of the industries concerned. We already reviewed some rather critical evidence about the performance of state industries in the last section, so it is clear that this argument has some force. However, other objectives have also played an important part, and the net result has sometimes been contrary to what one might have expected from efficiency arguments alone. These other objectives included the government's desire to make Britain a 'share-owning' society by encouraging widespread public participation in some of the larger public share issues; to raise revenue for the government and help to keep the

PSBR down; and last but not least, to weaken some of the major public-sector trade unions which, especially during the 1970s, were perceived as 'holding the nation to ransom'.

The effects of privatization depend on the supply and demand conditions in the industry both before and after the proposed changes are made, as Beesley and Littlechild (1986) explain. On the demand side, the size of the market and its rate of growth are both important, since expanding industries often allow new entry to occur and a larger industry in any case offers the possibility of greater consumer benefits through producing efficiently. On the supply side, cost conditions and technological change affect whether one or more firms can be economically viable in any particular market. Furthermore, those industries where considerable efforts have been made recently to lower costs are the least attractive to privatize, in that the additional benefits are probably not large. Based on these considerations, Beesley and Littlechild classified Britain's nationalized industries according to their cost and demand conditions and hence suggested a list of priorities for privatization, depending on the expected net benefits. Although finding that the privatization of the manufacturing parts of the nationalized industry sector would probably be beneficial, it was suggested that the greatest benefits would arise from privatizing the CEGB, the National Coal Board, British Rail, the Post Office, and British Telecom. Interestingly, only the last of these has so far been tackled by the government (see Table 12.4), though the government has announced its intention to privatize electricity supply commencing in 1990.

To an increasing extent, the social benefits of privatization have been offset by the government's desire to raise revenue from the sale of public sector assets. Table 12.5 shows the contribution made to government revenue by these sales. Clearly, in the early years the revenue raised in this way was very small, indeed smaller than envisaged, and many sales were delayed; but more recently it has increased sharply and it is expected to continue at about the present level for some years.

TABLE 12.5. *Sales of public sector assets,*
*1979/80 to 1989/90*

| Year | Total asset sales[a] (£m) |
|------|---------------------------|
| 1979/80 | 377 |
| 1980/1 | 405 |
| 1981/2 | 494 |
| 1982/3 | 488 |
| 1983/4 | 1139 |
| 1984/5 | 2171 |
| 1985/6 | 2707 |
| 1986/7 | 4460 |
| 1987/8 | 5139 |
| 1988/9 | 6100 (estimated) |
| 1989/90 | 5000 (planned) |

[a] Nationalized industries plus a few smaller items

*Sources*: Kay, Mayer and Thompson (1986); Economic Progress Report, Nov.–Dec. 1986; Public Expenditure White Papers (various years).

The higher revenue from asset sales in the last few years partly reflects the larger size of the industries being privatized now, but also has to do with the regulatory regimes being established for them, amounting to the creation of large, new private monopolies. For instance, in the case of British Telecom (BT), the chosen solution was to privatize the company as a single unit, rather than to create separate regional companies, or distinct companies offering local and long-distance services but using a common network. Some competition has been encouraged, affecting two areas of British Telecom business. The first concerns equipment connectable to the telephone network, such as telephones themselves, answering machines, modems, and so on. Previously BT had a monopoly over such supplies, but this is no longer the case: a wide range of other companies now provide equipment which can be connected to the network, the only requirement being certification from the DTI that the equipment in question meets the appropriate technical and safety standards. The second kind of competition comes from Mercury, a new private company set up to offer an alternative service to BT on certain trunk routes, mainly for business communications traffic, but also becoming available to domestic customers.

BT's economic behaviour, and its competitive environment, are regulated by OFTEL, the Office of Telecommunications. However, it was widely argued at the time of BT's privatization that the company retained too much monopoly power: this raised the share price and hence benefited the public revenue, but is of doubtful benefit to telephone users in general. Indeed it is far from obvious that a weakly regulated private-sector near-monopoly is to be preferred to a nationalized company, on either economic or social grounds. The privatization of BT in its existing form, therefore, reflects the government's political objectives as much as its desire to promote efficiency.

As far as efficiency is concerned, promoting competition is likely to be at least as influential as privatization *per se*, a point illustrated by developments in the bus industry since 1980. Rather than selling the National Bus Company back to the private sector, the long-established mechanism for regulating entry and allocating routes was largely dismantled, subject only to checks on such matters as passenger safety. This deregulation occurred in two stages. The first stage was a consequence of the 1980 Transport Act, which liberalized long-distance coach services. Although the state companies retained a dominant share of the market and increased their profits, substantial new entry did occur and prices fell on many routes. In addition, the quality and frequency of service increased. As Davis (1984) points out, some of the new firms soon fell by the wayside but not without forcing what appears to be a sustained improvement in the services offered by the remaining companies. While British Rail sought to avoid loss of business by offering special prices to certain groups (e.g. young people), the railways appeared to be net losers from bus deregulation; however, equally clearly, many consumers of bus services have gained substantially. One factor which helped the already established companies was their preferential access to existing city-centre bus terminals; this may change if the deregulation of long distance coaching is taken any further.

In 1986, the second stage of bus deregulation occurred. On this occasion it was applied to local bus services, with estabished and new operators competing to provide services on various routes. The new arrangements have been in operation for too short a time to permit a proper appraisal of their impact on costs, profitability and quality of service. But it is worth pointing out that some of the early 'horror stories' of buses racing for passengers, or completely clogging town centres, quickly disappeared from the headlines as the system settled down. One problem has remained, however, namely a general confusion about bus timetables as long-established arrangements to coordinate transport in many areas faded away. In the longer term, frequent changes in timetables and poor presentation of information to the public may encourage more people to use their cars, or to switch to the railways. Overall, though, the deregulation of public transport is an interesting alternative to the offer of shares to the public: the government gains no revenue, but significant gains in efficiency do seem to be achieved.

## 7. Conclusion

As should be all too apparent from the account presented above, the history of nationalization in Britain since the war is a rather disappointing one. In its initial conception, nationalization was seen as the solution to a pressing problem, and was welcomed with anticipation and excitement by politicians and public alike; and the public corporation was regarded as the most appropriate institutional expression of this solution. At different times the problem was understood in very different ways, depending on the industry being examined and its relation to the rest of the economy, or indeed to external markets. But the same solution—nationalization—was put forward time after time, not unlike the mechanical repetition of a mathematical formula.

For administrators, and even more so for politicians facing ever lengthening policy agendas, this conception of nationalization was like a dream come true. Unfortunately, it was only a dream, and very slowly and painfully the old and long-standing illusions have been shattered. On the left, very little has yet been put in the place of the now outdated ideas, and this has opened up space—both ideological and in terms of concrete policies—for the privatization programme of the present government to be initiated and take root. This programme has met with astonishingly weak, divided, and ineffectual opposition both inside and outside Parliament, a natural expression of the bankruptcy of the post-war model of nationalization.

Why, then, did the model fail, as it undoubtedly has done? This is not the place for a lengthy exegesis, but a few comments based on our earlier discussion are in order:

First, as we noted above, the model tacitly assumed that a change of ownership and the establishment of a public corporation would solve the problems of the industry concerned; but a change of ownership *per se* actually changes very little, and in any case a solution should surely depend on the particular nature of the problem.

Second, once an industry was nationalized, ministers could feel that they had 'dealt with it'; however, within a short time they were faced with demands for resources from the new managers, based on their assessment of the industry's requirements, and so further political intervention became unavoidable. One effect of such intervention was to weaken the industry's incentives to produce efficiently and to provide a good service, with consequences that are clear in the statistical record (see the fifth section). Associated with this was the frequent failure to implement the recommendations of major reports on various nationalized industries; at least partly for fear of the political consequences.

Third, the existence of many industries in the state sector, often quite closely related (especially in energy and transport), might have been expected to give rise to a degree of planning, to ensure reasonably well coordinated development in the absence of the market signals which are supposed to achieve such coordination in the private sector. Very little planning developed, however, and to a large extent each industry made its own demand, cost, and investment forecasts, independently of what the others were doing. We regard this as an opportunity missed, a chance to ensure that Britain's nationalized industry sector should provide maximum benefit to the community. It seems that the organizational form chosen for the nationalized industries was not a very suitable vehicle for the sort of coordination we would have liked to see.

Fourth, the model became a kind of dogma, in the sense that its existence both in the reality of various industries, and in the public consciousness, inhibited creative thinking about the alternative organizational structures or regulatory frameworks for industry. It is quite remarkable, for example, that every instance of nationalization carried out in the 1960s and 1970s applied virtually the same model, even though the industries being nationalized were in very different sectors and faced very different problems from those nationalized just after the war, predominantly in basic industries and infrastructure. Given this, whatever one may think about the merits of privatization (which is in danger of becoming another dogma), one can at least be grateful that the present campaign has widened the parameters for the debate about public ownership of industry.

Fifth, for the workforce of the nationalized industries, the established model had serious shortcomings. After nationalization, the model gave workers more or less the traditional adversarial position in relation to management, and focused their attention on the traditional concerns of bargaining about wages and conditions. While the economy was performing reasonably well and the public sector growing, this was an acceptable, if not especially imaginative or radical situation. But in later years, increasing economic pressure on the nationalized industries forced management to cut costs by reducing employment, in some instances very sharply. However justified this might have been in strict economic terms, it is not surprising that it resulted in severe disenchantment among the workforce, especially in view of their lack of opportunity to participate actively in the restructuring process (except as its victims).

To sum up, therefore, Britain's approach to nationalization, which was initially very appealing politically, as well as being based on a clear, simple, and administratively neat model, eventually ran up against an increasing number of serious difficulties which could not be resolved merely by tinkering with the established model. This model has had its day.

# 13

# Trade Unions and Industrial Relations*

## R. RICHARDSON

As earlier chapters have demonstrated, successive UK governments have been much more active in seeking to manage the economy since the Second World War than they were previously. As their involvement became more extensive, and as the degree of their success became more questionable, there was a search for the source of our relative economic failure. Among the favourite candidates were the trade unions and the peculiar patterns of industrial relations in the UK, but the diagnoses that lay behind this conclusion were not normally the result of sustained and systematic scientific analysis. Even the most far-reaching enquiry, that of the Donovan Commission (1968), suffered at many points from *ad hoc* reasoning and seriously limited vision. Nevertheless, a whole series of legislative changes have been introduced, many of them destined to be scrapped soon after the next change in government, seeking to alter the power of trade unions and improve the functioning of industrial relations institutions.

These legislative changes, or at least some of them, might well have been entirely appropriate for the purposes for which they were designed. A theme of this chapter is that the limited hard evidence that was and is available, as opposed to anecdotes and newspaper headlines, gives surprisingly slender support to the view that trade unions or industrial relations arrangements were themselves major contributors to our economic difficulties. Of course, the legislative changes were not prompted solely by the desire to overcome economic difficulties. But to the extent that they were a response to economic malfunctioning, they had, and continue to have, only relatively meagre support from the work of social scientists. It remains entirely possible that further work could provide more substantial support, but in its absence the safest conclusion is that many of the large charges levied against trade union activities and our institutional arrangements are 'not proven'.

It must be stressed at the outset that our knowledge on all of these matters is extremely limited. For the 1970s and 1980s there is a large and rapidly growing amount of basic information available, together with some increasingly searching analysis of labour markets and of industrial relations behaviour. The corresponding data and work for the first 25 years after the War simply do not exist, so that judgements about historical patterns and changing trends have to be qualitative and highly tentative.

The plan of the chapter is first to describe and explain the growth of union membership since 1945. It will then be appropriate to say something about the institutions of industrial relations in the UK, and changes in them. We shall then consider the impact of unions and union growth on two key objectives of economic

* I would like to thank Steve Dunn, John Kelly, Ben Roberts, and two referees for their comments on an earlier draft.

policy, the rate of economic growth and the rate of inflation. We shall finish the chapter with a brief discussion of whether industrial relations in the UK entered a new era in the 1980s, one in which the task of managing the economy has become significantly easier.

## The Growth of Trade Unions over the Post-War Period

The first column of Table 13.1 shows how the total number of trade union members in the UK has changed since 1945. It will be seen that total union membership has increased by more than 40 per cent over the period as a whole and that it has fluctuated by sizeable amounts within the period. As the size of the labour force has also changed substantially, it is appropriate to standardize union membership growth in some way. A conventional way of doing this is to express union membership as a percentage of the number of employees in employment plus the unemployed. This conventional measure of aggregate trade union 'density' was originally chosen in part because, before the Second World War, the trade unions were prominent in the provision of unemployment relief and very influential in its administration. As a result, workers quite often retained their union membership even when they were out of work. Some union members, many of those in the printing or entertainment trades, for example, still do this. Most, however, do not do so for more than a very short time and union membership is now very much tied to having a job. It is therefore probably more meaningful to measure aggregate union density by trade union membership as a percentage of employees actually in work. The second column of Table 13.1 shows how this measure has changed since 1945. It is worth noting that the more conventional measure moved in very much the same way as our preferred measure until unemployment began to rise sharply in the early 1970s.

It will be seen that aggregate union density changed very little until the late 1960s, i.e. the total number of trade union members increased more or less at the same rate as the number of employees in work. After the late 1960s, however, there was a rise in aggregate density at a pace that was probably unprecedented in British history except for the two world wars. It will also be seen that there was an even sharper fall after 1979, and that by the mid-1980s the absolute level of density was back to its level of the very early 1970s. This latter phase is reminiscent of the inter-war years when, between 1925 and 1933, total union membership fell by about 20 per cent.

Trade union membership has become far more extensive in the post-war period. This is not merely saying that aggregate density has grown. What has also happened is that the penetration of trade unions has become much more widespread. The small changes in aggregate density between 1945 and 1969 are quite misleading if they are taken to mean that very little was happening to the patterns of trade union membership. In fact, the reverse was the case. Trade union membership has always varied very much between industries and occupations. In 1945, union membership was notably strong among manual workers in certain manufacturing and extractive industries. It was also fairly strong among some white collar workers, particularly in the public sector, for example in local and central government. In many other areas, however, it was negligible.

In the 1950s and 1960s, some of the heavily unionized industries and trades began to shrink. The number of coal-miners, for example, stayed fairly level until the late

TABLE 13.1. *Trade Union membership, 1945–1985*

| Year | Total membership (thousands) | Aggregate density (percentage) | Number of trade unions |
|------|------|------|------|
| 1945 | 7,875 | 45 | 781 |
| 1947 | 9,145 | 46 | 734 |
| 1949 | 9,138 | 45 | 742 |
| 1951 | 9,535 | 46 | 735 |
| 1953 | 9,527 | 45 | 720 |
| 1955 | 9,741 | 45 | 704 |
| 1957 | 9,829 | 45 | 685 |
| 1959 | 9,623 | 43 | 668 |
| 1961 | 9,916 | 43 | 646 |
| 1963 | 10,067 | 43 | 607 |
| 1965 | 10,325 | 44 | 630 |
| 1967 | 10,194 | 45 | 606 |
| 1969 | 10,479 | 46 | 565 |
| 1971 | 11,135 | 51 | 525 |
| 1973 | 11,456 | 50 | 519 |
| 1975 | 12,026 | 53 | 470 |
| 1977 | 12,846 | 57 | 481 |
| 1979 | 13,289 | 57 | 453 |
| 1981 | 12,106 | 56 | 414 |
| 1983 | 11,236 | 53 | 394 |
| 1985 | 10,716 | 50 | 373 |

*Sources*: Estimates of trade union members and even of the number of trade unions are somewhat unreliable, and official sources sometimes disagree with one another. The estimates for total membership are taken from Bain and Elsheikh (1976, pp. 134–5) for the years up to 1965 and from the *Department of Employment Gazette* for later years; the density estimates use these membership figures and estimates for the number of employees in work taken from *British Labour Statistics, Historical Abstract 1886–1968*, for the years up to 1968, from the *DE Gazette, Historical Supplement No. 1* (August 1984), for the years 1969–83, and from the *DE Gazette* for 1985; the estimates of the number of trade unions are taken from various issues of the *DE Gazette*—it should be noted that the official definition of a trade union has changed from time to time and that *Gazettes* in successive years frequently give materially different estimates.

1950s and then began to fall rapidly; by 1968 there were nearly 350,000 fewer people employed in the coal-mines than there had been ten years earlier. Similarly, the number of people employed on the railways and in the textile industries fell sharply. In other cases, even though the total numbers employed in particular industries did not fall, the occupational composition changed away from manual workers towards white collar workers. These structural changes all worked to reduce the aggregate number of trade union members substantially. At the same time, however, trade union membership was becoming more common in groups where it had previously been much lower. Density patterns were by no means uniform across industries and occupations by the mid-1980s, but they were a lot closer together than had been the case at the end of the Second World War.

Table 13.2 gives some statistical support to this proposition. The figures are not

TABLE 13.2. *Union density by industry in Great Britain, 1948 & 1979*

| Industry | Density 1948 (%) | Density 1979 (%) |
|---|---|---|
| Food and drink | 43 | 65 |
| Tobacco | 60 | 96 |
| Chemicals | 35 | 60 |
| Metals & engineering | 55 | 80 |
| Cotton & man–made fibres | 78 | 98 |
| Other textiles | 39 | 47 |
| Leather, leather goods and fur | 33 | 28 |
| Clothing | 38 | 41 |
| Footwear | 77 | 81 |
| Bricks and building materials | 35 | 62 |
| Pottery | 61 | 72 |
| Glass | 45 | 65 |
| Timber and furniture | 45 | 35 |
| Paper and board | 37 | 57 |
| Printing and publishing | 76 | 94 |
| Other manufacturing | 39 | 43 |
| Coal mining | 86 | 97 |
| Other mining & quarrying | 57 | 43 |
| Gas | 73 | 90 |
| Electricity | 64 | 99 |
| Water | 57 | 93 |
| Construction | 46 | 37 |
| Distribution | 16 | 15 |
| National government | 53 | 91 |
| Local government & education | 69 | 77 |
| Health services | 43 | 74 |
| Post & telecommunications | 87 | 100 |
| Railways | 89 | 98 |
| Road transport | 93 | 100 |
| Sea transport | 75 | 96 |
| Port & inland water transport | 93 | 83 |
| Air transport | 39 | 85 |
| Insurance, banking & finance | 39 | 55 |
| Entertainment | 71 | 112 |
| Fishing | 48 | 20 |
| Agriculture, horticulture & forestry | 22 | 23 |
| Miscellaneous services | 5 | 7 |

*Source*:   Price and Bain (1983).

completely reliable, principally because not even the trade unions always know with a high degree of accuracy in which industries their members actually work. It is also the case that many trade unions do not have accurate and up-to-date measures of the total number of their members. It is even true that certain unions, from time to time, have reported membership figures which they knew to be somewhat inflated, in order, for example, to secure more seats on the TUC General Council. These qualifications having been made, it will be seen from Table 13.2 that the tendency over the 35 years following the Second World War was one of evening-out the levels of trade union membership density by industry.

*Explaining Trade Union Membership Growth*

Analysts have devoted much effort to explaining these developing patterns of union membership. Some have focused on why aggregate density levels have changed, while others have sought to explain the pattern of union membership by industry or occupation. The principal work on aggregate membership patterns in the UK is that by Bain and Elsheikh (1976; see also Richardson, 1977 and 1978; Bain and Elsheikh, 1978; Alison Booth, 1983; and Carruth and Disney, 1988). Bain and Elsheikh take a very long period, 1890 to 1970, and investigate the statistical association between changes in aggregate membership and various measures of business cycle pressures, such as unemployment, inflation, and changes in average money wages.

Various criticisms have been made of Bain and Elsheikh's work. Some of the data, especially for the earlier years, are very poor and may well cause the results to be distorted; the very large structural changes that have taken place in the labour force are not brought explicitly into the analysis, and their omission might lead to incorrect inferences being made; the theorizing linking membership decisions to the business cycle factors is very tenuous and sometimes highly unsatisfactory; finally, there is no investigation of the possibility that the business cycle measures are themselves influenced by changing patterns of union membership. In spite of these potential defects, however, Bain and Elsheikh's model was quite successful by some statistical criteria. Subsequent work by Booth (1983) and Carruth and Disney (1988) made further technical refinements to the basic model and arrived at somewhat different conclusions. Booth found that density tended to rise (a) when prices and average money wages were growing fast and (b) when unemployment was low and falling. Carruth and Disney agreed that union membership went up when unemployment was falling but concluded that membership fell when real wage growth was strong. They also suggested that union membership growth has tended to be stronger, other things equal, when non-Conservative Governments have been in office. Both of these recent specifications predict a significant fall in aggregate density after 1979, which is precisely what took place.

A different perspective on trade union membership patterns is to seek to explain cross sectional patterns, for example the changing structure of membership between industries and occupations. An early treatment of this question was by Bain (1970), who analysed the relatively fast post-war increase in union membership among white collar workers. One notable feature of post-war membership patterns has been that new kinds of workers, ones steadily further up the occupational hierarchy, have joined unions. A possible reason for this is that such workers came under increasing pressure, either in the degree to which they felt able to exercise effective workplace control or because their relative earnings began to slip. Another possibility, perhaps linked to the first, is that social inhibitions against collective behaviour were being eroded. With the post-war growth in social mobility, for example, increasing numbers of non-manual workers came from family backgrounds where union membership had been common. By the 1970s, virtually all occupational levels had some measure of unionization and there was much less of a class connotation attached to membership and union activity than there had previously been.

A different cross-sectional approach to the explanation of union membership patterns is exemplified by a recent survey of British industrial relations arrangements (Daniel and Millward, 1983), which found that trade union membership was strongly associated with establishment size—the larger the number of workers in a given place of work, the more likely was union presence and the higher was union density. There are, of course, many exceptions to this relationship. Some firms with sizeable plants (IBM is a well-known example) are not unionized at all, while many small ones are. But, on average, size is strongly associated with union membership. Why is this?

One answer focuses on pay. Most people would say that workers join unions principally because they want to secure higher wages, and that effective collective action is seen to make this more likely. There is also substantial evidence showing that larger establishments tend to pay higher wages than do smaller firms. This does not necessarily mean that the higher wages are the result of unions, however. Wages may be higher in larger establishments for a number of reasons; for example, bigger establishments often have to recruit from a wider geographical radius and need to compensate workers for the greater commuting involved. Further, unions are not a sufficient reason for higher wages. Presumably all workers want higher wages, and if it took only trade union membership to get them, all workers would rush to join unions. If higher wages are to explain the link between establishment size and union density, there must be some additional argument. One possibility is that many large establishments have some degree of monopoly power in their product markets and therefore earn higher than normal profits. There may be more potential for union success in such situations, they may be able to wrest some of the monopoly profits away from the employer and raise wages above the level which a competitive employer could afford.

The argument that unions flourish in larger establishments because they are more able to secure higher wages there suffers from the difficulty that an employer generally pays the same wage to a worker whether or not he or she is a union member. As far as the purely self-interested individual worker is concerned, the best possible arrangement would be for everyone else in the firm to combine into a union, to bear all the costs of doing so, and to win a wage increase which is automatically passed on to him or her, the non-member, or so-called free rider. The strict implication of this line of argument is that workers will generally wait for others to form a union and that, as a consequence, no union will ever be formed. The reply must be either that unions provide at least some services whose provision can be confined to union members or that the actions of many workers are not dominated by the kind of individualistic calculus assumed in the above argument. Both of these possibilities are in practice likely to be true.

Workers do not join unions solely to get higher wages and fringe benefits. They also join to get more control over their conditions of work. This might refer to manning rules, the kind of work they are expected to do, the pace of work, the procedures that have to be gone through when changes are to be instituted, disciplinary rules, etc. It is undoubtedly true that these conditions have always been of major significance to many workers, who in turn believe that unions substantially affect the degree to which control *vis-à-vis* management can be achieved. It is also the case that some of these control measures can be and are confined to union members. If a foreman acts in a way which union members feel to be arbitrary they often have recourse, via their shop steward, to formal and effective complaints procedures. They will also have a variety of protective arrangements if they are asked to do something they think is not legitimate. The 'nonner' may be in a much more exposed position. There is therefore often a significant insurance benefit to being a union member.

As with higher earnings, virtually all workers prefer more protection and job control to less. Why then is union membership so heavily related to establishment size? One possibility is that protection is felt by workers to be more urgent in larger establishments because their control would otherwise be especially weak or their position particularly vulnerable, say because of different forms of technology in large establishments or because of a special sensitivity to business-cycle movements. This view lies behind a Marxist position, which stresses the 'alienation' of workers in 'modern' factories, often equated with larger, more anonymous ones. A somewhat different view would stress the inevitably bureaucratic nature of larger concerns, where rules of all kinds have to be formalized, where it is inevitable that various groups produce representatives. From this group-consciousness and these representatives, it is only a relatively short step to formal trade unions. This second view is consistent with the first, but it is also consistent with all sorts of conditions, both material and other, being much better in the larger firms.

A final reason why union density is high in large establishments stresses not the special pay-off from unionization in larger establishments but the relatively low cost of organizing a union in such workplaces. Compare the position of a union seeking to organize a factory of 2,000 workers with one seeking to organize a set of 200 retail shops each employing 10 workers. The advantage in the former situation is obvious. Also, formal organization may lapse in smaller establishments, but in larger concerns this would be unusual.

None of this is to imply that employers generally recognize unions very willingly, certainly not in the private sector. Some writers suggest that employer recognition has historically been one of the most important factors determining union membership patterns, but this is often the case only tautologically. Obviously, recognition is a considerable aid to union growth—it signifies, for example, that the employer is no longer root and branch hostile to the union. But recognition has itself usually been the result of pressure, and often of sustained pressure, from the workers and the unions. Recognition is often not an independent factor but an index of the appetite for, or determination to secure, trade union services.

Union membership is also associated with factors other than size of establishment. Daniel and Millward (1983) showed that density tended to be higher in establishments which were parts of larger companies, in workplaces in the public sector, and in workplaces where most of the workers were male. Unfortunately, there are no corresponding earlier surveys on these issues so we cannot say whether the associations have changed over time. It does seem very likely, however, that plant size has been strongly associated with unionization throughout the whole of the post-war period.

Less precise approaches can supplement these statistical time series and cross-sectional attempts to explain trade union membership patterns. During the Second World War, for example, union membership mushroomed, strongly encouraged by pressures from the government to maximize the war effort. More significantly, shop stewards' committees were established in new areas. When the War ended, these provided an important organizational base from which further extensions could be won, especially as labour markets were generally tight. Union membership also became steadily less controversial in the post-war period. The desire for higher wages and greater control had always been present but unions were increasingly seen as a practical and legitimate way of securing advances. Most people in an environment hostile to unions, and where union membership is controversial, do not have so strong a commitment to collective action as to sacrifice much in order to secure union recognition. When it can be secured relatively easily, however, and when union membership in adjacent trades, firms, or occupations becomes visible, then people will opt for it for themselves as well.

By the end of the 1970s the major areas where unions were not prominent were the service industries in the private sector, particularly among the smaller firms. Elsewhere union membership was becoming very much the norm and the battle to unionize seemed to have been won. From the start of the 1980s, however, union membership suffered a very considerable setback. Some of this fall in aggregate density, illustrated in Table 13.1, was due to the relatively severe recession in the manufacturing industries. These were highly unionized so that any disproportionate decline there had a powerful impact on the average density level for the economy. Density figures industry by industry, or occupation by occupation, show a more stable pattern.

## The Closed Shop

A closed shop is an arrangement whereby an employee is required to belong to a designated union in order to hold his or her job. Some closed shops, the pre-entry type, require the worker to be a member of the union before starting the job. The other type, the post-entry closed shop, is generally thought to be much more common and requires the worker to join the union shortly after being hired. All of these arrangements, especially the post-entry kind, may well have exceptions to the rule of mandatory membership, for example on religious grounds. The first major study of the closed shop in post-war Britain was by McCarthy (1964) and it concluded that the closed shop tended to be found where it was almost a necessity if trade unionism was to function at all. As McCarthy put it, the closed shop required 'an additional readiness to take positive collective action' against the free riders, and it was seen as a rather exceptional trade union weapon.

Subsequent studies, carried out in the late 1970s, found that closed shop coverage had greatly increased during the 15 years after McCarthy had done his work (see, for example, S. Dunn, 1981). They also concluded that the more extensive patterns of the closed shop were not the result of the kind of pressures and exceptional circumstances that McCarthy had enumerated but came instead principally from a desire by both unions and employers to tidy up their arrangements. No doubt the main pressure came from the unions, who wished to increase their own financial health, eliminate the disliked free rider, and make collective action somewhat more solid. But the employer, it was claimed, could frequently see some gain in administrative tidiness from having all his employees directly covered by collective agreements. It was also suggested that the employer was anyway not convinced that granting a closed shop in a situation where density was already very high was terribly costly, especially if the unions were pressing for it with some force. It is estimated that by the end of the 1970s, about 25 per cent of the workforce was employed in closed shops. According to Millward and Stevens (1986) the percentage fell thereafter, and reached 18 per cent by 1984. The fall was thought to have been more because of the heavy recession in the industries where closed shops were common than because closed-shop agreements were torn up.

*The Number of Unions*

Table 13.1 above shows that the growing number of union members has been concentrated in a shrinking number of unions. While the number of members has substantially increased since 1945, the number of unions has halved. Some of the decline has come about because many very small unions have been wound up. In addition there has been a large number of union mergers, especially since the passage of the Trade Union (Amalgamations etc.) Act of 1964, which greatly eased the administrative obstacles facing those who wished to merge. The pattern of mergers is not always easy to explain, but they very often seem to be a sign of organizational distress rather than of purposeful planning. Frequently, for example, they reflect the falling membership and financial difficulties that come from industrial decline.

This very extensive merger activity has not obviously resulted in a more 'rational' pattern of union representation. There are some exceptions, for example in the printing trades and some of the textile industries, but very frequently there has been only a very modest industrial logic in union mergers. When a merger partner has been chosen, it has sometimes seemed that the personal wishes of the senior union officials concerned have been more important than the industrial logic of the situation. The result is that the morphology of union membership by the mid-1980s was at best only marginally clearer than it had been 20 or 30 years previously.

## A Brief Survey of Industrial Relations Institutions in the UK

By the end of the Second World War, very many wage packets in the private sector were determined through a process of multi-employer collective bargaining. This means that minimum conditions were laid down for an industry or area as a whole and had wide currency, at least as a basis, for the levels of pay set in many firms. Under these arrangements, employers were represented by employers associations and the workers were usually represented by committees of a number of trade unions. A conventional view at the time was that this represented a fine example of institutional maturity. It was widely seen to be an efficient method of establishing pay rates and of avoiding the 'chaos' and turbulence of fractured bargaining.

The principal objectives of such collective bargaining at that time were still to set wages and hours of work. Most of the other aspects of the employment relationship, for example manning rules, overtime arrangements or grievance procedures, were usually outside its purview. This does not mean that these other aspects were always decided by management prerogative. Work group pressures and 'custom and practice' were powerfully in evidence in many plants, and formalized negotiations on many of these issues were by no means unknown on a workplace basis.

As time passed, the authority of the multi-employer agreements began to wane, and the locus of collective bargaining began to shift. National agreements continued to be signed but they were supplemented to an increasing extent by less formal, local, plant-based negotiations. This development is usually thought to have been mainly a result of very tight labour markets and the growing power of shop stewards, with the growth of union recognition during the Second World War having been very important in providing a base from which the shop stewards could expand. Tight labour markets meant that employers were prepared to bid up the wage in an attempt to secure more labour. Given that industry-wide negotiations tended to reflect to some extent the conditions of those parts of the country where labour was relatively abundant, there was a persistent tendency for nationally bargained wages to be somewhat too low for employers in the other parts of the country. The consequence was that the second level of bargaining began to develop, particularly in these latter areas. One reflection of this by the late 1950s and early 1960s was the growing concern with 'wage drift', the tendency for the growth in actual earnings progressively to outstrip the growth in wages agreed in collective bargaining sessions at the national level.

This growth of multiple-level bargaining both reflected and contributed to the development of the growing power of shop stewards. Under a system of national bargaining, it was the national union leaders who were prominent on the union side. With workplace bargaining, however, the power was increasingly transferred to union representatives within individual companies or establishments, that is the shop stewards. This did not merely affect wage negotiations. In a context of generally tight labour markets, and given the quite natural ambitions of workers and shop stewards, the scope and range of bargaining issues began to widen. Industrial relations arrangements therefore become progressively more complex.

The extension of two-tier bargaining posed some problems for employers so, in an attempt to regain greater control, they encouraged a move to formal single-employer bargaining, either at the corporate level or, more usually, at the plant level. By 1980, Daniel and Millward found that in the private sector, single plant bargaining was the most important level of pay bargaining for 30 per cent of employees; corresponding numbers for the other forms were 21 per cent for multi-employer associations and 18 per cent for single-employer bargaining at the corporate level. Twenty-six per cent of workers had their pay determined by managers, which implied an absence of collective bargaining, and 5 per cent had their pay fixed by Wages Councils.

In addition to changes in the locus of bargaining there have also been a large number of changes in wage payment systems in the post-war period. Sisson and Brown (in Bain, 1983) concluded that there was a major decline in traditional piece-rate systems in favour of time-based schemes. This was part of a movement away from individual to group-based incentive schemes. Sisson and Brown note, for example, that in the late 1960s and early 1970s there was a move to 'measured daywork', a time-rate payment system with work studied output standards and no variable bonus. These subsequently became unpopular with managements and were followed by systems using bonuses linked to productivity or value added. The basic data are not very good in this area but according to the New Earnings Survey, the extent of payment-by-results (as measured by the percentage of total earnings received in this form) declined only slightly, from 11.4 per cent in 1968 to 9.1 per cent in 1987.

### The Donovan Commission

The movement from national bargaining to national plus workplace bargaining was at the heart of the findings of the Donovan Commission, a Royal Commission set up by the Labour Government in 1965, shortly after it came to power. Labour had come into office with an image of being a modernizing, reforming administration, and one of the areas that was very widely seen to be ripe for reform was industrial relations. Three industrial relations issues were seen to be of particular importance. The first was the phenomenon of unofficial or unconstitutional strikes; an 'unofficial' strike is one that is not officially recognized by the union, while 'unconstitutional' means that not all the agreed procedural steps have been followed by the workers. The second issue was the growing problem of wage inflation. The third issue was the belief that restrictive labour practices were an important reason for labour productivity continuing to grow more slowly in the UK than elsewhere in Europe. It was widely believed that industrial relations reforms could help to deal with these issues, but this belief posed two problems for the new government.

The first problem was that there was no well-established consensus as to the nature of such reform, either inside the Labour Party or outside. The second problem, even more difficult to resolve, came from the fact that the Labour Party had long had a very complex and delicate relationship with the trade union movement. Many Labour MPs were sponsored by trade unions, much of the Party's finance came from the union movement, many of its supporters and voters were union members, and it relied heavily on the unions for organizational support in general elections. It would not wish to alienate so powerful an ally and had to tread very carefully. In the area of industrial-relations reform above all, it would have been extremely imprudent for a Labour Government simply to announce its intentions, even if it had them worked out. The obvious response was to appoint a powerful Royal Commission, partly in the hope that a strong consensus view would emerge from its deliberations.

The Report of the Commission stressed the growing importance of what it termed the 'informal' system of industrial relations. This certainly referred to workplace bargaining, but more specifically it meant workplace bargaining which did not proceed via clearly laid down, written procedures. The Commission concluded, albeit with only very modest formal evidence, that the manner in which this informality had appeared had contributed to a number of economic and industrial relations difficulties, notably wage drift, unofficial strikes, and low productivity growth. It was strongly in favour of extending collective bargaining, both in the sense of bringing more workers under its operation and in widening the range of issues, both substantive and procedural, over which bargaining would take place. Most of all, however, the Commission advocated the use of formal factory agreements as a way of repairing the damage which it saw as a consequence of the higgledy-piggledy growth of informality. Its view was founded on a belief that both sides in industry have their own legitimate interests and that most people will act 'sensibly' most of the time if they are given the right institutions through which to express their points of view. Extensive and formalized, that is 'orderly', collective bargaining at the workplace was seen by the Commission as the right institution.

Most of the members of the Donovan Commission were also firm believers in the merits of what is normally termed 'voluntarism'. This meant that they did not wish to have legislation laying down precise statutory limits and obligations on industrial relations matters. They preferred instead to have the parties concerned arrive at arrangements that were mutually agreeable and which reflected local conditions. The Commission, therefore, did not wish formal factory agreements to become required by law. It preferred persuasion to legal obligation.

There was clearly a considerable extension of formal procedural agreements after the mid-1960s. Some part of this growth no doubt reflected the feeling among many managers that order should replace uncertainty, and would have happened even if the Donovan Commission had never been appointed. Another part of it was probably stimulated by Donovan. But perhaps the greatest part was encouraged by a whole series of legislative Acts, most of which came after the Donovan Commission reported. The twists and turns in this legislative history vividly illustrate the complexities of industrial relations affairs.

### Pre-Donovan Reform

As was noted above, voluntarism was the tradition in British industrial relations, supported by unions and employers alike. But by the mid-1960s, governments were becoming sufficiently concerned with the operation of labour markets and industrial relations events to feel that some reforms were imperative. The first important example of these reforms was the Industrial Training Act of 1964, an attempt to remedy what were thought to be serious and pervasive shortages of skilled workers. It was widely felt that individual employers were reluctant to train workers because they expected the workers, once trained, to be poached by other firms. The result, it was believed, was that far too few workers were being trained. The Act therefore set up Industrial Training Boards (ITBs) in many industries and empowered them to impose a levy on the payroll of each firm. The proceeds of this levy were then to be spent on providing training.

The ITBs were symptomatic of a developing tendency towards 'corporatism', an approach to industrial and economic affairs that was to become much more important later in the 1960s and 1970s. Corporatism reflected the growing legitimacy of trade unions, the belief that they represented interests that should formally be recognized and taken into account when making decisions. It typically resulted in institutions where employers, unions, and governments met to consult and take action. In the case of the ITBs the main operating decisions did not directly involve the government but they gave unions a foothold in an area that had previously been very largely the preserve of employers.

The next important piece of legislation which chipped away at the principle of voluntarism was the Redundancy Payments Act of 1965. Before the passage of this Act, there seems to have been only fairly patchy bargaining between employers and unions on redundancy terms, for example on the amount of compensation to be paid to workers whose services were no longer needed. The Act made provision for workers declared redundant to be given a lump sum payment, the size of which was to depend on the worker's age, the length of time he had been working in his job, and the level of his earnings. Part of the lump sum was to be paid directly by the employer and part was to come from the Redundancy Fund, which was to be financed from a payroll levy imposed on all private sector employers. The Redundancy Payments Act, like the earlier Industrial Training Act, seems to have given an impetus to the extension of collective bargaining. Many unions have subsequently negotiated much better redundancy terms for their members than are laid down in the statutory schedule. They are also now more likely to have a role in the redundancy process itself, for example in helping to determine precisely who should be made redundant and what length of notice should be given.

*Post-Donovan Industrial Relations Reform*

The Industrial Training and Redundancy Payments Acts were early examples of the erosion of voluntarism, but they were not particularly contentious, in part because they were not directed towards the core issues of industrial relations. The situation changed dramatically once the Donovan Commission had reported in 1968, because the Commission obviously had addressed many of the core issues in a way which made the Labour Government of the day feel that it had to respond. This caused them considerable embarrassment because, in spite of the Donovan deliberations, the trade unions generally clung fiercely to the principle of voluntarism, that is to the belief that industrial relations change should result only from agreement between the parties directly concerned and not be imposed by statute. By 1969, however, the Labour Government felt that some change had to be imposed, so widespread was the view that there were too many damaging unofficial strikes and that unregulated industrial relations was a major contributor to inflation and slow growth.

The government, therefore, published a White Paper, *In Place of Strife*. This accepted much of the Donovan analysis but wished in a very limited way to go down the statutory road. For example, it proposed that employers be required to recognize and negotiate with unions, on pain of otherwise being faced with legally binding arbitration, and encouraged the appointment of worker–directors to company boards. Much more contentious was the proposal that the Secretary of State for Employment would have the power to impose a 'conciliation pause' of 28 days in the event of an unconstitutional strike; the Secretary of State was also to be given the power, in some carefully defined circumstances, of requiring a ballot before a strike. These proposed powers were backed up by sanctions, including the possibility of prison for recalcitrant strikers.

On any dispassionate analysis it is hard to see that these proposals, in themselves, would have had a substantial effect on industrial relations behaviour. They were, however, an assault on voluntarism in a particularly sensitive area and they aroused so much hostility among trade union leaders and in the Parliamentary Labour Party that they had to be dropped, in circumstances which were politically highly embarrassing for the government.

After the Labour Party lost the succeeding election, the Conservative Government passed the Industrial Relations Act of 1971. This was a very complicated piece of legislation and constituted a much more systematic attack on voluntarist arrangements. Employees were to be given the legal right to belong, or not to belong, to a trade union and were to be eligible for compensation against unfair dismissal; collective bargaining was normally to be legally enforceable, there was to be machinery to resolve disputes over claims for trade union recognition, and a requirement on employers to provide certain information to workers and unions; the new concept of 'unfair industrial practices' was created and compensation was to be paid to those injured by them; trade unions and Employers Associations were required to be registered; new agencies, including a National Industrial Relations Court, were set up; and the Secretary of State for Employment was to be given powers to issue restraining orders, lasting 60 days, in certain types of industrial action. The broad intention of this legislation was to bring industrial relations into the law in a fairly detailed way. The underlying belief was that if collective agreements became legally enforceable, and if the rights and obligations of the parties became clear in law, then industrial relations would become more orderly. The principal immediate point of attack was the unofficial or unconstitutional strike.

The legislation aroused enormous controversy and a level of trade union opposition which was unparalleled in the post-war period. In other circumstances it might well have had a very significant effect on industrial relations but its actual effects were more important for politics than for industrial relations or economic policy. It aroused so much political animosity that it was immediately scrapped when the Labour Party resumed power in 1974, an event which was itself directly caused by a national strike in the coal-mines. There followed a series of Acts which very considerably strengthened the position of the trade unions. The first of these was the Trade Union and Labour Relations Act of 1974, which repealed the 1971 Act but re-enacted, with some amendments, the unfair dismissals provisions of that Act and provided legal immunities for those carrying out certain kinds of industrial action.

This was followed in 1975 by the Employment Protection Act which established some new industrial relations machinery and provided new legal rights for employees. The most important new piece of machinery was the Advisory, Conciliation and Arbitration Service (ACAS), which *inter alia* was to help unions gain recognition, offer conciliation services to help settle disputes, offer industrial relations advice to all parties, conduct enquiries into industrial relations matters, and issue codes of practice. The rights granted to employees included maternity leave and the right of shop stewards to be given reasonable time off, with pay, to pursue industrial relations duties. An employer who proposed to declare redundancies was required to give advance notification to its employees and to consult with any recognized trade unions as soon as possible.

The general effect of these and other Acts, notably the 1974 Health and Safety at Work Act, as well as other actions by the Labour Government, was greatly to strengthen the position of workers, shop stewards, and trade unions *vis-à-vis* the employer. As Table 13.1 shows, their passage coincided with a great upsurge in trade union membership and it is not unreasonable to attribute at least part of this increase to the legislation. It cannot be said, however, that the legislation was aimed at the economic problems that had earlier been of so much concern. The legislation did nothing directly to reduce strikes, raise productivity, or lower inflation.

By 1979 the pendulum of British politics had begun to swing decisively away from Labour, and the Conservative Government elected in that year pursued a very different strategy from that of Mr Heath in the early part of the decade. Instead of one major and comprehensive Act, they passed three important but relatively small-scale pieces of legislation by the end of their second term of office in early 1987. Taken together, these probably had a significant effect on the conduct of industrial relations but it is not easy to be confident about this because the economy was at the same time subject to very considerable shocks which would themselves normally be expected to change industrial relations behaviour. The first of these Acts was the Employment Act of 1980. Among other things, this sought to encourage secret ballots on whether to call a strike and for the election of trade union officials, gave a measure of protection to those workers who did not wish to join a closed shop, placed narrower limits on what constituted lawful picketing, and restricted the legality of 'secondary' industrial action, that is action at a workplace other than one's own.

The Employment Act of 1982 put further limits on the closed shop, reduced the legal immunities enjoyed by trade unions, and restricted the definition of lawful trade disputes to those involving workers and their own employer about pay and working conditions. Finally, the Trade Union Act of 1984 sought to affect the way in which trade unions conducted their own affairs. Its main provisions required senior union officials to be elected by secret ballot and made trade unions' legal immunity for organizing industrial action conditional on the holding of secret ballots.

These pieces of legislation again brought industrial relations into the law courts— they once more gave trade unions a legal personality, and thereby put union funds at risk from court action. They also inhibited trade unions from employing a range of weapons some of them had long been accustomed to use, and brought union members more directly and continuously into the conduct of union affairs. For example, following the passage of the legislation quite a number of strike ballots were 'lost' by the union, that is the members voted not to go on strike. This is not to imply that they would necessarily have gone on strike under the old procedures, nor that they would always have been denied the opportunity to express their views in a secret ballot. Nor does the requirement to hold a secret ballot necessarily benefit the employer. When the membership vote strongly for strike action, for example, the employer cannot so easily use the argument that there is no grievance and that the union leaders have not got their members behind them. There have certainly been occasions when managers felt their negotiating position was weakened by ballot results.

### The Consequences of More Formal Industrial Relations

The great volume of legislation since the mid-1960s undoubtedly affected the degree to which industrial relations arrangements became formalized. Daniel and Millward's authoritative industrial relations survey clearly indicated that there was a high level of formalization in many areas of employer/union relations by 1980. This meant that there were written agreements on industrial relations procedures and a relatively clear delineation of how things were to be done. The survey also concluded that there had been a fairly rapid growth in formalization over the previous five to ten years, that is since Donovan had reported. It is generally believed that this change was in good part a response to legislative changes which required employers to have more formalized arrangements in a number of areas. Whether, as Donovan implied, this growth in formalization contributed to an increase in labour productivity or to a reduction in either wage drift or unofficial strikes is a very open question. Certainly no one has provided strong evidence that this was the case, while some work has argued against it. Thus, Blanchflower and Cubbin (1986) used the 1980 survey data in an attempt to explain the pattern of strikes between establishments. They found that the existence of more formal industrial relations arrangements went along with a greater, not a lesser, frequency of strikes. As is so often the case, there is no unambiguous interpretation of this finding. It could be, for example, that greater formalization was a response to a high underlying strike propensity; alternatively, the formalization could, in spite of Donovan's analysis, actually have increased strikes. Whatever the true interpretation, these findings give no direct support to the Donovan position.

## Industrial Relations and Economic Policy

As was noted above, trade union actions and industrial relations arrangements have frequently been blamed for at least some of the poor industrial performance of the UK, as well as our tendency to be a relatively high inflation country. Three specific themes have been the impact of strikes, the resistance to change (particularly to technological innovation), and our inefficient wage-setting machinery. These will be discussed in turn.

### Strikes

In spite of its being a staple of public discussion, Britain's strike problem has been greatly exaggerated. One indication of this comes from comparing Britain with other countries. The data are not always strictly comparable but the best available evidence suggests that by international standards the UK is affected only to an average extent by strike activity. This is not to deny that strikes are costly and wasteful, nor that particular firms or industries have been severely damaged by them. But, in spite of the very considerable political debate they have generated, strikes can hardly in aggregate have led directly to the damaging economic consequences frequently claimed. Table 13.3 shows some strike statistics for the post-war period. A number of points stand out. First, the number of working days lost through strikes has persistently been very small when compared with the number of days worked in a year. In a typical year, less than a tenth of one per cent of the total available worktime has been lost through strikes. Expressed another way, the average worker has been on strike for no more than two to four hours a year.

In one important respect this is a misleading image because the average worker was not on strike in any one year. In most years, well over 90 per cent of workers were not involved in strike activity at all. A second point is that strike activity has displayed something of a cyclical pattern in the post-war period. A number of studies have shown that strikes tended to become more frequent when unemployment was relatively low and inflation was relatively high. A third point is that in many years when there was a particularly large total of working days lost the statistics were heavily affected by a single large dispute. A series showing working days lost which excluded the largest strike in the year would have a very much more even pattern than that shown in the second column of Table 13.3.

Given that strike activity has been relatively small and highly concentrated in relatively few industries it is not surprising that it has been difficult to identify a substantial link between strike rates and the patterns of economic growth. There are obvious examples of strike proneness and poor industrial performance. The motor car industry, for example, has had a clear tendency to suffer from a large number of very often small strikes throughout much of the post-war period. It is also an industry where performance levels and production have tended to fall

TABLE 13.3. *Strikes in the post-war
period, 1947–1985*

| Year | No. of strikes | Working days lost (thousands) |
|------|----------------|-------------------------------|
| 1947 | 1721 | 2433 |
| 1949 | 1426 | 1807 |
| 1951 | 1719 | 1694 |
| 1953 | 1746 | 2184 |
| 1955 | 2419 | 3781 |
| 1957 | 2859 | 8412 |
| 1959 | 2093 | 5270 |
| 1961 | 2686 | 3046 |
| 1963 | 2068 | 1755 |
| 1965 | 2354 | 2925 |
| 1967 | 2116 | 2787 |
| 1969 | 3116 | 6846 |
| 1971 | 2228 | 13551 |
| 1973 | 2873 | 7197 |
| 1975 | 2332 | 6012 |
| 1977 | 2737 | 10142 |
| 1979 | 2125 | 29474 |
| 1981 | 1344 | 4266 |
| 1983 | 1364 | 3754 |
| 1985 | 903 | 6402 |

*Sources*:   Durcan *et al.* (1983) for the years 1947–73; *DE
Gazette* (August 1986) p. 324, for the years
1975–85.

behind those in the rest of Europe. To establish this association is not the same
thing as establishing a strong causal connection, however. No doubt industrial
unrest hurt the UK motor car industry, but the extent of the damage done, in
comparison with that caused by other factors, is extremely difficult to establish.
The problem here is that strikes are very public, noticeable events. They can
readily be pointed to as self-inflicted wounds. This does not mean that they are in
the first rank of importance.

There have been very many attempts to explain strike patterns in the UK, a fact
which itself suggests that the problem has resisted explanation. The tradition
among industrial relations experts has emphasized the fact that strikes, their
causes, and their incidence, are an exceedingly variable phenomenon (see, for
example, Knowles, 1952). Almost anything can be the cause of a strike and, among
most industrial relations academics, there has perhaps been a reluctance to simplify
or generalize on the issue, except to advocate changes in industrial relations
machinery. Thus, Durcan and his colleagues (Durcan *et al.*, 1983) examined strike
patterns over the period 1946–73 in a number of industries and concluded that
changes in the method of setting wages were very important influences on strike
patterns. The coal-mining industry provides a good illustration of their approach.

In the early post-war period a very large majority of the nation's officially
recorded strikes occurred in the coal-mining industry. For the most part these were

relatively short and small-scale strikes but cumulatively they were both directly important and suggestive of deeper and more substantial causes of inefficiency. One of the features of the coal-mining industry is that output is heavily affected by very local conditions. Even within a single pit there will be variations in geological conditions, either from face to face or from week to week, which cause output and productivity to alter substantially. It has therefore been a tradition in the industry that at least some of this variation should be reflected in wages. This in turn led to large numbers of disputes as to whether the precise variation in wages sought by management was justified or was too great. Partly for this reason, and partly because the major union in the industry had a very strong preference for a single 'rate for the job' being established as widely as possible, a new system of setting wages began to be introduced in the mid-1960s. This led to more stable and uniform wages and to an erosion of certain wage differentials. One result, it is claimed by Durcan and his associates, was a sharp reduction in the number of strikes. It can also be argued that another consequence was the reappearance of national strikes in the coal industry. There were two such strikes in the early 1970s, following which management reintroduced a significant degree of wage variability via productivity schemes and area bonus systems. This process was accelerated after the third and largest national strike, which ended in 1985.

Economists have usually taken a very different line from industrial relations academics when seeking to explain strike patterns. A large number of studies have been published, some of them focusing on variations in strike incidence over time, and others seeking to explain the variation in strikes among different industries or plants. Most of the time-series work seeks to relate strike outbreaks to at least two key factors, namely the rate of unemployment and the rate of increase in real wages. Other factors, for example the use of incomes policy, will often be added to the analysis but unemployment and real wages are nearly always present. Their inclusion can be justified in a variety of ways. Perhaps the most general justification is to see the unemployment rate as an index of trade union bargaining strength, or more precisely as an index of what unions and their members see as their bargaining strength *vis-à-vis* the employer. When unemployment is high, unions see their relative bargaining strength as low, and vice versa. The real wage change variable may be seen as an index of worker grievances. The argument would be that workers form an adaptive view of how much of an increase in real wages they are currently legitimately entitled to, or can in practice get. This means that they will look at the increases they and others have had in recent years, placing a higher weight on the more recent increases, and see how they are doing against the trend. If they have been doing well against the trend they will be relatively satisfied, have relatively mild grievances, and not be so likely to initiate strike action. Such a model was applied to UK data (Pencavel, 1970) with some success.

Other economists have employed similar variables but starting from the proposition that strikes take place when both sides are in some way ignorant about the position and resolve of the other party. The key question then becomes, in what circumstances is such ignorance more likely? It can be plausibly argued, for example, that the two sides have distinctly different information around the peak of the business cycle. Employers will be tending to look to the future and will be seeing the beginning of a deceleration in orders. They will therefore become more pessimistic and more resistant to high wage claims. The workers on the other hand will see the recent improvements signified by a buoyant economy and will be extrapolating them into the future. The possibilities of a clash resulting in a strike are obvious.

Recent cross-sectional work on strikes by economists is exemplified by Blanch-flower and Cubbin (1986). They follow a number of theoreticians in believing that strikes can be explained by models drawn from 'game theory'; these are seen to give a framework for classifying the role of such influences on strikes as mistakes, malice, political opportunism, weak management, militant unions, and poor institutional arrangements. Using 1980 cross-sectional data, Blanchflower and Cubbin conclude that strikes were more likely in large plants, and in those where payment-by-results wage systems were employed, and where there was multi-unionism. Further, the presence of formal procedures and joint consultative committees were both positively associated with strike frequency. This might mean that such institutions were a response to high strike propensities or, by introducing unnecessary rigidities and delays into industrial relations dealings, a cause of them. If the latter is the correct interpretation, the recommendations of the Donovan Commission would be undermined.

The two approaches, the time-series and the cross-sectional are basically complementary. The structural variables emphasized in the cross-sectional analysis do not usually change very much from year to year, whereas strike patterns do. The cross-sectional work, therefore, is seeking to understand why certain industries or plants tend to be 'strike prone' year in and year out, while others are more or less strike free. The time series work seeks to explain why turbulence is high in some years but not in others.

Another interpretation of strike patterns stems from the work of political scientists. One of the more interesting strike patterns is the bunching of strikes in certain longer periods, for example in certain decades. Table 13.3 shows, for example, that strikes were unusually high in the 1970s. Is this just a reflection of, for example, bad information being acute at that time or of particular patterns of unemployment and real wage changes? One view, most powerfully expressed for the UK by Cronin (1979), is that there are different factors at work. In this view there are, from time to time, strike 'waves' which are best seen as an expression of deep-seated struggles for power, not just in the workplace but in society at large. One version of this story would incorporate Kondratieff Waves, that is long-run phases of economic expansion and decline. In this interpretation, certain social groups who had previously been relatively powerless begin to feel more confident as the long cycle upturn proceeds. This increase in confidence takes some time to germinate but when it appears it begins to find expression in political and social life in a whole variety of ways, all of which involve a questioning of previous standards and mores, which at any time usually reflect the views of dominant groups in society. The previously powerless begin to struggle to gain the recognition which they sense their changed economic significance and position holds out for them. One industrial relations corollary of this might well be an extension of unionization, as workers begin to feel more confident in collective action. A second industrial relations corollary, one that is obviously linked to the first, is a greater preparedness to embark on strike action. After a while, it is claimed, the long cycle begins to peak and the power position of the rising groups comes under threat. At the same time, resistance from the previously powerful groups becomes fiercer because they are less able to pass on, for example to consumers, the costs of the struggle. This model implies that strikes will tend to become more frequent at some point during the long cycle upswing, and that strike waves will be most common around the peak of long economic cycles. For the UK this fits in well with the strike wave of the 1970s and the sharp fall in strike activity in the 1980s. The perspective here is not with the changes in strike activity from year to year but from, say, decade to decade. It is sensitive to the possibility that over time there are substantial changes in the background parameters within which strike decisions are taken (see also Screpanti, 1987).

## Labour Productivity

Just as with the analysis of strikes, there is a range of views about the impact of trade unions on labour productivity in the UK. One frequently expressed view is that British unions have contributed to low productivity because of a traditional reluctance to agree to new working methods, for example new technology, in turn because of fears that their control of the work process would be reduced. This was manifestly the case in certain industries, for example in the printing industries, most notably in Fleet Street (Jenkins, 1979). In more typical circumstances, unions are said to have used their power not to block new methods totally but either to slow down their introduction or to dilute their impact and make their costs greater.

A specific variant of this general story is the possibility that the frequency of multi-unionism makes innovation more difficult. Multi-unionism, the existence of more than one recognized trade union in an establishment, is by no means confined to the UK but it has assumed particularly complex forms here. It has long been normal in manufacturing for more than one union to be recognized by management and for different kinds of workers to have their own separate union. This has given rise to demarcation problems, 'who does what', which can become especially acute when new methods of production are being contemplated.

The charge that unions in general, and the structure of UK unions in particular, have seriously impeded economic growth has been a constant of public policy debate in the post-war years, indeed in the pre-war years too. But careful and systematic research on the question was rather slow in coming. Such work did begin to appear by the mid-1970s, however, and the authors are by no means always in agreement. A powerfully argued statement of the view that unions have contributed to the slow pace of industrial advance in the UK was recently published by Correlli Barnett (1986). This was based on a series of case studies and concentrated on conditions during the Second World War. More recent studies have directly sought to hold technology, management style, and type of product constant. For example, case studies of plants in multi-national firms or modern steel plants in different countries have tended to conclude that output per worker in the UK is much lower than on the Continent. They often attribute much of the observed labour productivity difference to factors like demarcation rules, which in turn are often seen to be a consequence of multi-unionism.

Pratten (1976) concluded from a comparison of British, West German, and Swedish plants that more than 30 per cent of the large observed difference in output per worker was due to industrial relations factors. Unfortunately, he did not provide detailed reasoning, so the accuracy of his judgement cannot readily be assessed (see Nichols, 1986). Again, studies in the motor-car and steel industries in the mid-1970s purported to show similar relationships. The quality of the data in these studies is very hard to assess from what is publicly available and it is wise to be very cautious before accepting their implications.

A contrary position on some of these issues comes from Davies and Caves (1987). For the mid-1960s and mid-1970s, they identified a sample of manufacturing industries in both the UK and the USA, measured productivity levels and productivity changes, and correlated the resulting differences with some measures of trade union activity or structure. If the critics of unions are correct, the weakly unionized sectors in the UK should have had productivity levels much closer to those elsewhere than did the strongly unionized sectors. Davies and Caves discovered very large and varied differences in labour productivity between the two countries—the best eight industries in the UK achieved about 60 per cent of their American counterparts' productivity in 1977, while the worst eight achieved less than 30 per cent. Davies and Caves then sought to explain these differences, and the corresponding patterns for 1967. Among the candidates to explain the patterns was a set of variables seeking to capture different aspects of industrial relations. After extensive testing it was found that industrial relations factors were never among the most important explanations but that some such factors did have a secondary role, especially in the earlier period. By 1977, however, even this relatively marginal impact was found to have disappeared.

A third approach perhaps goes even further in absolving unions and industrial relations practices from any blame for low productivity growth in the UK. Lintner et al. (1987) carried out a survey of managers in the British engineering industry, who were strongly of the view that trade unions had only rarely been an impediment to the introduction of new technology.

Some writers have tried to take this one step further and have drawn on American work which suggests that unions might even have raised labour productivity in the UK. The argument here is that unions act as the agents of their members, and communicate the otherwise hidden grievances of workers to management, with the result that workers are more contented with their conditions in unionized plants and are more productive. There is virtually no published empirical support for this proposition in the UK.

On the contrary, recent developments and research have tended to conclude that unions have been a factor behind slow productivity growth in the post-war period. For example, it is well known that certain motor-car manufacturing companies that have plants both in the UK and elsewhere have tended to switch production away from the UK in the post-war period. They did this even when wage rates were relatively low in the UK. The obvious conclusion is that UK productivity was thought by senior management to be low, even within firms where technology, product, and management could not differ very much. Another piece of evidence supporting the view that unions seriously inhibited industrial performance for much of the post-war period is the record of productivity growth since 1979 in manufacturing industry. The very deep recession in manufacturing clearly put the trade unions very much on the defensive, and made them relatively powerless to stop management from introducing the changes which they wanted to introduce for a very long time. A recent case study of part of the coal industry supports this interpretation (Richardson and Wood, 1989). Following its victory in the 1984/5 miners' strike, management in the coal industry reasserted its authority, tightened performance standards, shed very large amounts of labour, nibbled away at entrenched custom and practice, and introduced some changes in the wage payment systems. This was seen to have led to a remarkable increase in output per worker, which rose by more than 50 per cent over a three-year period in the industry as a whole. The implication that union strength had previously contributed to a lowering of labour productivity is further supported by a recent view of the studies in this area (Metcalf, 1989), which concludes that 'we can be pretty sure of the (negative) direction of the effect that unions have on labour productivity'.

## Trade Unions, Inflation, and Wages

It was a persistent underlying policy theme between the end of the Second World War and the late 1970s that trade unions had a powerful impact on wages in Britain. This was said to be the case in two separate but linked ways. First, it was claimed, trade unions distorted the structure of wages and thereby inhibited the efficient allocation of labour; second, it was claimed, unions were an engine of inflation. These claims are reviewed in turn.

By the early 1950s there began to be agitation for a more 'rational' wage structure, that is for wages to reflect current demand-and-supply influences rather than what were seen to be a whole series of historical and institutional excrescences accumulated over the years and distorting the efficient allocation of labour. Trade unions were thought to be prominent among the sources of distortion. For many years it was not possible directly to estimate the impact of the trade unions on the wage structure because we did not have satisfactory data on the extent of union membership by industry or occupation. By the mid-1970s, however, more or less suitable data began to be available and a whole series of estimates have now been made. The early estimates often found quite large union differentials, some higher than 35 per cent (Metcalf, 1977). More recently, however, as statistical techniques and data have become more refined, the typical conclusion, perhaps surprisingly, is that trade union density or membership is not powerfully associated with wages. One widely regarded estimate (Stewart, 1983) is that a wholly unionized work group would typically earn no more than an extra 5 or 10 per cent than an otherwise similar but wholly ununionized work group. By extension of this approach, some analysts have concluded that the typical union/non-union differential increases when the economy is in recession and decreases in times of prosperity.

Some argue that this kind of calculation understates the impact of unions because the wage increases they in fact secure are then transmitted to the non-unionized, and thus escape detection. This may be true but it is exceptionally difficult to establish, and if it is true it means that unions are less important as a source of inefficient wage structures than as a source of inflationary pressures. The alternative interpretation is that unions, like many other monopolizing elements, cannot enjoy very substantial 'excess' returns indefinitely because of substitution possibilities elsewhere. Thus, if unions organizing the industries engaged in foreign trade were to raise the price of labour they would soon face such severe competition from abroad that their gains would be quickly eroded. In the more sheltered trades the process might take much longer. In the printing industry, for example, it has arguably lasted for decades; with new technology, it seems now to be on the run.

The disquiet about the structure of wages was rarely an important focus of public policy concern outside the period in the mid-1960s when there was a National Board for Prices and Incomes (see Fels, 1972). But there has been a deep and persistent worry about average money wages that has affected almost all governments in the post-war period. Underpinning this has been the view that inflation is a cost-push phenomenon largely instigated or continued by trade unions. By the early 1960s governments were very conscious of wage drift, the tendency of actual earnings to grow faster than national wage settlements, and began to see it as resulting from the lack of order in industrial relations institutions. This general view was given some support by Hines (1964) in a reply to Phillips's famous analysis of the impact of unemployment on average money wages. Hines concluded that the best single explanation of changing wages was changing levels of trade union membership. His argument was that more urgent grievances led to higher membership, because trade unions were seen to be the channel through which wage increases could be achieved. Hines's analysis was extensively discussed by economists in the late 1960s and early 1970s, and although it was heavily revised his basic finding could not readily be refuted.

The emphasis on trade unions as an engine of inflation lay behind some of the attempts, discussed above, to reduce the number of unofficial strikes. The more direct attack on the problem, however, came from the variety of attempts by post-war governments to make a success of incomes policies. An incomes policy is an attempt to replace market wage determination arrangements by centrally administered ones. Sir Stafford Cripps was a pioneer in this area with his voluntary wage pause of 1947. Thereafter the weapon was not used again until the Conservative Government tried it in 1962. But it was not until the Labour Government of the 1960s that there was a thoroughgoing commitment to incomes policies. Subsequently there was a variety of experiments under Mr Heath in the early 1970s and under Mr Wilson and Mr Callaghan in the mid- and late 1970s. The precise form of incomes policy varied substantially between these experiments. Some were backed by statutory powers, while others were voluntary; some had flat-rate norms, others permitted percentage increases, while others used more complex formulae; some allowed wage increases above the norm for stated reasons, while others tolerated no exceptions; some were introduced on their own, while others were used in conjunction with price controls and/or limitations on dividends; some were accompanied by fiscal and monetary contraction, while others had economic expansion as a quid pro quo.

The consensus among analysts of these experiments is that they largely failed. Why otherwise were they scrapped? More formal, econometric analysis suggests that, at best, they had only a small effect except perhaps temporarily. The key question is why? What accounts for their breakdown? This is not a trivial question. It lies at the heart of economic policy, for the failure of incomes policies has undoubtedly contributed very substantially to the underlying increase in the level of unemployment we have experienced since the mid-1960s.

There are three hypotheses for why incomes policies failed. The first, and vaguest, is that there was inadequate consent. This is a slippery concept but in part it refers to a widespread lack of agreement about the desirability and legitimacy of incomes policies. In fact, opinion polls have consistently shown considerable approval of the principle of incomes policies among the population at large, which must mean that part of the required consent in fact existed. But inadequate consent also implies a willingness to adhere to the collective constraint of the incomes policy norm. Here there was manifestly much less consent. Many groups of workers were able to secure more for themselves than was permitted under the terms of the policy and were not prepared to forgo their opportunity. Others, perhaps fearing that they would be left behind, were not prepared to take the chance.

This leads on to the second hypothesis, the possibility that the industrial relations institutions worked against success in this area. British industrial relations are highly fragmented and decentralized, and bargaining is taking place somewhere all through the year. In some other countries, bargaining is highly centralized and most groups agree their contracts at the same time. Many believe that the particular institutional forms in the UK were decisive factors behind wage push.

The third possible reason for the failure of incomes policies is held to be the absence of credible sanctions on those who violated the norm. In some policy phases there were sanctions, even the possibility of going to prison! But it is generally believed that the sanctions were rarely credible to many of those involved in the negotiations and that consequently all that was required to evade the policy was an exercise in ingenuity.

## Conclusions

Industrial relations have been closer to the heart of economic policy in the UK than in almost any other country in the world in the post-war period. Even today, the amount of time spent in the average news broadcast on industrial relations issues and events is surprisingly large. In the absence of hard evidence to the contrary it is unwise to dismiss this absorption as having no counterpart in reality. But it must be said again that there is a surprising dearth of solid work to support the view that defective industrial relations machinery has been a core reason for the poor post-war performance of the UK economy. The above survey certainly does not demonstrate this, whether on the importance of strikes, the extent to which labour productivity and innovation have been held back by recalcitrant unions or the degree to which unions have caused inflation. Perhaps the best way to conclude this chapter is to consider the claim that Britain began to enjoy a distinctly new style of industrial relations in the 1980s and, if it did, what that implies about what went before (see Richardson and Wood, 1989, for a more extended treatment).

For many industrial relations academics, their subject is the study of institutions. For them it is natural to test for the existence of a new era by looking to see whether there have been radical institutional changes. For example, have employers withdrawn union recognition, have single-union deals replaced multi-unionism, is the closed shop withering away, are shop stewards having facilities taken away from them by employers, and is the locus and content of collective bargaining changing substantially? There is no doubt that some such changes have taken place but Batstone and Gourlay (1986) and, perhaps to a lesser extent, Millward and Stevens (1986) were explicit, but not unqualified, in their judgements that there were few profound changes in industrial relations institutions in the first half of the 1980s. Batstone and Gourlay, for example, noted that although union membership had fallen, density had not changed much, the closed shop had hardly diminished, the number of shop stewards per 1,000 members had, if anything, risen, and union recognition had rarely been withdrawn. In short, formal trade union organization was intact, though a little bruised in certain areas.

Perhaps the key question raised by this kind of evidence is how much it tells us. Maybe the turbulence of the early 1970s taught managers that a frontal attack on union organization and well-established institutions was a losing tactic, and that it was far more effective to turn the flank by seeking to change industrial relations outcomes from largely unaltered forms. This suggests a different way of judging whether there is a new industrial relations, one that concentrates on the outcomes from the industrial relations system.

The UK economy, particularly the manufacturing part, began to enter a very severe recession in 1979, and managers were faced with exceptionally great pressures. Markets were falling, costs were rising, and profits were disappearing. Employers responded in a variety of ways, including plant closures and large scale redundancies (manufacturing employment fell by 28 per cent from 7.1m. in June 1979 to 5.1m. in June 1987).

As a corollary of this slimming down, output per worker rose fast by historic standards. Some indication of this was provided in a study by Ray (1987), which concluded that output per worker in manufacturing in Great Britain rose faster after 1980 than in other major industrial countries (the US, Japan, France, W. Germany, Italy, Belgium, and the Netherlands). Although productivity was estimated to have remained much lower in absolute terms than in these countries, it rose faster, sometimes by a very significant amount; output per worker in W. Germany, for example, was estimated to be only 80 per cent greater than in Britain in 1986, as opposed to 150 per cent greater in 1980.

In part, the increase in output per worker was an arithmetic consequence of some of the least productive facilities being closed down. In addition, there seems to have been a sharp and genuine rise in output per worker from new methods of production and working practices. Some of this was associated with technical change embodied in new capital equipment, even though a deep recession is not normally associated with a rapid rise in investment. An additional element was due to workers doing things more effectively, in other words to some combination of job redesign, scrapping of custom and practice, new manning levels, increased flexibility, reduced demarcation, and increased effort. This would often be seen as a sign of a reduced control by the workforce over the labour process, as a diminution of the strength of labour, and it could well have occurred even though formal industrial relations and trade union organization had been largely unaffected.

As Table 13.3 shows, there was also a sharp fall in the incidence of strikes in the 1980s. This too would often be taken as symptomatic of a decline in labour's strength. Turning to a third industrial relations outcome, pay, a new state of industrial relations would be indicated by pay levels which departed from those explained by conventional models. The puzzle here is that, if anything, real earnings have grown very rapidly in the 1980s given, for example, the level of unemployment and vacancies. Indeed, the rapid and sustained increase in pay might itself be an explanation for the low level of strikes. On the face of it, rapid wage increases could indicate strong unions. In the context of the other changes, a better interpretation might be that there was indeed a new industrial relations, but that it was new in some unexpected aspects.

The following is highly speculative but it seems to be consistent with the evidence. It starts with the well-known fact that at the end of the 1970s the UK was, by European standards, a low productivity/low wage economy. The depth of the recession meant that very many more companies were put under so unusual a degree of pressure that they had to engage in an 'agonizing reappraisal'. The consequent weakness of organized labour, together perhaps with industrial relations legislation hostile to trade unions and a small number of well publicized industrial relations events, gave managers the opportunity to push effectively for changes in work practices. In securing their objectives, it was sensible for managers not to bargain too hard on wages because the gains in productivity they could secure were more than enough to offset the higher wage costs. Just as in the 1960s, a concession on wages was a lubricant for productivity deals, but this time much more of the negotiated productivity gain was delivered. In a sense, the wage awards might be seen as a way in which managers retained more control over the continuing process of securing the productivity deals. In this story, the three outcomes of the industrial relations process, productivity, wages, and strikes, hang together and all point to a new industrial relations. It is consistent with, but does not rely on, any great importance of various new institutional forms like human resource management, employee share ownership schemes, quality circles, joint consultation, and 'communication' devices.

None of these developments necessarily indicates a change in underlying attitudes. The 'them and us' division in British industry might well be as profound today as it has always been. But if the claim that industrial relations has entered a new era were to mean merely that unions are temporarily weak, so that when business conditions improve sufficiently there will be a return to the status quo ante, it would not be very interesting. It must mean more than that. The claim for novelty must imply durable and substantial changes, at least in the outcomes of the industrial relations system, and that the future will be different from the past.

# 14

# Social Welfare since the War

### R. M. PAGE

## Introduction

Two issues which have been of perennial interest to economic and social historians will be addressed in this chapter. First, attention will be given to changes in average living standards in the post-war period. For example, was there an improvement in economic well-being? Was the nation better housed and educated? Did citizens enjoy improved levels of health and increased life expectancy? The role played by economic and social policy in these areas will be highlighted. Second, and closely related to these questions, distributional issues will be examined. Was there a movement towards greater degrees of equality in the distribution of income and wealth? Was there less poverty? Again, the impact of social and economic policy in this sphere will be alluded to.

In terms of both living standards and distribution one would expect to be able to record significant changes of an 'optimistic' kind in the past 40 years. The relatively high rate of domestic economic growth (especially up until the mid-1970s) is one of the main reasons for such an expectation. Rapid growth is not only a key determinant of average living standards but can also have important distributional effects (i.e. it can act as a springboard for government welfare initiatives.) Conversely, slow or non-existent growth is likely to have a negative impact in these areas. Living standards may stagnate or fall whilst painless forms of welfare expansion cease to be viable (Beckerman, 1979).

Another reason why we might anticipate 'optimistic' forms of change relates to the emergence of much more favourable political attitudes (both Labour and Conservative) towards state welfare. The Beveridge Report (Beveridge, 1942), is often regarded as a landmark in this respect. Although a rather 'reluctant' collectivist (George and Wilding, 1985, ch. 3), Beveridge was nevertheless convinced that planning was required to counter the inability or unwillingness of the market to meet some of the basic needs of citizens. For instance he felt it was imperative for government to reduce the economic and social misery caused by mass unemployment, if necessary by the direction of industry.

In his scheme for social security Beveridge sought to bring coherence to a system which was fragmented, administratively complex (private insurance companies and the friendly societies were still involved in the day-to-day operation of existing social insurance provision), and unpopular. Although Beveridge's proposals were less than enthusiastically received in some government circles they struck a sympathetic chord with the general public (Kincaid, 1973). Beveridge believed that his scheme would remove one of the giant evils which had blighted British society (despite the general rise in living standards) throughout the twentieth century, namely, want. Crucially, though, he stressed that the success or otherwise of this scheme would be dependent on effective forms of action in three other areas—the pursuit of full employment, the setting up of a national health service, and the introduction of family allowances.

Social insurance was to be the cornerstone of Beveridge's plan. He proposed the introduction of a comprehensive, nationally administered scheme which would be easily understood by the public. The scheme (based on subsistence and flat-rate principles) was intended to provide protection against predictable 'risks' such as unemployment, marriage, maternity, old age, sickness, and disability. It was recognized, however, that a means-tested national assistance scheme would need to be retained for those who would not be covered by the main programme.

Although Beveridge's proposals formed the basis for the post-war social security programme they were not implemented in their entirety. For example, Beveridge's contention that benefit entitlements should be open-ended (i.e. as long as the need persisted) was rejected in favour of fixed-payment periods (for instance, unemployment benefit was limited to 30 weeks). Moreover, marriage grants and benefits for marital breakdown were deemed impractical.

The new scheme quickly ran into trouble. One main problem was the relationship between insurance and means-tested benefits. In 1948 the rate for the latter proved to be relatively more generous than the former because it could be topped up with a rent allowance. As a result by 1951 over a million insurance recipients with no additional personal resources were claiming means-tested (poverty) benefits—a situation which Beveridge had been determined to prevent.

The pursuit of equality through social reformism (based on the principle of universalism rather than selectivity) was the hallmark of the 1945–51 Labour Government. It was firmly believed that determined action on the part of government could bring about fundamental economic and social change in society. Initiatives were undertaken in areas such as public-sector housing, health, and education in an effort to counter the disadvantages suffered by working-class people.

It is important to note that Labour's programme of social reform tended to be accepted, sometimes somewhat grudgingly, by the Conservative opposition. For example the coming of the National Health Service is often regarded as a triumph of socialist ideology in the face of powerful political and professional opposition. However, this interpretation of events is open to question (Klein, 1983). By 1939 there was a common acceptance that major changes in health care were required. Debate centred around the question of which policies would be most effective in this regard given the diverse and often conflicting interests of local and central government, the medical profession, the friendly societies, and other interested parties. The 1944 White Paper, which was introduced by Willink (after an earlier 'plan' had been scuppered by the medical profession—Willcocks, 1967), attempted to resolve these underlying tensions by accommodating the wishes of influential parties as far as possible. Amongst the proposals in this document were national responsibility for the service with a large measure of local control; the establishment of new joint authorities to run the hospitals whilst leaving local clinics and related services in the hands of local authorities; the incorporation of the voluntary sector into the public domain by means of financial inducements; strong medical representation on decision making bodies; and greater flexibility in terms of the GP service, especially in relation to health centres and the system of remuneration.

Not surprisingly, a compromise document of this kind attracted criticism from the various interest groups concerned. An amended document was accordingly published in 1945 which retained the local insurance committees (these were to have been replaced by a new central body), took account of GPs' wishes for greater autonomy, increased local control over hospital services, and provided the voluntary hospitals with a more central role in the planning of services. Although the return to power of a Labour Government in 1945 ensured that these proposals were not implemented, the newly appointed Minister of Health (Bevan) did not introduce any substantial changes in health-care policy. Although attacked by both the Conservative party and the medical profession Bevan was able, eventually, to secure the co-operation of both the hospital sector (by granting concessions to the Royal Colleges—special status for teaching hospitals, independent governing bodies, pay beds, and merit awards) and, after protracted negotiations, with GPs and their representative, the BMA. (Assurances concerning the method of remuneration (capitation fees rather than salaries) and professional autonomy (limitations on local authority control) were needed to secure acceptance in this area.) It can be concluded that opposition tended to be restricted in the main to administrative detail rather than principle.

One of the major achievements of the post-war Labour Government was the way in which it succeeded in changing the political agenda. As a result of their endeavours the Conservative Party, under the guidance of luminaries such as Butler, were forced to adjust their approach to economic and social policy. As Deakin (1987) notes:

Butler's approach was . . . subtle. By copious reference to the past history of his party, its undogmatic character and openness to new ideas, he laid the foundation for a substantial shift in the direction of policy. In essence this shift brought the Conservatives closely into line with their opponents' position on all the major issues of social policy and most economic priorities beside. (pp. 47–8)

Accordingly, the Conservatives moved from being enthusiastic free marketeers to one-nation 'pragmatists' capable of running welfare capitalism more efficiently than their rivals. Their main source of disagreement with Labour was over the question of equality. Unlike Labour they believed that the success, or otherwise, of welfare reformism should be judged by the degree to which want was diminished rather than by more 'unrealistic' and 'undesirable' goals such as a reduction in equality. Indeed, during their lengthy term of government in the 1950s and 1960s (1951–64) the Conservatives endeavoured to remove want by a judicious mix of private and public initiatives.

Although Labour's pursuit of equality remained paramount during their next period of government (1964–70) their performance in this respect left much to be desired. Their social programmes tended to be inappropriate (the construction of large, impersonal, high-rise housing estates), ineffective (the failure to eradicate poverty), and unduly paternalistic (a reluctance to consult and involve service users). In short, despite the growth in social expenditure results were disappointing.

Concern about the appropriateness of the government's role in social and economic policy began to re-emerge in the late 1960s (the 'Selsdon' approach—Harris and Seldon, 1979, ch. 4). By the early 1970s it had become increasingly popular to argue that government was being overloaded (King, 1976; Brittan, 1975, 1977). These theorists contended that the impact of Keynesianism (which had legitimized deficit financing) coupled with continued growth had fostered a climate in which government was being expected to meet the ever-increasing demands of citizens. Importantly, government was seen as unwilling to resist such demands (even when they recognized the adverse economic repercussions) because of possible electoral difficulties. These fears about overload were exacerbated in the early 1970s—a period which had been marked by expansionary economic policies (tax cuts, rapid growth in public spending) and supply 'shocks' (the OPEC price rises). The resulting increases in inflation and balance-of-payments problems led to the introduction of much tighter money-supply targets—a policy which led inevitably to curbs on public sector borrowing and, as a consequence, welfare expenditure. By the mid-1970s even senior members of the Labour Party were forced to admit that 'the party was over' and that painful and difficult choices would have to be made about welfare expenditure. Labour's own attempts to prune public expenditure in the mid-1970s failed to quell anxieties about the state of the British economy and it took IMF 'intervention' in 1976 to restore 'confidence'. Increasingly, public expenditure was now being regarded not as a vital instrument for social reform and the avoidance of mass unemployment but, rather, as a fetter on economic prosperity.

The resurgence of anti-collectivist (George and Wilding, 1985) ideas, which are based firmly on supply-side economics, had a major impact in undermining state welfarism. For commentators such as Hayek (1960, 1978), Friedman (1962), Friedman and Friedman (1980), Seldon (1981), and Murray (1984) the creation of the welfare state gave rise to serious economic and social difficulties. The shift towards collectivism was deemed to have quickened the pace of industrial decline, destroyed personal incentives, and undermined the work ethic.

In terms of deindustrialisation, Bacon and Eltis (1976) contended that the productivity gains of the 1960s and 1970s were not used as a springboard for further economic development. Instead, spare labour capacity was absorbed into the service side of the economy (particularly the public sector). The lack of further productivity improvements in what was now a declining industrial sector (which was expected to support a rapidly expanding 'non-productive' sector) led inevitably, it is alleged, to a sharp fall in investment, profitability, and overall economic activity. The reversal of this trend was deemed to be dependent on major cutbacks in state welfare expenditure.

The higher rates of taxation required to fund the expansion of state welfare was also considered to have had an adverse effect on Britain's economic performance. This assertion appears to be extremely difficult to substantiate. The available evidence seems to suggest that the disincentive effect of higher taxation was relatively insignificant except in the case of top-rate payers and those caught in the poverty trap (i.e. individuals who need a substantial rise in income to compensate for the loss of other benefits) (Royal Commission on the Taxation of Profits and Income, 1954; Brown and Levin, 1974).

The social security scheme was also criticized for undermining the work ethic. Such benefits were considered to be little more than a subsidy for strikers and an inducement to idleness. However, in terms of the state subsidy theory of strikes there seems to be scant evidence to suggest that there was any positive correlation between the provision of such benefits and the rate of strike activity or the willingness to strike (Gennard and Lasko, 1974, 1975; W. J. Cole, 1975). Similarly, with the possible exception of semi-skilled or unskilled men with very large families, the link between social security payments and workshyness cannot be substantiated (Report of the National Assistance Board, 1956; Department of Employment, 1974; Hill, 1976; Moylan and Davies, 1980, 1981).

The anti-collectivists also contended that state welfare services (especially those provided free at the point of use) were wasteful and inefficient. Such services were deemed to encourage consumers to make frivolous demands because of the absence of a controlling price mechanism whilst providers were seen as having no incentive to control costs because the Treasury acts as a beneficent guarantor. Not surprisingly, therefore, the anti-collectivists were firmly of the belief that citizens' welfare needs can best be met by the informal (other family members) and voluntary sectors and the private market rather than by the state. Accordingly, they contended that major changes are required in current welfare policies. For example, in terms of income support measures they argue that individuals should be encouraged to insure privately against risks such as unemployment and predictable contingencies such as old age. The duty of government should be restricted solely to the relief of destitution (means-tested subsistence benefits on the basis of need). Private medical insurance (which would require an element of compulsion in order to counter 'free-riding') is seen as the solution to citizens' health needs whilst the phasing out of subsidies and rent controls is viewed as the most appropriate means of increasing availability and choice in housing. However, it is accepted that taxpayers should continue to underwrite the cost of compulsory schooling on grounds of social (inculcation of appropriate values/attitudes) and economic (acquisition of productive skills) expediency.

For the anti-collectivists, then, the welfare state represents little more than a misguided form of social engineering which has led to the undermining of work incentives, the conspicuous waste of scarce economic resources for non-productive purposes, the inefficient delivery of vital services, a diminution of personal freedom and a threat to political stability.

The tenets of anti-collectivism have firmly underpinned successive Conservative administrations since 1979. During the first two terms of what has come to be known as 'Thatcherism' (Hall and Jacques, 1983) welfare spending, with the notable exception of housing, has not, despite rhetoric to the contrary, been drastically cut back. In fact, public spending has actually been increasing under the Conservatives (see Table 14.1). Even after allowance is made for inflation we find that expenditure in 1986/7 was 14 per cent higher in real terms than in 1978/9. The Conservatives' lack of success in this regard can be linked to various factors ranging from successful attempts on the part of local authorities to resist the imposition of cuts (a policy which is rapidly coming to an end as a result of reductions in central government support, rate capping, and the inability of councils to raise further loans on the private market), automatic stabilizers (i.e. non cash limited budgets such as unemployment benefits and Supplementary Benefit/Income Support) and demographic changes (increased number of old people).

However, the welfare state is coming under much more sustained attack during the Thatcher Government's third term. Reforms in the social security and education systems coupled with iniquitous measures such as the 'Poll Tax' lend credence to the view that the major assault upon the welfare state is only just beginning in earnest—a theme which will be returned to in the concluding section. In the interim an attempt will be made to evaluate the impact of post-war welfarism. To this end

TABLE 14.1. *UK public expenditure 1978/9 to 1986/7*
(£bn., 1986/7 prices)

|  | 1978/9 | 1983/4 | 1986/7 | Percentage growth 1978/9–1986/7 |
|---|---|---|---|---|
| Social security | 34.2 | 41.8 | 46.5 | +36 |
| Education | 17.6 | 18.0 | 18.7 | +6 |
| Health | 15.1 | 17.6 | 18.8 | +24 |
| Defence | 14.6 | 17.6 | 18.6 | +28 |
| Housing | 8.8 | 5.0 | 4.0 | −55 |
| Personal social services | 2.8 | 3.2 | 3.5 | +28 |
| Overseas aid | 1.4 | 1.2 | 1.2 | −15 |
| Other[a] | 33.7 | 34.3 | 34.6 | +3 |
| Total | 128.0 | 138.6 | 145.9 | +14 |
| National income | 334.8 | 348.5 | 380.1 | +14 |

[a] Does not include debt interest and does not include privatization as negative spending.

*Source*: J. Hills (1987), Table 1.

attention will be given to developments in the areas of income, wealth, and living standards; housing; education; health and, finally, poverty and income support. Such a review will enable some form of assessment to be reached about the achievements, and failings, of the post-war welfare state.

### Income, Wealth, and Living Standards

Any assessment of developments in the field of social welfare must give due attention to the distribution of income and wealth and the standard of living within society. Clearly those who command high salaries or possess large wealth holdings (far from mutually exclusive groups) are likely to enjoy higher standards of living, increased security, greater freedom of choice, and a substantial degree of potential, or actual, power and influence in society. Indeed, the extent to which income and wealth differences have narrowed is often regarded as an important test of the success, or otherwise, of post-war 'welfarism'. In this section I will look, first, at the distribution of income and wealth and then go on to consider changes in living standards.

### (i) *Income*

Any discussion of the distribution of income and wealth is likely to be deficient to some extent given the difficulties involved in data collection and interpretation (Atkinson, 1974; Pond, 1983; Playford and Pond, 1983; O'Higgins, 1985). Accordingly, the general overview which follows should be treated with a certain amount of caution.

As Table 14.2 indicates, the share of pre- and post-tax income has not changed markedly at various points of the distribution spread in the years between 1949 and 1981/2.

It can be seen that the position of the lowest 50 per cent on the income

TABLE 14.2. *Percentage shares of income before and after income tax received by given groups*

| Percentage share before income tax | 1949 | 1954 | 1964 | 1970/71 | 1974/5 | 1981/2 |
|---|---|---|---|---|---|---|
| Top 1 | 11.2 | 9.3 | 8.2 | 6.6 | 6.2 | 5.7 |
| Top 10 | 33.2 | 30.1 | 29.1 | 27.5 | 26.6 | 26.2 |
| Next 40 | 43.1 | 46.9 | 48.2 | 49.0 | 49.2 | 50.0 |
| Bottom 50 | 23.7 | 22.0+ | 22.7+ | 23.5 | 24.2 | 23.8 |
| after income tax | | | | | | |
| Top 1 | 6.4 | 5.3 | 5.3 | 4.5 | 4.0 | 3.9 |
| Top 10 | 27.1 | 25.3 | 25.9 | 23.9 | 23.2 | 23.1 |
| Next 40 | 46.4 | 48.4 | 48.9 | 49.9 | 49.8 | 50.3 |
| Bottom 50 | 26.5 | 26.3+ | 25.2+ | 26.1+ | 27.0 | 26.6 |

+ Estimated

*Sources*: Rubinstein (1986a), p. 80; Halsey (1988), pp. 151–2.

distribution scale has remained constant in terms of both pre- and post-tax income. Although the position of the top 10 per cent has declined over time this fall will bring little comfort to egalitarians. As the Royal Commission on the Distribution of Income and Wealth (1980) pointed out, 'successive falls in the share received by the top tenth have been largely retained in the top half of the spread' (p. 8). Clearly, the progressive nature of the income-tax system has only had a relatively modest effect in terms of reducing inequality. It would appear that the 'positive' impact of direct taxation has been offset to a large degree by the 'negative' effect of indirect taxation. Moreover, Playford and Pond (1983) contend that changes in the direct taxation systems have actually halted the relative decline of high income groups. For example, between 1959 and 1976/7 the bottom 40 per cent of the distribution scale experienced a four-fold increase in their tax burden compared to just 26 per cent for the richest decile.

The position of lower income groups has deteriorated still further over the past decade due in no small measure to the desire of successive Conservative administrations to bolster inequality. As Table 14.3 shows in the period from 1976 to 1985 the total household income share of the bottom 20 per cent has fallen by:

* *63 per cent in terms of original income* (i.e. income from employment, occupational pensions, investments, and gifts).
* *16 per cent in disposable income* (i.e. a measure of income which takes into account income tax and National Insurance payments as well as the effects of state benefits).
* *20 per cent in final income* (i.e. the amount of disposable income which remains after the payment of indirect taxes such as VAT and rates as well as imputed income to represent government expenditure on services such as health and education).

In contrast, the top fifth of the population have experienced gains of 14 per cent in original income, 11 per cent in disposable income, and 10 per cent in final income.

The disparity between high and low income groups is likely to be even more

TABLE 14.3. *Distribution of total household income, 1976–1985*

| | Share of income by household group (%) | | | |
| --- | --- | --- | --- | --- |
| | Bottom 20% | Bottom 40% | Top 40% | Top 20% |
| Original income | | | | |
| 1976 | 0.8 | 10.2 | 71.0 | 44.4 |
| 1981 | 0.6 | 8.7 | 73.3 | 46.4 |
| 1983 | 0.3 | 7.0 | 75.2 | 48.0 |
| 1986 | 0.3 | 6.0 | 77.6 | 50.7 |
| % change in income share | | | | |
| 1976–86 | −63% | −41% | +9% | +14% |
| Disposable income | | | | |
| 1976 | 7.0 | 19.6 | 62.2 | 38.1 |
| 1981 | 6.7 | 18.8 | 63.5 | 39.4 |
| 1983 | 6.9 | 18.8 | 63.6 | 39.6 |
| 1986 | 5.9 | 16.9 | 66.3 | 42.2 |
| % change in income share | | | | |
| 1976–86 | −16% | −14% | +7% | +11% |
| Final income | | | | |
| 1976 | 7.4 | 20.1 | 61.9 | 37.9 |
| 1981 | 7.1 | 19.5 | 62.6 | 38.6 |
| 1983 | 6.9 | 19.1 | 63.3 | 39.3 |
| 1986 | 5.9 | 17.3 | 65.6 | 41.7 |
| % change in income share | | | | |
| 1976–86 | −20% | −14% | +6% | +10% |

*Sources*:   Walker and Walker (1987), p. 36; *Social Trends*, 19, Table 5. 18.

marked if one takes into account such factors as tax avoidance and evasion, fringe benefits, and relative price changes. Although the extent of tax evasion and avoidance is extremely difficult to ascertain, it has been estimated that about 20 per cent of the entire tax yield (£4bn.) was lost as a result of avoidance and evasion in 1981 (Playford and Pond, 1983).

The effects of inflation are also likely to be hardest felt by the poorer sections of the community. In a survey of the period 1956–74, Piachaud (1978) found that the poorest 5 per cent of families experienced price rises which were 26 per cent above the rate for all families and nearly 31 per cent above the rate in the richest 5 per cent of families.

Post-war measures to reduce income inequalities have not been particularly dramatic. A contemporary example (Fig. 14.1) provides an illustration of the limited impact of welfare measures in terms of reducing inequality. If income were equally distributed each household quintile would receive 20 per cent of total income. However, it can be seen that the poorest income quintile receive virtually no 'original' income (0.3 per cent 1985) whilst the richest receive 49 per cent (1985). The effect of taxes and, more significantly, benefits does modify the situation but only in the modest way. The poorest 20 per cent increase their share of income to 5.6 per cent (1985) whilst the richest fifth suffer a 6 per cent decline (43 per cent).

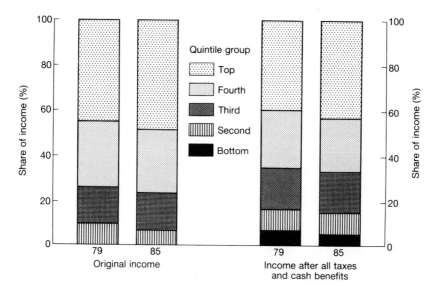

FIG. 14.1. *Effects of tax and cash benefits on income distribution in 1979 and 1985*
*Source*: J. Hills (1987), Fig. 2b, p. 9.

Clearly, if more fundamental forms of redistribution are desired then increased state regulation of market incomes will be required (O'Higgins, 1985).

Finally, it should be noted that there is some evidence to suggest that the income distribution pattern in the UK has been more egalitarian than in a number of other developed nations (USA, West Germany, Japan, Canada, and France) during the past 40 years (Stark, 1977).


(ii) *Wealth*

There has been a notable reduction in wealth inequalities during this century though the pattern of change has tended to be from the very rich to the rich rather than from rich to poor. As can be seen from Table 14.4 the richest 1 per cent of the population have seen their share of total wealth decrease by nearly 2/3 between 1923 and 1984. However, the 'wealth holdings' of the richest 20 per cent have not declined markedly.

The top 1 per cent of the population still own 21 per cent of all marketable wealth—nearly as much as the bottom 75 per cent. Even when allowance is made for occupational and state pension rights (a contentious issue—Pond, 1983; Kay and King, 1986) one still finds a marked disparity between rich and poor.

Those who defend the existing disparities in wealth have often suggested that any radical form of redistribution would only provide minimal financial advantages to the less well off. However Pond (1983), in an examination of 1979 data casts doubt on this assertion. He calculates that in that year every adult over the age of 18 would have had marketable wealth of some £12,000 (after the repayment of

TABLE 14.4. *Distribution of wealth in
England and Wales 1923–84*

| | Top 1% | Top 5% | Top 10% | Top 20% | Bottom 80% |
|---|---|---|---|---|---|
| 1923 | 60.9 | 82.0 | 89.1 | 94.2 | 5.8 |
| 1928 | 57.0 | 79.6 | 87.2 | 93.1 | 6.9 |
| 1938 | 55.0 | 76.9 | 85.0 | 91.2 | 8.8 |
| 1950 | 47.2 | 74.3 | — | — | — |
| 1953 | 43.6 | 71.1 | — | — | — |
| 1958 | 41.4 | 67.8 | — | — | — |
| 1960 | 33.9 | 59.4 | 71.5 | 83.1 | 16.9 |
| 1965 | 33.0 | 58.1 | 71.7 | 85.5 | 14.5 |
| 1968 | 33.6 | 58.3 | 71.6 | 85.1 | 14.9 |
| 1970 | 29.7 | 53.6 | 68.7 | 84.5 | 15.5 |
| 1971 | 28.4 | 52.3 | 67.6 | 84.2 | 15.8 |
| 1972 | 31.7 | 56.0 | 70.4 | 84.9 | 15.1 |
| 1976 | 25.0 | 46.0 | 60.0 | 77.0 | 23.0 |
| 1984 | 21.0 | 39.0 | 52.0 | 75.0[a] | 25.0[a] |

[a] Figure refers to top 25% and bottom 75% respectively.

*Source*:  F. Field (1983), p. 11; Royal Commission on the Distribution of
Income and Wealth (1980); T. Stark (1988).

mortgages, debts, and other liabilities) if strict egalitarianism had been adhered to rather than the rather meagre sum of £1,200 which was the actual share of the lowest 50 per cent of the population in that year. Of course, the question of what constitutes an acceptable level of wealth inequality is ultimately an ideological one. Those who wish to retain existing disparities often cite reasons of desert (reward for enterprise and endeavour) and economic efficiency (i.e. the benefits which accrue to the nation as a whole from individual forms of wealth generation) as justification. Certainly it might be easier to defend existing wealth inequalities if such differences could be explained in such ways.

However, it is clear that the rich (especially the very rich) have tended, in the main, to acquire their wealth through inheritance (which then provides the basis for further accumulation) rather than from their own entrepreneurial activity (Harbury and Hitchins, 1979; Rubinstein, 1981). Wealth taxes (Estate Duty/Capital Gains Tax (1975)/Inheritance Tax (1986) ), which have been advocated on grounds of equity (those with sizeable incomes and wealth holdings are better able to bear the burden of taxation than those with modest resources), economic efficiency (disincentive effects are likely to be far less for wealth as opposed to income taxes), and egalitarianism (undesirability of excessive disparity in wealth and power in society) have proved largely ineffectual as redistributive mechanisms (G. P. Marshall, 1980). As Table 14.5 shows the revenue raised from these transfer taxes has been quite modest. Indeed the £608m. collected from Estate Duty and Capital Transfer Tax in 1983/4 was equivalent to just a ½ per cent increase in the standard rate of income tax (Kay and King, 1986). The limited redistributive impact of these wealth taxes is due in large part to the numerous loopholes and exemptions in the legislation. For example, no tax is payable on a lifetime gift provided that the donor survives for a further seven years.

TABLE 14.5. *Revenue from transfer taxes*
(£m.)

|         | Estate duty | Capital transfer tax |
|---------|-------------|----------------------|
| 1963/4  | 312         | —                    |
| 1973/74 | 412         | —                    |
| 1976/7  | 124         | 259                  |
| 1977/8  | 87          | 311                  |
| 1978/9  | 46          | 317                  |
| 1979/80 | 32          | 404                  |
| 1980/1  | 27          | 423                  |
| 1981/2  | 17          | 480                  |
| 1982/3  | 15          | 499                  |
| 1983/4  | 9           | 599                  |

*Source*: Kay and King (1986), Table 4.5.

In the absence of more radical measures to reduce wealth inequalities (Annual Wealth Tax) it seems highly unlikely that there will be any marked changes in this area in the foreseeable future. Indeed, results from an opinion poll in the mid-1980s appear to indicate that there is little public appetite for change (*New Society*/London Weekend Television, 1986). Although 70 per cent of those polled felt that the gap between rich and poor was too wide, only 58 per cent favoured redistributing from rich to poor whilst only a minority supported the introduction of a wealth tax (42 per cent) or a limitation on individual wealth (33 per cent). More perturbing for egalitarians was the finding that those most likely to benefit (social class DE) or accept the need (Labour party supporters) for a limitation on individual wealth were only lukewarm in their support for this measure. Only 42 per cent of the former and 44 per cent of the latter favoured this policy.

Finally, as with income measures, it has proved extremely difficult to compare the distribution of wealth in Britain with other developed nations. For example, in one of the few studies undertaken, Harrison (1979) (in a detailed review of ten countries) only felt able to make tentative comparisons between Britain, the USA, and Canada. As Table 14.6 indicates the distribution of wealth is more highly concentrated at the top of the range in Britain than in either the USA or Canada. Two factors may account for this trend according to Harrison—the greater preponderance of public-sector housing in Britain and 'the fact that inheritance continues to feature prominently as a cause of persistent large fortunes' (Harrison, 1979, p. 38).

TABLE 14.6. *The distribution of wealth in Canada, USA, and Britain*

| Country and year | Share of the top | | |
|------------------|------|------|------|
|                  | 1%   | 5%   | 10%  |
| Canada, 1970 (households) | 21.6% | 45.7% | 59.8% |
|                           | (18.0%) | (39.2%) | (53.1%) |
| USA, 1969 (individuals)   | 25.1% | 43.7% | 53.0% |
| Britain, 1970 (individuals) | 30.1% | 54.3% | 69.4% |

*Source*: Harrison (1979), p. 34.

(iii) *Living Standards*

There is a substantial amount of evidence to suggest that living standards have improved in the post-war period (Toland, 1980; Halsey, 1987). For example, as Table 14.7 illustrates, GDP has increased from £2226/head in 1951 to £4465/head in 1983. Male manual workers (aged 21 or over) have experienced a near two-fold increase in their real wages over the same period (£60 in 1951; £111 in 1983) as well as a four-hour reduction in their working week. Moreover, holiday entitlements, which were either non-existent or of short duration in 1951, are now both more widespread and generous.

These improvements in real incomes have enabled increasing numbers of people to purchase a range of consumer durables which were once regarded as unobtainable luxuries. By 1983 94 per cent of households owned a fridge, 80 per cent a washing machine, 81 per cent a colour TV, and 57 per cent a deep freezer. For many working-class women now in their fifties and sixties the availability of such goods is often regarded as miraculous when they reflect back on the 'primitive' and back-breaking forms of washing and cleaning they once undertook. It should be remembered, though, that certain groups (one-parent families, the elderly) in society are much less likely to possess a number of these goods.

Citizens have also derived benefit from the development of easy care fabrics, detergents and an improved range of fresh and pre-packaged foods (though dietary 'habits' are still a source of some concern). Developments such as these and those mentioned previously have led commentators such as Burnett (1986) to conclude that the improvement in post-war living standards has been nothing less than remarkable:

There can be little doubt that in the years between 1945 and 1975 the English people as a whole were more prosperous than at any comparable period in the past, were able to achieve higher living standards, better housing, clothing and diet, more leisure and more material possessions than they had enjoyed before. These improvements in living standards were most marked in the working classes who, by contrast with their position before the war, benefited from practically full employment, a well-developed system of social security, and wages which moved ahead of the relatively low rates of inflation. Those who gained most in economic terms were the clerical occupations, semi-skilled and unskilled workers, all of whom increased their real earnings more than the average, and considerably more than professional and some other 'middle class' groups. (p. 281)

Of course one should not understate the improvements in general living standards since the war. These developments must, however, be set against less desirable changes which have occurred in society such as increasing crime rates, environmental pollution, and the loss of such intangibles as community spirit. For example, is it worth having a home full of the latest electrical gadgetry if you are afraid to leave it unattended even for a short period of time because of the possibility of theft (Maxfield, 1984)? Moreover, the material advantages of the majority (such as car ownership) may often have an adverse effect on the quality of life of less privileged minorities (congested and dangerous roads, reductions in public transport services, fewer local stores as out-of-town 'warehouse' shopping becomes more commonplace). Furthermore, even the possession of items such as central heating is no guarantee that those on low income can afford to use them. Externalities such as these need to be balanced against improvements in general living standards. Who, after all, wants to live in a society where a burglar alarm is a necessity, where people are frightened

TABLE 14.7. *Trends in the UK economy*

| | 1931 | 1951 | 1961 | 1966 | 1971 | 1976 | 1981 | 1985 |
|---|---|---|---|---|---|---|---|---|
| Gross domestic product at market prices | | | | | | | | |
| 1980 prices (£bn.) | | 112 | 148 | 171 | 195 | 220 | 228 | 253 |
| Index (1980 = 100) | | 49 | 64 | 74 | 85 | 96 | 99 | 110 |
| Per head (£) | | 2,226 | 2,811 | 3,138 | 3,495 | 3,918 | 4,037 | 4,465 |
| Percentage of men in manual occupations[a] | 77 | 72 | | | 62 | | 58 | |
| Percentage of women in manual occupations[a] | 76 | 64 | | | 53 | | 44 | |
| Percentage of total in manual occupations[a] | 77 | 70 | | | 59 | | 52 | |
| Average weekly hours of work[a,b], for full-time male manual employees | 48[d] | 48 | 48 | 46 | 46 | 45 | 44[b] | 44 |
| Percentage of manual employees[c] with basic holiday entitlement of over[c] weeks | | | | | 4 | 81 | 98 | 100 |

[a] Great Britain only.
[b] At April. Prior to 1983 data cover males aged 21 or over; since then they cover males on adult rates.
[c] Employees covered by national collective agreements or Wages Council Orders.
[d] October 1938.

*Source: Social Trends*, 17, p. 15.

to walk in their local streets, where public services continue to decline, and where the social event of the week is a meeting of the Neighbourhood Watch?

## Housing

In this section attention will be given to changes in the size and importance of the main housing of tenure as well as to more general qualitative ('fitness', amenities, over-crowding, sharing) and quantitative (numbers of dwellings and households) issues.

### Changes in the Main Housing Tenures

#### Owner-Occupation
There has been a dramatic rise in owner-occupation in the post-war period (26 per cent of all dwellings in 1945, 47 per cent in 1966, 62 per cent in 1985). A major reason for this increase was that house purchase, supported by Building Society advances, became more commonplace amongst higher paid manual workers (though the bias towards those of higher socio-economic status still remains—see Table 14.8). This form of tenure is now recognized as the most 'popular' and desirable form of tenure by all the major political parties, though the Conservatives' enthusiasm for a property-owning democracy is most notable in this regard. Conservative administrations have sought continually to boost owner-occupation by a series of measures which increased the financial attractiveness of this form of tenure. For example, since the later 1970s the Conservatives have adopted a vigorous council house sales policy in an attempt to increase home ownership amongst lower income groups. In 1970 a mere 6,000 council homes were sold. In contrast, between 1979 and 1984 nearly 700,000 properties were sold off (11.5 per cent of the total stock). The introduction of the Housing Act in 1980 (which extended to all tenants of three or more years standing the right to buy their homes at a discount of between 33 per cent and 50 per cent) and the Housing and Building Construction Act of 1984 (which increased the maximum discount to 60 per cent whilst reducing the qualifying period from three to two years) were instrumental in this development.

The advantages of owner-occupation are now well recognized. This form of tenure offers increased independence and security (though the degree of security is open to question given the growth in repossessions; see Ford, 1985) and recent attempts to limit assistance to owner-occupiers who receive means-tested benefits (Matthews and Tierney, 1985). In addition, owner-occupation provides considerable financial advantages (a hedge against inflation and an investment which grows in value). Owner-occupiers are able to obtain tax relief on mortgage interest, which is of particular advantage to those who pay tax at a higher rate. There has been a quite phenomenal growth in this form of public 'expenditure' (£300m. in 1971 to £2,750m. in 1984). Moreover, owner-occupiers are not required to pay capital gains tax (a tax on the difference between the purchase and sale price of a capital asset) and, as such, are able to make substantial financial gains by buying and selling property. This exemption was estimated to have 'cost' the treasury some £2,500m. in lost revenue in 1984. As Glennerster (1985) rightly surmises, owner-occupation has become 'a combined form of pension, life assurance and tax avoidance' (p. 195).

TABLE 14.8. *Tenure by economic activity status of head of household, 1986*

| | Owner occup'd | | Rented | | | | | |
| | Owned outright | With m'tgage | With job/ bus. | LA/ new town | Hous'g assoc/ co-op | Unfurn. Priv. | Furn. Priv. | Base (=100%) |
|---|---|---|---|---|---|---|---|---|
| *Economically active heads:* | | | | | | | | |
| Professional | % 13 | 76 | 4 | 2 | 0 | 2 | 2 | 468 |
| Employers & managers | % 15 | 71 | 5 | 5 | 1 | 2 | 1 | 1,309 |
| Intermediate non-manual | % 13 | 65 | 1 | 9 | 2 | 5 | 5 | 725 |
| Junior non-manual | % 15 | 57 | 2 | 18 | 1 | 4 | 4 | 513 |
| Skilled manual & own-account non-professional | % 16 | 54 | 1 | 23 | 2 | 3 | 1 | 2,165 |
| Semi-skilled manual & personal service | % 11 | 37 | 6 | 37 | 3 | 4 | 3 | 805 |
| Unskilled manual | % 16 | 21 | 0 | 49 | 5 | 5 | 3 | 221 |
| Economically inactive heads | % 42 | 6 | 0 | 41 | 3 | 7 | 1 | 3,638 |
| Total | % 25 | 38 | 2 | 27 | 2 | 5 | 2 | 9,844 |

*Note*: Excluding members of the Armed Forces, full-time students, and those who have never worked. These categories total, respectively 50, 56, and 124.

*Source*: *General Household Survey* (1986), Table 6.14.

## Council Housing

Council housing has had a rather chequered history in the post-war era. The rapid expansion in the period immediately after the war gradually tailed off with the result that this sector has declined in importance in recent decades (Forest and Murie, 1987).

The Second World War had exacerbated the perennial problems of homelessness, overcrowding, and poor-quality accommodation. During the war some 500,000 homes had been destroyed or irreparably damaged whilst a further 3½ million homes were in need of urgent repair. In the face of this problem the incoming Labour Government launched an ambitious housing drive. The Local Authority role in this initiative was substantial. With the aid of cheap loans and increased subsidies, Local Authorities were encouraged to build relatively high-quality accommodation for a wider cross-section of income groups (prior to the 1949 Housing Act Local Authorities had only been permitted to construct houses for the 'working class'). This programme proved fairly successful (900,000 homes were built by 1951 pre-dominantly in the public sector)—though initial projections were not met for a variety of reasons ranging from a shortage of building materials to balance of payments difficulties.

Although the succeeding Conservative administrations acknowledged the importance of maintaining a substantial building programme—some 370,000 homes were built in 1954—they were firmly of the opinion that the free market was the most appropriate way of meeting housing needs in 'normal' circumstances (new owner-occupation housing increased from 12 per cent of total output in 1951 to 56 per cent by 1959). As a result attempts were made to restrict public-sector programmes (subsidies were only permissable for slum clearance not general purposes from the late 1950s); rents were increased (The Housing Finance Act, 1972); councils discouraged from building new public housing (1988 Housing Act). In contrast, Labour Governments have attempted to promote modest house-building programmes when they adjudge the economic climate to be favourable (public sector completions rose, for instance, from 11,500 in 1974 to 147,300 in 1977). In addition, they have sought to defend (to some extent) the interests of council tenants as is indicated by their decision to restore Local Authorities' rights to determine their own rent levels following the financial pressure which had been exerted on tenants by the 'Fair Rents' policy of the early 1970s.

The outlook for public-sector housing (and for those low income groups who rely on this form of provision) is now extremely bleak. The Housing Act of 1988 is particularly significant in this respect given that it seeks to undermine the role of Local Authorities as providers of rented accommodation (Ginsburg, 1989).

*Privately Rented Accommodation*

The spectacular rise in owner-occupation referred to earlier has been matched by an equally remarkable decline in the privately rented sector (which was by far the most dominant form of tenure at the turn of the century) in the past 40 years. Immediately after the war private renting was by far the most common form of tenure (61 per cent in 1947). By 1961 this figure had almost been halved (31 per cent) and by the mid-1980s it had declined to just 9 per cent (mainly unfurnished tenancies).

Rent controls have often been identified as the principal reason for this decline. These controls were first introduced in 1915 to placate munitions workers in Glasgow. Although these controls were modified in later years (for example, controls were abolished on all new buildings after 1918), there were still some 4m. controlled dwellings at the beginning of the war. These controls, which were strengthened to some extent during the war years, remained largely unaltered until the 1957 Rent Act, which authorized rents to be decontrolled on properties with a rateable value of over £30 a year in England and Wales (£40/year in Greater London) and also permitted increased rent levels in properties which were to remain controlled. In addition, 'new lets' could be decontrolled—a policy which encouraged unsavoury forms of landlordism (Rachmanism).

This 'pro-landlord' legislation was redressed to some extent by the introduction of regulated tenancies (a procedure by which 'unfurnished' tenants and landlords of a formerly decontrolled house could apply for a fair rent assessment) under the 1965 Rent Act (the 1974 Rent Act extended this protection to the furnished sector).

The contention that uneconomic rent levels were the prime cause of the sharp decline in the privately rented sector is misleading. Two other factors are of greater importance. First, renting on the private market was becoming increasingly unattractive given the financial advantages of owner-occupation. Second, there was little incentive for entrepreneurs to invest in housing for rent, especially given that their depreciation costs could not be offset against tax.

The differences in housing tenure are of importance when considering the achievements or shortfalls in the area of housing. In general, owner-occupiers enjoy the highest standard of security and comfort whilst the position of council tenants is less favourable though their position is preferable to most of those who rent privately (Burke, 1981; Lansley, 1979). Any assessment of the post-war housing situation should address both qualitative and quantative issues.

## The Quality of Housing

Qualitative assessments of housing provision involve such dimensions as the 'fitness' of dwellings, the level of amenities and the degree of overcrowding and sharing. Each of these issues will be examined in turn.

### Unfit or Sub-Standard Housing

Any definition of unfitness is likely to be contested. For example, the Housing Repairs and Rents Act of 1954 defined 'unfitness' solely in relation to the physical condition of the property (degree of damp, access to natural light/ventilation, water supply and drainage). No allowance was made for the more intangible needs which were only afforded official recognition in the Parker Morris Report (Department of the Environment, 1961). Acknowledging the changes which had occurred in society, this report stressed the need for increased space within the home (larger kitchens, improved storage facilities) as well as better heating systems (Burnett, 1986).

The extent of unsatisfactory (i.e. statutory unfitness) and substandard (property lacking one or more basic amenities) housing has been falling sharply. For example, in 1931 there were 7½ million unsatisfactory homes. Some fifty years later there were just 2.1 million such dwellings (11 per cent of the total stock). Growing material prosperity has been a significant factor in this process. For example, in 1951 over half of all households were without a fixed bath and 8 per cent were without a WC of any kind. By 1981 these figures had fallen rapidly to 1.9 per cent and 0.3 per cent respectively (see Table 14.9). However, further progress is required in other areas. For example, some 33 per cent of homes (predominantly those occupied by lower income groups) are still without central heating.

Moreover, in the case of play space, Townsend (1979) estimated (on the basis of his 1968 'Poverty' survey, in which respondents were asked whether their children had an indoor play area that was adequate to ensure that neighbours were not inconvenienced with noise) that children in nearly one million households, especially in poorer families, were disadvantaged in this respect (p. 486).

### Overcrowding

Arriving at a satisfactory definition of overcrowding is also problematic. The legal definition of overcrowding (which ignores a 'reasonable' bedroom standard) can mean that a two-parent family with two children living in accommodation with one bedroom, a kitchen, and a dining room is deemed to be adequately housed (George and Wilding, 1984). More recent official estimates of overcrowding (Census; General Household Survey) have, however, tended to adopt more appropriate measures (i.e. the number of persons per habitable room or the 'bedrooms' standard—a

TABLE 14.9. *Housing conditions in Great Britain: availability of amenities*
(%)

|  | 1951 | 1961 | 1966 | 1971 | 1981 |
|---|---|---|---|---|---|
| Households entirely without certain amenities |  |  |  |  |  |
| Fixed bath | 37.6 | 22.4 | 15.4 | 9.1 | 1.9 |
| Water closet |  |  |  |  |  |
| internal or external | 7.7 | 6.5 | 1.7 | 1.1 | 0.3 |
| internal | — | — | 18.4 | 11.5 | 2.7 |
| Hot water tap | — | 21.8 | 12.5 | 6.5 | — |
| Households sharing certain amenities |  |  |  |  |  |
| Fixed bath | 7.5 | 4.4 | 4.1 | 3.2 | 1.2 |
| Water closet |  |  |  |  |  |
| internal or external | 14.9 | 6.7 | 6.4 | 4.1 | — |
| internal | — | — | 4.4 | 3.1 | 1.1 |
| Hot water tap | — | 1.8 | 2.0 | 1.9 | — |

*Source: Social Trends,* 16, Table 8.5.

bedroom should be provided for: (i) a married couple, (ii) each adult over 21, (iii) two persons of the same sex aged 10 to 21). As can be seen from Table 14.10 the extent of overcrowding using this first measure (persons/habitable room) is slowly declining. For example, the proportion of densely occupied households (more than one person per room) has declined from 4 per cent to 2 per cent during the period from 1971 to 1983 largely, it has to be said, due to a reduction in household size and the increase in one-person households). However, some 3 per cent of households are still below the 'bedroom' standard (see Table 14.11).

TABLE 14.10. *Persons per room: 1971 to 1986*
(%)

| Persons per room | 1971 | 1973 | 1975 | 1977 | 1979 | 1980 | 1981 | 1982 | 1983 |
|---|---|---|---|---|---|---|---|---|---|
| Under 0.5 | 37 | 39 | 39 | 41 | 41 | 42 | 42 | 43 | 44 |
| 0.5 to 0.65 | 25 | 24 | 25 | 25 | 26 | 26 | 25 | 26 | 25 |
| 0.66 to 0.99 | 24 | 24 | 23 | 24 | 23 | 23 | 23 | 22 | 23 |
| 1 | 9 | 8 | 8 | 7 | 7 | 7 | 7 | 7 | 7 |
| Over 1 to 1.5 | 4 | 4 | 3 | 3 | 2 | 2 | 2 | 2 | 2 |
| Over 1.5 | 1 | 1 | 0 | 0 | 0 | 0 | 0 | 0 | 0 |
| Base = 100% | 11,990 | 11,647 | 12,096 | 11,978 | 11,484 | 11,718 | 12,002 | 10,238 | 9,993 |
| Mean persons per room | — | — | 0.57 | 0.55 | 0.57 | 0.57 | 0.56 | 0.56 | 0.56 |

*Sources:*   General Household Survey (1982), Table 5.2.
General Household Survey (1983), Table 6.25.
General Household Survey (1986), Table 6.25.

TABLE 14.11. *Difference from bedroom standard by tenure, Great Britain, 1986* (%)

| | Owner Occupied | | Rented | | | | | Total |
|---|---|---|---|---|---|---|---|---|
| | Owned outright | With m'tgage | With job/ bus | LA/ new town | Hous'g assoc/ co-op | Unfurn. private | Furn. private | |
| Bedrooms: | | | | | | | | |
| 1 or more below standard | 1 | 3 | 3 | 6 | 4 | 3 | 10 | 3 |
| Equals standard | 16 | 26 | 29 | 45 | 76 | 34 | 65 | 31 |
| 1 above standard | 40 | 43 | 39 | 36 | 116 | 35 | 20 | 39 |
| 2 or more above standard | 43 | 29 | 29 | 14 | 5 | 29 | 6 | 27 |
| Base = 100% | 2,502 | 3,825 | 249 | 2,683 | 200 | 477 | 199 | 10,135 |

*Source*: *General Household Survey* (1986), Table 6.26.

## Degree of Sharing

Improvements have also occurred in terms of the numbers of households which have been forced to share accommodation and/or essential amenities. As Table 14.12 indicates the number of households sharing dwellings has fallen by well over half between 1951 and 1976. Similarly, the proportion of households having to share basic amenities such as a bath or WC has fallen sharply between 1951 and 1981 (see Table 14.9). Not surprisingly, those in the poorest housing sector (privately rented) experience this form of disadvantage most acutely.

TABLE 14.12. *Households sharing dwellings: England & Wales* (thousands)

| Type of household | 1951 | 1971 | 1976[a] |
|---|---|---|---|
| Multi-person households | 1,442 | 380 | 275 |
| One-person households | 430 | 440 | 375 |
| Concealed[b] households | 935 | 426 | 360 |
| Total | 2,807 | 1,246 | 1,010 |

[a] Estimated.
[b] Household within a household (e.g. family sharing more relatives).

*Source*: George and Wilding (1984), p. 29.

## The Quantity of Housing

The ratio of dwellings to households has gradually improved over the post-war period. As can be seen from Fig. 14.2 the housing shortage which existed in 1951 had been largely 'overcome' by 1961 (when a rough parity between dwellings and households was achieved). Moreover, by the mid-1980s dwellings had outstripped the number of households by over one million. Of course, these improvements must be put into perspective. It must be remembered that second homes, holiday residences, and unfit dwellings are all included as part of the housing stock. Accordingly, the amount of 'available' housing is likely to be much less than one might be led to expect from the basic figures. For example, in 1981 over 50 per cent of the vacant dwellings were either being renovated or being used as second or holiday homes (*Social Trends*, 17, p. 138). In addition, there may be a marked disparity in the balance between dwellings and households in particular locations. Clearly, the 'fixed' nature of the housing stock makes it extremely difficult to counter major shortfalls in short- or even medium-term supply. Furthermore, it should be noted that official estimates of the number of households are likely to be misleading as they make no allowance for those prospective householders who are 'involuntarily' sharing the household of another (e.g. married couples sharing with relatives).

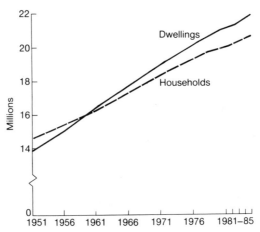

FIG. 14.2.   *Households and dwellings 1951–1985 (Great Britain)*

*Note*:   Estimates of the stock in England are based on the 1971 and 1981 Censuses. Estimates for Wales and Scotland prior to 1981 are based on the 1971 and earlier Censuses. Dwellings figures are at end year and households at mid year. Households figures are estimates from households projections.

*Source*:   *Social Trends*, 17, Table 8.2.

In the light of these and other factors it is not altogether surprising, therefore, that homelessness has proved to be a persistent rather than transitory problem since 1945. In the immediate aftermath of the war it was felt that homelessness would be a temporary phenomenon which would gradually fade away with the onset of the new housebuilding programme. Accordingly, the response to homelessness tended to be of a short-term, minimalist kind (Part III accommodation under the 1948 National Assistance Act). The persistence of homelessness in subsequent decades resulting from the relaxation of rent controls, the sale of rented housing, and the reduction in public-sector building served to underline the inadequacy of provision in this sphere (Greve *et al.*, 1971; Glastonbury, 1971). Although some modest efforts (e.g. the Housing (Homeless Persons) Act 1977) have been made to improve the situation of the homeless in the more recent past, the situation of this group remains extremely bleak (Grosskurth and Stearn, 1986).

One of the main problems with homelessness is the difficulty of comparing the incidence of this phenomenon over time (changes in legal definitions are important in this regard). However, it is possible to examine the extent of homelessness over short time sequences. For instance, in 1978 some 53,000 households were deemed to be homeless by Local Authorities. This figure had risen to over 95,000 by 1985—an 80 per cent increase. In addition, the number of households living in temporary accommodation had risen from 2,500 in 1966 to 14,000 by 1985. It would seem safe to conclude that the extent of homelessness (notwithstanding definitional disputes) in the 1980s is as problematic as it was in the 1950s.

## Education

The steady increase in the level of resources devoted to the educational section (see Table 14.13) has provided the basis for a number of significant initiatives in this sphere of the welfare state. The most important of these developments will be identified in the first part of this section as a prelude to an overall assessment of the achievements and shortcomings in this field.

TABLE 14.13. *General government expenditure on education 1948–1983 UK*

|  | Expenditure at current prices | Expenditure at 1948 prices | | Expenditure as percentage of GNP |
|---|---|---|---|---|
|  | (£m) | (£m) | Index (1948 = 100) |  |
| 1948 | 284 | 284 | 100 | 2.4 |
| 1950 | 347 | 307 | 108 | 2.6 |
| 1955 | 547 | 367 | 129 | 2.8 |
| 1960 | 917 | 458 | 161 | 3.6 |
| 1965 | 1,585 | 563 | 198 | 4.4 |
| 1970 | 2,532 | 705 | 248 | 4.9 |
| 1975 | 6,626 | 905 | 319 | 6.3 |
| 1980 | 12,121 | 935 | 329 | 5.3 |
| 1983 | 15,583 | 943 | 332 | 5.2 |

*Source:* Halsey (1988), Table 6.6.

## Educational Developments

### The Pre-School Sector

The rapid expansion in nursery education which occurred during the war (there were 19,000 school places by 1946) as a result of the government's desire to adopt a more active role in the care of infants did not lead to the development of universal provision in this area during the early years of peacetime. As M. E. David (1980) remarked:

In 1945 the Labour government stressed that a comprehensive system of nurseries had to be worked out with the welfare authorities, to determine their character, needs and custom. The assumption was that such facilities would be needed only in certain circumstances, where mothers needed to work or children needed care and protection because of inadequate mothering. Indeed, LEAs had only been granted permissive powers in the 1944 ACT: nursery schooling was not to be universally available. (p. 76)

This uncertainty about the need for nursery schooling has been a feature of the post-war period. As a result, this service has always been extremely vulnerable to public expenditure cuts and restricted development. For example, in the late 1950s and early 1960s LEAs were instructed to halt any proposed expansion of nursery-school provision on grounds of cost. Similarly, the increase in nursery education demanded by the Plowden Committee (Department of Education and Science, 1967) in an effort to combat the social and economic deprivation experienced by working class children, failed to materialise. Although Urban Aid initiatives in the late 1960s facilitated a modest initial expansion in nursery provision (10,000 new places were created by 1969) this development was short lived. By 1971 a mere 18,000 places had been created—a figure which only served to emphasize the impossibility of reaching Plowden's targeted figure for 1975 (500,000 places—see Mortimore and Blackstone, 1982). By the mid-1980s just under 57 per cent of all children aged three or four were receiving pre-school education—a figure which compares unfavourably with most of our European neighbours (New and David, 1986).

The nursery-school sector, which is administered by the DES, competes with a variety of 'non-educational' services such as playgroups, day nurseries, and child-minders. This diversity of provision reflects, in part, the lack of a cohesive strategy for the under-fives. It has not been generally accepted that *all* children should receive pre-school education *or* that substitute care should be provided as of right to all parents who request it. This ambivalence has continued to stifle the develop-ment of the nursery school sector.

*Primary Education*

Many of the reforms which have occurred in primary education since the war have not come about as a result of specific policy initiatives of a dramatic kind. As M. Hill (1984) explains:

Many primary schools have been transformed over the last twenty to thirty years from formal institutions in which uniformed children sat in straight rows in classes streamed on the basis of tests of educational ability, to very informal places where pupils move about or work together in little clusters drawn from mixed ability classes. The gradual elimination of selection at eleven-plus has clearly contributed to this 'liberation' of the primary schools. It is an interesting example of a change that developed from the bottom and has never required any formal recognition in legislation, which may nevertheless be regarded as a major policy development. (pp. 181–2)

The Plowden Report—*Children and their Primary Schools* (DES, 1967) was arguably the most influential post-war document on primary education. During the late 1950s and early 1960s concern was being expressed about the negative impact of the home and local environment on the educational performance of primary schools (Douglas, 1964). It was believed that children living in such areas were likely to be educationally deprived. To counter this problem Plowden proposed the introduction of special Educational Priority Areas. These EPAs were to be selected on the basis of such factors as housing conditions, the proportion of claimants and one-parent families and the incidence of poor school attendance. Designated schools (which were intended to become better than average) were to be provided with increased equipment budgets and other grants as well as more teaching staff (who were to be paid higher salaries). Despite attempting to achieve equality of outcome (rather than just equality of opportunity), this Report produced few practical gains—a failure which can be linked in large part to the limited theoretical underpinnings of this proposal. As Halsey (1972) argued, a fundamental weakness of the EPA scheme was the assumption that the problem to be addressed was one of cultural deprivation and educational failings rather than 'structural' impediments.

## Secondary Education

The secondary-school sector has been the subject of continuous review since 1945. Education, along with many other areas of social policy, figured prominently in wartime reconstruction plans. There was general agreement that all children should receive 'free' secondary school education until the age of 15. It is important that children came to be seen increasingly as an economic asset which could either be usefully 'exploited' or squandered. For example, the Spens Committee (Board of Education, 1938) contended that education should be linked far more closely to the world of work—a theme which resurfaced in the Norwood Report (Secondary Schools Examinations Council, 1943) and a subsequent White Paper *Educational Reconstruction* (Board of Education, 1943). The 1944 Education Act endorsed the Norwood Committee's recommendation that children should be educated according to their aptitude in one of three types of school—grammar (more academically inclined children, destined for careers in the professions, higher administrative and managerial positions), technical and secondary modern (more 'practically' minded children who would join the world of work at comparatively early ages in semi-skilled or unskilled occupations).

These changes did little, however, to placate those who were concerned about the effectiveness of the educational system with regard to both the economic needs of the nation and the personal aspirations of children themselves. These problems were addressed in two influential reports in the late 1950s and early 1960s. The Crowther Report (Central Advisory Council for Education, 1959) was set up to consider the post-compulsory educational needs of children and young people. Recognizing that the 80 per cent of children who left school before the age of 16 did so because of a lack of opportunity rather than personal choice, Crowther recommended the extension of courses, the raising of the school leaving age to 16 by the late 1960s, the development of more applicable forms of examination; and the expansion of county colleges and further education opportunities.

The Newsom Report, *Half Our Future* (CACE, 1963), was concerned with children lower down the age and ability range (i.e. 13 to 16-year-olds of average or less than average ability). This report documented the educational deprivation of this group (greater likelihood of attending an overcrowded and poorly maintained school—40 per cent of secondary modern buildings were in severe disrepair; frequent staff changes—50 per cent of male teachers served for a period of under three years; a restricted curriculum). To counter these problems Newsom, like Crowther, recommended the raising of the school leaving age. In addition, more imaginative programmes were demanded as well as improved facilities and better motivated and rewarded teachers.

A number of subsequent initiatives can be linked, to a greater or lesser extent, to these two reports. The school leaving age was eventually raised to 16—albeit rather belatedly (1972). The development of the CSE examination ensured that far greater numbers of children left school with some form of qualification. For example, in 1967 only 36 per cent of English school leavers achieved one or more passes in a public examination. By 1984 this had increased to over 90 per cent (see Table 14.14).

TABLE 14.14. *Proportions of children passing GCE and CSE examinations*
(%)

|  | 1964/65 | 1984/85 |
|---|---|---|
| *English school leavers obtaining* |  |  |
| 1 or more A-level pass: | 12.9 | 17.1 |
| 5 or more GCE 0 level or CSE grade 1 | 20.3 | 26.9 |
| 1 or more GCE 0 level or CSE grade 1 | 36.0 | 54.7 |
| No graded examination pass | 64.0 | 9.4 |

*Source*: Sanderson (1987), Table 1.

The expansion of comprehensive schooling since the mid-1960s has also strengthened the position of 'average' pupils. As Table 14.15 demonstrates there has been a dramatic switch to this form of schooling in recent decades.

TABLE 14.15. *Pupils in secondary education (England)*
(%)

|  | 1971 | 1981 | 1985 |
|---|---|---|---|
| *Maintained secondary schools*: |  |  |  |
| Middle deemed secondary | 1.9 | 7.0 | 6.8 |
| Modern | 38.0 | 6.0 | 4.7 |
| Grammar | 18.4 | 3.4 | 3.2 |
| Technical | 1.3 | 0.3 | 0.1 |
| Comprehensive | 34.4 | 82.5 | 84.5 |
| Other | 6.0 | 0.9 | 0.7 |
| Total pupils (= 100%) |  |  |  |
| (thousands) | 2,953 | 3,840 | 3,526 |

*Source*: *Social Trends*, 17, Table 3.3.

*Higher Education*

The need to expand higher education provision was clearly accepted in the post-war period. For example, the Robbins *Committee on Higher Education* (1963) asserted that the future economic prosperity of the nation could be threatened if investment in higher education was neglected. The Committee recommended that higher education should be provided for all those (with the necessary aptitude) who required it. The proposed increase in provision was to be achieved by an increase in the number of, and places at, universities (the new universities were to play an important part in this process) and by the development of polytechnics and colleges of education. By 1970/1 the number of full-time students enrolled in higher education totalled some 457,000—a twofold increase since 1962/3 (217,000). Further growth has occurred in subsequent decades. In 1984/5 there were nearly 590,000 full-time students. In addition, there has been a substantial rise in the number of part-time students from 165,000 in 1970/1 to 320,000 in 1984/5. Women now make up an increasingly important proportion of this sector (14 per cent in 1970/1, 34 per cent in 1984/5).

One of the major success stories in higher education since the war has been the Open University, which has provided a range of high quality 'distance learning' degree and vocational courses for a fairly wide cross-section of the public. In particular, the OU has attempted to cater for older age groups who had previously left school without any formal qualifications (P. Hall, Land, Parker, and Webb, 1975).

In common with all other areas of public expenditure the higher education system has been subject to increased central government scrutiny over the past decade or so. In the future it would appear that all institutions in this sector will have to give even greater priority to issues such as efficiency and government-prescribed priorities if they wish to retain even a reduced level of public funding.

*Achievements*

There have been a number of achievements in the education field since the war—a number of which have been referred to previously (e.g. the growth of comprehensivization). Four further achievements are worthy of note. First, there would appear to have been a substantial improvement in the quality of teachers in both the primary and secondary school sector—at least in terms of the rather crude indicator of educational attainment. For example, some 23 per cent of current primary school teachers (1984/5) are graduates compared to just 3 per cent in 1950. In the secondary-school sector the number of graduate teachers has increased from about 30 per cent in 1950 to 61 per cent in 1984/5. It should be noted, though, that graduate teachers are more likely to be found in grammar and 'full range' comprehensive schools rather than other institutions (DES, 1979).

Training programmes for teachers have also become more rigorous. Courses are provided for a longer period of time and all teachers who have been appointed since 1968 are now expected to be fully qualified if they wish to work in state primary or secondary schools (though a reversal of this trend is likely in the 1990s to combat a teacher 'shortage').

The second achievement is the general improvement in the educational standards of school pupils. Although a number of commentators—most notably the authors of the Black papers on education (Cox and Dyson, 1971; Cox and Boyson, 1975)—have argued vehemently that there has been a rapid decline in attainment and a corresponding increase in the number of ignorant, undisciplined school leavers since the advent of comprehensivization the limited evidence available tends to contradict such a gloomy assessment. In terms of literacy, the Bullock Report (DES Committee of Inquiry, 1975) concluded that the reading standard (measured at ages 11 and 15) had improved steadily in the period from 1948 to 1960 and then stabilized in the subsequent decade. This favourable impression of the impact of increased state involvement in education was confirmed by another DES report (1978) which commented favourably on the improvement in reading standards in the period from 1955 to 1976. In addition, as was noted earlier, educational certification has also improved—an improvement which has been sustained (see Table 14.14). Particularly encouraging is the fall in the proportion of pupils who leave school without any form of qualification whatsoever. One disturbing feature of the current situation, though, is the fact that 'disadvantaged' pupils from low-income/ethnic-minority households continue to be overrepresented in the underachievement categories (Swann Report, *Education for All*, 1985). This suggests that education is unlikely to be a sufficient vehicle to redress wider forms of inequality in society.

Despite evidence to the contrary fears about declining educational standards have persisted in the 1970s (the Great Debate instigated by the Labour Government under Callaghan) and 1980s (a principal aim of the Conservative's 1988 Education Act was to improve standards by means of benchmark testing at the ages of seven, eleven, fourteen, and sixteen).

Improvements in pupil–teacher ratios and class sizes can be regarded as a third achievement of the post-war education system. Between 1946 and 1987 the pupil–teacher ratio decreased from 32.5:1 to 21.8:1 in primary schools and from 21.4:1 to 15.4:1 in secondary schools. Class sizes have also fallen. In 1950 40 per cent of primary schools had class sizes of between 30 and 40 pupils (30 per cent had classes in excess of 40). By 1987 these figures had fallen to 22.7 per cent and 0.8 per cent respectively. A similar trend has also occurred in secondary schools. In 1950, 46 per cent of such schools had class sizes of between 35 and 40 pupils (7 per cent had classes of over 40). By 1981 the former figure had fallen to 8.5 per cent and the latter to 1.1 per cent.

Finally, the raising of the school leaving age can be regarded as a· positive educational initiative (though see Landymore, 1985, for a contrary opinion). This development has contributed to the growth of certification and has also served to encourage 'potential leavers' to stay on at school after the age of 16. Moreover, RSLA helps to equalize the level of education received by children from different social backgrounds thereby increasing the possibility of greater equality in future earnings levels.

It should also be noted that there is some evidence to suggest that the expansion of both compulsory and further education has helped to reduce the dispersal of earnings (Routh, 1980). In the case of RSLA, Blaug *et al.* (1980) estimate that this policy may have reduced the dispersal of earnings by as much as 15 per cent.

*Shortcomings*

Two major criticisms have been levelled at the education system since 1945. First, it is alleged that the system has failed to halt Britain's economic decline. Second, the education sector has failed to reduce class inequalities to any significant extent. The first of these criticisms will not be pursued here as this issue has been discussed in Chapters 1 and 9.

In considering this second criticism it is clearly open to question whether the education system can, or even should, be expected to reduce inequalities in society. However, what cannot be denied is that the reduction of inequality has been a major feature of post-war educational policy, particularly under Labour administrations.

In *The Strategy of Equality*, Le Grand (1982) examined the notion of educational equality in relation to resources, use, costs, and outcomes. His analysis makes sombre reading for social reformers. Le Grand found that households in the top 20 per cent of the income distribution scale receive nearly three times more in terms of educational expenditure than those in the lowest 20 per cent (adjustments for household composition—i.e. eliminating non-educational consumers such as the elderly—would have only marginally improved this situation). Moreover, if this assessment is related to occupation a similar picture emerges. The highest socio-economic group (made up of professionals, employers, and managers) receive 50 per cent more educational expenditure per person than those in the lowest group (comprised of semi/unskilled workers). Although this latter group receives marginally more expenditure in the compulsory sector (up to the age of 16), the position is markedly reversed in relation to post-16 secondary schooling (higher-lower ratio (HLR) 2:1), further education (HLR, 3:1), and university education (HLR, 5:1).

As these figures indicate, there are also significant class inequalities in the use of educational resources. Throughout the post-war period evidence from various sources indicates that children from the highest socio-economic classes are more likely to attend nursery schools; study (in increasing numbers) at primary and secondary independent schools and be over-represented in the 16-to-19 population of grammar schools. For example, Halsey *et al.* (1980) found that pupils from social classes I and II were much more likely to stay on at school than their lower-social-class counterparts. Similar findings emerged in relation to university education.

Despite the rapid expansion of free educational provision and the student grant system (which has come under serious threat in recent years as its 'real' value continues to decline), the 'costs' of education remain a key source of inequality. Unlike their middle-class peers, working-class children are often faced with insurmountable financial and other problems if they wish to pursue their education. In particular, the lack of mandatory grants for 16-to-18-years-olds (coupled with the prospect of student loans) has increased the likelihood that working-class children and their parents will continue to regard the short-term 'costs' of additional education as prohibitive.

Finally, in terms of Le Grand's final measure—outcomes—it is clear that the expansion of education has not had a significant effect on social mobility (Goldthorpe, 1980). Children from middle-class families still stand a four times better chance of securing a 'middle-class' occupation and income level than those from working-class backgrounds. Although increased educational opportunity has undoubtedly enabled more working-class children to become upwardly mobile (duration of education is positively related to higher earnings; George and Wilding, 1984) progress has been disappointing. As Le Grand (1982) concludes:

The ability of public expenditure on education to achieve equality appears to be limited, however the latter is defined. The provision of free education has created neither equality of use, cost, public expenditure nor outcome. Indeed, it is possible that in some cases it may actually have promoted greater inequality. The reason for this appears to be the pervasive influence of the structure of broader social and economic inequality, a structure that itself seems largely impervious to educational reform. (p. 79).

## Health and Health Care

There can be little doubt that there have been substantial improvements in the health of the nation in the post-war period. Improved living standards coupled with effective forms of medical intervention have enabled greater numbers of people to live longer. In terms of life expectancy a female born in 1985 can expect to live to the age of 77 and a male to the age of 71. The comparative figures for 1951 were 71 years and 66 years respectively (see Table 14.16).

One of the key reasons for this improvement has been the successful fight against a number of infectious diseases (see Table 14.17). Immunization programmes have proved to be highly significant in this respect in the case of both diptheria (introduced in 1942) and polio (1957). The less impressive performance in relation to a disease such as whooping cough is due in large part to fluctuations in the number of children being immunized.

Infant mortality has continued to decline since the war. In 1950 there were nearly 26 deaths per 1000 live births. By 1986 this figure had been substantially reduced (9.4/1000). This reduction can be explained by such factors as the shift towards smaller family sizes (which tend to be associated with lower infant mortality) and more effective forms of clinical practice. However, there is no room for complacency in this area. A number of other European countries have been much more successful in reducing their infant mortality rate (see Table 14.18).

In terms of adult mortality there have been notable changes in the principal causes of death. Circulatory diseases and cancer have grown in importance whilst infectious and respiratory diseases have declined in significance (see Figure 14.3). Moreover, there has been a dramatic increase in one type of circulatory disease (coronary artery). In 1951 the rate for men was 248 per million for women 175 per million. By 1987 these figures had risen to 359 per million and 270 per million respectively. Smoking, diet, and blood pressure have been identified as three of the most common 'causes' of this increase. Moreover, cigarette smoking has also been linked with lung cancer—another major modern killer. In 1951 lung cancer was responsible for 51 deaths per million for men and 9 per million for women. By 1987 the rate for men had doubled (102/m.) whilst the rate for women had quadrupled (41/m.).

It is possible to suggest that the general improvement in life expectancy and infant survival in the post-war period has been due in part to increases in the level of resources being devoted towards health care. The NHS has been a particularly favoured area of government expenditure. Between 1950 and 1980 resource levels in this sector have doubled in real terms while overall public spending only increased by 150 per cent (see Table 14.19).

TABLE 14.16. *Expectation of life: from birth and from specific ages (UK)*

| | Males | | | | | | | Females | | | | | | |
|---|---|---|---|---|---|---|---|---|---|---|---|---|---|---|
| | 1906 | 1931 | 1951 | 1961 | 1971 | 1981 | 1985 | 1906 | 1931 | 1951 | 1961 | 1971 | 1981 | 1985 |
| **Expectation of life[a]** | | | | | | | | | | | | | | |
| At birth | 48.0 | 58.4 | 66.2 | 67.9 | 68.8 | 70.8 | 71.5 | 51.6 | 62.4 | 71.2 | 73.8 | 75.0 | 76.8 | 77.4 |
| At age | | | | | | | | | | | | | | |
| 1 year | 55.0 | 62.1 | 67.5 | 68.6 | 69.2 | 70.7 | 71.3 | 57.4 | 65.1 | 72.1 | 74.2 | 75.2 | 76.6 | 77.0 |
| 10 years | 51.4 | 55.6 | 59.1 | 60.0 | 60.5 | 62.0 | 62.5 | 53.9 | 58.6 | 63.6 | 65.6 | 66.5 | 67.8 | 68.2 |
| 15 years | 46.9 | 51.1 | 54.3 | 55.1 | 55.6 | 57.1 | 57.6 | 49.5 | 54.0 | 58.7 | 60.6 | 61.6 | 62.8 | 63.3 |
| 20 years | 42.7 | 46.7 | 49.5 | 50.4 | 50.9 | 52.3 | 52.8 | 45.2 | 49.6 | 53.9 | 55.7 | 56.7 | 57.9 | 58.4 |
| 30 years | 34.6 | 38.1 | 40.2 | 40.9 | 41.3 | 42.7 | 43.2 | 36.9 | 41.0 | 44.4 | 46.0 | 47.0 | 48.2 | 48.6 |
| 40 years | 26.8 | 29.5 | 30.9 | 31.5 | 31.9 | 33.2 | 33.7 | 29.1 | 32.4 | 35.1 | 36.5 | 37.3 | 38.5 | 38.9 |
| 45 years | 23.2 | 25.5 | 26.4 | 26.9 | 27.3 | 28.5 | 29.0 | 25.3 | 28.2 | 30.6 | 31.9 | 32.7 | 33.8 | 34.2 |
| 50 years | 19.7 | 21.6 | 22.2 | 22.6 | 23.0 | 24.1 | 24.6 | 21.6 | 24.1 | 26.2 | 27.4 | 28.3 | 29.2 | 29.6 |
| 60 years | 13.4 | 14.4 | 14.8 | 15.0 | 15.3 | 16.3 | 16.6 | 14.9 | 16.4 | 17.9 | 19.0 | 19.8 | 20.8 | 21.0 |
| 65 years | 10.8 | 11.3 | 11.7 | 11.9 | 12.1 | 13.0 | 13.2 | 11.9 | 13.0 | 14.2 | 15.1 | 16.0 | 16.9 | 17.2 |
| 70 years | 8.4 | 8.6 | 9.0 | 9.3 | 9.5 | 10.1 | 10.3 | 9.2 | 10.0 | 10.9 | 11.7 | 12.5 | 13.3 | 13.6 |
| 75 years | 6.4 | 6.4 | 6.7 | 7.0 | 7.3 | 7.6 | 7.9 | 7.1 | 7.4 | 8.0 | 8.7 | 9.4 | 10.2 | 10.4 |
| 80 years | 4.9 | 4.8 | 4.8 | 5.2 | 5.5 | 5.7 | 5.9 | 5.4 | 5.4 | 5.8 | 6.3 | 6.9 | 7.4 | 7.6 |

a Further number of years which a person could expect to live.

*Source:* *Social Trends*, 19, Table 7.2.

TABLE 14.17. *Number of notified cases of diphtheria,*
*whooping cough, measles, and poliomyelitis in*
*England and Wales, 1940–1981*

|  | Diphtheria | Whooping cough | Measles | Poliomyelitis |
|---|---|---|---|---|
| 1940 | 45,479 | 53,545 | 407,468 | 1,066 |
| 1945 | 17,595 | 62,663 | 445,412 | 853 |
| 1950 | 962 | 157,752 | 367,598 | 7,760 |
| 1955 | 155 | 79,101 | 693,740 | 6,331 |
| 1960 | 49 | 58,030 | 159,315 | 378 |
| 1965 | 27 | 12,945 | 502,066 | 94 |
| 1970 | 22 | 16,598 | 307,408 | 7 |
| 1975 | 11 | 8,910 | 143,024 | 3 |
| 1979 | 2 | 30,808 | 77,386 | 8 |
| 1980 | 3 | 21,131 | 139,486 | 3 |
| 1981 | 2 | 19,395 | 52,974 | 6 |

*Source*: Butler and Vaile (1984), Table 3.8.

The extent to which this growth in spending accurately matches consumer demand has been a highly contentious issue. Free marketeers have consistently objected to tax-financed health care (Treasury support for the NHS has never fallen below 70 per cent of total expenditure) on the grounds that state allocations merely reflect political or professional preferences rather than the choices of consumers (Seldon, 1981; Harris and Seldon, 1979). Clearly, it is extremely difficult to decide what constitutes an appropriate resource level for the NHS. Given the increasing number of elderly people, changes in the pattern of disease (more chronic illness), the rising cost of medical technology, increased consumer/professional expectations, and the labour-intensive nature of the service (which leads to an upward pressure on costs given that wages tend to rise faster than prices) there is a continuous demand for increased resource allocations. Indeed, even a real increase in the level of resources devoted to the NHS may prove inadequate (because of demographic factors and technological advance) to prevent a reduction in the level of service provision. For example, Iliffe (1985) contends that the 5.7 per cent real growth in input volume for current expenditure in the hospital and community health services between 1978/9 and 1984/5 was insufficient to prevent the level of provision deteriorating.

Those pressing for increased resources to be devoted to the NHS point to international evidence in order to further their case. As Table 14.20 indicates the UK currently comes near the bottom of a list of EEC countries in terms of proportionate GDP spending on health care. Moreover, this Table also shows that the additional resources devoted to health care in the UK between 1960 and 1983 are relatively modest when compared to many other EEC countries. Of course the relatively low level of resources devoted to health care in Britain does not necessarily mean that the service offered is inferior. There are good grounds for arguing that the NHS is extremely cost effective. For example, the administrative costs of the NHS (5 per cent of total expenditure) compare favourably with those pertaining in France (9–10 per cent), West Germany (9–10 per cent) and the United States

TABLE 14.18. Perinatal and infant mortality in Europe, 1960–1975

| | Perinatal mortality per 1,000 live births | | | | Infant mortality per 1,000 live births | | | |
|---|---|---|---|---|---|---|---|---|
| | 1960 | 1975 | % Decrease 1960–75 | Annual % decrease 1971–5 | 1960 | 1975 | % Decrease 1960–75 | Annual % decrease 1972–5 |
| England & Wales | 33.5 | 17.9* | 46.5++ | 4.1 | 21.8 | 14.2* | 34.3++ | 4.5 |
| Scotland | 38.1 | 18.5* | 51.3++ | 5.1 | 26.4 | 14.8* | 43.0++ | 5.4 |
| Sweden | 26.2 | 11.1 | 57.7 | 7.3 | 16.6 | 8.3 | 50.0 | 7.7 |
| Norway | 24.0 | 14.2 | 40.8 | 5.1 | 18.9 | 11.1 | 41.3 | 2.0 |
| Denmark | 26.5 | 12.7* | 52.1+ | 5.5 | 21.5 | 10.3* | 52.0++ | 3.9 |
| Finland | 25.3 | 13.9+ | 45.0** | 5.9 | 21.0 | 11.0+ | 47.6** | 1.4 |
| Netherlands | 25.6 | 14.0 | 45.3 | 4.3 | 16.5 | 10.6 | 35.7 | 3.1 |
| France | 31.8 | 19.5+ | 38.7** | 4.8 | 27.4 | 11.1 | 59.8 | 10.2 |
| W. Germany | 36.3 | 19.4 | 46.5 | 4.8 | 33.8 | 19.7 | 41.6 | 4.5 |
| (E. Germany) | — | (17.6) | — | — | — | (15.9) | — | (3.4) |
| USA | 29.4 | 20.7 | 29.2 | — | 26.0 | 16.1 | 38.1 | 4.3 |

*1976   +1974   ++1960   **1960–74

Source: Townsend and Davidson (1982), Table 20.

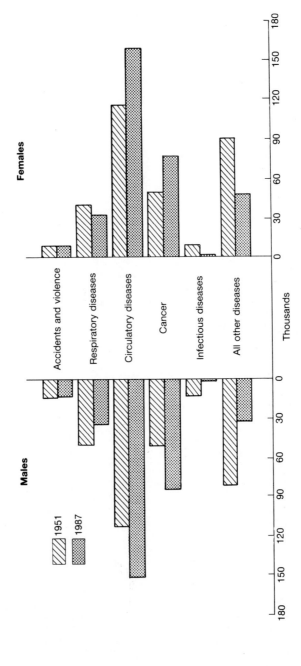

**FIG. 14.3.** *Selected causes of death: by sex, 1951 and 1987 (UK)*
*Source: Social Trends, 19. Table 7.4.*

TABLE 14.19. *National health service expenditure, 1950–1980 (UK)*

| Year | NHS expenditure at 1975 prices (£m.) | Percentage change on previous year | NHS expenditure as % of GDP at market prices | NHS expenditure as % of total government expenditure |
|------|------|------|------|------|
| 1950 | 2,553 |      | 3.7 | 18.4 |
| 1955 | 2,668 | +2.9 | 3.0 | 14.8 |
| 1960 | 3,059 | +3.3 | 3.4 | 17.1 |
| 1965 | 3,460 | +4.5 | 3.6 | 17.0 |
| 1970 | 3,998 | +3.6 | 3.9 | 17.3 |
| 1975 | 4,865 | +6.2 | 4.9 | 18.3 |
| 1980 | 5,432 | +2.4 | 5.1 | 21.2 |

*Source*:  Butler and Vaile (1984), p. 53.

(15–20 per cent). However, given that hospital waiting lists, to cite just one example, have remained high (Yates, 1987) there would appear to be valid grounds for demanding an increased level of funding. The question remains whether this should come from general taxation or an increase in private provision (private subscribers have increased from 2.3 per cent of the population in 1967 to 7.8 per cent in 1984—(The Politics of Health Group, 1982).

TABLE 14.20. *European health care comparisons*

| Health care expenditure in the European community as a percentage of GDP, 1982 | | Changes in the share of GDP devoted to health care 1960–1983 (EEC) | |
|------|------|------|------|
| Country | % | Country | % |
| France | 9.3 | France | +5.0 |
| Netherlands | 8.7 | Netherlands | +4.9 |
| Germany | 8.2 | Ireland | +4.3 |
| Ireland | 8.2 | Italy | +3.5 |
| Italy | 7.2 | Germany | +3.4 |
| Denmark | 6.8 | Belgium | +3.1 |
| Spain | 6.3 | Denmark | +3.0 |
| Belgium | 6.2 | UK | +3.0 |
| UK | 5.9 | Greece | +2.3 |
| Portugal | 5.7 | Portugal | +1.8 |
| Greece | 4.4 | Spain | N.A. |

*Sources*:  Radical Statistics Health Group (1987), Tables 5.1 and 5.2.

The growth in the level of health resources referred to earlier has led to numerous changes in the range and quantity of medical activity. For example, during the period from 1951 to 1985 the number of GPs and dentists have increased substantially whilst list sizes have fallen (see Table 14.21). It would be misleading, however, to draw any firm conclusions from such statistics. The apparent improvement in the

GP service may prove illusory given the increased proportion of elderly patients (who require more frequent consultations and home visits). Indeed, the overall level of service for many patients might be declining. Crucially, increases in the number of staff are often required to *maintain* rather than *improve* the service. Similarly, an apparent decrease in provision of, say, hospital beds would not necessarily signal a deterioration in service. In recent years more patients have been treated despite the reduction of bed availability (i.e. increased throughput).

Of course, it is perfectly possible to argue that even more patients could have been treated if more beds had been kept open. Moreover, the reduction in hospital-based recuperation might prove detrimental to the long-term health prospects of patients.

Crucially, then, increased activity in health care since the war should not be regarded as a satisfactory measure of the effectiveness, or otherwise, of the service. It is vital to consider the outcomes of medical intervention rather than outputs.

This distinction between outputs and outcomes lies at the heart of any assessment of the achievements of the NHS since 1948. As has been argued general levels of health care in the nation have improved. However, such an outcome cannot be attributed solely to the performance of health services. Demographic, epidemilogical, 'cultural', economic, and political factors are all likely to have played a part in determining the overall level of health.

In considering the impact of the NHS it is perhaps most useful to consider how successful it has been in achieving its objective of reducing inequalities in the pattern of ill health and service provision.

## 1. *Inequalities in Health*

There is substantial evidence to suggest that class inequalities in health and ill health have persisted since the war (Townsend and Davidson, 1982; Whitehead, 1987). If one examines the mortality rates for different sections of society it is clear that there is a sizeable gap between social class I and V (see Table 14.22). Crucially, it appears that the relative situation of the unskilled has actually worsened since the inception of the NHS—a conclusion which has been challenged by both Le Grand (1985) and Illsley (1986, 1987). The reliability of official data—most notably mortality rates—lies at the heart of this issue. The apparent widening of the class gap can be said to be a reflection of the changing composition of the various categories (social class I has increased from 1.8 per cent of the economically active male population in 1931 to 5.7 per cent in 1981 whilst social class V has decreased from 12.9 per cent to 5.6 per cent over the same period) rather than a further deterioration in the position of the lowest group. In short, there has been an absolute decrease in the incidence of premature death in all social classes. However, this trend is not reflected in inter-class comparisons not least because the contemporary composition of a shrunken unskilled class is more likely to contain a greater concentration of the most 'sickness prone' members of the community. Nevertheless, the importance of class inequalities should not be understated. As Table 14.23 demonstrates it is still the case that only two out of every three working class men actually reach pensionable age.

The limited evidence available relating to class differences in morbidity since the

TABLE 14.21. *General medical, pharmaceutical, and dental services, UK (selected years, 1961–1985)*

| | General medical and pharmaceutical services | | | | | | General dental services | | |
|---|---|---|---|---|---|---|---|---|---|
| | No. of doctors' in practice[a] (thousands) | Average number of patients per doctor (thousands) | Prescriptions dispensed[b] (millions) | Average cost per prescription (£s) | Average number of prescriptions per person | Average prescription cost per (£s) | Number of dentists in practice (thousands) | Average number of persons per dentist (thousands) | Average number of courses of treatment per dentist (thousands) |
| 1951 | 20.18[c] | 2.48[c] | 256.2[c] | 0.19[c] | 5.1[c] | 0.96[c] | 11.28[c] | 4.40[c] | 1.10[c] |
| 1961 | 23.56 | 2.25 | 233.2 | 0.41 | 4.7[c] | 1.91[c] | 11.89 | 4.41 | 1.36 |
| 1971 | 24.00 | 2.39 | 304.5 | 0.77 | 5.6 | 4.28 | 12.45 | 4.47 | 1.97 |
| 1976 | 25.38 | 2.29 | 360.5 | 1.58 | 6.5 | 10.22 | 13.60 | 4.11 | 2.25 |
| 1981 | 27.49 | 2.15 | 370.0 | 3.46 | 6.6 | 22.97 | 15.19 | 3.67 | 2.23 |
| 1982 | 28.06 | 2.10 | 383.3 | 3.83 | 6.9 | 26.37 | 15.71 | 3.56 | 2.21 |
| 1983 | 28.66 | 2.06 | 389.2 | 4.17 | 7.0 | 29.16 | 16.19 | 3.49 | 2.19 |
| 1984 | 29.14 | 2.04 | 395.6 | 4.42 | 7.1 | 31.38 | 16.68 | 3.39 | 2.18 |
| 1985 | 29.66 | 2.01 | 393.1 | 4.77 | 7.0 | 33.42 | 16.97 | 3.33 | 2.17 |

[a] Unrestricted principals only.
[b] Prescriptions dispensed by general practitioners are excluded. The number of such prescriptions in the UK is not known precisely but in England and Wales during 1985 totalled some 22.6m.
[c] Estimated.

*Source: Social Trends*, 17, Table 7.27.

TABLE 14.22. *Mortality of men (aged 15–64) by occupational class (1930s–1980s)*
(standardized mortality ratios)

|  | 1930–32 | 1949–53[a] | 1959–63 | | 1970–72 | | 1979–83 |
|---|---|---|---|---|---|---|---|
|  |  |  | unadjst | adjst[b] | unadjst | adjst[b] | unadjst |
| Professional | 90 | 86 | 76 | 75 | 77 | 75 | 66 |
| Managerial | 94 | 92 | 81 | — | 81 | — | 74 |
| Skilled manual & | | | | | | | |
| non-manual | 97 | 101 | 100 | — | 104 | — | 98 |
| Partly skilled | 102 | 104 | 103 | — | 114 | — | 114 |
| Unskilled | 111 | 118 | 143 | 127 | 137 | 121 | 159 |

[a] Corrected figures as published in Registrar General's Decennial Supplement, England and Wales 1961; Occupational Mortality Tables (London: HMSO, 1971), p. 22.
[b] Occupations in 1959–63 and 1970–2 have been reclassified according to the 1950 classification.

*Source*: Carr-Hill (1987), Table 1.

TABLE 14.23. *Social class and survival for males in
England and Wales 1951–1981*

| % who survive to: | 45 yrs | 55 yrs | 65 yrs | 75 yrs | 85 yrs |
|---|---|---|---|---|---|
| 1951 manual | 93.4 | 83.4 | 67.2 | 37.3 | 7.7 |
| non-manual | 94.2 | 86.9 | 69.5 | 44.3 | 14.5 |
| 1971 manual | 94.6 | 87.1 | 67.1 | 38.1 | 8.7 |
| non-manual | 96.0 | 90.1 | 75.2 | 47.4 | 15.8 |
| 1981 manual | 95.2 | 88.4 | 71.2 | 43.2 | 11.5 |
| non-manual | 96.7 | 92.0 | 80.3 | 54.5 | 18.2 |

*Source*: Hart (1987), Table 2.

war also tends to suggest that those from semi or unskilled backgrounds are more disadvantaged than those from professional or managerial groups. Such differences have been found in relation to long-standing illness (Whitehead, 1987), height and obesity (Knight, 1984), blood pressure (Rose and Marmot, 1981) and low birth weight (Macfarlane and Mugford, 1984).

## 2. *Inequalities in Provision*

A second way of evaluating the performance of the NHS relates to the provision of services. Has the NHS managed to achieve a more equitable distribution of medical services? In terms of GP consultations it has proved to be rather difficult to draw any firm conclusions about class differences. For example, evidence from the General Household Survey tends to suggest that, in general, people from lower socio-economic groups tend to make greater use of GP services than their more prosperous counterparts. However, if allowance is made for need rather than strict usage then the picture tends to be reversed (Brotherston, 1976). Indeed, the greater the weight attached to factors such as reported sickness or absence from work due to sickness the more clear cut it becomes that the semi-skilled and unskilled make less use of GP services (Forrester, 1976). Moreover, within the consultation process itself there is evidence to suggest that middle-class patients obtain a better quality of service as measured by the information conveyed and obtained (Cartwright and O'Brien, 1976). In addition, an earlier study by Cartwright (1964) found that GPs tended to know more about, and took greater interest in, the personal circumstances and needs of their middle-class rather than working-class patients. As Townsend and Davidson (1982) conclude on this issue:

The data are limited and further analyses remain to be carried out, but what is available suggests that the level of consultation among partly skilled and unskilled manual workers does not appear to match their need for health care. (pp. 79–80)

With regard to the use of hospital provisions there is very little class-related evidence. The data which has been collected tends to suggest that whilst there are no significant class variations in terms of out-patient attendance there does appear to be a greater likelihood that working-class citizens will be admitted to hospital than their middle-class counterparts—a finding which reflects their greater proneness to illness and injury (Townsend and Davidson, 1982).

There is more conclusive evidence to suggest that working-class people make less use of preventative services—with the possible exception of health visiting (DHSS, 1980a)—than the middle classes. For example, working class women are much less likely than their middle-class counterparts to receive ante-natal treatment; attend family planning clinics or receive screening for cervical cancer (Douglas and Rowntree, 1949; Gordon, 1957; Cartwright, 1970; Bone, 1973; DHSS, 1980a). Other evidence indicates that working-class people make less use of dental and chiropody services (Bulman et al., 1968; Clarke, 1969; Gray et al., 1970). In addition, working-class children are less likely to be immunized or receive dental treatment than their middle-class peer group (Blaxter, 1981).

Cultural or behavioural factors are often assumed to be the principal cause of this disparity. However, class factors are of more importance in this regard. For example, the under-utilization of health services by working-class children tends to reflect the external pressure exerted on their parents. As H. Graham (1984) explains:

where money is short, the costs and benefits of any action must be carefully weighed. Where the costs, however marginally, outweigh the benefits, a mother cannot always afford to take advantage of health service for herself and her family. Even with a National Health Service which is free at the time of use, the indirect costs can be prohibitive. (p. 54)

Regional disparities in the provision of health care have also proved to be a persistent problem for the NHS (as it was for its predecessors). Substantial variations in the distribution of financial and manpower resources persist across the country—disparities which cannot be justified on grounds of medical need. Indeed, there is good evidence to suggest that an 'inverse care law' tends to operate (i.e. in areas of greatest need one tends to find major deficiencies in supply; see Tudor-Hart, 1971; Noyce et al., 1974). For example, West and Lowe (1976), in a study of child health services in 15 Hospital Board Regions (now reorganized) in England and Wales, found a negative correlation between the numbers of GPs and health visitors and 'need' indicators such as infant mortality and still-birth rates.

Attempts have been made to reduce such inequalities. For example, the Resource Allocation Working Party (Department of Health and Social Security, 1976, 1980*b*) has attempted gradually to reduce regional disparities by promoting the idea that a greater proportion of additional resources should be diverted to those regions with the greatest needs as measured by such indicators as the number of children, elderly people, and women, and prevailing standardized mortality rates. The application of this formula, though generally welcomed, has, however, attracted both theoretical (the inappropriateness of certain indicators) and practical (the adverse effect on those deprived areas situated in relatively prosperous regions) objections (Ham, 1982). As yet RAWP has only proved modestly successful. Moreover, some of the more specific policies which were introduced to encourage practitioners to work in deprived locations such as the Designated Area scheme for GPs (Butler *et al.*, 1973; Butler, 1980) have proved equally disappointing. Importantly, the rights of practitioners to live and work in areas of their choice have always taken precedence over the rights of local communities to enjoy an adequate level of provision.

It would appear then that the NHS has not been particularly successful in reducing either health inequalities or disparities in the provision of services. However, it would be inappropriate to conclude that the NHS has been largely irrelevant to the well-being of citizens. In comparison to the pre-war situation the supply of health care has indeed been 'revolutionized'. The poorest groups in our society no longer have to rely upon highly stigmatized (and often extremely rudimentary) forms of medical treatment. Instead, like the rest of the population, they now have a much better chance of obtaining high-quality medical and nursing assistance at the time of need.

As George Godber, a pioneer of post-war health care points out, the NHS 'is imperfect, has included many mistakes and often achieved less than one hoped it would. It still does not have in-built review of quality, especially in medicine, it is underfunded and now too much focussed on reducing costs. Yet it has achieved more for the resources invested in it than any of the numerous services I know' (quoted in M. Dean, 1988).

This positive assessment of the NHS would appear to be shared by the general public, who have indicated in a number of surveys that they are strongly in favour of, and satisfied with, the NHS (Cartwright, 1964; Cartwright and Anderson, 1981; Bosanquet, 1984; Brook *et al.*, 1989). Not surprisingly, therefore, reforms which are seen to pose a threat to the basic ethos of the service such as the 1989 White Paper *Working for Patients* are likely to prove extremely unpopular. For all its shortcomings the NHS has captured the hearts and minds of the British population thus providing one of the greatest sources of comfort for collectivists.


**Poverty and Income Support**

In this section the issue of poverty, and the measures which have been introduced to counter it, will be addressed.

*The Notion of Poverty*

There is a considerable divergence of opinion concerning what actually constitutes poverty. The major definitional dispute centres around the question of whether poverty should be regarded as an 'absolute' or 'relative' phenomenon. Those who favour an absolutist approach regard poverty as the absence of the basic requirements for physical subsistence such as food, shelter, clothing, and heating. This approach is generally associated with the work of some of the earlier social investigators such as C. Booth (1903) and Rowntree (1901, 1918, 1941)—though see Veit-Wilson's (1986) reservations in this regard. For example, Rowntree (1901) utilized the work of leading nutritionists in order to devise a poverty threshold. In the case of a family of five (two adults, three children) living in York it was estimated that a weekly income of 21s. 8d. would be necessary in order to cover the cost of food (purchased at the cheapest shops), rent (average prevailing rate), and other essential items such as soap. A family was deemed to be in *primary* poverty if their income level fell below this threshold or, alternatively, in *secondary* poverty if some part of an otherwise adequate income had been absorbed by 'non-essential' expenditure. From this basis Rowntree calculated that 9 per cent of the population of York were living in primary poverty. Although this figure had doubled according to evidence obtained in a later study (in which a more generous interpretation of basic needs was adopted in 1941), the problem of poverty was adjudged to have all but withered away by 1950 (2 per cent).

The major advantage of absolute measures is the possibility of achieving an accurate measure of poverty which can be used comparatively over time. However, even the most tightly drawn absolute definitions are unable to overcome the problem of arbitrariness. For example, questions can be raised about the supposed objectivity of Rowntree's survey in the mid-1930s. Although Rowntree consulted the BMA in an effort to devise a scientific dietary standard he was prepared to override such advice if it conflicted with his own views. Unlike the BMA, Rowntree saw no reason why the poor should be granted an allowance for fresh milk or ready baked bread when there were 'acceptable' alternatives (condensed milk, homemade bread).

The limitations of absolute measures has led some commentators to stress the importance of examining poverty from a 'relative' standpoint. According to Townsend,

Individuals, families and groups in the population can be said to be in poverty when they lack the resources to obtain the types of diet, participate in the activities and have the living conditions and amenities which are customary, or are at least widely encouraged or approved, in the societies to which they belong. (Townsend, 1979, p. 31)

Acceptance that the definition of poverty will vary according to time and place inevitably leads one to question whether this notion can usefully be distinguished from broader concepts such as inequality or deprivation. It could be argued, for instance, that in any unequal society the least well-off will always be relatively poor. Townsend (1979) rejects this assertion.

Inequality, however, is not poverty. Even if inequalities in the distribution of resources are successfully identified and measured, those in the lowest 20 per cent or 10 per cent, say, are not necessarily poor. For example, the 20 per cent with the lowest incomes in Sweden are not so badly placed as the corresponding 20 per cent in the United States. (p. 57)

Townsend (1987) has also drawn attention to the importance of distinguishing between poverty and deprivation.

Deprivation may be defined as a state of observable and demonstrable disadvantage relative to the local community or the wider society or nation to which an individual, family or group belongs. The idea has come to be applied to conditions (that is, physical, environmental and social states or circumstances) rather than resources and to specific and not only general circumstances, and therefore can be distinguished from the concept of poverty. (p. 125)

For Townsend (1987) the term poverty should be reserved solely for a severe form of income deprivation.

It is assumed in this conceptualisation (deprivation) that a certain point in descending the scale of income or resources deprivation is likely to grow disproportionate to further loss of resources and that this 'threshold' properly marks the beginning of a state of objective poverty. (p. 131)

Townsend (1979) has favoured what is commonly referred to as a 'behavioural' approach to relative poverty (Piachaud, 1987). Broadly, this involves an attempt to find a point on a household resource scale where it is difficult for a family to engage in commonly accepted customs and activities (style of living indicators). By comparing his own deprivation index (Townsend, 1979, Table 63) with household income levels (weighted according to family size) Townsend was able to demonstrate that the 'objective' poverty line (i.e. a point at which an incremental loss of income results in a sharp rise in the level of deprivation) was approximately 50 per cent higher than prevailing supplementary benefit allowances (the 'official' poverty line).

In contrast to Townsend, other researchers (Van Praag et al., 1982; Mack and Lansley, 1985) have adopted a social consensus approach to the study of poverty. This approach places far greater emphasis on public rather than expert or official conceptions of poverty (Piachaud, 1987; Veit-Wilson, 1987). For example, Mack and Lansley (1985) equated their definition of poverty (an enforced lack of socially perceived necessities) with the absence of three or more 'essential' requirements (see Mack and Lansley, Table 47). Extrapolating from their survey findings these researchers estimate that 12 per cent of the adult population (5m. people) could be said to be living in poverty on this basis. Although Mack and Lansley express serious reservations about the existence of a clearly defined poverty threshold, their findings do lend credence to Townsend's 150 per cent benchmark referred to above.

*The Extent of Poverty*

Estimates of the extent of poverty should always be treated with caution given the diverse assumptions and methodologies which underpin them. Townsend (1979) provides a useful illustration of the different estimates that can be arrived at in his study of poverty in the late 1960s. As can be seen from Table 14.24 the percentage of the population in poverty ranged from 6.1 per cent (3.32m.) according to the 'official' standard to 22.9 per cent (12.46m.) if one adopts Townsend's own deprivation standard.

Although 'official' estimates of poverty have a number of weaknesses they do at least provide a basis for some form of comparison over time. As Figure 14.4

TABLE 14.24. *Percentages and numbers in poverty*
*according to three standards*
(UK 1968/9)

| Poverty standard | Percentage of population | Estimated number of non-institutionalized population |
|---|---|---|
| State's standard (SB) | 6.1 | 3.32m. |
| Relative income standard[a] | 9.2 | 5.00m. |
| Deprivation standard[b] | 22.9 | 12.46m. |

[a] Households having an income of less than 50% of the mean for their type.
[b] Households having an income of less than a level below which deprivation tends to increase disproportionately as income diminishes.

*Source:*  Townsend (1979), Table 7.1.

illustrates the problem of poverty has not, contrary to Beveridge's expectations, withered away. In 1948 some one million claimants were dependent on National Assistance; by 1984 there had been a four-fold increase. This rise in the absolute number of claimants can be accounted for in various ways. For example, the failure of (or unwillingness to pursue) full employment policies has led to a sharp rise in the number of unemployed claimants. In 1984 there were two million such claimants

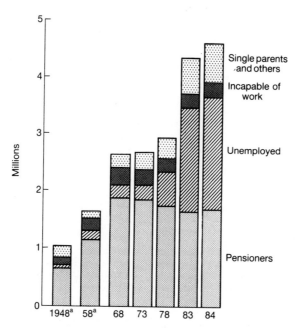

FIG. 14.4. *Supplementary benefit (income support) claimants, Great Britain*
*Source:*  *Social Trends*, 17, Table 5.7.

compared to a figure of 220,000 in 1968 and just 50,000 in 1948. Importantly, the unemployment insurance scheme (which did not include an adequate allowance for housing costs) has proved to be a less than satisfactory method of preventing poverty even in times of relatively low unemployment. By 1985 only 18 per cent of claimants were relying solely on unemployment benefit as a means of state income support (47 per cent in 1961).

The growth in 'unforeseen' poverty is another reason for the sharp increase in the numbers of claimants. For instance, there has been a large increase in the numbers of single-parent families—a group which finds it extremely difficult to secure an independent income given the dearth of child-care facilities and suitable job opportunities. By 1984 some 518,000 single parents (caring for a further 850,000 children) were receiving regular SB payments.

### Living Standards of the Poor

Although the levels of means-tested benefits are notoriously difficult to measure over time (Cooke and Baldwin, 1984) evidence suggests that the allowance of a single householder receiving supplementary benefit has doubled in real terms and maintained a degree of comparability with average male manual workers' earnings since 1948 (see Table 14.25). A similar conclusion can be drawn in relation to a single person receiving unemployment benefit on a retirement pension (see Table 14.26).

TABLE 14.25. *The level of supplementary benefit for a single householder relative to prices and earnings, 1948–1984*

| | Equivalent November 1984 prices (£) excl. housing costs | | As % of average male manual earnings | |
| --- | --- | --- | --- | --- |
| | Ordinary rate | Long-term rate | Ordinary rate | Long-term rate |
| July 1948 | 13.01 | 13.01 | 17.6 | 17.6 |
| January 1958 | 15.85 | 15.85 | 17.8 | 17.8 |
| November 1969 | 23.88 | 23.88 | 19.2 | 19.2 |
| November 1979 | 26.58 | 34.43 | 17.7 | 22.9 |
| November 1983 | 27.83 | 35.41 | 18.0 | 22.9 |
| November 1984 | 28.05 | 35.70 | 17.6[a] | 22.5[a] |

[a] Estimated.

*Source*: Bradshaw and Deacon (1986), Table 4.6.

The rise in the real value of benefits does not, of course, necessarily mean that the living standards of the poor have markedly improved. Importantly, the price of necessities (itself a rather 'elastic' concept) may rise at a much faster rate than general prices (F. Williams, 1977; Godfrey and Bradshaw, 1983). Moreover, the testimonies of claimants themselves suggest that the state minimum falls far short of any contemporary notion of adequacy (Burgess, 1980), a view confirmed by the most recent evidence which indicates that the 'real' living standards of the poorest

TABLE 14.26. *The level of standard rates of retirement pensions and unemployment benefit for a single person relative to prices and earnings, 1948–1984* (selected years)

|  | Equivalent November 1984 prices (£) | | As % of average male manual earnings | |
|---|---|---|---|---|
|  | Unemployment benefit | Retirement pension rate | Unemployment benefit | Retirement pension rate |
| July 1948 | 14.93 | 14.93 | 19.1 | 19.1 |
| January 1958[a] | 18.79 | 18.70 | 19.7 | 19.8 |
| November 1969 | 25.78 | 25.78 | 20.0 | 20.2 |
| November 1979 | 27.93 | 35.17 | 17.9 | 22.5 |
| November 1983 | 28.39 | 35.73 | 18.2 | 22.9 |
| November 1984 | 28.45 | 35.80 | 17.9[b] | 22.5[b] |

[a] February for unemployment benefit.
[b] Estimated.

*Source:* Bradshaw and Deacon (1986), Table 4.6.

groups in society are actually declining (Child Poverty Action Group, 1988; House of Commons, Social Services Committee, 1988).

## The State's Response to Poverty

As was noted in the introduction it was the Beveridge Report on Social Insurance which formed the basis for the first concentrated attack upon poverty after the war. Although some of the incoming Labour Government's measures were more generous than Beveridge had envisaged (pensions were paid without a 'phase-in' period) many were less favourable (insurance benefits, which failed to take account of the wartime rise in inflation and did not include a rent allowance, fell below subsistence level as did the newly created family allowances). The failure to devise an effective insurance-based income-support scheme at that time has led to a vast increase in the proportion of people (3 per cent 1948, 12 per cent 1981) dependent on means-tested benefits, which have proved to be a highly ineffective instrument for dealing with poverty. The major disadvantage with means-tested benefits is the level of take-up. As countless official and other studies have indicated, many of those in greatest need have been reluctant to claim this form of assistance despite having a clear entitlement (Ministry of Pensions and National Insurance, 1966; Moss, 1969, 1970; Cohen and Tarpey, 1982). The reasons for non-claiming are complex and inter-related. They include stigma (Page, 1984), inadequate forms of information, poor publicity, and the 'costs' (time, money) of claiming. Although it is difficult to be precise about the extent of non take-up it is unquestionably a problem of some magnitude. For example, according to a recent government estimate the take-up rate (case-load based) for supplementary benefit was just 76 per cent (DHSS, 1988). This shortfall is of some magnitude. In 1983 it was estimated that unclaimed Supplementary Benefit totalled some £570m.—a figure which represents an average individual loss of £8.40/week (DHSS, 1987).

Universal benefits (allowances provided for all those within a particular social category regardless of income or savings) are a much more effective way of combating poverty. However, these benefits have been criticized for failing to distinguish between the needy and non-needy. For example, in a study of social-security spending in the mid-1970s Beckerman and Clark (1982) suggested that this form of expenditure was successful not only in reducing the numbers of poor people in the population from 22.7 per cent to 3.2 per cent but also in narrowing the 'poverty gap' (the level of resources which needs to be distributed to poor households to lift them out of poverty) from £5,885m. to £250m. However, they estimate that only 40 per cent of the social-security budget was being directed towards the reduction of this poverty gap (between 1974–6). The remainder of the budget was swallowed up by the non-poor (42 per cent) or those who were only in need of a smaller allowance to lift them out of poverty (18 per cent). This 'leakage', which could not be attributed solely to universalism (means-tested payments to income units within non-poor households were also partly responsible), was not adjudged to be of a significant enough magnitude to warrant a fundamental change in the social-security system (though see Dilnot et al., 1984 for a contrary viewpoint).

The argument concerning the relative merits of means-testing and universalism is clearly an important one. The main advantage of the former is that it allows resources to be targeted on the poor rather than the non-poor. An illustration of the positive effect of such selectivity is provided in Fig. 14.5 which shows how the savings accruing from a reduction in a universal allowance of £2 per week cut in child benefit could improve the situation of poorer groups (i.e. by transferring these savings to means-tested benefits such as Income Support and Family Credit). As this figure demonstrates the bottom 30 per cent of the population gain at the expense of the relatively better off 70 per cent. However, as Hills (1988) reminds us, means-tested programmes are plagued by take-up problems and high adminis-trative costs. In addition they pose a threat to both horizontal redistributive goals (e.g. from childless couples to families) and social cohesion (the poor become seen as a distinct and separate group).

Although the social security system has failed to deal with the problem of relative poverty it should be recognized that certain policy initiatives have improved the economic situation of a number of disadvantaged groups in the population to a limited extent. Family Income Supplement (now Family Credit) was introduced in 1971 in an effort to help the 'working' poor. Such claimants were provided with an allowance which represented half the difference between their gross income and a prescribed 'need' level. By March 1986 some 200,000 people were in receipt of this benefit—a large number of whom were single parents (84,000). Like other means-tested benefits FIS has suffered from the problem of take up (only 65 per cent in 1983). This benefit has also been criticized for failing to tackle the underlying problem of low pay (Jordan, 1974).

The financial needs of disabled people have also been recognised (though only in the very recent past). Previously this group was only entitled to insurance benefits if they had adequate contribution records (an unlikely scenario given the economic and social barriers which blight the life changes of this section of the community). How-ever, since the early 1970s a range of modest disability benefits have been introduced:

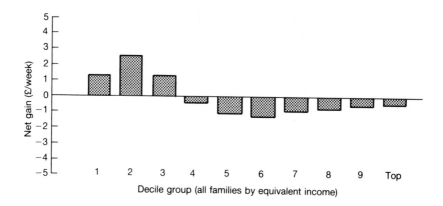

FIG. 14.5. *Switch to means-tested child support*
*Source:* Hills (1988), Fig. 11A.

1971: *Invalidity Benefit*—an 'indirect' contributory allowance payable to those who continue to require support after their entitlement to sickness benefit has ended.

1971: *Attendance Allowance*—a non-contributory benefit for those requiring constant care.

1975: *Non-Contributory Invalidity Pension (NCIP) and Housewives' Non-Contributory Invalidity Pension (HNCIP)*—a benefit for those ineligible for Invalidity Benefit.

1976: *Mobility Allowance*—a non-contributory benefit for those with severe walking difficulties.

1976: *Invalid Care Allowance*—a non-contributory allowance for those caring for someone in receipt of Attendance Allowance (married women excluded from eligibility until 1986).

1984/5: *Severe Disablement Allowance*—a non-contributory benefit which replaced NCIP and HNCIP, though the disability test was made more severe.

A number of criticisms have been made about these benefits. First, the benefit levels have proved inadequate to meet the expenses incurred by disabled people and their carers. Accordingly, the close association between poverty and disability has remained. Second, the eligibility tests for these benefits have been unacceptably harsh. For example, 82,000 initial or renewal claims for Attendance Allowance were rejected or withdrawn in 1985. Third, these benefits, like so much of the social security system, have tended to discriminate against women. For instance, married and cohabiting women were originally excluded from receiving NCIP. In an attempt to rectify this anomaly a new benefit (HNCIP) was introduced solely for this group of women. However, the eligibility criteria were stricter. An HNCIP claimant had to prove not only that she was incapable of work outside the home but also that she was unable to cope with 'normal household duties'.

Attempts have also been made to improve the financial circumstances of the elderly poor. There was substantial evidence in the 1950s and 1960s which suggested that large numbers of elderly people were not claiming means-tested benefits to which they were entitled (Cole and Utting, 1962; Townsend, 1963; Ministry of Pensions and National Insurance, 1966). In an effort to counter this problem the Labour Government of the mid-1960s introduced various social security reforms. Under the new Supplementary Benefit scheme (1966) allowances and 'disregards' were uprated and more comprehensive and appropriate forms of administration instigated (elderly claimants could opt to visit the SB office if they disliked home visits; reappraisals of circumstances were to be undertaken on a yearly rather than six-monthly basis). It was acknowledged, though, that the problem of poverty in old age could only be effectively countered by a major improvement in the basic pension. Accordingly, legislation was prepared along these lines in 1970 (based on the imaginative document *National Superannuation and Social Insurance* (1969) ). However, these plans were scuppered by the return of a Conservative administration, whose own remedy (The Social Security Act 1973—based on a white paper entitled *Strategy for Pensions* (1971) ) also fell foul of a changed political climate (Kincaid, 1975).

There were a number of differences between Conservative and Labour approaches to retirement pensions. Labour wanted a more generous basic pension with an earnings-related supplement which took greater account of the needs of disadvantaged groups (women, ethnic minorities) whilst the Conservatives favoured a more modest basic pension with the possibility of 'private' additions. The 1975 Social Security Act (which took effect from 1978) represented something of a compromise. The basic pension entitlement (which was more generous than the Conservatives would have wished) was supplemented by a fairly generous earnings-related addition (SERPS). As a concession to the Conservatives, companies were permitted to opt out of the state scheme provided that their own level of provision was at least as generous.

One of the underlying assumptions of SERPS, namely that the cost of the scheme would fall upon a relatively smaller working population during the first part of the next century, has been a source of concern to more recent Conservative administrations whose social security reforms in the late 1980s led to the introduction of a less generous form of pension provision (Silburn, 1985).

The modification of SERPS was only part of the Conservatives' social security reform in the 1980s. This policy initiative was intended to deal with the problem of poverty by adhering more firmly to the principle of selectivity. Resources are to be diverted to those in greatest need (such as families with dependent children) by means of a reduction in the incomes of the 'not so poor' (especially young people)— a policy which has been roundly condemned by egalitarians (Silburn, 1985; Bennett, 1987). Clearly, any poverty policy which is designed with the sole intention of producing a more 'rational' form of an existing income distribution pattern is unlikely to encompass the notion of relativity referred to earlier. As Alcock (1987) has noted, acceptance of the relative dimensions of poverty necessitates a qualitatively different kind of state support:

Rather than responding ex post facto to the problem caused by the existing distribution of wealth and resources, the state would have to intervene directly in that distribution in order to redistribute from those with more to those with less. And to do this social security policy would have to encompass not only the benefits paid to those without other resources, but also the wages and taxes paid by everybody else. For without change in wage and taxation policy there will be no resources to redistribute to those receiving benefits. (p. 142)

What conclusions, then, can be reached about poverty and income support measures in the post-war period? Clearly, the answer to this question will depend in large part upon the definition and measurement of poverty adopted. If one accepts the official guideline (the Supplementary Benefit/Income Support standard) then there is evidence which suggests that although the numbers in poverty have grown disproportionately in relation to the population in general (Piachaud, 1988) their living standards have 'improved' and maintained some comparability with average male manual workers' earnings. In contrast, those who believe that the 'official' poverty line underestimates the true extent and degree of poverty are likely to maintain that the living standards of the poor remain unacceptably low. Opinion is also likely to differ over the question of the effectiveness, or otherwise, of the state's response to poverty. Much of the debate has centred around the relative merits of universal or selective measures. However, the universal-selective debate tends to deflect attention away from a much more fundamental question, namely the role of social security (and indeed the welfare state itself) within the wider society. Crucially, the meeting of human need in the form of income support, health, or housing has always been tempered by considerations of costs, incentives, labour discipline, and self-help. In brief, social policy measures have always tended to be subservient to wider economic considerations.

## Social Welfare since 1945: A Concluding Assessment

This chapter has charted some of the major developments in the area of social welfare since the war. Many of these changes have been of a 'progressive' kind. In the sphere of housing supply has gradually outstripped the numbers of households, home ownership has risen dramatically, the number of unsatisfactory and substandard dwellings have decreased as has the level of overcrowding and enforced sharing. In terms of health and health care services it is noticeable that life expectancy has continued to rise whilst the converse is the case (until very recently) with childhood mortality rates. The steady growth in NHS expenditure has led to increased staff recruitment, an improved range of treatments, and a general rise in the level of activity. In education there have been improvements in pupil/teacher ratios, class sizes, and standards (reading, writing, and accreditation) as well as in the level of opportunities. More generally, there have been marked improvements in general living standards (at least in terms of measurements such as real wage rates and possession of consumer durables).

On the 'debit' side, the problem of poverty (at least in its relative form) has persisted as has that of homelessness. Indeed, the extent of homelessness is likely to increase in future decades given the continuing decline of private or public-sector property to rent and the spiralling cost of owner-occupation for first-time buyers (which is already restricted to those with substantial inheritances or savings in much of London and the South East). Other shortcomings include the failure to counter class inequalities in the fields of health and education and the absence of a more egalitarian distribution of income and wealth.

A useful way of assessing the achievements, or otherwise, of post-war welfarism is to explore the extent to which the aspirations of the social reformers of the 1940s actually materialized. To this end attention will be given to two distinctive (though somewhat interrelated) approaches to social welfare—reluctant collectivism and Fabian socialist (George and Wilding, 1985).

The reluctant collectivist approach to social welfare is exemplified by the work of Beveridge, most notably in his report on Social Insurance. Although some commentators (Pinker, 1979; Barnett, 1986) have expressed reservations about whether Beveridge should be regarded as a reluctant collectivist, there would appear to be enough evidence to support a classification of this kind. The reluctant collectivists are characterized by their commitment to individualism and freedom—values which they believe are best preserved by a competitive economic system. However, it is accepted that government has a vital role to play in regulating the worst excesses of the free market—though much intervention should be restricted to the protection of a citizen's basic living standards. More ambitious objectives such as the pursuit of egalitarianism are rejected on the grounds that this would stifle individual initiative and enterprise.

This contingent collectivism is clearly evidenced in Beveridge's Report on Social Insurance. According to Beveridge,

The State should offer security for service and contribution. The State in organising security should not stifle incentive, opportunity, responsibility; in establishing a national minimum, it should leave room for voluntary action by each individual to provide more than that minimum for himself and his family. (Report on Social Insurance and Allied Services (1942), Para. 9, pp. 6–7).

Beveridge's flat-rate insurance scheme (bolstered, where necessary, by means-tested assistance) was not designed to bring about a fundamental shift in the distribution of income. Its sole objective was to ensure that the living standards of citizens did not fall below a socially acceptable (subsistence) minimum. As was noted earlier, the success or otherwise of this system of income support was deemed to be dependent on other 'preventative' measures such as the pursuit of full employment policies, the introduction of a National Health Service, and Family Allowances.

It would appear, then, that the welfare objective favoured by the reluctant collectivists is the achievement of satisfactory minimum standards not only in the area of income support but also in such fields as health care, education, and housing. Clearly, given the changeable nature of minimum standards it is extremely difficult to assess whether this reluctant collectivist goal has been achieved in the post-war period. However, as has been noted in the previous sections of this chapter, there would appear to be sufficient evidence to support the assertion that minimum standards have been achieved in one or two key areas. In particular, enormous strides have been made in health care and education, where many would argue that acceptable levels of provision have been established. The picture is less satisfactory with regard to housing. Although improvements have been forthcoming in this area the level of homelessness and the reluctance of both Labour and Conservative Governments to regard the provision of accommodation as a basic right are major deficiencies.

The most telling indictment of the reluctant collectivist approach is the failure to eradicate poverty. Although it can be argued that the non-implementation of some of Beveridge's proposals reduced the overall effectiveness of his Social Insurance scheme it would be wrong to place too great an emphasis on this particular shortcoming. Of far greater importance was the underlying weakness of the scheme as a whole. As Williams and Williams (1987) contend:

Poverty cannot be abolished by social insurance because the politically congenial technique of social insurance cannot be extended to cover the whole field of income maintenance. It was certain that a Beveridge-style flat rate insurance scheme could not do the job because, as long as flat rate contributions were levied, the insurance fund would never have a substantial and elastic revenue base from which dependence could be supported. (p. 175)

It is evident that any effective attack on poverty required a for greater degree of government intervention than the reluctant collectivists were prepared to countenance. This unwillingness to support a greater degree of government intervention is the Achilles' heel of reluctant collectivist welfarism as it effectively stifles the possibility of achieving a satisfactory social minimum.

The pursuit of minimum standards in the welfare field was also a short-term policy objective for post-war Fabian Socialists (Crosland, Titmuss, Townsend). However, unlike the reluctant collectivists, they also believed that state welfare could, and should, be used for the purpose of reducing the level of inequality in society. For the Fabians the welfare state provided a means of ensuring that all citizens (especially the poorest members of society) would enjoy a decent standard of living throughout their lives and have access to important resources such as education and health care. Such goals were to be achieved by means of a progressive tax system which would provide the financial basis for redistributive social expenditure.

The welfare state was also seen to have a wider social purpose. It was envisaged that the solidarity and mutual aid which had surfaced during wartime could be maintained and extended by means of collective provision. The welfare state would lead, it was hoped, to a welfare society in which co-operation and altruism flourished. For example, Titmuss (1973) considered that the coming of the National Health Service was nothing less than 'the most unsordid act of British social policy in the twentieth century'. It 'had allowed and encouraged sentiments of altruism, reciprocity and social duty to express themselves; to be made explicit and identifiable in measurable patterns of behaviour by all social groups and classes' (pp. 254–5).

The optimism of the Fabians has been badly shaken by developments over the past 40 years. Despite improvements in the basic level of welfare provision there is little evidence to suggest that the goal of greater equality has been reached. Indeed, it is one of the ironies of the welfare state that the middle class have tended to gain as much, if not more, from the various social programmes than the working class. Le Grand (1987) provides an illustration of this trend in Table 14.27. Excluding housing, it can be seen that the richest 20 per cent of the population derive equal or greater advantage from certain forms of public expenditure than their poorer counterparts.

Disparities of this kind might tempt some egalitarians to press for the introduction

TABLE 14.27. *The distribution of public expenditure on the British social services*

| Service | Ratio of expenditure per person in top fifth to that per person in bottom fifth |
|---|---|
| *Pro-poor*: | |
| Council housing (general subsidy and rent rebates)[a] | 0.3 |
| Rent allowances | not available |
| Equal nursery education | not available |
| Primary education | 0.9 |
| Secondary education, pupils over 16 | 0.9 |
| *Pro-rich*: | |
| National health service | 1.4[b] |
| Secondary education, pupils over 16 | 1.8 |
| Non-university higher education[c] | 3.5 |
| Bus subsidies | 3.7 |
| Universities | 5.4 |
| Tax subsidies to owner-occupiers | 6.8 |
| Rail subsidies | 9.8 |

[a] The estimates pre-date the introduction of housing benefit.
[b] per person ill.
[c] Polytechnics, colleges of education, technical colleges.
*Source*: Le Grand (1987), Table 5.1.

of welfare policies which are targeted towards the poor rather than the better off. However, such a step might prove counter-productive. It can be argued that the retention of the middle class as consumers (rather than just as providers) of state welfare might be instrumental in securing the long-term 'legitimacy' of such provision. Without middle-class involvement it is possible that even the rather modest and unsatisfactory gains achieved by the disadvantaged since the war (alleviation of absolute poverty, reasonable minimum living standards) might be reversed (Le Grand, 1987). Moreover, the gradual exclusion of middle-class state welfare recipients is almost certain to increase rather than decrease the level of class divisiveness within society. If such a scenario is to be avoided even the most radical of egalitarians may be forced to concede, however grudgingly, that universal services (bolstered by positive forms of selectivity; see Titmuss, 1968) should not be jettisoned.

The evidence of the past 40 years suggests, then, that the pursuit of real equality requires radical change in the distribution of primary income and wealth rather than welfare reforms (Le Grand, 1982; O'Higgins, 1985). The limits of state welfare are being increasingly recognized by contemporary Fabians. For example, Wilding (1986) in a recent commentary on the welfare state asserts:

What is abundantly clear is that simple provision of state health or education services free at the point of use has not, and cannot, achieve equality of opportunity or outcome in health or in education. Such goals are only achievable by a wide range of policies to do with income, housing, diet, working conditions, and so on. To blame the health and education services for not achieving such equality is unrealistic. (pp. 128–9).

The failure to appreciate the limitations of state welfarism has been a major weakness of Fabian Socialist thought. The contention that progressive government action could overcome underlying economic relations has proved unfounded. Moreover, the Fabians too readily assumed that the pursuit of Keynesian economic policy would inevitably continue to reproduce the conditions in which state welfare could be painlessly expanded. This illusion was finally shattered in the mid-1970s when faltering economic performance led to a major reappraisal of the role and purpose of state welfare. The Fabian expectation that the welfare state would have become virtually immune to any form of attack or retrenchment was rudely shattered as cuts were imposed in various programmes. Importantly, even the unquestioned allegiance of the disadvantaged could not be relied upon during this hour of need. Over the decades those dependent on state welfare have voiced criticisms about poorly conceived policies, undue paternalism, inflexible forms of administration, and inappropriate forms of provision. Although certain programmes have retained their popularity (Bosanquet, 1984; Taylor-Gooby, 1987) it remains largely the case that public support for the welfare state is conditional rather than automatic. In the absence of a more developed collectivist ideology it seems reasonable to assume that state welfare will only prosper in those societies such as Sweden where the economy remains buoyant or, at least, relatively successful (Mishra, 1984).

The overt attacks on the welfare state over the past decade have highlighted the need for a more concerted defence of collectivism on the part of the Fabians. As Halsey (1987) has remarked:

a new version of the two nations has appeared in the last decade in the form of a widening division between a prosperous majority in secure and increasingly well remunerated employment by contrast with a depressed minority of the unemployed, the sick, the old, and the unsuccessful ethnic minorities. (p. 17)

Given the evidence of the last 40 years, which suggests that the welfare state cannot radically transform a market economy, the Fabians must it would appear (given their rejection of the revolutionary struggle) endeavour to enlist popular support for more realizable objectives (such as the attainment of high-quality basic provision) which do not run contrary to the capitalist ethic.

Finally, it should be remembered that any assessment of social welfare developments since the war depend, ultimately, on which side of the divide you happen to be situated (or where your sympathies lie). For those on the wrong side of this divide the evidence of the past 40 years would seem to indicate that the pursuit of 'welfarism' is likely to have only a limited positive impact on one's life chances. Clearly, the establishment of a welfare society will require a more fundamental form of economic and social change in society.

# Bibliography

AARONOVITCH, S., and SAWYER, M. (1975), 'Mergers, Concentration and Growth', *Oxford Economic Papers*, 27, 136–55.

ACTON SOCIETY TRUST (1956), *Management Succession* (London).

ADDISON, P. (1975), *The Road to 1945: British Politics and the Second World War* (London: Jonathan Cape).

ADVISORY, CONCILIATION AND ARBITRATION SERVICE (1988), *Labour Flexibility in Britain: The 1987 ACAS Survey* (London).

AHLSTROM, G. (1982), *Engineers and Industrial Growth* (London: Croom Helm).

ALCOCK, P. (1987), *Poverty and State Welfare* (London: Longman).

ALDCROFT, D. H. (1968), *British Railways in Transition* (London: Macmillan).

—— (1984), *Full Employment: The Elusive Goal* (Brighton: Wheatsheaf).

—— (1986), *The British Economy, the Years of Turmoil 1920–51* (London: Wheatsheaf).

ALDINGTON, LORD (1985), *Report from the Select Committee on Overseas Trade: House of Lords: Session 1984/5* (London: HMSO).

ALLEN, G. C. (1966), *The Structure of Industry in Britain*, 2nd edn. (London: Longmans).

—— (1968), *Monopoly and Restrictive Practices* (London: George Allen & Unwin).

—— (1979), 'Policy Towards Competition and Monopoly', in G. C. Allen (ed.), *British Industry and Economic Policy* (London: Macmillan), 155–70.

ALLSOPP, C. J. (1982), 'Inflation', in A. Boltho (ed.), *The European Economy* (Oxford: Oxford University Press), 72–103.

—— (1985a), 'The Assessment of Monetary and Fiscal Policy in the 1980s', *Oxford Review of Economic Policy*, 1, 1–20.

—— (1985b), 'International Macroeconomic Policy', in D. J. Morris (ed.), *The Economic System in the UK*, 3rd edn. (Oxford: Oxford University Press), 581–623.

ALLSOPP, C. J., and MAYES, D. G. (1985), 'Demand Management in Practice', in D. J. Morris (ed.), *The Economic System in the UK*, 3rd edn. (Oxford: Oxford University Press), 398–443.

ARGY, V. (1980), *The Post-War International Monetary Crisis: An Analysis* (London: Allen & Unwin).

ARMSTRONG, H. W. (1978), 'Community Regional Policy: A Survey and Critique', *Regional Studies*, 12, 511–28.

—— (1983), 'The Assignment of Regional Policy Powers within the European Community', in A. M. El-Agraa (ed.), *Britain within the European Community: The Way Forward* (London: Macmillan), 271–98.

—— (1986), 'The Division of Regional Industrial Policy Powers in Britain: Some Implications of the 1984 Policy Reforms', *Government and Policy, Environment and Planning C*, 4, 325–42.

ARMSTRONG, H. W., and FILDES, J. (1988), 'Industrial Development Initiatives in England and Wales: The Role of District Councils', *Progress in Planning*, 30, Pt. 2, 87–155.

ARMSTRONG, H. W., and TAYLOR, J. (1985a), *Regional Economics and Policy* (Oxford: Philip Allan, Deddington).

—— (1985b), 'Regional Policy', in G. B. J. Atkinson (ed.), *Development in Economics* (Ormskirk), 35–62.

—— (1986), 'Regional Policy: Dead or Alive?', *Economic Review*, 4, 2–7.

ARTIS, M. J. (1972), 'Fiscal Policy for Stabilisation', in W. Beckerman (ed.), *The Labour Government's Economic Record* (London: Duckworth).

—— (1978), 'Monetary Policy Part II', in F. T. Blackaby (ed.), *British Economic Policy 1960–74* (Cambridge: Cambridge University Press), 258–303.

ARTIS, M. J., and CURRIE, D. (1981), 'Monetary Targets and the Exchange Rate', *Oxford Economic Papers*, supplement, 33, 176–200.

ARTIS, M. J., and LEWIS, M. J. (1981), *Monetary Control in the United Kingdom* (Eddington: Philip Allan).

—— (1985), 'Inflation in the United Kingdom', in V. Argy and J. Neville (eds.), *Inflation and Unemployment: Theory, Experience and Policymaking* (London: Allen & Unwin), 200–20.

ARTIS, M. J., and NOBAY, A. R. (1969), 'Two Aspects of the Monetary Debate', *National Institute Economic Review*, Aug., 49, 33–51.

ARTIS, M. J., and TAYLOR, M. (1989), 'Abolishing Exchange Control: The UK Experience', CEPR Discussion Paper, 294.

ASHCROFT, B., and TAYLOR, J. (1979), 'The Effect of Regional Policy on the Movement of Industry in Great Britain', in D. Maclennan and J. B. Parr (eds.), *Regional Policy: Past Experience and New Directions* (Oxford: Martin Robinson), 43–64.

ASSOCIATION OF DISTRICT COUNCILS (1984), 'Economic Development Initiatives and Innovations', Best Practice Paper, 6.

ATKINSON, A. B. (1974), *Unequal Shares*, rev. ed. (Harmondsworth: Penguin).

ATKINSON, A. B., GORDON, J. P. F., and HARRISON, A. (1989), 'Trends in the Shares of Top Wealth Holders in Britain, 1923–1981', *Oxford Bulletin of Economics and Statistics*, 51, 315–32.

AYLEN, J. (1988), 'Privatisation of the British Steel Corporation', *Fiscal Studies*, 9, 3, 1–25.

BACKUS, D., and DRIFFILL, J. (1986), 'Inflation and Unemployment', *American Economic Review*, 75, 530–8.

BACON, R., and ELTIS, W. A. (1976), *Britain's Economic Problem: Too Few Producers* (London: Macmillan).

—— (1978), *Britain's Economic Problem: Too Few Producers*, 2nd edn. (London: Macmillan).

BAILEY, M. J. (1982), *Workers, Jobs and Inflation* (Washington, DC: Brookings Institution).

BAILY, R. (1968), *Managing the British Economy: A Guide to Economic Planning in Britain Since 1962* (London: Hutchinson).

BAIN, G. S. (1970), *The Growth of White-Collar Unionism* (Oxford: Oxford University Press).

—— (ed.) (1983), *Industrial Relations in Britain* (Oxford: Blackwell).

BAIN, G. S., and BACON, R. (1988), 'The Labour Force', in A. H. Halsey (ed.), *British Social Trends since 1900* (London: Macmillan), 97–128.

BAIN, G. S., and ELSHEIKH, F. (1976), *Union Growth and the Business Cycle* (Oxford: Blackwell).

—— (1978), 'Trade Union Growth: A Reply', *British Journal of Industrial Relations*, 16, 99–102.

BAIN, J. S. (1956), *Barriers to New Competition* (Cambridge, Mass.: Harvard University Press).

BAIROCH, P. (1968), *La population active et sa structure* (Brussels: OECD).

BALASSA, B. (1979), 'Export Composition and Export Performance in the Industrial Countries', *Review of Economics and Statistics*, 61, 604–7.

BALL, R. J., and BURNS, T. (1976), 'The Inflation Mechanism in the UK', *American Economic Review*, 66, 467–84.

—— (1978), 'Stabilisation Policy in Britain 1964–81', in M. V. Posner (ed.), *Demand Management* (London: Heinemann).

BANK OF ENGLAND (1966), 'Official Transactions in the Gilt-Edged Market', *Bank of England Quarterly Bulletin*, 6, 141–8.

—— (1969), 'The Operation of Monetary Policy since the Radcliffe Report', *Bank of England Quarterly Bulletin*, 9, 448–74.

—— (1970a), *Statistical Abstract* (London: Bank of England).

—— (1970b), 'The Importance of Money', *Bank of England Quarterly Bulletin*, 10, 159–98.

—— (1971a), 'Monetary Management in the United Kingdom', *Bank of England Quarterly Bulletin*, 11, 37–47.

—— (1971b), 'Key Issues in Monetary and Credit Policy', *Bank of England Quarterly Bulletin*, 11, 196–98.

—— (1971c), 'Competition and Credit Control', *Bank of England Quarterly Bulletin*, 11, 189–93.

—— (1971d), 'Sykes Memorial Lecture', *Bank of England Quarterly Bulletin*, 11, 477–81.

—— (1972), 'The Demand for Money in the United Kingdom: A Further Investigation', *Bank of England Quarterly Bulletin*, 12, 43–55.

—— (1978), 'Reflections on the Conduct of Monetary Policy', *Bank of England Quarterly Bulletin*, 18, 31–7.

—— (1979), 'Monetary Base Control', *Bank of England Quarterly Bulletin*, 19, 149–59.

—— (1980), 'Methods of Monetary Control', *Bank of England Quarterly Bulletin*, 20, 428–9.

—— (1981a), 'Monetary Control: Next Steps', *Bank of England Quarterly Bulletin*, 21, 38–9.

—— (1981b), 'Monetary Control—Provisions', *Bank of England Quarterly Bulletin*, 21, 347–50.

—— (1982a), 'The Supplementary Special Deposits Scheme', *Bank of England Quarterly Bulletin*, 22, 74–85.

—— (1982b), 'The Role of the Bank of England in the Money Market', *Bank of England Quarterly Bulletin*, 22, 86–94.

—— (1982c), ' "Overfunding" and Money Market Operations', *Bank of England Quarterly Bulletin*, 22, 201.

—— (1983), 'Setting Monetary Objectives', *Bank of England Quarterly Bulletin*, 23, 200–15.

—— (1984a), 'The Variability of Exchange Rates: Measurement and Effects', *Bank of England Quarterly Bulletin*, 24, 346–9.

BANK OF ENGLAND (1984b), *The Development and Operation of Monetary Policy 1960–1983* (Oxford: Clarendon Press).

—— (1984c), 'Funding the PSBR 1952–83', *Bank of England Quarterly Bulletin*, 24, 482–92.

—— (1984d), 'Aspects of U.K. Monetary Policy', *Bank of England Quarterly Bulletin*, 24, 474–81.

—— (1986), 'Financial Change and Broad Money', *Bank of England Quarterly Bulletin*, 26, 499–507.

—— (1987), 'The Instruments of Monetary Policy', *Bank of England Quarterly Review*, 27, 365–370.

BANK OF ENGLAND and HM TREASURY (1980), *Monetary Control*, Cmd. 7858 (London: HMSO).

BARBER, J., and WHITE, G. (1987), 'Current Policy and Problems from a UK Perspective', in P. Dasgupta and P. Stoneman (eds.), *Economic Policy and Technological Performance* (Cambridge: Cambridge University Press), 24–50.

BARKER, T. S. (1976), 'Imports', in T. S. Barker (ed.), *Economic Structure and Policy with Applications to the British Economy* (London: Chapman Hall), 162–73.

BARNA, T. (1945), *Redistribution of Incomes through Public Finance in 1937* (London: Oxford University Press).

BARNETT, C. (1986), *The Audit of War* (London: Macmillan).

BARRY, E. (1965), *Nationalization in British Politics* (London: Cape).

BARTLETT, B. (1985), 'Supply-Side Economics: Theory and Evidence', *National Westminster Bank Quarterly Review*, 18–29.

BARTLETT, B. and ROTH, T. (1984); *The Supply-Side Solution* (London: Macmillan).

BATCHELOR, R. A., MAJOR, R. L., and MORGAN, A. D. (1980), *Industrialisation and the Basis for Trade* (National Institute for Economic and Social Research, Cambridge: Cambridge University Press).

BATSTONE, E. (1986), 'Labour and Productivity', *Oxford Review of Economic Policy*, 2, 32–43.

—— (1988), *The Reform of Workplace Industrial Relations* (Oxford: Clarendon Press).

BATSTONE, E., and GOURLAY, S. (1986), *Unions, Unemployment and Innovation* (Oxford: Blackwell).

BAUMOL, W. J. (1982), 'Contestable Markets: An Uprising in the Theory of Industry Structure', *American Economic Review*, 72, 1–15.

BEAN, C. R. (1981), 'An Economic Model of Manufacturing Investment in the UK', *Economic Journal*, 91, 106–21.

BEAN, C. R., LAYARD, R., and NICKELL, S. J. (eds.) (1987), *The Rise in Unemployment* (Oxford: Blackwell) (originally issued as a special number of *Economica*).

—— (1986), 'The Rise in Unemployment: A Multi-Country Study', *Economica*, 53, S1–S22.

BEAUMONT, P. B. (1977), 'Assessing the Performance of Assisted Labour Mobility Policy in Britain', *Scottish Journal of Political Economy*, 24, 55–65.

—— (1979), 'An Examination of Assisted Labour Mobility Policy', in D. Maclennan and J. B. Parr (eds.), *Regional Policy: Past Experience and New Directions* (Oxford: Martin Robertson), 65–80.

BECK, G. (1951), *A Survey of British Employment and Unemployment 1927–1945*, privately printed by Oxford University Institute of Statistics and Economics.

BECKERMAN, W. (1965), *The British Economy in 1975* (Cambridge: Cambridge University Press).

—— (ed.) (1972), *The Labour Government's Economic Record 1964–1970* (London: Duckworth).

—— (1979), *Slow Growth in Britain* (Oxford: Clarendon).

—— (1985), 'How the Battle against Inflation Was Won', *Lloyds Bank Review*, 155, 1–17.

BECKERMAN, W., and CLARK, S. (1982), *Poverty and Social Security in Britain since 1961* (Oxford: Oxford University Press).

BECKERMAN, W., and JENKINSON, T. (1986), 'What Stopped the Inflation? Unemployment or Commodity Prices?', *Economic Journal*, 96, 39–54.

BEECHING, R., LORD (1963), *British Railways Board, the Reshaping of British Railways* (Beeching Report) (London: HMSO).

BEENSTOCK, M. (1983), *The World Economy in Transition* (London: Macmillan).

BEESLEY, M., and LITTLECHILD, S. (1986), 'Privatisation: Principles, Problems and Priorities', in J. A. Kay *et al.* (eds.), *Privatisation and Regulation—The UK Experience* (Oxford: Oxford University Press), 35–57.

BEGG, D. K. H. (1984), *Economics: British Edition* (London: McGraw-Hill).

—— (1987), 'Fiscal Policy', in R. Dornbusch and R. Layard (eds.), *The Performance of the British Economy* (Oxford: Oxford University Press), 29–63.

BELL, D. N. F., and KIRWAN, F. X. (1979), 'Return Migration in a Scottish Context', *Regional Studies*, 13, 101–11.

BENJAMIN, D. K., and KOCHIN, L. A. (1979a), 'What Went Right with Juvenile Unemployment Policy between the Wars: A Comment', *Economic History Review*, 2nd Ser. 32, 523–8.

—— (1979b), 'Searching for an Explanation of Unemployment in Interwar Britain', *Journal of Political Economy*, 87, 441–78.

BENNETT, F. (1987), 'What Future for Social Security?', in A. Walker and C. Walker (eds.), *The Growing Divide* (London: CPAG), 120–8.

BEVERIDGE, W. H. (1942), *Social Insurance and Allied Services*, Cmd. 6404 (London: HMSO).

—— (1944), *Full Employment in a Free Society* (London: George Allen & Unwin).

BISPAM, J. (1986), 'Growing Public Sector Debt: A Policy Dilemma', *National Westminster Bank Quarterly Review*, 52–67.

BISWAS, R., JOHNS, C., and SAVAGE, D. (1985), 'The Measurement of Fiscal Stance', *National Institute Economic Review*, 113, 50–64.

BLACKABY, F. T. (ed.) (1978a), *British Economic Policy 1960–74* (Cambridge: Cambridge University Press for the National Institute of Economic and Social Research).

—— (ed.) (1978b), *De-Industrialisation* (London: Heinemann).

—— (1978c), 'Incomes Policy', in F. T. Blackaby (ed.) *British Economic Policy 1960–74* (Cambridge: Cambridge University Press), 360–401.

—— (1979), *The Future of Pay Bargaining* (London: Heinemann).

BLACKBURN, K., and CHRISTENSEN, M. (1989), 'Monetary Policy and Policy Credibility', *Journal of Economic Literature*, 27, 1–45.

BLAIR, A. R. (1987), 'The Relative Distribution of United States Direct Investment: The UK/EEC Experience', *European Economic Review*, 31, 1137–44.

BLANCHFLOWER, D., and CUBBIN, J. (1986), 'Strike Propensities at the British Workplace', *Oxford Bulletin of Economics and Statistics*, 48, 19–39.

BLAUG, M., DOUGHERTY, C., and PSACHAROPOULOS, C. (1980), *The Distribution of Schooling and the Distribution of Earnings: Evidence From the British ROSLA 1972* (London: London School of Economics).

BLAXTER, M. (1981), *The Health of the Children* (London: Heinemann).

BOARD OF EDUCATION (1938), *Secondary Education* (Spens Report), (London: HMSO).

—— (1943), *Educational Reconstruction* (London: HMSO).

BOARD OF TRADE (1948), *Distribution of Industry*, Cmd. 7540 (London: HMSO).

BOLTHO, A. (ed.) (1982*a*), *The European Economy: Growth and Crisis* (Oxford: Oxford University Press).

—— (1982*b*), 'Economic Growth', in A. Boltho (ed.), *The European Economy* (Oxford: Oxford University Press), 9–37.

BOND, M., and KNOBL, A. (1982), 'Some Implications of North Sea Oil for the UK Economy', *IMF Staff Papers*, 29, 363–97.

BONE, M. (1973), *Family Planning Services in England and Wales* (London: HMSO).

BOOTH, ALAN (1983), 'The Keynesian Revolution in Economic Policy Making', *Economic History Review*, 36, 102–23.

BOOTH, ALISON (1983), 'A Reconsideration of Trade Union Growth in the United Kingdom', *British Journal of Industrial Relations*, 21, 379–91.

BOOTH, A., and PACK, M. (1985), *Employment, Capital and Economic Policy in Great Britain 1918–1939* (London: Blackwell).

BOOTH, C. (1903), *Life and Labour of the People in London* (London: Macmillan), 17 vols.

BORRIE, SIR G. (1987), 'Competition, Mergers and Price Fixing', *Lloyd's Bank Review*, 164, 1–15.

BOSANQUET, N. (1984), 'Social Policy and the Welfare State', in R. Jowell and C. Airey (eds.), *British Social Attitudes: The 1984 Report* (Aldershot: Gower), ch. 4.

BOSWORTH, B. P., and LAWRENCE, R. Z. (1982), *Commodity Prices and the New Inflation* (Washington, DC: Brookings Institution).

BRADSHAW, J., and DEACON, A. (1986), 'Social Security', in P. Wilding (ed.), *In Defence of the Welfare State* (Manchester: Manchester University Press), 81–97.

BRADY, R. A. (1950), *Crisis in Britain: Plans and Achievements of the Labour Government* (Cambridge: Cambridge University Press).

BRANSON, W. H., and BUITER, W. H. (1983), 'Monetary and Fiscal Policy with Flexible Exchange Rates', in J. S. Bhandari and B. H. Putnam (eds.), *Economic Interdependence and Flexible Exchange Rates* (Cambridge: MIT Press).

BRANT, J. (1984), 'Patterns of Migration From the 1981 Census', *Office of Population Censuses and Surveys, Population Trends*, 35, 23–30.

BRECHLING, F. P. R. (1967), 'Trends and Cycles in British Unemployment', *Oxford Economic Papers*, 19, 1–21.

BRISTOW, J. A. (1968), 'Taxation and Income Stabilisation', *Economic Journal*, 78, 299–311.

BRITTAN, S. (1969), *Steering the Economy* (London: Secker and Warburg).

—— (1971), *Steering the Economy: The Role of The Treasury* (Harmondsworth: Penguin).

—— (1975), 'The Economic Contradictions of Democracy', *British Journal of Political Sciences*, 5, 1, 129–59.

—— (1977), 'Can Democracy Manage an Economy?', in R. Skidelsky (ed.), *The End of the Keynesian Era* (London: Macmillan), 41–9.

BRITTAN, S., and LILLEY, P. (1977), *The Delusion of Incomes Policy* (London: Temple Smith).

BRITTON, A. (1983), 'The Economic Policy and Prospects', in J. Kay (ed.), *The Budget of 1983* (London: Blackwell).

BROADBERRY, S. N. (1984), 'Fiscal Policy in Britain during the 1930s', *Economic History Review*, 37, 95–106.

—— (1986), *The British Economy between the Wars: A Macroeconomic Survey* (Oxford: Blackwell).

—— (1987), 'Crowding Out or Crowding In? The British War Economy 1939–45' (paper given to Cliometrics Conference, Illinois).

BROOK, L., JOWELL, R., and WITHERSPOON, S. (1989), in *Social Trends 19* (London: HMSO), 13–22.

BROOKS, S., CUTHBERTSON, K., and MAYES, D. G. (1986), *The Exchange Rate Environment* (London and Sydney: Croom Helm).

BROTHERSTON, J. (1976), 'Inequality: Is It Inevitable?', in C. O. Carter and J. Peel (eds.), *Equalities and Inequalities in Britain* (London: Academic Press).

BROWN, A. J. (1972), *The Framework of Regional Economics in the United Kingdom* (Cambridge: Cambridge University Press).

BROWN, A. J., and J. DARBY (1986), *World Inflation since 1950: An International Comparison* (Cambridge: Cambridge University Press).

BROWN, C. J. F., and SHERIFF, T. D. (1978), 'De-industrialisation: A Background Paper', in F. T. Blackaby (ed.), *De-industrialisation* (London: Heinemann), 233–62.

BROWN, C. V., and LEVIN, E. (1974), 'The Effects of Income Taxation on Overtime: The Results of a National Survey', *Economic Journal*, 84, 833–48.

BROWNING, P. (1986), *The Treasury and Economic Policy 1964–85* (London: Longmans).

BRUNNER, K., and MELTZER, A. H. (1976), 'Government, the Private Sector and "Crowding Out" ', *The Banker*, 126, 765–9.

BRUNO, M., and SACHS, J. D. (1985), *The Economics of Worldwide Stagflation* (London: Blackwell).

BRYANT, R. C. (1980), *Money and Monetary Policy in Interdependent Nations* (Washington, DC: Brookings Institution).

BUCK, T. W., and ATKINS, M. H. (1976), 'Capital Subsidies and Unemployed Labour, a Regional Production Function Approach', *Regional Studies*, 10, 215–22.

BUCKLEY, P. J., and CASSON, M. (1976), *The Future of the Multinational Enterprise* (London: Macmillan).

BUCKLEY, P. J., and ENDERWICK, P. (1985), *The Industrial Relations Practice of Foreign Owned Firms in Britain* (London: Macmillan).

BUDD, A. (1978), *The Politics of Economic Planning* (Manchester: Manchester University Press).

BUDD, A., and DICKS, G. (1982), 'Inflation: A Monetarist Interpretation', in A. Boltho (ed.), *The European Economy* (Oxford: Oxford University Press), 104–31.

BUITER, W. (1985), 'A Guide to Public Sector Debt and Deficits', *Economic Policy*, 1, 13–61.

BUITER, W., and MILLER, M. H. (1981a), 'Monetary Policy and International Competitiveness: The Problem of Adjustment', *Oxford Economic Papers*, 33, supplement, 143–75.

BUITER, W., and MILLER, M. H. (1981b), 'The Thatcher Experiment: The First Two Years', *Brookings Papers on Economic Activity*, 2, 315–79.

—— (1983), 'Changing the Rules: Economic Consequences of the Thatcher Regime', *Brookings Paper*, 2, 305–65.

BULMAN, J. S., RICHARDS, N. D., SLACK, G. L., and WILLCOCKS, A. J. (1968), *Demand and Need for Dental Care* (Oxford: Oxford University Press).

BURGESS, M. (1980), *Living from Hand to Mouth*, Poverty Pamphlet 50 (London: Child Poverty Action Group/Family Service Units).

BURKE, G. (1981), *Housing and Social Justice* (London: Longman).

BURN, D. (1978), *Nuclear Power and the Energy Crisis: Politics and the Atomic Industry* (London: Macmillan).

BURNETT, J. (1986), *A Social History of Housing 1815–1984*, 2nd edn. (London: Methuen).

BURNS, T. (1988), 'The U.K. Government's Financial Strategy', in W. A. Eltis and P. J. N. Sinclair (eds.), *Keynes and Economic Policy* (London: Macmillan), 428–47.

BURTON, J. (1985), *Why No Cuts?*, Hobard Paper 105 (London: Institute of Economic Affairs).

BUSINESS STATISTICS OFFICE (1987), *Census of Production, 1984* (London: HMSO).

BUTLER, J. R. (1980), *How Many Patients?* (London: Bedford Square Press).

BUTLER, J. R., and VAILE, M. S. B. (1984), *Health and Health Services* (London: Routledge & Kegan Paul).

BUTLER, J. R., BEVAN, J. M., and TAYLOR, R. C. (1973), *Family Doctors and Public Policy* (London: Routledge & Kegan Paul).

BUTTON, K. J. (1985), 'New Approaches to the Regulation of Industry', *Royal Bank of Scotland Review*, December, no. 148, 18–34.

BUXTON, N. K., and ALDCROFT, D. H. (eds.) (1979), *British Industry between the Wars* (London: Scolar Press).

CABLE, J. R. (1980), 'Industry and Commerce', in A. R. Prest and D. J. Coppock (eds.), *The UK Economy: A Manual of Applied Economics*, 8th edn. (London: Weidenfeld & Nicolson), 181–236.

CABLE, J. R., and STEER, P. (1978), 'Internal Organisation and Profit: An Empirical Analysis of Large UK Companies', *Journal of Industrial Economics*, 27, 13–30.

CAIRNCROSS, A. (1985), *Years of Recovery—British Economic Policy 1945–51* (London: Methuen).

—— (1986), *Economics and Economic Policy* (London: Basil Blackwell).

—— (1987), 'Prelude to Radcliffe Monetary Policy in the United Kingdom 1948–57', *Rivista di Storia Economia*, 4, 2–20.

—— (1989), *The Robert Hall Diaries 1947–53* (London: Hyman).

—— and EICHENGREEN, B. (1983), *Sterling in Decline: The Devaluations of 1931, 1949 and 1967* (London: Blackwell).

CALMFORS, L., and DRIFFILL, J. (1988), 'Bargaining Structure, Corporatism and Macroeconomic Performance', *Economic Policy*, 6, 13–62.

CAPIE F., and COLLINS, M. (1983), *The Interwar British Economy* (Manchester: Manchester University Press).

——, AND WEBBER, A. (1985), *A Monetary History of the United Kingdom 1870–1982*, vol. 1: *Data, Sources and Methods* (London: Allen & Unwin).

CARLSON, K. M., and SPENCER, R. W. (1975), 'Crowding Out and Its Critics', *Federal Reserve Bank of St Louis Review*, 57 (December), 2–17.

CARR-HILL, R. (1987), 'The Inequalities in Health Debate: A Critical Review of the Issues', *Journal of Social Policy*, 16, 4, 509–42.

CARRUTH, A., and DISNEY, D. (1988), 'Where Have Two Million Trade Union Members Gone?', *Economica*, 55, 1–19.

CARTER, C. (ed.) (1981a), *Industrial Policy and Innovation* (London: Heinemann).

—— (1981b), 'Reasons for Not Innovating', in C. Carter (ed.), *Industrial Policy and Innovation* (London: Heinemann) 21–31.

CARTWRIGHT, A. (1964), *Human Relations and Hospital Care* (London: Routledge & Kegan Paul).

—— (1970), *Parents and Family Planning Services* (London: Routledge & Kegan Paul).

CARTWRIGHT, A., and ANDERSON, R. (1981), *General Practice Revisited* (London: Tavistock).

CARTWRIGHT, A., and O'BRIEN, M. (1976), 'Social Class Variations in Health Care', *The Sociology of the NHS*, Sociological Review Monograph 22 (Keele: University of Keele).

CASSON, M., and ASSOCIATES (1986), *Multinationals and World Trade* (London: Allen & Unwin).

CAVES, R. E. (ed.) (1968), *Britain's Economic Prospects* (London: Allen & Unwin).

—— (1982), *Multinational Enterprise and Economic Analysis* (Cambridge: Cambridge University Press).

CENTRAL ADVISORY COUNCIL FOR EDUCATION (CACE) (1959), *15 to 18*, Crowther Report (London: HMSO).

—— (1963), *Half Our Future*, Newsom Report (London: HMSO).

CENTRAL STATISTICAL OFFICE, *Annual Abstract of Statistics* (various issues) (London: HMSO).

—— *Economic Trends: Annual Supplement* (various issues) (London: HMSO).

—— (1986), *Social Trends 16* (London: HMSO).

—— (1987), *Social Trends 17* (London: HMSO).

—— (1988), *UK National Accounts* (London: HMSO).

—— (1989), *Social Trends 19* (London: HMSO).

CHANDLER, A. D. (1980), 'The Growth of the Transnational Industrial Firm in the United States and the United Kingdom: A Comparative Analysis', *Economic History Review*, 33, 396–410.

CHANDLER, SIR G. (1984), 'The Political Process and the Decline of Industry', *Three Banks Review*, no. 141, 3–17.

CHANNON, D. F. (1973), *The Strategy and Structure of British Enterprise* (London: Macmillan).

CHATTERJI, M., and WICKENS, M. R. (1982), 'Productivity, Factor Transfers and Economic Growth in the UK', *Economica*, 49, 21–38.

—— (1983), 'Verdoorn's Law and Kaldor's Law: A Revisionist Interpretation', *Journal of Post-Keynesian Economics*, 5, 397–413.

CHESTER, D. N. (1951), 'The Central Machinery for Economic Policy', in D. N.

Chester (ed.), *Lessons of the British War Economy* (Cambridge: Cambridge University Press).

CHILD POVERTY ACTION GROUP (1988), *Poverty: The Facts* (London: CPAG).

CHIPLIN, B., and WRIGHT, M. (1987), *The Logic of Mergers* (London: Institute of Economic Affairs).

CHOURAQUI, J.-C., and PRICE, R. E. (1985), 'Fiscal and Monetary Strategy, in V. Argy and J. Neville (eds.), *Inflation and Unemployment: Theory, Experience and Policymaking* (London: Allen & Unwin), 105–33.

CHRYSTAL, K. A. (1979), *Controversies in British Macroeconomics* (Oxford: Philip Allan).

—— (1984), 'Dutch Disease or Monetarist Medicine? The British Economy under Mrs Thatcher', *Federal Reserve Bank of St Louis Review*, 66, 5, May.

CHRYSTAL, K. A., and ALT, J. E. (1979), 'Endogenous Government Behaviour: Wagner's Law or Gotterdammerung?', in S. T. Crook and P. J. Jackson (eds.), *Current Issues in Fiscal Policy* (London: Martin Robertson).

—— (1981a), 'Some Problems in Formulating and Testing a Politico-Economic Model of the United Kingdom', *Economic Journal*, 91, 730–6.

—— (1981b), 'Public Sector Behaviour: The Status of the Political Business Cycle', in D. Currie, R. Nobay, and D. Peel (eds.), *Macroeconomic Analysis* (London: Croom Helm).

—— (1983), *Political Economics* (Brighton: Wheatsheaf).

CLARE GROUP (1982), 'Problems of Industrial Recovery', *Midland Bank Review*, 9–16.

CLARK, J. M. (1940), 'Toward a Concept of Workable Competition', *American Economic Review*, 30, 241–256.

—— (1961), *Competition as a Dynamic Process* (Washington, DC: Brookings).

CLARKE, M. (1969), *Trouble with Feet*, Occasional Papers on Social Administration 29 (London: Bell and Sons).

CLARKE, R. (1984), 'Profit Margins and Market Concentration in UK Manufacturing Industry: 1970–6', *Applied Economics*, 16, 57–71.

—— (1985), *Industrial Economics* (Oxford: Blackwell).

CLARKE, R., and DAVIES, S. W. (1983), 'Aggregate Concentration, Market Concentration and Diversification', *Economic Journal*, 93, 182–92.

CLARKE, R., DAVIES, S., and WATERSON, M. (1984), 'The Profitability–Concentration Relation', *Journal of Industrial Economics*, 32, 435–50.

CLEGG, H. (1971), *How to Run an Incomes Policy and Why We Made Such a Mess of the Last One* (London: Heinemann).

—— (1979), *The Changing System of Industrial Relations in Great Britain* (Oxford: Blackwell).

Cmd. 1337 (1961), *Financial and Economic Obligations of the Nationalized Industries* (London: HMSO).

Cmd. 3437 (1967), *Nationalised Industries: A Review of Economic and Financial Objectives* (London: HMSO).

Cmd. 4755 (1971), *A Strategy For Pensions* (London: HMSO).

Cmd. 9453 (1985), *Education for All*, Swann Report (London: HMSO).

Cmd. 9474 (1985), *Employment: The Challenge for the Nation* (London: HMSO).

Cmd. 9835 (1986), *Profit Related Pay* (London: HMSO).

COASE, R. H. (1950), *British Broadcasting: A Study in Monopoly* (London: London School of Economics and Political Science).

COATES, D. (1980), *Labour in Power? A Study of the Labour Government, 1974–79* (London: Longman).

COATES, D., and HILLARD, J. (eds.) (1987), *The Economic Revival of Modern Britain* (Aldershot: Edward Elgar).

COATES, K. (ed.) (1979), *What Went Wrong? Explaining the Fall of the Labour Government* (London: Spokesman Books).

COHEN, C. D. (1971), *British Economic Policy 1960–69* (London: Butterworths).

COHEN, R., and TARPEY, M. (1982), *The Trouble with Take-Up* (London: Islington People's Rights).

COLE, D., and UTTING, J. E. G. (1962), *The Economic Circumstances of Old People*, Occasional Papers on Social Administration 4 (Welwyn: Codicote Press).

COLE, W. J. (1975), 'Research Note: The Financing of the Individual Striker: A Case Study in the Building Industry', *British Journal of Industrial Relations*, 13, 1, 94–7.

COLEMAN, D. C., and MACLEOD, C. (1986), 'Attitudes to New Techniques: British Businessmen, 1800–1950', *Economic History Review*, 39, 588–611.

COMMISSION OF THE EUROPEAN COMMUNITIES (1981a), *Study of the Regional Impact of the Common Agriculture Policy*, Regional Policy Series, 21 (Brussels).

—— (1981b), *Deglomeration Policies in the European Community—A Comparative Study*, Regional Policy Series, 18 (Brussels).

COMMISSIONER FOR THE SPECIAL AREAS (1936), *Report 1936*, Cmd. 5090 (London: HMSO).

—— (1937), *Report 1937*, Cmd. 5595 (London: HMSO).

COMMITTEE OF INQUIRY INTO THE GAS INDUSTRY (1945), Hayworth Report, Cmd. 6699 (London: HMSO).

COMMITTEE ON THE WORKING OF THE MONETARY SYSTEM (Radcliffe Committee) (1959), *Report*, Cmd. 827 (London: HMSO).

COMMITTEE ON HIGHER EDUCATION (1963), *Higher Education*, Robbins Report, Cmd. 6684 (London: HMSO).

COMMITTEE TO REVIEW THE FUNCTIONING OF FINANCIAL INSTITUTIONS (Wilson Committee) (1980), Cmd. 7937 (London: HMSO).

CONFEDERATION OF BRITISH INDUSTRY (1977), *Britain Means Business* (London: CBI).

COOKE, K., and BALDWIN, S. M. (1984), *How Much Is Enough: A Review of the Supplementary Benefits Scales* (London: Family Policy Studies Centre).

COOPER, R. N., and LAWRENCE, R. Z. (1975), 'The 1972–75 Primary Commodity Boom', *Brookings Papers on Economic Activity*, 3, 671–715.

COOPERS AND LYBRANDS ASSOCIATES (1985), *A Challenge to Complacency: Changing Attitudes to Training* (London: MSC/NEDO).

CORDEN, W. M. (1958), 'The Control of Imports: A Case Study in the United Kingdom Import Restrictions of 1951–52', *Manchester School*, 26, 181–221.

COSH, A. D., HUGHES, A., and SINGH, A. (1980), 'The Causes and Effects of Takeovers in the United Kingdom: An Empirical Investigation for the Late 1960s at the Microeconomic Level', in Mueller, D. C. (ed.), *The Determinants and Effects of Mergers* (Mass.: Oelgeschlager, Gunn and Hain), 227–70.

COSH, A. D., HUGHES, A., LEE, K., and SINGH, A. (1989), 'Institutional Investment, Mergers and the Market for Corporate Control', *International Journal of Industrial Organization*, 7, 73–100.

COURAKIS, A. S. (1981), 'Monetary Targets: Conceptual Antecedents and Recent

Policies in the US, UK and West Germany', in A. S. Courakis (ed.), *Inflation, Depression and Economic Policy in the West* (London: Mansell), 259–357.

COWLING, K. (1982), *Monopoly Capitalism* (London: Macmillan).

COWLING, K. (1983), 'Excess Capacity and the Degree of Collusion: Oligopoly Behaviour in the Slump', *Manchester School*, 51, 341–59.

COWLING, K., and SUGDEN, R. (1987), *Transnational Monopoly Capitalism* (Brighton: Wheatsheaf).

COWLING, K., and WATERSON, M. (1976), 'Price-Cost Margins and Market Structure', *Economica*, 43, 267–74.

COWLING, K., STONEMAN, P., CUBBIN, J., CABLE, J., HALL, G., DOMBERGER, S., and DUTTON, P. (1980), *Mergers and Economic Performance* (Cambridge: Cambridge University Press).

COX, C. B., and BOYSON, R. (eds.) (1975), *Black Paper 1975* (London: Dent).

COX, C. B., and DYSON, A. E. (eds.) (1971), *The Black Papers on Education* (London: Davis-Paynter).

CRAFTS, N. F. R. (1985), *British Economic Growth during the Industrial Revolution* (Oxford: Clarendon Press).

CRAFTS, N. F. R. (1987), 'Long Term Unemployment in Britain in the 1930s', *Economic History Review*, 2nd ser. 40, 418–32.

CRAFTS, N. F. R., and THOMAS, M. (1986), 'Comparative Advantage in UK Manufacturing Trade 1910–1936', *Economic Journal*, 96, 629–45.

CRAWFORD, P., FOTHERGILL, S., and MONK, S. (1985), 'The Effect of Business Rates on the Location of Employment', Industrial Location Research Group, Department of Land Economy (Cambridge: University of Cambridge).

CREEDY, J. (ed.) (1981), *The Economics of Unemployment in Britain* (London: Butterworths).

CRIPPS, T. F., FETHERSTON, M. J., and GODLEY, W. A. H. (1978), 'Simulations with the Cambridge Economic Policy Group Model', in M. V. Posner (ed.), *Demand Management* (London: Heinemann), 9–34.

CRONIN, J. (1979), *Industrial Conflict in Modern Britain* (London: Croom Helm).

CROSLAND, C. A. R. (1956), *The Future of Socialism* (London: Cape).

CROSS, R. (1982), *Economic Theory and Policy in the UK* (Oxford: Martin Robertson).

CROUCH, R. L. (1963), 'A Re-examination of Open Market Operations', *Oxford Economic Papers*, July, NS 15, 81–94.

CROWTHER COMMITTEE (1971), *Consumer Credit: Report of the Committee* (London: HMSO).

CURRY, B., and GEORGE, K. D. (1983), 'Industrial Concentration: A Survey', *Journal of Industrial Economics*, 31, 203–55.

DALY, A., HITCHENS, D. M., and WAGNER, K. (1985), 'Productivity, Machinery and Skills in a Sample of British and German Manufacturing Plants: Results of a Pilot Inquiry', *National Institute Economic Review*, 111, 48–61.

DANIEL, W. W. (1987), *Workplace Industrial Relations and Technical Change* (London: Frances Pinter).

DANIEL, W. W., and MILLWARD, N. (1983), *Workplace Industrial Relations in Britain* (London: Heinemann).

DARBY, J., and WREN-LEWIS, S. (1988), 'Trends in Manufacturing Labour Productivity', National Institute of Economic and Social Research, Discussion Paper 145.

DAVID, M. E. (1980), *The State, the Family and Education* (London: Routledge & Kegan Paul).

DAVID, P. A. (1977), 'Invention and Accumulation in America's Economic Growth: A Nineteenth Century Parable', in K. Brunner and A. H. Meltzer (eds.), *International Organization, National Policies and Economic Development* (Amsterdam: North Holland), 177–97.

DAVIES, G., and DAVIES, J. (1984), 'The Revolution in Monopoly Theory', *Lloyds Bank Review*, July, 38–52.

DAVIES, S. W., and CAVES, R. E. (1987), *Britain's Productivity Gap* (Cambridge: Cambridge University Press).

DAVIS, E. (1984), 'Express Coaching since 1980: Liberalisation in Practice', *Fiscal Studies*, 5, 1, 76–86.

DAWKINS, P. J. (1980), 'Incomes Policy', in W. P. J. Maunder (ed.), *The British Economy in the 1970s* (London: Heinemann), 61–85.

DEACON, D. (1982), 'Competition Policy in the Common Market: Its Links with Regional Policy', *Regional Studies*, 16, 53–63.

DEAKIN, B. M., and PRATTEN, C. F. (1987), 'Economic Effects of YTS', *Department of Employment Gazette*, 95, 491–7.

DEAKIN, N. (1987), *The Politics of Welfare* (London: Methuen).

DEAN, M. (1988), 'A Charter for Health', *The Guardian*, 1 July.

DEANE, P. (1979), 'History of Inflation', in D. Heathfield (ed.), *Perspectives of Inflation* (London: Macmillan).

DEARDEN, S. (1986), 'EEC Membership and the UK's Trade in Manufactured Goods', *National Westminster Quarterly Review*, February, 15–25.

DEARDOFF, A. V., and STERN, R. M. (1983), 'The Effects of Domestic Tax/Subsidies and Import Tariffs on the Structure of Protection in the United States, United Kingdom and Japan', in J. Black and L. A. Winters (eds.), *Policy Performance in International Trade* (London: Macmillan).

DELL, E. (1973), *Political Responsibility and Industry* (London: Allen & Unwin).

DEMSETZ, H. (1973), 'Industry Structure, Market Rivalry and Public Policy', *Journal of Law and Economics*, 16, 1–9.

—— (1982), 'Barriers to Entry', *American Economic Review*, 72, 47–57.

DENNIS, G. E. J. (1980), 'Money Supply and Its Control', in P. Maunder (ed.), *The British Economy in the 1970s* (London: Heinemann), 35–60.

DENNISON, S. R. (1939), *The Location of Industry and the Depressed Areas* (London: Oxford University Press).

DEPARTMENT OF ECONOMIC AFFAIRS (1965), *The National Plan*, Cmd. 2764 (London: HMSO).

DEPARTMENT OF EDUCATION AND SCIENCE (1967), *Children and their Primary Schools*, Plowden Report, vol. i (London: HMSO).

—— (1978), *Primary Education in England* (London: HMSO).

—— (1979), *Aspects of Secondary Education in England* (London: HMSO).

—— (1981), *Report by H.M.I. on the Effects on the Education Service in England of Local Authority Expenditure Policies—Financial Year 1980–81* (London: DES).

DEPARTMENT OF EDUCATION AND SCIENCE, COMMITTEE OF ENQUIRY (1975), *A Language for Life*, Bullock Report (London: HMSO).

DEPARTMENT OF EMPLOYMENT (1974), 'Characteristics of the Unemployed, Sample Survey June, 1973', *Department of Employment Gazette*, 82, 211–21.

DEPARTMENT OF EMPLOYMENT (1989), *Employment Gazette* (London: HMSO).

—— *Employment Gazette* (London: HMSO) (various issues).

DEPARTMENT OF EMPLOYMENT AND PRODUCTIVITY (1971), *British Labour Statistics: Historical Abstract 1886–1968* (London: HMSO).

DEPARTMENT OF ENERGY (1988), *Privatising Electricity*, Cmd. 322 (London: HMSO).

DEPARTMENT OF HEALTH (1989), *Working for Patients*, Cmd. 555 (London: HMSO).

DEPARTMENT OF HEALTH AND SOCIAL SECURITY (1976), *Sharing Resources for Health in England* (London: HMSO).

—— (1980*a*), *Inequalities in Health*, The Black Report (London: DHSS).

—— (1980*b*), *Report of the Advisory Group on Resource Allocations* (London: DHSS).

—— (1987), *Social Security Statistics 1987* (London: HMSO).

—— (1988), *Social Security Statistics 1988* (London: HMSO).

DEPARTMENT OF INDUSTRY (1974), *The Regeneration of British Industry*, Cmd. 5710 (London: HMSO).

DEPARTMENT OF PRICES AND CONSUMER PROTECTION (1978), *A Review of Monopolies and Mergers Policy*, Cmd. 7198 (London: HMSO).

—— (1979), *A Review of Restrictive Trade Practices Policy*, Cmd. 7512 (London: HMSO).

DEPARTMENT OF THE ENVIRONMENT (1961), *Homes for Today and Tomorrow*, Parker-Morris Report (London: HMSO).

DEPARTMENT OF TRADE AND INDUSTRY (1971), *Report of the Committee on Consumer Credit* (Crowther Committee) (London: HMSO).

—— (1983*a*), 'Company Analysis of Direct Exporters in 1981', *British Business*, 27 May.

—— (1983*b*), *Regional Industrial Development*, Cmd. 9111 (London: HMSO).

—— (1988*a*), *DTI—The Department for Enterprise*, Cmd. 278 (London: HMSO).

—— (1988*b*), *Review of Restrictive Trade Policies Policy* (London: HMSO).

—— (1989*a*), *Acquisitions and Mergers of Industrial and Commercial Companies*, Business Monitor Series, MQ7.

—— (1989*b*), *Monthly Review of External Trade Statistics* (London: HMSO).

DICKEN, P. (1986), *Global Shift* (London: Harper and Row).

DILNOT, A. W., and KELL, M. (1988), 'Top Rate Tax Cuts and Incentives: Some Empirical Evidence', *Fiscal Studies*, 9, 70–92.

DILNOT, A. W., KAY, J. A., and MORRIS, C. N. (1984), *The Reform of Social Security* (Oxford: Oxford University Press).

DIMSDALE, N. H. (1981), 'British Monetary Policy and the Exchange Rate, 1920–1938', *Oxford Economic Papers*, 33, Supplement, 306–49.

DONOVAN COMMISSION (1968), *Royal Commission on Trade Unions and Employers' Associations, 1965–1968* (London: HMSO).

DORNBUSCH, R. (1976), 'Expectations and Exchange Rate Dynamics', *Journal of Political Economy*, 84, 1161–76.

—— (1989), 'Credibility, Debt and Unemployment: Ireland's Failed Stabilisation', *Economic Policy*, 8, 173–210.

DORNBUSCH, R., and FISCHER, S. (1984), *Macroeconomics*, 3rd edn. (London: McGraw-Hill).

—— (1988), *Macroeconomics*, 4th edn. (London: McGraw-Hill).

DOUGLAS, J. W. B. (1964), *The Home and the School* (London: MacGibbon and Kee).

DOUGLAS, J. W. B., and ROWNTREE, G. (1949), 'Supplementary Maternal and Child Health Services', *Population Studies*, 3, 205–26.

DOW, J. C. R. (1964), *The Management of the British Economy 1945–60* (Cambridge: (Cambridge University Press).

DOW, J. C. R., and SAVILLE, I. D. (1988), *A Critique of Monetary Policy and British Experience* (Oxford: Oxford University Press).

DOZ, Y., and PRAHALAD, C. K. (1988), 'Quality of Management: An Emerging Source of Global Competitive Advance?', in N. Hood and J. Vahlne (eds.), *Strategies in Global Competition* (London: Croom Helm), 345–69.

DUNN, M. (1979), *The Penguin Guide to Real Draught Beer* (Harmondsworth: Penguin).

DUNN, S. (1981), 'The Growth of Post-Entry Closed Shops in Britain since the 1960s', *British Journal of Industrial Relations*, 19, 275–96.

DUNNING, J. H. (1958), *American Investment in British Manufacturing Industry* (London: Allen & Unwin).

—— (1986), *Japanese Participation in British Industry* (London: Croom Helm).

DURCAN, J. W. *et al.* (1983), *Strikes in Post-War Britain* (London: Allen & Unwin).

EATWELL, J. (1982), *Whatever Happened to Britain?* (London: Duckworth).

ECKSTEIN, O. (1981), *Core Inflation* (London: Prentice Hall).

EDELSTEIN, M. (1982), *Overseas Investment in the Age of High Imperialism: The United Kingdom, 1850–1914* (London: Methuen).

EFTA (1969), *The Effects of EFTA on the Economies of Member States* (EFTA).

ELLIOT, R. (1978), 'Industrial Relations and Manpower Policy', in F. T. Blackaby (ed.), *British Economic Policy 1960–74* (Cambridge: Cambridge University Press).

ENGLANDER, A. S., and MITTELSTADT, A. (1988), 'Total Factor Productivity: Macro-economic and Structural Aspects of the Slowdown', *OECD Economic Studies*, 10, 7–56.

ETHIER, W. J. (1983), *Modern International Economics* (New York and London: Norton).

EVANS, A., and EVERSLEY, D. (1980), *The Inner City: Employment and Industry* (London).

EVANS, M. J. (1982), *The Truth about Supply-Side Economics* (London: Basic Books).

EVELY, R., and LITTLE, I. M. D. (1960), *Concentration in British Industry* (Cambridge: Cambridge University Press).

FEINSTEIN, C. H. (1972), *National Income, Expenditure and Output of the United Kingdom, 1855–1965* (Cambridge: Cambridge University Press).

—— (ed.) (1983), *The Managed Economy: Essays in British Economic Policy since 1929* (Oxford: Oxford University Press).

—— (1988), 'Economic Growth since 1870: Britain's Performance in International Perspective', *Oxford Review of Economic Policy*, 4, 1, 1–13.

FELDSTEIN, M. (ed.) (1980), *The American Economy in Transition* (Chicago, Ill.: University of Chicago Press).

FELLNER, W. (1979), 'The Credibility Effect and Rational Expectations: Implications of the Gramlich Study', *Brookings Papers on Economic Activity*, 2, 167–90.

FELLNER, W. (1980), 'The Valid Core of Rationality Hypotheses in the Theory of Expectations', *Journal of Money, Credit and Banking*, 12, 763–87.

FELS, A. (1972), *The British Prices and Incomes Board* (Cambridge: Cambridge University Press).

FERGUSON, P. R. (1985), 'The Monopolies and Mergers Commission and Economic Theory', *National Westminster Bank Review*, September, 30–40.

—— (1988), *Industrial Economics: Issues and Perspectives* (London: Macmillan).

FIELD, F. (ed.) (1983), *The Wealth Report—2* (London: Routledge & Kegan Paul).

*Financial Times* (1989), 'EC Competition Policy', 12 April.

FINEGOLD, D., and SOSKICE, D. W. (1988), 'The Failure of Training in Britain: Analysis and Prescription', *Oxford Review of Economic Policy*, 4, 3, 21–53.

FISCHER, S. (1987), 'Monetary Policy', in R. Dornbusch and R. Layard (eds.), *The Performance of the British Economy* (Oxford: Oxford University Press), 6–28.

FLANAGAN, R. J., SOSKICE, D. W., and ULMAN, L. (1983), *Unionism, Economic Stabilization and Incomes Policies: The European Experience* (Washington, DC: Brookings Institution).

FLEMING, J. M. (1962), 'Domestic Financial Policies under Fixed and under Floating Exchange Rates', *IMF Staff Papers*, 9, 369–79.

FLEMING, M. C. (1980), 'Industrial Policy', in W. P. J. Maunder (ed.), *The British Economy in the 1970s* (London: Heinemann), 141–68.

FLORENCE, P. SARGANT (1953), *The Logic of British and American Industry* (London: Routledge & Kegan Paul).

FORD, J. (1985), 'High Short Term Mortgage Debts', *Roof*, 6.

FOREMAN-PECK, J. S. (1979), 'Tariff Protection and Economies of Scale: The British Motor Industry before 1939', *Oxford Economic Papers*, 31, 237–56.

—— (1983), *A History of the World Economy: International Economic Relations since 1850* (Brighton: Wheatsheaf).

FORESTER, T. (1979), 'Neutralising the Industrial Strategy', in K. Coates (ed.), *What Went Wrong?* (London: Spokesman Books), 74–94.

FORREST, R., and MURIE, A. (1987), 'The Pauperisation of Council Housing', *Roof*, Jan. Feb., 20–3.

FORRESTER, D. P. (1976), 'Social Class Differences in Sickness and General Practitioner Consultations', *Health Trends*, 8, 29.

FORSYTH, P. J., and KAY, J. A. (1980), 'The Economic Implications of North Sea Oil Revenue', *Fiscal Studies*, 1, 1–18.

FOSTER, J. I. (1974), 'The Relationship between Unemployment and Vacancies in Great Britain 1958–72: Some Further Evidence', in D. Laidler and D. Purdy (eds.), *Inflation and Labour Markets* (Manchester: Manchester University Press).

—— (1976), 'The Redistributive Effect of Inflation on Building Society Shares and Deposits, 1961–74', *Bulletin of Economic Research*, 28, 67–76.

FOTHERGILL, S., and GUDGIN, G. (1982), *Unequal Growth: Urban and Regional Employment Change in the UK* (London: Heinemann).

FOTHERGILL, S., GUDGIN, G., KITSON, M., and MONK, S. (1984), 'Differences in the Profitability of the UK Manufacturing Sector between Conurbations and Other Areas', *Scottish Journal of Political Economy*, 31, 72–91.

FOX, A. (1985), *History and Heritage: The Social Origins of the British Industrial Relations System* (London: Allen & Unwin).

FRANKS, J. R., and HARRIS, R. S. (1986), 'Shareholder Wealth Effects of Corporate

Takeovers: The UK Experience 1955–1985', London Business School, Institute of Finance and Accounting Discussion Paper, 95–86.

FRANKS, J. R., HARRIS, R., and MAYER, C. (1988), 'Means of Payment for Takeovers: Results for the UK and US', in Auerbach, A. (ed.), *Corporate Takeovers: Causes and Consequences* (Chicago, Ill.: University of Chicago Press), 221–63.

FREEMAN, C. (1978), 'Technical Innovation and British Trade Performance', in F. T. Blackaby (ed.), *De-Industrialisation* (London: Heinemann), 56–73.

—— (1982), *The Economics of Industrial Innovation* (London: Frances Pinter).

FREEMAN, R. B. (1988), 'Labour Market Institutions and Economic Performance', *Economic Policy*, 6, 63–80.

FREY, B. S., and SCHNEIDER, F. (1978), 'A Politico-Economic Model of the United Kingdom', *Economic Journal*, 88, 243–53.

—— (1981), 'A Politico-Economic Model of the UK: New Estimates and Predictions', *Economic Journal*, 91, 737–40.

FRIEDMAN, M. (1953), *Essays in Positive Economics* (Chicago, Ill.: Chicago University Press).

—— (1956), 'The Quantity Theory of Money: A Restatement', in M. Friedman (ed.), *Studies in the Quantity Theory of Money* (Chicago, Ill.: Chicago University Press), 3–21.

—— (1957), *A Theory of the Consumption Function* (Princeton, NJ: National Bureau of Economic Research).

—— (1959), *A Program for Monetary Stability* (New York: Fordham University Press).

—— (1962), *Capitalism and Freedom* (Chicago, Ill.: University of Chicago Press).

—— (1968), 'The Role of Monetary Policy', *American Economic Review*, Mar., 58, 1–17.

—— (ed.) (1969), *The Optimum Quantity of Money and Other Essays* (Chicago, Ill.: Aldine).

—— (1977), 'Nobel Lecture: Inflation and Unemployment', *Journal of Political Economy*, 85, 451–77.

—— (1980), Memorandum on Monetary Policy submitted to the Treasury and Civil Service Committee, HC720, Session 1979–80 (London: HMSO), 55–61.

FRIEDMAN, M., and FRIEDMAN, R. (1980), *Free to Choose*, (Harmondsworth: Penguin).

FRIEDMAN, M., and SCHWARTZ, A. J. (1969), 'Money and Business Cycles', repr. in M. Friedman (ed.), *The Optimum Quantity of Money* (London: Macmillan), 189–235.

FUKAO, M., and HANAZIKI, M. (1986), 'Internationalization of Financial Markets: Some Implications for Macroeconomic Policy and for the Allocation of Capital', OECD Working Paper 37.

GALBRAITH, J. K. (1952), *American Capitalism: The Concept of Countervailing Power* (Boston: Houghton Miflin).

GAMBLE, A. M., and WALKLAND, S. A. (1984), *The British Party System and Economic Policy 1945–1983* (Oxford: Clarendon Press).

GARRATY, J. A. (1978), *Unemployment in History: Economic Thought and Public Policy* (New York: Harper and Row).

GARSIDE, W. R. (1977), 'Juvenile Unemployment and Public Policy between the Wars', *Economic History Review*, 2nd ser. 30, 322–45.

—— (1980), *The Measurement of Unemployment: Methods and Sources 1850–1979* (Oxford: Blackwell).

GENNARD, J., and LASKO, R. (1974), 'Supplementary Benefit and Strikers', *British Journal of Industrial Relations*, 12, 1–25.

—— (1975), 'The Individual and the Strike', *British Journal of Industrial Relations*, 13, 346–70.

GEORGE, K. D., and WARD, T. S. (1975), *The Structure of Industry in the EEC: An International Comparison* (Cambridge: Cambridge University Press).

GEORGE, V., and WILDING, P. (1984), *The Impact of Social Policy* (London: Routledge & Kegan Paul).

—— (1985), *Ideology and Social Welfare*, rev. edn., (London: Routledge & Kegan Paul).

GEROSKI, P. (1981), 'Specification and Testing of the Profits-Concentration Relationship: Some Experiments for the UK', *Economica*, 48, 279–88.

GIBSON, N. S. (1964), 'Special Deposits as an Instrument of Monetary Policy', *Manchester School of Social and Economic Studies*, 32, 239–59.

GINSBURG, N. (1989), 'The Housing Act, 1988 and its Policy Context: A Critical Commentary', *Critical Social Policy*, 9, 1, 56–81.

GLASTONBURY, B. (1971), *Homeless Near a Thousand Homes* (London: Allen & Unwin).

GLENNERSTER, H. (1985), *Paying for Welfare* (Oxford: Blackwell).

GLYNN, S., and BOOTH, A. (eds.) (1987), *The Road to Full Employment* (London: Allen & Unwin).

GODFREY, C., and BRADSHAW, J. (1983), 'Inflation and the Poor', *New Society*, 65, 247–8.

GODLEY, W. (1977), 'Inflation in the United Kingdom', in L. B. Krause and W. S. Salant (eds.), *Worldwide Inflation: Theory and Relevant Experience* (Washington, DC: Brookings Institution), 449–92.

GOLDTHORPE, J. H. (1980), *Social Mobility and Class Structure in Modern Britain* (Oxford: Clarendon).

GOODHART, C. A. E. (1973), 'Monetary Policy in the United Kingdom', in K. Holbik (ed.), *Monetary Policy in Twelve Industrial Countries* (Boston, Mass: Federal Reserve Bank of Boston), 465–524.

—— (1978), 'Money in an Open Economy', in P. Ormerod (ed.), *Economic Modelling* (London: Heinemann), 143–167.

—— (1981), 'The Problems of Monetary Management in the UK', in A. S. Courakis (ed.), *Inflation, Depression and Economic Policy in the West* (London: Mansell), 111–43.

—— (1984), *Monetary Theory and Practice: The U.K. Experience* (London: Macmillan).

—— (1986), 'Financial Innovation and Monetary Control', *Oxford Review of Economic Policy*, 2, 4, 79–102.

—— (1989), 'The Conduct of Monetary Policy', *Economic Journal*, June, 99, 293–346.

GORDON, I. (1957), 'Social Status and Active Prevention of Disease', *Monthly Bulletin of the Ministry of Health*, 10, 9, 59–61.

GORDON, R. J. (1980), 'Postwar Macroeconomics: The Evolution of Events and Ideas', in M. Feldstein (ed.), *The American Economy in Transition* (Chicago, Ill.: University of Chicago Press), 101–62.

—— (1982*a*), 'Inflation, Flexible Exchange Rates and the Natural Rate of Unemployment', in M. J. Baily (ed.), *Workers, Jobs and Inflation* (Washington, DC: Brookings Institution), 89–158.

—— (1982*b*), *Macroeconomics*, 4th edn. (London: Little, Brown and Co.).

GOURVISH, T. R. (1986), *British Railways 1948–73* (Cambridge: Cambridge University Press).

—— (1987), 'British Business and the Transition to a Corporate Economy: Entrepreneurship and Management Structures', *Business History*, 29, 18–45.

GOWLAND, D. (1982), *Controlling the Money Supply* (London: Croom Helm).

GRAHAM, A. (1972), 'Industrial Policy', in W. Beckerman (ed.), *The Labour Government's Economic Record 1964–1970* (London: Duckworth), 178–217.

GRAHAM, E. M. (1978), 'Transatlantic Investment by Multinational Firms: A Rivalistic Phenomenon?', *Journal of Post-Keynesian Economics*, 1, 82–99.

GRAHAM, H. (1984), *Women, Health and the Family*, (Brighton: Wheatsheaf).

GRANT, W. (1982), *The Political Economy of Industrial Policy* (London: Butterworths).

GRASSMAN, S. (1980), 'Long Term Trends in the Openness of National Economies', *Oxford Economic Papers*, 32, 123–33.

GRAY, P. G., *et al.* (1970), *Adult Dental Health in Britain* (London: HMSO).

GREAT BRITAIN (1980), *Report of the Committee to Review the Functioning of Financial Institutions* (London: HMSO).

GREVE, J., PAGE, D., and GREVE, S. (1971), *Homelessness in London* (Edinburgh: Scottish Academic Press).

GRIBBIN, J. D. (1978), 'The Post-War Revival of Competition as Industrial Policy', Government Economic Service Working Paper 19.

GRIBBIN, J. D., and UTTON, M. A. (1986), 'The Treatment of Dominant Firms in UK Competition Legislation', in H. W. De Jong and W. G. Shepherd (eds.), *Mainstreams in Industrial Organisation* (Dordrecht: Kluwer Academic Publishers), 243–72.

GROSSKURTH, A., and STEARN, J. (1986), 'They Call it Colditz', *Roof*, Jan. Feb., 9–13.

GROVE, J. W. (1962), *Government and Industry in Britain* (London: Longmans).

GRUBB, D., JACKMAN, R., and LAYARD, R. (1982), 'Causes of the Current Stagflation', *Review of Economic Studies*, 49, 195–204.

HAGUE, D., and WILKINSON, G. (1983), *The IRC—An Experiment in Industrial Intervention: A History of the Industrial Reorganisation Corporation* (London: Allen & Unwin).

HALL, P., LAND, H., PARKER, R., and WEBB, A. (1975), *Change, Choice and Conflict in Social Policy* (London: Heinemann).

HALL, S. and JACQUES, M. (eds.) (1983), *The Politics of Thatcherism* (London: Lawrence and Wishart).

HALL, S. G., and ATKINSON, F. (1983), *Oil and the British Economy* (London: Croom Helm).

HALL, S. G., HENRY, B., and HERBERT, R. (1986), 'Oil Prices and the Economy', *National Institute Economic Review*, 116, 38–44.

HALSEY, A. H. (1972), *Educational Priority*, vol. i, Department of Education and Science (London: HMSO).

—— (1987), 'Social Trends since World War II', *Social Trends 17* (London: HMSO) 11–19.

—— (ed.) (1988), *British Social Trends since 1900*, 2nd edn. (London: Macmillan).

HALSEY, A. H., HEATH, A. F., and JUDGE, J. (1980), *Origins and Destinations* (Oxford: Clarendon).

HAM, A. (1981), *Treasury Rules* (London: Quartet Books).

—— (1982), *Health Policy in Britain* (London: Macmillan).

HAMEL, G., and PRAHALAD, C. K. (1988), 'Creating Global Strategic Capability', in N. Hood and J. Vahlne (eds.), *Strategies in Global Competition* (London: Croom Helm), 5–39.

HANNAH, L. (1974), 'Takeover Bids in Britain before 1850: An Exercise in Business Pre-History', *Business History*, 16, 65–77.

—— *The Rise of the Corporate Economy*, 2nd edn. (London: Methuen).

HANNAH, L., and KAY, J. A. (1977), *Concentration in Modern Industry* (London: Macmillan).

—— (1981), 'Symposium on Bias and Concentration', *Journal of Industrial Economics*, 29, March, 305–13.

HARBERGER, A. C. (1954), 'Monopoly and Resource Allocation', *American Economic Review*, 44, 77–87.

HARBURY, C. D., and HITCHENS, D. M. W. N. (1979), *Inheritance and Wealth Inequality in Britain* (London: Allen & Unwin).

HARDIE, C. J. M. (1977), 'Anti-Trust Policy', in D. J. Morris (ed.), *The Economic System in the UK* (Oxford: Oxford University Press), 393–414.

HARE, P. (1984), 'The Nationalized Industries', in P. Hare and M. Kirby (eds.), *British Economic Policy* (Brighton: Wheatsheaf).

—— (1985), *Planning the British Economy* (London: Macmillan).

HARE, P., and KIRBY, M. W. (eds.) (1984), *An Introduction to British Economic Policy* (Brighton: Wheatsheaf).

HARRIS, R., and SELDON, A. (1979), *Over-Ruled on Welfare* (London: Institute of Economic Affairs).

HARRISON, A. (1979), *The Distribution of Wealth in Ten Countries*, Royal Commission on the Distribution of Income and Wealth, Background Paper 7 (London: HMSO).

HART, N. (1987), 'Social Class Still Reigns', *Poverty*, 67, Summer, 17–19.

HART, P. E. (1979), 'On Bias and Concentration', *Journal of Industrial Economics*, 27, 211–26.

—— (1981), 'Symposium on Bias and Concentration', *Journal of Industrial Economics*, 29, March, 315–20.

HART, P. E., and CLARKE, R. (1980), *Concentration in British Industry 1935–75* (Cambridge: Cambridge University Press).

HART, P. E., and MORGAN, E. (1977), 'Market Structure and Economic Performance in the United Kingdom', *Journal of Industrial Economics*, 25, 177–93.

HART, P. E., UTTON, M. A., and WALSHE, G. (1973), *Mergers and Concentration in British Industry* (Cambridge: Cambridge University Press).

HARTLEY, K. (1977), *Problems of Economic Efficiency* (London: Allen & Unwin).

HARVEY, D. R., and THOMSON, K. J. (1985), 'Costs, Benefits and the Future of the Common Agricultural Policy', *Journal of Common Market Studies*, 24, 1–20.

HATTON, T. J. (1988), 'Institutional Change and Wage Rigidity in the UK, 1880–1985', *Oxford Review of Economic Policy*, 4, 74–86.

HAY, D. A. (1985), 'Competition and Industrial Policies', *Oxford Review of Economic Policy*, 3, Autumn, 27–40.

HAYEK, F. A. (ed.) (1935), *Collective Economic Planning* (London: Routledge & Kegan Paul).

—— (ed.) (1944), *The Road to Serfdom* (Chicago, Ill.: University of Chicago Press).

—— (1960), *The Constitution of Liberty* (London: Routledge & Kegan Paul).

—— (1978), *New Studies in Philosophy and Economics and the History of Ideas* (London: Routledge & Kegan Paul).

HAYWARD, J., and NARKIEWICZ, O. (eds.) (1978), *Planning in Europe* (London: Croom Helm).

HEALD, D. (1980), 'The Economic and Financial Control of UK Nationalized Industries', *Economic Journal*, 90, 243–65.

—— (1984), 'Privatisation: Analysing Its Appeals and Limitations', *Fiscal Studies*, 5, 1, 36–46.

HEATH, J. B. (1961), 'Restrictive Practices and After', *Manchester School*, 29, 173–202.

HENDERSON, SIR H. D. (1947), 'Cheap Money and the Budget', *Economic Journal*, 57, 265–71.

HENDERSON, P. D. (1952), 'Development Councils: An Industrial Experiment', in G. D. N. Worswick and P. H. Ady (eds.), *The British Economy, 1945–50* (Oxford: Clarendon Press), 452–62.

HENDERSON, P. D. (1977), 'Two British Errors: Their Probable Size and Some Possible Lessons', *Oxford Economic Papers*, 29, 186–94.

HENRY, S., and ORMEROD, P. (1978), 'Incomes Policy and Wage Inflation', *National Institute Economic Review*, 31–9.

HEWER, A. (1980), 'Manufacturing Industry in the 1970s', *Economic Trends*, 320, 97–109.

HICKS, SIR J. R. (1947), 'The Empty Economy', *Lloyds Bank Review*, 5, 1–13.

—— (1975), 'What is Wrong with Monetarism', *Lloyds Bank Review*, 118, 1–13.

HILL, M. (1976), 'Can We Distinguish Voluntary from Involuntary Unemployment?', in G. Worswick (ed.), *The Concept and Measurement of Industry Unemployment* (London: Allen & Unwin).

—— (1984), *Understanding Social Policy*, 2nd edn. (Oxford: Basil Blackwell and Martin Robertson).

HILL, T. P. (1979), *Profits and Rates of Return* (Paris: OECD).

HILLS, J. (1984), 'Public Assets and Liabilities and the Presentation of Budgetary Policy', in M. Ashworth, J. Hills, and N. Morris (eds.), *Public Finance in Perspective* (London: Institute for Fiscal Studies), 5–49.

—— (1987), 'What Happened to Spending on the Welfare State', in A. Walker and C. Walker (eds.), *The Growing Divide* (London: CPAG), ch. 10, 88–100.

—— (1988), *Changing Tax: How the System Works and How to Change It* (London: Child Poverty Action Group).

HINE, R. C. (1985), *The Political Economy of European Trade* (Brighton: Wheatsheaf).

HINES, A. G. (1964), 'Trade Unions and Wage Inflation in the United Kingdom, 1893–1961', *Review of Economic Studies*, 31, 221–52.

HITIRIS, T. (1978), 'Effective Protection and Economic Performance in UK Manufacturing Industry, 1963 and 1968', *Economic Journal*, 88, 107–20.

HM TREASURY (1945), *Statistical Material Presented during the Washington Negotiations*, Cmd. 6707 (London: HMSO).

—— (1947), *Economic Survey for 1947*, Cmd. 7046 (London: HMSO).

—— (1960), *Report from the Select Committee on Nationalised Industries*, H. C. 254 (London: HMSO).

—— (1961), *Financial and Economic Obligations of the Nationalised Industries*, Cmd. 1337 (London: HMSO).

—— (1967), *Nationalised Industries: A Review of Economic and Financial Objectives*, Cmd. 3437 (London: HMSO).

—— (1974), *The Regeneration of British Industry*, H. C. 1117 (London: HMSO).

—— (1978), *The Nationalised Industries*, Cmd. 7131 (London: HMSO).

—— (1986), 'Nationalised Industries', *Economic Progress Report*, no. 185, July–Aug., 5–7.

—— (1989), *The Government's Expenditure Plans 1989–90 to 1991–92*, Cmd. 601 (London: HMSO).

HM TREASURY/DEPARTMENT OF INDUSTRY (1975), *An Approach to Industrial Strategy*, Cmd. 6315 (London: HMSO).

HOLLAND, S. (1972), *The State as Entrepreneur* (London: Weidenfeld & Nicolson).

—— (1975), *The Socialist Challenge* (London: Quartet Books).

HOLMANS, A. E. (1970), 'The Role of Local Authorities in the Growth of Public Expenditure in the United Kingdom', in A. K. Cairncross (ed.), *The Managed Economy* (Oxford: Blackwell), 149–63.

HOLMES, M. (1982), *Political Pressure and Economic Policy: British Government 1970–1974* (London: Butterworth).

HOLMES, P. (1978), *Industrial Pricing Behaviour and Devaluation* (London: Macmillan).

HOLTERMANN, S. E. (1973), 'Market Structure and Economic Performance in UK Manufacturing Industry, 1963 and 1968', *Economic Journal*, 88, 107–20.

HOUSE OF COMMONS, SOCIAL SERVICES COMMITTEE (1988), 4th Report, *Families on Low Income: Low Income Statistics*, Session 1987–8 (London: HMSO).

HOUSE OF LORDS (1985), *Report from the Select Committee on Overseas Trade* (London: HMSO).

—— (1986), *Select Committee on Science and Technology, Report on Civil Research and Development*, vol. i (London: HMSO).

HOUTHAKKER, H. S., and MAGEE, S. P. (1969), 'Income and Price Elasticities in World Trade', *Review of Economics and Statistics*, 51, 111–25.

HOWSON, S. (1987), 'The Origins of Cheaper Money 1945–47', *Economic History Review*, 40, 433–52.

HUFBAUER, G. (1983), 'Subsidy Issues after the Tokyo Round', in W. R. Cline (ed.), *Trade Policy in the 1980s* (London: MIT), 327–61.

HUGHES, A. (1989), 'The Impact of Merger', in J. A. Fairburn and J. A. Kay (eds.), *Mergers and Merger Policy* (Oxford: Oxford University Press), 30–98.

HUGHES, A., and KUMAR, M. S. (1984), 'Recent Trends in Aggregate Concentration in the United Kingdom Economy', *Cambridge Journal of Economics*, 8, 235–50.

HUTCHISON, T. W. (1968), *Economics and Economic Policy in Britain 1946–66* (London: George Allen & Unwin).

ILIFFE, S. (1985), 'The Politics of Health Care: The NHS Under Thatcher', 14, Winter, 57–72.

ILLSLEY, R. (1986), 'Occupational Class, Selection and the Production of Inequalities in Health', *Quarterly Journal of Social Affairs* 2, 2, 151–65.

—— (1987), 'Bad Welfare or Bad Statistics', *Poverty*, 67, 16–17.

INDUSTRIAL TRANSFERENCE BOARD (1928), *Report*, Cmd. 3156 (London: HMSO).

INTERNATIONAL MONETARY FUND, *International Financial Statistics Yearbook* (various issues) (Washington, DC: IMF).

JACKSON, D., TURNER, H. A., and WILKINSON, F. (1972), *Do Trade Unions Cause Inflation?*, Department of Applied Economics Occasional Paper 36 (Cambridge: Cambridge University Press).

JENKINS, S. (1979), *Newspapers: The Power and the Money* (London: Faber and Faber).

JENKINSON, T. (1987), 'The Natural Rate of Unemployment: Does it Exist', *Oxford Review of Economic Policy*, 3, 3, 20–6.

JERVIS, F. R. (1971), *The Economics of Mergers* (London: Routledge & Kegan Paul).

JEWKES, J., SAWERS, D., and STILLERMAN, R. (1958), *The Sources of Invention* (London: Macmillan).

JOHNSON, D. G. (1965), *World Agriculture in Disarray* (London: Macmillan).

JOHNSON, H. G. (1976), 'The Monetary Approach to the Balance of Payments', in J. A. Frenkel and H. G. Johnson (eds.), *The Monetary Approach to the Balance of Payments* (London: Allen & Unwin), 145–67.

—— (1977), 'Theory and Policy: Explanations and Policy Implications', *Economica*, 44, 217–29.

JOHNSTON, R. B. (1983), *The Economics of the Euro-Dollar Market* (London: Macmillan).

JONES, C. (1987), *Tariff and Non-Tariff Barriers to Trade*, Government Economic Service Working Paper 97 (London: HMSO).

JONES, I. (1988), 'An Evaluation of YTS', *Oxford Review of Economic Policy*, 4, 1, 54–71.

JONES, R. (1987), *Wages and Employment Policy 1936–1985* (London: Allen & Unwin).

JORDAN, B. (1974), *Poor Parents*, (London: Routledge & Kegan Paul).

JUNANKAR, P. N. (1981), 'An Econometric Analysis of Unemployment in Great Britain, 1952–75', *Oxford Economic Papers*, 33, 387–400.

KALDOR, N. (1966), *Causes of the Slow Rate of Growth of the United Kingdom* (Cambridge: Cambridge University Press).

KAMIEN, M., and SCHWARTZ, N. L. (1982), *Market Structure and Innovation* (Cambridge: Cambridge University Press).

KAREKEN, J. H. (1968), 'Monetary Policy', in R. E. Caves and Associates (eds.), *Britain's Economic Prospects* (London: Allen & Unwin), 68–103.

KATRAK, H. (1982), 'Labour Skills, R and D and Capital Requirements in the International Trade and Investment of the United Kingdom 1968–78', *National Institute Economic Review*, 101, 38–47.

KAY, J. A., and BISHOP, M. (1988), 'The Impact of Privatization on the Performance of the UK Public Sector', paper presented to the Conference of European Industrial Economists, Rotterdam.

KAY, J. A., and KING, M. (1978), *The British Tax System* (Oxford: Oxford University Press).

—— (1986), *The British Tax System*, 4th edn. (Oxford: Oxford University Press).

KAY, J. A., MAYER, C., and THOMPSON, D. (eds.) (1986), *Privatisation and Regulation—The UK Experience* (Oxford: Oxford University Press).

KEEBLE, D., OWENS, P. L., and THOMPSON, C. (1982), 'Regional Accessibility and Economic Potential in the European Community', *Regional Studies*, 16, 419–32.

KEEGAN, W., and PENNANT-REA, R. (1979), *Who Runs the Economy?* (London: Maurice Temple Smith).

KELF-COHEN, R. (1961), *Nationalization in Britain* (London: Macmillan).

—— (1973), *British Nationalisation 1945–1973* (London: Macmillan).

KENNEDY, C. M. (1952), 'Monetary Policy', in G. D. N. Worswick and P. H. Ady (eds.), *The British Economy 1945–50* (Oxford: Clarendon Press), 188–207.

—— (1962), 'Monetary Policy', in G. D. N. Worswick and P. H. Ady, *The British Economy in the Nineteen Fifties* (Oxford: Clarendon Press), 301–25.

KENNEDY, W. P. (1987), *Industrial Structure, Capital Markets and the Origins of British Economic Decline* (Cambridge: Cambridge University Press).

KEYNES, J. M. (1936), *The General Theory of Employment Interest and Money* (London: Macmillan).

—— (1940), 'How to Pay for the War', repr. in *Keynes Collected Writings*, ix. 367–439 (London: Macmillan).

—— (1979), *Collected Writings*, xxiv, *Activities 1944–6: The Transition to Peace* (London: Macmillan).

KHALILZADEH-SHIRAZI, J. (1974), 'Market Structure and Price-Cost Margins in UK Manufacturing Industries', *Review of Economics and Statistics*, 54, 64–76.

KINCAID, J. C. (1973), *Poverty and Equality in Britain* (Harmondsworth: Penguin).

KING, A. (1976), *Why Is Britain Becoming Harder to Govern?* (London: BBC).

KIRBY, M. W. (1977), *The British Coalmining Industry, 1870–1946* (London: Macmillan).

—— (1984), 'Industrial Policy in Britain', in P. Hare and M. W. Kirby (eds.), *An Introduction to British Economic Policy* (Brighton: Wheatsheaf), 93–109.

—— (1987), 'Industrial Policy', in S. Glynn and A. Booth (eds.), *The Road to Full Employment* (London: Allen & Unwin), 125–39.

KLEIN, R. (1983), *The Politics of the National Health Service* (London: Longman).

KNIGHT, I. (1984), *The Heights and Weights of Adults in Great Britain* (London: HMSO).

KNOWLES, K. (1952), *Strikes—A Study in Industrial Conflict: With Special Reference to the British Experience 1911–47* (Oxford: Blackwell).

—— (1962), 'Wages and Productivity', in G. D. N. Worswick and P. H. Ady (eds.), *The British Economy in the Nineteen Fifties* (Oxford: Clarendon Press), 502–36.

KOGUT, B. (1988), 'Country Patterns in International Competition: Appropriability and Oligopolistic Agreement', in N. Hood and J. Vahlne (eds.), *Strategies in Global Competition* (London: Croom Helm), 315–40.

KOTTIS, A. (1972), 'Mobility and Human Capital Theory', *Annals of Regional Science*, 6, 41–60.

KUMAR, M. S. (1984), *Growth, Acquisition and Investment* (Cambridge: Cambridge University Press).

LABOUR PARTY (1943), British Labour's Reconstruction Programme, *The Old World and the New Society*.

LABOUR PARTY (1964), *Let's Go with Labour for the New Britain* (Election Manifesto).

LABOUR PARTY (1976), *Report of the Annual Conference of the Labour Party* (London: Labour Party).

LAIDLER, D. (1976), 'Inflation in Britain: A Monetarist Perspective', *American Economic Review*, 66, 485–500.

—— (1985), 'Monetary Policy in Britain: Success and Shortcomings', *Oxford Review of Economic Policy*, 1, 1, 35–43.

LAIDLER, D., and PARKIN, M. (1975), 'Inflation: A Survey', *Economic Journal*, 85, 741–809.

LANDYMORE, P. J. A. (1985), 'Education and Industry since the War', in D. J. Morris (ed.), *The Economic System in the UK*, 3rd edn., ch. 22 (Oxford: Oxford University Press), 690–717.

LANGE, O., and TAYLOR, F. M. (1938), *On the Economics of Socialism* (repr., New York: McGraw-Hill, 1964).

LANSLEY, S. (1979), *Housing and Public Policy* (London: Croom Helm).

LARKEY, P., STOLP, C., and WINER, M. (1981), 'Theorizing about the Growth of Government: A Research Assessment', *Journal of Public Policy*, 1, 157–220.

LAWSON, N. (1984), *The British Experiment*, The Fifth Mais Lecture, City University Business School, mimeo.

LAYARD, R. (1986), *How to Beat Unemployment* (Oxford: Oxford University Press).

LAYARD, R., and NICKELL, S. J. (1985), 'The Causes of British Unemployment', *National Institute Economic Review*, 111, 62–85.

—— (1986), 'Unemployment in Britain', *Economica*, 53, S121–S169.

—— (1987), 'The Labour Market', in R. Dornbusch and R. Layard (eds.), *The Performance of the British Economy* (Oxford: Oxford University Press).

LAYARD, R., METCALF, D., and NICKELL, S. (1978), 'The Effect of Collective Bargaining on Relative and Absolute Wages', *British Journal of Industrial Relations*, 16, 287–308.

LEAK, H., and MAIZELS, A. (1945), 'The Structure of British Industry', *Journal of the Royal Statistical Society*, 108, 142–99.

LEE, C. H. (1979), *British Regional Employment Statistics, 1841–1971* (Cambridge: Cambridge University Press).

LE GRAND, J. (1982), *The Strategy of Equality* (London: George Allen & Unwin).

—— (1985), *Inequalities in Health: The Human Capital Approach*, Welfare State Programme no. 1. (London: London School of Economics).

—— (1987), 'The Middle-Class Use of the British Social Services', in R. E. Goodin and J. Le Grand, *Not Only the Poor*, ch. 5 (London: Allen & Unwin).

LERUEZ, J. (1978), 'Macro-Economic Planning in Mixed Economies: The French and British Experience', in J. Hayward and N. Olga (eds.), *Planning in Europe* (London: Croom Helm), 26–52.

LEWCHUK, W. (1987), *American Technology and the British Vehicle Industry* (Cambridge: Cambridge University Press).

LEYLAND, N. H. (1952), 'Productivity', in G. D. N. Worswick and P. H. Ady (eds.), *The British Economy 1945–50* (Oxford: Clarendon Press), 381–98.

LIEPMANN, K. (1960), *Apprenticeship: An Enquiry into Its Adequacy under Modern Conditions* (London: Routledge & Kegan Paul).

LINDBECK, A., and SNOWER, D. (1985), 'Explanations of Unemployment', *Oxford Review of Economic Policy*, 1, 2, 34–59.

LINTNER, V. G. *et al.* (1987), 'Trade Unions and Technological Change in the UK Mechanical Engineering Industry', *British Journal of Industrial Relations*, 25, 19–29.

LIPSEY, R. J. (1960), 'Does Money Always Depreciate', *Lloyds Bank Review*, 58, 1–13.

—— (1983), *An Introduction to Positive Economics*, 6th edn. (London: Weidenfeld & Nicolson).

LITTLECHILD, S. C. (1986), *The Fallacy of the Mixed Economy*, 2nd edn. (London: Institute of Economic Affairs).

—— (1989), 'Myths and Merger Policy', in J. A. Fairburn and J. A. Kay (eds.), *Mergers and Merger Policy* (Oxford: Oxford University Press), 301–25.

LIVINGSTONE, J. M. (1966), *Britain and the World Economy* (Harmondsworth: Penguin).

LLEWELLYN, J., and POTTER, S. (1982), 'Competitiveness and the Current Account', in A. Boltho (ed.), *The European Economy* (Oxford: Oxford University Press), 132–58.

LOMAX, D. F. (1982), 'Supply-Side Economics: The British Experience', *National Westminster Bank Quarterly Review*, 2–15.

LONDON AND CAMBRIDGE ECONOMIC SERVICE (LCES) (1971), *The British Economy: Key Statistics 1900–1970* (London: Times Newspapers).

LONG, F. (1981), *Restrictive Business Practices, Transnational Corporations and Development* (London: Macmillan).

LORD, A. (1976), 'A Strategy for Industry', Sir Ellis Hunter Memorial Lecture 8, University of York.

LORD, J. S. (1981), 'Unemployment Statistics in Britain', in J. Creedy (ed.), *The Economics of Unemployment in Britain* (London: Butterworths), 335–54.

LUCAS, R. E. (1973), 'Some International Evidence on Output Employment Tradeoffs', *American Economic Review*, June, 63, 326–34.

LUFFMAN, G. A., and REED, R. (1984), *The Strategy and Performance of British Industry 1970–80* (London: Macmillan).

LYDALL, H. (1959), 'The Long Term Trend in the Size Distribution of Income', *Journal of the Royal Statistical Society*, Ser. A, 122, 1–37.

LYONS, B. R. (1981), 'Price-Cost Margins, Market Structure and International Trade', in D. Currie, D. Peel, and W. Peters (eds.), *Microeconomic Analysis* (London: Croom Helm).

McCALLUM, J. D. (1979), 'The Development of British Regional Policy', in D. Maclennan and J. B. Parr (eds.), *Regional Policy, Past Experience and New Directions* (Oxford: Martin Robertson), 3–41.

—— (1983), 'Inflation and Social Consensus in the Seventies', *Economic Journal*, 93, 784–805.

McCALLUM, R. B., and READMAN, A. (1947), *The British General Election of 1945* (Oxford: Oxford University Press).

McCARTHY, W. E. G. (1964), *The Closed Shop in Britain* (Oxford: Blackwell).

McCloskey, D. N. (1970), 'Did Victorian Britain Fail?', *Economic History Review*, 23, 446–59.

McCombie, J. S. L. (1983), 'Kaldor's Laws in Retrospect', *Journal of Post-Keynesian Economics*, 5, 414–29.

McCormick, B. J. (1979), *Industrial Relations in the Coal Industry* (London: Macmillan).

McCracken, P. *et al.* (1977), *Towards Full Employment and Price Stability* (Paris: OECD).

McCrone, G. (1969), *Regional Policy in Britain* (London: Allen & Unwin).

—— (1971), 'Regional Policy in the European Community', in G. R. Denton (ed.), *Economic Integration in Europe* (London: Weidenfeld & Nicolson), 194–219.

MacDonald, D. F. (1960), *The State and the Trade Unions* (London: Macmillan).

Macfarlane, A., and Mugford, M. (1984), *Birth Counts: Statistics of Pregnancy and Childbirth* (London: HMSO).

Mack, J., and Lansley, S. (1985), *Poor Britain* (London: Allen & Unwin).

Macmillan, H. (1972), *Pointing the Way 1959–61* (London: Macmillan).

—— (1973), *At the End of the Day 1961–3* (London: Macmillan).

Maddison, A. (1982), *Phases of Capitalist Development* (Oxford: Oxford University Press).

—— (1987), 'Growth and Slowdown in Advanced Capitalist Economies: Techniques of Quantitative Assessment', *Journal of Economic Literature*, 24, 649–98.

—— (1989), *The World Economy in the Twentieth Century* (Paris: OECD).

Maizels, A. (1963), *Industrial Growth and World Trade* (Cambridge: National Institute of Economic and Social Research).

Mann, M., and Scholefield, T. (1986), 'Recent Trends in UK Concentration', in Confederation of British Industry, *Issues in UK Competition Policy* (London: CBI), 10–15.

Mansfield, E. (1969), *Industrial Research and Technological Innovation: An Econometric Analysis* (London: Longman, Green).

Marks, M. (1980), 'State and Private Enterprise', *Business Economist*, 11, 5–15.

Marquand, D. (1988), *The Unprincipled Society* (London: Cape).

Marquand, J. (1980), 'Measuring the Effects and Costs of Regional Incentives', Government Economics Service Working Paper 32.

Marshall, A. (1920), *Industry and Trade*, 3rd edn. (London: Macmillan).

Marshall, G. P. (1980), *Social Goals and Economic Perspectives* (Harmondsworth: Penguin).

Matthews, K., and Minford, A. P. (1987), 'Mrs Thatcher's Economic Policies 1979–1987', *Economic Policy*, 5, 57–102.

Matthews, R., and Tierney, M. (1985), 'Don't Rely on the Safety Net', *Roof*, May/June, 13–14 and 19.

Matthews, R. C. O. (1968), 'Why Has Britain Had Full Employment since the War?', *Economic Journal*, 78, 555–69.

—— (1970), 'Full Employment Since the War—A Reply', *Economic Journal*, 80, 173–6.

Matthews, R. C. O., Feinstein, C. H., and Odling-Smee, J. (1982), *British Economic Growth, 1856–1973* (Stanford, Calif.: Stanford University Press).

MAUNDER, W. P. J. (ed.) (1980), *The British Economy in the 1970s* (London: Heinemann).

MAURICE, R. (ed.) (1968), *National Accounts Statistics: Sources and Methods* (London: HMSO).

MAXFIELD, M. G. (1984), *Fear of Crime in England and Wales*, Home Office Research Study 78 (London: HMSO).

MAYER, C. P., and MEADOWCROFT, S. A. (1985), 'Selling Public Assets: Techniques and Financial Implications', *Fiscal Studies*, 6, 4, 42–56.

MAYES, D. G., and BUXTON, A. (1988), 'R and D and Trade Performance', paper presented to the Conference of European Industrial Economists, Rotterdam.

MAYNARD, G. (1988), *The Economy Under Mrs Thatcher* (Oxford: Blackwell).

MEADE, J. E. (1948), 'Financial Policy and the Balance of Payments', *Economica*, 15, 101–15.

MEEKS, G. (1977), *Disappointing Marriage: A Study of the Gains from Merger* (Cambridge: Cambridge University Press).

MEEKS, G., and MEEKS, J. G. (1981), 'Profitability Measures as Indicators of Post-Merger Efficiency', *Journal of Industrial Economics*, 29, June, 335–43.

METCALF, D. (1977), 'Unions, Incomes Policy and Relative Earnings in Britain', *British Journal of Industrial Relations*, 15, 157–75.

—— (1988a), 'Unions and Productivity', London School of Economics, mimeo.

—— (1988b), 'Water Notes Dry Up: The Impact of the Donovan Reform Proposals and Thatcherism at Work on Labour Productivity in British Manufacturing Industry', paper presented to British Universities Industrial Relations Association Conference, Cambridge.

—— (1989), 'Trade Unions and Economic Performance', *London School of Economics Quarterly*, Spring.

METCALF, D., NICKELL, S. J., and FLOROS, N. (1982), 'Still Searching for an Explanation of Unemployment in Interwar Britain', *Journal of Political Economy*, 90, 386–99.

METHVEN, M. J. (1975), 'The Office of Fair Trading and Industry', *The Business Economist*, 7, Summer, 45–50.

MIDDLEMAS, K. (1979), *Politics in Industrial Society: The Experience of the British System Since 1911* (London: André Deutsch).

—— (1983), *Industry, Unions and Government: Twenty-One Years of NEDC* (London: Macmillan).

MIDDLETON, R. (1981), 'Constant Employment Budget Balance and British Budgetary Policy 1929–39', *Economic History Review*, 34, 266–86.

—— (1985), *Towards the Managed Economy* (London: Methuen).

MILLER, M. H. (1981), 'The Medium Term Financial Strategy: An Experiment in Coordinating Fiscal and Monetary Policy', *Fiscal Studies*, 2, 2, 50–60.

MILLWARD, N., and STEVENS, M. (1986), *British Workplace Industrial Relations 1980–1984* (Aldershot: Gower).

MILWARD, A. S. (1984), *The Reconstruction of Western Europe, 1945–51* (London: Methuen).

MINFORD, A. P. (1980), Memorandum on Monetary Policy Treasury and Civil Service Committee HC720 Session 1979–80 (London: HMSO), 131–43.

—— (1983), *Unemployment: Cause and Cure* (Oxford: Blackwell).

MINISTRY OF HEALTH (1944), *A National Health Service*, Cmd. 6502 (London: HMSO).

MINISTRY OF LABOUR (1934), *Reports of Investigations into Industrial Conditions in Certain Depressed Areas*, Cmd. 4728 (London: HMSO).

MINISTRY OF LABOUR AND NATIONAL SERVICE (1947), *Report for the Years 1939–1946*, Cmd. 7225 (London: HMSO).

MINISTRY OF PENSIONS AND NATIONAL INSURANCE (1966), *Financial and Other Circumstances of Retirement Pensioners* (London: HMSO).

MINISTRY OF RECONSTRUCTION (1944), *Employment Policy*, Cmd. 6527 (London: HMSO).

MISHRA, R. (1984), *The Welfare State in Crisis* (Brighton: Wheatsheaf).

MITCHELL, B. R. (1975), *European Historical Statistics, 1750–1970* (London: Macmillan).

—— (1988), *British Historical Statistics* (Cambridge: Cambridge University Press).

MOLYNEUX, R., and THOMPSON, D. (1987), 'Nationalised Industry Performance: Still Third Rate?', *Fiscal Studies*, 8, 1, 48–82.

MONOPOLIES AND MERGERS COMMISSION (1966), *Household Detergents* (London: HMSO).

—— (1968a), *Man Made Cellulosic Fibres* (London: HMSO).

—— (1968b), *Barclays Bank Ltd., and Martins Bank Ltd., Report on the Proposed Merger* (London: HMSO).

—— (1975), *Contraceptive Sheaths* (London: HMSO).

—— (1979), *Ice Cream and Water Ices* (London: HMSO).

—— (1983), *National Coal Board*, Cmd. 8920 (London: HMSO).

—— (1987), *The Monopolies and Mergers Commission* (London: MMC/COI).

MOORE, B., and RHODES, J. (1973), 'Evaluating the Effects of British Regional Economic Policy', *Economic Journal*, 83, 87–110.

MOORE, B., RHODES, J., and TYLER, P. (1977), 'The Impact of Regional Policy in the 1970s', *Centre for Environmental Studies Review*, 1, 67–77.

—— (1986), 'The Effects of Government Regional Economic Policy', Department of Trade and Industry (London: HMSO).

MORGAN, A. (1988), *British Imports of Consumer Goods: A Study of Import Penetration* (Cambridge: Cambridge University Press).

MORGAN, K. O. (1984), *Labour in Power 1945–51* (Oxford: Oxford University Press).

MORRIS, D. J. (1983), 'Industrial Policy', in D. J. Morris (ed.), *The Economic System in the UK*, 2nd edn. (Oxford: Oxford University Press), 523–45.

—— (ed.) (1985), *The Economic System in the UK*, 3rd edn. (Oxford: Oxford University Press).

MORRIS, D. J., and STOUT, D. K. (1985), 'Industrial Policy', in D. J. Morris (ed.), *The Economic System in the UK*, 3rd edn. (Oxford: Oxford University Press), 851–94.

MORRISON, H. (1933), *Socialisation and Transport* (London: Constable).

MORTIMORE, J., and BLACKSTONE, T. (1982), *Disadvantages and Education* (London: Heinemann).

MOSLEY, P. (1984), *The Making of Economic Policy* (Brighton: Harvester).

MOSS, P. (1969), *Welfare Rights Project '68* (Liverpool: Merseyside Child Poverty Action Group).

Moss, P. (1970), *Welfare Rights Project Two* (Liverpool: Merseyside Child Poverty Action Group).

Mottershead, P. (1978), 'Industrial Policy', in F. T. Blackaby (ed.), *British Economic Policy 1960–1974* (Cambridge: Cambridge University Press), 418–83.

Moylan, S., and Davies, B. (1980), 'The Disadvantages of the Unemployed', *Employment Gazette*, 88, 8, 830–2.

—— (1981), 'The Flexibility of the Unemployed', *Department of Employment Gazette*, 89, 1, 29–33.

Muellbauer, J. (1986), 'Productivity and Competitiveness in British Manufacturing', *Oxford Review of Economic Policy*, 2, i–xxv.

Mulroy, R. (1973), 'Iatrogenic Disease in General Practice: Its Incidence and Effects', *British Medical Journal*, 2, 407–10.

Mundell, R. A. (1962), 'The Appropriate Use of Monetary and Fiscal Policy for Internal and External Balance', *IMF Staff Papers*, 9, 70–9.

—— (1963), 'Capital Mobility and Stabilisation Policy under Fixed and Flexible Exchange Rates', *Canadian Journal of Economics and Political Science*, 29, 475–85.

Murray, C. (1984), *Losing Ground: American Social Policy 1950–1980* (New York: Basic Books).

Musgrave, A., and Peacock, A. T. (eds.) (1962), *Classics in the Theory of Public Finance* (London: Macmillan).

Musgrave, R. A., and Musgrave, P. B. (1968), 'Fiscal Policy', in R. E. Caves (ed.), *Britain's Economic Prospects* (London: Allen & Unwin).

Narendranathan, W., Nickell, S. J., and Stern, J. (1985), 'Unemployment Benefits Revisited', *Economic Journal*, 95, 307–29.

National Assistance Board (1957), *Report of the National Assistance Board, 1956*, Cmd. 181 (London: HMSO).

National Board for Prices and Incomes (1967), *Report No. 34 Bank Charges*, Cmd. 3292 (London: HMSO).

National Economic Development Council (1963*a*), *Conditions Favourable to Faster Growth* (London: NEDO).

—— (1963*b*), *Growth of the United Kingdom Economy to 1966* (London: HMSO).

National Economic Development Office (1975), *Finance for Investment* (London: NEDO).

—— (1976*a*), *Cyclical Fluctuations in the UK Economy* (London: NEDO).

—— (1976*b*), *A Study of UK Nationalized Industries* (London: NEDO).

—— (1982), *Industry Policy in the UK: Memorandum by the Director General* (London: NEDO).

—— (1983), *Innovation in the UK* (London: NEDO).

—— (1987), *The Making of Managers* (London: NEDO).

National Superannuation and Social Insurance (1969), Cmd. 3883 (London: HMSO).

Neild, R. R. (1979), 'Managed Trade between Industrial Countries', in R. L. Major (ed.), *Britain's Trade and Exchange Rate Policy* (London: Heinemann).

New, C., and David, M. (1986), *For the Children's Sake* (Harmondsworth: Penguin).

New Society/London Weekend Television (1986), 'The Rich in Britain', *New Society*, 77, 1234.

NEWBOULD, G. (1970), *Management and Merger Activity* (Liverpool: Guthstead).

NEWELL, A., and SYMONS, J. S. V. (1989), 'The Passing of the Golden Age', London School of Economics, Centre for Labour Economics Discussion Paper no. 347.

NICHOLAS, T. (1986), *The British Worker Question* (London: Routledge & Kegan Paul).

NICKELL, S. J. (1986), 'Why Is Wage Inflation in Britain So High?', *Oxford Institute Applied Economics Discussion Paper* no. 15.

NOBAY, A. R. (1987), 'Interest Rate Parity and Debt Management in the Fixed Exchange Rate UK', mimeo for Oxford Seminar.

NOYCE, J., SNAITH, A. H., and TRICKEY, A. J. (1974), 'Regional Variations in the Allocation of Financial Resources to the Community Health Services', *Lancet*, 1, 554–7.

O'BRIEN, D. P., HOWE, W. S., WRIGHT, D. M., and O'BRIEN, J. R. (1979), *Competition Policy, Profitability and Growth* (London: Macmillan).

ODLING-SMEE, J. C., and RILEY, C. (1985), 'Approaches to the PSBR', *National Institute Economic Review*, 113, 65–80.

O'DONNELL, A. T., and SWALES, J. K. (1977), 'Regional Elasticities of Substitution in the United Kingdom in 1968: A Comment', *Urban Studies*, 14, 371–7.

O'DONNELL, A. T. (1979), 'Factor Substitution, the CES Production Function and UK Regional Economies', *Oxford Economic Papers*, 31, 460–76.

OFFICE OF FAIR TRADING (1975, 1980, 1981, 1987), *Annual Report of the Director General of Fair Trading* (London: HMSO).

—— (1986), *Anti-Competitive Practices* (London: OFT).

OFFICE OF POPULATION CENSUSES AND SURVEYS, SOCIAL SURVEY DIVISION (1985), *General Household Survey 1983* (London: HMSO).

—— (1989), *General Household Survey 1986* (London: HMSO).

OGILVY, A. A. (1982), 'Population Migration between Regions of Great Britain 1971–1979', *Regional Studies*, 16, 65–73.

O'HIGGINS, M. (1985), 'Welfare, Redistribution, and Inequality—Disillusion, Illusion and Reality', in P. Bean, J. Fems, and D. Whynes (eds.), *Defence of Welfare*, ch. 8 (London: Tavistock).

OLSON, M. (1982), *The Rise and Decline of Nations: Economic Growth, Stagflation and Social Rigidities* (New Haven, Conn.: Yale University Press).

—— (1983), 'The Political Economy of Comparative Growth Rates', in D. C. Mueller (ed.), *The Political Economy of Growth* (New Haven, Conn.: Yale University Press), 7–52.

OPIE, R. (1972), 'Economic Policy and Growth', in W. Beckerman (ed.), *The Labour Government's Economic Record 1964–1970* (London: Duckworth), 157–77.

ORGANISATION FOR ECONOMIC CO-OPERATION AND DEVELOPMENT (1970), *National Accounts of OECD Countries, 1950–1968* (Paris: OECD).

—— (1984), *Competition and Trade Policies, Their Interaction* (Paris, OECD).

—— (1986), *Historical Statistics, 1960–1984* (Paris: OECD).

—— (1987), *Economic Survey of the United Kingdom 1986/7* (Paris: OECD).

—— (1988), *Historical Statistics, 1960–1987* (Paris: OECD).

—— (1989a), *Historical Statistics, 1960–1987* (Paris: OECD).

—— (1989b), *Quarterly Labour Force Statistics* (Paris: OECD).

OULTON, N. (1987), 'Plant Closures and the "Productivity Miracle" in Manufacturing', *National Institute Economic Review*, 121, 53–9.

PAGE, R. M. (1984), *Stigma* (London: Routledge & Kegan Paul).

PAISH, F. W. (1950), 'The Cheap Money Policy', in F. W. Paish (ed.), *The Post War Financial Problem* (London: Macmillan), 16–35.

—— (1962), *Studies in an Inflationary Economy: The United Kingdom 1948–1961* (London: Macmillan).

PANIC, M. (ed.) (1976), *UK and West German Manufacturing Industry, 1954–1972: A Comparison of Performance and Structure* (London: NEDC), 137–60.

—— (1978), 'The Origins of Increasing Inflationary Tendencies in Contemporary Society', in F. Hirsh and J. H. Goldthorpe (eds.), *The Political Economy of Inflation* (London: Martin Robertson).

PARKIN, M., and SUMNER, M. (eds.) (1972), *Income Policy and Inflation* (Manchester: Manchester University Press).

PARKIN, M., and BADE, R. (1983), *Modern Macroeconomics*, 2nd edn. (Scarborough, Ontario: Prentice Hall).

—— (1986), *Modern Macroeconomics*, 3rd edn. (Deddington: Philip Allan).

PATEL, P., and PAVITT, K. (1987), 'The Elements of British Technological Competitiveness', *National Institute Economic Review*, 122, 72–83.

—— (1988), 'The Technological Activities of the UK: A Fresh Look', in A. Silberston (ed.), *Technology and Economic Progress* (London: Macmillan), 113–54.

PAVITT, K. (1976), 'The Choice of Targets and Instruments for Government Support of Scientific Research', in A. Whiting (ed.), *The Economics of Industrial Subsidies* (London: HMSO).

PAVITT, K., and SOETE, L. (1982), 'International Differences in Economic Growth and the International Location of Innovation', in H. Giersch (ed.), *Emerging Technologies* (Tubingen: Mohr), 105–33.

PAVITT, K., ROBSON, M., and TOWNSEND, J. (1987), 'The Size Distribution of Innovating Firms in the UK, 1945–83', *Journal of Industrial Economics*, 35, 297–316.

PEACOCK, A., and WISEMAN, J. (1961), *The Growth of Public Expenditure in the UK* (Princeton, NJ: Princeton University Press).

PECK, M. J. (1968), 'Science and Technology', in R. E. Caves and Associates, *Britain's Economic Prospects* (London: Allen & Unwin), 448–84.

PEDEN, G. C. (1983), 'Sir Richard Hopkins and the "Keynesian Revolution" in Employment Policy 1929–45', *Economic History Review*, 36, 281–96.

—— (1985), *British Economic and Social Policy: From Lloyd George to Margaret Thatcher* (Oxford: Philip Allan).

PENCAVEL, J. (1970), 'An Investigation in Industrial Strike Activity in Britain', *Economica*, 37, 239–56.

PHELPS-BROWN, E. H. (1975), 'A Non Monetarist View of the Pay Explosion', *Three Banks Review*, 105, 3–24.

—— (1977), 'What is the British Predicament?', *Three Banks Review*, December, 3–29.

—— (1983), *The Origins of Trade Union Power* (Oxford: Oxford University Press).

PHILLIPS, A. (1972), 'An Econometric Study of Price Fixing, Market Structure and Performance in British Industry in the Early 1950s', in K. Cowling (ed.), *Market Structure and Corporate Behaviour* (London: Gray-Mills).

PIACHAUD, D. (1978), 'Inflation and Income Distribution', in F. Hirsch and J. H.

Goldthorpe (eds.), *The Political Economy of Inflation* (London: Martin Robertson), 88–116.

—— (1987), 'Problems in the Definition and Measurement of Poverty', *Journal of Social Policy*, 16, 2, April, 147–64.

—— (1988), 'Poverty in Britain, 1899–1983', *Journal of Social Policy*, 17, 3, 335–49.

PICKERING, J. F. (1983), 'The Causes and Consequences of Abandoned Mergers', *Journal of Industrial Economics*, 31, 267–81.

PINKER, R. A. (1979), *The Idea of Welfare* (London: Heinemann).

PISSARIDES, C. A. (1980), 'British Government Popularity and Economic Performance', *Economic Journal*, 90, 569–81.

PITFIELD, D. E. (1978), 'The Quest for an Effective Regional Policy 1934–1937', *Regional Studies*, 12, 429–44.

PLAYFORD, C., and POND, C. (1983), 'The Right to Be Unequal: Inequality in Incomes', in F. Field (ed.), *The Wealth Report—2* (London: Routledge & Kegan Paul), 34–55.

PLIATZKY, L. (1982), *Getting and Spending* (Oxford: Blackwell).

PODOLSKI, T. M. (1986), *Financial Innovation and the Money Supply* (Oxford: Blackwell).

POLITICAL AND ECONOMIC PLANNING (1960), *Growth in the British Economy* (London: Allen & Unwin).

POLITICS OF HEALTH GROUP (1982), *Going Private: The Case against Private Medicine* (The Politics of Health group).

POLLARD, S. (1982), *The Wasting of the British Economy: British Economic Policy 1945 to the Present* (London: Croom Helm).

—— (1983), *The Development of the British Economy 1914–80*, 3rd edn. (London: Edward Arnold).

POND, C. (1983), 'Wealth and the Two Nations', in F. Field (ed.), *The Wealth Report—2* (London: Routledge & Kegan Paul), 9–33.

PORTER, J. H. (1979), 'Cotton and Wool Textiles', in N. K. Buxton and D. H. Aldcroft (eds.), *British Industry between the Wars* (London: Scolar Press), 25–47.

POUNC (1972), Post Office Users' National Council Report, January.

PRAIS, S. J. (1976, 1980), *The Evolution of Giant Firms in Britain*, 1st edn. and preface to 2nd impression (Cambridge: Cambridge University Press).

—— (1981), *Productivity and Industrial Structure* (Cambridge: Cambridge University Press).

PRATTEN, C. F. (1976), *Labour Productivity Differentials within International Companies* (Cambridge: Cambridge University Press).

—— (1984), *Applied Macroeconomics* (Oxford: Oxford University Press).

PRATTEN, C. F., and ATKINSON, A. G. (1976), 'The Use of Manpower in British Manufacturing Industry', *Department of Employment Gazette*, 84, 571–6.

PRESSNELL, L. S. (1986), *External Economic Policy since the War*, vol. i: *The Post-War Settlement* (London: HMSO).

PREST, A. R. (1968), 'Sense and Nonsense in Budgetary Policy', *Economic Journal*, 78, 1–18.

PREST, A. R., and COPPOCK, D. J. (eds.) (1984), *The UK Economy: A Manual of Applied Economics*, 10th edn. (London: Weidenfeld & Nicolson).

PRICE, R., and BAIN, G. S. (1983), 'Union Growth in Britain: Retrospect and Prospect', *British Journal of Industrial Relations*, 21, 46–68.

PRICE, R. W. R. (1978), ' "Public Expenditure" and "Budgetary Policy" ', in F. T. Blackaby (ed.), *British Economic Policy 1960–74* (Cambridge: Cambridge University Press), 77–134, 135–217.

PRYKE, R. (1971), *Public Enterprise in Practice* (London: MacGibbon and Kee).

—— (1981), *The Nationalised Industries* (Oxford: Martin Robertson).

—— (1982), 'The Comparative Performance of Public and Private Enterprise', *Fiscal Studies*, 3, 2, 68–81.

PRYOR, F. (1972), 'An International Comparison of Concentration Ratios', *Review of Economics and Statistics*, 54, 130–40.

RADCLIFFE REPORT. *See* Committee on the Working of the Monetary System.

RADICAL STATISTICS HEALTH GROUP (1987), *Facing the Figures* (London: Radical Statistics).

RAVENSCROFT, D., and SCHERER, F. M. (1988), *Mergers, Sell-Offs and Economic Efficiency* (Washington, DC: Brookings Institution).

RAY, G. (1987), 'Labour Costs in Manufacturing', *National Institute Economic Review*, 120, 71–4.

REDFERN, P. (1985), 'Profile of Our Cities', *OPCS Population Monitor*, 30, 21–32.

REDWOOD, J. (1980), *Public Enterprise in Crisis* (Oxford: Blackwell).

REDWOOD, J., and HATCH, J. (1982), *Controlling Public Industries* (Oxford: Blackwood).

REES, G. L. (1963), *Britain and the Post-War European Payments System* (Cardiff: University of Wales Press).

REES, R. D., and MIALL, R. H. C. (1979), 'The Effects of Regional Policy on Manufacturing and Capital Stock within the UK', Government Economic Service Working Paper 26.

REID, D. J. (1945), *Coal Mining: Report of the Technological Advisory Committee* (Reid Report), Cmd. 6610 (London: HMSO).

—— (1977), 'Public Sector Debt', *Economic Trends*, 283, 100–9.

REID, M. (1982), *The Secondary Banking Crisis 1973–75* (London: Macmillan).

REITH, J. C. W. (1924), *Broadcast over Britain* (London: Hodder and Stoughton).

—— (1926), The Memorandum: Crawford Broadcasting Committee. (Lindsay, SAE., 27th Earl Crawford), Cmd. 2599 (London: HMSO).

REPORT COMMISSION ON THE TAXATION OF PROFITS AND INCOME (1954), Second Report, Cmd. 9105 (London: HMSO).

RICHARDSON, R. (1977), 'Trade Union Growth', *British Journal of Industrial Relations*, 15, 279–82.

—— (1978), 'Trade Union Growth: A Rejoinder', *British Journal of Industrial Relations*, 16, 103–5.

RICHARDSON, R., and WOOD, S. (1989), 'Productivity Change in the Coal Industry and the New Industrial Relations', *British Journal of Industrial Relations*, 27, 33–55.

RIDDELL, P. (1985), *The Thatcher Government* (London: Martin Robertson).

ROBBINS, L. C. (1947), 'Inquest on the Crisis', *Lloyds Bank Review*, 6, 1–27.

ROBBINS, LORD (1963), Committee on Higher Education, *Report*, Cmd. 2154 (London: HMSO).

ROGOW, A. A. (1955), *The Labour Government and British Industry 1945–51* (Westport, Conn.: Greenwood Press).

ROGOW, A., and SHORE, P. (1955), *The Labour Government and British Industry* (Oxford: Blackwell).

ROLLINGS, N. (1985), 'The "Keynesian Revolution" and Economic Policy-Making: A Comment', *Economic History Review*, 2nd ser. 38, 95–100.

ROSE, G., and MARMOT, M. G. 'Social Class and Coronary Heart Disease', *British Heart Journal*, 45, 1, 13–19.

ROSE, H. (1986) 'Changes in Financial Innovation in the U.K.', *Oxford Review of Economic Policy*, Winter, 2, 4, 18–39.

ROSTAS, L. (1948), *Comparative Productivity in British and American Industry* (Cambridge: Cambridge University Press).

ROUTH, G. (1980), *Occupation and Pay in Britain, 1906–1979* (London: Macmillan).

ROWNTREE, B. S. (1901), *Poverty: A Study of Town Life* (London: Macmillan).

—— (1918), *The Human Needs of Labour* (London: Nelson).

—— (1941), *Poverty and Progress* (London: Longmans, Green and Co.).

ROWTHORN, R. E., and WELLS, J. R. (1987), *Deindustrialization and Foreign Trade* (Cambridge: Cambridge University Press).

ROYAL COMMISSION ON THE DISTRIBUTION OF INCOME AND WEALTH (1979), *Report* (London: HMSO).

—— (1980), *An A to Z of Income and Wealth* (London: HMSO).

ROYAL COMMISSION ON THE DISTRIBUTION OF THE INDUSTRIAL POPULATION (1940), *Report* (Barlow Report), Cmd. 6153 (London: HMSO).

ROYAL COMMISSION ON TRADE UNIONS AND EMPLOYERS' ASSOCIATIONS (1968), *Report*, Cmd. 3683 (London: HMSO).

RUBINSTEIN, W. D. (1981), *Men of Poverty. The Very Wealthy in Britain since the Industrial Revolution* (London: Croom Helm).

—— (1986a), *Wealth and Inequality in Britain* (London: Faber & Faber).

—— (1986b), 'Education and the Social Origins of British Elites, 1880–1970', *Past and Present*, 112, 163–207.

RYDER, D. (SIR) (1975), *British Leyland: The Next Decade*, H. C. 342 (London: HMSO).

SACHS, J. D. (1979), 'Wages, Profits and Macroeconomic Adjustment: A Comparative Study', *Brookings Papers on Economic Activity*, 2, 269–319.

SANDBERG, L. G. (1981), 'The Entrepreneur and Technical Change', in R. C. Floud and D. N. McCloskey (eds.), *The Economic History of Britain since 1700*, vol. ii (Cambridge: Cambridge University Press), 99–119.

SANDERSON, M. (1972a), *The Universities and British Industry, 1850–1970* (London: Routledge & Kegal Paul).

—— (1972b), 'Research and the Firm in British Industry, 1919–1939', *Science Studies*, 3, 107–51.

—— (1987), *Educational Opportunity and Social Change in England* (London: Faber & Faber).

—— (1988), 'Education, and Economic Decline 1890 to the 1980s', *Oxford Review of Economic Policy*, 4, 38–50.

SANKEY, J., 1st VISCOUNT (1919), *Sankey Coal Industry Commission*, 1st Stage, Cmd. 359, 2nd Stage, Cmd. 360 (London: HMSO).

SARGENT, T. J., and WALLACE, N. (1976), 'Rational Expectations and the Theory of Economic Policy', *Journal of Monetary Economics*, 2, 169–83.

SAUL, S. B. (1979), 'Research and Development in British Industry from the End of the Nineteenth Century to the 1960s', in T. C. Smout (ed.), *The Search for Wealth and Stability* (London: Macmillan), 114–38.

SAUNDERS, C. (1975), *From Free Trade to Integration in Western Europe?* (London: Chatham House: PEP).

SAVAGE, C. I. (1966), *An Economic History of Transport* (London: Hutchinson and Co.).

SAVAGE, D. (1979), 'Monetary Targets and the Control of the Money Supply', *National Institute Economic Review*, Aug., 99, 44–52.

—— (1980), 'Some Issues of Monetary Policy', *National Institute Economic Review*, Feb., 91, 78–85.

SAWYER, M. C. (1985), *The Economics of Industries and Firms*, 2nd edn. (Beckenham: Croom Helm).

SAYERS, R. S. (1957), *Central Banking after Bagehot* (Oxford: Oxford University Press).

—— (1958), *Modern Banking*, 4th edn. (London: Oxford University Press).

SCHUMPETER, J. A. (1942), *Capitalism, Socialism and Democracy* (New York: Harper and Row).

SCOTT, M. (1963), *A Study of UK Imports* (Cambridge: Cambridge University Press).

SCOTTISH OFFICE (1988), *Privatisation of the Scottish Electricity Industry*, Cmd. 327 (London: HMSO).

SCOULLER, J. (1987), 'The United Kingdom Merger Boom in Perspective', *National Westminster Bank Review*, May, 14–30.

SCREPANTI, E. (1987), 'Long Cycles in Strike Activity', *British Journal of Industrial Relations*, 25, 99–124.

SECONDARY SCHOOLS EXAMINATIONS COUNCIL (1943), *Curriculum and Examinations in Secondary Schools* (The Norwood Report) (London: HMSO).

SELDON, A. (1981), *Wither Welfare State?*, Occasional Paper 60 (London: Institute of Economic Affairs).

SHANKS, M. (1977), *Planning and Politics: The British Experience, 1960–1976* (London: Political and Economic Planning/Allen & Unwin).

SHAW, R. W., and SIMPSON, P. (1984), 'The Impact of Monopolies Commission Inquiries in Changing Market Structure and Profitability: A Preliminary Assessment', University of Stirling Working Paper.

—— (1986), 'The Persistence of Monopoly: An Investigation of the Effectiveness of the United Kingdom Monopolies Commission', *Journal of Industrial Economics*, 34, June, 355–72.

SHELDRAKE, J., and VICKERSTAFF, S. (1987), *The History of Industrial Training in Britain* (Aldershot: Avebury).

SHEPHERD, W. G. (1972), 'Structure and Behaviour in British Industries, with US Comparisons', *Journal of Industrial Economics*, 20, 35–54.

—— (1982), 'Causes of Increased Competition in the US Economy, 1939–1980', *Review of Economics and Statistics*, 64, 613–26.

—— (1984), 'Contestability vs Competition', *American Economic Review*, 74, 572–87.

SHIELDS, J. (1988), 'Controlling Household Credit', *National Institute Economic Review*, Aug., 125, 46–55.

SHINWELL, E. (1955), *Conflict without Malice* (London: Oldhams).

SHONFIELD, A. (1959), *British Economic Policy since the War* (Harmondsworth: Penguin).

SILBURN, R. (ed.) (1985), *The Future of Social Security* (London: Fabian Society).

SINFIELD, A. (1981), *What Unemployment Means* (Oxford: Martin Robertson).

SINGH, A. (1971), *Takeovers* (Cambridge University Press).

—— (1975), 'Takeovers, Natural Selection and the Theory of the Firm: Evidence from the Postwar UK Experience', *Economic Journal*, 85, 497–515.

SINGLETON, J. (1986), 'Lancashire's Last Stand: Declining Employment in the British Cotton Industry, 1950–1970', *Economic History Review*, 39, 92–107.

SISSON, K., and BROWN, W. (1983), 'Industrial Relations in the Private Sector: Donovan Re-visited', in G. S. Bain (ed.), *Industrial Relations in Britain* (Oxford: Blackwell), 137–54.

SJAASTAD, L. A. (1962), 'The Costs and Returns of Human Migration', *Journal of Political Economy*, supplement, 70, S80–S93.

SKIDELSKY, R. (ed.) (1977*a*), *The End of the Keynesian Era: Essays on the Disintegration of the Keynesian Political Economy* (London: Macmillan).

—— (ed.) (1977*b*), 'The Political Meaning of the Keynesian Revolution', in R. Skidelsky (ed.), *The End of the Keynesian Era* (London: Macmillan), 33–40.

SMITH, A. (1970), *The Wealth of Nations (1776)* (Harmondsworth: Penguin).

—— (1937), *An Inquiry into the Nature and Causes of the Wealth of Nations (1776)* (New York: Macmillan).

—— (1976), *An Inquiry into the Nature and Causes of the Wealth of Nations (1776)* (Oxford: Clarendon Press).

SMITH, A. D., HITCHENS, D. M., and DAVIES, S. W. (1982), *International Industrial Productivity: A Comparison of Britain, America and Germany* (Cambridge: Cambridge University Press).

SMITH, D. (1987), *The Rise and Fall of Monetarism: The Theory and Politics of an Economic Experiment* (London: Pelican Books).

SMITH, S. R., WHITE, G. M., OWEN, N. C., and HILL, M. R. (1982), 'UK Trade in Manufacturing: The Pattern of Specialisation during the 1970s', Government Economic Service Working Paper No. 45 (London: DTI).

SMOUT, T. C. (ed.) (1979), *The Search for Wealth and Stability: Essays in Economic and Social History Presented to M. W. Flinn* (London: Macmillan).

SOLVELL, O. (1988), 'Is the Global Automobile Industry Really Global?', in N. Hood and J. Vahlne (eds.), *Strategies in Global Competition* (London: Croom Helm), 181–208.

SOSKICE, D. (1978), 'Strike Waves and Wage Explosions, 1968–70: An Economic Interpretation', in C. Crouch and A. Pizzorno (eds.), *The Resurgence of Class Conflict in Western Europe* vol. ii: *Comparative Analysis* (London: Macmillan), 219–46.

SPENCER, P. D. (1986), *Financial Innovation Efficiency and Disequilibrium: Problems of Monetary Management in the UK 1971–81* (Oxford: Oxford University Press).

STAFFORD, J. B. (1970), 'Full Employment Since the War—Comment', *Economic Journal*, 80, 165–72.

STARK, T. (1977), *The Distribution of Income in Eight Countries*, Royal Commission on the Distribution of Income and Wealth, Background Paper 4 (London: HMSO).

—— (1988), *A New A–Z of Income and Wealth* (London: Fabian Society).

STEEDMAN, H. (1988), 'Vocational Training in France and Britain: Mechanical and Electrical Craftsmen', *National Institute Economic Review*, 126, 57–70.

STEUER, M. D. *et al.* (1973), *The Impact of Foreign Direct Investment in the United Kingdom* (DTI: HMSO).

STEVENS, R. B., and YAMEY, B. S. (1965), *The Restrictive Practices Court: A Study of the Judicial Process and Economic Policy* (London: Weidenfeld & Nicolson).

STEWART, M. (1978), *Politics and Economic Policy in the UK since 1964* (London: Pergamon Press).

STEWART, M. (1983), 'Relative Earnings and Individual Union Membership in the UK', *Economica*, 50, 111–25.

STOREY, D. J. (1982), *Entrepreneurship and the New Firm* (London).

STOUT, D. K. (1981), 'The Case for Government Support of R & D and Innovation', in C. Carter (ed.), *Industrial Policy and Innovation* (London: Heinemann).

STRANGE, S. (1971), *Sterling and British Policy: A Political Study of an International Currency in Decline* (Oxford: Oxford University Press).

STURGESS, B., and WHEALE, P. (1984), 'Merger Performance Evaluation: An Empirical Analysis of a Sample of UK Firms', *Journal of Economic Studies*, 2, 33–45.

SUPPLE, B. E. (1984), 'No Bloody Revolutions but for Obstinate Reactions: British Coalminers in Their Context 1919–20', in D. C. Coleman and P. Mathias (eds.), *Enterprise and History: Essays in Honour of Charles Wilson* (Cambridge: Cambridge University Press).

—— (1986), 'Ideology and Necessity: The Nationalisation of Coal Mining, 1916–46', in N. McKendrick and R. B. Outwaite (eds.), *British Life and Public Policy: Essays in Honour of D. C. Coleman* (Cambridge: Cambridge University Press).

—— (1987), *History of the British Coal Industry*, vol. iv: *1913–1946* (Oxford: Oxford University Press).

SURREY, M. J. C., and ORMEROD, P. A. (1978), 'Demand Management in Britain 1964–81', in M. V. Prosner (ed.), *Demand Management* (London: Heinemann), 101–25.

SUTHERLAND, A. (1969), *The Monopolies Commission in Action* (Cambridge: Cambridge University Press).

SWANN, D. (1978), *The Economics of the Common Market*, 4th edn. (London: Penguin).

SWANN, D., O'BRIEN, D. P., MAUNDER, W. P., and HOWE, W. S. (1974), *Competition in British Industry* (London: George Allen & Unwin).

SWANN REPORT. See Cmd. 9453.

SWORDS-ISHERWOOD, N. (1980), 'British Management Compared', in K. Pavitt (ed.), *Technical Innovation and British Economic Performance* (London: Macmillan), 88–99.

SYKES, F. (1923), *Report of the Sykes Broadcasting Committee*, Cmd. 1951 (London: HMSO).

TAYLOR, A. J. (1972), *Laissez-Faire and State Intervention in Nineteenth-Century Britain* (London: Macmillan).

TAYLOR, C. T. (1978), 'Why is Britain in a Recession?', *Bank of England Quarterly Bulletin*, 18, 38–47.

TAYLOR, J., and BRADLEY, S. (1983), 'Spatial Variations in the Unemployment Rate: A Case Study of North West England', *Regional Studies*, 17, 113–24.

TAYLOR-GOOBY, P. (1987), 'Citizenship and Welfare', in R. Jowell, S. Witherspoon, and L. Brook (eds.), *British Social Attitudes: The 1987 Report* (Aldershot: Gower), 1–28.

TEECE, D. J. (1981), 'Internal Organisation and Economic Performance: An Empirical Analysis of the Profitability of Principal Firms', *Journal of Industrial Economics*, 30, Dec., 173–99.

—— (1978a), 'Monetary Policy, Part I', in F. T. Blackaby (ed.), *British Economic Policy 1960–74* (Cambridge: Cambridge University Press), 208–57.

—— (1978b), 'Policies Aimed at Improving the Balance of Payments', in F. T. Blackaby (ed.), *British Economic Policy 1960–74* (Cambridge: Cambridge University Press), 304–53.

TEW, J. H. B. (1985), *The Evolution of the International Monetary System 1945–85*, 3rd edn. (London: Hutchinson).

THIRLWALL, A. P. (1979), 'The Balance of Payments Constraint as an Explanation of International Growth Rate Differences', *Banca del Lavora Quarterly Review*, 128, 44–53.

—— (1986), *Balance of Payments Theory and the United Kingdom Experience*, 3rd edn. (London: Macmillan).

THOMPSON, G. (1986), *The Conservatives' Economic Policy* (London: Croom Helm).

TILLY, R. H. (1986), 'German Banking, 1850–1914: Development Assistance for the Strong', *Journal of European Economic History*, 15, 113–52.

TITMUSS, R. M. (1968), *Commitment to Welfare* (London: George Allen & Unwin).

—— (1973), *The Gift Relationship* (Harmondsworth: Penguin).

TOBIN, J. (1963), 'Commercial Banks as Creators of Money', in D. Carson (ed.), *Banking and Monetary Studies* (Homewood, Ill.: Irwin), 408–19.

TOLAND, S. (1980), 'Social Commentary: Changes in Living Standards Since the 1950's', in Central Statistical Office, *Social Trends*, 10, 13–38.

TOLLIDAY, S. (1987), *Business, Banking and Politics: The Case of British Steel, 1918–1939* (Cambridge, Mass.: Harvard University Press).

TOMLINSON, J. (1982), *The Unequal Struggle? British Socialism and the Capitalist Enterprise* (London: Methuen).

—— (1984), 'A Keynesian Revolution in Economic Policy-Making?', *Economic History Review*, 2nd ser. 37, 258–62.

—— (1985), *British Macroeconomic Policy Since 1940* (London: Croom Helm).

TOOZE, M. (1976), 'Regional Elasticities of Substitution in the United Kingdom in 1968', *Urban Studies*, 13, 34–44.

TOWNSEND, P. (1963), *The Family Life of Old People* (Harmondsworth: Penguin).

—— (1977), *The Family Life of Old People* (London: Macmillan).

—— (1979), *Poverty in the United Kingdom* (Harmondsworth: Penguin).

—— (1987), 'Deprivation', *Journal of Social Policy*, 16, 2 Apr., 125–46.

TOWNSEND, P., and DAVIDSON, N. (eds.) (1982), *Inequalities in Health* (Harmondsworth: Penguin).

TREASURY AND CIVIL SERVICE COMMITTEE (1980), *Memoranda on Monetary Policy 1979–80* (London: HMSO).

—— (1981), *Report on Monetary Policy Session 1980/81* (London: HMSO).

TUDOR-HART, J. (1971), 'The Inverse Care Law', *Lancet*, 405–12.

TURNER, P. P. (1980), 'Import Competition and the Profitability of United Kingdom Manufacturing Industry', *Journal of Industrial Economics*, 29, 155–66.

TURVEY, R. (1971), *Economic Analysis and Public Enterprises* (London: Allen & Unwin).

TWOMEY, J., and TAYLOR, J. (1985), 'Regional Policy and the Interregional

Movement of Manufacturing Industry in Great Britain', *Scottish Journal of Political Economy*, 32, 257–77.

UTTON, M. A. (1970), *Industrial Concentration* (Harmondsworth: Penguin).

—— (1971), 'The Effects of Mergers on Concentration: UK Manufacturing Industry 1954–65', *Journal of Industrial Economics*, 20, 42–58.

—— (1972), 'Some Features of the Early Merger Movements in British Manufacturing Industry', *Business History*, 14, Jan., 51–60.

—— (1974), 'On Measuring the Effects of Industrial Mergers', *Scottish Journal of Political Economy*, 21, 95–121.

—— (1975), 'British Merger Policy', in K. D. George and C. Joll (eds.), *Competition Policy in the UK and EEC* (Cambridge: Cambridge University Press).

—— (1979), *Diversification and Competition* (Cambridge: Cambridge University Press).

UTTON, M. A. (1982), *The Political Economy of Big Business* (Oxford: Martin Robertson).

—— (1986), *Profits and the Stability of Monopoly* (Cambridge: Cambridge University Press).

UTTON, M. A. and MORGAN, A. D. (1983), *Concentration and Foreign Trade* (Cambridge: Cambridge University Press).

VAN ARK, B. (1990), 'Comparative Levels of Labour Productivity in Postwar Europe: Some Evidence for Manufacturing', *Oxford Bulletin of Economics and Statistics*, forthcoming.

VANDERKAMP, J. (1972), 'Migration Flows, Their Determinants and the Effects of Return Migration', *Journal of Political Economy*, 80, 1012–31.

VAN PRAAG, B., HAGENAARS, A., and VAN WEEREN, H. (1982), 'Poverty in Europe', *Review of Income and Wealth*, 28, 345–59.

VEIT-WILSON, J. H. (1986), 'Paradigms of Poverty: A Rehabilitation of B. S. Rowntree', *Journal of Social Policy*, 15, 1, 69–99.

—— (1987), 'Consensual Approaches to Poverty Lines and Social Security', *Journal of Social Policy*, 16, 2, 183–211.

VICKERS, J. (1985), 'Strategic Competition Among the Few—Some Recent Developments in the Economics of Industry', *Oxford Review of Economic Policy*, 1, Autumn, 39–62.

VICKERS, J., and YARROW, G. (1988), *Privatization: An Economic Analysis* (Cambridge, Mass: MIT Press).

VICKERSTAFF, S. (1985), 'Industrial Training in Britain. The Dilemmas of a Neo Corporatist Policy', in A. Cawson (ed.), *Organised Interests and the State* (London: SAGE Publications), 45–64.

WADHWANI, S. (1989), 'The Effect of Unions on Productivity Growth, Investment and Employment: A Report on Some Recent Work', Centre for Labour Economics, London School of Economics, Discussion Paper 356.

WALKER, A., and WALKER, C. (eds.) (1987), *The Growing Divide* (London: Child Poverty Action Group).

WALKLAND, S. A. (1984), 'Economic Planning and Disfunctional Politics in Britain, 1945–1983', in A. M. Gamble and S. A. Walkland (eds.), *The British Party System and Economic Policy* (Oxford: Clarendon Press), 92–151.

WALSHE, G. (1974), *Recent Trends in Monopoly in Great Britain* (Cambridge: Cambridge University Press).

WALTERS, A. A. (1986), *Britain's Economic Renaissance: Margaret Thatcher's Reforms, 1979–1984* (Oxford: Oxford University Press).

WARD, R., and ZIS, G. (1974), 'Trade Union Militancy as an Explanation of Inflation: An International Comparison', *Manchester School*, 42, 46–65.

WARD, T. S., and NIELD, R. R. (1978), *The Measurement and Reform of Budgetary Policy* (London: Heinemann).

WARD-PERKINS, C. N. (1952), 'Banking Developments', in G. D. N. Worswick and P. H. Ady (eds.), *The British Economy, 1945–1950* (Oxford: Clarendon Press), 208–23.

WARWICK UNIVERSITY INSTITUTE OF EMPLOYMENT RESEARCH (1986), *Review*, vol. ii (Coventry).

WEBB, M. G. (1973), *The Economics of Nationalized Industries* (London: Nelson).

—— (1976), *Pricing Policies for Public Enterprises* (London: Macmillan).

WELLS, S. J. (1964), *British Export Performance: A Comparative Study* (Cambridge: Cambridge University Press).

WEST, R. R., and LOWE, C. R. (1976), 'Regional Variations in Need for and Provision and Use of Child Health Services in England and Wales', *British Medical Journal*, 843–6.

WHITEHEAD, M. (1987), *The Health Divide, Inequalities in Health in the 1980s* (London: Health Education Council).

WICKS, M. (1987), *A Future for All* (Harmondsworth: Penguin).

WILDING, P. (ed.) (1986), *In Defence of the Welfare State* (Manchester: Manchester University Press).

WILES, P. J. D. (1952), 'Pre-War and War-Time Controls', in G. D. N. Worswick and P. H. Ady (eds.), *The British Economy 1945–1950* (Oxford: Clarendon Press), 101–24.

WILLCOCKS, A. J. (1967), *The Creation of the National Health Service* (London: Routledge & Kegan Paul).

WILLIAMS, F. (ed.) (1977), *Why the Poor Pay More* (London: Macmillan).

WILLIAMS, K., and WILLIAMS, J. (1987), *A Beveridge Reader* (London: Allen & Unwin).

WILLIAMS, K., WILLIAMS, J., and THOMAS, D. (1983), *Why Are the British Bad at Manufacturing?* (London: Routledge & Kegan Paul).

WILLIAMSON, J. H., and WOOD, G. E. (1976), 'The British Inflation: Indigenous or Imported?' *American Economic Review*, 66, 520–31.

WILLIAMSON, O. E. (1965), 'Innovation and Market Structure', *Journal of Political Economy*, 73, 67–73.

—— (1968), 'Economics as an Anti-Trust Defense: The Welfare Trade-Offs', *American Economic Review*, 58, Mar., 18–31.

—— (1972), 'Dominant Firms and the Monopoly Problem: Market Failure Considerations', *Harvard Law Review*, 85, 1512–31.

—— (1977), 'Economies as an Anti-Trust Defense Revisited', in A. P. Jacquemin and H. W. De Jong (eds.), *Welfare Aspects of Industrial Markets* (Leiden: Martinus Nijhoff), 237–71.

WILSON COMMITTEE. *See* Committee to Review the Functioning of Financial Institutions.

WILSON, H. (1974), *The Labour Government 1964–70: A Personal Record* (Harmondsworth: Penguin).

WINCH, D. (1972), *Economics and Policy* (London: Hodder & Stoughton).

WINCHESTER, D. (1983), 'Industrial Relations in the Public Sector', in G. S. Bain (ed.), *Industrial Relations in Britain* (Oxford: Blackwell).

WINTERS, L. A. (1976), 'Exports', in T. S. Barker (ed.), *Economic Structure and Policy with Applications to the British Economy* (London: Chapman Hall), 131–61.

—— (1987), 'Britain in Europe: A Survey of Quantitative Trade Studies', *Journal of Common Market Studies*, 25, 315–36.

WOOD, G. E., and WILLIAMSON, J. H. (1976), 'The British Inflation: Indigenous or Imported', *American Economic Review*, 66, 520–31.

WORSWICK, G. D. N. (1984), 'The Great Recessions: The 1980s and 1930s in Britain', *Scottish Journal of Political Economy*, 31, 209–28.

WORSWICK, G. D. N., and ADY, P. H. (eds.) (1952), *The British Economy 1945–1950* (Oxford: Clarendon Press).

WORSWICK, G. D. N., and ADY, P. H. (eds.) (1962), *The British Economy in the Nineteen Fifties* (Oxford: Clarendon Press).

WRIGHT, J. F. (1979), *Britain in the Age of Economic Management: An Economic History since 1939* (Oxford: Oxford University Press).

YATES, J. (1987), *Why Are We Waiting?* (Oxford: Oxford University Press).

YOUNG, S., and LOWE, A. V. (1974), *Intervention in the Mixed Economy: The Evolution of British Industrial Policy 1964–72* (London: Croom Helm).

ZEITLIN, J. (1987), 'From Labour History to the History of Industrial Relations', *Economic History Review*, 40, 159–84.

ZIS, G. (1975), 'Inflation: An International Monetary Problem or a National Social Phenomenon', *British Journal of International Studies*, 1, 98–118.

# Name Index

# Subject Index